THE HISTORY AND THEORY OF INTERNATIONAL LAW

Remaking Central Europe

THE HISTORY AND THEORY OF INTERNATIONAL LAW

General Editors

In the past few decades the understanding of the relationship between nations has undergone a radical transformation. The role of the traditional nation-state is diminishing, along with many of the traditional vocabularies which were once used to describe what has been called, ever since Jeremy Bentham coined the phrase in 1780, 'international law'. The older boundaries between states are growing ever more fluid, new conceptions and new languages have emerged which are slowly coming to replace the image of a world of sovereign independent nation states which has dominated the study of international relations since the early nineteenth century. This redefinition of the international arena demands a new understanding of classical and contemporary questions in international and legal theory. It is the editors' conviction that the best way to achieve this is by bridging the traditional divide between international legal theory, intellectual history, and legal and political history. The aim of the series, therefore, is to provide a forum for historical studies, from classical antiquity to the twenty-first century, that are theoretically informed and for philosophical work that is historically conscious, in the hope that a new vision of the rapidly evolving international world, its past and its possible future, may emerge.

PREVIOUSLY PUBLISHED IN THIS SERIES

The Battle for International Law
South-North Perspectives on the Decolonization Era
Edited by Jochen von Bernstorff and Philipp Dann

Rewriting the History of the Law of Nations
How James Brown Scott Made Francisco de Vitoria the Founder of International Law
Paolo Amorosa

To Reform the World
International Organizations and the Making of Modern States
Guy Fiti Sinclair

The New Histories of International Criminal Law
Retrials
Edited by Immi Tallgren and Thomas Skouteris

Sovereignty
A Contribution to the Theory of Public and International Law
Hermann Heller, edited and introduced by David Dyzenhaus

Law and the Political Economy of Hunger
Anna Chadwick

Remaking Central Europe

The League of Nations and the Former Habsburg Lands

Edited by

PETER BECKER AND NATASHA WHEATLEY

OXFORD
UNIVERSITY PRESS

OXFORD
UNIVERSITY PRESS

Great Clarendon Street, Oxford, OX2 6DP,
United Kingdom

Oxford University Press is a department of the University of Oxford.
It furthers the University's objective of excellence in research, scholarship,
and education by publishing worldwide. Oxford is a registered trade mark of
Oxford University Press in the UK and in certain other countries

First Edition published in 2020

Impression: 3

Published in the United States of America by Oxford University Press
198 Madison Avenue, New York, NY 10016, United States of America

British Library Cataloguing in Publication Data

Data available

Library of Congress Control Number: 2020942417

ISBN 978–0–19–885468–5

DOI: 10.1093/oso/9780198854685.001.0001

Printed and bound by
CPI Group (UK) Ltd, Croydon, CR0 4YY

Acknowledgements

This volume has roots in a conference we organized in Vienna in 2015 under the title, 'After Empire: The League of Nations and the Former Habsburg Lands'. We thank all those who participated in our conversations that December, as well as those who joined the project subsequently. The conference was co-sponsored by the Austrian Institute of Historical Research at the University of Vienna and the Laureate Research Program in International History at the University of Sydney, led by Professor Glenda Sluga. We are most grateful to both institutions for their financial and administrative support: their investment enabled and nurtured a collective project on this scale. We owe particular thanks to Glenda Sluga: not only for the generous funding from her Australian Research Council Laureate Fellowship, but for her many-sided contributions to the conceptualization of this project, her intellectual companionship and moral support, and indeed her own pioneering work in linking (Central) European and international history.

We gratefully acknowledge the excellent and extensive editorial work done by Stephan Stockinger on many of the chapters, and the Austrian Institute of Historical Research for funding his work. We also extend warm thanks to Birgit Aubrunner, who did a marvellous job with the conference logistics, and to Petra Latschenberger, who heroically wrestled the citations into conformity.

Peter Becker
Natasha Wheatley

Series Editors' Preface

The years which followed the Paris Peace Conference of 1919 have recently come to be seen as beginning of a distinctly new epoch in the history of the West and arguably of the entire globe. A little over a century earlier, in 1815, the 'Great Powers' had gathered in Vienna to create what the Prussian diplomat Friedrich von Gentz had called optimistically the 'Areopagus of Europe'. It ushered in what has come to be called the 'Century of Vienna' which brought a largely unprecedented degree of peace to Europe itself—even as it had unleashed an era of conquest and subjection across much of the rest of the globe. In 1914 this finally collapsed and with it went the belief that the European states could by themselves dominate most of the world. The League of Nations, which was created in 1919, although in no real sense a league, was intended to build not only a new European order, but also a truly 'new international order'. A new set of institutions and new legal order, and new forms of international governance, were created to replace the older, chaotic, and always unstable 'balance of powers' and the 'congress system' which had previously kept the 'Great Powers' from entirely annihilating each other. One of the vanquished of the war was the Austro-Hungarian Empire, and with its collapse went the entire political social and legal structure of Central and Eastern Europe.

The subsequent reconstruction of the area was, as Peter Becker and Natasha Wheatley explain here, a process which was heavily dependent upon the new institutions of international governance set up by the League of Nations. At the same time, however, it was both a challenge to them, and was challenged by them. The First World War had been a conflict between empires as much as between nation-states, and in some respects it had been a conflict *over* empire. The new areopagus of the globe certainly espoused new, more liberal objectives, than had any of its predecessors: 'self-determination' (for some); a committee for refugees; a health organization; a slavery commission; a commission for the study of the legal status of women; a series of 'Minorities Treaties' to secure the rights, religious, civil, and cultural, of all peoples; and it made a provision for a Permanent Court of International Justice. The Germans and the Italians complained bitterly that this was conducted under the aegis, and very largely on behalf, of some of the victorious allies, and as a means, in part at least, of allowing the British and the French in particular to expand their global influence. All of these aspects of the new order which the League sought to create had a lasting impact on the former Hapsburg lands. Most of the literature on the post-war settlements, however, has tended to overlook the experience of Central and Eastern Europe, which in the aftermath of the war went from being, as the editors say, 'a highly integrated economic and political region into a cluster of new states behind new walls'.

Remaking Central Europe is the first sustained attempt to analyse the relationship between the League's 'new order', and the emergence of the new states created in the ruins of the Austro-Hungarian Empire. It was, in more general terms, an encounter, sometimes consensual, sometimes conflictual, between a new brand of internationalism and emergent post-imperial nationalism. For much of its history, this encounter between the universalist ambitions of the League, and the 'local particularisms' of the states it sought to manage, constituted, as the editors say, not a 'static opposition' but rather a 'dynamic historical process'. Yet that process was always, at some level, a fraught one, for it touched on the still amorphous notion of state sovereignty which, in the aftermath of the war became—and, it might be said, has remained ever since—the principal obstacle in the path of any attempt to create a truly international political order. The League's claim to oversee the rights of minorities (discussed here by Börries Kuzmany), the attempt to control crime across borders (see the chapters by David Petruccelli and Martina Steer), the bid to create international health organizations (Sara Silverstein), and international scientific communities (Michael Burri), as well as the need to heal the crippled economies of the region (Nathan Marcus), all placed severe limitations on the self-declared sovereignty of the new states of central and eastern Europe, which were clearly critical to their status and their identity as states. Some of the same problems which arose out of this encounter between the local and international at the political and the legal level persist to this day, as the League's structures of international control were replaced first by the brutal impositions of the Third Reich, followed by those of the Soviet Union, and now, at least in the imagination of the new ultranationalists, by the regulatory and monetary controls imposed by the European Union.

The chapters in *Remaking Central Europe* offer a rich and varied discussion of the emergence of the post-imperial world within Europe, and a series of detailed accounts of how the relationship between the national and the international, the local, and the universal, evolved in the aftermath of 1919. It is a relationship which still shapes and threatens the European order to this day.

Anthony Pagden

Table of Contents

PART II REMAKING TERRITORIES AND BORDERS

Editors' Biographies

Peter Becker is Professor of Austrian History in the Department of History at the University of Vienna. Before moving to Vienna, he held a professorship at the European University Institute in Florence, where he started his research on the history of modern state and governance especially of the Habsburg monarchy and on the cultural history of public administration. In Vienna, he developed a research focus on the engagement of the Habsburg monarchy and the successor states with the new international order. He is the editor of the open access yearbook *Administory. Journal for the History of Public Administration*, published with Sciendo since 2016.

Natasha Wheatley is an Assistant Professor in the Department of History at Princeton University. Prior to joining the Princeton faculty, she completed her PhD at Columbia University and was an ARC Postdoctoral Research Fellow at the University of Sydney. Her article 'Spectral Legal Personality in Interwar International Law' received the 2018 Surrency Prize from the American Society for Legal History, and a volume titled *Power and Time*, edited together with Dan Edelstein and Stefanos Geroulanos, is published by Chicago University Press in 2020. She has held fellowships in Vienna, Cambridge, and elsewhere, and was a Fellow at the Wissenschaftskolleg zu Berlin for the 2019–20 academic year.

List of Contributors

Dr Antal Berkes
Lecturer in Public/International Law, Brunel Law School, Brunel University London

Dr Michael Burri
Lecturer, FMA, Temple University

Dr Katja Castryck-Naumann
Senior Researcher, Department 'Entanglements and Globalization', Leibniz-Institute for the History and Culture of Eastern Europe, Leipzig

Professor Patricia Clavin
Professor of International History, Faculty of History, University of Oxford

Dr Madeleine Dungy
Visiting Lecturer, College of Humanities, École Polytechnique Fédérale de Lausanne

Dr Johannes Feichtinger
Senior Research Associate, Austrian Academy of Sciences

Dr Börries Kuzmany
Assistant Professor of Modern History of Central and Eastern Europe, Department of East European History, University of Vienna

Dr Sarah Lemmen
Assistant Professor, Department of Modern and Contemporary History, Universidad Complutense de Madrid

Dr Nathan Marcus
Senior Lecturer, Department of General History, Ben-Gurion University of the Negev

Dr Zoltán Peterecz
Associate Professor, Institute of English and American Studies, Eszterházy Károly University

Dr David Petruccelli
Assistant Professor, Department of History, Dartmouth College

Dr Sara Silverstein
Assistant Professor, Department of History and Human Rights Institute, University of Connecticut

Dr Glenda Sluga
Professor of International History and Capitalism, Department of History and Civilization (HEC), European University Institute/ARC Laureate Fellow, University of Sydney

Dr Martina Steer
Adjunct Professor, History, University of Vienna

List of Abbreviations

AAAS	Archive of the Austrian Academy of Sciences
ADMAE	*Archives Diplomatiques du Ministère des Affaires Étrangères*
AIDP	International Association of Penal Law (*Association internationale de Droit Pénal*)
ALoN	Archive of the League of Nations
ARA	American Relief Administration
AUV	Archive of the University of Vienna
BoE	Bank of England
CARA	Council for At-Risk Academics
CEIP	Carnegie Endowment for International Peace
ERC	European Research Council
IAA	International Association of Academies
ICC	International Chamber of Commerce
ICHS	International Committee of Historical Sciences
ICIC	International Commission on Intellectual Cooperation
ICPC	International Criminal Police Commission
IECI	International Educational Cinematographic Institute
IFC	International Financial Commission
IFLNS	International Federation of League of Nations Societies
IIIC	International Institute of Intellectual Cooperation
ILO	International Labour Organization
IMF	International Monetary Fund
IPU	Inter-Parliamentary Union
IR	International Relations
IRC	International Research Council
KPIPE	Karl Polanyi Institute of Political Economy
LNA	League of Nations Archive Geneva
LNHO	League of Nations Health Organization
LoN	League of Nations
LRCS	League of Red Cross Societies
LSE	London School of Economics
MAT	Mixed Arbitral Tribunals
NEM	nutritional equivalent of milk
NGO	non-governmental organization
OECD	Organisation for Economic Co-operation and Development
OIPH	Office of International Public Health (originally *Office International d'Hygiène Publique*)
PCIJ	Permanent Court of International Justice
POW	Prisoner of War

RSDRP	Russian Social Democratic Labour Party
SAP	Structural Adjustment Program
SCF	Save the Children Fund
SCIU	Save the Children International Union
SHS	Kingdom of Serbs, Croats, and Slovenes
TB	tuberculosis
TNA FCO	The National Archives/Foreign Commonwealth Office
UIA	International Union of Academies
UIC	International Union of Railways
UN	United Nations
UNESCO	United Nations Educational, Scientific and Cultural Organization
WHO	World Health Organization
WTO	World Trade Organization

Introduction

Central Europe and the New International Order

Peter Becker and Natasha Wheatley

Over the last two decades, the 'new international order' of 1919 has rapidly grown into an expansive new area of research across multiple disciplines and fields.[1] With the League of Nations at its heart, the interwar settlement has been rediscovered as the foundational moment of our contemporary global order: its innovations in international organization, international law, national and social rights, colonial governance, state making, financial coordination, and humanitarianism shaped the world we know today.[2] No longer preoccupied exclusively with the League as

[1] For new overviews and handbooks in several languages see United Nations Library (ed), *The League of Nations 1920–1946, Organization and Accomplishments: A retrospective of the First Organization for the Establishment of World Peace* (United Nations 1996); Paul David, *Histoire de la Société des Nations: l'esprit de Génève: vingt ans d'efforts pour la paix* (Ed. Slatkine 1998); Marit Fosse, *La Société des Nations: ou l'histoire d'une institution moderne oubliée* (Edition Diva 2005); Ruth Beatrice Henig, *The League of Nations* (Haus Publishing Ltd 2010); Isabella Löhr, *Völkerbund* (Leibniz-Inst. f. Europ. Geschichte 2015); John Fox, *The League of Nations: From Collective Security to Global Rearmament* (United Nations 2012); Michel Marbeau, *La Société des Nations: vers un monde multilatéral: 1919–1946* (Presses universitaires François-Rabelais 2017). For new research tools see Anigue H M van Ginneken, *Historical Dictionary of the League of Nations* (Scarecrow Press 2006); *La Société des Nations: Bibliographie* (Bibliothèque de l'ONUG [2010]); *Commentaire sur le pacte de la Société des Nations* (Bruylant 2015).

[2] Key works include: Susan Pedersen, 'Back to the League of Nations' (2017) 112/4 American Historical Review 1091; Patricia Clavin, *Securing the World Economy: The Reinvention of the League of Nations, 1920–1946* (Oxford University Press 2013); Erez Manela, *The Wilsonian Moment: Self-Determination and the International Origins of Anticolonial Nationalism* (Oxford University Press 2007); Susan Pedersen, *The Guardians: The League of Nations and the Crisis of Empire* (Oxford University Press 2015); Antony Anghie, 'Colonialism and the Birth of International Institutions: Sovereignty, Economy, and the Mandate System of the League of Nations' (2002) 34/3 New York University Journal of International Law and Politics 513; Megan Donaldson, 'The League of Nations, Ethiopia, and the Making of States' (2020) 11/1 Humanity 6; Mark Mazower, 'Minorities and the League of Nations in Interwar Europe' (1997) 126/2 Daedalus 47; Mark Lewis, *The Birth of the New Justice: The Internationalization of Crime and Punishment, 1919–1950* (Oxford University Press 2014); Bruno Cabanes, *The Great War and the Origins of Humanitarianism, 1918–1924* (Cambridge University Press 2014); Daniel Gorman, *The Emergence of International Society in the 1920s* (Cambridge University Press 2012); Keith Watenpaugh, 'The League of Nations' Rescue of Armenian Genocide Survivors and the Making of Modern Humanitarianism, 1920–1927' (2010) 115/5 American Historical Review 1315; Daniel Lacqua, 'Transnational Intellectual Cooperation, the League of Nations, and the Problem of Order' (2011) 6/2 Journal of Global History 223; Tomoko Akami, 'A Quest to be Global: The League of Nations Health Organization and Inter-Colonial Regional Governing Agendas of the Far Eastern Association of Tropical Medicine 1910–25' (2016) 38/1 International History Review 1; Madeleine Dungy, 'Writing Multilateral Trade Rules in the League of Nations' [2020, forthcoming] Contemporary

Peter Becker and Natasha Wheatley, *Introduction* In: *Remaking Central Europe.* Edited by: Peter Becker and Natasha Wheatley, Oxford University Press (2020). © the many contributors. DOI: 10.1093/oso/9780198854685.003.0001

an organ of collective security or with the reasons 'why the League failed', this new literature instead explores its role in structuring policy-making across a wide variety of fields.

No region experienced the many-sided effects and implications of this new order more intimately than Central and Eastern Europe, which turned from a highly integrated economic and political region into a cluster of new states behind new walls.[3] With the collapse of the imperial states that had structured the region for centuries in 1918, a new political, social, and legal order needed to be created,[4] and this process unfolded in intimate dialogue with the new institutions of international governance set up by the Allied peacemakers to guarantee their post-war settlement. At the same time, Central and Eastern Europe became the key test case for those institutions: problems of financial collapse, national minorities, endemic disease, and humanitarian aid emerged as domains where the League's identity and authority were defined and tested.

Remaking Central Europe presents the first study of this intricate and reciprocal relationship between the new international order of 1919 and the new regional order in Central and Eastern Europe.[5] It analyses the co-implication of these two orders as both the Habsburg successor states and the League's agencies sought to build their capacity, character, and power out of the rubble of collapsed empires and world war. Relations between the new states and the new international bodies

European History; Simon Jackson and Alanna O'Malley (eds), *The Institution of International Order: From the League of Nations to the United Nations* (Routledge 2018).

[3] Cf. Quinn Slobodian, *Globalists: The End of Empire and the Birth of Neoliberalism* (Harvard University Press 2018), chap. 1. This observation takes up the catchy title of the first chapter: 'A World of Walls' (27). See also Natasha Wheatley, 'Central Europe as Ground Zero of the New International Order' (2019) 78/4 Slavic Review 900.

[4] Exciting new work on the refashioning of the region into ostensibly national states includes: Larry Wolff, *Woodrow Wilson and the Reimagining of Eastern Europe* (Stanford University Press 2020); Dominique Kirchner Reill, *The Fiume Crisis: Life in the Wake of the Habsburg Empire* (Harvard University Press 2020); Steven Seegel, *Map Men: Transnational Lives and Deaths of Geographers in the Making of East Central Europe* (University of Chicago Press 2018); Volker Prott, *The Politics of Self-Determination: Remaking Territories and National Identities in Europe, 1917–1923* (Oxford University Press 2016); Marcus M. Payk and Roberta Pergher (eds), *Beyond Versailles: Sovereignty, Legitimacy, and the Formation of New Polities After the Great War* (Indiana University Press 2019). There were well-known attempts to fashion the region into a new supranational bloc, for example the Briand plan for European integration under the umbrella of the League, explored in Jean-Luc Chabot, *Aux origines intellectuelles de l'Union européenne: L'idée d'Europe unie de 1919 à 1939* (Presses Universitaires de Grenoble 2005); on Briand cf. Gérard Unger, *Aristide Briand: Le ferme conciliateur* (Fayard 2005). Another broadly discussed plan was put forward by Richard Nikolaus Coudenhove-Kalergi under the heading *Paneuropean Union*. See Anita Ziegerhofer, *Botschafter Europas: Richard Nikolaus Coudenhove-Kalergi und die Paneuropa-Bewegung in den zwanziger und dreißiger Jahren* (Böhlau 2004).

[5] To our knowledge, the only publication that has examined more than one Central European state and its relation to the League of Nations deals with Czechoslovakia and Poland: Isabelle Davion, 'Das System der kollektiven Sicherheit im Praxistest: Polen und die Tschechoslowakei im Völkerbund' (2015) 63 Vierteljahrshefte für Zeitgeschichte 167. Her article does not engage, however, with the question of the political, cultural, and institutional legacies of Habsburg rule but focuses instead on the role of the League in appeasing border conflicts between the two states as a very peculiar kind of Habsburg legacy.

were constitutive and simultaneously riven with ambivalence, and illustrate a set of foundational historical conundrums for those engaged in the practice of international history. How have international frameworks and imperatives shaped nation- and state-building, and vice versa? How have these imperatives and frameworks dealt with the legal, cultural, institutional legacies of the empires from which the new states emerged? And how do regionally specific problems and experiences become abstracted into international benchmarks and precedents? As editors, our aim has been no less than to introduce a new research agenda. Together, the essays we have brought together frame the tension between the ostensible universalism of international orders and the specificity of local particularisms less as a static opposition than a dynamic historical process.

Four central interventions lie at the heart of *Remaking Central Europe*. The first concerns the *legacies of empire*. An influential stream of scholarship on the interwar international order has explored its imperial debts. Historians have revealed how key internationalist thinkers, as well as the central architects of the League of Nations and its mandate system, drew models and practices from the British Empire into the sphere of international organization.[6] Yet the new order of 1919 arguably took shape on the ground most palpably in Central and Eastern Europe, where international organizations and actors worked in the shadow not of the British Empire, but the Austro-Hungarian one.[7] *Remaking Central Europe* thus explores how one supranational order, built upon multinational dynastic rule, segued into another, founded upon the dual premise of national states and international oversight. It traces, for the first time, the interwar legacies of Habsburg imperial order—especially in the fields of law, administration, and science—in the landscape of an international order rather than in the successor states.[8] International and transnational responses to the region's challenges confronted the legacies of Habsburg rule across a range of planes and scales, including social and scientific networks, epistemic communities, legal concepts, fiscal structures,

[6] These included figures like General Smuts, Alfred Zimmern, and Frederick Lugard. See for example Mark Mazower, *No Enchanted Palace: The End of Empire and the Ideological Origins of the United Nations* (Princeton University Press 2013); Pedersen, *The Guardians* (n 2); Jeanne Morefield, '"A Liberal in A Muddle": Alfred Zimmern on Nationality and Commonwealth' in David Long and Brian C. Schmidt (eds), *Imperialism and Internationalism in the Discipline of International Relations* (SUNY Press 2004). More broadly, see also new work on empire and internationalism like Miguel Bandeira Jerónimo and José Pedro Monteiro (eds), *Internationalism, Imperialism and the Formation of the Contemporary World: The Pasts of the Present* (Palgrave Macmillan 2017) and Sean Andrew Wempe, *Revenants of a Fallen Empire. Colonial Germans, the League of Nations, and the Redefinition of Imperialism, 1919–1933* (Oxford University Press 2019).

[7] See here also Slobodian, *Globalists* (n 3), which anchors the emergence of neoliberal, that is, ordoglobalist, economic thinking in the theoretical and political reflection of Viennese intellectuals after the end of the Great War.

[8] On this aspect cf. Paul Miller and Claire Morelon (eds), *Embers of Empire: Continuity and Rupture in the Habsburg Successor States after 1918* (Berghahn 2018); and in a more cultural vein, Magdalena Baran-Szołtys and Jagoda Wierzejska (eds), *Continuities and Discontinuities of the Habsburg Legacy in East-Central European Discourses since 1918* (Vienna University Press 2020).

trans- and supranational political imaginaries, horizons of expectation, and spaces of experience.

We thus offer a new perspective not only on the League's new order—one less beholden to Anglo-American lineages—but also on the afterlives of imperial rule in Central Europe. Rather than focus on Habsburg nostalgia, or on ethnic conflict, or the internal dynamics and memory politics of the successor states,[9] we frame the question of imperial afterlives as one of supranational or transnational governance, spanning not only formal political structures but also civil society, professional disciplines, and political vocabularies.[10] Our approach thus opens up a new, unsentimental, and non-provincial history of the empire's disappearance that is closely engaged with current developments in the fields of international and transnational history.

In uncovering a new Central European nexus to the relationship between empire and international order, we do not present Habsburg rule in Europe as commensurable with (for example) British or French imperial rule in the wider world. These imperial histories—and their legacies—vary widely.[11] What is commensurable, we suggest, is the process in which ideas and practices derived from the management of diversity in imperial settings and within a multi-national European state are transported into the domain of international law and order. We are especially interested in the particularity of these Habsburg ideas and practices and their subsequent international afterlives, for example regarding the management of ethnic, linguistic, and religious difference (from the empire's 'nationalities' into interwar 'minorities') and the mechanisms and imaginary of multi-level government.

The second central intervention resides in our *regional approach*.[12] In highlighting the common legal, institutional, and cultural inheritance shared by

9 Cf. Mark Cornwall and John Paul Newman (eds), *Sacrifice and Rebirth: The Legacy of the Last Habsburg War* (Berghahn 2016).

10 On business elites over the cusp of 1918, see Máté Rigó, 'The Long First World War and the Survival of Business Elites in East-Central Europe: Transylvania's Industrial Boom and the Enrichment of Economic Elites' (March 2917) 24/2 European Review of History/Revue européenne d'histoire 250. The continued effect of previous borders in newly established or expanded states, like in Poland, could be seen as another instance of imperial afterlife, which was strongly felt especially in Poland. Cf. Béatrice von Hirschhausen and others (eds), *Phantomgrenzen: Räume und Akteure in der Zeit neu denken* (Wallstein 2015). For a fresh look at the changing role of civil society vis-à-vis international governance see Cecilia M. Lynch, *Beyond Appeasement: Interpreting Interwar Peace Movements in World Politics* (Cornell University Press 2018) esp. chaps. 1–3.

11 On a comparative history of European Empires cf. Jörn Leonhard and Ulrike von Hirschhausen (eds), *Comparing Empires: Encounters and Transfers in the Long Nineteenth Century* (Vandenhoeck & Ruprecht 2011).

12 For a fine example of a differently structured regional approach, see Alan McPherson and Yannick Wehrli (eds), *Beyond Geopolitics. New Histories of Latin America at the League of Nations* (University of New Mexico Press 2015). Indeed, a regional approach to the League has been pursued mainly with regard to Latin America. See also Thomas Fischer, *Die Souveränität der Schwachen: Lateinamerika und der Völkerbund, 1920–1936* (Franz Steiner Verlag 2012). Our volume thus ties Central European history into methodological trends shaping international and global history across other world regions. For a regional study of one domain of the League's activity—namely, the mandates system—see Cyrus Schayegh and Andrew Arsan (eds), *The Routledge Handbook of the History of the Middle East Mandates* (Routledge 2015).

the successor states, our volume probes the possibility and plausibility of treating the domain of former Habsburg rule as a (more or less coherent) region. This optic allows us to transcend an older generation of scholarship that tended to focus on the relationship between a single (nation-)state and an international organization or question.[13] Rather than pre-presume the uniqueness of each particular national predicament or perspective, this volume makes analytic space for the common issues and challenges that confronted the new states as they constructed both their internal architecture and external standing. It also carries forward the most sophisticated new work on the Habsburg Empire with the recovery of the institutions and interests that tied Central Europeans into a common cultural and political world.[14]

Some international innovations—like the minorities treaties—had a distinct regional hue from the outset; others—like the international management of national economies—became connected to the region's particular problems as first Austria, then Hungary submitted to the fiscal oversight of the League in exchange for financial aid.[15] Several key challenges besetting the new Central European states—especially epidemics and other health questions, trade, and international crime—blithely transgressed sovereign borders, and demanded regional responses. Those responses in turn ran up against and relied upon networks, relationships, and bodies of knowledge inherited from the era of Habsburg rule.

In thinking across these cases, *Remaking Central Europe* asks: to what extent can we consider this region a single site for questions of international order during this period? In presenting this regional coherence as a historical question, we propose a new tripartite analytical frame—*national-regional-international*—that takes the mutual implication of these scales as a key point of departure.[16]

Our third (and related) intervention moves towards an *integrated history of the interwar order in Europe*. The regional perspective allows us to explore the

[13] These country studies look increasingly at the interrelation between national politics, civil society, and the international order. See especially Carlo Moos, *Ja zum Völkerbund—Nein zur UNO: Die Volksabstimmungen von 1920 und 1986 in der Schweiz* (Chronos; Editions Payot 2001); Helen McCarthy, *The British People and the League of Nations: Democracy, Citizenship and Internationalism, c. 1918–45* (Manchester University Press 2011); Elisabetta Tollardo, *Fascist Italy and the League of Nations, 1922–1935* (Palgrave Macmillan 2016).

[14] See especially Pieter Judson, *The Habsburg Empire: A New History* (Harvard University Press 2016); John Deak, *Forging a Multinational State: State Making in Imperial Austria from the Enlightenment to the First World War* (Stanford University Press 2015).

[15] See Clavin, *Securing the World Economy* (n 2) chap. 1; Nathan Marcus, *Austrian Reconstruction and the Collapse of Global Finance, 1921–1931* (Harvard University Press 2018); Zoltán Peterecz, *Jeremiah Smith, jr. and Hungary, 1924–1926: The United States, the League of Nations, and the Financial Reconstruction of Hungary* (Versita 2013).

[16] We thus take up the conceptual advances made by Sandrine Kott and look at the 'régimes circulatoires' structuring the exchange between the international, national, and local levels. In contrast with Kott's approach, we collect a series of essays with the same regional and temporal focus, with the aforementioned analytical benefits. Sandrine Kott, 'Les organisations internationales, terrains d'étude de la globalisation: Jalons pour une approche socio-historique' (2011) 52 Critique internationale 9. More generally, see also Cyrus Schayegh's exploration of 'spatial layeredness' or 'transpatialization' in *The Middle East and the Making of the Modern World* (Harvard University Press 2017).

entanglement of different areas of the League's activity—often through the mobilization of policy specific networks of state and non-state actors. In drawing these various studies together, our volume exposes the connections between different regional challenges and their remedies, rather than tracing a single subject area like health or law or finance. By contrast, much of the new work on the international order pursues a singular institutional wing (like the International Labour Organization (ILO) or the mandates system) or a singular category (like humanitarianism, white slavery, or civil society support).[17] The multi-author format is thus crucial to our conceptualization of the topic, because it enables us to transcend the limits of individual scholarly expertise and show how fiscal, national, social, health, intellectual, and political crises twisted and melted together in unpredictable ways, sometimes involving overlapping personnel. If this interconnectedness proved especially visible on the ground in Central Europe, then the regional approach suggests ways of writing histories that are not beholden to the League's own categorization of different domains of governance and organization of knowledge. In this way, *Remaking Central Europe* has the potential to open up new methodological pathways for histories of international order in different times, places, and fields.

The fourth and final intervention focuses on the relationship between *nationalism and internationalism*, especially in relation to *sovereignty*, *supranational governance*, and *European integration*. Recent works of international history have sought to undo the traditional binary between nationalism and internationalism by arguing for their close historical and conceptual connection.[18] Interwar Central Europe arguably offers an unparalleled testing ground for these claims.[19] In the condensed span of a few short decades, the region experienced revolutionary nationalization *and* internationalization: in the same moment that the nation-state model triumphed over multinational empire, the Allies launched an unprecedented experiment in international organization that seemingly claimed the right to modify or check traditional sovereignty in various ways. By granting the nascent League of Nations the power to oversee the rights of minorities in the new states, the peace treaties enshrined this tension in the foundational moment of the new

[17] To mention just a few contributions from a rich and inspiring literature: R.M. Douglas, Michael D. Callahan, and Elizabeth Bishop (eds), *Imperialism on Trial: International Oversight of Colonial Rule in Historical Perspective* (Lexington 2006); Clavin, *Securing the World Economy* (n 2); Sandrine Kontt and Joëlle Droux (eds), *Globalizing Social Rights: The International Labour Organization and Beyond* (Palgrave 2013); McCarthy, *The British People and the League of Nations* (n 13) ; Daniel Maul, *The International Labour Organization: 100 Years of Global Social Policy* (de Gruyter 2019); Pedersen, *The Guardians* (n 2).

[18] Glenda Sluga, *Internationalism in the Age of Nationalism* (University of Pennsylvania Press 2013); Mark Mazower, *Governing the World: The History of an Idea* (Penguin 2012); Guy Fiti Sinclair, *To Reform the World: International Organizations and the Making of Modern States* (Oxford University Press 2017).

[19] As we see so vividly in Quinn Slobodian's analysis of economists' desire to 'encase' inner-state policies in an international regulatory system. Slobodian, *Globalists* (n 3).

European order. The range of ways in which the functions of the state might be managed or even turned over to international organizations expanded still further when the League's financial reconstruction of Austria and then Hungary became test cases with global resonance. The paradoxes involved in these dual imperatives surfaced in myriad ways across the various faces of the interwar settlement. As some actors toiled to construct new state borders, others simultaneously developed new techniques for transcending them. Perhaps more than any other region, interwar Central Europe compels us to view the twinned process of state-building/nationalization and internationalization in the same historical frame.

Through this conceptualization of the topic, *Remaking Central Europe* seeks novel paths of connection between interwar Central Europe and other major historiographies, including global governance and European integration. In presenting new studies on episodes like the international management of the Austrian and Hungarian economies, for example, our study ties interwar Europe into the larger literature on global governance and financial supervision. The former Habsburg lands emerge as key workshops for international prerogatives and techniques that still structure relationships between many parts of the developing world and the international community, including peacekeeping, humanitarian intervention, international monetary loans, and regulatory oversight.

The same is true for European integration. As the European Union has grown institutionally and become pivotal to Europe's economic future and its standing in world affairs, public and academic appetite for new interpretations of Europe's collective past, present, and future have expanded rapidly. Historians have looked back to the Austro-Hungarian Empire, the German customs union, or even the Holy Roman Empire in pursuit of enlightening precedents and pre-histories for contemporary European integration. Even for an understanding of the dynamics of disintegration under the spell of resurgent nationalism,[20] it can be rewarding to cast a critical eye at the end of the Habsburg Empire and even at the beginning of the new international order in the 1920s. *Remaking Central Europe* channels this interest into the plastic and formative moment in which older techniques of supranational organization—namely, the rule of a multi-national state—directly confronted the modern techniques of transnational administration and regulation over multiple national-states that characterize European (and global) governance today. We thus provide a new, subtle space for thinking about the history of European integration between different forms of coercion and different forms of agency, without privileging either a simple history of imperial/international control, nor a whiggish account free from the frictions and paradoxes that characterized the period in question.

[20] See Christian Karner and Monika Kopytowska (eds), *National Identity and Europe in Times of Crisis: Doing and Undoing Europe* (Emerald 2017); Ivan T. Berend, *Against European Integration: The European Union and its Discontents* (Routledge 2019).

A New History of Internationalism and Governance in the Habsburg Lands

The League was derided already during its lifetime for not living up to its bold claims of stabilizing a new world order in which peace would prevail and armament races would be consigned to the past. As Susan Pedersen and others have argued, the failure of this utopian vision obscures our view of all that the League did transform. It actually relied already on the 'solidarity of facts' that Robert Schuman would later promote as the starting point of European integration in 1950.

International collaboration in the provision of common goods[21] such as health care, environment, infrastructure, education, research, and security was restructured around the League of Nations after the war.[22] Rather than focus solely on the more familiar story of cooperation between states, we turn to the less studied question of how expert and civil society networks were redrawn under the influence of the new political situation. Our focus on the successor states of the Habsburg Empire provides a penetrating lens for a thorough discussion of continuities and changes in the ways in which these networks collaborated with governments and with supranational agencies. Did the Habsburg monarchy leave a legacy not just in the legal underpinnings of state action and personal transactions but also with respect to the networks of governance? This question has the potential to open a Pandora's box of studies on regional identity from a governance perspective.

Our exploration of the interaction between expert and civil society networks and international agencies offers the opportunity to look not just at the resilience of networks of governance in the provision of common goods at the state level. It also helps identify continuities and ruptures in a single state's networking with international agencies. This is one of the legacies that extended across a range of planes and scales, including social and scientific networks, epistemic communities, legal concepts, fiscal structures, trans- and supranational political imaginaries, horizons of expectation, and spaces of experience.

Interestingly, the Habsburg Monarchy was comparatively disengaged from many international initiatives.[23] This does not mean that expert groups and civil society organizations in the Habsburg monarchy refrained from international networking. On the contrary, we only need to think of the peace movement, the philanthropic networks and their fight against the white slave trade, and the

[21] See Adrienne Héritier (ed), *Common Goods: Reinventing European and International Governance* (Rowman & Littlefield 2002).

[22] See, for example, Anna-Katharina Wöbse, *Weltnaturschutz: Umweltdipomatie in Völkerbund und Vereinten Nationen, 1920–1950* (Campus Verlag 2011).

[23] See Peter Becker, 'Von Listen und anderen Stolpersteinen auf dem Weg zur Globalisierung: Die Habsburgermonarchie und der Internationalismus des 'langen' 19. Jahrhunderts' in Barbara Haider-Wilson, William Godsey, and Wolfgang Mueller (eds), *International History in Theory and Practice* (ÖAW 2017).

internationally well-connected medical profession.[24] The Habsburg Monarchy and the Austrian republic provided formal support for these international activities only in rare instances, such as the creation of the forerunner of today's Interpol in the 1920s under the auspices of Johann Schober, president of the Vienna police and federal chancellor.[25] Looking at the ways in which the successor states positioned themselves towards the involvement of their expert communities and civil society organizations with the League of Nations also casts light on the legacy of the Habsburg Monarchy in this field.

When the League's agencies started to generate tools to respond to the main challenges of the interwar period, they also turned to the toolbox of the Habsburg empire. This was the case particularly in developing strategies to govern the minority problem. The experience of the Habsburg Monarchy in dealing with nationality rights had a strong impact on this discussion, which translated nationality rights into minority rights.[26]

In examining the resilience of institutional, legal, cultural, and social practices in the successor states of the Habsburg Empire through the lens of the League of Nations, we do not ignore the enormous ruptures brought about by war and by the peace treaties of 1919–20. The frequently discussed schisms of the war years—including the assault on civil society during wartime emergency measures, the rapid expansion of the state in the economic field, the radicalization of nationalist sentiments, and the breakup of a political, economic, financial, and cultural space—were aggravated by the region's experience of a new world of walls, where borders suddenly impeded the flow of goods and people.[27] This constellation of developments and their challenges provides the backdrop against which *Remaking Central Europe* traces continuities from the Habsburg Monarchy into the successor states. We have organized this discussion into two major sub-sections: 'Remaking Actors and Networks' and 'Remaking Territories and Borders'.

Part I, 'Remaking Actors and Networks', analyses various actors and networks circulating through the 'multiverse' of the League.[28] Operating at the intersection of state and civil society, these transnational networks of governance bore the imprint of the Habsburg Empire, and often reacted against it. They were communities of expertise that had to adapt to a new landscape of sovereign states, often 'rescaling' their projects in ways that allow us to explore different forms of

[24] For the fate of these networks into the interwar era, see the chapters of Michael Burri, Sara Silverstein, Katja Castryck, and Martina Steer in this volume.

[25] See the chapter of David Petruccelli in this volume; as well as Jens Jäger, *Verfolgung durch Verwaltung: Internationales Verbrechen und internationale Polizeikooperation, 1880–1933* (UVK Verlagsgesellschaft mbH 2006); Mathieu Deflem, *Policing World Society: Historical Foundations of International Police Cooperation* (Oxford University Press 2002).

[26] See the chapter of Börries Kuzmany in this volume, as well as Natasha Wheatley, 'Making Nations into Legal Persons between Imperial and International Law: Scenes from a Central European History of Group Rights' (2018) 28 Duke Journal of Comparative and International Law 481.

[27] See the chapters of Peter Becker and Madeleine Dungy in this book.

[28] For the League as a 'multiverse,' see Clavin, *Securing the World Economy* (n 2).

'internationalization'—and its discontents. These actors and networks include technical experts, diplomats, doctors and medical professionals, and scholars.[29] In tracking patterns of continuity, change, and adaptation in particular policy fields,[30] Part I reveals how these actors rebuilt the infrastructure of governance in the wake of imperial collapse, made complex processes visible to policy makers and lay persons,[31] and thereby affected the reach of the League's agencies into the new states of the interwar order. This dynamic is clearly on display in Sara Silverstein's study of the League's innovations in international health and the central role played by Polish doctor Ludwik Rajchman.[32] Katja Castryck's comparative analysis of Albert Apponyi and Ludwik Rajchman introduces an important differentiation to our discussion of the way in which networks of bureaucrats, politicians, and scientific experts were drawn into the work of the League. Technical expert networks around the policy field of public health harnessed different state and civil society support than political networks that collected around League activities directed towards a lasting peace.[33] While public health emerged on the international level as an institutional practice, reflecting past methods and future forms of multi-level governance, the peace initiatives of the League continued to be based on the workings of a more traditional mélange of diplomats, politicians, and state-based associations. The legacy of pre-war international networks involving state and non-state actors alike was felt strongly in efforts to control international crime, drug traffic,

[29] Much of the innovative new scholarship on the League of Nations is informed by advances in science studies and in the study of expert communities and their role in international organizations. Already in 1992, Peter Haas proposed the concept of an *epistemic community* to better understand the shared definition of problems and of the best analytical means to tackle them: Peter Haas, 'Introduction: Epistemic Community and International Policy Coordination' (1992) 46 International Organization 1; on the use of this concept cf. exemplarily Daniel Laqua, 'Internationalisme ou Affirmation de la Nation? La cooperation intellectuelle transnationale dans l'entre-deux guerre' (2011) 52 Critique internationale 51; Patricia Clavin and Jens-Wilhelm Wessel, 'Transnationalism and the League of Nations: Understanding the Work of Its Economic and Financial Organisation' (2005) 14 Contemporary European History 465.

[30] For other policy fields such as environmental issues, city planning and forestry, see for example Wöbse, *Weltnaturschutz* (n 22); Martin Bemmann, 'Das Chaos beseitigen: Die internationale Standardisierung forst- und holzwirtschaftlicher Statistiken in den 1920er und 1930er Jahren und der Völkerbund' (2016) 57 Jahrbuch für Wirtschaftsgeschichte / Economic History Yearbook 545; Phillip Wagner, *Stadtplanung für die Welt? Internationales Expertenwissen* 1900–1960 (Vandenhoeck & Ruprecht 2016).

[31] On the visualization of economic processes see Slobodian, *Globalists* (n 3) chap. 2; on the visualization of the spread of epidemic disease see Heidi J.S. Tworek, 'Communicable Disease. Information, Health, and Globalization in the Interwar Period' (2019) 124 American Historical Review 813, 816f and 829–832.

[32] On the role of Central European public health experts in shaping public health as an international policy field see more generally: Iris Borowy, *Coming to Terms with World Health: The League of Nations Health Organisation 1921–1946* (Peter Lang 2014); Josep Lluis Barona Vilar, *The Rockefeller Foundation, Public Health and International Diplomacy, 1920–1945* (Pickering & Chatto 2015).

[33] These more technical activities of the League, as Susan Pedersen ('Back to the League' (n 2) 1108) has argued, responded to challenges regarding humanitarian, medical, and internal security matters that could not be resolved by newly formed nation-states and voluntary organizations. Depending on the policy fields, different networks were mobilized.

and the 'white slave trade'.[34] That said, the only field in which an Austrian polity ever gained a leading role within the 'international life' (Alfred Fried) of the pre- and post-war years was the field of policing. The International Criminal Police Commission (ICPC), founded in 1923, developed close ties to the League without ever being fully integrated into its technical departments.[35] Collaboration in the field of internal security and crime prevention had already a long tradition[36] when Johann Schober, long time president of the Vienna police and several times Federal Chancellor of the Austrian Republic, founded the ICPC. David Petruccelli's chapter situates this important field of international collaboration within contemporary practices and discourses, which included the League but were not restricted to it.

Central to our research agenda are not only the protagonists of governance, but also the techniques and strategies they used. We argue that Central Europe emerged as a key laboratory for new genres of supranational oversight and new international 'remedies', with lasting—and global—consequences.[37] The League of Nations developed new techniques for crisis management, as the Austrian and Hungarian loans—analysed here by Nathan Marcus and Zoltán Peterecz—illustrate especially sharply.[38] In this case, the toolbox of the League contained new instruments such as the delegation of sovereignty. This approach posed a bold political challenge to both Austria and Hungary and required massive political work since the relevant states needed to secure the support of crucial political actors.[39] In other words, the remaking of strategies on the *international* level required an

[34] Cf. exemplarily Paul Knepper, *International Crime in the 20th Century: The League of Nations Era, 1919–1939* (Palgrave Macmillan 2011).

[35] Jens Jäger, *Verfolgung durch Verwaltung: Internationales Verbrechen und internationale Polizeikooperation 1880–1933* (Konstanzer Universitätsverlag 2006); Cyrille Fijnaut, 'The International Criminal Police Commission and the Fight Against Communism, 1923–1945' in Mark Mazower (ed), *Policing of Politics in the Twentieth Century: Historical Perspectives* (Berghahn 1997); Jan Selling, 'The Obscured Story of the International Police Commission: Harry Södermann and the Forgotten Context of Antiziganism' (2017) 42 Scandinavian Journal of History 329.

[36] Cf. Tiago Marques, *Crime and the Fascist State, 1850–1940* (Routledge 2016) esp. chap. 1.

[37] On the lasting influence of the Austrian rescue mission on future interventions in state finance cf. Patricia Clavin, 'The Austrian Hunger Crisis and the Genesis of International Organization after the First World War' (2014) 90 Internationale Affairs 265; cf. also Peter Berger, *Im Schatten der Diktatur: die Finanzdiplomatie des Vertreters des Völkerbundes in Österreich, Meinoud Marinus Rost van Tonningen 1931–1936* (Böhlau 2000); and forthcoming work by Jamie Martin.

[38] These two case studies are part of recent scholarship's shift from themes of appeasement and security to the League's lesser known role in rebuilding international cooperation after the war. Within this fresh look at the League, humanitarian and financial questions have assumed a particular prominence, as Susan Pedersen argues in 'Back to the League' (n 2) 1108–1112. On the new modes of intervention in state finances, see Clavin and Wessel, 'Transnationalism and the League of Nations' (n 29); Michel Fior, *Institution globale et marchés financiers la Société des Nations face à la reconstruction de l'Europe, 1918–1931* (P. Lang 2008); Yann Decorzant, *La Société des Nations et la naissance d'une conception de la régulation économique internationale* (P. Lang 2011); Yann Decorzant, 'La Société des Nations et l'apparition d'un nouveau réseau d'expertise économique et financière (1914–1923)' (2011) 52 Critique internationale 35; Clavin, *Securing the World Economy* (n 2).

[39] For previous research in this field, see Jürgen Nautz, *Unterhändler des Vertrauens: Aus den nachgelassenen Schriften von Sektionschef Dr. Richard Schüller* (Verlag für Geschichte und Politik 1990); Zoltán Peterecz, *Jeremiah Smith, jr. and Hungary, 1924–1926: the United States, the League of Nations, and the Financial Reconstruction of Hungary* (De Gruyter 2013).

adaptation on the *national-state* level to secure their functioning. At the same time, the agencies of the League used tools developed by the pre-war Habsburg monarchy and translated them into new interwar frames of reference, such as the aforementioned governance of minority issues. Sometimes, the cultural and material devastation wrought by the war meant that techniques developed in earlier periods now needed to be deployed on a much larger scale, as we can see in examples such as the children's aid mission in Vienna.[40] This is featured in Michael Burri's study of nutrition as an object and mode of international governance, where the Austrian paediatrician Clemens Pirquet was instrumental in linking Austrian and international intellectuals, philanthropists, and policy makers; and in the rebuilding of scholarly networks between the former enemy nations explored in Johannes Feichtinger's essay on Austria and international intellectual cooperation. Feichtinger brings to bear on our understanding of the Central European region recent studies of the work and impact of the International Institute of Intellectual Co-operation,[41] the role of the League in the development of intellectual property rights,[42] and institutionalization of collaboration in educational policy.[43] He recovers the expectations, visions, and frustrations connected to the League's intellectual cooperation programme and its role in restructuring national academic networks. Upscaling philanthropic missions and intellectual exchange obviously required more stable networks and institutions, which were gradually developed at the state and the supranational level.

Part II, 'Remaking Territories and Borders', examines a major paradox of the interwar period: the concurrent erection and transcending of state borders.[44] On

[40] On the American Hunger Aid, see Franz Adlgasser, *American individualism Abroad: Herbert Hoover, die American Relief Administration und Österreich, 1919–1923* (VWGÖ 1993).

[41] Cf. Jean-Jacques Renoliet, *L'UNESCO oubliée: La Société des Nations et la coopération intellectuelle (1919–1946)* (Publication de la Sorbonne 1999); Hans Manfred Bock, 'Europa als konkrete Utopie? Zum intellektuellen Umfeld der deutschen Vertretung im Internationalen Institut für geistige Zusammenarbeit in Paris 1927–1933' in Hans Manfred Bock (ed), *Topographie deutscher Kulturvertretung im Paris des 20. Jahrhunderts* (Narr 2010); Ute Lemke, '"La femme, la clandestine de l'histoire": Margarete Rothbarth—ein Engagement für den Völkerbund' (2012) 37 Lendemains 45; Jimena Canales, 'Einstein, Bergson, and the Experiment that Failed: Intellectual Cooperation at the League of Nations' (2005) 120/5 Modern Language Notes 1168; Corinne A. Pernet, 'Twists, Turns and Dead Alleys: The League of Nations and Intellectual Cooperation in Times of War' (2014) 12 Journal of Modern European History 342; Jo-Anne Pemberton, 'The Changing Shape of Intellectual Cooperation: From the League of Nations to UNESCO' [2012] Australian Journal of Politics and History 34; Daniel Laqua, 'Transnational intellectual Cooperation, The League of Nations, and the Problem of Order' (2011) 6/2 Journal of Global History 223.

[42] Isabella Löhr, 'Der Völkerbund und die Entwicklung des internationalen Schutzes geistigen Eigentums in der Zwischenkriegszeit' (2006) 54 Zeitschrift für Geschichtswissenschaft 900.

[43] Eckhardt Fuchs, 'Der Völkerbund und die Institutionalisierung transnationaler Bildungsbeziehungen' (2006) 54 Zeitschrift für Geschichtswissenschaft 888.

[44] We follow the lead of Susan Pedersen, who pointedly asked in her survey article, 'how the League handled the tricky dual task of protecting the populations and legitimating the borders of the states created or recreated in 1919' Pedersen, 'Back to the League of Nations' (n 2) 1099; cf. also Carole Fink, *Defending the Rights of Others: The Great Powers, the Jews, and International Minority Protection, 1878–1938* (Cambridge University Press 2004).

the one hand, the fledgling successor states invested intellectual, political, fiscal, and military resources in the construction of new sovereign frontiers (both literal and metaphoric). On the other, they were simultaneously bound up in a series of League experiments that eclipsed or altered traditional sovereign prerogatives, and in many senses diluted those state frontiers. An imperial territoriality was dismantled, and a new political territorialization gradually emerged out of the duelling imperatives of nationalization and internationalization. Not coincidentally, it was an initiative from Vienna that sought to revive the right of citizens to trade freely through the region, despite the myriad new borders now obstructing the flow of goods, capital, and people. Here the preservation of an imperial spatiality required bold new international treaties that managed the rights of foreign commercial agents. Patterns of continuity and change tangled together in complicated ways, as Madeleine Dungy's chapter on international commerce reveals. In other cases, the League was turned into an arbiter, balancing competing interests and the messy consequences of the new borders, as when the League oversaw the sorting of people and property into different national categories in the optants' disputes, explored here by Antal Berkes. Peter Becker interrogates how passports—those quintessential microcosms of the intersection of sovereignty and mobility—came into their own as an international policy question, when the war turned a world characterized by open borders into a 'world of walls'.[45]

The strategies deployed by Central European states to secure their newly established borders were intensively discussed within political and economic circles. Civil society and business interests used the League to push their governments in a different direction. Civil society groups were strongly involved in the prevention of the victimization of eastern European women in the so-called white slave trade, as Martina Steer argues. As with the international history of passports, efforts to combat the traffic in women and children reveal all too well that the alliance between non-state actors and the League as an international organization had only a limited ability to influence the policy of states. This was particularly the case if and when states used the shield of sovereignty to avoid changes in strategy.

The same held true in the field of minority protection, where the newly established states in Central Europe had accepted international contractual obligations. The internationally reinforced imperative to grant protection to minorities in the new nation-states suggested to many jurists that rights and autonomy needed to be considered in non-territorial terms—a case explored in Börries Kuzmany's

[45] Slobodian, *Globalists* (n 3) chap. 1; on the passport question in the League of Nations see the remarks in Susan F. Martin, *International Migration: Evolving Trends from the Early Twentieth Century to the Present* (Cambridge University Press 2014) 46–48. For a critical perspective on the apparent golden age of free mobility, see Tara Zahra, *The Great Departure: Mass Migration from Eastern Europe and the Making of the Free World* (Norton 2016).

chapter on non-territorial autonomy. Kuzmany's contribution shifts our historical focus from the actual working of the minorities section of the Secretariat and its limitations[46] towards an analysis of the potential of this system to reshape ethnic and political identities,[47] especially given their link to nationality politics during the Habsburg era.[48] Our concentration on Central Europe sharply exposes the internal asymmetries of the minorities protection regime, with only some European states—the new Central European states—required to sign minorities treaties.[49] Across these domains of governance and many others, the edges of sovereignty were drawn and contested between the legacy of the Habsburg empire and spatial demands of the new international order.

Reflecting on states in the post-war system of international relations would be futile if we did not study the ways in which the new states positioned themselves and forged distinctive international identities within this new framework. Sarah Lemmen's chapter tackles the lack of studies of relations between the successor states and the League of Nations[50] with a case study of the Czechoslovak republic, one of the most active members of the League of Nations. In contrast to the strictly international relations perspective chosen by Miklós Zeidler for the Hungarian case,[51] Lemmen excavates the broad international, even global outlook of the

[46] Christoph Gütermann, *Das Minderheitenschutzverfahren des Völkerbundes* (Duncker & Humblot 1979); Christian Raitz von Frentz, *A Lesson Forgotten: Minority Protection under the League of Nations; The Case of the German Minority in Poland, 1920–1934* (Lit Verlag 1999); Martin Scheuermann, *Minderheitenschutz contra Konfliktverhütung? Die Minderheitenpolitik des Völkerbundes in den zwanziger Jahren* (Verlag Herder-Institute 2000); Fink, *Defending the Rights of Others* (n 44) 282. An important strand of scholarship also explores the connection between the minorities treaties and the emergence of the international human rights regime after the Second World War. See especially: Mark Mazower, 'The Strange Triumph of Human Rights, 1933–1950' (2004) 47 Historical Journal 379. For one of the more successful incarnations of interwar minority protection, see also Brendan Karch, 'A Jewish "Nature Preserve": The League of Nations Minority Protections in Nazi Upper Silesia' (2013) 46/1 Central European History 124.

[47] On the second aspect cf. Gerhard Seewann, 'Grenzüberschreitender Minderheitenschutz 1919–1941: Patronagestaat Deutschland, Heimatstaat Ungarn und der Völkerbund' in Enikö Dácz (ed), *Minderheitenfragen in Ungarn und in den Nachbarländern im 20. und 21. Jahrhundert* (Nomos 2013).

[48] See also Wheatley, 'Making Nations into Legal Persons between Imperial and International Law' (n 26).

[49] Pedersen, 'Back to the League' (n 2) 1099–1103; cf. also Manfred Mohr (ed), *Friedenssichernde Aspekte des Minderheitenschutzes in der Ära des Völkerbundes und der Vereinten Nationen in Europa* (Springer 1996); Carole Fink, 'Minority Rights as an International Question' (2000) 9 Contemporary European History 385; Nicolas Nachtigall-Marten, *Der Minderheitenschutz des Völkerbundes in Vardar-Mazedonien: Mazedonische Identitäten im Spiegel der Völkerbundakten, 1920–1939* (VDM Verlag 2009); Jane Cowan, 'Who's Afraid of Violent Language?: Honour, Sovereignty, and Claims-Making in the League of Nations' (2003) 3 Anthropological Theory 271.

[50] Cf. James S. Pacy, *Hungary, the League of Nations and the Assassination of King Alexander of Yugoslavia: A Study of the Resolution of an International Political Crisis* (University Microfilms 1979); Peter Burian, *Österreich und der Völkerbund* (Böhlau 1992); Miklós Zeidler, 'Hungary and the League of Nations' in Eniko Dácz, Christina Griessler, and Henriett Kovács (eds), *Traum vom Frieden—Utopie oder Realität? Kriegs- und Friedensdiskurse aus historischer, politologischer und juristischer Perspektive, (1914–2014)* (Nomos 2016).

[51] Miklós Zeidler, 'The League of Nations in Hungary's Thinking about Foreign Policy' (2017) 53 Hungarian Quarterly 170.

Czechoslovak republic, where the League of Nations played an important, but certainly not an exclusive role. This contribution moves the discussion of the role of the League of Nations within the new international order beyond the more conventional consideration of appeasement, international security and great power politics.[52] Small states can be nodes of global order, too.

[52] Cf. Pedersen, 'Back to the League' (n 2) 1093–1906. More recent studies include Martyn Housden, *The League of Nations and the Organisation of Peace* (Pearson Longman 2012); Sami Sarè, *The League of Nations and the Debate on Disarmament (1918–1919)* (Edizioni Nuova cultura 2013); Erin K. Jenne, *Nested Security Lessons in Conflict Management from the League of Nations and the European Union* (Cornell University Press 2015).

1
Habsburg Histories of Internationalism

Glenda Sluga

> This allows us to sum up the lessons of history. Internationalism the feature of our time, is not a new thing, but rather the rule. Nationalism was the new thing. For a time internationalism was in eclipse. Now we are back to it again.
>
> Karl Polanyi, 'Nationalism and Internationalism', *c.* 1945.[1]

In 1945, the Vienna-born intellectual Karl Polanyi was in London typing up lecture notes on *Nationalism and Internationalism*, insisting on his view of a past in which internationalism was 'the rule', and nationalism was 'the new thing'.[2] At first glance, Polanyi's historical perspective seems counterintuitive, particularly in the context of more familiar historical narratives of modern political progress as the progress of national-states. Even the fate of Polanyi's own *multi-national* imperial birthplace appeared to undermine his argument. The 1919 Treaty of St Germain-en-Laye that established the new League of Nations also determined the demise of the defeated Austro-Hungarian empire, granting *post-hoc* international recognition to its seceding national-states: the Austrian, Hungarian, Polish, and Czechoslovak republics, and a Kingdom of Serbs, Croats, and Slovenes. If anything, at the least these developments reinforced wartime characterizations of the Habsburg empire as the *ancien* antagonist of the post-1919 modern national future.[3] Even more radically, I want to argue that the Habsburg and Austrian history of internationalism leads to a different pattern altogether, of the persistent *intersections* of imperial, international, and national politics.

By situating Polanyi's thinking in the context of the new historiography of internationalism which turns on studies of the League of Nations, this chapter explores these points of ideological and institutional intersection in the Habsburg

[1] Karl Polanyi, Lecture—'Nationalism and Internationalism'—Notes, n.d. [annotated typed lecture notes], 9 pp., (Con_18_Fol_35), in Archive Catalogue—'Listing of archival material', Karl Polanyi Digital Archive, Karl Polanyi Institute of Political Economy (KPIPE), Concordia University, California; available online at <http://hdl.handle.net/10694/684> accessed 13 April 2020.

[2] Polanyi is remembered today for *The Great Transformation: The Political and Economic Origins of Our Time* (Farrar & Rinehart 1944).

[3] For this background, see Glenda Sluga, 'Bodies, Souls and Sovereignty: The Austro-Hungarian empire and the legitimacy of nations' (June 2001) 1/2 Ethnicities 207.

Glenda Sluga, *Habsburg Histories of Internationalism* In: *Remaking Central Europe.* Edited by: Peter Becker and Natasha Wheatley, Oxford University Press (2020). © the many contributors. DOI: 10.1093/oso/9780198854685.003.0002

and Austrian past. Half a century after Polanyi, international historians are delving into the archives of international institutions, piecing together a new historical framing of the modern era that draws closer the fates of nations, empires, and an internationalism that was not simply a by-product of Marxist thought. To be sure, on this new view, the 1880s, the same decade in which Polanyi was born, ushered in a 'new internationalism'. As evidence, contemporaries pointed to multiplying international organizations, international laws, and practices.[4] The adherents of this new internationalism placed their faith in progress and peace in international practices (such as intergovernmental conferences on protective labour regulations), international law (most memorably the Hague peace congresses of 1899 and 1907), and the assemblies of endless international organizations (think of the International Council of Women, and the all-male Inter-Parliamentary Union). But this new internationalism was perched on the horizon both to the right and left of contemporary political expectations, it coincided with imperial consolidation of territorial ambitions, and was connected to the rising fortunes of nationalism across that same European and colonial landscape.

In 1919, from this view of Europe as an *International land*, the Geneva-based League of Nations was a belated manifestation of the mainstream political status of nationalism and internationalism, and a persistent imperialism. The Covenant of the League of Nations—like the equally novel Geneva-based International Labour Organization—reinforced and renewed the late nineteenth-century emphasis on 'international co-operation', 'international peace and security', 'international law as the actual rule of conduct among Governments,' and 'the maintenance of justice and a scrupulous respect for all treaty obligations in the dealings of organised peoples with one another'.[5] In the context of the havoc wreaked by the violence of a nationalist war, however, we can detect a heightened sense of urgency surrounding the internationalist expectations heaped on a new international order.

As the arrival of this collection of essays underscores, the history of League-based internationalism has rarely been considered in the context of the Austro-Hungarian, Habsburg, or Austrian pasts. This is despite the close conjunction between the rise of the League and decline of the Habsburg empire. That conjunction is evident in the Treaty conditions which juxtaposed the dismantling of the Habsburg empire and the invention of the League of Nations. It is also reflected in the life of the Jewish bourgeois Polanyi, who, as a young intellectual in Budapest, could not ignore the 'supranational' claims surrounding the form and function of the new intergovernmental organization (even though its jurisdiction was firmly

[4] For an overview, see Glenda Sluga, *Internationalism in the Age of Nationalism* (University of Pennsylvania Press 2013); see also her 'Remembering 1919: international organizations and the future of international order' (January 2019) 95/1 International Affairs 25.

[5] See 'The Covenant of the League of Nations', The Avalon Project—Documents in Law, History and Diplomacy, Lillian Goldman Law Library, Yale Law School, online at: <http://avalon.law.yale.edu/20th_century/leagcov.asp>.

demarcated by the sovereignty of member-states). Nor is it a coincidence that in 1919, Robert Musil, the writer so closely identified with the new Austrian republic, mused on the importance of 'creating a world-political goal!'[6] Musil defined that goal as 'the task of the impulses that have grouped themselves around the idea of a League of Nations'. At a time when Habsburg imperial federalism had been dismantled in the interest of new nation states, Musil set the League idea against 'the evil destiny that attaches itself to the organization of mankind into states'.[7]

By the mid-twentieth century, Polanyi was formulating his distinctive view of nationalism and internationalism against the background of two devastating world wars, *and* the creation of a second more ambitious intergovernmental body, the United Nations Organization. At around the same time, in 1942, Musil died, while in exile in Geneva, leaving behind his masterpiece, *The Man without Qualities*. Although written in the interwar, Musil's novel was set in the prewar of 1913. It mapped out a political and social landscape in which imperial, national, and international imaginaries mingled, and the idea of '*Weltösterreich*'—conventionally translated into English as 'Global Austria'—became a slogan for proclaiming Austria the 'true home of the human spirit everywhere'. Even as the irony in Musil's tone seems to announce itself, we can also hear in *Weltösterreich* echoes of Musil's own internationalist thinking. It captures the prewar feel of intersecting imperial and international imaginaries, of what Musil describes as 'the need to simulate a unity that could govern all of humanity's highly varied activities', but which he also announces as 'lost' 'because the disparity of interests in society had grown so great'.[8]

As I pick my way through the documentary debris of a Habsburg/Austrian past, Musil's conceptualization of *Weltösterreich*/Global Austria is a useful provocation. Drawing from the expanding historiography of international ideas and institutions, on the one hand, and the uncollected evidence of people and politics of the Habsburg empire-*cum*-Austrian republic, on the other, my intention here is to gauge the political, cultural, and economic significance of these strands of the 'new internationalism' in the history of the Habsburg empire, and its afterlife. Overall, this approach allows me to address the broader aims of this breakthrough volume. In this context I emphasise the affinities between the post-First World War history of internationalism and Austria's prewar experience with diversity and multinationality, nowhere more obvious than in the ambitions attached to *Weltösterreich*.

[6] Robert Musil, '"Nation" as Ideal and as Reality (1921)' in Robert Musil, *Precision and Soul: Essays and Addresses* (Burton Pike and David S. Luft, ed. and tr., University of Chicago Press 1990) 101, 115.

[7] Robert Musil, '*Anschluss* with Germany (1919)' in Musil *Precision and Soul* (n 6) 90, 91.

[8] Musil, *Man Without Qualities* (Pan Macmillan 2017) 104.

I. The New Internationalism

The late nineteenth-century European trend to intergovernmental meetings, and 'public international unions' for the discussion of labour and health policies, and the setting of international standards, inspired some observers to see a pattern: the progress of the world was towards larger and more inclusive forms of governance, even towards an 'international land'.[9] As Peter Becker has noted, not all these developments were part of the experience of the Habsburg empire, where international congressing, for example, was relatively unfamiliar.[10] However, in *The Man Without Qualities,* Robert Musil left it to the aristocratic *salonnière* Diotima, a character meant to represent a passing political order, to conceive of a future *Weltösterreich* in the image of the new internationalism. The circumstances, in this case, were the pre-First World War plans for the anticipated (and fictional) seventieth jubilee of the accession of the Austro-Hungarian Emperor Franz Josef as the 'Emperor of Peace' in 1918. In the real prewar period too, individual Habsburg imperial subjects took cameo roles in the denouement of international 'progress' throughout Europe. Some of them, such as the Prague-born Baroness von Suttner—a woman of mixed class descent—have since become central to narratives of internationalism's general appeal, including its pacifist and progressivist liberal connotations.

In 1891 Bertha von Suttner established the first pacifist society in the Habsburg empire, the Austrian Society of Friends of Peace. In addition, she convinced the Swedish Alfred Nobel (an enamoured dynamite manufacturer) to fund a peace prize in his name. Less well-known is her work organizing non-governmental participation in the Hague peace congresses of 1899 and 1904, which established the legal framework for limiting war technologies and arsenals, and the idea of war crimes. In all these contexts, Suttner stood out as a woman leading a network of organizations and actors espousing an international future that would take institutional and legal forms. In general terms, Suttner represents a prewar Austrian-identified generation committed to civil society and international law to the ends of peace, the motifs and characters of which (including herself) made appearances in the storyline of *The Man without Qualities.*[11]

Among this prewar generation too were the Austrian lawyers who became proponents of international law as the core of a new internationalism. Like Suttner, the Vienna University law professor Heinrich Lammasch was no political radical.

[9] See Alfred Hermann Fried, *Das internationale Leben der Gegenwart* (B.G. Teubner 1908).

[10] Peter Becker, 'Von *Listen* und anderen Stolpersteinen auf dem Weg zur Globalisierung. Die Habsburgermonarchie und der Internationalismus des „langen" 19. Jahrhunderts' in Barbara Haider-Wilson, William D. Godsey, and Wolfgang Mueller (eds), *Internationale Geschichte in Theorie und Praxis/International History in Theory and Practice* (Internationale Geschichte/International History 4, Verlag der Österreichischen Akademie der Wissenschaften 2017).

[11] Musil, *Man Without Qualities* (n 8) 18.

Unlike Suttner (who died in June 1914), Lammasch also personally connected the prewar Habsburg history of internationalism with the postwar creation of the League of Nations. Through this period his views combined a conservative monarchism and Christian socialism with faith in the wisdom and power of international legal codes and practices. We can also use Lammasch's law career, as well as legal thinking, as a template for understanding many of his legal contemporaries in Western Europe and across the Atlantic. Their typical *curriculum vitae* would include attendance at both Hague congresses (in his case as Austro-Hungarian legal adviser), and employment at the Hague-based Permanent Court of International Arbitration (in 1911, Lammasch was president).[12] Lammasch also linked his professional past with membership of international associations, in his case, the Inter-Parliamentary Union, and Suttner's Austrian Peace Society, although she thought him *too* legalistic.[13] For all their differences, Suttner's and Lammasch's transnational networks continuously brought them together in the prewar, most prominently in their separate election to bodies of the New York-based Carnegie Foundation for International Peace—another bastion of the new internationalist trend.

Neither the impetus of such internationalist associations, nor the political influence or elite transnational networks of figures such as Lammasch and Suttner, was of course enough to prevent the outbreak of war in 1914. Even so, during the war, conservative and progressive Austrian men and some women (although not Suttner, who died in 1914), continued to ply these same social and political, or legal 'international' routes. The hub of these developments was across the English channel. Within a year of the continental conflict, the efforts of British intellectuals (mainly classicists) and politicians led to the emergence of British societies devoted to the establishment of a League of Nations as a form of international government. By 1918, a number of these societies had unified as the League of Nations Union, and established a model emulated throughout the empire, to the extent that in former colonies such as Australia the League was often confused with British imperial aims. In Europe, local versions were created that were often linked intellectually and personally to the British versions. Thus Austrians were not alone in copying the idea for a League of Nations association, but they were among the first continental Europeans to do so. (A German League of Nations union had appeared slightly earlier, in 1918.) As significantly, an Austrian version of the League of Nations Union made its appearance against the background of the demise of the Habsburg empire.

At the Vienna centre of this phase of the history of internationalism were Lammasch (by then in his sixties), and Joseph Redlich, a jurist and Vienna university law professor. In 1918 both men had roles in the short-lived Habsburg 'cabinet

[12] A.H.F., 'Heinrich Lammasch' (April 1920) 22/1 Die Friedens-Warte 8.

[13] For more on the importance of pacifist organizations, see Daniel Laqua, 'Pacifism in fin-de-siècle Austria: the politics and limits of peace activism' (March 2014) 57/1 Historical Journal 199.

of liquidation'. Redlich, like Lammasch, was part of an expanding network of international lawyers, and personally close to the English intellectuals at the heart of British internationalism, while his American peers described him as a federalist 'child of the Enlightenment'. The anglophile Redlich was briefly Minister of Finance to Lammasch's Prime Minister in this last cabinet of the Austro-Hungarian empire. Later, Redlich would assume a role in the League 'system' as Deputy Judge of the Permanent Court of International Justice at the Hague (1930–36). Amy Ng has argued that Redlich regarded the League of Nations as unworkable because it had no true Anglo-American support—the United States having opted not to join. However, in this early period, before the reticence of the American state was formalized, Redlich's investment was less ambivalent, even if never ostentatious.[14] As for Lammasch, he published an essay entitled 'The Peace Alliance of States', which advocated the mandatory adoption of 'procedures serving the peaceful settlement of disputes as recommended by the Hague Peace Conferences', and the institution of 'an organization of states with as wide-ranging participation as possible'.[15] One scholar suggests that Lammasch was even prepared to conceive of new limitations to the sovereignty of states, 'including not only their right to war but also the right to decide when they want to resort to the use of force'.[16]

The origins of the Austrian League of Nations movement were rooted in the combination of such intellectual and institutional trends. Ideas were fostered in the foment of local wartime associations, many of which espoused expectations contiguous with the pacifist, legal, and economic trends of prewar, law-focused internationalism.[17] In Vienna this included not only lawyers, but also businessmen, at times together. The *Meinl* group was a political circle of Austrian intellectual pacifists established by the businessman Julius Meinl, to serve 'as a platform for public debates and for peace initiatives aiming at the termination of World War I'. Alternatively, Redlich was key in an Austrian version of the Fabians, touting a 'humane' version of socialism, and the more populist *Para Pacem* movement, which was set up to further understanding among peoples, as '*Völkersverstandigung*'.[18]

The story of the Austrian *Völkerbundliga*, headquartered at Burgring 9, Vienna 1, with its sections on economics, rights, transport, press, education, teaching, and ethics, draws us into this almost exclusively male world of politicians, lawyers, and university professors. That exclusivity is particularly apparent when we compare

[14] Amy Ng, *Nationalism and Political Liberty: Redlich, Namier and the crisis of Empire* (Oxford Historical Monographs, Clarendon Press 2004 [& Oxford Scholarship online 2010]).

[15] See Erich Kussbach, 'Heinrich Lammasch, Scholar of Public International Law and Austrian Statesman' (2004) 1/2 Miskolc Journal of International Law 64, 3.

[16] Kussbach, ibid, 3–4.

[17] Helen McCarthy, *The British People and the League of Nations: Democracy, Citizenship and Internationalism c.1918–45* (Manchester University Press 2011); Thomas Richard Davies, 'Internationalism in a Divided World: The Experience of the International Federation of League of Nations Societies, 1919–1939' (April 2012) 37/2 Peace & Change 227, 246.

[18] One of the most famous Fabians was Michael Hainisch, who was later elected Federal President of Austria.

the Austrian and English League of Nations associations—as Helen McCarthy has shown, the English version owed its grass-roots foundations to women's advocacy groups.[19] In Austria that was not the case. Instead, the formation of the *Völkerbundliga* resonated within the networks of Lammasch and Redlich, each of whom was involved in the amalgamation of local pacifist groups into a single Austrian League of Nations society. The overriding intention was to move away from advocacy of a sentimental and humanitarian pacifism towards a more overtly political program promulgating 'the idea of an international peace organisation'. That said, the association's origins were markedly inauspicious, as Redlich's diary records (with characteristic brevity): on 5 February 1919, a retired Habsburg diplomat in his seventies named Constantine Dumba held an 'incredibly silly' meeting of a so-called League of Nations Committee; 'first Dumba spoke, then me; there were approximately 100 people present'.[20] Although Redlich felt he could not go along with the limited Dumba's nonsense, two weeks later an Austrian League of Nations society was formally constituted.

Newly ennobled and implanted in the Austrian Herrenhaus, Constantin Dumba was also part of the *Para Pacem* network, the influence of which was reflected in the Liga's original name: *Österreichischen Liga Für Völkerbund und Völkersverstandigung*. Only later was the society known by a name that echoed the League of Nations—*Österreichischen Völkerbundliga*.[21] Dumba assumed the association's presidency and clung on to the role for two decades.[22] Redlich, despite his disdain for Dumba, became one of two vice-presidents, along with the economist Josef Schumpeter, Lammasch's academic protegé.[23] Lammasch took on the role of the Liga's honorary president, although based at a distance in Salzburg. In some contexts, the *Völkerbundliga* was reinvented as a progressive, even radical, association that would work towards 'a far-reaching reorganisation of the League of Nations', from a body 'promoted by the victors for the permanent protection of their booty into a true League of Peace, in which all civilized nations—victors and vanquished and neutrals alike—would be equal members'.[24]

Völkerbundliga was not the only Austrian body inspired by an internationalist mood and interest in ever-larger political units on the imperative of peace. In early 1919, new ideas for League-inspired groupings were common—from a *Deutschösterreichisch-Italienische Liga*, proposed by Councilor Grunhut from the

[19] McCarthy, *The British People* (n 17) chapters 6 & 7.

[20] See Redlich's diary, F. Fellner (ed), *Schicksalsjahre Österreichs 1908–1919: Das politische Tagebuch Josef Redlichs, II. Band 1915–1919* (Verlag Hermann Böhlaus Nachf 1954) 492.

[21] Österreichischen Völkerbundliga, *Heinrich Lammasch und der Völkerbund. Die Gedenkfeier der Österreichischen völkerbundliga für ihren Ehrenpräsidenten* (Verlag der Österreichischen Liga für Völkerbund und Völkerverständigung 1920).

[22] Constantin Dumba, *Memoirs of a Diplomat* (foreword by Joseph Redlich, George Allen & Unwin 1933) 314.

[23] While the Ministerial Councillor and pacifist Arthur Miller was appointed the Liga's Secretary-General and Friedrich Moc, its Treasurer: Dumba, ibid, 315.

[24] Dumba, ibid, 316.

Ministry of Labour, to a League for a Free Economy suggested by the entrepreneur Meinl.[25] Then there was the *Institut für Kulturforschung* (also known as the Institute for Research of Mankind) established in 1915 by a relatively unknown figure, Erwin Hanslik, to promote *Weltkultur und Weltpolitik*. Hanslik's concept became the hallmark of a wartime Austrian and German publication series and drew in men of the cultural and political calibre of Walter Rathenau, Georg Simmel, Oskar Kokoschka, and Egon Schiele.[26] In 1920, with a League of Nations in operation, and Austria reduced to national status, Hanslik renamed his cause the Institute for World Culture (World-Science, Art and Education), boasting its own *Weltkulturgesellschaft* (or Society for World Culture).

Hanslik ran the Institute and wrote around twenty books on Geography, Sociology, Anthropology, and Politics with 'the unity of civilization' as their common theme. Within and across these categories he drew on the new *Völkerpsychologie*, as well as on social data on the status of women and levels of education, as tools for distinguishing between people. This was of course only one intellectual trend out of which the idea of a *Weltkultur* was born during the war, and from which connections to the League were made in the postwar.[27] As importantly, Hanslik repeatedly emphasised the 'world' context of Austria: '*Die Menschheit*', he argued, '*ist des Österreichers wahres Vaterland*' ['humanity is the true fatherland of Austrians'], or '*Österreich ist ein viel verwickelterer Kosmos des Zusammenlebens als alle westlichen Einzelstaaten*' ['Austria is a more complex cosmos of cohabitation than all the Western states'].[28]

In the mode of the *Völkerbundliga*, the legitimacy of Hanslik's World Culture Institute drew on the weight of its representative expertise rather than the actual number of members. During the last years of the war 1917, the Institute attracted the likes of Otto Wagner and Gustav Klimt, as well as Josef Hoffmann, Oskar Strand, Joseph Matthias Hauer, and Adolf Loos.[29] (The Institute continued to claim Klimt, Wagner, and Schiele as honorary members even after they died.) At the same time it relied on the financial support of the industrialist, art lover, and philanthropist, Dr Victor Ritter von Bauer. Hanslik took the role of one of its Scientific

[25] Diary entry for Sonntag 23 März [Sunday, 23 March] in Fellner, *Schicksalsjahre Österreichs* (n 20) 106.

[26] Exploring the new 'Weltkultur Gemeinschaft'—this was the work, in the main, of Erwin Hanslik (published in Munich), the Society for World Culture, or, originally, the wartime-established Institut für Kulturforschung [Institute for Cultural Investigation]. LONA, section 10C, 718963, 1916, 'World Culture and World Politics: Austrian Signature Series', edited by the Institut für Kulturforschung in Vienna and Ernst Jadh in Berlin, and published by F. Brudmann in Munich.

[27] The series was published by Bruckmann Verlag, München, in 1916. Individual books featured maps, onto which Hanslik visualised data regarding geology, climate, and the demography of a world population, divided into geographical settlement areas East and West Urvölker, Europe, India, and East Asia.

[28] LONA, section 10C, 718963, 1917, by Professor Dr Erwin Hanslik of the Institut für Kulturforschung: a/ 'Austria: Earth and Spirit'; b/ 'Humanity Through 30 World Maps'.

[29] This institution connected in 1917 with Stockholm to create a Büro für Kulturforschung and brought Schiele into the circle.

directors (*Wissenschaftliche Leitung*), while Dresden-based Kokoschka was named Artistic director (*Künstlerische Leitung*).[30]

In 1920 Hanslik and Kokoschka decided to approach the League of Nations in Geneva on behalf of the *Weltkulturgesellschaft*, working in the first instance through the Austrian embassy in London. They hoped that they could use Austrian diplomats to offer the League the Institute's help in realizing a world cultural mission—on the assumption that the League was in pursuit of this same mission. They wrote to the League's Secretary-General that they would help the League of Nations work for 'a consciousness of the unity of the world so far nonexistent on the continent of Europe'. The Institute for World Culture would generate that consciousness among people of diverse languages through Kokoschka's concept of 'visual consciousness': 'a uniform international system of education based on Object-Teaching conceived on the foundation of its work', which they presented as 'WORLD SCIENCE' (the capitalization was theirs). The League of Nations' executive was invited 'to join the Society, to facilitate the creation of an International Institute for World Culture', and to grant its representatives 'exterritorial' status—a concept that resonated both diplomatic norms and prewar Habsburg conceptions of cultural identity disconnected from territorial sovereignty.[31]

While it is clear that League bureaucrats were not interested in the *Institut für Kulturforschung*, Hanslik and Kokoschka's ambitions offer further evidence of the Habsburg-inflected international imaginaries that reached into different corners of society and politics in the lands of the former empire, during the war and after. Hanslik and Kokoschka argued that Vienna and the Habsburg empire were beacons 'showing the direction in which this old outpost of civilization may once more be called upon to perform an important function in the future organisation of the world'—intimating that it might represent major League functions, both in symbol and practice.[32] From this view, as in the case of the British League societies, which were as likely to reference the British empire, among Austrian league supporters there was a conscious connection between the Habsburg imperial past and international future. The Austrian idea of *Weltösterreich* resonated the experiences of the Habsburg empire as an amalgam of diverse nationalities.

It is somewhat ironic, then, that in 1919 the twin principles of the new international order—nationality on the one hand, and the League of Nations on the other—generated actual new patterns for the organization of the lands of the former Habsburg empire that undermined the international ambitions associated

[30] Edmund Küttler (a student of Orientalism and Ethnography, and PhD from the University of Vienna) was the other 'Scientific Director'.

[31] LONA, section 13, 7521, 13 October 1920, letter from the Austrian Legation, London, to the Secretary General of the League of Nations.

[32] LONA, section 13, series 4601–10500: a/ undated, Society for World Culture, Vienna, 1; and b/, 1920, letter from Professor Dr Erwin Hanslik and Oskar Kokoschka, of the Society for World Culture, to the Chief Secretary of the League of Nations, 1.

with *Weltösterreich*. Even in this context, the Habsburg experience could be invoked as having set precedents for the League of Nations. Dumba, for instance, happily took credit for the League's emphasis on minority representation. At the World Union's meeting in Vienna, in 1921 (the first to which the still pariah Austrians were invited), he claimed Austrians were 'the first to touch on the important question of minorities'.[33] In celebrating this achievement, Dumba declared his own version of a nation-based international vision:

> Each people has a kind of natural right to cherish and reverence these intellectual ideals by which the soul finds expression. [...] it is the duty of all lovers of peace to defend their imperishable heritage [...] the only way which leads to lasting peace.[34]

The impact of the League version of nation-based internationalism is obvious in the ways in which the multiplication of pro-League organizations within the new Central European nations both mirrored and distorted the national question in the older imperial order. We still know little about each of these societies, or the multiple motivations of their members, except that an association with League unions (as much as membership of the actual League of Nations) was regarded as a useful instrument for sovereign ambitions and recognition.[35] In June 1923 the seventh conference of the International Federation of League Unions held in the Vienna Hofburg was eagerly attended by new League societies representing minorities within the rump Austrian republic, as well as the nation states that had been carved out of the territory of the former Habsburg empire. The new Czecho-Slovakia was represented at the conference by two bodies: the Czecho-Slovak and the Czecho-Slovak German Associations. Both 'followed with a close assiduity' the work of the League of Nation's Commission of Minorities.[36] At the 1926 International Federation annual conference, the number of league societies carrying a Czecho-Slovak banner had multiplied to four: the Czecho-Slovak National Association for the League of Nations, the *Deutsche Liga für Völkerbund und Völkerverstandigung in der Tschechoslovakischen Republik*, the Hungarian League for the League of Nations in the Czech Republic, and the Jewish Association for the League of Nations in Czech-Slovakia.[37] Meanwhile the Austrian delegation itself fielded two groups: the *Österreichischen Völkerbundliga* and the *Judische Völkerbundliga*

33 Dumba, *Memoirs of a Diplomat* (n 22) 320.

34 Ibid, 321.

35 LONA, section 22, 12579, 8 June 1921, bulletin of the 5th conference of the International Federation of League of Nations Societies; LONA, section 22, 30323, 23 June 1923, programme for the 7th congress of the International Federation of League of Nations Societies.

36 The stories of the creation of the Czechoslovak League of Nations Association (like that of the Hungarian one, and others in the former Habsburg lands after empire) remain to be told. LONA, section 22, 24444, 12594, 1922, report of the International Federation of League of Nations Societies, 19.

37 Societé de la Paix Chelcicky, section 22, 30323, 23 June 1923, programme for the 7th congress of the International Federation of League of Nations Societies; LONA, section 22, 37074, 12594, 27 June 1924, programme for the 8th congress of the International Federation of League of Nations Societies;

für Österreich.[38] The following year, the Austrian delegation was split between the *Österreichischen Völkerbundliga*, the *Judische Völkerbundliga für Österreich*, and the Slavic Minorities Association.[39]

By contrast, the Habsburg biographies of Austrian supporters of the League of Nations also resonated a distinctive multi-national and trans-national past: Dumba was of Greek-Austrian bourgeois origins as well as being the last Habsburg ambassador to the United States, under Wilson's regime; Karl Polanyi was the Jewish son of a railway entrepreneur, whose real name Pollacsek spoke to his diverse Habsburg origins; Redlich could be described as Moravian, Jewish, German; Hanslik was born in 1889 in Galicia, in the bilingual *slawisch–deutsch* town of Bielitz/Biala, to a Roman Catholic factory worker and a washerwoman. Hanslik's educational background too counted in his formation as a 'world'-focused internationalist, as he went on to study in Vienna under Professor Eduard Suess, a liberal politician, professor of paleontology, and coiner of the term 'biosphere'.[40] Then there is Robert Musil himself. Born in 1880 in Klagenfurt, of a noble family with connections to the Hungarian lands of Transylvania and Czech-inflected Bohemia, Musil was on the cusp of his thirtieth year when the League of Nations was established. As we have already seen, his writing from that time reveals an engagement with the ideas that led to the League's creation. The sense of a League *zeitgeist* appears in his essay from that time, 'Anschluss with Germany' (1919), as 'the spirit of humanity which is rising up on all sides', and as 'the movement that has now begun in reaction to war and social injustice [that] has assumed the forms of the League of Nations'. On Musil's view, what stood in the way of this spirit was 'the state—not as an administrative organism, but as a spiritual-moral entity'.[41]

As significantly, Musil evaluated the actually existing League of Nations as 'an association of states [that] reveals itself as ever more grotesque' because it manifested the national more than the international; 'nothing', he explained, 'more

LONA, section 22, 52205, 12594, May 1926, the League of Nations Societies and their International Federation.

38 The Society of Austrian Jews had applied for League of Nations membership in 1924, at the 8th conference of the International Federation (its delegates included Dr I. Margulies and Dr Karbach), LONA, section 22, 37074, 12594, 27 June 1924, programme for the 8th congress of the International Federation of League of Nations Societies.

39 Delegates from the Austrian League included Constantin Dumba (chairman and former ambassador), Joseph L. Kunz (secretary), Friedrich Spitzer (assistant director of the Austrian bank Creditanstalt), Dr Stolz (professor at the University of Innsbruck), Ernst Mumelter (former district chief of Bozen), Robert Breza (Ministerialrat), Alain Stuchly-Lux. Delegates from the Jewish League included Dr Goldhammer, Dr Davied Rothblum and Dr Oskar Karbach. Delegates from the Slavic Minorities Association included Anton Machat (municipal councillor of Vienna) and Arthur Kantor. LONA, section 22, 59176, 12594, 24 May 1927, programme for the 11th congress of the International Federation of League of Nations Societies.

40 Franz Smola, 'Vom "Menschenbewusstsein" zum neuen Menschenbild—Egon Schiele und der Anthropogeograph Erwin Hanslik' in Leander Kaiser and Michael Ley (eds), *Die ästhetische Gnosis der Moderne* (Passagen Verlag 2008) 123.

41 Robert Musil, 'Anschluss with Germany (1919)' in Musil, *Precision and Soul* (n 6) 90; 91.

nefarious stands in the way of a natural ordering of human society than the arrogance that the two ideals of nation and state show toward human beings'.[42] His diary entries for this period reveal him closely parsing the implications of the new international world order, and the statehood version of nation and nationalism it entrenched: 'The "Idea" of world unity was so alien to "Realpolitik" thinking with its orientation toward nationalism and the state, it seemed so utopian to them, that they were obviously unable to give it serious consideration.'[43]

It could be argued that, at the end of the First World War, the Habsburg-induced cultural internationalism of men such as Hanslik and Kokoschka, and even Musil, was more ambitious than the political internationalism of the League of Nations itself. Hanslik's Institute presented the League's (British) Secretary-General with the idea of Vienna's specific 'international mission', owing to its 'geographical situation, [...] its ancient culture evolved out of a mutual penetration of different races'. It was League bureaucrats who simply dismissed the Institute's plans as premature.[44]

II. 'Austria [and] What the League has done for Austria'[45]

In 1919, the particular circumstances of the League's invention coinciding with the Habsburg empire's demise drew ambivalent reactions. Redlich's diary denounced the American president Woodrow Wilson as a doctrinaire without any heart who had discredited the League project. Dumba recalled that 'The great majority of Austrians would hear nothing of the League of Nations of which the Covenant formed the opening clause of the fateful peace treaties'.[46] This included Part IV of the Treaty of Versailles, which required the Habsburg monarchy to give up territory, economic rights and interests inside and outside Europe. In effect this meant that in Morocco a French Protectorate replaced Habsburg rule, and mining, property, shares and banks were all passed on to the French. In Egypt, Britain benefited. In Siam and China, Austria-Hungarian leases were returned to the sovereign state. Each of these territorial re-occupations reminds us, firstly, that *Weltösterreich* stood for Austria as an imperial-colonizing space, not simply the aspirations of Habsburg or Austrian subjects for international status and internationalist thinking. Secondly, the demise of the Habsburg empire did not coincide with the demise of imperialism overall: other European empires assumed Austrian privileges. Indeed, the League of Nations mandate system saw the transfer of the colonies

42 Robert Musil, '"Nation" as Ideal and Reality (1921)' in ibid, 115.

43 From 'Notebook 19: 1919 to 1921', in Mark Mirsky (ed), Robert Musil, *Diaries 1899–1941* (Philip Payne sel., tr., an.; Basic Books 1999) 269.

44 The decision was taken by the Deputy Secretary-General, Nitobe: LONA, section 13, 7521, 13 October 1920, letter from the Austrian Legation, London, to the Secretary-General of the League of Nations.

45 This is the title of a British League of Nations Union pamphlet, 1923.

46 Dumba, *Memoirs of a Diplomat* (n 22) 315.

of the defeated powers to the trust of victor powers (British, French, Australian, New Zealand, Japanese), and the League's Permanent Mandates Commission was given the weak role of moral 'guardian'.

The tension between an imperial and international League of Nations percolated through other arenas of postwar Austrian life, most prominently when the League was invited to intervene in Austria's "Hunger Catastrophe". The path to this experiment in international economic governance was prepared by Dumba, who used the 1921 meeting of the International Federation of the League of Nations' societies in Vienna to ask for financial assistance—a loan from the Entente of $US250,000,000.[47] A year later, in October 1922, the League of Nations itself stepped in on the formal request of Ignaz Seipel, President and Chancellor of the new Austria. For the first time in international history, an inter-governmental organization offered immediate food aid along with a long-term plan for capital supplies from financiers, who presented their motivation as an 'humanitarian impulse'.[48]

The economic historian Patricia Clavin has argued that the financial reconstruction of Austria constituted a crucial episode in the League's reinvention of itself as the instrument of a 'liberal, capitalist world order', and as the guarantee of the 'common economic needs' that would stabilize international relations to 'make the world anew and to guarantee peace'.[49] The League of Nations package—the so-called Geneva Protocol—offered Austria fiscal assistance in exchange for 'a rigorous programme of fiscal retrenchment'. That is, Austria was required to cut food subsidies and slash state expenditure. The League's financial 'dictatorship', as Clavin describes it, was overseen by the League-appointed Commissioner General, Alfred Rudolph Zimmerman, a former mayor of Rotterdam, who exercised extraordinary powers 'to determine when and where Seipel's government disbursed or cut expenditure'.[50] Within six months, the Geneva Protocol had helped stabilize Austria's economy, and within a year the national budget was in black, although at the expense of the larger population. Regardless, League officials touted Austria as a success story and used it as a template for tackling other economic crises in Hungary and Germany in the 1920s. The British League of Nations Union announced the League intervention as a prime example of 'Self-help and international co-operation'; 'the League alone', it said, 'had sufficient moral authority to induce Austria to make the first difficult but necessary steps towards self-help'. Financial experts—including the American banker J.P. Morgan, and the Governor

[47] LONA, section 22, 10490, 1921, meeting between representatives of the Italian, German, Austrian, Hungarian and Bulgarian League of Nations Unions, 2.

[48] Patricia Clavin, 'The Austrian hunger crisis and the genesis of international organization after the First World War' (March 2014) 90/2 International Affairs 265, 271.

[49] Clavin, 'The Austrian hunger crisis' (n 48) 265–266.

[50] Ibid, 266; 276–7.

of the Bank of England Montagu Norman—were celebrated as the heroes of the operation.[51]

While the League of Nation's economic intervention was invited by the Austrian government, its austerity policy further corroded 'Austrian attitudes towards international cooperation and with regard to internationalism'.[52] Austrian Social Democrats, including the key architects of the more innovative conceptions of nationality in the old empire, Otto Bauer and Karl Renner, came out swinging against the League. Each spoke up in the Austrian parliament against the Geneva Protocol and its 'enslavement' of the Austrian people.[53] In their view, Geneva and its 'general komissar' were quasi colonial powers imposing a'bourgeois capitalist order'.[54]

Consideration of the diverse strands of Habsburg and Austrian engagement with international ideas, institutions, and practices—including the spectrum of left- and right-wing internationalist thought—as well as the complexity of the League's own bureaucracy, prevents us from too simple a reduction of the League's significance as simply capitalist or elitist, or even as a proxy for the victor imperial powers.[55] These nuances of intersecting prewar internationalisms and their unpredictable meeting points in post-imperial Austrian economic life were also in evidence at the 1927 League-organized World Economic Conference, when the Bohemian-born Emmy Freundlich was given a voice (because an international women's association insisted she be invited).[56] Freundlich was a prominent social democrat in the era of imperial Austria, and a leader of the international cooperative movement. She had close connections with English socialist and cooperative organizations, which she herself thought of as closely identified with the aims of the League, as she argued in 1927: 'To co-operators the birth of the League of Nations represented the dawn of a new era, because they were convinced that the League, though a government creation, would gradually come more and more under popular influence'.[57] Freundlich's aim in making this identification of mutuality, was to argue for a 'new economic evolution' leading to a 'democratic cooperative' method of the economic organization at a world level, 'a fixed tradition that women should take part in all discussions that concern the human race as a whole'.[58] The detail of that economic

[51] See League of Nations Union, *Austria. What the League has done for Austria* (League of Nations Union November 1923) 10.

[52] Clavin, 'The Austrian hunger crisis' (n 48) 277.

[53] *'Der Genfer Knechtungsvertrag [contract that enslaves people] und die Sozialdemokratie Rede des Abgeordneten Otto Bauer auf dem Socialdemokratischen Parteitag in Wien am 14 Oktober 1922'* (Verlag der Wiener Völksbuchandlung 1922).

[54] Karl Seitz, *Die Schmach von Genf und die Republik* (Verlag der Wiener Völksbuchandlung 1922) 31.

[55] See the essays in Glenda Sluga and Patricia Clavin (eds), *Internationalisms: A Twentieth-Century History* (Cambridge University Press 2016 [online 2017]).

[56] See Glenda Sluga, 'Women, feminisms and twentieth-century internationalisms' in ibid, 61.

[57] LONA, section 10C, 59187, 46431, 5 May 1927, International Economic Conference, Record of the Third Plenary Sessions Speeches given by Zimmerman (Netherlands), Freundlich (Austria), von Siemens (Germany), and Shidachi (Japan); LONA, 48847, 1926 Mission of Mlle Radziwill to Vienna, I 1604 5801 580.

[58] Ibid.

organization was reducing custom tariffs *and* 'economic governance of prices, as well as representation for women and consumers' through cooperative societies.[59]

Evidence of the engagement of 'non-state actors' as well as state actors with the League of Nations indicates that through the interwar the League continued to be a focus of international thinking in the lands of the former Habsburg empire. A range of economic, cultural, and political Austrian interests sought and found a platform in internationalism under a Habsburg or *Weltösterreich* umbrella in the first decades of the twentieth century: not only Freundlich's cooperative ideal, but also Vienna-born Friedrich Hayek's influence as a League consultant on business statistics in this period, and the organizations in the region whose members imagined the League as an instrument of free trade, the cause pursued by the Austrian jurist and politician Franz Klein, and by Dumba, when he directed the *Völkerbundliga* to lobby for a European customs union.

Despite the social, political and economic provocations of the Geneva Protocol, there is a longer through-line of political and economic imaginaries which reinforced the relevance of internationalism in that area. Often those imaginaries drew on a vision of the Habsburg empire as the beacon of the international future rather than the past. In the interwar and after, however, Vienna, rather than Austria, became the more common focus of these deliberate connections between the imperial past and an international future. In 1927 there were explicit moves by local governments to relocate the League of Nation's seat to Vienna. Although in the Habsburg period Vienna had been an unlikely centre of international congressing, in the interwar the city was an eager host of international events: including the 1921 International Women's Conference; the 1922 International Postal Union Conference; and the 1926 Paneuropa Congress; as well as the annual meetings of the International Federation of League Societies. From the Geneva side, bureaucrats and delegates who complained about the Swiss city's climate, bad transportation, and its constrictive political atmosphere, were not averse to the prospect of Vienna as home—Vienna, it was argued, was full of empty palaces that could even save the League money.[60] The appeal of Vienna lost its traction only once the League of Nations had taken the decision to build the Palais des Nations on Lake Geneva—the expansive building that, belatedly, became the iconic image of interwar internationalism. That said, Vienna still occasionally, and briefly grabbed headlines: in 1932 when it was mooted as the site of the League's Disarmament conference; and in late 1944, at the hand of the British progressive intellectual Dorothy Thompson who touted Vienna as the *natural* home for the League's replacement.[61]

[59] E. Freundlich, 'The Coöperative Movement in the Present World Order' (1935) 180/1 The ANNALS of the American Academy of Political and Social Science 119.

[60] See Andreas Resch and Dieter Stiefel, 'Vienna: The Eventful History of a Financial Center' in Gunter Bischof (ed), *Global Austria: Austria's Place in Europe and the World* (Innsbruck University Press 2011) 117.

[61] Eric Frey, 'Konferenzplatz Wien: Vienna as an International Conference Site' in Bischof, *Global Austria* (n 60) 147.

Should we imagine that by the mid-twentieth century Hanslik's vision of Vienna as a world centre was coming to the fore? Not quite. International Vienna carried mixed messages. Seipel wanted Vienna as the capital of a 'reconstructed Austro-Hungarian Monarchy, a Central European empire'.[62] Polanyi, for his part, would record 1944 as a time when internationalism (even as the rule) had been reduced 'to an exclusivist and imperialist ideology, a vehicle of oppression rather than emancipation'.[63] By then, Hanslik, who had been institutionalized at the Am Steinhof, a Vienna institution for *Geistes und Nervenkranke*, was one of 3200 patients deported to Hartheimin Oberösterreich. There he was killed, a victim of Nazi anti-internationalist ideology that systematically murdered psychiatric patients.[64]

III. Conclusion

Through the first half of the twentieth century, individuals from the Habsburg lands were keen inventors as well as interpreters of the main trends of the new liberal internationalism. Their efforts, like the League of Nations and the complex of organizations and networks that it encompassed in the interwar years take us—as it took so many of its adherents and employees—back and forth across a sea of international objectives, methods and obstacles. Swathes of this social history of the internationalist past and its imperial and nationalist inflections has long remained unexplored terrain. Bringing together what we do know adds to the existing historiography of internationalism the evidence of a spectrum of political and intellectual elites from the left and right of European politics engaged with the promise of internationalism, whether in its political, cultural, or economic manifestations. In the lawyer Lammasch's posthumously published 1920 *Völkermord oder Völkerbund?*, a critique of the League was layered in arguments about its failure to meet the expanse of his expectations.[65] 'An effective "league of peace"', Lammasch supposed, 'must transform the 'recommendations' of the [1899 and 1907] Hague [Peace] Conferences into legal obligations, it must embrace within its jurisdiction all disputes, including those affecting vital interests as well as those hitherto regarded as justiciable, and it must create a sanction to enforce the observance of the law.'[66] Lammasch associated ambitions for the League with a longer history of international thinking, perpetual peace, and a *Weltrepublik*. But he also inserted the urgency of those ambitions in the contemporary context of the postwar, '[t]he

[62] Ignaz Seipel, *Nation und Staat* (Braumüller 1916) 322.

[63] Karl Polanyi, Lecture—'Nationalism and Internationalism'—Notes, n.d., (Con_18_Fol_35), in Archive Catalogue—'Listing of archival material', Karl Polanyi Digital Archive (KPIPE).

[64] Franz Smola, 'Vom "Menschenbewusstsein" zum neuen Menschenbild' (n 40) 124.

[65] Dr. Heinrich Lammasch, *Völkermord oder Völkerbund?*, written for a German-speaking audience, with a preface by Prof. Hans Sperll, University of Vienna (Martinus Nijhoff 1920).

[66] Ibid, 8.

devastation and depopulation of Europe, the brutalization of Nations, the demise of European culture'. The body he imagined was nothing like the real League; it was a 'powerful organization,' an 'all civilized [*sic*] countries comprehensive League of Nations,' with the power 'to compel the nations, their differences and conflicts,' in order to avoid 'physical and moral genocide'.[67]

Although Austria rarely appears in historical accounts of the creation of the League, during the late imperial era, its citizens debated, discussed, and promoted their views of internationalism and its scope in relation to an empire imagined as *Weltösterreich*. Lammasch's words echo the resonant imperialism integral to interwar institutionalised internationalism, with its knee-jerk distinction between 'civilized' and un-civilized countries, and, in the Austrian case, Habsburg nostalgia. In the latter case (as was also true of enduring British imperial imaginaries), imperial government was idealised as a landscape of national diversity managed in ways commensurate with the unifying aims of internationalism. *Völkermord oder Völkerbund?* can be read as a view onto the Habsburg empire as a *Völkerbund*, and its intellectual life as an alternative rendering of a model for making nationalism and internationalism compatible.

There are echoes of this view of the internationalist potential of prewar and postwar Austria in the prewar writing of Robert Musil, who, in 1912, took a circumspect view of the latent possibilities of the empire and the 'secret idea' it harboured: 'It is not the idea of the state, not the dynastic principle, not the idea of a cultural symbiosis of different peoples (Austria could be a world experiment)'.[68] However, postwar nation-state Austria, on his view, was 'grotesque', 'nothing but a particular clearcut case of the modern world'.[69]

If we return to Karl Polanyi, his place in this history draws our attention back to the still misunderstood engagement of socialists with the ambitions of prewar and interwar internationalism.[70] In the immediate postwar Polanyi was in Budapest, where, Redlich duly alleged in his diary, he was a 'member/leader of the Budapest bolsheviks and *Führer des Galilei*-Clubs'.[71] While Redlich's account of his compatriot's sympathies has been questioned, in 1942, the story Polanyi told of internationalism as 'the rule' premised a liberal, rather than Marxist, internationalism. On Polanyi's historical view, internationalism had its high point in the early nineteenth century, when a Mazzinian vision of nationhood simultaneously embraced 'international brotherhood'.

67 A.H.F., 'Heinrich Lammasch' (n 12) 8.

68 Musil, 1912, cited in Stefan Jonsson, *Subject without Nation: Robert Musil and the History of Modern Identity* (Duke University Press 2000) 267–8.

69 Robert Musil, 'Little Notebook without a Number: At the latest 1916, to 1918–1919', in Philip Payne (ed), *Diaries 1899–1941* (Basic Books 1999) 193, 201.

70 See Patrizia Dogliani, 'The Fate of Socialist Internationalism' in Sluga and Clavin, *Internationalisms* (n 55) chapter 3.

71 Joseph Redlich, 'Freitag 2. Mai' in Fellner, *Schicksalsjahre Österreichs* (n 20) 342.

There were of course other versions of Austrian socialist internationalism, as we have seen in the case of Emmy Freundlich (who also reminds us that not all international thinkers were men). A distinctive bureaucratic, rather than economic emphasis, encouraged the liberal (imperial/national) internationalism of Egon Ranshofen-Wertheimer, an avowed Austrian Social Democrat. In 1944, Ranshofen-Wertheimer promoted the now all-but defunct League as a model for a new kind of postwar international organization, alongside the example of institutional multi-national governance set by the Habsburg empire itself.

Born in 1894, in Ranshofen, upper Austria, a Catholic with Jewish roots, Egon Ranshofen was twenty when the First World War broke out. He would recall of his time as 'a frontline soldier' that the experience of three gruelling years in three European theatres of war made him vow never to forget what he had gone through along with millions of his contemporaries: 'While I was not a League of Nations man, I was a believer in international organisation'.[72] In 1930, Ranshofen actually took up employment at the League of Nations, remaining there for ten years in its Social Questions section, but he had never, he claimed, 'felt the urge to watch the League in action, nor belonged to a League of Nations Association, nor even so much as looked into a League document'. Nevertheless, during the final years of the Second World War, this former League employee turned his hand to writing a study of the League secretariat and its achievements as a guide to the formation of the League's successor organization, the United Nations. The rather dull-titled *The International Secretariat—A Great Experiment in International Administration* (1944) referred the reader back to the example of a 'multinational civil service' that had been in existence for hundreds of years in the Centre of Europe.[73] This was the only reference that Ranshofen indulged in resuscitating 'the Austrian experience'. But he took the moment to issue an historical lesson. If that experience 'had been studied by the pioneers of the League Secretariat', he insisted,

> [I]t might have suggested that existing cleavages even strong disaffection, can be counterbalanced or more than counterbalanced by a common administrative loyalty, by common social and material conditions. This might have conveyed the important lesson that supranational loyalty was possible even if full harmony among the members composing the international organisation should not be achieved. But who could have expected the League's creators to ponder this lesson of the past at the very moment when the Dual Monarchy

[72] Ranshofen-Wertheimer and Egon F., *The International Secretariat: A Great Experiment in International Administration* (Carnegie Studies in the Administration of International Law and Organization 3, Carnegie Endowment for International Peace 1945) ix.

[73] Ibid, 77–9.

had dissolved into her component parts under the impact of the explosive forces of nationalism.[74]

By the mid-twentieth century the different strands of intellectual and political and economic thought that fed nostalgia for *Weltösterreich*, and vice-versa, had become—at least in the minds of those who could remember—the fabric of internationalism on a UN-scale. The League did take on some lessons from the Habsburg past. By 1929, the Council of the League of Nations adopted as policy the suggestions of the Austrian *Völkerbundliga*: minority complaints should be published and brought to the attention of every member of the League and thereby given a hearing in the public opinion of the whole world. We could even argue that if Hanslik had lived to see the end of the war, he would have heard the resonant tones of his much earlier ambitions in the 'world citizenship' cultural program of the UN in its early years, and in UNESCO's own post-Second World War cultural internationalism.

These developments took form through the actions and thinking of individuals, women and men. *Weltösterreich* coincided with the moment of *Weltkultur*, world citizenship and world government, thanks to the intellectual and political work of Habsburg/Austrian subject/citizens. Even world government was the idea of another Habsburg citizen, the Budapest-born Rosika Schwimmer, who conjured the movement out of disillusionment with the League's limitations, and on the foundations of her personal statelessness in a nation state bound world that discriminated against women.[75] When we return to such examples of unequal diversity, the significance of internationalism in the Habsburg context also makes sense, even its permeation of the narrative arc in Musil's *The Man Without Qualities*—as it moves from the *Weltösterreich* of the aristocratic Diotima's peace campaign, to the intertwined fate of Rachel, 'Diotima's housemaid, a poor Jewish girl from remote Galicia', and Soliman, 'a young African' servant 'usually referred to as the Moor'. As war descends, they become lovers, and pose for us the most radical possibility of a future *Weltösterreich* world, 'the Austrian-African-Jew'.[76]

The imposing patterns of the first half of the twentieth century were of mutually reinforcing and messily conjoining waves of nationalism and internationalism. When we survey the imperial and republican phases of internationalism, Polanyi and Musil represent the more high-profile examples of a broader array of bourgeois and aristocratic, imperial and post-imperial, Central European contemporaries who were more likely to identify their Habsburg past and present *with* an international future, than *against* it. The voices of the working class were more likely to

74 Ibid, 78.

75 See Glenda Sluga, 'Women, feminisms and twentieth-century internationalisms', in Sluga and Clavin, *Internationalisms* (n 55).

76 Jonsson, *Subject without Nation* (n 68) 245.

associate themselves with an alternative socialist internationalism, or 'Red Vienna', and oriented away from the League as an instrument of international capitalism as much as international cooperation. In sum, the Habsburg/Austrian past was embedded in international developments and the simultaneously international/imperial/national legacies of the 1919 peace. From some perspectives that past is still considered a world experiment that 'anticipates fundamental features of the concepts of hybridity, border culture and métissage'.[77]

[77] Ibid, 265.

PART I

REMAKING ACTORS AND NETWORKS

2
Clemens Pirquet
Early Twentieth-Century Scientific Networks, the Austrian Hunger Crisis, and the Making of the International Food Expert

Michael Burri

I. The Birth of the Food Expert Out of the Spirit of War

Few public figures emerged from the political, professional, and human wreckage of the First World War better situated to contribute to the future of the new Austrian Republic than the pioneer of allergy research Clemens von Pirquet. Thanks to his development of the 1907 'Pirquet test', a groundbreaking diagnostic innovation that uses a skin reaction to establish a positive indication for tuberculosis, Pirquet possessed stellar scientific credentials and high name recognition abroad. Locally, as director of the Children's Hospital at University of Vienna (*Universitäts-Kinderklinik*), said to be the largest and most modern in the world when he presided over its opening in 1911, Pirquet occupied an exemplary position in a long tradition of medical elites in Vienna.[1] And though the wartime crisis reduced his usual staff of seven assistants to just one, he himself remained shielded from military service.[2] Privately, Pirquet had written to an American colleague in 1915, asking for his assistance in keeping the United States neutral during the war. But publicly, Pirquet remained a notably subdued Austrian patriot, largely advocating for public health campaigns against tuberculosis and smallpox.[3]

This chapter traces the professional ascent of Clemens Pirquet, the subdued patriot of 1915, who, while remaining director of the *Kinderklinik*, would subsequently become a central figure in the international postwar humanitarian relief effort in Austria, and a contributing expert at the League of Nations Health Organization in the 1920s. During the hunger crisis that gripped early postwar Vienna, Pirquet administered American Relief Administration (ARA) resources for all Austria,

[1] Karl H. Spitzy and Inge Lau, *Van Swietens Erbe. Die Wiener Medizinische Schule heute in Selbstdarstellungen* (Maudrich 1982) 64. The standard overview on the medical tradition is Erna Lesky, *The Vienna Medical School of the 19th Century* (L. Williams and I. S. Levij trs, JHU Press 1976).
[2] Richard Wagner, *Clemens von Pirquet: His Life and Work* (JHU Press 1968) 117.
[3] See, for example, *Neue Freie Presse* [16 January 1915] 15. *Mährisches Tagblatt* [2 March 1915] 7.

Michael Burri, *Clemens Pirquet* In: *Remaking Central Europe.* Edited by: Peter Becker and Natasha Wheatley, Oxford University Press (2020). © the many contributors. DOI: 10.1093/oso/9780198854685.003.0003

even to the exclusion of the Austrian government in determining where and how these resources would be distributed. In addition, Pirquet had the satisfaction of employing his own Pirquet System of Nutrition for the delivery of ARA food relief. Prior to 1914, Pirquet had worked in the United States, making valuable personal contacts at Johns Hopkins, and he spent the war years enduring the Allied food blockade in Austria. As a matter of personal history, the postwar ascent of Pirquet suggests how greatly prewar international networks mattered, particularly as public health initiatives became internationalized following the war, and how research expertise linked to wartime exigencies could be mobilized for in the international postwar context. As a scientific matter, the ascent of Pirquet underscores the importance of depersonalized data and statistics for the emerging (American) postwar model of public health, as experts in science, public policy, and emergency aid sought to universalize the ideal of humanitarian relief around the figure of the child. Of course, the distinction between the personal and the scientific was never straightforward. The Rockefeller Foundation funded much that contributed to the new model of public health, and those who advised the Foundation knew Pirquet. Meanwhile, the local and personal also mattered, as Pirquet was engaged in a bitter rivalry with the Socialist leadership of 1920s Vienna. In 1929, Pirquet committed suicide, and an account of his remarkable ascent must also take note of this definitive setback. Pirquet first drew international attention through his humanitarian relief work after 1918. For as Bruno Cabanes has noted, the scale of the postwar crisis made experts as well as careers.[4] And yet, the professional ascent of Pirquet began during the hungry years of the First World War in Austria.

An axiom of recent scholarship is that hunger, and the struggle to access food, became the defining civilian wartime experience on the Austrian home front.[5] Though subjected to the same Allied naval food and agricultural supply blockade imposed on Germany in 1914, Austrians simply had less to eat than their German counterparts. Statistics presented in late 1918, for example, showed that during the wartime period when most goods were rationed the maximum legal caloric value of ration cards for individuals in Berlin and Munich was 1,400 per day, in Vienna 740.[6] Inadequate planning by the Austrian government was largely to blame. Shortly after the outbreak of war, for example, the military initiated large purchases of goods, but avoided coordinating these with civilian authorities. Such

[4] Bruno Cabanes, *The Great War and the Origins of Humanitarianism, 1918–1924* (Cambridge University Press 2014).

[5] On the food crisis, see Marion Breiter, 'Hinter der Front. Zur Versorgungslage der Zivilibevölkerung im Wien des Ersten Weltkriegs' (1994) 50 Jahrbuch des Vereins für die Geschichte der Stadt Wien 229. Maureen Healy, *Vienna and the Fall of the Habsburg Empire: Total War and Everyday Life in World War I* (2004, reprint, Cambridge University Press, 2006). Hans-Georg Hofer, 'Ernährungskrise, Krankheit, Hungertod: Wien (und Österreich-Ungarn) im Ersten Weltkrieg' (2013) 31 Medizin, Gesellschaft und Geschichte 33.

[6] John W. Boyer, *Culture and Political Crisis in Vienna. Christian Socialism in Power 1897–1918* (University of Chicago Press 1995) 421.

purchases shook commodity markets, leading to price inflation and eventually to the introduction of price ceilings on foodstuffs. In early 1915, Hungary responded to these ceilings by announcing that it would stop the export of cereal grains and corn to Austria.[7] Though Austria-Hungary had been more or less self-sufficient in food production before the war, the food supply chain for Austria depended on Hungarian imports. Without those imports, foodstuff markets began to collapse, and mounting failures engulfed Austrian efforts to respond. Food was not just a political issue, as Maureen Healy has observed, it '*was* the political issue of the day'.[8] Conflicts over food production and distribution undercut appeals to shared sacrifice and accelerated social disintegration. Meanwhile, the home front became a battle zone. As one Austrian woman wrote to her husband, who was held in a Russian POW camp, 'I have lost all hope that I and your only child will ever see you again, because we are going to die of starvation'.[9]

The hunger crisis at home elevated those bold or gifted enough to confront it to the status of national hero. In April 1918, Chair of the recently created Joint (civilian and military) Food Committee, General Ottokar Landwehr, ordered the Austrian seizure of a Romanian maize shipment destined for Germany in order to provide food relief for Vienna, a gesture that infuriated the German high command, at the time, and later nearly earned Landwehr a monument in Vienna.[10] Landwehr gave the plain-spoken title *Hunger* to his memoirs of the final two war years. But actions such as his, uncertainly situated between courage and despair, were seldom risked—at least by government officials. More characteristic of the crisis situation was the rising prestige and place of scientists who worked on nutrition and food policy. Shortly after the outbreak of war in 1914, for example, German scientists anchored by the food scientist and physiologist Max Rubner presented a comprehensive plan to meet the challenges of wartime nutrition, promising that 'through correct action, Germany will also be invincible in the realm of feeding its people'.[11] Where food is a matter of national concern, the scientist of nutrition will be destined to play a conspicuous role in the destiny of the nation. In the December 1914 speech he delivered to the Reichstag, Rubner warned Germany's leaders of 'political nutritional encirclement' (*politische Ernährungseinkreisung*), while also

[7] Hans Loewenfeld-Russ, *Die Regelung der Volksernährung im Kriege* (Yale University Press 1926) 48–50.

[8] Healy, *Habsburg Empire* (n 5) 63.

[9] Ibid, 41.

[10] General Landwehr, *Hunger. Die Erschöpfungsjahre der Mittelmächte 1917/1918* (Almathea 1931) 190–192. General Landwehr, Associated Press, 'Vienna Honors Officer Who Saved its Rolls' *New York Times* (New York, 1 June 1924) 3.

[11] Paul Eltzbacher (ed), *Die deutsche Volksernährung und der englische Aushungerungsplan. Eine Denkschrift* (Vieweg 1914) iv. For Rubner's contributions to the German war effort, see Daniel Schmidt, 'Zwischen Expertise und Propaganda. Max Rubner und die Kriegsernährung im Ersten Weltkrieg' in Theo Plesser and Hans-Ulrich Thamer (eds), *Arbeit, Leistung und Ernährung* (Franz Steiner 2012).

offering a series of measures—including his *bête noire*, eating fewer sandwiches—that would defend the country in the war of starvation.[12]

The war helped redefine nutrition as an issue of national security, even as Rubner's theory of the calorie drew upon pre-existing state-building trends that had begun to facilitate the 'state's supervision of the welfare and conduct of whole populations'.[13] This redefinition also ensured that the food crisis would help produce a growing cadre of medical and public health professionals with the expertise to manage it. Characteristic of the new group of nutrition experts was the Austrian physiologist Arnold Durig, a figure Sigmund Freud once described as a man of 'sympathetic disposition and uncommon integrity'.[14] With physicians made greatly in demand by war, Durig was drafted in 1914, and led the Department of Internal Medicine at the Fortress Hospital in Sarajevo before becoming the commanding officer of the Military Hospital in Grinzing, the largest such hospital in Austria.[15] Though his greatest passion prior to 1914 had been for his research on exercise and high altitude, Durig represented an Austrian counterpart to the German scientists and food experts who had rallied to defend their country, as he turned his attention early in the war towards the problem of providing adequate nutrition to the civilian population.[16] Once established, the nutrition expert remained in the postwar years. A champion of Rubner and his calorie-based approach to human nutritional requirements, Durig called for a more systematic statistical investigation into food consumption in his 1918 inaugural lecture as head of the Institute of Physiology at the University of Vienna, and continued to shape public policy on food in the years ahead.[17]

The case of Durig underscores how intellectually nimble scientists could retailor their research agenda to fit the wartime hunger emergency. When the hunger emergency outlasted the war, their research agenda could, once again, be hemmed to suit

[12] On Rubner's 'irrational sandwich', see Corinna Treitel, 'Max Rubner and the biopolitics of rational nutrition' (2008) 41 Central European History 1, 5–10. On the Reichstag speech, Treitel, Ibid, 19.

[13] Nick Cullather, 'The foreign policy of the calorie' (2007) 112/2 American Historical Review 337, 348. Treitel notes that 'rational nutrition had a decisively international valence', and Rubner presented his research at both the 1907 and 1912 manifestations of the International Congress for Hygiene and Demography, with the American President William Taft providing an enthusiastic welcoming address to the 1912 Congress. Treitel, 'Max Rubner' (n 12) 17.

[14] Sigmund Freud, *The Question of Lay Analysis. Conversations with an Impartial Person* (first published Postscript 1927, James Strachey tr, 1959; W. W. Norton and Company 1990) 87. Durig is regarded as Freud's 'impartial person', in this classic defence and explanation of psychoanalysis. See Gerhard Benetka and Karl Fallend, 'Der „Unparteiische" in Sigmund Freud's "Frage der Laienanalyse", Prof. Arnold Durig (1872–1961)' (2002) 49 Werkblatt. Zeitschrift für Gesellschaftskritik 118.

[15] Gerhard Oberkofler, 'Arnold Durig (1872–1961)' (1972) 24/3–4 Montfort: Zeitschrift für Geschichte und Gegenwart Vorarlbergs 582, 587.

[16] Martin Burtscher and others, 'Arnold Durig (1872–1961): Life and work. An Austrian pioneer in exercise and high altitude physiology' (2012) 13/3 High Altitude Medicine & Biology 224, 224. Arnold Durig, 'Die Volksernährung während des Krieges' (11 March 1915) 27/9–10 Das Österreichische Sanitätswesen 250.

[17] Arnold Durig, 'Physiologie als Unterrichtsgegenstand. Erhebungen über die Ernährung der Wiener Bevölkerung' (2 November 1918) Wiener Medizinische Zeitschrift 1925.

postwar exigencies and postwar careers. But the figure of Durig also highlights the reputational risks attached to wartime success in the military hierarchy. In 1920, he became a secondary target in an investigation into the use of electroshock therapy on shell-shocked soldiers. Though primarily directed by Julius Wagner-Jauregg, the head of the municipal clinic for Psychiatry and Nervous Diseases, electroshock therapy had also been employed at the Grinzing Military Hospital commanded by Durig.[18] Favoured with a civilian post during the war, Pirquet had no such ethical or ideological questions circling him: he had conducted research, and he had cared for children. As alleviating the hunger crisis moved from a national wartime necessity to a postwar international humanitarian imperative, Pirquet was well positioned. He could easily be classified as outside the 'old guard of professors who were militant nationalists' that the initiatives of American public health philanthropy in particular sought to avoid.[19] His side-stepping of the German Max Rubner probably also helped. Not that release from military service guaranteed an enduring research agenda—even for Pirquet. In his early wartime clinical work on nutrition, Pirquet profiled himself as an advocate of the increased sugar in the diet of children, dismissing objections that sugar ruined teeth or hurt the stomach: 'We don't yet know how to make proper use of this staple food product of our country.'[20]

Pirquet quickly abandoned sugar as an expanded food source.[21] But he remained committed to developing a scientifically grounded method to ensure that each individual received the nutrition they needed. Indeed, by 1916, Pirquet had begun to fashion the research framework that would underpin his system of nutrition and constitute the public health legacy that he would continue to defend for the remainder of his life.[22] This framework, the Pirquet System of Nutrition, was anchored in two numerical quantifications, that of individual nutritional state and that of the nutritional value of food. The first quantification, the 'Pelidisi number', was reached by applying a mathematical formula to sitting-height and weight measurements of children or adults recorded during a physical examination. The

[18] Kurt Robert Eissler, *Freud as an Expert Witness* (Christine Trollope tr, IU Press 1986) 45–46. Gilles Tréhel, 'Sigmund Freud, Julius Wagner von Jauregg, Arnold Durig, Julius Tandler' (2013) 87/7 L'Information psychiatrique 587.

[19] Paul Weindling, 'Public health and political stabilisation: The Rockefeller Foundation in Central and Eastern Europe between the Two World Wars' (1993) 31/3 Minerva 253, 255.

[20] Clemens Pirquet, 'Ernährung des Kindes während des Krieges' (31 July 1915) 31 Wiener Medizinische Wochenschrift 1169, 1171.

[21] On the wartime search for new sources of nutrition, see Martin Franc, 'Bread from Wood: Natural Food Substitutes in the Czech Lands during the First World War' in Ina Zweiniger-Bargielowska, Rachel Duffett, and Alain Drouard (eds), *Food and War in the Twentieth Century Europe* (Ashgate 2011). Franz Vojir, 'Ersatzlebensmittel im Ersten Weltkrieg in Österreich' in Herbert Matis, Juliane Mikoletzky, and Wolfgang Reiter (eds), *Wirtschaft, Technik und das Militär 1914–1918* (LIT 2014).

[22] Clemens Pirquet, 'Die Milch als Nahrungseinheit (System der Ernährung I.)' (1916) 14 Zeitschrift für Kinderheilkunde 197. In fact, Pirquet did not immediately abandon his advocacy for sugar in children's diet. Thus, in 1915, he had recommended milk with 17 per cent dissolved sugar for babies (Pirquet 'Ernährung des Kindes während des Krieges' [n 20] 1171), the same percentage he administered to a research cohort of children in January 1918. Clemens Pirquet, *System der Ernährung* (4 vols, Springer Verlag 1919) 2:317; 319.

examining physician also recorded a supplemental quantification, *Sacratama*, based on skin tension, muscular development, and other more subjective measurements, and *Sacratama* provided a confirmation of the Pelidisi number. The second quantification, the NEM (nutritional equivalent of milk), expressed the nutritional value of individual food items using fat, sugar, and other elements of one gram of milk as a nutritional baseline.[23]

Such numerical quantifications replaced subjective individual expressions of satiety with a scientific determination of what nutrition an individual required in order to be in a state of health. A range of Pelidisi numbers and categories—e.g. children below 90 'very undernourished', between 91 and 94 'poorly nourished'—now rendered individual nutritional state 'legible'.[24] These quantifications also removed the food expert from the political and public policy issues of supply and distribution; that is, from wartime issues. As Pirquet told a sympathetic audience in Berlin, the further development of food policy 'must make available to every single citizen that amount of foodstuffs that they require for the maintenance of their life and for completing their assigned tasks'.[25] The Pirquet System of Nutrition, which by mid-1917 was being tested in three separate Austrian locations, was designed as the public health arm of this policy.[26]

The Pirquet System of Nutrition formed an essential prerequisite for the accelerated rise of Clemens Pirquet in the early postwar period. But this was not the only such prerequisite. Another was the network of transatlantic connections that Pirquet had made prior to 1914. Mark Mazower has described the roughly thirty years prior to the outbreak of the First World War as 'perhaps the apogee of technical and scientific internationalism'.[27] Strengthened by a growing number of international conferences, specialized professional associations, and other forms of cooperation, this internationalism also enabled an idealized vision of science as a borderless, non-national practice with scientists forming an avant-garde of globally interconnected elites. In such a scenario, Clemens Pirquet may be said to have belonged to the prewar avant-garde. Of course, the nationalist barbarism of the First World War demonstrated how easily global networks could be shattered—and how much else that made up everyday life could simply disappear. In Austria,

[23] The biography of Pirquet, written by Richard Wagner, his former assistant at the *Kinderklinik*, remains the standard for a contextualization of the contemporary science together with an explanation of the Pirquet System of Nutrition. See Wagner, *Clemens von Pirquet* (n 2) 121–151.

[24] Cullather, 'The Foreign Policy of the Calorie' (n 13) 338.

[25] Clemens Pirquet, 'Ergebnisse der Kinderernährung nach einem neuen System' [2 February 1918] Wiener Medizinische Wochenschrift 217, 218.

[26] Experiments were conducted at Pirquet's *Kinderklinik*, a daycare centre, and a military hospital. Clemens Pirquet, 'Praktische Durchführung des Ernährungs-Systems' in Clemens Pirquet (ed), *System der Ernährung. Zweiter Teil* (4 vols, Berlin, 1919). Franz von Groer, 'In einer Kinderkrippe' in Pirquet, *System der Ernährung* (n 26) 325–340. Edmund Nobel, 'In einem Militärspitale' in Pirquet, *System der Ernährung* (n 26) 340–358.

[27] Mark Mazower, *Governing the World. The History of an Idea, 1815 to the Present* (Penguin Press 2012) 106.

what remained were political instability, economic distress, and an enduring hunger crisis. But instability, distress, and crisis are the elements of a third essential prerequisite. For as Patricia Clavin has argued, it was just this convergence of factors that placed Austria at the centre of new internationalist interest. In the coming years, Austria would successfully export its national crisis to the world and become a rallying point for postwar internationalism as embodied in the League of Nations.[28] In that development, Pirquet would play an exemplary role, first in connection with the American Relief Administration's relief effort to Austria and subsequently with the League of Nations Health Committee. 'Violence', Marx famously observed, 'is the midwife of history'. The war with its aftermath enabled and accelerated the postwar career of Clemens Pirquet in public health. But that career was also deeply embedded in the years leading to 1914.

II. Building Prewar Networks in Europe and the United States

Born in 1874 in Hirschstetten, near Vienna, Clemens Pirquet grew up in an aristocratic family perhaps more distinguished by its international outlook than by its contributions to medicine. His father Peter Zeno Freiherr (Baron) Pirquet served in the Austrian parliament as a representative of the liberal landowners' party (*Landeigner-Partei*), though today he is more often recalled for his early support of the international peace and arbitration movement. The London-based International Peace and Arbitration Society, for example, counted Peter Pirquet among its eight Austrian adherents in 1882.[29] Of greater consequence politically, Pirquet figured largely in the Inter-Parliamentary Union (IPU), a transnational association founded in 1889. The IPU sought to unite parliamentarians from different governments to support a peace agenda, especially in the form of arbitration, which has been described as 'perhaps the single most influential strand of internationalism' before 1914.[30] Pirquet officially led the Austrian delegation from 1892 to 1904, and organized the IPU conference held in Vienna in 1903, with the conference the following year scheduled for St. Louis, USA.[31] In Austria, as Daniel Laqua has argued, inter-parliamentarianism and pacifism were closely aligned, with Pirquet active both in the IPU and the Austrian Peace Society (*Österreichische Friedensgesellschaft*).[32] And of course, it was Pirquet, who, in his capacity as a

[28] Patricia Clavin, 'The Austrian hunger crisis and the genesis of international organization after the First World War' (2014) 90/2 International Affairs 265.

[29] Daniel Laqua, 'Pacifism in fin-de-siècle Austria: The politics and limits of peace activism' (2014) 57/1 The Historical Journal 229, 202.

[30] Mazower, *Governing the World* (n 27) 83.

[31] Ralph Uhlig, *Die Interparlamentarische Union 1889–1914* (Franz Steiner Verlag 1988) 132; 297–304.

[32] Laqua, 'Pacifism in Fin-de-siècle Austria' (n 29) 204.

member of the IPU, nominated the Austrian recipient of the 1905 Nobel Peace Prize, Bertha von Suttner.[33]

On the maternal side, Pirquet could also claim a noble and, indeed, very Viennese pedigree. His mother, Flora Freiin (Baroness) von Pereira-Arnstein was the great-granddaughter of Fanny von Arnstein (1758–1818), the celebrated Jewish patroness whose salon in Vienna welcomed the great figures of her day, including Madame de Staël, Talleyrand, and Rahel Varnhagen, while her grandmother was the accomplished pianist and salon hostess Henriette von Pereira-Arnstein (1780–1859). Together with her husband, Pereira-Arnstein had converted to Catholicism in 1805, and the young Pirquet followed a Catholic calling not uncharacteristic of an Austrian aristocrat, studying theology first in Innsbruck and then in Leuven. The American historian Carl Schorske established the 'fin-de-siécle Vienna' research agenda based upon the proposition that in Vienna cultural modernism represented a retreat from political to the psychological realm, and that this process could be traced to the failure of Austrian liberalism.[34] But the trajectory of Pirquet might be described as one in which the father finds himself abandoned at the altar of liberalism, only to have the son renew his vows to rationalism in the study of medicine. By 1900, in any case, Pirquet had completed his medical degree in Graz, studying with Theodor Escherich. In 1902, Escherich became head of the St. Anna's Children's Hospital in Vienna, with the mandate to build a new clinic, and he promoted Pirquet to clinical assistant there in 1903. Pirquet's breakthroughs on serum sickness, allergy, and tuberculosis quickly followed. Meanwhile, construction on the new *Universitäts-Kinderklinik* began in 1910, but Escherich did not live to see it open, dying suddenly in 1911. Shortly thereafter, Pirquet was appointed Escherich's successor, ensuring that Pirquet would achieve scientific and institutional significance before the age of forty.

Pirquet always recognized that his development of the tuberculin skin test conferred upon him the status of scientific royalty.[35] Locally, of course, tuberculosis represented a much-feared scourge, and the Austrian physicians whose discoveries are landmarks in the fight against it are memorialized in the Viennese landscape—*Auenbruggergasse* (Leopold Auenbrugger), *Schrötter-von-Kristelli* monument (Leopold Schrötter), and *Skodagasse* (Joseph Škoda), and Julius Tandler still looms large today for the public health campaign he led against tuberculosis as the socialist municipal Councilman for Public Welfare during the years of 'Red Vienna', even as the reductions in mortality rates in that period have tended to overshadow

[33] Official Web Site of the Nobel Prize, 'Nomination Database', <http://www.nobelprize.org/nomination/archive/show.php?id=8420>.

[34] Carl Schorske, *Fin-de-Siècle Vienna* (Alfred A. Knopf Inc. 1981).

[35] As the writer of the long reflection on Pirquet life that appeared after his death observed, 'Pirquet was very aware of the consequences of his discovery and returned again and again to it in his future work.' Zapperl, 'Clemens Pirquet' (1929) 11 Separatabdruck aus der Wiener Medizinischen Wochenschrift 4.

the significant progress made before the turn of the century.[36] But if tuberculosis was already known locally since the era of Joseph II as the *Wiener Krankheit* (Viennese disease), by 1900, health and medical experts from around the world had begun to establish and share a framework that made it possible to understand tuberculosis as an 'international' disease. A critical contribution to this understanding took place in the 1890s, when at its congresses in Vienna, Chicago, and Bern, the International Institute of Statistics developed a standard international nomenclature for causes of death, a nomenclature that would be adopted at its next meeting in Paris, where twenty-six countries were in attendance.[37] A second, related precondition for the internationalization of tuberculosis is the general increase in all forms of cross-border scientific association—congresses, meetings, and international networking—that occurred towards the end of the nineteenth- and into the twentieth-century. The annual average of international scientific conferences in the 1870s was twelve, by the 1890s, thirty.[38]

A critical turn in the career of Pirquet that followed his development of the tuberculin skin test came with an invitation to the International Tuberculosis Meeting, convened in Washington, D.C. in October 1908, where he presented a paper on cutaneous tuberculin reaction in postmortem examinations.[39] By design, the Washington meeting targeted research contributions from abroad. Homer Folks, who served on its Committee on Print and Publication, underscored this focus years later, recalling that, 'the experience of the leading cities and countries of the world was placed on exhibit'.[40] Recent scholars, too, have linked the International Union for the Study of Tuberculosis with the 1908 meeting, noting how advances on the continent 'spurred US reformers to evaluate European models of tuberculosis'.[41] As William Welch, the president of the section on tuberculosis put it in his welcome speech, 'every effort has been made to assure the truly international character of this Congress [. . .] Over seventy percent of the papers on the program of Section I are contributed by participants from foreign countries.'[42]

[36] Elisabeth Dietrich-Daum, *Die "Wiener Krankheit." Eine Sozialgeschichte der Tuberkulose in Österreich* (Verlag für Geschichte und Politik 2007) 136–137.

[37] World Health Organization, International Classifications of Diseases for Mortality and Morbidity Statistics, History, <http://www.who.int/classifications/icd/en/HistoryOfICD.pdf>. Calls for a standard nomenclature for causes of death had been made previously, and such calls predated successful agreements in the 1850 to produce international standards in setting measurement units and standards. Robert P. Crease, *World in the Balance. The Historic Quest for an Absolute System of Measurement* (W. W. Norton & Company Inc. 2011) 128–129.

[38] Mazower, *Governing the World* (n 27) 106.

[39] Clemens Pirquet, 'Erfahrungen über die Kutane Tuberkulinreaktion an 200 Obduzierten Kindern' in *Transactions of the Sixth International Congress on Tuberculosis* (vol 2, Fell 1908) 258.

[40] Homer Folks, 'Tuberculosis Associations and Relief Agencies' in Savel Zimand (ed), *Public Health and Welfare. The Citizens' Responsibility. Selected Papers of Homer Folks* (1933 Macmillan, 1958) 274.

[41] Paul Weindling, 'From Moral Exhortation to the New Public Health, 1918–45' in Esteban Rodríguez-Ocaña (ed), *The Politics of the Healthy Life. An International Perspective* (European Association for the History of Medicine and Health Publications 2002) 113; 117.

[42] *Transactions of the Sixth International Congress on Tuberculosis* (vol 1, Fell 1908) 2.

Paul Weindling remarks that William Welch emerged from the Washington meeting strengthened by the internationalist agenda he had helped promote there.[43] Of course, like many other physicians of his generation, Welch himself had studied in Germany and Vienna, the latter of which he called 'the conventional Mecca of American practitioners'.[44] But in 1908, Welch sought to bring European expertise to the United States for the newly established Department of Pediatrics at Johns Hopkins Medical School, and he offered Pirquet a professorship in that department, together with the position of the first Pediatrician-in-Chief of the Harriet Lane Home for Invalid Children at Johns Hopkins. Pirquet accepted. Known as the grandfather of American pathology, immortalized in a heroic portrait by American painter John Singer Sargent, an essential figure in the modelling of the American approach to public health, and much else, Welch would become an influential friend, colleague, and promoter of Pirquet. Welch, for example, sat on the board of the American Association for Study and Prevention of Infant Mortality, and Pirquet was appointed to a three-year term on its Board of Directors, at the Association's first annual meeting in November 1910. Pirquet would retain this board position, even as he took a leave of absence from Baltimore to accept a professorship in Breslau.[45] In his Vienna study, Pirquet kept a picture of Welch on horseback in China against the background of the tombs of the Ming Dynasty, and it is difficult to overstate his importance for Pirquet in the post-Johns Hopkins years.[46]

III. From Relief to Public Health: The American Model, Made in Austria

Reporting on the memorial service that the Austria-America Society and the Austro-American Institute of Education organized for Pirquet following his unexpected death in 1929, the *Neues Wiener Journal* pointed to what had enabled Pirquet to succeed in organizing the celebrated ARA children's relief action a few years previously. 'Pirquet', as the writer put it, 'had the trust of the Americans'.[47] Indeed. And that trust had its beginnings in the scant year Pirquet had spent in Baltimore. But if the war disrupted transatlantic networks of scientific exchange between the United States and the Central Powers, the postwar deepening of the Austrian hunger crisis, together with the American preference to use food aid as

43 Weindling, 'From Moral Exhortation' (n 41) 117.

44 Thomas Bonner, *American Doctors and German Universities: A Chapter in International Intellectual Relations, 1870–1914* (University of Nebraska Press 1963) 69. Bonner estimates that between 1870 and 1914 more than 10,000 American physicians had some kind of medical study in Vienna.

45 American Association for Study and Prevention of Infant Mortality, *Transactions of the First Annual Meeting* (Johns Hopkins University 9–11 November 1910) 3; 5.

46 Wagner, *Clemens von Pirquet* (n 2) 76.

47 'Trauerkundgebung für Professor Pirquet' [9 March 2016] *Neues Wiener Journal* 9.

a tool of foreign policy, virtually ensured that Pirquet would reconnect with that network.[48] In fact, the relief administrators, public health experts, and others who were the first to arrive in Vienna, following the November Armistice, to plan the *Amerikanische Kinderhilfsaktion* insisted upon the participation of Pirquet. In January 1919, Pirquet took part in all scheduled meetings with representatives of the 'Mission of the Allies and the United States for dealing with food problems in Vienna', meetings that established the framework for the May 1919 launch of the *Hilfsaktion*.[49] Herbert Hoover himself had dispatched this group to Vienna, and its leader, Dr Alonzo Taylor, paid a visit to the *Kinderklinik*.[50] And of Clare M. Torrey, Director of the ARA Austrian Mission who arrived in May 1919, Franz Adlgasser has noted that Pirquet was 'from the beginning the [his] closest adviser'.[51]

In Austria, the ARA fastened itself to Pirquet as its General Commissioner, and until the de facto end of the *Kinderhilfsaktion*, negotiated for 1 August 1922, it never abandoned him. Starting in mid-May 1919, with 60,000 (NEM) meals served at locations across Vienna, by July 1919, the *Hilfsaktion* programme provided more than 100,000 (NEM) meals in Vienna alone, and at its height in late 1920 and 1921, the monthly average in Vienna was 160,000; in Austria, 300,000.[52] That same programme captured anthropometric (*Pelidisi*) measurements for 418,412 children, between October 1920 and January 1921, and as a follow-up, 379,864 measurements in spring 1922—an enormous data set.[53] Originally envisioned to continue for three months, ARA leaders decided to extend the *Kinderhilfsaktion* after a Europe-wide meeting of representatives in Prague, at which the Austrian relief organization was described as 'the best led and operated, as absolutely "perfect"'.[54] What earned the *Kinderhilfsaktion* such tributes, and also moved the ARA to fundamentally insist upon its autonomy from the City of Vienna, and practically speaking, the Austrian state, was the scientific rationale

48 American humanitarian action in Belgium during 1914 set the course for the connection between wartime food and foreign policy that would continue beyond the war. Branden Little, 'Humanitarian Relief in Europe and the Analogue of War, 1914–1918' in Jennifer D. Keene and Michael S. Neiberg (eds), *Finding Common Ground. New Directions in First World War Studies* (Brill 2011). On American food policy, maintaining peace in Austria, and the Hungarian revolution, see Franz Adlgasser, 'The Roots of Communist Containment: American Food Aid in Austria and Hungary after World War I' in Günter Bischof, Anton Pelinka, and Rolf Steininger (eds), *Austria in the Nineteen Fifties* (Transaction Publishers 1995).

49 Franz Adlgasser, *American Individualism Abroad. Herbert Hoover, die American Relief Administration und Österreich, 1919–1923* (PhD, diss., University of Salzburg 1993) 100.

50 Suda Lorena and Ralph Hawell Lutz (eds), *Organization of American Relief in Europe, 1918–1919* (Stanford University Press 1943) 111–112.

51 Adlgasser, *American Individualism Abroad* (n 49) 103.

52 Friedrich Reischl, *Wiens Kinder und Amerika. Die amerikanische Kinderhilfsaktion 1919*, Hrsg. Vom Deutschösterreichischen Jugendhilfswerk in Wien (Gerlach & Wiedling 1920) 95–100; 151–152. *American Relief Administration European Children's Fund. The Organization and Distribution System in Austria* (Vienna: 1 October 1920) 3.

53 Clemens Pirquet, 'Schülerspeisung als Teil der allgemeinen Ernährungsfürsorge' in Clemens Pirquet (ed), *Volksgesundheit im Krieg* (vol 1, Hölder-Pichler-Tempsky 1926).

54 Clemens Pirquet, 'Die amerikanische Hilfsaktion in Österreich, Teil I' (1 May 1920) 19 Wiener Medizinische Wochenschrift 854, 855.

of the Pirquet System of Nutrition. Indeed, anyone who has consulted the official Austrian record of the *Amerikanische Hilfsaktion* in the hope of finding a record of lives saved, or a moving chronicle of the humanitarian spirit, will have been disappointed. Presented here, rather, is a detailed account of the methodology of the Pirquet system of feeding and measurement, accompanied by pre- and postwar mortality statistics, and above all Pelidisi tables.[55] Recalling these contributions of the Vienna child-feeding programme to the ARA relief effort, Herbert Hoover wrote in his 1951 memoirs that 'they developed a series of easy tests of whether a child was undernourished and when it was reasonably restored. We adopted these tests in all our European child-feeding operations.'[56] Hoover's recollection inflated the European scope of the Pirquet programme, which was implemented only in a few instances outside Austria. But it accurately registered, decades later, the perceived place of the Pirquet system within the European child relief effort and its significance to the ARA.

In early 1920, William Welch himself stepped into the leadership of a fundraising campaign to provide food and material support for medical scientists in Vienna, and persuaded the Rockefeller Foundation to contribute $10,000 towards its goal.[57] Delivered directly to Pirquet at the *Kinderklinik* by Paris-based Rockefeller representative Linsley R. Williams, this support had apparently been requested by Pirquet in an appeal addressed directly to Welch and Simon Flexner.[58] Founding president of the Board of Scientific Directors at the Rockefeller Medical Institute, Welch seems to have exercised his influence with the board and the officers of the Foundation on more than one occasion to help steer resources or goodwill towards Pirquet. When, for example, Alonzo Taylor travelled to Vienna to negotiate on behalf of the ARA, he ensured the participation of Pirquet in the negotiations, while also reporting to Wickliffe Rose, director of the International Health Board at the Rockefeller Foundation, that 'this situation calls for sympathetic engagement and encouragement'.[59]

Such sentiments could be said to belong to a script written by Welch for Taylor. Of course, Pirquet himself also did his part in the always difficult task of winning Rockefeller support. During his visit to Central Europe in the summer of 1920, Foundation Secretary Edwin Embree wrote of the Vienna operation that he had 'the finest impression of the work' there, and that 'marvelous results' were produced with limited American oversight.[60] The internal history of Rockefeller Foundation

[55] See Reischl, *Wiens Kinder und Amerika* (n 52) and *Die Amerikanische Hilfsaktion in Österreich* (Vienna 1921).

[56] Herbert Hoover, *The Memoirs of Herbert Hoover. The Years of Adventure 1874–1920* (Macmillan 1952) 394.

[57] Rockefeller Archive Center (hereafter RAC) RF RG 3, Folder History 2, Box 11, Series 900, 3426–3429.

[58] RAC RF RG 3, Folder History 2, Box 11, Series 900, 3437. *Wiener Zeitung* [18 August 1920] 3.

[59] RAC RF RG 3, Folder History 2, Box 11, Series 900, 3591.

[60] Edwin R. Embree, Log of Journey to Europe, 19 July 1920, RAC RF RG 12, Officers' Diaries, FA391.

observes that the fact that Embree 'had been deeply impressed with the work of the American Relief Administration' figured greatly in the Foundation's decision to contribute $1 million to the ARA in December 1920.[61] Together with the contribution to the Welch-led Committee for Relief of Viennese Medical Scientists, this was the final appropriation of the Rockefeller Foundation to emergency postwar relief. And as with that previous appropriation, the board made it grudgingly, as a 'deliberate exception' to Foundation policy to cease emergency relief.[62] But this would not be the last time where, in matters concerning Pirquet, Foundation policy would be stretched to fit.

Pirquet's approach to nutrition shaped how postwar food relief came to be defined, both locally and beyond, even as Austria itself constituted a focus of keen international interest, and a place where an extraordinary number of organizations from around the world were active in providing emergency assistance.[63] Though the Rockefeller Foundation declined further grants for short-term relief, it provided a highly visible endorsement of the approach of Pirquet by elevating him within its funding infrastructure. Thus, in Austria, as elsewhere in postwar Central Europe, the Foundation underwrote programmes designed to ensure that university medical facilities would continue—at least at a subsistence level. Funds were then made available, primarily for medical education, laboratory supplies, and British and American medical publications. In Austria, Pirquet and his team received and allocated these funds, deciding, for example, which applicants would receive Rockefeller travel fellowships and what items the faculties at the medical schools in Graz and Innsbruck would be allowed to purchase.[64] When in 1921, the Rockefeller Foundation approved a $60,000 contribution to the *Kinderklinik*, one of two such grants that year designated to be distributed among the three Austrian medical schools, neither Graz nor Innsbruck ever saw the actual money. Béla Schick, Pirquet's assistant at the *Kinderklinik*, simply did all the purchasing and arranged delivery.[65]

Not that the Rockefeller Foundation could not refuse Pirquet. Embree, for example, rejected an appeal for the NEM-based cafeteria for university faculty, the Professor's Table, because it did not align with the Foundation's focus on 'medical and public health'.[66] Still, the Rockefeller approach was to work with elite individuals in their respective scientific fields, and in that respect, of course, Pirquet

[61] RAC RG 3, Folder History 2, Box 11, Series 900, 3441.
[62] Ibid.
[63] On these organizations, see Friedrich Reischl, 'Die fremden Hilfsaktionen in Österreich. Ein Bild ihrer Tätigkeit und eine Ernährungs-Studie' Separatabdruck aus 'Ernährungskunde', *Österr. Almanach für Ernährung 1921–1922* (Salzer 1921).
[64] Vincent to Pearce, 22 November 1922, RAC RF, RG 1.1, Folder 121–122, Box 16, Series 700A.
[65] Pirquet to Williams, 6 April 1921, RAC RF RG 1.1, Folder 4, Box 1, Series 705. Uhlenhuth to Pearce, 21 October 1921, RAC RF RG 1.1, Folder 5, Box 1, Series 705. Stoughton to Pirquet, 21 August 1921, RAC, RF, RG 1.1, Folder 4, Box 1, Series 705.
[66] Pirquet to Embree, 7 June 1921, RAC, RF, RG 1.1, Folder 4, Box 1, Series 705.

qualified. Moreover, he was not reckoned among the professorial ancien règime that the Foundation sought to displace.[67] Pirquet and the Vienna *Kinderklinik* thus became a de facto Foundation headquarters for Austria, with an occasional claim to Central European influence. Indeed, the log Edwin Embree compiled from his July 1920 interview with Pirquet reads like a rough draft of the agenda that the Rockefeller Foundation would purse in Central Europe over the next six years.[68] And for a short time, even the stationery Pirquet used for official Foundation-related correspondence read 'Rockefeller Foundation in Austria, Zentralbureau Kinderklinik', with Frederic F. Russell, the Paris-based Rockefeller Director of the International Health Board, identified as Chair, and Pirquet listed as Vice-Chair. The New York office soon objected, however, and requested a letterhead that suggested a less direct connection between the Foundation and the *Kinderklinik*.[69] Rarely, at least outside Ludwik Rajchman in Poland, did the Rockefeller Foundation permit their grantees such autonomy. If the arrangement did create some discomfort for Foundation officers, it also worked.

But in the early 1920s, the Rockefeller Foundation had broader public health ambitions for Central Europe. These ambitions, which emerged slowly and would eventually be remade in the funding they devoted to the international public health agenda at the League of Nations, were shaped by several factors. Some were, roughly speaking, geopolitical. Paul Weindling, for example, has noted the broad vision guiding intervention in the Habsburg successor states as one of a 'middle Europe based upon a recognition of even justice with international team play substituted for German domination', while also keeping in check the spread of communism from the Soviet Union.[70] But as with the ARA, Rockefeller Foundation officers were physicians and public health administrators attentive to geopolitics, not geopolitical strategists attentive to public health. Early officer recommendations for Foundation help may have presented an expanded range of possibilities—for example, Edwin Embree's late 1920 'Medical Education and Nurse Training Report' quite reasonably indicated the desirability of programmes for scientific agriculture—but such recommendations all sought improved general health, even as they increasingly narrowed to a focus on initiatives within a public health

[67] As Richard Pearce wrote to George Vincent, President of the Rockefeller Foundation, 'I repeat that I would prefer to count on forward-looking men such as Pirquet and Reuter rather than existing "heads of departments".' Reuter was a forensic specialist in Graz. Pearce to Vincent, 28 November 1922. RAC RF RG 1.1, Folder 121–122, Box 16, Series 700A.

[68] Edwin R. Embree, Log of Journey to Europe, 19 July 1920, RAC RF RG 12, Officers' Diaries, FA391.

[69] For the actual letterhead, see Schick to Russell, 23 January 1921, RAC RF RG 1.1, Folder 4, Box 1, Series 705. On the issue of what the stationery should look like, see Russell to Pirquet, 21 February 1921. RAC, RF, RG 1.1, Folder 4, Box 1, Series 705; Russell to Pirquet, 11 March 1921. RAC RF RG 1.1, Folder 4, Box 1, Series 705.

[70] Weindling cites this phrase from a report prepared by Wickliffe Rose and Selskar Gunn during their February 1920 trip to Czechoslovakia. Paul Weindling, 'Public Health and Political Stabilisation' (n 67) 253.

framework.[71] That framework, as it acquired shape in Central Europe, might be described as a transplant of the School of Hygiene and Public Health at Johns Hopkins University that the Foundation had built and endowed. The School had opened in 1918 with William Welch as director, and in conceiving that institution Wickliffe Rose had said that its plan 'should be formulated with a view to its beginning not on the scale of its ultimate character, but rather on that of its minimum requirements'.[72] As in Baltimore, the Rockefeller Foundation would provide the minimum requirements for public health institutions. With time, the ultimate character of those institutions would manifest itself.

In these calculations, Vienna occupied a special place. On the one hand, Austria lacked the economic strength to merit private philanthropic investment in science that could be used to leverage government funding. Together with the fact that Austria was not seen as lacking an adequate public health infrastructure, this meant that the Foundation never sought to establish the centralized state institutes of public health and hygiene there as they did in other Habsburg successor states.[73] Such institutes were funded, for example, by the Foundation's International Health Board in Czechoslovakia ($377,000, July 1921), in Poland ($212,500, January 1922), and in Hungary ($245,00, 1925).[74] Still, Vienna possessed some advantages over other locations. One was that the Foundation tended to consider the Viennese medical facilities and personnel superior to those in other parts of the former monarchy.[75] Another was that Foundation officers generally expected Vienna to emerge as a regional centre. As Richard Pearce, Director of the Foundation's Division of Medical Education, put it, 'After all, it is only Vienna which will become, if after all this is possible for any university in Austria, the medical center in that part of the world'.[76] And reputation mattered. Rockefeller Foundation leaders in particular felt loyalty to the Medical School in Vienna, even as they tended to see past achievements as belonging to the present. When asked for his input, Simon Flexner, a Foundation trustee, student of Welch, and a personal friend of John

71 Edwin R. Embree, 'Medical Education and Nurse Training Report Prepared by Edwin R. Embree, Secretary of Rockefeller Foundation, Following a Visit by him to 11 Countries of Europe [June–October, 1920]'. RAC RF RG 12, Officers' Diaries, FA391.

72 Cited in Raymond B. Fosdick, *The Story of the Rockefeller Foundation* (Harper and Brothers 1952) 41.

73 Benjamin Page argues that Rockefeller Foundation officers arrived more slowly at their plan for public health and hygiene institutes in Central Europe than Weindling and others have claimed. Benjamin B. Page, 'The Rockefeller Foundation and Central Europe: A reconsideration' (2002) 40/3 Minerva 265.

74 In the immediate postwar period, the International Health Board helped establish sixteen schools of public health, from Brazil to Yugoslavia. Elizabeth Fee, *Disease and Discovery. A History of the Johns Hopkins School of Hygiene and Public Health, 1916–1939* (1987; Johns Hopkins University Press 2016) 220. Schools in Central Europe were densely concentrated and can be plotted as forming a single contiguous line from the Black Sea to the North Sea.

75 Richard M. Pearce, 'Report on the Distribution of 100,000 for the Rehabilitation of the Universities of Central Europe' (30 March 1921) RAC RF RG 1.1 Folder 121,22, Box 16, Series 700.

76 Pearce to Gregg, 19 February 1926. RAC, RF, RG 1.1, Folder 5, Box 1, Series 705.

D. Rockefeller Jr., said of the School that it 'was unequaled and unapproached in graduate clinical work' and that 'its staff, its facilities, its access to clinical and cadaver material and its tradition cannot be replaced by any center'.[77]

In considering possibilities for action in postwar Central Europe, Rockefeller Foundation officers generally recognized the instability of the political, historical, and public health situation. But in this instability, they also found confirmed the correctness of the Foundation's emerging public health agenda. As Pirquet told Edwin Embree in July 1920, no one could predict what would happen next in the Habsburg successor states. Governments to the south and east were in a violent flux. The next months might bring a reunification of nations in an Austro-Hungarian confederation, or they might bring further subdividing of those governments. They could bring a restoration of monarchies, or Bolshevism might spread across Europe. Nevertheless, in such a situation, much could still be accomplished. 'Whatever the governments, whatever the national boundary lines', Pirquet concluded, 'man's enemy, disease, will be foiled only by a careful, well-planned, scientific attack'.[78]

In the coming years, Pirquet would continue to circulate in expert networks where Rockefeller Foundation officers and their grantees also moved, and to devote himself to work closely aligned to the priorities of the Rockefeller Foundation. For the Foundation, Pirquet had the pedigree, the elite recognition, and the transatlantic connections that meant that they could never quite be done with him. For Pirquet, the Rockefeller Foundation represented the ideal champion for his system of nutrition, which would constitute one part of the 'scientific attack' in the postwar world, where disease would now replace other men as the enemy. True, Austria presented a particular kind of emergency situation, but the Pirquet system could be applied to conditions of undernutrition or malnutrition anywhere, whether in Asia, Eastern Europe, or the United States. Indeed, with its numerical abstraction of the body and nutrition, the system programmatically excluded context. And of course, American foundations were always interested in operationalizing scientific innovation for public health.[79] Whether his innovation would, in fact, be operationalized remained an open question.

[77] Edwin R. Embree, Log of Journey to Europe, 12–13 July, 1920, RAC RF RG 12, Officers' Diaries, FA391.

[78] Edwin R. Embree, Log of Journey to Europe, 19 July 1920, RAC RF RG 12, Officers' Diaries, FA391.

[79] Paul Weindling, 'American Foundation and the Internationalizing of Public Health' in Susan Gross Solomon, Lion Murard, and Patrick Zylberman (eds), *Shifting Boundaries of Public Health. Europe in the Twentieth Century* (University of Rochester Press 2008).

IV. Fractured Public Health Politics in Vienna: Pirquet versus Tandler

One setting where the approach of Pirquet had encountered significant resistance from the outset was in the postwar public health agenda of Julius Tandler (1869–1936), the Austrian physician and politician, who was named both Undersecretary of State for Public Health and Director of the (State) Office of Public Health in May 1919, before leaving the latter position in November 1920 to become Vienna City Councilman for Public Welfare under the municipal Socialist government. This resistance was rooted in both the local Viennese context and in divergent conceptions of how to maintain and improve public health after 1918. Focused on individual nutritional health, the Pirquet programme moved in three distinct and interrelated steps. First, it delivered a formula to quantify nutritional health, the Pelidisi number. Second, using that quantification, it proposed a health baseline, namely, the Pelidisi categories of 'very undernourished', 'poorly nourished', and so forth. Third, it offered a standardized means, the NEM-system, to elevate the nutritional state of individuals who fell below a particular baseline.

Pirquet's undertaking might be described as a 'postwar' scientific system, in the sense that both a particular scientific method and the war years had shaped it. Its intended result was an overall improvement in public health, measured by a rise in aggregate Pelidisi numbers, and the Pirquet system evaluated individuals and programme success independently from social criteria. A small fee of 30 to 50 hellers was requested from children who received meals at ARA kitchens, but this amount was viewed as a symbolic contribution and reflected only 2.5 per cent of the actual cost of the meal.[80] Consistent with this approach, moreover, the Pirquet system was open. As its reports and promotional materials always stressed, the ARA meal programme was available to any school-age child whose Pelidisi number made them eligible—regardless of 'nationality', religious confession, or 'economic need of the family'.[81] Universal accessibility belonged to the design of public health proposed by the Pirquet system, and practically speaking, this mattered a great deal in Austria, where postwar inflation and the collapse of the Habsburg state hit the middle-class harder than the working class, the relationship between nutritional health and social standing did not correlate in the old ways.[82]

[80] This is Pirquet's calculation, based on a 50-heller meal. Clemens Pirquet, 'Die amerikanische Hilfsaktion in Österreich, Teil II' (8 May 1920) 20 Wiener Medizinische Wochenschrift 908, 908. Elsewhere it is reported that a request of 30 hellers was made for the ARA meal. Reischl, *Wiens Kinder und Amerika* (n 52) 90.

[81] Reischl, *Wiens Kinder und Amerika* (n 52) 90. For two contemporary observations of the economic and social situation, see Charles à Court Repington, *After the War* (Houghton Mifflin Co. 1922) 132–153. Stephen Graham, *Europe—Whither Bound?* (Appleton 1922) 103–113.

[82] Fritz Weber, 'Zusammenbruch, Inflation und Hyperinflation' in Helmut Konrad and Wolfgang Maderthaner (eds), *Das Werden der ersten Republik… der Rest ist Österreich* (vol 2, Carl Gerold's Sohn Verlagsbuchhandlung KG 2008).

If the Pirquet system merits the description 'postwar', the approach of Tandler might be characterized as 'post-Habsburg'. For Tandler, maintaining and improving public health after 1918 meant grasping the concept of health broadly. Infant mortality, tuberculosis, alcoholism, and other issues, he believed, were urgent public health matters. But to address these issues, they needed to be understood as rooted in their social context, where the larger interpretive framework is poverty, together with Habsburg legacies of neglect in social welfare. Under Tandler's leadership, Socialist Vienna would link public health and social circumstances and reverse those legacies. As Tandler put it later, 'Perhaps in no other city as Vienna are the relationships [between social and medical improvements] so clearly recognized and consequently so thoroughly worked through.'[83] Thus, while Tandler saw new housing construction in Vienna as a decisive blow against tuberculosis, and in 1922, accused the Christian Socialist party of having done nothing for sixty to eighty years to eradicate the disease, Pirquet was publishing an article on the 'Nutritional Treatment of Tuberculosis'.[84] Nor can the divergent approaches of Tandler and Pirquet be represented as a dispute over the use scientific methods in public health. Tandler deployed statistics to represent the condition of populations just as Pirquet did. But whereas Pirquet's team arranged Pelidisi numbers into tables, with, for example, a Pelidisi number below 90 considered 'very undernourished' according to the Pirquet system, Tandler framed the public health situation in terms of material requirements. Thus, under the title *Existenzminimum*, his Office of Public Health published and updated tables that presented the subsistence costs in Austrian currency for food and other essentials in various Austrian cities.[85]

Of course, such divergent approaches also yielded different solutions to problems of human health. Already during wartime in Austria, for example, two basic policy responses directed to the problem of undernourished children had emerged. One gradually developing response consisted in the Pirquet System of Nutrition. The other response, the 'Children to the Countryside' (*Kinder aufs Land*) action, owes its origins to the last Austrian Emperor Charles I who underwrote the initiative as part of his *Kaiser Karl-Wohlfahrtswerk* starting in the summer of 1918. Here, under imperial auspices, 64,805 undernourished children were transported to the nutritionally well-provisioned Hungarian countryside for a recuperative stay of several weeks.[86] Together with the Pirquet programme, this initiative was expanded after 1918, though under the patronage of the Austrian state and the

[83] Julius Tandler, 'Wohlfahrtswesen und Gesundheitsamt' in Volksgesundheitsamt der Gemeinde Wien (ed), *Das Österreichische Gesundheitswesen* (Wirtschafts-Zeitungs-Verlag-Gesellschaft 1930) 81, quoted in Britta I. McEwen, 'Welfare and eugenics: Julius Tandler's *Rassenhygienische* vision for interwar Vienna' (2010) 41 Austrian History Yearbook 170, 178.

[84] Karl Sablik, *Julius Tandler. Mediziner und Sozialreformer* (2nd edn, Peter Lang 2010) 252. Clemens Pirquet, 'Nutritional treatment of tuberculosis' (1 February 1922) 115/3 New York Medical Journal 121.

[85] See, for example, Mitteilungen des Volksgesundheitsamtes 10 (27 August 1921) 450.

[86] *Die Amerikanische Hilfsaktion in Österreich* 1921: 1.

Tandler-led Office of Public Health. The Office organized recuperative trips for children to the Austrian countryside. It also coordinated, and partly sponsored, 'Kinder ins Ausland', a larger programme that arranged recuperative stays for children outside Austria. In implementing this programme, which in July 1920, for example, organized trips to ten countries, from Denmark to Rumania, for 17,782 children, the Office managed logistics, tracked participants, and negotiated bilateral agreements with the foreign countries and organizations who participated in the programme.[87] Children in the programme were selected according to a variety of criteria, including social and religious ones.[88] An enormous cooperative undertaking, the 'Kinder ins Ausland' initiative sent 247,450 children abroad between 1919 and 1923, and foreshadowed campaigns that removed children from urban areas during and after the Second World War.[89]

As an aid programme for children, the 'Kinder ins Ausland' initiative reflected the socialist view of public health and its continuities with traditional conceptions of social assistance. Known both internally and to the public as an '*Erholungsaktion*', or 'recuperation campaign', the programme's purpose was to allow the entire child to 'recuperate', not simply to feed the child. When the child returned home, and sometimes it did not, the recuperation ended and the campaign envisioned no continuing treatment.[90] Such an approach clashed directly with the scrupulous monitoring of the open access Pirquet system, and Pirquet and his circle rarely mentioned their own efforts without also criticizing recuperative programmes. Indeed, already in 1919, Pirquet had underscored their failings in improving nutritional health. When those children who ate tastier meals during their recuperative stays return to their parents, he observed, they refused the coarse fare offered at home and subsequently lost their newly gained weight. Children receiving the less flavourful NEM meals in the Pirquet system, by contrast, experienced no such negative side effects and continued to gain weight with the food that was available at home.[91] Nor were hybrid efforts that sought to mix elements of the ARA Pirquet system with recuperative programmes rated much better. In 1921, the Austrian ARA newsletter described a hybrid project in Styria, in which one group

[87] Österreichisches Staatsarchiv/Archiv der Republik (ÖStA/AdR), Bundesministerium für soziale Verwaltung (BMfsV), Aktionen "Kinder ins Ausland" im Monate Juli 1920, 1920, K1665.

[88] Friedrich Reischl, 'Der Professorentisch' (May 1921) 46–50 Mitteilungen der American Relief Administration 235.

[89] ÖStA/AdR, BMfsV, 'Zusammenfassung über die in den Jahren 1919–1923 abgegangenen österreichischen Erholungstransporte' 1924, K1850. Friederike Kind-Kovács describes the scope of wartime and postwar recuperative campaigns in Austria-Hungary and indicates the connection to the Second World War. Friederike Kind-Kovács, 'The "other" child transports: World War I and the temporary displacement of needy children from Central Europe' (2013) 15 Revue d'histoire de l'enfance "irrégulière" 75.

[90] ÖStA/AdR, BMfsV, Aktionen "Kinder ins Ausland" im Monate Juli 1920, 1920, K1665. Tara Zahra addresses the 'lost' children of wartime relief efforts who chose not to return home. Tara Zahra, *The Lost Children. Reconstructing Europe's Families after World War II* (Harvard University Press 2011) 37.

[91] Clemens Pirquet, 'Der Ernährungszustand der Wiener Kinder' (Neujahr 1919) 1 Wiener Medizinische Wochenschrift 6, 8. Pirquet, *System der Ernährung* (n 22) 2:314.

of children were lodged in the countryside and received NEM meals, while another group was placed in farming households to eat there. As the newsletter drily put it, '[i]n general, the farmer was hostile'.[92] By 1926, in a retrospective article on postwar aid to children, the critique was more pointed, lengthier, and scientifically grounded. Sending children abroad, as the ARA publicist Friedrich Reischl noted, was psychologically stressful for the children, disruptive of their education, an opportunity for them to be exploited in household work, expensive, and as two research studies showed, of little lasting value for the children.[93]

For its part, the *Amerikanische Kinderhilfsaktion* confronted Tandler with a variety of challenges. One of these was ideological. For in addition to improving housing conditions and advancing new initiatives in public health, Tandler, like others in the leadership of 'Red Vienna', considered strengthening the feeling of self-responsibility among the working-class to be an essential task of socialism. His campaign to fight the spread of tuberculosis, for example, also questioned the moral character of those who were sick with tuberculosis, but refused to stay away from children.[94] Consistent with that principle, Tandler objected to giving free, or low-cost, meals to children because it diminished a primary duty of the parents in caring for their children, and as he said, 'we . . . have seen the feeling of responsibility of parental caregivers in the course of the last years disappear sufficiently'.[95] Such local anxieties of 'pauperization by charity', in particular the concern that parents would no longer feel a responsibility to feed their children when the American programme ended, were registered by ARA leadership, but it was felt that the crisis outweighed the concern, and somehow the Austrians would manage.[96] As a politician, Tandler also encountered difficulties in accommodating the high-profile ARA programme led by Pirquet. The name *Amerikanische Kinderhilfsaktion* conveyed the impression to constituents that Vienna and Austria were being sustained by charity. The contributions of the city and country—50 per cent of programme food costs paid in the form of flour, with Vienna covering two-thirds of these costs starting in August 1920—simply disappeared in the public relations campaign.[97] Politically speaking, the city of Vienna received virtually no credit.

But with the Pirquet-led ARA *Amerikanische Kinderhilfsaktion* Tandler faced a still larger challenge. From the outset, the ARA programme insisted on two absolute principles in working with the Austrian government and its representatives. First, the power of decision for the programme finally resided with the

[92] Friedrich Reischl (ed), *Mitteilungen der American Relief Administration 41–43* (Verlag des Generalkommissariates der A.K.H.A. April 1921) 223–224.

[93] Friedrich Reischl, 'Die Ausländische Kinderhilfe in Wien' in Clemens Pirquet (ed), *Volksgesundheit im Krieg* (vol 1, Hölder-Pichler-Tempsky 1926) 363, 366–371.

[94] Sablik, *Julius Tandler* (n 84) 252.

[95] Ibid, 192.

[96] Clare M. Torrey, 'For the children of Austria (Report)' (20 June 1919) 14 American Relief Administration Bulletin 16.

[97] Adlgasser, *American Individualism Abroad* (n 49) 141–143. Sablik, *Julius Tandler* (n 84) 192.

Americans. Second, 'owing to the urgency of the situation [...] the executive of the American organization shall be subject to the control of no department of the city of Vienna'.[98] In short, the city of Vienna, a political and administrative unit that functioned virtually as a state within a state at the time, had no authority over the vast relief operations of Pirquet. When ARA officials had observed that Pirquet's programme 'the best led and operated' in Vienna, they expressed an official position, and also, their low estimation of the government-directed recuperative initiatives, 'Kinder ins Ausland' and 'Kinder aufs Land'. And where the ARA went, the Rockefeller Foundation followed. A general principle of the Foundation was to remove itself from local politics, even as it applied this principle unevenly, cooperating with governments in Czechoslovakia, Hungary, and Poland. In Austria, the Rockefeller Foundation cooperated with the municipally averse Pirquet. While its officers occasionally interviewed Tandler as part of their due diligence, Foundation resources stayed away.

It is fitting that the final chapter of the *Amerikanische Kinderhilfsaktion* in Austria belongs to both Tandler and Pirquet. As the emergency phase of the ARA relief effort concluded in mid-1921, plans were drawn up to expand its reach and place the effort on a more permanent legal basis. One ARA option that gained support called for a new organization to administer a compulsory meal programme for school children and for this initiative to be authorized by new child-feeding legislation at the federal level. Tandler led the resistance to this proposal, calling instead for a feeding programme that would be conducted by municipalities with the assistance of the federal government and state provinces. Relief to children would feature a 'strengthened social component', according to the plan of Tandler, and it would reduce the number of children reached.[99] As his biographer Karl Sablik describes it, Tandler 'pulled out all the stops' to replace foreign and private ARA relief with a local and public programme built on self-reliance, including mobilizing the support of parents' councils from the socialist-oriented Free School (Freie Schule).[100] The ARA initially balked at the proposed changes, but eventually supported May 1922 legislation passed by the Austrian *Nationalrat* and *Bundesrat* that officially 'continued' the feeding programme. According to the new plan, the city of Vienna would take over the feeding of 20,000 children on 1 August 1922 but delays prevented the programme from ever taking place. Cooperation between the ARA and the Austrian state officially ended on 1 June 1923.

To be sure, Tandler and Pirquet knew the necessity of cooperation, and their status and ambition frequently placed them in shared space. In February 1920, for example, both represented Austria at the Geneva 'Congress of Children's Relief

98 Geist to Reumann, 12 June 1919, cited by Adlgasser, *American Individualism Abroad* (n 49) 108.
99 Adlgasser, *American Individualism Abroad* (n 49) 151–152.
100 Sablik, *Julius Tandler* (n 84) 192.

Agencies for Countries Affected by War'.[101] Together, they also sat on official committees, such as one that included Sigmund Freud that received a one million crown ($200,000) contribution for children's relief from his New York brother-in-law Eli Bernays.[102] And the founding of the Austrian Society for Public Health in 1926 (*Die Österreichische Gesellschaft für Volksgesundheit*), in which both participated, was an organization itself designed to reconcile opposing public health agendas in Vienna. But animosity between the two ran deeply, and it was hardly a secret. Richard Pearce, Director of the Rockefeller Foundation's Division of Medical Education, wrote in his report on Vienna to his Associate Director, Alan Gregg, that 'I suppose you understand that Tandler is a bitter antagonist of von Pirquet, the former representing the extreme socialistic point of view and the latter the aristocratic, and that this has been one of the difficulties in the University of Vienna'.[103] Tandler had not always endeared himself to the Rockefeller Foundation, once telling Allan Embree, at an event hosted by Pirquet, that a 'sewerage worker should have more pay than a university professor because his work is more disagreeable'.[104] Still, the conflict between Pirquet and Tandler manifested itself across postwar Vienna. In his reply to Pearce, Gregg simply registered the obvious, writing to his superior, '[i]ncidentally, Tandler's position in Vienna was clear to me'.[105]

Today, Julius Tandler is widely viewed as the engineer of postwar public health advances in Vienna, while the contributions of postwar private initiatives, including the ARA and the Rockefeller Foundation, from which Tandler was excluded have little place in the history of those advances. In that, perhaps, there may be an equal measure of fairness and irony. After all, scholars have charged those private initiatives with serving as a Trojan horse for other, undeclared agendas, among them, imperialism, models of American public health, moral pedagogy (American), and communist containment.[106] But what the addition of Pirquet to the context of Tandler adds is a richer and more nuanced picture of the local expertise that contributed to the reconstruction of postwar Austria and, as Herbert Hoover suggested, to Europe. It brings to view, as well, an open Austrian public health model—progressive, vigorous, and engaged with international philanthropic networks and experts—that flourished parallel to the social approach of Red Vienna, and indeed, improved that approach by challenging it. The postwar

[101] 'Abschrift eines Berichtes der österreichischen Gesandtschaft in Bern vom 3. März 1920 an das Staatsamt für Aeusseres. Kongress der Kinderhilfswerke in Genf.' Österreichisches Staatsarchiv/Archiv der Republik (ÖStA/AdR/BMfsV), Bundesministerium für soziale Verwaltung, Karton 1664, 1920.

[102] Letter: Sigmund Freud to Sándor Ferenczi, 22 April 1920. Ernst Falzeder and Eva Brabant (eds), *The Correspondence of Sigmund Freud and Sándor Ferenczi, Volume 3, 1920–1933* (Belknap Press 2000) 17.

[103] Pearce to Gregg, 19 February 1926. RAC, RF, RG 1.1, Folder 5, Box 1, Series 705.

[104] Edwin R. Embree, Log of Journey to Europe, 24 July 1920, RAC RF RG 12, Officers' Diaries, FA391.

[105] Gregg to Pearce, 2 March 1926. RAC, RF, RG 1.1, Folder 5, Box 1, Series 705.

[106] E.R. Brown, 'Public health and American imperialism: Early Rockefeller programs at home and abroad' (1976) 66 American Journal of Public Health 897. Zahra, *The Lost Children* (n 90) 39–40. Adlgasser, 'The Roots of Communist Containment' (n 48).

campaign in Austria that sent children elsewhere in Europe to recuperate, for example, certainly energized an international discourse of humanitarianism.[107] But this campaign, no less than the ARA initiative led by Pirquet, was grounded in a series of social, scientific, and public health assumptions. The bold claims of the Pirquet System of Nutrition to quantify nutritional health also serve as a reminder of the intense competition not only to participate in the 'humanitarian', but to define what constituted 'relief'.

V. From Vienna to Geneva—and Back Again

Had he cast a backwards glance at his leadership of the *Kinderhilfsaktion* as its end was fixed in August 1922, Clemens Pirquet might have concluded that things did not look all that bad. True, he had not realized his hope of expanding the programme and continuing his research. But he could fairly have ascribed this outcome to the dark workings of local politics. If many had connected the programme's termination with the ending of the postwar emergency crisis in Austria, he might also have watched Austrian hyperinflation reach its highest levels in July and August 1922 with a told-you-so foreboding.[108] Moreover, he could still consider his ARA work, which had reestablished his scientific prominence, reconfigured his study of tuberculosis, and applied his wartime research on nutrition, as a success. Indeed, as awareness of the scope of the Austrian hunger crisis grew, so did professional recognition of the Pirquet System of Nutrition. In fact, Pirquet had spent some months of that crisis in the United States, delivering the Cutter Lecture at Harvard University in December 1921, the Silliman Lectures at Yale University, also during December and in January 1922. In addition, though the NEM component had met with particular scrutiny, advocates of Pirquet's method stressed the importance of his 'system', and researchers in San Francisco had generated interesting results on the basis of Pelidisi numbers and *sacratama* determinations they collected from 1,282 local school children there.[109] Finally, looking ahead, Pirquet could hope that the prewar scientific networks to which he had turned in the postwar Austrian crisis might once again be mobilized to create a new context, equal to his stature, where his research on nutrition would regain its international relevance. Public health Europe was moving from a state of emergency towards the new normal. Opportunities were moving, too.

[107] See Kind-Kovács, 'The "Other" Child Transports' (n 89). Other relief agents also contributed to the 'internationalizing' of the Austrian hunger crisis. On the important role of the Quakers, see Sheila Spielhofer, *Stemming the Dark Tide. Quakers in Vienna 1919–1942* (William Sessions 2001) 4–63.

[108] Nathan Marcus, 'Hyperinflation as a Catalyst of Transformations: Path dependence through accelerated dynamics in post-First World War Austria' (2016) 23/4 European Review of History-Revue Européenne d'Histoire 595.

[109] William E. Carter, 'The Pirquet System of Nutrition and its Applicability to American Conditions' (1921) 77/20 Journal of the American Medical Association 1541.

In 1926, a new opportunity reached Pirquet when Ludwik Rajchman, director of the League of Nations Health Organization (LNHO), invited him to join the Committee of Health Experts on Child Welfare. The Health Committee of the LNHO had been recently tasked with the preparation of an Infant Mortality Report, a Report that constituted one of the few concrete actions to address child health at the League, despite the adoption of the landmark 'Declaration of the Rights of the Child' by the League Assembly in 1924.[110] Established in June 1921, first provisionally, and then on a permanent basis, the LNHO is a complex organizational entity. Iris Borowy, its chronicler, has observed that while 'seemingly an institutional entity, it is to some extent a convenient symbol for a group of men and a process'.[111] Through the Health Committee, this group oversaw the operation of the League's health work, gripped by the sense that their activities should not just administer the existing state of affairs, but create a better world. The LNHO 'lacked tradition, precedence, and a stable framework', as Borowy notes, but that bestowed a freedom of action.[112] For Pirquet, this freedom of action mattered. It provided access to external financial resources that enabled him to travel largely at his discretion, and to invite international public health experts to Vienna to learn about his work at the *Kinderklinik*.[113] More importantly, perhaps, it permitted him to envision his new work with the Infant Mortality Report as part of a natural trajectory that would reach its zenith on an international stage in Geneva at the League of Nations. And as long as Pirquet was alive, his Vienna public health nemesis Julius Tandler had no role in LNHO activities.[114]

As one who acquired a worldwide reputation for his tuberculosis test, and then achieved perhaps a yet more elevated celebrity through his scientific work on nutrition during the Austrian hunger crisis, Clemens Pirquet possessed the great gift of adaptability. But during the 1920s Pirquet largely pursued the path charted by the postwar work he had done in Vienna, and his cooperation with the LNHO, may be seen as a continuation of that work in several ways. The first is the central role of the Rockefeller Foundation in shaping the purpose of the LNHO.[115] Guided by its International Health Board and Medical Sciences Division, the

[110] Iris Borowy, *Coming to Terms with World Health. The League of Nations Health Organisation 1921–1946* (Peter Lang 2009) 184. The Health Committee was charged with addressing 'infant mortality', despite the founding of the Child Welfare Committee in 1924, which might have been expected to channel the two-decade-old international infant welfare movement. On the difficulties in constructing a children's agenda at the League, see Dominique Marshall, 'The construction of children as an object of international relations: The Declaration of Children's Rights and the Child Welfare Committee of the League of Nations, 1900–1924' (1993) 7 The International Journal of Children's Rights 103.

[111] Borowy, *Coming to Terms with World Health* (n 110) 32.

[112] Ibid.

[113] On travel, see, for example, Pirquet to Olsen, 5 October 1927. League of Nations Archive (LNA) / Box R974 / Class 12b / Ser 46927 / Doc 5113b.

[114] Sablik, *Julius Tandler* (n 84) 302–303.

[115] Paul Weindling, 'Philanthropy and world health: The Rockefeller Foundation and League of Nations Health Organisation' (1997) 35 Minerva 269.

Foundation increasingly believed that the development of science was connected to international action, and beginning in 1922, provided a sizable annual subvention for the LNHO—in 1924, for example, 40 per cent of its entire budget—to support public health activities much like those it had advanced in Central Europe.[116] The second is the transfer of postwar expertise from Central Europe to Geneva, in the form of a new cadre of public health experts. This cadre includes, above all, Rajchman, whose widely praised leadership in Poland of the Rockefeller-funded Warsaw Institute for Public Hygiene had been a stepping-stone to the League, but also others, such as Rajchman's countryman Witold Chodźko and the Croat Andrija Štampar. The third is a newly rigorous approach to statistical data as a substantive element in the exchange of public health information undertaken by the LNHO. The Rockefeller Foundation supported such an approach, directing funding in June 1922 to support statistics-based work and epidemiological intelligence.[117] It is in this third area that Pirquet intended to demonstrate to his League of Nations colleagues the vast potential of what in Vienna he had only just begun.

A gifted leader, whose professional background in Anglo-American institutions of public health echoed that of Pirquet, Rajchman believed that the LNHO should work to advance the sharing of health data across member countries. His vision of LNHO activities, as he expressed it in 1922 to Eric Drummond, the League's Secretary General, was that the health secretariat 'should be a clearing-house for national health administrations, review national reports and collect and standardize epidemiological data. It should conduct surveys, help create international biological standards […] Agreements also should be promoted on child welfare, tuberculosis, venereal diseases and perhaps opium'.[118] The exchange of epidemiological intelligence at a March 1922 LNHO-led conference in Warsaw represented an early realization of this vision. The Warsaw conference, which brought together representatives from all European countries except Albania and Portugal, proceeded from the principle that all member countries had a shared interest in being informed about potential disease threats. But the exchange of information could always find new justifications. In January 1923, the LNHO recruited the American statistician Edgar Sydenstricker to establish its statistical service. Working with Sydenstricker, Rajchman updated existing publications on notifiable diseases, while also introducing a new series of reports that would systematically study the organization of health administrations in different countries, as well as the conditions in which health data was collected.[119] Such study, Rajchman hoped,

[116] 'Minutes of the Sixth Session', Held in Paris, 26 May to 3 June 1923: 13. LNA R821/12b/11346/29313.

[117] Paul Weindling, 'Philanthropy and World Health' (n 115) 274.

[118] Rajchman to the Secretary-General, 20 January 1922. LNA 12b/18772.

[119] Paul Weindling, 'From Moral Exhortation to the New Public Health, 1918–45' in Esteban Rodríguez-Ocaña (ed), *The Politics of the Healthy Life. An International Perspective* (EAHMH Publications 2002) 113, 120. Borowy, *Coming to Terms with World Health* (n 110) 103.

would lead to increased uniformity in health data. By October 1923, nine countries had submitted their reports, with Hermann Schrötter, assisted by the statistician Siegfried Rosenfeld, contributing the survey of public health services in Austria.[120]

Sydenstricker himself had co-authored a comparative statistical analysis of three indices of physical well-being that included the Pelidisi approach and could have attested to the statistical temperament that the clinician Pirquet would bring to the LNHO project. In any case, Pirquet had already publicly endorsed the LNHO as a clearinghouse for health data sharing and as an authoritative agent for the international standardization of nomenclature. One area of advance in standardization, he wrote in a March 1926 article describing the work of the Health Committee to an Austrian audience, was in 'mortality statistics, which previously among different countries were in many cases scarcely comparable'.[121] Mortality statistics would form the basis of the Infant Mortality Report, though some cause-of-death classifications, such as 'stillbirth', remained elusive, and the report largely built upon the model of the cross-country surveys of public health services.[122] Initial members of the Committee of Child Health Experts were Pirquet, Dame Janet Campbell (Great Britain), Arthur Collett (Norway), Robert Debré (France), Corrado Gini (Italy), Evert Gorter (Netherlands), and Fritz Rott (Germany). The American Taliaferro Clark, employed by the United States Public Health Office in Paris and a co-author with Sydenstricker of the comparative statistical analysis that had included the Pirquet system, joined the planning process. Additional national reports were envisaged from Latin America and elsewhere. Altogether, the Committee would convene four times to plan and coordinate their reports, including once in Vienna, from 26–27 September 1927. The inaugural planning meeting took place on 27 September 1926 in Geneva.

In joining the Committee of Child Health Experts Pirquet found himself among both clinicians and statisticians, and such hybrid entities expressed the dual origins of the LNHO. Its early collation and sharing of epidemiologic intelligence acknowledged the central role of statistics, while physicians and health workers in the field collected real-time data via physical examinations. Ideally, the Infant Mortality Report would proceed in similar fashion. Clinicians would examine the exact cause of every infant death for a one-year period, while statisticians would make manifest statistical anomalies in ways that helped produce an understanding of the factors that contributed to lower infant mortality rates. Early in the design

[120] Hermann Schrötter, *Public Health Services in Austria* (League of Nations Health Organisation 1923).

[121] Clemens Pirquet, 'Die Leistungen des Völkerbundes auf dem Gebiete der Hygiene' (13 March 1926) 11 Wiener Medizinische Wochenschrift 340, 340.

[122] Pirquet himself later sought to have the category of 'stillbirth' removed from the Austrian report on infant mortality, Pirquet to Rajchman, 17 March 1927. LNA R974/12b/46927/5113b. On the particular definitional complexities of 'stillbirth' as a statistical category, see Iris Borowy, 'Counting Death and Disease: Classification of Death and Disease in the Interwar Years, 1919–1939' (2003) 18/3 Continuity and Change 457, 461–462; 466–467.

stage, the British statistician Major Greenwood was retained to review and evaluate the project, and Committee members identified a number of promising areas for investigation. For example, it was known that where the proportion of births to population was high, infant mortality also tended to increase.[123] Yet, this was not always the case: some countries had high rates of birth to population and also lower infant mortality rates. Why? Likewise, 'Investigations carried out at The Hague showed the remarkable fact that poverty among certain classes of the people was not necessarily a factor in infant mortality'.[124] Again, why? Such questions would merit the Committee's attention.

True to his recent experience with the *Amerikanische Kinderhilfsaktion*, Pirquet believed that infant mortality should be studied by bundling standardized observations of clinicians into statistical information. In this respect, Pirquet stood for the greater incorporation of statistics into the practice of physicians. Of course, in Vienna, he had been surrounded by clinicians, not statisticians. In Geneva, statisticians were not only better represented, but their value had been administratively authorized by the LNHO, so that the conflict between those who favoured a statistical report and those who sought medical insights became more acute. When the statistician Corrado Gini, the Italian member of the Committee, tendered his resignation, for example, Pirquet lamented his departure, noting that the south Italian conditions added a unique dimension to the Infant Mortality Report. Still, in the letter he wrote to fellow physician Rajchman, he expressed both professional solidarity and a theory regarding Gini's action, pointing out that Gini 'was a pure statistician who showed little understanding for our medical outlook'.[125] Indeed, in Geneva, Pirquet advocated from the first planning meeting what he described as more than a 'statistical report', if by statistics one means only numbers. What Pirquet sought was a close study of the 'method of feeding' children and, if they died, cause of death. This, he argued, was more accurate than 'mere statistics'.[126]

Such an emphasis on method of feeding echoed the original proposal on infant mortality, which requested the Health Organization 'to investigate infant mortality from the point of view of feeding in infancy'.[127] But this emphasis also recalls the NEM-system Pirquet had administered during the postwar hunger crisis in Austria. Indeed, the participation of Pirquet with the LNHO might be narrowly defined as an effort to uproot the Pirquet System of Nutrition from its emergency relief context and to replant it in the new ground of international public

[123] 'Health Organisation. Committee on Health Experts on Child Welfare'. Meeting held at 4:30 pm, Tuesday 28 September 1926. LNA R975/12b/46927/54409, 'Conférence d'Experts en matière de protection de l'enfance. Procès verbaux des séances de la 1ère session septembre 1926'. P. 2.
[124] Ibid.
[125] Pirquet to Rajchman, 5 March 1927. LNA R974/12b/46927/5113b.
[126] 'Health Organisation. Committee on Health Experts on Child Welfare'. Meeting held at 4:30 pm., Tuesday 28 September 1926, p4. LNA R975/12b/46927/54409.
[127] 'Infant Mortality and Child Welfare. Resolutions of the Health Committee'. LNA R972/12B/46927/48719.

health. After all, according to the Pirquet System, the clinician would conduct a series of measurements and a subjective evaluation to yield a Pelidisi number and a Sacratama determination that would express the nutritional state of the child; the NEM-kitchen, in turn, would serve well-measured but not too tasty meals that improved the nutritional state of the child. Here, the statistician tracked the nutritional progress of individual children, aggregated Pelidisi data, and evaluated feeding results.

Likewise, Pirquet's proposed close study of the 'method of feeding' at the LNHO would enable an identification of nutritional factors in infant mortality—with his NEM-system standing by as the implicit corrective to deficient nutritional factors. And Pirquet pushed repeatedly with Rajchman to include standardized measuring of school-aged children in connection with the work of the Infant Mortality Report.[128] As always, Rajchman was willing to review a proposal from a respected colleague—in this case what amounted to a plan to internationalize the Pelidisi index. In March 1927, however, Otto Olsen, the German LNHO Secretariat, travelled to Austria to discuss with Pirquet the upcoming September Committee meeting in Vienna, and he quickly produced the project evaluation that gave Rajchman the administrative cover to reject Pirquet's proposal.[129] If measuring school-aged children to assess their nutritional state, as Pirquet proposed, was in fact difficult to justify within the context of the Infant Mortality Report, his approach with the Pelidisi index did fulfil the ambitions of the LNHO in others respects. For one, Pelidisi measurements provided the standardization of statistical procedures that the Rajchman-led LNHO sought. For another, they furnished a scientific alternative to data that would highlight social situation and poverty as factors to investigate in infant mortality. As British statistician Major Greenwood described the relevance of capturing poverty as a factor in his early letter that evaluated the proposed project of infant mortality, 'we don't want statistical calculations to tell us that if we could raise the general standard of living we could decrease mortality'.[130]

In this observation, Greenwood was largely endorsing the objective of the hunger relief programme led by Pirquet in postwar Austria. As the ARA 'Principles of Policy' had put it, '[t]he relief must be confined to averting actual starvation, the American Relief Administration not being concerned in the alleviation [sic] of poverty per se'.[131] Indeed, in a postwar Austria whose middle-class was devastated by economic upheaval, the Pirquet System of Nutrition was rigorously agnostic concerning social class. From this standpoint, the Pirquet System shared the universalist ideal that informed the establishment of Save the Children International

[128] Pirquet to Rajchman, 21 February 1927. Rajchman to Pirquet, 26 February 1927. LNA R972/12b/46927/48719.

[129] Otto Olsen, Definite Proposal, 19 March 1927. LNA R972/12b/46927/48719.

[130] Greenwood to Rajchman, 6 August 1926. LNA R972/12b/46927/52992.

[131] Cited in Adlgasser, *American Individualism Abroad* (n 49) 114.

Union in 1920 by Eglantyne Jebb, namely that child welfare should be pursued 'irrespective of race, country or creed'.[132] That ideal of a child in need of protection, a child abstracted from claims upon it by nation or family, was also the child imagined by the League in its 1924 'Declaration of Children's Rights'.[133]

But the Infant Mortality Report aimed to take the agnosticism of the Pelidisi index a step further. Measurement would now be fully decoupled from aid to the individual, and it was primarily statistical anomalies that would guide future policy. Confronted with this approach, the physician rebelled. Pirquet called for what he described as not 'mere statistics', but 'critical, clinical and medical statistics'.[134] Rajchman agreed, at least initially, summarizing what was planned by saying it should be 'medical, not statistical'. But the word of Rajchman was rarely final, and by the second Committee meeting, held at the League's Paris office in January 1927, the Committee had decided that the Report would focus more on the potential of immunization than nutrition. Pirquet, who knew how to communicate his displeasure, sent his assistant Edmund Nobel to this meeting, explaining half-heartedly to Rajchman that he was 'sick, or not so much sick, as stuck with a lingering cold'.[135]

Projects that did not showcase his own breakthroughs in nutrition science had never interested the former ARA General Commissioner Pirquet, though he certainly could be counted upon to fulfil his commitments. Agreements were already in place to hold the September 1927 meeting of the Committee of Child Health Experts in Vienna, a site choice that underscores the clout Pirquet had with the LNHO, which preferred its external events to be held in Paris or London. For the Vienna meeting, Pirquet planned for the Committee to convene at the *Kinderklinik*, and among other activities, the Austrian President Michael Hainisch would host a reception. Pirquet did place 'Standards and Measurement' on the programme agenda, in a final effort to promote the Pirquet System of Nutrition to the group.[136] But this, too, was soon lost. As the Infant Mortality Report shifted its agenda away from nutrition towards immunization, Pirquet increasingly replaced himself with his top assistant Edmund Nobel on the Committee, and he seems to have lost interest in the endeavour.[137]

Pirquet did continue to have occasional opportunities to promote his work in connection with the League. In 1927, for example, Saiki Tadasu, the Yale-educated,

132 Paul Weindling, 'From sentiment to science: Children's relief organisations and the problem of malnutrition in inter-war Europe' (1994) 18/3 Disasters 203.

133 On the return of the family in the postwar 'Geneva Declaration of the Rights of the Child' (1948) see Lara Bolzman, 'The advent of child rights on the international scene and the role of the Save the Children International Union 1920–45' (2008) 27/4 Refugee Survey Quarterly 26.

134 'Health Organisation. Committee on Health Experts on Child Welfare.' Meeting held at 4:30 pm, Tuesday, 28 September 1926, P. 5. LNA R975/12b/46927/54409.

135 Pirquet to Rajchman, 14 January 1927. LNA R974/12b/46927/5113b.

136 'Program' LNA R976/12b/46927/55953.

137 League of Nations, Geneva, *Report on the Conference of Infant Health Experts* (League of Nations, Geneva, 3 October 1927).

Japanese specialist in nutrition delivered a lecture at the *Kinderklinik* that was reported upon in the press.[138] Saiki was a central figure in League's Asia-focused programme on nutrition. He had lectured under its auspices on nutrition in the USA, Argentina, Brazil, and Chile, and he had also prepared a report on nutrition and Japan for the League in 1926.[139] As Pirquet wrote Rajchman, he hoped to demonstrate the particulars of his NEM-system and nutrition for diabetic children to Saiki.[140] Still, for the most part, Pirquet's cooperation with the League had ended. As for the Infant Mortality Report on Austria, the LNHO had to remind Pirquet to complete it. Of his work with Geneva, only a few travel assignments and some writing remained.[141]

In retrospect, it might be said of Pirquet and his activities with the League of Nations that he failed because he wished to sit on two chairs at once. His gift for numbers, as manifested in his anthropometric Pelidisi index and his prescient sense that big data mattered, put him at the table with the LNHO's Committee of Child Health Experts. But in the infant mortality report they finally agreed to produce, Pirquet found no place to express his identity as a clinician and doctor to children. Meanwhile, the role of paediatrician limited his ability to express himself as a scientist. And the possibility of such a role did, in fact, present itself for Pirquet at the League of Nations. His February 1920 trip to Geneva had the purpose of helping to shape the relief efforts of the newly created Save the Children International Union (SCIU). Pirquet subsequently remained close to its founders, Eglantyne Jebb and her sister Dorothy Buxton, even serving as the organization's president in 1927.[142] When the League of Nations established the Child Welfare Committee in 1924, SCIU with Jebb was granted a consultative status to the Committee, and Pirquet advised the Committee. Through the SCIU, Pirquet succeeded in formally bringing details of the Pirquet Nutrition System to the Child Welfare Committee and the LNHO.[143] Pirquet did care deeply about the welfare of children. But the emotional appeal of the SCIU, which Jebb herself acknowledged, did not resonate deeply with the scientist Pirquet. Pirquet may have tried to sit in two chairs at the League, but in truth neither one—infant mortality nor child welfare—fit him very well.[144]

Through the war and the early postwar period Pirquet had transformed himself into an international expert in nutrition—and he had a résumé that could not be

[138] Letter from Pirquet to Rajchman, 19 February 1927. LNA R930/12b/34884/55726.

[139] Josep L. Barona, *The Problem of Nutrition. Experimental Science, Public Health and Economy in Europe 1914–1945* (Peter Lang 2010) 30.

[140] Letter from Pirquet to Rajchman, 27 January 1927. LNA R930/12b/34884/55726.

[141] Pirquet to Rajchman, 12 December 1927. LNA R974/12b/46927/5113b.

[142] On Geneva trip, see 'Abschrift eines Berichtes der österreichischen Gesandtschaft in Bern vom 3. März 1920'.

[143] Patricia T. Rooke and Rudy L. Schnell, '"Uncramping Child Life:" International Children's Organisations, 1914–1939' in Paul Weindling (ed), *International Health Organisations and Movements, 1918–1939* (Cambridge University Press 1995) 176 , 185.

[144] Ibid, 182.

challenged. Had the LNHO sought to establish a research programme around nutrition, he might have flourished at the League. But a report on infant mortality was hardly the place to test hypotheses regarding nutrition and the nutritional state of individuals. For its part, the Child Welfare Committee was largely excluded from developing its own agenda for nutrition research.[145] Indeed, as great as the obstacles to humanitarian relief had been, reaching agreement on a shared League agenda to study nutrition proved greater. No Nutrition Commission existed at the League in the 1920s, even though by 1926, the LNHO had decided to add nutrition science to its programme.[146] And before interest in nutrition research surged in the 1930s, the LNHO issued few reports on nutrition, with none between 1929 and 1931; before issuing fifteen such reports between 1932 and 1934.[147]

Meanwhile, the broader move in nutrition research away from minimum diets of fats and protein towards optimum diets that maximized vitamins and minerals, confronted the Pirquet System of Nutrition with additional challenges. Tailored to the war and postwar crisis, the NEM formula had addressed survival, not well-being, and the formula offered little to a discussion focused on how to remedy nutritional deficiencies. Likewise, the *Sacratama* measurement was insufficient and had been dismissed as too subjective. Into the 1930s, only the Pelidisi number, a body mass index, remained, and it continued to be referenced in League documents.[148] The Pirquet System itself, however, had become obsolete.

Thanks to his discovery of the 'Pirquet test' for tuberculosis at a relatively young age, Clemens Pirquet earned the lifetime burden of a professional success that he could never again hope to equal. At the same time, he internalized the lessons of this success. One of these lessons was a deep distrust of compromise, a preference to win the game rather than to play it. Socialist Vienna of the 1920s eagerly sought to displace him, but he also seems to have removed himself. It is remarkable to consider, for example, that as Socialist leadership stepped into the spotlight, Pirquet was virtually absent from the Fourth International Conference on Child Welfare, organized by SCIU, held in Vienna in October 1924.[149] That was his moment. The 'Declaration of Children's Rights' was on the verge of being adopted by the League

[145] Dominque Marshall, 'The Rise of Coordinated Action for Children in War and Peace. Experts at the League of Nations, 1924–1945' in Davide Rodogno, Bernhard Struck, and Jakob Vogel (eds), *Shaping the Transnational Sphere* (Berghahn 2014).

[146] Marta A. Balinska, *For the Good of Humanity. Ludwik Rajchman*—Medical Statesman (1995, CEU Press 1998) 73.

[147] Paul Weindling, 'The Role of International Organizations in Setting Nutritional Standards in the 1920s and 1930s' in Harmke Kamminga and Andrew Cunningham (eds), *The Science and Culture of Nutrition, 1840–1940* (Rodopi 1995) 319, 323.

[148] See, for example, 'The most suitable methods of detecting malnutrition due to the economic depression, conference held at Berlin from December 5th to 7th, 1932' (1933) 2/1 Quarterly Bulletin of the Health Organisation 116.

[149] *IVᵉᵐ Congrès international des Oeuvres de l'Enfance, Vienne-Budapest 6–11 October 1924* (Geneva: Union International de Secours aux Enfants). For a report of the event, which seems to have included everyone but Pirquet, see 'Willkommengruß an die Internationale Vereinigung für Kinderhilfe' [7 October 1924] *Neue Freie Presse* 7.

of Nations in November, and Vienna had been selected as the Conference site because the city had drawn international attention for the humanitarian relief efforts there. Roughly put, the Conference celebrated the achievement of Pirquet. But as elsewhere, where his own achievements were not recognized in the manner he saw as appropriate, take, Pirquet often simply said 'no'.

It was a distrust of compromise that may have been not only professional but existential. In October 1925, news reports carried a story about an accident that had befallen Pirquet while he attended a conference in Karlsbad. Apparently, under the influence of painkillers, Pirquet had inadvertently jumped out of a hotel window, suffering a broken leg and other injuries.[150] When, altogether unexpectedly, Pirquet joined his wife in committing suicide in 1929, media reports revised their earlier description of the Karlsbad, now calling it an 'earlier suicide attempt'.[151] A contemporary reassessment of Clemens Pirquet suggests the continuities and discontinuities of scientific networks across the years prior to and following the First World War, as well as how those networks contributed to postwar careers. Such an assessment also points to the hard realities of local politics in 1920s Vienna. But not all the challenges Pirquet struggled with were scientific. Twenty years later, on the anniversary of his death in 1949, the writer of a commemorative article in Vienna's *Arbeiter-Zeitung* recalled Pirquet in emotional terms, noting that 'many of us, who as children of the First World War suffered from hunger, exhaustion, and sickness owe their life and health to his activity'.[152] The saviour of Austria's children, Clemens Pirquet left behind a legacy of national and international dimension because he had helped others. But Pirquet, too, needed help.

150 'Als Opfer eines Traumes', [3 October 1925] Volksfreund 2.

151 'Das Ehepaar Pirquet hat wahrscheinlich Selbstmord begangen. Frühere Selbstmordversuche—Das Testament am Todestag geschrieben' *Das Kleine Blatt* (Vienna 2 March 1929) 7.

152 J.P., 'Ein großer Arzt und Kinderfreund' [6 June 1949] *Arbeiter-Zeitung* 8.

3

Reinventing International Health in East Central Europe

The League of Nations, State Sovereignty, and Universal Health

Sara Silverstein

I. Introduction

In March 1919 the Paris Peace Conference's governing Council learned that east central European officials intended to ask the assembled states for assistance in combatting a typhus epidemic.[1] Faced with this request from the states they had delivered into existence, the international authorities in Paris began shuffling responsibility. The Council declared itself unable to assist. In the moment of establishing modern international institutions, the Council determined that such cooperation between governments should address issues of common, cross-border, concern. Social crises they defined as domestic problems. They passed the appeal for assistance in the anti-typhus campaign to humanitarian relief organizations.[2]

The Paris Council's decision set the precedent for its successors, the League of Nations and the League's governing Council. Social action within the League was an ambivalent proposition in its early years. The League of Nations had a Social Section but that branch was designed to function best when focusing on issues of a particularly international nature, such as drug trafficking or trafficking in women and children.[3] Fears of compromising state sovereignty and of obligating members to invest in caring for the citizens of other states set limitations on the League's areas of activity.

By the League's second decade of existence, its Health Organization had led a transformation in the meaning of international collaboration. Officials from the western powers envisioned the League's health branch operating along restricted lines, similar to the Social Section. Health received little attention in Paris, despite

[1] Herbert Hoover, *An American Epic: Famine in Forty-Five Nations, Organization Behind the Front, 1914–1923*, vol. II (Chicago: Henry Regnery Co. 1960) 441.
[2] Ibid, 441–443.
[3] Social Section: Daniel Gorman, *The Emergence of International Society in the 1920s* (Cambridge: Cambridge University Press 2014) 21–51.

Sara Silverstein, *Reinventing International Health in East Central Europe* In: *Remaking Central Europe.*
Edited by: Peter Becker and Natasha Wheatley, Oxford University Press (2020). © the many contributors.
DOI: 10.1093/oso/9780198854685.003.0004

the decimating influenza pandemic that engulfed the conference. It would take nearly two years after the League of Nations began operations for it to establish a health section. Even then, western officials eschewed the idea of this branch's involvement in social policy. Instead, they defined it as a meeting of the League's security objectives with limited humanitarian relief concerns. For them, international health was a question of inter-institutional politics and diplomacy.[4]

In practice, it would be their counterparts in east central Europe who shaped what the League Health Organization and the principles of international health would become. In addition to security and humanitarian relief, they introduced collaboration and mutual assistance between states, directing it towards expanding health services. In eastern Europe, international health became part of the resources for state-building. This different resonance in the post-imperial states quickly found its way into the League Health Organization. It would eventually contribute to a broader re-interpretation of the League of Nations' objectives.

The director of the League Health Organization was decisive in setting this course. Ludwik Rajchman assumed the post in November 1921, holding it until 1939 and emerging as a forceful personality in international health and in internationalism more generally.[5] Rajchman, who was Polish, was trained as a physician, a bacteriologist, and an epidemiologist in the Habsburg empire, the Russian empire, and in France. Before the First World War, he led a research laboratory in London. He returned to Warsaw in 1918 to become the chief epidemiologist of the new Polish state.[6] The head of the League's Social Section, Rachel Crowdy, advocated for Rajchman's appointment to the Health Organization after she viewed his work combatting the typhus epidemic in Poland during the early years of Polish independence.[7]

Rajchman and his Polish colleagues made this typhus epidemic a persistent challenge to restrictions on the League's involvement in domestic social problems. The epidemic intensified in 1919 and 1920, precisely at the moment of debate over whether the League would house a health branch, and what form such a branch would take. The appeals from Rajchman and his colleagues for assistance would weight the balance of the debate towards an international health organization with a capability for practical intervention.[8] When League officials finally approved one form of humanitarian intervention, Rajchman—now a member of the League's

[4] On west's intergovernmental and inter-institutional politics of establishing the League Health Organization: Francesca Piana, 'Humanitaire et politique, in medias res: le typhus en Pologne et l'Organisation international d'hygiène de la SDN (1919–1923)', *Relations Internationales*, vol. 138, no. 2 (2009) 23–38.

[5] Jean Monnet, *Memoirs*, trans. Richard Mayne (London: Collins 1978) 103.

[6] Rajchman, 'Autobiografia', Institut Pasteur (IP) RAJ.A1; Marta Balińska, *For the Good of Humanity: Ludwik Rajchman Medical Statesman* (Budapest: Central European University Press 1995) 29–34.

[7] League of Nations (LoN) S.861/2966: Rachel Crowdy to Ludwik Rajchman (16 July 1921); Telegram from Rajchman to Crowdy (27 July 1921); Rajchman to Crowdy (28 July 1921).

[8] Reception of Polish crisis in western international health negotiations: Piana, 'Humanitaire et politique' (n 4).

Epidemic Commission—quickly changed the very terms of that relief, using funds channelled through the League to support the development of Poland's health services. Crowdy and the advisory board of the Epidemic Commission understood this use of the League's anti-epidemic contributions when they toured Poland in the spring of 1921.[9]

Ludwik Rajchman would not define the League Health Organization as humanitarian, observing that the problem with humanitarian relief programmes was that they inherently had an end-date. The Health Organization, he promised in 1922, would not depart when the crisis abated but would assist a country until its health service 'can stand on its own feet'.[10] It was a model rooted in the post-imperial realities of east central European state-building. Over the following seventeen years, he expanded on this idea in company with a like-minded network of public health experts from across this region. Geneva replaced imperial Vienna as a hub for their collaboration. Their interest in utilizing internationalism for the benefit of smaller states resulted in the Health Organization creating a precedent and a programme for the League of Nations to expand its involvement in technical 'development'. In doing so, they redefined human security and the role of international cooperation.[11]

II. Conditions of an International Health Institution

From the western perspective, the League of Nations Health Organization originated in an inter-institutional and intergovernmental history. It involved the politics of the League of Nations, of the International Office of Public Health, and of the several Red Cross organizations (given to their own internecine struggles at the time), as well as the governments principally of Britain, France, and the United States. The prolonged debate tracked the League's expansion from a security organ to include humanitarian concerns. It helped when those concerns touched on security issues, as did the threat of infectious disease crossing borders and fuelling social unrest. In this context, international activity revolved around moments of crisis, either security or humanitarian.[12]

Further east, the League Health Organization arose from practical concerns of building states from the shreds of empire and wartime devastation. Tomasz Janiszewski, the Polish Minister of Health who had appealed for assistance in

[9] 'Minutes of the first meeting of the advisory board' (15 April 1921) LNHO R.822/12B/12462/13436.

[10] Rajchman to Madsen (4 July 1922) League of Nations Health Organization (LNHO) R.820/12B/11346/23213X jacket 2.

[11] On League of Nations technical work in the 1930s: Sunil Amrith and Patricia Clavin, 'Feeding the World: Connecting Europe and Asia, 1930–1945', *Past & Present*, vol. 218, no. 8 (2013) 29–50.

[12] See: Piana, 'Humanitaire et politique' (n 4).

fighting the typhus epidemic, warned that international collaboration must take into account that the peoples of Europe held their wartime sacrifices 'as so many promissory notes' and that the new governments 'must reckon with the fact that what the majority wants is change in the direction of progress, in the conditions of our social and political life'.[13] Officials like Janiszewski, understanding collaboration through the lens of their imperial networks and shared administrations, perceived the League's international federation as a solution to postwar social instability.

The covenant establishing the League of Nations referenced healthcare only to confirm it as an internal responsibility of separate states and, in times of crisis, as a concern for philanthropic humanitarian relief organizations. The covenant stipulated that signatory states engaged to control infectious disease within their own borders, for the sake of preventing its spread. The document did not engage the League to offer assistance. Instead, it proposed the Red Cross societies would lead in addressing health crises.[14] Janiszewski despaired that references to health at the Paris Conference and in its documents were 'mere fragmentary observations of quite secondary importance'.[15]

Diplomats in Paris did not see health as an issue in need of their attention. On the one hand, there was the Red Cross. On the other, when international collaboration required the agreement of states, an International Office of Public Health (OIHP, its common acronym derived from its French name) already existed. The OIHP, established in Paris in 1907, represented the understanding of international health that existed at that time. Its mandate entailed data collection and gave it regulatory authority over conventions regarding quarantine and disease control related to international trade and travel.[16]

Nevertheless, there were advocates of consolidating all international activity within the League of Nations, including health administration. Certain voices amongst these suggested a new League health branch should involve the capability for practical intervention. Typhus in Poland was the central issue of the interventionist camp.[17] Ultimately, it would be in Poland, not in the inter-institutional debates in London or even among western advocates for intervention, that the shape of the potential operations of international public health would form.

[13] Tomasz Janiszewski, 'The Versailles Treaty and the question of Public Health', *The International Journal of Public Health*, vol. 2 (1921) 141.

[14] 'Covenant of the League of Nations', Article 25.

[15] Janiszewski, 'Versailles Treaty', 145 (n 13).

[16] OIHP's history and activities, politics of existing organizations and League of Nations: Piana, 'Humanitaire et politique', 25–26, 33–35 (n 4); Iris Borowy, *Coming to Terms with World Health* (Frankfurt: Peter Lang 2009) 27–28, 41–43, 54–65.

[17] Ibid.

III. Humanitarian Relief and International Collaboration in a Sovereign State

Ludwik Rajchman's experience during the typhus epidemic in Poland illustrated the limitations of humanitarian relief and suggested alternative paths for international assistance. In Poland, foreign humanitarian relief projects failed when they were reluctant to engage the governing institutions. The directors of the principal international humanitarian mission to Poland, sponsored by the American Relief Administration, expected to operate within a sovereignty vacuum. Such humanitarian organizations anticipated that they would offer their services when there was no state to protect the destitute people, or when the state was incapable of doing so. However, Poland lacked resources but it did not lack expertise. Its officials wanted to expand the reach and effectiveness of government institutions, rather than find temporary relief. The American Typhus Expedition's failure was framed against other humanitarian agencies who, once on the ground in Poland, joined Polish authorities in making a case that Poland's government required international support from fellow governments—not from emergency philanthropic contributions—to secure the socio-economic stability that would arrest the typhus epidemic.

Polish authorities rejected humanitarianism that failed to acknowledge their state's independent authority. They did not see accepting, or requesting, international assistance as inherently invasive. Western authorities feared the implications for the state of international involvement in social issues. In Poland, far from seeing international assistance as an undermining interference, officials repeatedly experimented with methods of using internationalism to bolster Polish sovereignty.

On numerous issues, the Polish government sought in the League of Nations an ally in state-building. At the same time, it disregarded the mechanisms of international governance when interests conflicted. Poland's reluctance to accept borders decided by international negotiation put the country in a difficult position with regard to the League of Nations into the early 1920s. The Polish-Soviet War (1919–1921) was directly relevant to the typhus epidemic. The war both aggravated the conditions for this disease, among others, and also brought territories and refugees infected with typhus into Poland. The western powers took an ambivalent view of Poland's conflict with Soviet Russia over their shared border. By the winter of 1919–1920, the Allies effectively distanced themselves, decrying Polish motives.[18] To further complicate the matter, Poland was not only involved in border conflicts with a non-League member but also with Czechoslovakia and

[18] Margaret MacMillan, *Paris 1919: Six Months that Changed the World* (New York: Random House 2003) 221; Jerzy Borzęcki, *Soviet-Polish Peace of 1921 and the Creation of Interwar Europe* (New Haven: Yale University Press 2008) 7, 78, 103–104.

Lithuania. Some politicians believed the League of Nations should explicitly forbid a conflict they interpreted as Polish aggression.[19] Opponents of granting League assistance to Poland for the anti-typhus campaign expressed concern regarding these ongoing wars.[20]

While their compatriots created this first challenge to the League of Nations' authority, other Poles turned to the League for assistance fighting typhus, controlling the refugee population, and even confirming Poland's international stature. In December 1920, the president of Poland appealed to the League of Nations to intervene against Austria's plans to expel Jewish refugees from Galicia into Poland.[21] In the same year, the League considered a petition for the young Polish state to be recognized as a tutor of democracy, overseeing a Crimean mandate.[22] The anti-typhus campaign proved to be Poland's most successful early engagement with the League of Nations.

In these cases, the Poles joined other leaders from newly established central and eastern European states in delineating relationships between sovereignty and international cooperation that were distinct from those that limited their larger partners in the League. The political assumptions and economic interests of the great powers who dominated the League's formation did not pre-determine the shape of internationalism the smaller states envisioned. Theirs was unscripted, responsive to changing conditions, and utilitarian.

Poland's first appeal for assistance during the Paris Peace Conference led to major philanthropic relief missions from the United States and from western Europe. A year later, the typhus epidemic appeared to have worsened and Polish health experts and diplomats renewed their requests for intergovernmental assistance. The American Relief Administration and the League of Red Cross Societies both sent anti-typhus commissions to Poland in August 1919.[23] For the next eight months, Polish authorities made the most of this assistance. However, it quickly became apparent that the relationship between the Poles and their foreign relief was not going to be simple. Polish health authorities were in the midst of establishing a Ministry of Health. They had their own infectious disease experts and their own plans for the anti-typhus campaign. The head of the League of Red Cross Societies

[19] Norman Davies, *White Eagle, Red Star: The Polish Soviet War, 1919–1920* (New York: St. Martin's Press 1972) 83–85, 89–95; Borzęcki, *Soviet-Polish Peace*, 29–30, 64–65, 78, 108 (n 18); Timothy Snyder, *The Reconstruction of Nations: Poland, Ukraine, Lithuania, Belarus* (New Haven: Yale University Press 2003) 52–72; T. Shaw, House of Commons Debate, 17 June 1920, *Hansard*, vol. 130, 1557–1564.

[20] Archives Diplomatiques Courneuve (AFMFA) SDN 1579: Letter from the Minister of France in Poland to the Minister of Foreign affairs (27 Dec. 1921); Président de la commission des finances to Monsieur le Président du Conseil (7 Februaury 1922).

[21] J. J. Paderewski to the League of Nations Council (11 Dec. 1920) LoN R.586/11/9557/9557.

[22] This petition reached the League from the Crimean Tatars and it is unclear what involvement the Poles had in formulating this petition. LoN R.572/11/4328/4328.

[23] ARA typhus expedition: Alfred E. Cornebise, *Typhus and Doughboys: The American Polish Typhus Relief Expedition, 1919–1921* (Newark: University of Delaware Press 1982) 51; LRCS: 'Report of a Medical Commission to Poland', *Bulletin of the League of Red Cross Societies*, vol. 1, no. 4 (October 1919).

(LRCS) adjusted to this situation, while the head of the American Expedition fell into a power struggle with Polish authorities.

The American Relief Administration's Typhus Relief Expedition arrived with much-needed supplies and with a leader who believed himself to be the controlling authority of anti-typhus operations in Poland. Herbert Hoover, director of the American Relief Administration, delegated Harry Gilchrist of the United States Army Medical Corps to lead the Typhus Expedition. Gilchrist brought with him thirty-two officers and 500 enlisted men, as well as sanitary equipment, clothing, soap, and beds. The Americans were not volunteering this materiel. They required the Polish government to purchase the majority of these medicines and other supplies, totalling $4 million, at a favourable rate from American army surpluses.[24] The programme thus directed Poland's meagre resources away from the country.

Unlike Gilchrist, the head of the League of Red Cross Societies felt his own limitations in representing an organization that had no money.[25] An LRCS team conducted an initial survey in August 1919. In January 1920, the LRCS followed this advance unit with two representatives and made appeals to its member societies for supplies.[26] The LRCS mission's mandate was to coordinate relief efforts between the Red Cross societies present in Poland and to consult with the Polish government.[27]

Henry Shaw, who led the LRCS mission, admitted that operations did not begin as he and Harry Gilchrist had expected. They had assumed the foreign relief workers would manage the anti-typhus campaign in Poland, given that the Poles had indicated themselves unable to address the problem without assistance. Instead, they discovered they were subordinate to the Polish Ministry of Health. Shaw reported that they found the Poles 'a proud and also very capable people, believing implicitly in their ability to manage their own affairs and jealous of anything like outside interference. What they wanted and asked for was material assistance and not advice.'[28]

Shaw responded diplomatically. He offered Red Cross inspectors to the Ministry for auxiliary reports from the field and focused his own efforts on coordinating

[24] By March 1920, Poland had already purchased four million dollars' worth of supplies from the United States for the anti-typhus campaign: Gilchrist, 'Memorandum: Poland Typhus Situation and International Action', LNHO R.812/12B/1719/3659; The American Army soon reduced the personnel numbers to nineteen officers and seventy-five enlisted men. Gilchrist, 'Memorandum'. American anti-typhus operations: Cornebise, *Typhus*, 51–76 (n 23); 'Prace Ministerstwa Zdrowia Publicznego na terenie międzynarodowym', 1–2, Archiwum Polskiej Akademii Nauk (PAN) III-77/10; Piana, 'Humanitaire et politique', 29–30 (n 4).

[25] Harry Plotz, 'Report to Doctor Justus Goldman' (18 June 1820) JDC NY AR191921/4/36/3/260.

[26] 'League in Poland', *Bulletin*, vol. 1, no. 10 (May 1920) 13.

[27] They arrived in early winter 1920: 'League in Poland', *Bulletin*, vol. 1, no. 10 (May 1920) 13 (n 26); Witold Chodźko, 'Prace Ministerstwa Zdrowia Publicznego na terenie międzynarodowym', 1, PAN III-77/10.

[28] 'League in Poland', *Bulletin*, vol. 1, no. 10 (May 1920) 13 (n 26).

the many smaller voluntary organizations.[29] Shaw consoled himself for his lack of greater usefulness with the opera in Warsaw, which he found to be 'one of the very best I have ever seen both as to singers, orchestra and stage setting'.[30] Where Gilchrist saw chaos and an untutored people, Shaw encountered a culture that he recognized as European and experts who were amongst the leaders in their fields.

Gilchrist, increasingly impatient, tried to sidestep the Polish Ministry of Health's authority. He advised that Poland form a new body to manage all official anti-typhus work. His proposal revolved on removing the anti-typhus programme from the Ministry of Health's jurisdiction, which would give him an opportunity to gain greater influence.[31]

Polish officials understood that ceding authority would be the antithesis of extending their ability to govern and of the state development needed to check typhus. Instead of allowing Gilchrist to have his way, they would use his proposed anti-typhus commission and the foreign resources available to it as part of their own state-building. The Minister of Health, Witold Chodźko, agreed to a centralized commission. He agreed it would be a useful method to overcome lack of coordination between various ministries, and civilian and military authorities.[32] But Chodźko made sure to place a Pole in charge, confirming Polish control of operations in their own country.[33] In this instance, Habsburg legacy reinforced Chodźko's position. Chodźko, Rajchman, and Janiszewski had all worked within the Habsburg health administration and now the Polish Ministry of Health recruited another Habsburg official, Emil Godlewski, to lead its Special Epidemic Commission.[34]

Gilchrist, having been sidelined from the Special Commission, made a request in March 1920 for an international committee to assume control of anti-typhus operations in Poland.[35] He conceded a Pole might head the commission, but

[29] Shaw to Williams (4 May 1920) Rockefeller Foundation (RF) 1.1/789/2/11; Cornebise, *Typhus*, 70 (n 23).

[30] Shaw to Williams (4 May 1920) RF 1.1/789/2/11, RF 1.1/789/2/11.

[31] Ibid; cf. Paul Weindling, *Epidemics and Genocide in Eastern Europe, 1890–1945* (Oxford: Oxford University Press 2000) 144.

[32] Witold Chodźko, 'Stan Polski pod względem zdrowotnym podczas wojny', (1923) 24, PAN III-77/10.

[33] Shaw to Williams (4 May 1920) RF 1.1/789/2/11. The Special Polish Epidemic Commission (NNK for *Naczelny Nadzwyczajny Komisariat do Walki z Epidemiami*) was established in March 1920.

[34] Jacek Majchrowski, *Kto był Kim w Drugiej Rzeczypospolitej* (Warsaw: Polska Oficyna Wydawnica 'BGW' 1994) 35, 511; Urszula Perkowska, 'Działalność Społeczna Profesora Emila Godlewskiego Juniora', *Archiwum Historii I Filozofii Medycyny*, vol. 64, no. 1 (2002) 1–22; Witold Chodźko, 'Stan Polski pod względem zdrowotnym podczas wojny', 24 (1923) PAN III-77/10; Heiner Fangerau and Irmgard Müller, 'Scientific exchange: Jaques Loeb (1859–1924) and Emil Godlewski (1875–1944) as representatives of a transatlantic developmental biology', *Studies in the History and Philosophy of Biological and Biomedical Sciences*, vol. 38 (2007) 614.

[35] Gilchrist, 'Memorandum: Poland Typhus Situation and International Action', (11 March 1920) LNHO R.812/12B/1719/3659. The American Red Cross supported Gilchrist in challenging Polish competency: Piana, 'Humanitaire et politique', 31, n 42 (n 4); 'Typhus as general Distress in Eastern Galicia and West Ukraine, visit of Cuthbert Clayton to East Galicia (Little Poland) and West Ukraine from Jan 4th to Jan 23rd, 1920', LNHO R.812/12/1719/3377.

he clearly meant that this international body would surpass the authority of the Polish Ministry of Health or other institutions of the Polish government, acting as an international board of directors, overseeing and tutoring Polish activities.[36] As Shaw had recognized, the Poles were not prepared to compromise their sovereignty in this way.

Rejecting Gilchrist's latest proposal, the Polish health authorities renewed their appeal to the League of Nations for intergovernmental assistance. In doing so, they forged a new model for international collaborative assistance.

In April 1920, Ludwik Rajchman and Witold Chodźko travelled to London to present their case at the conference undertaking the question of establishing a League Health Organization.[37] By this time, it was evident that the experiment of bringing the LRCS and the American expedition to Poland had accomplished little.[38] An American foreign relief officer who worked with both organizations stated that the American anti-typhus expedition in particular 'has accomplished absolutely nothing in Poland'.[39] Even the much-hailed supply of American equipment that Gilchrist's expedition brought with them had broken down by the spring of 1920.[40] Indeed, despite relief efforts, the winter of 1919-1920 had the highest incidence of typhus cases yet.[41]

The western intergovernmental community remained reluctant to make a commitment to domestic engagement in Poland. In February 1920, the president of the League of Nations Council, fearing that the League would be drawn into addressing the typhus epidemic in Poland, dispatched a letter to the LRCS. Ignoring this organization's actual presence in Poland, the president, at the time former British Prime Minister Arthur Balfour, requested the LRCS provide relief to Poland and coordinate the various humanitarian groups that had responded to the crisis.[42]

36 Gilchrist, 'Memorandum: Poland Typhus Situation and International Action' (11 March 1920) LNHO R.812/12B/1719/3659.

37 Witold Chodźko 'Prace Ministerstwa Zdrowia Publicznego na terenie międzynarodowym', 2, PAN III-77/10.

38 Weindling also notes this relation between Polish independence and Gilchrist's failure: *Epidemics*, 144 (n 31).

39 Harry Plotz, 'Report to Doctor Justus Goldman' (18 June 1820) JDC NY AR191921/4/36/3/260.

40 Ibid.

41 Weindling, *Epidemics*, 432 (n 31); 'Epidemic Commission: Minutes of the first meeting of the advisory board, held in Warsaw, 15 April 1921' (n 9); Henry Shaw to Linsly Williams, 4 May 1920, RF 1.1/789/2/11; 'Note sur le Typhus en Pologne' (21 June 1920) AFMFA SDN 1578; 'Report presented to the chamber of deputies in France by the finance commission about conditions in Poland' (7 Dec. 1921) AFMFA SDN 1578; 'The Epidemic of Typhus in Poland. Document du Conseil 40 (Dated for the archives 10 April 1920) AFMFA SDN 1578; 'European Health Conference held at Warsaw from March 20th to 28th, 1922' (League of Nations, 3 April 1922); 'How to Organise Relief in Poland' by Dr. Brodowicz, countersigned by Mr. Jaroszynski, Polish RX Commissioner for the Volhynian Front, *Bulletin of the League of Red Cross Societies*, vol. 1, no. 10 (May 1920) 15.

42 *League of Nations Official Journal*, vol. 1 (Geneva 1920) 68. He acted so precipitously that the preparatory material circulated to Council members at the beginning of March for their upcoming meeting included Balfour's letter to the LRCS with an apology for not consulting his colleagues before sending it, which he had done supposedly 'owing to the urgency of the matter'; 'Prevention of Disease in Eastern Europe', AFMFA SDN 1578, 1.

Calling on the Red Cross in this way satisfied the League of Nations' obligation in a health-related crisis, as laid out in the organization's covenant. Even if Balfour were naïve of the LRCS's ongoing presence in Poland, the timing and urgency of his request was striking. It suggested his desire to avoid greater League involvement.

Balfour wrote that it fell to charitable associations to fill the 'vast field' of need in Poland. The LRCS replied that they resolved to extend their activities in Poland only upon receiving League of Nations assurance that they could rely on governments—rather than philanthropy—for supplies of 'such essentials as food, clothing and transportation which must be given if the peoples are to live and be restored to a condition of self-support'.[43] The LRCS's letter to Balfour concluded with an apocalyptically evocative expression of hope that the League of Nations' limitations 'will not prevent such action before it is too late for the salvation of humanity and civilization'.[44]

The LRCS was proposing an early theory of mutual assistance between governments, administered by the League of Nations. A change had occurred since the humanitarian anti-typhus work on the battle front during the war. Now, the anti-typhus relief occurred within a state. The state had a government and that government had a Ministry of Health. The Ministry of Health formulated policy and managed resources. International relief projects had to work with that Ministry, complementing its projects and resources.

At the conference in London, Ludwik Rajchman took the stage with a report on the Polish government's anti-typhus campaign.[45] He detailed the existing measures the Ministry of Health was taking to fight typhus: the Special Commission, hospitals, sanitary brigades, quarantine stations, delousing programmes, and provision of food and fuel.[46] He described their three new branches of the Special Commission along the eastern front, at Lwów, Vilnius, Łuck, and Płoskirów.[47] His presentation made clear that the Polish Ministry of Health had a plan to undertake substantial anti-epidemic and public health action but lacked the resources to pursue their operation, and that it was these resources they requested.

The conference delegates recommended that the League of Nations create a commission to coordinate donations of resources and personnel from foreign governments to the Polish government, with additional support from the LRCS.[48] Utilization of resources and personnel would be under the jurisdiction of the

[43] 'Resolution', LRCS to League Council, AFMFA SDN 1578, 18.

[44] William Rappard, Secretary-General of the LRCS, to Arthur Balfour (10 March 1920) AFMFA SDN 1578, 17.

[45] For more on the perspective of the international humanitarian actors at and around the conference, see: Piana, 'Humanitaire et politique', 31 (n 4).

[46] 'Typhus in Poland: Report of the Health Conference on this Subject', LNHO R.812/12B/1719/3980, 4–5; 'Minutes of the meeting of the Conference held at the Ministry of Health, London', (13–16 April 1920) LNHO R.811/12B/126/4124.

[47] Ibid, annex 1, 4; cf. Piana, 'Humanitaire et politique', 31 (n 4).

[48] Ibid, 2, 4–7.

Polish Ministry of Health, while a medical commission representing the League would be based in Poland to consult.[49] Such support would bolster the Ministry of Health's projects without usurping its authority.

Meeting in Rome in May 1920, the Council of the League of Nations took up this recommendation. Having received the experts' recommendation, they still had to determine the feasibility of such a project as part of the League. They would also have to assess the terms under which the League could request contributions from its members in such a matter.[50] Exactly a year before, the Council of the Paris Peace Conference had declared itself unable to address the domestic problems of Europe, explicitly the typhus epidemic in Poland.[51]

The Council trod lightly in this preliminary year of the League's existence. Balfour warned in presenting the issue that he was 'very uneasy' about taking up the proposal to assist Poland. He feared that a misstep in how they invited the contributions of member states could 'do great harm' and undermine 'the whole idea of that common international action which is the very basis of the League of Nations'.[52] Any action they took in the Polish case would set a precedent for the League's future involvement in social or other domestic issues.[53] What they had to do before they could request funds from their members states, Balfour determined, was to legitimate the decision they made by rendering it as an 'example of some generally accepted principle'. Security and humanitarian ethics might provide such common grounds, he suggested: 'But has the Council either the right or the authority to commit the League to so great an innovation of international practice?'[54] The Council voted in favour of a League of Nations Epidemic Commission, while the future form of its Health Organization remained ambiguous.

IV. From Relief to State-Building

Although there was hesitant progress towards an anti-typhus campaign in Poland, an international crisis provoked a more definite response. Shortage of funds prevented the League's Epidemic Commission from accomplishing a great deal during its first year, while the typhus epidemic remained a domestic Polish crisis.

[49] Ibid, 6; cf. Marta Balińska, 'Assistance and Not Mere Relief: The Epidemic Commission of the League of Nations, 1920–1923', ed. Paul Weindling, *International Health Organizations and Movements, 1918–1939* (Cambridge: Cambridge University Press 1995) 81, 84–86.

[50] Britain, France, Italy, and Japan were permanent members of the Council, while Belgium, Brazil, Greece, and Spain began filling their three-year tenure in 1920. It was these eight members who had to ratify the creation of an epidemic commission and the appeal to member nations for funds. See also Piana's discussion of the Epidemic Commission's origins: Piana, 'Humanitaire et politique', 32–33 (n 4).

[51] Hoover, *An American Epic*, vol. 2, 443 (n 1).

[52] Balfour, 'International Assistance to Poland' (15 May 1920) LNHO R.812/12B/1719/4456. This speech did not make it into the official record.

[53] Ibid.

[54] Ibid.

Altogether, after a full year, the Epidemic Commission had received only £74,559 of the two million pounds the League Council determined to be the minimum required for any efficient contribution, and the three to four million the experts had deemed necessary.[55]

Despite these limitations, Ludwik Rajchman—now co-director of the League Epidemic Commission—busied himself assisting the Polish government's existing programmes.[56] With restricted resources, he and his British co-director focused on development rather than relief. Instead of purchasing more materiel from the American army or accepting British credits to purchase British products, as philanthropic contributions had required, funds channelled through the League enabled the international Commission to promote Polish industry. They looked to Łódź for wool and cotton goods, manufactured beds with iron and coal from Silesia, and produced sera for vaccinations at Rajchman's National Institute of Public Health in Warsaw.[57]

A renewed perception of international crisis allowed the Epidemic Commission to take on new life in April 1921, one month after Poland and Soviet Russia signed the Treaty of Riga.[58] This vigour served to reinforce the pattern of development that Rajchman had already set. The end of the war marked the transition of the typhus epidemic in Poland from a domestic to an international crisis enmeshed in the west's fears of communism and in its uncertain relationship with the Soviet Union.

The reason for reinvigorating the Epidemic Commission lay in the Treaty of Riga's terms. The treaty absorbed land and people of several nationalities into Poland. In the previous two years, typhus control had figured in the Polish government's efforts to distinguish their country from Russia and present it as European. Now they stood to absorb recently Russian territories with a high incidence of typhus.[59] Additionally, the treaty also provided for repatriation of prisoners of war and civilian populations who had been displaced during the recent

[55] Britain finally released its contribution of £50,000 in January 1921, after the Commission had raised only £14,493. The preceding contributions came from Siam, Sweden, Switzerland, and Belgium. Austria, Finland, Peru, and Albania contributed small sums in February and March. The non-European contributions are notable. The LRCS also gave £10,000 over the course of 1920–1921 and donated clothes. 'Second rapport annual de l'activité de la commission' (1 August 1922) LNHO R.822/12B/12462/26297X; "Report presented to the chamber of deputies in France by the finance commission about conditions in Poland' (7 December 1921) AFMFA SDN 1579.

[56] 'Typhus in Poland: Report by the Medical Commissioner of the League of Nations, 24 June 1920', AFMFA SDN, 1578.

[57] Ibid.

[58] Borzęcki's, *Soviet-Polish Peace* (n 18) is a comprehensive and nuanced study of the peace. Original treaty: 'Traktat Pokoju Między Polską a Rosją i Ukrainą, podpisany w Rydze dnia 18 marca 1921 roku'. Document available here: <http://www.irekw.internetdsl.pl/traktat_ryski/> (6/28/16).

[59] The Epidemic Commission believed that the most heavily infected regions were Novogrodek, Polesia, and Volhynia: 'Report on the state of the anti-epidemic campaign in Poland' (15 March 1922) LNHO R.822/12B/12462/19917. On destruction in the region during the Polish-Soviet War: 'Epidemic Commission: Minutes of the first meeting of the advisory board, held in Warsaw' (n 9); 'Report of the Special Commission on Typhus in Poland' by Thorvald Madsen, Henri Pottevin, and Norman White (29 November 1920) AFMFA SDN 1578.

war and the preceding Great War.[60] In 1921, authorities estimated 500,000 to 600,000 people—of mixed national identity but claiming Polish citizenship based on their residence under the preceding empires—awaited repatriation from Soviet Russia to Poland.[61] Later, official records would place the number of repatriates into Poland between April 1921 and June 1922 at 1.1 million.[62] This population transfer marked the beginning of a new phase of relations between Poland and the Soviet Union. Via the typhus epidemic, Poland put this relationship at the centre of its interactions with the rest of Europe in a way that it had not achieved while at war with the Soviets. This redirected struggle with the Soviet Union and the refugees crossing the border (whom the health officials avoided referring to as repatriates in their correspondence with the League), brought new international support to the Polish health administration.[63]

The month after the Treaty of Riga, an international advisory board for the League Epidemic Commission toured Poland. Rachel Crowdy was at its head. It was shortly after this trip that Crowdy recruited Rajchman to direct the League Health Organization.[64] During this visit, the Polish government, the Epidemic Commission, and the advisory board all agreed that the incidence of typhus had decreased by 78 per cent between the Januaries of 1920 and 1921, despite wartime conditions.[65] There were only 7,000 notified typhus cases in January 1921.[66] Nevertheless, the advisory board determined the number of cases remained 4000 per cent above recorded typhus data from 1905 to 1911 and continued to produce fatality rates above the disease's average.[67] They concluded the League of Nations should redouble its efforts to provide the Polish government with funds and supplies to pursue its anti-typhus campaign.[68]

[60] Borzęcki, *Soviet-Polish Peace*, 239 (n 18). The provision was in fact signed in February.

[61] 'Minutes of the first meeting of the advisory board' (n 9). Borzęcki, *Soviet-Polish Peace*, 244 (n 18); Kateryna Stadnik, 'The Repatriation of Polish Citizens from Soviet Ukraine to Poland in 1921–2', eds. Nick Baron and Peter Gatrell, *Homelands: War, Population and Statehood in Eastern Europe and Russia, 1918-1924*, (London: Anthem Press 2004) 135–136.

[62] Borzęcki, *Soviet-Polish Peace*, 244 (n 18); Stadnik, ibid.

[63] Examples of language in Polish reports: Archiwum Akt Nowych AAN MOS 90, 'Repatriacja ludności polskiej ze Związku Radzieckiego. Dzienniki Urzędowe Nadzwyczajnego Komisarza do Spraw Walki z Epidemiami, sprawozdania, protokół, raporty, telegramy, wnioski, 1921-1922'. International reports frequently use only the term 'refugee' although sometimes both appear, as in this internal memo: Memo from Rajchman to Gauthier (13 Feb. 1922) LNHO R.822/12B/12462/26383X.

[64] The other members of the advisory board were Edouard Frick, the International Committee of the Red Cross' delegate to Russia, Dr. Frédéric Ferrière of the ICRC, Thorvald Madsen, who would shortly become president of the League Health Committee, and Charles-Edward Amory Winslow, who had established the Department of Public Health at Yale University and represented the League of Red Cross Societies. Rachel Crowdy, '"La Lutte Contre le Typhus en Europe Orientale" (4 May 1921) LNHO R.822/12B/12462/12462. Winslow: Norman Howard-Jones, *International Public Health between the Two World Wars—The Organizational Problems* (Geneva: World Health Organization 1978) 34.

[65] 'Epidemic Commission: Minutes of the first meeting of the advisory board', 3, 8 (n 9). The Epidemic Commission meeting noted there were 168,000 recorded cases of typhus in 1920. Weindling supports this number: *Epidemics*, 432 (n 31).

[66] 'Minutes of the first meeting of the advisory board, held in Warsaw' (n 9).

[67] Ibid, 8.

[68] Ibid, 2.

Even though the epidemic had waned in Poland, Rajchman and his Polish colleagues presented the Epidemic Commission's visiting board members with evidence that typhus continued to ravage Russia and that the population exchange could continuously reintroduce the disease. The Epidemic Commission's advisory board re-affirmed that its role would be to support the Polish anti-typhus campaign's plan.[69]

The Polish Special Commission had decided the most effective method would be to focus attention on building hospitals.[70] It had already created fifty hospitals of fifty beds each, and provided supplies.[71] The continuing plan involved specific attention to the east. Constructing institutions in the eastern borderlands contributed to state-building in a nationally-contested region where work could only begin belatedly in the spring of 1921.[72] They would focus on increasing the number of hospitals, baths, and disinfecting stations in the districts along the border.[73] Their programme involved establishing fifty hospital beds for infectious disease in each county in Galicia, 100 for each in central and western Poland, and 200 each in the eastern counties.[74] In total, they planned 117 new infectious disease hospitals, 54 hygiene centres for delousing, and 353 mobile disinfecting units.[75] In supporting these plans, the advisory board determined 'that future expenditure should be made wherever possible along lines which will further the permanent development of the general health organization in Poland'.[76] This conclusion acknowledged the work as development rather than temporary humanitarian relief.

This conceptualization did not appear in the renewed appeals for contributions from foreign governments. The applications took a new direction in framing the humanitarian cause and the threat, focusing on the refugees who threatened to carry typhus into Poland. References to typhus already present in Poland decreased, directing attention towards preventing infection from Russia. Developments in the eastern districts, now termed the 'sanitary zone', fell under the category of protecting against disease the refugees might carry. The west's increasing recognition of Poland as a sovereign state corresponded to receding emphasis on Poland as itself a source of typhus. The narrative of its self-sacrifice in humanitarian relief for refugees and to protect the west from typhus enabled an intergovernmental collaboration that eschewed the complicated problems of foreign investment in domestic issues while pursuing the same programme. Renewed attention allowed the Polish

69 'Report on the state of the anti-epidemic campaign in Poland' (15 March 1922) LNHO R.822/12B/12462/19917.

70 Ibid.

71 'La Lutte Contre le Typhus en Europe Orientale' (4 May 1921) LNHO R.822/12B/12462/12462.

72 On beginning work in the region in spring of 1921: 'Report on the state of the anti-epidemic campaign in Poland' (15 March 1922) LNHO R.822/12B/12462/19917.

73 Sanitary zone and the Epidemic Commission: cf. Balińska, 'Assistance', 92 (n 49).

74 'Epidemic Commission: Minutes of the first meeting of the advisory board, held in Warsaw' (n 9).

75 'Minutes of the first meeting', 8 (n 9); See also Piana's discussion: 'Humanitaire et politique', 35–36 (n 4).

76 'Minutes of the first meeting' (n 9).

health administration to pursue the plan their Special Commission had already deemed necessary, creating permanent Polish institutions that would outlast international interest in the refugee crisis.

V. From Relief to Welfare

The relief to development transition that occurred in Poland was not unique among the post-imperial states. Public health leaders across the region articulated and acted on a similar concern. Establishing healthcare institutions as part of expanding mechanisms of the state quickly led to questions of the state's welfare responsibilities and a citizen's social rights. Humanitarian projects, of both domestic and international origin, catalysed the state's welfare objectives and became part of its governance structures. A similar phenomenon following wartime sacrifices in Britain and France transformed the state by inspiring new expectations of citizenship.[77] Further east, the process was much closer to the core of the state's legitimacy and the practical growth of institutions that confirmed its authority. The League Health Organization would introduce a similar principle to international objectives.

In Poland, international relief efforts sponsored the emergence of Polish-planned institutions and extended the state's governance capabilities. However, humanitarian relief contributed to state development in more than one way. In Czechoslovakia, international relief efforts established programmes and institutions for which the state gradually assumed responsibility. This method echoed the working model of the American-based Rockefeller Foundation, which preferred to invest in a country's long-term growth, eschewing short-term relief projects and grants. The fit between the Rockefeller Foundation and the Czechoslovak Ministry of Health and its counterparts in other countries was not entirely smooth, as the Foundation preferred to target specific diseases than address broader public health. All the same, the Czechoslovak Ministry of Health received encouragement from a Rockefeller official who spent two years embedded in their office.[78] At the same time, responding to a request from Ludwik Rajchman, the Rockefeller Foundation invested a substantial grant in the League of Nations Health Organization on the same model.[79] The Rockefeller officials and Rajchman shared an understanding that the international community would eventually assume financial responsibility for the Health Organization's programmes, as the new states were assuming

[77] Bruno Cabanes, *The Great War and the Origins of Humanitarianism, 1918-1924* (Cambridge: Cambridge University Press 2014); Jay Winter (ed.) *Capital Cities at War: Paris, London, Berlin 1944-1919*, vols. 1 & 2 (Cambridge: Cambridge University Press 1999 & 2007).

[78] Selskar Gunn's correspondence from Czechoslovakia: RF 1.1/712/2.

[79] Borowy, *Coming to Terms*, 136–138 (n 16).

responsibility for welfare. The funds gave the Health Organization independence within the League.

In Czechoslovakia, the transition from relief to welfare occurred with substantial international collaboration, proceeding rapidly in the period between the end of the war and January 1922, when Rajchman met with Czechoslovak health authorities in Prague. The relief projects in Czechoslovakia both contributed to establishing institutions of the state and to motivating several international humanitarian organizations to address long-term welfare programmes. The meeting of relief and welfare proved more fraught and contentious for the international bodies than it did for the state, superficially establishing a division between international organizations that dealt in relief and those that dealt in development.[80] This boundary would prove permeable repeatedly at the time and in subsequent decades.

In April 1920 Czechoslovakia nationalized health services, only two months after centralizing the government and its administration.[81] The Czechoslovak Ministry of Health's existence and efforts both at self-reform and general reform directed and confirmed the transition from relief to welfare. The Czechoslovak Red Cross and its president, Alice Masaryková, helped ensure that humanitarian projects were part of core state policy. Masaryková early undertook to reform social welfare within the new republic. Although she was the daughter of the country's first president, she was not merely a figurehead for the Red Cross, but used it as a platform from which to launch her reforms.[82] Nevertheless, the Red Cross's private nature was inherently limiting and Masaryková used her personal political connections and her own position as a member of parliament to establish government institutions from the Red Cross' projects and from those of international relief programmes. Masaryková began with child nutrition, making the case that child feeding programmes initiated by international relief should not end when Czechoslovakia as a country had recovered. She made it a principle that hungry children from impoverished families deserved food all the time, not only when the country was recovering from wartime devastation. Masaryková proposed that the state, with assistance from the national Red Cross, should assume responsibility for feeding programmes.[83] Beginning with food for children, they would extend their obligation to the health of their citizens.

Individuals leading missions coordinated by the American Relief Administration and the American Red Cross were enthusiastic about contribution they could make to the new state by establishing clinics and feeding programmes. Their superiors remained more hesitant about changing the objective of international relief in this

80 Selskar Gunn to Wickliffe Rose (16 April 1921) RF 1.1/712/2/11.

81 Hynek J. Pelc, MD, DPH, 'Organisation of the Public Health Services in Czechoslovakia, League of Nations Health Organisation' (1925) C.H.268, 10.

82 Examples of Alice Masaryková's work: RF 1.1/712/2/10-13.

83 Selskar Gunn, 'Public Health Situation in Czecho-Slovakia', (1920) RF 6.1/1.3/47/527.

way. It would be more effective, they believed, to keep relief and welfare separate. They could not justify prolonged programmes to their sponsors and boards once Czechoslovakia was stabilized.[84] At the same time, at the state level, Czechoslovak officials were learning to cooperate with private organizations—such as the Red Cross—but not to allow these private organizations to assert control over public programmes.[85]

The Czechoslovak Ministry of Health found international assistance also in pursuing its own internal reforms and in assuming authority from private organizations. Masaryková, whose mother was American and who had ties herself amongst the American elite, approached the Rockefeller Foundation for assistance. Masaryková's invitation persuaded the Rockefeller International Health Division to extend itself beyond its normal sphere of work, engaging itself in social health and in Europe after it had declared its first experiment in both these areas a failure.[86] Czechoslovakia caused the Foundation's officials to reconsider. It was, one official wrote, a 'clean slate' with the opportunity to change the lives of thirteen million people.[87]

The international exchange was not one-way. The Czechoslovak Ministry of Health benefited from international contributions, but it in turn served as part a network of similar institutions whose collaboration and mutual assistance internationalized social welfare. This network grew from comparable institutions—Ministries of Health and National Institutes of Hygiene—established in some form in every country across the post-imperial region.[88]

VI. Internationalizing a Regional Public Health Movement

Relief shading into welfare assumed a part in determining the nature of internationalism, as it did the formation of post-imperial states. A network of public health officials spanning east central Europe integrated the national and international projects. From Geneva, Ludwik Rajchman formalized this regional network with structure and resources from the League Health Organization's programme, and connected it to health experts in other post-imperial agrarian parts of the world.

[84] RF 1.1/712/2/11: Gunn to Rose (16 April 1921) Rose to Gunn (6 May 1921).

[85] Gunn to Rose, 10 April 1921, RF 1.1/712/2/11.

[86] John Farley, *To Cast Out Disease: A History of the International Health Division of the Rockefeller Foundation (1913-1951)* (Oxford: Oxford University Press 2004) 44.

[87] Selskar Gunn, 'Public Health Situation in Czecho-Slovakia', (1920) 45; RF 6.1/1.3/47/527; Gunn to Rose (19 Aug. 1919) RF 6.1/1.3/47/529.

[88] On the beginnings of public health administration in new states across the region: Andrija Štampar, 'Organisation of the Public Health Services in the Kingdom of the Serbs, Croats and Slovenes', LNHO, C.H.326 (1925); Hermann Schroetter, 'Public Health Services in Austria', LNHO C.825.M.314/C.H.141 (1923); Alexander de Dobrovits and Aladár de Fáy, 'Public Health Services in Hungary', LNHO, C.H.265 (1925); Hynek J. Pelc, 'Organisation of the Public Health Services in Czechoslovakia', (n 81).

Encompassing the former Habsburg empire, this network of experts followed channels created by the Habsburg public health administration. Very early in his tenure at the League Health Organization, Rajchman joined a small conference in Prague for the purpose of promoting cooperation among the public health experts of east central Europe.[89] This network would bring together people who had trained in the small number of Habsburg medical institutions, who had belonged to the centralized Habsburg health administration, and who shared analogous systems and challenges in the post-imperial states. The Czech physician who took the lead in the Prague meeting was Pavel Kucera. Kucera had been born in Moravia, now part of Czechoslovakia, and he was by 1922 the director of a projected National Institute of Hygiene in Czechoslovakia.[90] But he started his career as a professor in Cracow, which was at the time in Habsburg Galicia, at the university from which Rajchman received his medical degree.[91] Before Rajchman entered the League, Kucera and his colleagues in Prague had independently begun to consider a network of east central European health officers, calling their idea 'The Little Entente Public Health Committee' after the Little Entente alliance between Czechoslovakia, Romania, and Yugoslavia.[92] As they established their Ministry of Health and their National Institute of Hygiene, exchanging information with colleagues in the same situation seemed a natural part of their programme.

The Ministries of Health were themselves a continuity from the Habsburg empire, which—along with Germany—had established health ministries in the nineteenth century. In the west, Britain and France, whose voices were so prominent in the controversy over international health, did not establish Ministries of Health until 1919 and 1920 respectively, after the new states of Poland and Austria.[93] Prior to the war, the west had addressed its concerns with public health through specialized or localized administration.[94] Centralized administration and interconnected public health authorities belonged to the continental empires, and shaped the nature of post-imperial health administration in the successor states.

This legacy of centralization also created the health network within the region that influenced the League Health Organization after the First World War.

[89] Selskar Gunn, 'Report on Poland', (7–11 Jan. 1922) 1, RF 6.1/1.3/47/528.

[90] 'Prague: From Our Correspondent', *JAMA*, vol. 80, no. 4 (27 Jan. 1923) 266–267.

[91] Rajchman's background: Ludwik Rajchman, 'Autobiografia', 5. IP RAJ.A1 (n 6); Rajchman and Kucera: Selskar Gunn, 'Report on Poland', 1, RF/6.1/1.3/47/528; Kucera's biography: 'Prague', *JAMA*, vol. 80, no. 1 (27 Jan. 1923) 266.

[92] Selskar Gunn to Wickliffe Rose (6 Sept. 1921) RF 1.1/712/2/12. At this time, Yugoslavia was the Kingdom of Serbs, Croats, and Slovenes. For simplicity, this chapter will use 'Yugoslavia'.

[93] The British Ministry of Health was created by the Ministry of Health Act of 1919 [9 & 10 Geo. 5. Ch. 21], available at <http://www.legislation.gov.uk/ukpga/1919/21/pdfs/ukpga_19190021_en.pdf>; on the creation of the French ministry in 1920: 'Décret fixant les attributions du ministre de l'Hygiène, de l'Assistance et de la Prévoyance sociale', available in Vincent-Pierre Comiti (ed.) *Les textes fondateurs de l'action sanitaire et sociale* (ESF: Issy-les-Moulineaux 2002) 56; Marta Balińska, 'The National Institute of Hygiene and Public Health in Poland, 1918-1939', *Soc. Hist. Med.*, vol. 9, no. 3 (1996) 428–429.

[94] See Weindling, rise of specialist ministries of health a move away from policing toward social cohesion: Weindling, *Epidemics*, 141 (n 31).

Fundamental to Rajchman's purpose in building east central European collaboration was the medical training in the Habsburg empire. The shared experience and common ideas and values these medical schools instilled in their students preserved a transnational medical network as politics and even science became nationalized.[95] This system originated around 1745, as part of the modern state born from the Habsburg Enlightenment, and remained a tenet of the empire's governance structure. The metropole brought students in from the peripheries to train for roles as imperial officials in the healthcare administration.[96] Certain regions had their own medical schools, such as in the universities of Prague, Cracow, and Budapest, but the imperial authorities specifically denied other provinces the right to build new schools.[97] Medical education and the network it produced remained a method of centralization even while the Austrian Habsburg Ministry of Health itself began to decentralize elements of legislative and administrative authority in the late nineteenth century.[98]

Most successor states established their own centralized Ministries of Health. Fragmented from the empire's health administration, and now incorporating regions from surrounding states and empires, officials in each ministry shared a common process of consolidating legislation and practice across their states.[99] Czechoslovakia collected information from its various regions but also faced the problem that the western half of the country had sent all its public health statistics on to Vienna and the eastern half to Budapest. No data had been kept in Prague

[95] On medicine and the Habsburg Enlightenment: E. C. Spary, 'Centre and Periphery in the Eighteenth-Century Habsburg 'Medical Empire', *Studies in History and Philosophy of Biological and Biomedical Sciences*, vol. 43 (2012) 684–689. Within Vienna itself, the link between physicians and the medical school was so close that Erna Lesky argues it functioned along the lines of a medieval guild: Erna Lesky, *Vienna Medical School of the Nineteenth Century* (Baltimore: Johns Hopkins University Press 1976) 1; For effects of rising nationalism on science: Mitchell G. Ash and Jan Surman (eds.), *The Nationalization of Scientific Knowledge in the Habsburg Empire, 1848-1918* (New York: Palgrave Macmillan 2012); Petr Svobodný et al., 'Continuity and Discontinuity of Health and Health Care in the Czech Lands during two Centuries (1800-2000)', *Hygiea Internationalis*, vol. 4, no. 1 (2004) 91. On the nationalized teaching of medicine: Tatjana Buklijas, 'The Politics of *Fin-de-siècle* Anatomy', eds. Mitchell G. Ash and Jan Surman, *The Nationalization of Scientific Knowledge in the Habsburg Empire* (New York: Palgrave Macmillan 2012) 209–244; Tatjana Buklijas, 'Surgery and national identity in late nineteenth-century Vienna', *Studies in History and Philosophy of Biological and Medical Sciences*, vol. 38 (2007) 756–774.

[96] Spary, ibid, 685.

[97] Andrija Štampar, *Public Health in Jugoslavia*, report for the UCL School of Slavonic and East European Studies (1938) 39.

[98] Selskar Gunn, 'Public Health Situation in Czecho-Slovakia', (1920) 24, RF 6.1/1.3/47/527; Štampar, ibid, 1, 3; Aladár de Fáy and Alexander de Dobrovits, *Public Health Services in Hungary*, 265, 7 (n 88); 'Organisation des öffentlichen Sanitätsdienstes, No. 68', (30 April 1870) Database: *Alex: Historische Rechts- und Gesetzestexte Online*, <http://alex.onb.ac.at/cgi-content/alex?aid=rgb&datum=18700004&seite=00000125> accessed 8 May 2016; Gunn, 'Public Health Situation in Czecho-Slovakia' (1920) 24; Croatia fell under Hungarian rule in the Austro-Hungarian split but it maintained relatively more autonomy than most Hungarian territories by playing the authorities of Vienna and Budapest against one another, see: Charles and Barbara Jelavich, *The Establishment of the Balkan National States, 1804-1920* (Seattle: University of Washington Press 2000, original 1977) 247–265.

[99] Selskar Gunn, 'Public Health in Jugoslavia' (1924) 36, RF 6.1/1.3/46/524; Pelc, 'Organisation', 10 (n 81)

and the Ministry of Health began operations by trying to recover information about recent conditions in its own country from the two former capitals.[100] An entire division of the Yugoslav Ministry of Health's tripartite structure focused on researching existing legislation and preparing proposals for an eventual unified system. First officially, and later in practice, the Habsburg laws remained operational in both countries.[101]

Common legacies laid the foundation for a regional public health network of reformers. In these ministries, physicians welcomed the opportunity to assume prominent government positions to pursue their favoured reforms.[102] Within their separate Ministries of Health, these officials shared visions of the future, often mapping out new programmes that reflected textbook models of health administration before they accepted the necessity to prioritize and adapt based on local conditions and needs.[103] Officials looked to their neighbours in pursuing their ideals and learning to manage a health system. The example on the largest scale was the National Institute of Public Health that each country built, adopting the model of Ludwik Rajchman's institute in Warsaw.[104] This Polish model was distinct from its western counterparts, and mimicked by those in the east, in its unification of laboratory functions with practical public health engagement.[105] In turn, these institutes became the principal forum for exchange of information and ideas within the regional network. As the Ministries and ancillary institutes became established, it mattered that they were able to receive relevant information from their counterparts. Czechoslovakia needed to know the extent of typhus and cholera outbreaks in Poland, and Poland needed to know when smallpox in Czechoslovakia began to spread.[106] But, unlike existing international health collaboration, sharing data on contagious disease was only an aspect of the relationship. As one of Rajchman's Polish associates explained, he and his colleagues believed the agrarian countries of the region should cooperate more fully because they shared similar health challenges.[107]

[100] Selskar Gunn, 'Report of a Visit of Investigation to Czechoslovakia, 1919', 6–7, RF 6.1/1.3/47/529. Nationalizing information collection also made it accessible for international collection, one of the League Health Organization's roles: Borowy, *Coming to Terms*, 103–105 (n 16). On fighting regional disparity in Czechoslovak health standards: Hana Mášová and Petr Svobodný, 'Health and Health Care in Czechoslovakia 1918-1938: From Infectious to Civilisation Diseases', eds. Iris Borowy and Wolf D. Gruner, *Facing Illness in Troubled Times: Health in Europe in the Interwar Years, 1918-1939* (Frankfurt am Main: Peter Lang 2005) 165–205.

[101] Gunn, 1924 Report, 56 (n 99); Selskar Gunn to Frederick Russell (23 Dec. 1925); Selskar Gunn, 'Notes on Visit to Jugoslavia', (3–8 Feb. 1926): RF 1.1/710/2/11.

[102] On physicians assuming a role in the state: Keely Sauter-Halsted, *The Devil's Chain: Prostitution and Social Control in Partitioned Poland* (Ithaca and London: Cornell University Press 2015) ex. 333–334.

[103] Selskar Gunn, 'Report of a Visit of Investigation to Czecho-Slovakia, 1–14 June 1919', 5, RF 6.1/1.3/49/546.

[104] On the different institute approaches: Balińska, 'National Institute', 427–445 (n 93).

[105] Ibid.

[106] Selskar Gunn, 'Public Health Situation in Czechoslovakia, 1920' 38, RF 6.1/1.3/49/546.

[107] Czesław Wroczyński to Rajchman (3 March 1926) LNHO R.982/12B/50168X/50168.

Habsburg continuities made themselves felt in administration, legislation, and personnel. These elements provided the context for enduring interconnection among central European health programmes long after the period of immediate postwar relief had passed. Collaboration fostered an environment in which state-formation became part of regional initiatives, and those regional initiatives contributed to defining the structures and institutions of internationalism. These conduits brought the principles and methods of transitioning relief to welfare into the League Health Organization, ultimately originating a new practice of international development.

The regional public health network—the Little Health Entente—was an integral part of establishing government health operations in post-imperial Europe. Not one national health service introduced reforms in isolation, without the knowledge and discussion of counterparts in other countries and in Geneva. Rajchman continued to assist in formalizing this exchange through the League Health Organization, funding joint commissions, shared publications, study tour interchanges, and conferences. He worked in conjunction with the Rockefeller Foundation, but pointedly diverged from Rockefeller policy on the grounds that the east central European network had established better principles for uniting health with social welfare and development. He determined the League Health Organization's policy would be the extension of this model to other agrarian countries.[108]

VII. From Building States to Building Institutions

While the east central European health network influenced the shape of the international health programme, international support remained crucial for expanding national health services within their home countries. This continued engagement originated from the principles that Rajchman had absorbed into the League Health Organization and that Masaryková had persuaded the Rockefeller Foundation to adopt. The foreign contributions served to legitimate national health policy and institutions in the midst of contentious domestic politics. In Poland, the Ministry of Health's existence depended significantly on the typhus epidemic and the international recognition and support of the anti-typhus campaign. Soon after the League of Nations Epidemic Commission terminated, the Polish government pulled its support from the Ministry of Health, folding it into a subordinate department of another ministry.[109]

[108] Rajchman to George Newman (26 Aug. 1927) LNHO R.952/12B/41197/57656X; Teaching of Hygiene: Proceedings of 4th session of Committee at Warsaw (April 1926) LNHO R.861/12B/26435/51114X; 'Enseignement de l'hygiène', R.861/12B/26435/49913.

[109] 'Note sur le typhus en Pologne' (21 June 1920) AFMFA SDN 1578. Not all epidemic control was done by the Ministry of Health. In 1922, the Ministry of Health spent 7,360,446,513 Polish marks and other ministries (such as the Military, Ministry of Railways, and Department for Repatriation) spent an

The public health experts who formed the east central European network held government positions and initially placed great faith in state-building. At first, their international contacts offered resources that would bolster the state systems, working exclusively through the Ministries of Health. However, within a decade, they were beginning to use foreign resources to divorce their health institutions from government politics. Having determined a principle of universal healthcare when the states were new, they subsequently sought international support rather than relinquish their ideals. In turn, the League of Nations Health Organization, under Rajchman, responded by making healthcare a universal ideal and by supporting institutions that would make healthcare more readily available regardless of state policy. While the Health Organization continued to work with and support governments in their healthcare reforms, it also reached out to local health experts via its east central European public health network. In particular, eastern European health officials who had lost their jobs due to political opposition began by the early 1930s to turn their attention to colleagues in China. For the League Health Organization and its affiliates, their early faith in state-building evolved quickly into a concern with institution building. The state proved desirable but not sufficient to enact and protect their principles of healthcare. Institutions became their preferred mechanism for organizing society.

Within the unsettled federation of Yugoslavia's nations, international support for health services separated from centralized state politics. Later, it would be the Croatian doctors who had attempted this divorce who would become strong promoters of the League Health Organization's involvement in development programmes and who would manage both the official and unofficial parts of the Health Organization's operations in China.

Yugoslavia, like Poland and Czechoslovakia, experienced a transition from relief to welfare that was closely interwoven with international collaboration. The expansion of Yugoslav health services illustrated the utility of this support. Modern international humanitarian medical relief for civilians essentially began in Serbia, following the outbreak of the typhus epidemic in 1915.[110] After the war, Yugoslavia could most readily tap international resources for combatting malaria. The disease-specific campaign was the successor to emergency relief in justifying humanitarian

additional 4.2 billion polish marks on sanitary issues. 'Stan Polski pod względem zdrowotnym podczas wojny', 23, PAN III-77/10. The total budget for the Ministry of Health in 1923 was 26.5 billion Polish marks. In 1921 the Ministry of Health's budget was 1.09% of the entire state budget, and 1.24% in 1922. Apart from anti-typhus work, much of the Ministry's work focused on controlling infectious disease, but its programmes also included cancer, eye diseases, alcoholism, child health, maternal health, Witold Chodźko, 'Stan Polski pod względem zdrowotnym podczas wojny', (1923) 6, 8–10, 12, PAN III-77/10. Górny gives it as 0.9% of the total budget: Janusz Górny, 'Pierwsze Ministerstwo Zdrowia Publicznego w Rzeczypospolitej Polskiej w latach 1919-1923', *Zdrowie Publiczne*, vol. 87, no. 6 (June 1976) 488.

110 Weindling, *Epidemics*, 76, 87–91 (n 31); Ludwik Hirszfeld, *The Story of One Life*, trans. & ed. Marta Balińska (Rochester: University of Rochester Press 2010) 31, 34, 47; 'Epidemics in Roumania', *Warsaw Health Conference, 1922*, LNHO R.836/12B/19916/19920.

international involvement in domestic social concerns. As Poland did with typhus, the Yugoslav Ministry of Health used this campaign to get its own institutions off the ground. In 1921, the Yugoslav government formed a commission of Yugoslav and foreign physicians to study malaria in Macedonia and Dalmatia. It was headed by an Austrian malaria expert who had worked at the University of Vienna while the Yugoslav Director of Public Health had been a student there. The outcome of the malaria commission was an institute in the Macedonian capital, Skoplje, and a continuing engagement with international experts.[111]

Within a few years, Yugoslavia emerged as the leader of progressive healthcare reform, thanks to its vigorous, idealistic, and uncompromising director of public health, Andrija Štampar. Štampar advocated an intentional move from relief to rights: 'All our efforts made so far towards the promotion of public health have been considered as charity, as acts of humanity, and that is why the budget allotted for these efforts has been so small, for the understanding of charity can be found only among the few.'[112] Instead, Štampar insisted that the success of a democratic state depended on healthcare being a civil right.[113]

Yugoslavia, like Czechoslovakia, was made up of parts from both the Austrian and Hungarian sides of the Habsburg Monarchy. Like Poland, it was also made up of different empires. Much of its southern territory had belonged until recently to the Ottomans. Uniquely, its capital, Belgrade, had been the capital of the independent Kingdom of Serbia. The Director of Public Health was Croatian, born in a rural village of the Hungarian-governed Habsburg province of Slavonia. He had received his training in Vienna, as was typical under the Habsburg Monarchy.[114] Štampar believed strongly in the Yugoslav project. He insisted the physicians he employed rotate through the regions to become familiar with the entire country and learn to act as Yugoslav officials. Becoming director of the new Department of Racial, Public, and Social Hygiene in 1919, Štampar worked from the premise that a strong health service would help nationalize and democratize the country.[115]

Štampar worked pragmatically with the resources he could find. He began with malaria in part because it was a grave problem, but also because that was where

[111] Gunn, 1924 Report (n 99). On malaria in Macedonia: Sara Silverstein, 'The Periphery is the Centre: Some Macedonian Origins of Social Medicine and Internationalism', *Contemporary European History*, vol. 28, no. 2 (2019) 220–233; Patrick Zylberman, 'Mosquitos and Komitadjis: Malaria and Borders in Macedonia (1919-1938)', eds. Iris Borowy and Wolf D. Gruner, *Facing Illness in Troubled Times: Health in Europe in the Interwar Years, 1918-1939* (Frankfurt am Main: Peter Lang 2005) 305–343.

[112] Andrija Štampar, 'On Health Politics', *Serving the Cause of Public Health*, 60. Originally published in *Jugoslavenska njiva*, no. 29–31 (1919) 1–29.

[113] Štampar, 'Hygiene and the Cause of the World's Peace', annex to Štampar to Rajchman (3 Nov. 1924) LNHO R.853/12B/26249/27295X.

[114] Gunn, 1924 Report, 53 (n 99); Mirko Grmek, 'Introduction', *Serving the Cause of Public Health: Selected Papers of Andrija Štampar*, trans. M. Halar (Zagreb: Škola narodnog zdravlja, 1966) 5–16.

[115] Gunn, 1924 Report, 57 (n 99).

the money was. In particular, the Rockefeller Foundation favoured this disease-oriented approach, and the Foundation was the most important source of funds for healthcare projects.[116] Štampar was able to secure money for anti-malaria work while he considered 'he would probably have failed' if he had applied to do work in general public health from the beginning.[117] Indeed, the Rockefeller Foundation rejected his requests to fund general health centres and school clinics.[118] He rarely gave up, repeating his requests year after year.[119] But he focused his first clinics on malaria.[120] Gradually, he converted the anti-malaria clinics into comprehensive public health centres when money and personnel were available, and where local support made it possible.[121]

International collaboration took on new meaning in the autumn of 1924, when Štampar came under attack from political opposition in Belgrade. Štampar reported to Ludwik Rajchman at the League of Nations that his foes in Belgrade 'tried to show my associates in Macedonia as political agents which work against the Government'.[122] Sending Rajchman photographs of 'the so-called detrimental activity in Macedonia,' he bemoaned: 'I think that such people in any other country would be considered as benefactors and carried on the hands, and here we are estimated as enemies of the Government.'[123] Rajchman was an important source of support to Štampar at this time, and the two men maintained a frequent correspondence.[124] At that time, and at moments of later political tension, Štampar also explained to his benefactors in the Rockefeller Foundation that receiving money from abroad was more important than receiving the same sum from the Yugoslav government because the boost to morale 'has a greater value than financial aid'.[125]

Increasingly, Štampar used international funds to counter national politics. He first found this method successful in maintaining his programme in Macedonia against politics in Belgrade. He then applied it to a more comprehensive decentralization strategy. Rather than allowing Belgrade to dominate health policy in Yugoslavia, Štampar determined to run the public health administration from three major centres: Belgrade, Zagreb, and Skoplje.[126] He began seeking funds for a School of Public Health in Zagreb. What was notable was that the school was

[116] Rockefeller Foundation's public health methods: Farley, *To Cast Out Disease* (n 86).
[117] Gunn, 'Notes on Visit to Jugoslavia', 5–6 (n 101).
[118] W. Leland Mitchell, *Report on the Public Health Situation in Southern Yugoslavia (Macedonia)* Sept. 1926, 75, RF 6.1/1.3/48/539.
[119] Leland Mitchell to Gunn (17 Sept. 1926) RF 6.1/1.3/48/539.
[120] Gunn, 1926 Report, 5–6 (n 101).
[121] Ibid, 4–5; Mitchell to Gunn (17 Sept. 1926) RF 6.1/1.3/48/539.
[122] Andrija Štampar to Ludwik Rajchman (24 Dec. 1924) LNHO R.853/12B/26249/27295X.
[123] Ibid.
[124] 'Various Correspondence with Dr. Štampar', LNHO R.853/12B/26249/27295X; Ludwik Rajchman and Andrija Štampar's private papers at the Hrvatski Državni Arhiv [Croatian State Archives] (Record Group 831) and the Institut Pasteur Archives (Record Group RAJ).
[125] RF 1.1/710/2/11: Štampar to Gunn (20 Nov. 1924); Štampar to Gunn (17 July 1926); Gunn, 1926 Report, 10 (n 101).
[126] Mitchell, 1926 Report, 5–6 (n 118).

to be associated with the Zagreb Epidemiology Institute, rather than attached to the national Institute of Public Health in Belgrade, thereby securing Zagreb as a second hub.[127] The government made contributions toward the Zagreb school but it ultimately depended on local municipal and private fundraising in Zagreb, and funds from the Rockefeller Foundation.[128] Although Štampar remained part of the government, he was not a minister and therefore the Rockefeller Foundation found its policy of only supporting government programmes strained by the Zagreb school. The Foundation nonetheless acceded to Štampar's requests.[129] Contrary to the Rockefeller Foundation's hesitancy, Rajchman was enthusiastic about what this school represented in codifying an east central European model of public health.[130] By the early 1930s, Štampar was accusing the central government of methodically discriminating against the Zagreb school and he and his colleagues explicitly requested emergency funds from the Rockefeller Foundation on these grounds.[131]

When political opponents attacked Štampar again, they would say the king was dazzled because Štampar brought in foreign funds.[132] Štampar had indeed preserved his position for some time and attracted the king's support in part by portraying foreign interest and investment as legitimation of his work. In 1931, at what would prove the end of his government career, the intensifying political attacks specifically targeted his expenditure of those foreign funds.[133]

The end of his government career at home enabled Štampar to become an expert in the employ of the League Health Organization.[134] The principles he had espoused in Yugoslavia became increasingly prominent in the international health programmes. The Health Organization had begun to assume an advisory capacity in the development of national health services. In 1928, it had agreed to consult for the Greek Government. The director of the Zagreb School of Public Health was recruited to be one of the advisors, as well as one of Štampar's teachers from the

[127] Discussion of Zagreb School and Rockefeller Foundation funding: Željko Dugac, 'New Public Health for a New State: Interwar Public Health in the Kingdom of Serbs, Croats, and Slovenes (Kingdom of Yugoslavia) and the Rockefeller Foundation', eds. Iris Borowy and Wolf D. Gruner, *Facing Illness in Troubled Times: Health in Europe in the Interwar Years, 1918-1939* (Frankfurt am Main: Peter Lang 2005) 277–304.

[128] W. L. Mitchell, 'Trip to Jugo-Slavia' (25 Nov. 1925) 3–4, RF 1.1/710/2/11; Gunn to Russell (23 Dec. 1925): RF 1.1/710/2/11. The Department of Zagreb donated 200,000 dinars, the City of Zagreb would make an annual donation of 200,000 dinars, and the most substantial sum came from the Association of Banks in Zagreb, which was considering a donation amounting to 3,000,000 dinars ($50,000) annually. The Zagreb power company also donated the materials and labour for installing electrical fixtures.

[129] Gunn to Russell (15 Sept. 1924) RF 1.1/710/2/11; Farley, *Cast Out Disease*, 4 (n 86).

[130] Teaching of Hygiene: Proceedings of 4th session of Committee at Warsaw (April 1926) LNHO R.861/12B/26435/51114X; 'Enseignement de l'hygiène', R.861/12B/26435/49913.

[131] It seems that the Rockefeller officials may have originally gone along with the idea because they favoured decentralization for practical administrative reasons and therefore did not understand the underlying political motivation until later. Gunn to Russell (23 Dec. 1925): RF 1.1/710/2/11; Strode Diary (16–18 Feb. 1933) RF 12; Borčić to Gunn (16 April 1934): RF 1.1/710/1/6.

[132] George Radin to Gunn (30 July 1931) HDA, 831.3.

[133] Russell to Štampar (2 July 1931) RF 1.1/710/2/11.

[134] Andrija Štampar's Personnel File, LNHO S.886/3355; Rajchman had proposed this attachment by early 1929: Gunn diary (18 Feb. 1929) RF 1.1/710/2/11.

University of Vienna.[135] The government of Turkey also expressed interest in advice from the League Health Organization, and Rajchman began forming a plan in the late 1920s to export the east central European model of public health to South America. Specifically, he meant going beyond even the Rockefeller Foundation's programme for investment to offer international aid for addressing health within its socio-economic context.[136]

The League Health Organization would expand its cooperation with experts in South America, but the comprehensive development programme that Rajchman was beginning to envision found its focus in China. In 1929, the victorious party in a civil war reached out to the League Health Organization for assistance. The Chinese government was not seeking emergency relief but assistance in establishing institutions. Rajchman noted that Chinese officials had a particular interest in the newer European States—those of the east—which they 'closely identified with the League'.[137] Rajchman, Štampar, and Štampar's colleague from the Zagreb school became the core of a mission from the League and from representatives of the east central European model of public health and development.

VIII. Conclusion

Rajchman commenced the League Health Organization's engagement with China one decade after he had petitioned the League of Nations for assistance with the anti-typhus campaign in Poland. This time, there was no premise of temporary relief. The League was in China to assist in establishing the institutions of state.[138] But the League Health officials had learned from their decade of state-building in eastern Europe. Technically, the League's lead expert in China held a position analogous to that the Rockefeller Foundation's official had held in Czechoslovakia immediately after the First World War. However, Rajchman, Štampar, and other colleagues complemented this programme with prolonged visits to the country, during which time they worked with Chinese health experts on more local levels. They assisted in establishing local institutions based on principles of public welfare and universal health that aligned with the aspirations of the Chinese health experts, but did not always match the government's position.[139]

135 Correspondence and Reports on Reorganization of the Greek Public Health Service: LNHO R.5898/8A/8323/13315; LNHO R.5899/8A/8323/23480.

136 Rajchman to George Newman (26 Aug. 1927) LNHO R.952/12B/41197/57656X.

137 Memo from Rajchman to Secretary General Drummond (5 Feb. 1930) 17, LNHO R.5906/8A/10595/18022.

138 Ibid; 'Proposals for the National Government of the Republic of China for Collaboration with the League of Nations on Health Matters' (C.118.M.38, 1930) LNHO R.5906/8A/10595/18022.

139 Report by Andrija Štampar (1934) LNHO R.5721/50/7263/12695; 22nd Session of the Health Committee (6 Sept. 1935) Impressions of the Activities of the Health Institutions in the North-west Provinces of China with Recommendations for the Future (Presented to the National Health

The League Health Organization was operating on the premise of mutual-assistance between states with common concerns and common development objectives. It was the justification for international collaboration that the League's Council had explicitly rejected in 1920. In China, circumstances would push this form of internationalism rapidly to the fore. Following Japan's invasion of Manchuria on 18 September 1931, the League's source of authority as an arbiter of international security crumbled. In its wake, a new form of internationalism emerged from the collaboration between the League's smaller member states, its technical sections, and China's National Economic Council.

In Rajchman's opinion, it was not internationalism that had failed, but the internationalism of large powers whose conflicting interests prevented the mechanisms of international governance from functioning. Within the League, the invasion generally became a flashpoint for the divergence between the interests of great powers and smaller states, the latter arguing that the crisis was proof that the League had failed to substantiate its premise of equality among nations. Edvard Beneš, then foreign minister of Czechoslovakia and a member of the League Council, led the smaller states in demanding the League take action.[140] The affinity between the smaller states grew stronger and Rajchman remained close to what his secretary called a 'little Mafia' of League Secretariat members committed to evolving the League's international mission.[141]

Secretary General Sir Eric Drummond anticipated that when the League failed at peacekeeping, it would 'still go on doing technical and useful work in other domains'.[142] Surpassing Drummond's prediction, this side of the League would in fact grow substantially. While the social and technical sides could do little to address the invasion directly, they could assist China in recovering from devastating floods and famine. They strikingly based their methods on principles of reconstruction rather than relief alone. With the League of Nations discredited, the Health Organization's growing interest in reconstruction became the new face of the League.[143]

Administration, Nanking) by Dr. A Štampar, LNHO R.5710/50/6501; Andrija Štampar, 'Final Remarks on North West Health Programme', (March 1936) LNHO R.5710/50/6501/20156.

[140] The small states supporting China included Czechoslovakia, the Scandinavian states, Spain, Greece, Colombia, Bolivia, Ireland, and South Africa. Zara Steiner, *The Lights that Failed: European International History, 1919-1933* (Oxford: Oxford University Press 2005) 724–725, 741–742.

[141] Alfred Max, *Trente ans d'initiatives et d'affrontements*, 84–85, cited in Balińska, *Good of Humanity*, 97 (n 6).

[142] Drummond to Joseph Avenol (6 November 1931) Archives Diplomatiques: Avenol Papers, 24, cited in Balińska, *Good of Humanity*, 91–92 (n 6).

[143] Sara Silverstein, *Doctors as Diplomats: The Origins of Universal Healthcare in International Society* (Unpublished dissertation: Yale University 2016), chapter 3. On The League Health Organization in China, see also: Iris Borowy (ed.), *Uneasy Encounters: The Politics of Medicine and Health in China, 1900-1937* (Frankfurt am Main: Peter Lang 2009); Margherita Zanasi, 'Exporting Development: The League of Nations and Republican China', *Comparative Studies in Society and History*, vol. 49, no. 1 (Jan. 2007) 143–169.

The idea for a League of Nations Health Organization had originated in western Europe after the First World War as a proposal for consolidating international medical activity. The reality of establishing states and defining the benefits of citizenship in a post-imperial space pushed the Health Organization to undertake projects beyond anything the advocates of a League of Nations had imagined. The western impetus would have brought a relatively restricted form of international health into the League. It would have been a regulatory administration, focusing on data collection and bilateral sanitary conventions. At its most progressive, humanitarian concern would have prompted it to incorporate some emergency relief activities that the League's founders had suggested should rest with the Red Cross. Once the League's Council acceded to humanitarian relief, Polish health officials used that relief to establish the institutions of a national health service, allowing them to extend the arms of governance into nationally contested regions. It was an instance of institutions born out of crisis, but this time as part of a new internationalism. The typhus epidemic set the stage since the disease, associated with poverty and squalor, responded best to long-term measures. Elsewhere in east central Europe, health ministries absorbed humanitarian projects, using them both to define their welfare policy and to build the mechanisms to realize those objectives. Relief turned to welfare, and a passionate regional group of colleagues ensured that the League Health Organization continued to pursue these principles through international collaboration.

In the early years of the League Health Organization, these international projects worked closely with the states of east central Europe. By the late 1920s, international health offered support to public health experts who aspired to expand health services despite political opposition. Benefitting from international collaboration and themselves contributing actively through international networks, these experts were poised to extend their action from mutual assistance to international development. These reformers were idealists, but they were also pragmatic institution builders. They never had an idea that they did not try to envision as part of an institution, whether at the most local or widely global level. Both within states and internationally they established the institutions to make universal access to healthcare a realizable principle, and offered anyone who wanted it the help they needed to share this future.

4
Polycentric International Participation after the First World War

Experts from East Central Europe in and around the League of Nation's Secretariat

*Katja Castryck-Naumann**

The First World War accelerated the clash between the political orders of empire and nation. The emergence of the nation as a prime point of reference in politics and culture in Europe took until the mid-twentieth century, and imperial power continued to advance throughout the postwar period. In Central and Eastern Europe, the dissolution of the Habsburg, Ottoman, and Russian empires induced processes of nation state building, but this nationalization also collided with imperial legacies.[1]

At the same time, the war formed a watershed for a broad range of international activities, ushering in the collapse of prewar internationalism in some respects while also opening up new areas of cooperation. The League of Nations was established to preserve peace and collective security on a global scale, and it soon became active in a wide range of fields such as social, technical, economic, and cultural development. The League was based on the principle of state sovereignty, and the global order it epitomized was conceived as multiplying nation state-based political orders. There existed differing standpoints on who would be granted the right of self-determination, however—and what was more, the League rested on colonial structures, imperial interests, and transnational practices.[2]

Differing territorialities, that is, modes of political control through bounded spaces, coexisted at the level of state sovereignty as well as in the new international

* I would like to thank the editors and anonymous reviewers as well as Geert Castryck, Balint Varga, and Gilad Ben-Nun for their invaluable comments.

[1] Lutz Raphael, *Imperiale Gewalt und mobilisierte Nation: Europa 1914–1945* (C.H. Beck 2011); Zara Steiner, *The Lights that Failed: European International History, 1919–1933* (Oxford University Press 2005); Paul Miller and Claire Morelon (eds), *Embers of Empire: Continuity and Rupture in the Habsburg Successor States of 1918* (Berghahn 2018).

[2] Susan Pedersen, *The Guardians: The League of Nations and the Crisis of Empire* (Oxford University Press 2015); Sean Andrew Wempe, *Revenants of the German Empire: Colonial Germans, Imperialism, and the League of Nations* (Oxford University Press 2019); Patricia Clavin and Jens-Wilhelm Wessels, 'Transnationalism and the League of Nations: Understanding the work of its economic and financial organisation' (2005) 14/4 Contemporary European History 465.

Katja Castryck-Naumann, *Polycentric International Participation after the First World War* In: *Remaking Central Europe.* Edited by: Peter Becker and Natasha Wheatley, Oxford University Press (2020). © the many contributors.
DOI: 10.1093/oso/9780198854685.003.0005

order, and the shifts in both domains coincided and developed in close intertwinement with a variety of cross-border currents and non-territorial dynamics. This interaction had reciprocal effects. The changing scale of sovereignty had an impact on the conditions, forms of representation, and scopes of action in international politics. The adjustment of ties, networks, and practices between empires and nation states was echoed in the reordering of sovereignty. Even though political transformations often involved new orientations and repositioning in the global political landscape and brought about new geographies of international cooperation, many international actors from previous times persisted, adjusting their agendas and resources to the new political orders at home and in the international sphere. Overall, the reconstruction of international participation and cooperation after the First World War was a multifaceted, context-specific endeavour that heavily depended on individuals with their specific trajectories, leanings, and abilities.

Protagonists from the former Habsburg and Russian empires are instructive in this regard, especially the respective groups of experts and professionals involved. Their international careers reflected international practices from the imperial era as well as the post-imperial transformations, and their general biographies (that is their mobility and connections) point to a multiplicity of identifications. In some cases, their rationales and actions transcended national categorizations and the binary order of 'national/international', represented by diplomats and politicians.

Their (re-)gained sovereignty provided Poland, Czechoslovakia, and to a lesser degree, Hungary, with direct access to international politics. This opportunity also represented a challenge, however, for it could only be exploited successfully with the involvement of personnel familiar with the rules and dynamics of international negotiations. The finding, recruitment, and qualification of representatives in Geneva had to occur against the backdrop of the widespread destruction, starvation, epidemics, and violent conflict marking the beginning of the postwar period—and we should not forget that state power in East Central Europe initially continued to erode under these conditions.[3] Establishing offices abroad and nominating official delegates was one challenge,[4] but participating in the mushrooming number of commissions and the League's Secretariat was quite another. The recruitment of experts and professionals who had gained international experience before the war, maintained extensive cross-border networks, and could act confidently in international settings and negotiations was a path to quickly

[3] Tim Buchen and Frank Gelka (eds), *Akteure der Neuordnung: Ostmitteleuropa und das Erbe der Imperien, 1917–1924* (epubli GmbH 2016).

[4] On Czechoslovakia, see the contribution by Sarah Lemmen, Chapter 14 in this volume. In Budapest, significant reliance in terms of the new offices abroad was placed on diplomats who had been in the service of the Habsburg Monarchy, see: Éva Somogyi, 'Professionalisierung und Veränderung der nationalen Identität von ungarischen Beamten im gemeinsamen Ministerium des Äußern: Die nationale Identität der ungarischen Beamten' (2013) 119/1–2 Mitteilungen des Instituts für Österreichische Geschichtsforschung 136.

achieving a strong presence. Inter-imperial mobility and the little-known internationalization of societies in the Habsburg Empire and the Russian Empire thus found their way into the League of Nations.

Recent scholarship has acknowledged the crucial role played by the new states of Eastern and Central Europe in establishing the League and making it an authority in international affairs; it has also demonstrated the importance of international representation for the Polish and Czechoslovakian states.[5] We likewise know today that experts were drafted specifically to build new nation states because their interests coincided with those of the states to be formed. These experts often 'relied on a complex relationship between national and international affiliations, which they were well aware of and often intentionally employed'.[6] In general, the major role played by experts in establishing transnational and transregional networks within and around international organizations has been explored extensively.[7]

Less attention has been paid to the role of experts from Eastern Europe in the League of Nations, however—especially in the Secretariat and related commissions. The general revision of the history of the League over the past ten years has also shed new light on its administrative branch known as the Secretariat, the third organ alongside the General Assembly and the Council. Although its primary tasks were to implement the decisions made by the Assembly and the Council and manage the work of the entire organization, the Secretariat's scope of activity soon expanded. Within just a few years, technical sections dealing with economic and financial matters, social and health issues, and transport and communication were created—and expert commissions were attached to them. In effect, bodies came into being that far transcended the mainly technical tasks of the Secretariat.

One striking new feature of the administrative unit was that its staff were bound by loyalty to the League of Nations, with mechanisms in place to secure their 'detachment' from their home countries. The grand vision was to assemble a group of independent personnel dedicated to the aims of the organization.[8]

[5] Patricia Clavin, 'The Austrian hunger crisis and the genesis of international organization after the First World War' (2014) 90/3 International Affairs 265; Bruno Cabanes, *The Great War and the Origins of Humanitarianism 1918–1924* (Cambridge University Press 2014); see also the contribution by Sara Silverstein, Chapter 3 in this volume.

[6] Katrin Steffen, Martin Kohlrausch, and Stefan Wiederkehr (eds), *Expert Cultures in Central Eastern Europe: The Internationalization of Knowledge and the Transformation of Nation States since World War I* (fibre 2010) 21–22; Katharina Kreuder-Sonnen, 'From transnationalism to Olympic internationalism: Polish medical experts and international scientific exchange, 1889–1939' (2016) 25/2 Contemporary European History 207; Martin Kohlrausch, *Brokers of Modernity. East Central Europe and the Rise of Modernist Architects, 1910–1950* (Leuven University Press 2019).

[7] David Rodogno, Bernhard Struck, and Jakob Vogel (eds), *Shaping the Transnational Sphere: Experts, Networks, and Issues from the 1840s to the 1930s* (Berghahn Books 2014); Sandrine Kott and Joelle Droux (eds), *Globalizing Social Rights: The International Labour Organization and Beyond* (Palgrave MacMillan 2013); Wolfram Kaiser and Johan Schot, *Writing the Rules for Europe: Experts, Cartels, and International Organizations* (Palgrave Macmillan 2014); Daniel Laqua (ed), *Internationalism Reconfigured: Transnational Ideas and Movements between the World Wars* (I.B. Tauris 2011).

[8] Article 6 of the Covenant of the League of Nations does not state this innovative feature, but subsequent regulations introduced it. The size of the Secretariat was considerable; at its zenith in 1931, it comprised over 700 officers from 38 countries. Egon Ranshofen-Wertheimer, *The International Secretariat: A*

Many of the League's achievements such as protection schemes for refugees and children and the collection of information on a global scale were based on exchange and collaboration between diplomats and politicians on the one hand, and experts, technocrats, scholars, and activists on the other. Especially in and around the Secretariat, relations with agents from civil society were fostered.

More importantly, the Secretariat became powerful precisely because academics and experts were employed in considerable numbers. Their professional backgrounds gave them a strong position vis-à-vis the technical and administrative staff, and they had access to information that the political bodies of the League did not have. They produced information while conducting their daily affairs, correspondence, etc, but also collected scientific material, prepared commission work, and drafted reports. Several sections were directed by ambitious young men—and one by a woman—keen to develop their fields. They were able to do so thanks to the intimate knowledge they had in their areas of expertise as well as their professional alliances, which often went back to the prewar period.[9]

This contribution discusses two individuals whose postwar careers took them to the League, albeit along different routes and with different agendas: Ludwik Rajchman, a bacteriologist by profession who was hired as a medical officer and advanced to the office of director of the League of Nations Health Organization (LNHO), and Count Albert Apponyi, a high-ranking politician and diplomat who headed the Hungarian delegation to the League (1923–1933), served as expert in several commissions of the League, and led the Hungarian group in the International Federation of League of Nations Societies.

I have selected these two persons to depict the scope, variety, and multi-layered character of the international practice which East Central European agents brought to the League. As an appointed representative of his country, Apponyi, a leading figure of the Hungarian conservatives, represents both the field of official diplomacy of postwar Hungary and the as yet hardly recognized international practice before the war. Apponyi's roots were in the Inter-Parliamentary Union (IPU). It was developed as a result of the nineteenth-century peace movement and advocated for disarmament and the establishment of international arbitration. After many years as a member of its executive committee, Apponyi left the IPU before the First World War. Still interested in arms control and the peaceful resolution of conflicts, he worked for the League in the fields of disarmament and minorities,

Great Experiment in International Administration (Carnegie Endowment for International Peace 1945) 241–242; 358. See also Karen Gram-Skjoldager and Haakon A. Ikonomou, 'The construction of the League of Nations Secretariat: Formative practices of autonomy and legitimacy in international organizations' [2017] The International History Review; Haakon A. Ikonomou and Karen Gram-Skjoldager (eds), *The League of Nations. Perspectives from the Present* (Aarhus University Press 2019).

9 See among others Patricia Clavin, *Securing the World Economy: The Reinvention of the League of Nations, 1920–1946* (Oxford University Press 2013).

and was also involved in the area of intellectual cooperation. Meanwhile, the career of Rajchman, who was a committed socialist, began in international politics in 1919. Before then, he had been part of a transnationally connected scientific community. In the League of Nations, he was instrumental in establishing social health as a new area of activity, while also fundamentally transforming the rationale of traditional elements of international health that had developed in the nineteenth century. Accordingly, these two protagonists were involved with very different agendas and in different ways in the changing landscape of international organizations: one with a background in established realms of international politics, the other building up one of the original sectors of the League's work. For both of them, participating in the League was crucial, and both reflect the different constellations from which internationalization from East Central Europe enfolded after the end of the First World War. Both give evidence to the fact that international participation from this region was polycentric, shaped by continuities and new approaches, and, as we will see, evolved along territorial and non-territorial rationales.

The protagonists of this article also differed in terms of their strategies. Apponyi combined efforts for his own (nation) state with a commitment to cross-border cooperation as a way of addressing global problems, epitomizing a more traditional understanding of international politics. Rajchman built on the growing authority of expertise and professional networking in the international domain to conceptualize a new area of international work, and he used the new political order based on local, national, and international spheres of governance to organize a transnational production and circulation of knowledge as well as fields of activity where the different levels were closely circumscribed. The beginnings of the multi-level governance we know today can be made out in his vision of international health.

Both Rajchman and Apponyi were shaped by the imperial past and the post-imperial transformations in Eastern and Central Europe, and both were forced to adjust their international participation after the First World War. Yet they did so under fundamentally different circumstances: Apponyi was, before 1918, a member of various conservative and/or liberal parties, and after the 1918–1920 turmoil, he did not join the United Party (the governing party of the Horthy regime) but remained independent. He also remained a committed defender of Hungary's interests, and yet an active supporter of the League of Nations. His trajectory reminds us that the postwar territorial order restricted Hungary's position in international affairs and complicated the work of Hungarians in the League. Yet we will also see that by modifying his international work against the background of a politically isolated country, Apponyi was able to combine revisionist aims with a belief in international cooperation. By contrast, Rajchman—who came from Poland, which for many in Geneva represented the very spirit of the new world order—had a very different point of departure to begin with. In addition, he was part of a network of left-wing medical professionals and health experts from Eastern Europe who quickly gained influence on the international stage during the 1920s.

Both Apponyi and Rajchman were outstanding individuals with more room to manoeuvre than others, yet a direct comparison between them reveals different spaces of manoeuvre. Their varying scope of activity in part reflected the different fates of Hungary and Poland after the war, but it was even more closely related to the fact that Rajchman devised an original concept for international health that offered new directions for more traditional aspects of the field such as disease control and established several new domains such as social health from scratch. He was able to implement this approach thanks to his employment at the League Secretariat, a new body yet to be forged and shaped. From within the Secretariat, innovation following professional and technocratic agendas was easier; it was here that the League was most flexible. The commissions in which Apponyi was active offered less freedom to act since the involvement of state representatives, and national delegates made it harder to balance national and political motives with thematic, professional concerns.

The career trajectories of Rajchman and Apponyi reveal the League as a multilayered, polycentric body and tell us much about how the legacy of the Habsburg and Russian empires resonated within the organization. Furthermore, the two men's life stories are instructive in regard to the question of what made the Secretariat, and the League as a whole, so powerful. The professional expertise exemplified by Rajchman and Apponyi was one major element of this development. Yet they were also experts in a more practical or organizational sense of the word: they knew how to work 'the international'. Involvement in the mechanics of internationalism as it had begun to emerge since the 1870s gave them the experience needed to act in a fast-moving international arena. The realities of the Habsburg and Russian empires—especially their multiethnic societies, multilingualism, and trans-imperial professional mobility—enabled Rajchman and Apponyi to manage and connect the different rationales ranging from national and imperial/post-imperial to colonial and international reasoning that came together in the League.[10] In other words, their multifaceted imperial lives and careers[11] helped them to navigate the multicultural landscape of the League of Nations.

The capacities, strategies, practices, and connectivity of high-profile experts such as Rajchman and Apponyi were essential for the League's outreach, authority, and potential to make a difference in international politics. It was especially the capacity to understand, to connect, and at times to transcend prominent loyalties and attachments that became a major resource for the League. Historians of international organizations have recently discovered individuals whose mindset

[10] Sandrine Kott, 'International organizations: A field of research for a global history' (2011) 8/3 Zeithistorische Forschungen/Studies in Contemporary History 449.

[11] Tim Buchen and Malte Rolf (eds), *Eliten im Vielvölkerreich: Imperiale Biographien in Russland und Österreich-Ungarn (1850–1918)* (De Gruyter 2015); Teodora Daniela Sechel, 'Networks of medical knowledge in Eastern and Central Europe: Introduction to the thematic bloc' (2013) 30 East Central Europe 207.

and actions were not restricted to 'imperial', 'national', or '*inter*national' environments but who utilized, transcended, subverted, and connected these domains.[12] Although different terms have been used to describe these multiplex attachments, they all underline the capacity of (some) historical actors to operate along professional, technocratic, social, and cultural loyalties.[13] In effect, spaces emerged that were not only employed to organize territorial or ethnonational identities, but in which alternative rationales operating 'over, across, through, beyond, above, under, or in-between polities and societies' were at the fore.[14] This significant aspect of the empowerment of the League in international politics is revealed most clearly when individual life stories take centre stage.

In the following, I will combine an actor-based approach to international organizations with a focus on biographical trajectories to analyse continuities and discontinuities between prewar internationalism and the new international order. A traditional institutional analysis would carve out disruptions, for the League of Nations and its Secretariat were institutional novelties. Similarly, concentrating on prominent political orders and geopolitical constellations would highlight interruptions. By contrast, the biographical approach underlines the transformative power of the First World War along with the fact that the new postwar order was intensely permeated by experiences, practices, and networks from the previous order. It allows us to see how the post-imperial transformations in Central and Eastern Europe resonated within the League, shaping and interweaving international politics. Studying the trajectories of international experts with the political orders in flux after the war also helps us grasp the polycentric international participation after 1918 and the interplay of different levels of continuity and discontinuity. Besides, it shows an essential dimension of the continuing and changing connectedness of East Central Europe.[15]

12 Patricia Clavin, 'Introduction: Conceptualising Internationalism between the World Wars' in Daniel Laqua (ed), *Internationalism Reconfigured: Transnational Ideas and Movements between the World Wars* (I.B. Tauris 2011); Jessica Reinisch (ed), 'Agents of internationalism (Special Issue)' (2016) 25/2 Contemporary European History.

13 Madeleine Herren, 'Inszenierung des globalen Subjekts: Vorschläge zur Typologie einer transgressiven Biographie' (2005) 13 Historische Anthropologie; Glenda Sluga, 'Editorial: The transnational history of international organizations' (2011) 6/2 Journal of Global History 219; Sidney Tarrow, 'Rooted Cosmopolitans and Transnational Activists' in Sidney Tarrow (ed), *Strangers at the Gates: Movements and States in Contentious Politics* (Cambridge University Press 2012); Antje Dietze and Katja Naumann (eds), 'Situating transnational actors: Special Issue' (2018) 25/3–4 European Review of History.

14 Akita Iriye and Pierre-Yves Saunier (eds), *The Palgrave Dictionary of Transnational History: From the mid-19th Century to the Present Day* (Palgrave Macmillan 2009) xviii.

15 See on this also: Katja Castryck-Naumann (ed), *Transregional Connections in the History of East Central Europe* (De Gruyter 2021).

I. Ludwik Rajchman and the Development of a Multifaceted International Health Policy

Born in 1881 in Warsaw, then part of the Russian Empire, into an assimilated Jewish family belonging to the Warsaw bourgeoisie, Rajchman learned to mingle and communicate in a multilingual and multiconfessional environment as a child. His political orientation and strong sense of social responsibility developed early on. While still in school, he cofounded the Association of Urban and Rural Education, then eventually joined the Union of Young Socialists.[16] After finishing school, he studied Medicine at the Jagiellonian University in Habsburg Cracow. Unlike in the Russianized educational system in Congress Poland, instruction was given in Polish in the more liberal atmosphere in Galicia. Among Rajchman's tutors was Odo Bujwid, the founding father of Polish microbiology, who aroused his enthusiasm for bacteriology and shared his experience of competing scientific communities in bacteriological research and conflicting political loyalties. Bujwid had worked with Robert Koch in Berlin and Louis Pasteur in Paris. He had been fascinated instantly by the fierce opposition between their institutes, which was also perceived as a national rivalry in which Koch championed the German approach and Pasteur the French.[17] With some distance to this rivalry in Cracow, Bujwid made use of the knowledge and techniques acquired during his time in Berlin, as is apparent from his establishment of the Bacteriological Laboratory in 1886, while simultaneously incorporating what he had learned later in Paris—as he acknowledged by renaming the laboratory the Pasteur Institute. His research focused on developing a vaccine against rabies, and his practical work on the production of sera and vaccines made him well-known in the Polish hygiene movement and among czarist public health officers. While embracing the changes offered by Polish circles, Bujwid also made use of the opportunities provided by imperial officials. For example, he went to St. Petersburg to work at a newly founded institute for rabies research and served as head of the bacteriological station in Odessa before returning to Cracow when he was offered the Chair of Hygiene at Jagiellonian University. Traversing various national and imperial contexts, Bujwid 'maintained an open mind to the various possible "allies" for the promotion of his work. […] He did not exclusively commit his bacteriology to either the Polish national cause or the Tsarist Empire. […] [H]e did not commit his bacteriological style to either the "French" or the "German" side.'[18] While learning how to conduct bacteriological research from Bujwid, Rajchman thus also observed in his teacher the

[16] Marta A. Balińska, *For the Good of Humanity: Ludwik Rajchman—Medical Statesman* (CEU Press 1998) 12f.

[17] Kreuder-Sonnen, 'From Transnationalism to Olympic Internationalism' (n 6) 213f.

[18] Ibid, 218.

self-determined appropriation of knowledge from other places and a pragmatic manner of dealing with competing environments.[19]

Equally important was the fact that Bujwid introduced Rajchman to his family's socialist circles. Soon after his arrival in Cracow, Rajchman learned about the Open University (*Uniwersytet Ludowy im. Adamą Mickiewicza*) intended primarily for workers, and he soon became involved in setting up a Polish counterpart of the *Musée social* in Paris, a research and information centre on social policy where he obtained his first experiences with transferring organizational patterns and building institutions.[20] In Cracow, he also began working for the Polish Socialist Party. Inspired by Edward Józef Abramowski's concept of a 'moral revolution' and the philosophy of a civil society, Rajchman developed a firm belief in the 'necessity for political means for combating poverty and illness, and of founding institutions which, while providing help, can promote self-help'.[21] These ideas would later feature prominently in the conception of the LNHO.

In 1905, Rajchman returned to Warsaw to work in a hospital, opened his own laboratory, and continued his political activities, for which he would be arrested shortly thereafter. Released from prison thanks to financial support from his family, he transferred to the Pasteur Institute in Paris on a research grant from Kazan University, where he had graduated. In Paris, he conducted research into immunology under two Russian exiles, Élie Metchnikoff and Constantin Levaditi. During his time there, he increasingly realized that major illnesses such as typhoid fever, Spanish flu, syphilis, and tuberculosis were severe threats requiring preventive medicine and improved public health. In 1910, Bujwid recommended Rajchman for a position at the Royal Institute of Public Health in London, after which he worked at King's College and the London Hospital Medical College before becoming involved in health policy.[22]

His travel itinerary was a fairly typical example of scientific mobility in and beyond the Habsburg and Russian empires. Around the turn of the twentieth century, many Polish scientists travelled for the purposes of studying, conducting research, or engaging in international politics. Numbers vary, but we can assume that around half of the medical students from the era of the Polish partitions studied at a university outside of Poland, and many of them remained mobile for the rest of their careers.[23]

19 See also Katarina Kreuder-Sonnen, *Wie man Mikroben auf Reisen schickt: Zirkulierendes bakteriologisches Wissen und die polnische Medizin 1885–1939* (Mohr Siebeck 2018).

20 Balińska, *For the Good of Humanity* (n 16) 16f.

21 Ibid, viii.

22 Marta A. Balińska, 'Rajchman, Ludwik Witold' in Bob Reinalda, Kent J. Kille, and Jaci Eisenberg (eds), *IO BIO, Biographical Dictionary of Secretaries-General of International Organizations* <www.ru.nl/fm/iobio> accessed 24 August 2018.

23 Kreuder-Sonnen, 'From Transnationalism to Olympic Internationalism' (n 6) 207, footnote 17; Ruth Leiserwitz et al., 'Das unsichtbare Gepäck: Warschauer Studenten und Wissenschaftler des 19. Jahrhunderts als Akteure des Wissenschaftstransfers' in Ruth Leiserowitz, Stephan Lehnstaedt, Joanna Nalewajko-Kulikov, and Grzegorz Kryzwiec (eds), *Lesestunde/Lekcje czytania* (Neriton 2013).

With the Pasteur Institute and the Royal Institute of Public Health representing hubs of the international medical community, Rajchman naturally assembled a large personal network that he could later make use of at the LNHO. For example, he hired his Parisian colleagues Erich Knaffl-Lenz (as advisor to the Opium Commission) and Stefan Mutermilch. The latter was the designated specialist in bacteriological studies in Eastern Europe tasked with organizing the international collection of epidemiological information. While in London, Rajchman also met Thorvald Madsen, who would eventually become head of the Health Committee of the LNHO. Their close collaboration was crucial for enforcing the LNHO's innovative public health programme.

When the war ended, Rajchman immediately returned to Warsaw, where Witold Chodźko, head of the newly established Ministry of Health, offered him the directorship of the Department of Epidemiology. This was a huge responsibility given that Russia and the eastern parts of Poland were struck by typhoid epidemic in 1919, which caused broad international concern. Confronted with the need for action, Rajchman planned to establish a network of epidemic quarantine centres and founded the Central State Epidemiological Institute—which later became the State Institute of Hygiene (*Państwowy Zakład Higieny*), a centre of medical research and training—in November 1918. The Epidemiological Institute soon expanded to include all areas of public health and operate branches throughout the country, and simultaneously became a model for the establishment of public health institutions both within and beyond Central and Eastern Europe.[24]

When Rajchman heard that the Rockefeller Foundation was funding training for Czechoslovak physicians, he requested support for his institute as well. Although his application was unsuccessful, he was introduced to Wickliffe Rose, director of the Rockefeller International Health Board, and Selskar Gunn, director of the European Section Board. Both of these contacts would later prove to be beneficial to the activities of the LNHO. Rajchman's involvement in international health policy began to increase significantly in 1920. Even so, he remained in Poland, continuing his work as director of the State Institute of Hygiene in Warsaw until 1932 while developing a public health agenda for the entire Central and Eastern European region and beyond.[25] By this time, it was evident that Rajchman was a highly qualified scientist who was well-connected in the prewar scientific community, maintained contacts with health-related policymakers, and knew how to connect these different environments.

[24] Marta A. Balińska, 'The national institute of hygiene and public health in Poland 1918–1939' (1996) 9/3 Social History of Medicine 427. On the establishment of a Polish public health architecture, see Kreuder-Sonnen, *Wie man Mikroben auf Reisen schickt* (n 19) 139ff, 147ff; Katrin Steffen, 'Experts and the modernization of the nation: The arena of public health in Poland in the first half of the twentieth century' (2013) 61/4 Jahrbücher für Geschichte Osteuropas 574, 577–580.

[25] See the contribution by Sara Silverstein, Chapter 3 in this volume.

International prevention and control of diseases had been included in the statutes of the League of Nations as one of its lines of work, and in the spring of 1920, League members came together at a health conference for the first time. They established the Epidemics Commission—to which Chodźko and Rajchman were appointed—to tackle the ever-worsening sanitation problems in Eastern Europe.[26] At the same time, a temporary League Health Section was formed in the Secretariat, and Rajchman was approached to serve as medical officer. The permanent merging of this Health Section with the Health Committee in 1924 established the LNHO as an organization, and Rajchman would serve as its director until 1939.

Rajchman was appointed for various reasons. According to Iris Borowy, the main factor was his reputation as an effective and imaginative organizer. In addition, the position required sound medical training and research experience, multilingualism, enthusiasm for international cooperation, and familiarity with the most pressing health concerns.[27] Besides fulfilling all of these qualifications, Rajchman was a citizen of a newly established nation state, thereby symbolizing the new world order, and was also familiar with British and French scientific culture, which meant he enjoyed recognition from all sides.[28] Last but not least, he was also a strategist who could work with politically difficult constellations. Within the League of Nations and during his travels for it, he often faced national rivalries and diverse, sometimes even hostile parties, but he had learned from his former teacher and during his own career how to handle and mediate diverging interests.

These qualities were essential for a successful career in the League. Rajchman's ability to grasp situations and seize opportunities was already apparent from his response to Dame Rachel Crowdy, who had approached him unofficially in July 1921 to offer him the position in the Health Section. On the one hand, he presented himself modestly as being new to the field and in need of Crowdy's support in developing it. On the other hand, his enquiries regarding the job left no doubt as to his expectations concerning budgets and staff, and he frankly insisted on the possibility of remaining in Warsaw.[29] His directness and goal-oriented work would later elicit considerable criticism, but it served his purpose of building up the influence of the LNHO.

Rajchman's position as an employee of the League Secretariat was essential when it came to harnessing his expertise in 'working internationally'. His role in the LNHO is a telling example of the authority the League had attained as a result of the integration of experts in new institutional settings of international governance.

[26] On the Epidemics Commission and the establishment of the LNHO, see Francesca Piana, 'Humanitaire et politique, in medias res: le typhus en Pologne et l'Organisation Internationale d'Hygiène (1919–1923)' (2009) 138/2 Relations internationales 23.

[27] Iris Borowy, *Coming to Terms with Health: The League of Nations Health Organisation, 1921–1946* (Peter Lang 2009) 67.

[28] Neither the British nor the French would have accepted a national of the respective other country: Letter Dame Rachel Crowdy to Jean Monnet, 6 August 1921, LON S 861/2966.

[29] Letter Rajchman to Crowdy, 28 July 1921, ibid.

Rajchman epitomized the gravitas of a leading position in the Secretariat and the advantages of a cross-border trajectory in which experiences and networks from the prewar period and the post-imperial transformation in East Central Europe were intertwined.

In his interaction with the Health Committee in particular, Rajchman was able to carve out substantial power for himself and his colleagues in the Health Section. The Committee consisted of the president and nine members of the *Office International d'Hygiène Publique* (OIHP) as well as six other members appointed by the League Council and approved by the Committee itself. Officially, the Committee was in charge of approving programmes, while the Section was responsible for their implementation. Although Rajchman officially reported to the Committee, the relationship frequently ran vice versa in practice, with the Committee addressing issues introduced by Rajchman and taking decisions based on reports and proposals prepared under his guidance. Decisions by the Health Committee usually left ample room for interpretation in their implementation. Rajchman believed in direct communication and usually persuaded one or two key individuals to support his plans before presenting them to the Committee. He could not have persuaded the Committee to accept retroactive approval without persistent backing from within it, however. The Health Committee consisted of eminent scientists and leading theorists in social health such as René Sand and Andrija Štampar. Socializing health meant linking a social and political agenda to the medical-scientific one and viewing social reform as a prerequisite for improving health. In fact, orbiting the LNHO and the Rockefeller Foundation, doctors and health experts formed a network whose members were convinced—despite their divergent fields and different political agendas—that the conditions determining health mattered and that health was an issue for international activity.[30]

In addition to Chodźko, a long-term member of the Health Committee, Rajchman was also backed by Thorvald Madsen, the head of the committee. Madsen was an internationally respected bacteriologist and director of the *Statens Serum Institut* in Copenhagen; he shared Rajchman's ideas for increasing the influence of the LNHO. Once again, prewar professional contacts bore fruit, for Rajchman and Madsen knew each other from academic circles in London. In the League of Nations, they realized they shared fundamental ideas regarding the organization's agenda and became close collaborators and friends.[31]

[30] They thus fought for preventive measures, a combination of bacteriology and social hygiene, joint action between governments, insurance funds, scientists, and physicians, and international exchange as a prerequisite for effective action. See Paul Weindling, 'Philanthropy and world health: The Rockefeller Foundation and the League of Nations Health Organisation' (1997) 35/3 Minerva 269.

[31] Anne Hardy, 'Actions not Words: Thorvald Madsen, Denmark, and International Health, 1902–1939' in Iris Borowy and Anne Hardy (eds), *Of Medicine and Men: Biographies and Ideas in European Social Medicine between the World Wars* (Peter Lang 2008).

Another reason for Rajchman's rapid rise in influence was his ability to autonomously appoint junior staff and suggest candidates for permanent positions in the Health Section. Here, too, prewar networks and Rajchman's self-perception as a scientist came to the fore. For the most part, he recruited scientifically trained experts in public health, epidemiology, and statistics whom he either knew personally or who had been recommended to him by his circle of like-minded colleagues in and around the LNHO.[32] Rajchman's rootedness in this cross-border scientific cooperation within imperial structures ensured that the LNHO developed into a space that embodied a strong research orientation and institutionalized transnational forms of knowledge generation and dissemination.

A case in point is the epidemiological intelligence and public health statistical service provided by the League of Nations. It was based on the conviction that epidemics had to be understood from the perspective of populations, that is, in terms of their spread, development, and mortality. Vital statistics, especially statistical surveys and indexes, were considered fundamental. The typhoid epidemic brought home to League officials in Geneva the fact that there was no reliable international epidemiological intelligence service. One of the primary goals of the organizers of the LNHO from its very beginnings was therefore to work towards this end by establishing a centre for the collection and delivery of comparative information.

Building on the nineteenth-century diplomatic warning systems intended to quarantine and contain outbreaks of illnesses, the Health Section began to gather data on diseases—not (primarily) through diplomatic channels, but by contacting national health authorities as well as making use of telegraphic transmission and other new methods. In addition, systematic studies were planned to investigate the conditions under which data were collected, that is, the organization of the health administrations in different countries.

Two more far-ranging elements were also added: the *regular* provision of acute epidemiological data (which had previously only been provided during emergencies) and general indicators for the condition of public health systems.[33] These were bold ventures, since requests for this type of information increasingly challenged domestic control. Rajchman planned to use the data for further scientific investigation. His aim was to develop new, more standardized methods of data generation in order to integrate national information retrieval and to develop a model for public health systems. This was in keeping with his general objectives for the Health Section: international information, comparative research, and political regulation.[34]

[32] Iris Borowy, *Coming to Terms with Health* (n 27) 67f, 125.

[33] Patricia Anne Sealey, *The League of Nations Health Organization and the Evolution of Transnational Public Health* (DPhil thesis, Ohio State University 2011).

[34] Here and in the following paragraph, I follow Iris Borowy, *Coming to Terms with Health* (n 27) 103–105.

For this ambitious and risky endeavour, he appointed Edgar Sydenstricker, a brilliant statistician who had developed new methods for collecting data on morbidity. In early 1923, while on leave of absence from the United States Public Health Service, Sydenstricker envisioned the Health Section as a centre for statistical services and analysis with two aims: the gathering and immediate distribution of as much data as possible, and the collection of reliable data for scientific epidemiological studies. After consultations with colleagues from several statistical offices, Sydenstricker wrote a detailed work programme entailing the continuous compilation of epidemiological data for quick and easy exchange. Over 50 reports and six long-term reports on sanitary conditions in Eastern Europe had already been published and served as a springboard for the planned global inventory. Other areas were devoted to innovation, like the conceptualization of the LNHO as a clearing house and coordinating agency for public health statistics (in particular for Europe) that was to compile surveys of vital national and public health indexes, along with information on their origins and reports on the organization of health in different countries, and produce medical statistics for long-term use especially in research. One new approach in this context was the integration of national data already published in its respective countries of origin into tables and maps. This proposal by Rajchman and Sydenstricker was particularly critical, as it enabled comparisons.

It is remarkable how quickly their plans yielded results. Starting in 1923, monthly reports on notifiable diseases, national surveys of sanitary conditions and public health governance structures, and overviews of statistical systems and the gathering of public health indicators were published; Ignacy Wasserberg was put in charge of these (seemingly) technical publications. Initially, Rajchman had wanted Stefan Mutermilch to replace Stanisława Adamowicz (a qualified statistician who returned to Poland to direct the epidemiological department at the Ministry of Health and represented Poland at the General Assembly in 1936).[35] Mutermilch could have easily taken over her work on Russia and the whole of Eastern Europe, but Wasserberg brought other qualities to the Section. Born in Cracow in 1879, he studied medicine, psychology, and anthropology, receiving his MD in 1906 and a PhD in 1910. During the two years before being appointed to the LNHO, he worked at a small psychiatric clinic near Danzig as well as at a lunatic asylum in Philadelphia by way of a research appointment.[36] For Rajchman, he was the perfect choice: besides being intellectually prepared to critically read and edit national reports and serials, Wasserberg also spoke five languages (Polish, Russian, German, English, and French).[37]

[35] Kreuder-Sonnen, *Wie man Mikroben auf Reisen schickt* (n 19) 166. On Adamowicz's engagement in the international women's movement, see Iwona Dadej, *'Die Frau von Morgen': Frauenpolitisch tätige Akademikerinnen in Deutschland und Polen, 1918–1939* (DPhil thesis, Free University of Berlin 2015).

[36] Curriculum Vitae, 6 June 1921, LON S 903/3699.

[37] Rajchman to Secretary General, 22 June 1923, LON S 903/3699.

A year later, in 1924, another expert was added to the Section staff. Rajchman secured the approval of two to three temporary liaison officers to build contacts with health authorities. In the case of Evald (Ewald) Tománek, the initial work contract had a rather short probation period since Rajchman was actually looking for a vital statistician, also enquiring at the Rockefeller Foundation, which recommended Tománek. In the end he stayed with the Health Section from November 1924 until 1934, working mostly in the epidemiological intelligence and public health statistical service.[38] Tománek's trajectory is another of the many examples of educational and professional mobility in and beyond the Habsburg Monarchy as well as in the Russian and German empires. Born in 1884 in Morkovice near Brno, Tománek received his MD from the Bohemian Medical Faculty in Prague in 1909, after which he began working at the *Ärztliche Applikationsschule* (a military academy), the Institute for Forensic Medicine, and the Institute of Hygiene in Vienna. As soon as the war ended, he transferred to the Harvard Technological School of Public Health. Shortly thereafter, he found employment with the Czechoslovak Ministry of Health. By the time Rajchman contacted him in 1923, Tománek had returned to the US, working on vital statistics in Cambridge and making use of his language skills: he spoke Slovak, Czech, Russian, English, and French.[39]

With Wasserberg, Tománek, and several other medical experts on board, the Health Section was able to expand its publishing activities. Beginning in 1925, weekly reports were compiled; not long thereafter, handbooks on vital statistics were also being edited, each containing instructions on how to interpret and compare the national data submitted. Volumes on 15 European countries were completed quickly.[40]

One can easily imagine that this international collection of health knowledge and its transnational management prompted varied reactions. For example, when plans for an extended format of the Epidemiological Reports and Intelligence were announced, the British delegate to the Health Committee, George Buchanan, voiced criticism. He complained that the numbers were based on notification figures, not on real-life data. In a survey of different national data, countries such as Great Britain would therefore implicitly be penalized for not having an effective notification system.[41]

Nonetheless, the production of information in improved quality and greater quantities continued. The most ambitious undertaking was the International

[38] Rajchman an Tománek, 16 January 1924; Rajchman to General Secretary, 3 November 1924, LON S 893/3501.

[39] Curriculum Vitae, undated; Wilson to Wells, 18 December 1923, LON S 893/3501.

[40] Borowy, *Coming to Terms with Health* (n 27) 177f.

[41] Ibid, 104. See also the debates and negotiations concerning a comparable collection of mortality causes. While several governments set up their own expert commissions to evaluate and revise the International List of Death Causes compiled by the LNHO, others provided the requested data only reluctantly, ibid, 167ff.

Health Yearbook. Negotiations to implement a systematic documentation of the field began in 1927. During this process, the LNHO established itself as an authoritative centre for maintaining continuous records on world health. The yearbook played a crucial role in this context, since it was meant to complement the national reports with global surveys of legislative and administrative developments. Its first volume contained the results of the collaboration between 22 of the 23 contracted health administrations, and by the preliminary end of the endeavour in 1930, six volumes had been published. Though the results fell short of expectations, the yearbook's purpose and uniform cross-border collection of health information—among others by the use of a standardized questionnaire developed in the secretariat—which transcended the logics and interests of the national informants deserve credit. In the late 1930s, the Health Section introduced health indexes incorporating the registration of health, vitality, socioeconomic, and cultural milieus as well as sanitary services. As Ilana Löwy and Patrick Zylberman have pointed out, these indexes went beyond earlier surveys in terms of scale and their implementation of sophisticated statistical tools. Above all, different notions of 'public health' distinguished the projects: while many of the surveys focused on the elimination of specific diseases, the indexes included a wide range of indicators and conditions related to health; they introduced an 'era of large-scale intervention in public health and centralised strategic planning'.[42]

Moreover, much of the data collected bore the characteristics of research by including interpretation and the drawing of conclusions. These new ways of investigation brought about 'international meta-studies', which in turn contributed to the use of a uniform terminology through the LNHO's standardization programme.[43] In addition, data was now being gathered through new channels—not through diplomatic representations but through the cooperation of health administrations, national statistical bureaus, and medical field offices. In 1925, for example, the Czechoslovak Ministry of Health established a liaison office to communicate with the League of Nations, with Jaroslav Hrdlička responsible for submitting information to the LNHO.[44] His counterpart in the Health Section was Evald Tománek, who was responsible for communicating with officials in Prague on behalf of Edvard Beneš. This connection lasted beyond 1932, when Tománek became a key figure in developing collaboration between Czechoslovakia and the LNHO. It involved a sanitary survey of Slovakia and Subcarpathian Ruthenia, which Czechoslovakia had advocated and for which it requested the League to delegate one of its Section members to the State Institute of Hygiene as well as to arrange

42 Ilana Löwy and Patrick Zylberman. 'Medicine as a social instrument: Rockefeller Foundation, 1913–45' (2000) 31/3 Studies in History and Philosophy of Science, Part C: Studies in History and Philosophy of Biological and Biomedical Sciences 365, 371.

43 Borowy, *Coming to Terms with Health* (n 27) 285.

44 Shortly thereafter, a Hungarian liaison office was established; its relations with Polish authorities were close. See ibid, 140f.

training courses at home and abroad for health officials from the region. The proposal was accepted, since it was in line with the recommendations of the European Conference on Rural Hygiene organized by the LNHO in 1930.[45]

The rural hygiene programme was one of the largest LNHO endeavours and is a significant example of how Eastern and Southeastern European challenges informed international health—or in more general terms, how regional approaches developed into global models. Yet it also illustrates that Rajchman adapted to the new format of organizing international health. An interest in rural hygiene first emerged in 1928; from 1930 onwards, it became a focal area, with the Great Depression and its dramatic effects on the countryside contributing to this development. In early 1930, a Spanish proposal for a conference on the situation of rural hygiene in Europe reached the Health Committee. At the same time, a proposal was received from Hungary for the establishment of a health centre in Gödöllő, and the ministry in charge sought to turn the occasion into a larger event by organizing an international conference on the general tasks of such centres. The two proposals were discussed together and adopted by the Committee, and they continued to be viewed as interrelated. From the outset, rural hygiene was thus connected to health centres like the one in Gödöllő. While preparing the conference to be held in Budapest in October 1930, a model was agreed upon that would later be promoted worldwide. It stipulated action at multiple levels as well as a combination of state health and local autonomy: institutes of hygiene or central health administrations would be in charge, with district health centres and primary centres in villages acting as secondaries.[46] As with other programmes, Rajchman aligned the work of the LNHO with the emerging structure of governance. His commitment to transnational knowledge transfer notwithstanding, Rajchman built on and connected different levels of governance (local, regional, national, and international) in this regard. As a member of the subcommittee organizing a second conference on European rural health, he ensured that formats of health organization in the preferred multi-scale model remained on the agenda. One of the three main areas of recommendations prepared by the sub-committee that were eventually discussed at the conference in Geneva in July 1931 dealt with the provision of health services by way of a structure of local and regional health centres with a central health administration at the top.[47]

Internationalists are characterized as mediators, communicators, and brokers within and beyond their institutions who were frequently in fragile and ambivalent

[45] Rajchman to Secretary General, 9 November 1932, LON S 893/3501; Sara Silverstein, 'The Periphery is the Center. Some Macedonian Origins of Social Medicine and Universal Healthcare' (2019) 28/3 Contemporary European History 220.

[46] Borowy, *Coming to Terms with Health* (n 27) 329–336.

[47] Continuing interactions between the local, national, and international levels of activity are described in Susan Gross Solomon, Lion Murard, and Patrick Zylberman (eds), *Shifting Boundaries of Public Health: Europe in the Twentieth Century* (University of Rochester Press 2008).

positions.[48] This was the case with Rajchman as well: over the course of the 1930s, his scope of activity within the LNHO decreased due to the new composition of the Health Committee, in which personal antagonists increasingly worked against him, and due to his anti-fascist attitude, which clashed with the widespread support for appeasement policy within the League of Nations—especially under the new conservative secretary-general Joseph Avenol. In Poland, Rajchman also became the target of numerous attacks, and in 1932 his directorship of the National Institute of Hygiene was not renewed.[49] Nevertheless, his trajectory shows that those active in international settings could become key figures wielding substantial power as a result of their ability to build networks, direct knowledge transfer, and structure problems. The two aspects—room to manoeuvre and vulnerability—went hand in hand.

II. Albert Apponyi's Representation of Hungary at the League of Nations combining Revisionist Agendas with International Commitment

Albert Apponyi de Nagy-Apponyi was born into a noble family in Vienna in 1846. The Apponyis belonged to a small circle of noble families who were highly influential in Hungarian politics and Habsburg governance, and Albert continued this tradition. In 1872, after graduating in Law from Budapest and Vienna (including periods of study in Rome and Paris), he was elected to the Hungarian parliament, where he represented various national conservative parties almost continuously until his death in 1933.[50] A gifted speaker, he quickly rose to prominence in both domestic and international affairs. In the late 1870s, he took the reins of the National Party, which later became a catchment for the conservative opposition aiming at increasing the power of the Hungarian parliament and government within the Habsburg Monarchy. In 1918, Apponyi became speaker of the house of representatives, and from 1906 to 1910 (and again in 1917/18), he served as minister of education. Among other things, he is known for three education acts of 1907/08 (together referred to as Lex Apponyi) aiming at stronger influence of the state in elementary education, which at that time was largely organized by church congregations. The state subsidies for the prescribed improvement of the quality of instruction were, however, granted only when the language of instruction was Hungarian. In addition, all pupils had to learn Hungarian by the end of the fourth

[48] Isabella Löhr and Madeleine Herren, 'Being international in times of war: Arthur Sweetser and the shifting of the League of Nations to the United Nations' (2018) 25/3 European Review of History 535.

[49] Balińska, 'Rajchman, Ludwik Witold' (n 22).

[50] Friedrich Gottas, 'Apponyi, Albert Graf' in Mathias Bernath and Felix von Schroeder (eds), *Biographisches Lexikon zur Geschichte Südosteuropas, vol. 1* (Oldenbourg Wissenschaftsverlag 1974).

class. These steps towards a state-led and nationalizing education policy provoked fierce criticism.[51]

In international politics, Apponyi made a name for himself especially as leader of the Hungarian delegation to the Versailles Peace Conference (along with Pál Teleki and István Bethlen). It was he who submitted the Hungarian objections to the peace conditions to the convened victorious powers; the speech he delivered received broad acclaim.[52] After the signing of the Treaty of Trianon, he became a key figure in the revisionist movement that would soon dominate political sentiment in Hungary.[53] A revisionist agenda aiming at the consolidation of the Hungarian nation, which had an imperial and pro-Habsburg script, also informed his subsequent international activities as official representative at the League of Nations, dedicated advocate for disarmament, and chairman of the *Association hongroise des affaires étrangères et pour la Société des nations*, the Hungarian branch in the International Federation of League of Nations Societies (IFLNS), which hosted the 1931 international congress of organization.[54] Serving the national cause was in his case linked with a deep commitment to international cooperation for peace and understanding among nations. We know that in East Central Europe and beyond, participation in international organizations was partly linked with hopes for international recognition, which was considered as resource for building the nation state.

Apponyi's political work included a strong and lasting involvement in the Inter-Parliamentary Union (IPU), which was a pioneer of the Hague Conventions in 1899 and 1907, and the Permanent Court of Arbitration as well as his membership in the European Centre of the Carnegie Endowment for International Peace and the *Académie Diplomatique Internationale* in Paris. It is telling that he introduced the anniversary of the Hague Convention in 1899 as a commemoration day in schools,[55] and that he died in Geneva in 1933 just a few days after the opening of the World Disarmament Conference, which he had planned to attend.

[51] On the whole issue and what these laws meant in reality see: Joachim von Puttkamer, *Schulalltag und nationale Integration in Ungarn: Slowaken, Rumänen und Siebenbürger Sachsen in der Auseinandersetzung mit der ungarischen Staatsidee 1867–1914* (De Gruyter 2003).

[52] For his realistic assessment of the limited possibilities of the Hungarians, as well as for his personal account of the negotiations in Paris, see his autobiography: Albert Apponyi, *Erlebnisse und Ergebnisse* (Keil Verlag 1933) 237–246.

[53] Anikó Kovács-Bertrand, *Der ungarische Revisionismus nach dem Ersten Weltkrieg: Der publizistische Kampf gegen den Friedensvertrag von Trianon* (De Gruyter Oldenbourg 1997). On the images of the Habsburg Monarchy among Hungarian conservatives, see: Gergely Romscis, *The Memory of the Habsburg Empire in German, Austrian, and Hungarian Right-Wing Historiography and Political Thinking, 1918–1941* (Columbia University Press 2010).

[54] The association was founded in 1920 to explain and promote Hungary's foreign policy, on the one hand, and to promote the ideals of the League on the other. It was dissolved in 1948. See Jules de Pekár, 'L'Union Internationale des Associations pour la Société de Nations et la Hongrie' in Olivier D'Eöttevényi and George Drucker (eds), *La Hongrie dans les relations internationales* (Athenaeum 1935); Thomas R. Davies, 'Internationalism in a divided world: The experiences of the international federation of League of Nations Societies, 1919–1939' (2012) 37/2 Peace & Change 227.

[55] Ralph Uhlig, *Die Interparlamentarische Union 1889–1914* (Franz Steiner 1988) 286.

In the following, Apponyi's work and role in the IPU will be outlined to illustrate the experience, skills, and visions he brought with him when becoming involved in the League. The IPU was established in connection with the peace movement emerging in the nineteenth century. During the 1840s and 1850s, pacifists from different parts of Europe came together at peace congresses, and eventually the first peace societies were founded and united in international federations. In Central Europe, peacebuilding work was institutionalized in the 1890s: the Austrian Society of Friends of Peace (Österreichische Gesellschaft der Friedensfreunde, 1891) was followed by similar associations in Germany (Deutsche Friedensgesellschaft, 1892) and Hungary (Magyar Szent Korona Országainak Békeegyesülete, 1895). Nineteenth-century peace advocates shared the firm belief that lasting peace could be achieved only through international law and arbitration with the authority to regulate relations between states and mitigate conflicts. Differing opinions existed regarding the role of national governments in this process, however.[56] The IPU embodied the notion that people and their representatives should be proactive; for obvious reasons, nearly 100 parliamentarians from different countries founded the organization in 1889 at the *Exposition Universelle* in Paris as an approach to transnational representation of peoples. Until the beginning of the First World War, the IPU advocated for the creation of an international arbitration tribunal, the drafting of international law, arms control agreements, and the development of international private law. Eighteen congresses were held and numerous resolutions tabled by the growing membership, which reached 2,000 in 1906 and 3,000 in 1913—this meant that around a third of all parliamentarians from the 24 participating parliaments were involved in the organization.[57]

The Hungarian IPU committee was one of the first groups of parliamentarians to form in the mid-1890s. As early as 1895, the Hungarian section had more than 100 members, and this number had doubled by the 1910s, meaning that roughly a third of the members of the Hungarian Diet were involved in inter-parliamentary work.[58] During its early years, the Hungarian IPU section was directed by Mór Jókai; Apponyi took over in 1899 and remained in charge until 1913. According to Apponyi, one reason for the creation of the group was the rising tide of anti-Hungarian sentiment at previous IPU congresses. In preparation for the congress in Brussels in 1895, Rumanian delegates had tried to put the treatment of

[56] C. Roland Marchand, *The American Peace Movement and Social Reform, 1898–1918* (Princeton University Press 1972); Henriett Kovács, *Die Friedensbewegung in Österreich-Ungarn an der Wende zum 20. Jahrhundert* (Gabriele Schäfer Verlag 2009).

[57] Uhlig, *Interparlamentarische Union* (n 55) 899–902; Claudia Kissling, *Die Interparlamentarische Union im Wandel: Rechtspolitische Ansätze einer repräsentativ-parlamentarischen Gestaltung der Weltpolitik* (Peter Lang 2006) 31–82.

[58] Uhlig, *Interparlamentarische Union* (n 55) 105f, 903. The names of the Hungarian representatives in the office of the IPU can be found here: 'Congress and conference 1896' in the newspaper (1896) 5/8 Die Waffen nieder! 293–295. Albert Berzeviczy, the longtime president of the Hungarian Academy of Sciences and vice president of the house of representatives, served as Apponyi's deputy.

nationalities in Hungary on the agenda as a factor promoting war—and as a result, 131 Hungarian parliamentarians had constituted themselves as a group and member of the IPU. In Brussels, Jókai and Apponyi as representatives successfully lobbied to have the Romanian motion removed from the agenda. Moreover, their proposal to hold the next congress in Budapest was accepted.[59] This decision had nothing to do with the confrontation between the two countries, but was linked to the fact that it had been announced that the World Peace Congress in 1896 would be held in Budapest as well. Linking the two events was a way of joining forces. Although the conflicts between nationalities in the Hungarian half of the Habsburg Empire were visible at the Budapest congress,[60] Apponyi and other leading Hungarian parliamentarians used their influence as local organizers for something else, namely to table two far-reaching issues.

The first concerned the question of how to establish an international court of arbitration, since such an institution would rely on voluntary jurisdiction, that is, the conscious submission of the interstate conflict to an arbitrator. Although the need for such a mechanism was not a matter of debate within the IPU, its realization very much was. Two proposals were put forth: William Randal Cremer suggested a special committee to be convened by the IPU and tasked with persuading governments to act. Albert Berzeviczy requested national IPU groups to canvass for international arbitration within their respective parliaments and at an international congress of diplomats. The eventual compromise was for the IPU's executive board to take centre stage with a mandate to negotiate with European governments at a congress to establish international arbitration.[61] The proposal for a diplomatic meeting was subsequently considered to be a breakthrough in arbitration leading to the first Hague Peace Conference; and the Budapest IPU resolution proved useful for the drafting of an agreement to set up a permanent court.

As their second momentous act, and initiated by Apponyi as the person in charge of organizing the congress, the delegates passed an amendment to the IPU statutes (valid until 1908) under which the possibility of IPU membership could be offered to non-constitutional states. The Russian Empire, whose involvement in a European or even global peace framework appeared essential to Apponyi and others to ensure lasting peace, was the primary target of this endeavour. The importance of cooperation between the IPU and Russia was evidenced by the delegates endorsing an amendment to the statutes—a signal to Saint Petersburg that they would welcome a Russian representative in Budapest—on the eve of the conference. Their hopes were dashed, but even so, the IPU initiative is regarded as one

59 Kovács, *Die Friedensbewegung in Österreich-Ungarn* (n 56) 97f.

60 Not least at the symbolic level: of the 441 delegates from 15 countries, 143 came from Hungary. Ibid, 118.

61 Uhlig, *Interparlamentarische Union* (n 55) 234f.

of the reasons why Czar Nicholas II published a peace manifesto that would be instrumental in convening the Hague Conference of 1899.[62]

In the years that followed, Apponyi continued to shape the programme of the IPU and gain experience in political negotiations at the international level. Besides leading the Hungarian IPU group, he also served on the IPU executive board for many years. In this position, he proposed the establishment of an international press union to promote global collaboration for peace among parliamentarians and pacifists alike. Furthermore, he was deeply involved in the discussion about the organization's role, the creation of a legislative body as a continuation of the Hague Conventions, and the institutionalization of global governance in general.

In 1904, the US delegation proposed that future work should aim at establishing a world parliament; Paul Henri Balluet d'Estournelles de Constant put forth a similar proposal, namely for the creation of a 'Ministère International', at around the same time. The basic idea was to place a people's representation with legislative competence—in effect, the IPU—alongside permanent courts and a world government. Beginning in 1905, a study commission discussed these proposals. Beniamino Pandolfi and Philip Stanhope (later Lord Weardale and IPU president from 1912–22) spoke out in favour of focusing the IPU's attention on the continuation of the Hague Peace Conferences. Pandolfi considered such a permanent national congress of governments accompanied by a court to be sufficient. This intention to give the new world a strong governmental leaning deviated from previous ideas within the IPU, which had envisioned a triad of extra-parliamentary pacifism (peace societies), inter-parliamentary pacifism, and governments working together in a congress of the nations (a League of Nations of sorts). A fourth proposal came from Apponyi, who wished to anchor the IPU under international law as an international representative body with a moral function.[63] Ultimately, it was agreed to call for the Hague Conferences being convened regularly as a starting point for the institutionalization of a legislative body. The discussion had no practical consequences, and the IPU subsequently lost itself in internal reform debates. The devised scenarios were not entirely out of the picture, however; they would remain in the backs of the minds of the individuals shaping the League of Nations and other international organizations after the war.

Apponyi resigned as chair of the Hungarian IPU group in 1912 and left the executive committee a year later. Over the preceding nearly 20 years, he had become familiar with the inner workings of an international organization, knowledgeable regarding the ongoing debates about the institutionalization of international

[62] Ibid, 224–226.

[63] Ibid, 413ff; Christian L. Lange, *Union interparlamentaire: Résolutions des Conférences et Décisions principales du Conseil* (Misch et Thron 1911) 93f.

arbitration and global governance, and connected with wide circles of politicians and diplomats, many of whom would play a role in the postwar period.[64]

His thinking was also influenced by his perception of American political thought, which partly formed during his three visits to the United States. The first time he crossed the Atlantic was to attend the international meeting of the IPU in St. Louis in 1904, which was held in parallel with the World's Fair. During his stay there, he met President Theodore Roosevelt[65] as well as Nicolas Murray Butler, a leading figure in the US peace movement. When Apponyi visited the country again in 1912 during a lecture tour, his acquaintance with Butler was renewed and he was also introduced to the Carnegie Endowment for International Peace (CEIP), where Butler was head of the Division of Intercourse and Education. The leaders of the CEIP were emphatically liberal internationalists who advocated international law and arbitration as the basis for a peaceful world.[66] Shared beliefs led to further meetings between Apponyi and Butler as well as to other joint activities such as collaboration on the establishment of a Permanent Court of Arbitration. While impressed by the peace work in the United States, Apponyi gained the impression that there was little understanding for the situation and challenges in Europe.[67] To countervail this perceived problem, he returned to the US in 1924 on a lecture tour to explain the situation in postwar Central Europe. Ideas and knowledge travelled in both directions.

It is no surprise that the First World War left a significant mark on the peace movement, not to mention on the visions of a stable, peaceful international order. Apponyi abandoned his conviction that Russia would play a proactive role, which had been the reason for his intervention at the IPU conference in Budapest. He now promoted a European Union without Russia; in fact, he argued that permanent peace could be brought about only by means of a united bloc of Western and Central European countries.[68] His revised opinion echoed the mainstream post-1848 political discourse in Hungary, which suggested there were three conditions for a peaceful European (and global) order: the exclusion of Russia, a central

64 Albert de Berzeviczy, 'La Hongrie et l'Union Interparlementaire. Activité du feu comte Albert Apponyi' in Olivier D'Eöttevényi and George Drucker (eds), *La Hongrie dans les relations internationales* (Athenaeum 1935).

65 According to Apponyi's account, he used his conversation with Roosevelt to justify Hungarian national aspirations while assuring the president that this did not call into question the Habsburg Monarchy itself. This is noteworthy because in domestic politics, Apponyi belonged to the political wing that fought hard against the constitutional union. See: Apponyi, *Erlebnisse und Ergebnisse* (n 52) 148–152.

66 On Butler and the CEIP, see Joseph W. Winn, 'Nicholas Murray Butler, the Carnegie Endowment for International Peace, and the search for reconciliation in Europe, 1919–1933' (2006) 31/4 Peace & Change; Martin David Dubin, 'The Carnegie Endowment for International Peace and the advocacy of a League of Nations, 1914–1918' (1979) 123/6 Proceedings of the American Philosophical Society 356ff.; Dietmar Müller and Stefan Troebst (eds), *The 'Carnegie Report on the Causes and Conduct of the Balkan Wars of 1912/13': Philanthropy, Conflict Management and International Law* (CEU Press 2021).

67 Albert Apponyi, 'Amerikanische Eindrücke' (1911) 13/4 Die Friedenswarte 100.

68 Albert Apponyi, 'Der große westliche Block' (1915) 18/8 Die Friedenswarte 205.

position and mediating role for Hungary vis-à-vis Eastern and Southern Europe, and the need for a supranational organization of the peoples in Central Europe, be it in the form of the Habsburg Monarchy or a union of sovereign nations.

When the war ended—and especially with the Treaty of Trianon—the basis for continuing international collaboration changed radically for Apponyi and Hungarians in general. Assessments of the political needs of the country, which was politically isolated and experiencing a deep economic crisis, were torn between calls to find partners in the international arena (including the question whether Hungary should join the League) and efforts to renegotiate the territorial losses. On the one hand, the League of Nations was established at a moment when Hungary was at the peak of disappointed nationalism and counter-revolutionary sentiments. On the other hand, political decision-makers familiar with international politics knew only too well that the price for not joining the new international organizations would be high. Miklós Zeidler has pointed out that those in charge of determining Hungary's foreign policy were aware of the well-known phrase '*les absents ont toujours tort*'. They saw that the League was a forum in which they could work towards their goals—or would at least be involved in the decisions affecting the country. Indeed, the League Covenant contained regulations that could be invoked, especially Articles 8 and 10 on the reduction of armament and the protection of territorial integrity as well as Article 19 stipulating the reconsideration of international conditions that had become inapplicable or whose continuation might endanger world peace. The latter was viewed as a gateway to the revision of Trianon. In fact, three revisionist foreign policy goals seemed attainable by way of the League: the protection of Hungarian minorities in neighbouring states, equal rights for the country regarding armament, and a readjustment of its borders.[69]

In this context, Albert Apponyi encouraged rapprochement with the League and was charged with negotiating Hungary's membership. The application was submitted in May 1921 but subsequently withdrawn when it became clear that the prospects of acceptance at the next meeting of the Assembly were slim. The Little Entente as well as France were against the admittance of Hungary owing to its occupation of the city of Sopron and its vicinity and refusal to overthrow the Habsburg royalty. The situation was more favourable a year later when both of these reasons for objection had been resolved. In September 1921, the Assembly voted unanimously for Hungary to be admitted to the League of Nations.

A group of individuals thus had to be chosen to represent the country, and it included established politicians and diplomats, who attended the sessions of the

[69] Miklós Zeidler, 'Hungary and the League of Nations' in Enikő Dácz, Christina Griessler, and Henriett Kovácz (eds), *Traum vom Frieden—Utopie oder Realität? Kriegs- und Friedensdiskurse aus historischer, politologischer und juristischer Perspektive (1914–2014)* (Nomos 2016) 191. Mária Ormos, 'Magyarország belépése a Népszövetségbe'/Hungary's entrance into the League of Nations (1957) 91/1–4 Szazadok/Centuries.

Council and the Assembly or were part of the permanent representation, as well as experts from different backgrounds to participate in the commissions and the Secretariat.[70] Apponyi was an obvious choice to be one of the chief representatives, given his previous experience and status as well as his rhetorical and language skills; moreover, such a position was attractive to him. Judging by his account, however, his presence in Geneva was disappointing, at least at first. Given the cold shoulder by several old friends and colleagues from the IPU such as d'Estournelles de Constant in the Assembly sessions, Apponyi felt a painful awareness of Hungary's loss of status and recognition. But over time the atmosphere warmed, his isolation decreased, and his room for manoeuvre grew. Like before, he pursued two main approaches: serving Hungarian interests, in particular in the course of the optant disputes[71], and continuing international cooperation based on mutual assistance and shared interests. As a member of the League's International Commission on Intellectual Cooperation (ICIC), for example, he organized support for Hungary by emphasizing internationalism as a process of give and take for all parties. In 1924, he persuaded the ICIC to launch an international appeal for support for Hungarian scientists and intellectuals. Henri Bergson, president of the ICIC, invited universities and academies of sciences to send their publications to Hungary and develop lasting academic ties and collaboration. Apponyi made two arguments to justify the need for support. Firstly, he cited the international spirit and the fact that a similar appeal had been published to improve the situation in Austria, which was effective above all in strengthening understanding among nations. Secondly, he stressed the contribution of Hungarian culture and learning to the general development of the affected disciplines, pointing out their manifold contacts with colleagues across Europe as evidenced by their international academic careers.[72] We see here a more general imagination that Apponyi and others promoted at the time, that of Hungary as part of Europe which through throughout its history has been of great importance for European development.[73] Revisionist motives were at stake, too: at large, and in concrete terms since Apponyi had intended to include scholars who were members of the Hungarian minorities into the exchange

[70] According to Zeidler, no more than two or three Hungarian officers were employed at the Secretariat, with few short-term assistants at their side. For the year 1930, he counts 630 employees of whom 183 were Swiss, 142 British, and 104 French, compared to 20 Germans, 12 Poles, 6 Czechoslovakians, 6 Yugoslavs, 6 Austrians, 3 Hungarians, 3 Romanians, and one Bulgarian. See Miklós Zeidler, 'The League of Nations in Hungary's thinking about foreign policy' (2013) 53/205–206 The Hungarian Quarterly 191ff. The numbers are instructive as they indicate the different representation and standing of the successor states in Eastern and Central Europe in the Secretariat, but also in general.

[71] On these disputes, see the contribution by Antal Berkes, Chapter 12 in this volume.

[72] Daniel Laqua, 'Internationalisme ou Affirmation de la Nation? La Coopération Intellectuelle Transnationale dans l'entre-deux-Guerres' (2011) 52/3 Critique internationale 51, 57–58. See also the extended version of the article: Daniel Laqua, 'Internationalism and Nationalism in the League of Nation's Work for Intellectual Cooperation' in M.B. Jerónimo and J.P. Monteiro (eds), *Internationalism, Imperialism and the Formation of the Contemporary World* (Palgrave 2018).

[73] See on the discourses of historical legitimization in postwar-Hungary: Zsolt Nagy, *Great Expectations and Interwar Realities: Cultural Diplomacy in Horthy's Hungary* (CEU Press 2017).

of scientific literature. This agenda, however, was combined with and embedded in an international practice.

Apponyi remained an emphatic advocate of internationalism and the League. In January 1933, shortly before the World Disarmament Conference, he delivered a speech in Vienna entitled 'The Crisis in the League of Nations', most of which was later included in his memoirs. In it, he outlined three causes of the crisis: the Far East dispute, the world trade depression, and general disarmament. He partly related these to the fact that the organization was composed of representatives of individual nations who could not cease serving their own interests. 'Is one' he asked, 'to renounce the idea of a League representing great collective interest, as its Covenant declares, or are we to shut our eyes […] and go on living in a world of illusion?' Neither of these was the way forward, he continued: instead, one needs to take into account that the 'League is still in process of development'. The difficulty of mediating between national causes and the interests of the whole would persist, but according to Apponyi it would gradually diminish. Patriotic ideas would change—not through ideology but because 'nations will eventually weary of seeing their real interests sacrificed to antagonisms'. He concluded by stating, 'I believe in the League of Nations, not as it is, but as it will be'.[74]

III. Conclusion

As Susan Pedersen has pointed out, 'interwar internationalism depended more on structure than on faith: a genuinely transnational officialdom, and not visionaries or even statesmen, was at its beating heart'.[75] Officers and affiliated experts of the League of Nations created considerable scope of action for themselves as well as new institutional spaces such as the Secretariat's sections and related commissions. As shown above, this had much to with expertise, professional orientation, and skills obtained in international careers before the First World War and is connected to the past of Central and Eastern Europe.

The two individuals presented here differ in many respects; nevertheless, they highlight beyond their individual trajectories the legacy of the Habsburg Monarchy and the Russian Empire within the League of Nations after the war. Their work and careers in the League, like those of many others, were influenced by practices of internationalism and transnational contacts from the prewar period. At the same time, issues and problems of the post-imperial transformation in Central

[74] The quotations are taken from the English edition of his memoirs published under the title *The Memoirs of Count Apponyi* (Macmillan 1935) 291f, 294, 296, 301.

[75] Susan Pedersen, 'Back to the League of Nations' (2007) 112/4 The American Historical Review 1091, 1112.

and Eastern Europe were introduced. The League and its politics were shaped by continuities and discontinuities alike.

By linking international practices and transnational connections from the time of the Habsburg and Russian empires to national motives and the representation of post-imperial professional agendas, Apponyi and Rajchman contributed to the emergence of a new international order. Lasting until the 1930s, this order was characterized by the enforcement of national representation as a core principle based on the inclusion of Central and Eastern European imperial legacies, colonial structures, and new dynamics of cross-border entanglements.

In addition to the interplay of imperial, post-imperial and international undercurrents, the examples reveal a major resource that the League of Nations capitalized on to gain authority as a global organization. Essentially, it became the vanguard of a post-imperial world order because it was set up and run by individuals employed in the Secretariat or appointed to commissions who had learned to act and navigate successfully in the international sphere before the First World War. They were part of networks, had access to and produced various sources of information, and were able to adapt, mitigate, and connect different environments and scales of action. This competence and strategic capacity, which Rajchman acquired in trans-imperial scientific and medical networks and Apponyi promoted in his work for the Inter-Parliamentary Union, became a source of empowerment for the League. International officers and experts combined their technical expertise with their proficiency in conducting international work. By using and building on these two dimensions of expertise, the League was able to make a difference and become an agent of change.

At the same time, the selected biographies highlight the more general need to adapt and remake international practice and participation. Rajchman organized transnational knowledge production and transfer along with the new political order based on local, national, and international spheres of governance, connecting and arranging these different levels in original ways. Apponyi combined revisionist and national motives with a strong commitment to the League of Nations; in his eyes, international cooperation was the only way to contain and reduce national interests in the long run.

Especially in the League's Secretariat, and to a lesser degree in related committees, professional and technocratic rationales often enough balanced out national, (post-)imperial, and international motives and led to a change in practice. Action at the national, regional, and international level was seen as related and connected in multiple ways. In effect, multifaceted international policy fields formed in which sovereignty was embedded. This outlook helped to make the League flexible in regard to changing circumstances in the political order, and it resonates in the structures of global governance we know today. As we have seen, its long heritage is closely connected to internationalization and changing political orders in Central and Eastern Europe.

5

Austria, the League of Nations, and the Birth of Multilateral Financial Control

Nathan Marcus

The end of the Great War incurred far-reaching economic, financial, and political changes both in and beyond Europe. The United States rapidly emerged as the world's dominant economic power, entire Empires collapsed and communism conquered Russia. On the continent, the ruinous war had discredited ruling monarchs and elites in the eyes of veterans and widows, and gradual extension of the vote threatened the bourgeoisie's weakening grip on power. In Central and Eastern Europe new nation states emerged, but war raged on in Poland, communism took root in Hungary and, albeit briefly, even Munich, while border disputes in the Balkans remained precariously unresolved. For too many then in Central and Eastern Europe, the armistice failed to bring peacefulness as instead they continued to suffer from material depravation, political instability, and the continuation of armed conflicts. But despite the prevailing chaos, the Paris Peace Treaties had brought to life the League of Nations, a novel international organization that many hoped signified the dawn of a more peaceful and egalitarian era, one in which elites would have to respect women's and workers' minority and national rights and one in which nation states would strive to work together towards peace.

The League of Nations was charged with building and safeguarding a new and peaceful world order and within a few years it would boast among its earliest achievements the successful transition of Austria from monetary chaos to economic and financial stability. But initially its lofty tasks, besides a commitment to free trade, did not pertain to questions of economics or finance. Instead, the League focused its work on disarmament, national minorities, and the facilitation of peaceful solutions between conflicting states. This was partially because the sensitive and divisive question of reparations and war debts was still unsolved, but also because Britain feared giving the new institution any say on economic policy, whether domestic or foreign.[1] Still, not only was it in the realms of economics and

[1] Patricia Clavin and Jens-Wilhelm Wessels, 'Transnationalism and the League of Nations: Understanding the work of its economic and financial organisation' (2005) 14/4 Contemporary European History 465, 471. Patricia Clavin, *Securing the World Economy: The Reinvention of the League of Nations, 1926–1946* (Oxford University Press 2013).

Nathan Marcus, *Austria, the League of Nations, and the Birth of Multilateral Financial Control* In: *Remaking Central Europe*. Edited by: Peter Becker and Natasha Wheatley, Oxford University Press (2020). © the many contributors.
DOI: 10.1093/oso/9780198854685.003.0006

finance that the League displayed its first successes, but arguably these achievements incurred important legacies that carried over into the period after the Second World War. The innovations that the League of Nations' intervention in Austria brought to sovereign foreign borrowing, foremost the curtailment of power of predatory creditors, was an important step towards today's more considerate policies practiced by the International Monetary Fund (IMF) or the World Bank vis-à-vis sovereign nations.

As the post-war boom abated, leading bankers, who were historically engaged in trade finance, agreed that government action was necessary to ward off continued economic misery and the Bolshevik threat it contained for Europe. The Allies had necessarily cooperated on economic and financial questions during the war, but they had to be called into renewed action by a call from 150 bankers convening twice in Amsterdam during 1919.[2] Their one-page manifesto, published or reported on by major newspapers all around the world, called for an international conference to discuss and recommend changes in economic policy. By the autumn of 1920, the League of Nations had garnered enough support to convene almost 200 bankers, economists, and government experts to exchange their ideas at a conference in Brussels and propose how best to restore global trade and money flows. To prepare the conference, the League of Nations had founded an Economic and Financial Section, which subsequently published a series of policy papers by leading economists on the 'World's Monetary Problems', in which they endorsed price stability, gradual restoration of the gold standard, and the resumption of international lending. In Genoa in the spring of 1922, the British and French governments hosted a follow-up conference to Brussels that recommended balanced budgets and a gradual return to gold as the way for a return of international trade and capital flows.

At such conferences, focused on the economic future of Europe, the problem of Austria, plagued by hunger and hyperinflation, had always been prominent, not least because of the incessant efforts of the Austrian Foreign Ministry. The deteriorating economic situation in Austria and its potential risks for political stability in Central and Eastern Europe were a concern for the Allied powers, who were held responsible for creating a new state that many feared was economically unviable. The Viennese, who historically relied heavily on food and coal imports from vast areas now outside the country's borders, were already undernourished during the war and quickly fell victim to the Spanish flu and tuberculosis. Lifting the Allied Blockade in March 1919 pushed off starvation, but did little more, because supplies were expensive and hard to come by. Banking on western

[2] Yann Decorzant, 'La Société des Nations et l'apparition d'un nouveau réseau d'expertise économique et financière (1914–1923)' (2011) 52/3 Critique internationale 35. Yann Decorzant, 'Internationalism in the Economic and Financial Organisation of the League of Nations' in Daniel Laqua (ed), *Internationalism Reconfigured: Transnational Ideas and Movements Between the World Wars* (I.B. Tauris 2011).

sympathies that identified Vienna as part of their own cultural heritage, Austrian foreign policy was fatefully centred on obtaining foreign money and seemingly willing to risk ruining the country in order to get it. Desperately playing an already bad hand, Austrian diplomats never tired of stressing Vienna's unique cultural and commercial importance for the Danubian region and to raise the sceptre of the Bolshevik threat, which if unchecked, they warned, would lead to the collapse of human civilization in all of Central and Eastern Europe.

Unable to overcome the political deadlock that stalled Allied discussions on how to jointly help Austria, the victorious European Powers decided to let the League of Nations attempt a solution. In fact, as Clavin has shown, the League's intervention in Austria was preceded by foreign efforts to feed Vienna's starving population right after the war.[3] The American Relief Administration sold and distributed medical aid and material supplies all across Europe, with a large chunk of its deliveries going to Soviet Russia. Together with the American Child Welfare Mission it supplied thousands of soup kitchens across all of Central and Eastern Europe, thirty of which fed hungry Viennese.[4] But when the United States turned its back on the League of Nations and the Treaty of Versailles, it left the question of what to do with Austria to its European Allies, who eventually called upon the League of Nations to try to devise a solution. What both earlier and later interventions had in common was the conviction among Allied leaders that in order to preserve the peace in Central and Eastern Europe, economic conditions had to improve. But whereas food relief was considered a temporary and charitable practice, the Allies' wanted the League's plan to permanently wean Austria from foreign benevolence and help the new country regain economic strength to stand on its own feet.

At the end of 1920, the League's first General Assembly had approved the creation of a Joint Provisional Economic and Financial Committee, which eventually transformed into the more permanent Economic and Financial Section, the League Secretariat's largest. It worked independently but also towards and alongside the Financial Committee, which was made up of governmental experts (and its twin body, the Economic Committee), meeting several times a year and advising the League Council. While Austrian attempts to raise money abroad or at home floundered successively, the Secretariat's staff and the experts on the Financial Committee began working out a comprehensive intervention scheme that would stabilize Austria's prices, currency, and economy. They faced a myriad of interconnected problems, from the unsettled question of Austrian reparations and relief debts, to the dismemberment of the Austro-Hungarian National Bank and the unrestrained printing of Austrian currency. Since Austria was bankrupt, however, it

[3] Patricia Clavin, 'The Austrian hunger crisis and the genesis of international organization after the First World War' (2014) 90/2 International Affairs 265.

[4] Tibor Glant, 'Herbert Hoover and Hungary, 1918–1923' (2001) 8/2 Hungarian Journal of English American Studies 95 and *The American Relief Administration Bulletin No. 2, The Relief of the Children of Eastern Europe* (New York 1919).

was clear that money to pay for Austrian reconstruction would have to come from abroad, and that raised the sensitive question of foreign control, a question that is the focus of this chapter.

Sovereign states ceding control over fiscal policy and revenue streams to foreign creditors was a well-established practice. In the nineteenth century, poor countries raised money by selling bonds to private investors in London or Paris through the help of large banks. Bankrupt states or monarchs had to renegotiate with these foreign banks and private bondholders to raise new funds, and often ceded parts of their financial administration to foreign control in return for debt relief and fresh funding. The extent of foreign control in these debtor countries varied from case to case, but was always prone to abuse: in China after 1912, for example, revenues securing a foreign loan got deposited with foreign creditor banks, who in turn used these sums to influence China's economy and financial markets to service their own selfish goals.[5] More examples abound. In 1898, Russia, Great Britain and France guaranteed a foreign loan to bankrupt Greece, which accepted foreign control over important state monopolies and revenues by an International Financial Commission (IFC) staffed with foreign diplomats.[6] In Egypt, officially an Ottoman province, a financial commission was installed in 1876 to protect foreign bondholders, effectively excluding the destitute Khedive from administering his country's finances. The Ottoman Empire itself, after going bankrupt in 1876, accepted the control of a foreign-staffed Council of the Administration of Ottoman Public Debt over a wide variety of state revenues in return for an extensive debt reduction.[7] In all these cases, foreign creditor representatives were given various

[5] Linsun Cheng, *Banking in Modern China: Entrepreneurs, Professional Managers, and the Development of Chinese Banks, 1897–1937* (Cambridge University Press 2003).

[6] Previous attempts to establish foreign control of Greek revenues had failed. In 1843, British demands for control of state revenues were halted by the revolution. French opposition scuttled a second creditors' attempt in 1857 and the control commission then established was only tasked with overseeing budgetary planning and proposing repayment schemes, which were never realized. In 1898, Greece's parliament passed a law proposed by foreign representatives and Greek Finance Minister Stephan Streit to charge a separate company, the *Société de régie des revenus affectés au service de la dette publique hellénique*, with collecting certain state revenues for the IFC to service Greek foreign debt. There was lots of international 'outrage' after the IFC's establishment in 1898 (purposefully not named control), even though it saw itself as a 'true friend of Greece'. IFC calls to clamp down on tax evasion and smuggling or to implement administrative reforms were regularly ignored or rejected by parliament, but criticism in the IFC's public reports might have prevented the government from new risky financial undertakings. Commission members were quick to downplay their own role, claiming they simply provided a form of administrative stability. See: Korinna Schönhärl, *Finanziers in Sehnsuchtsträumen. Europäische Banken und Griechenland im 19. Jahrhundert* (Vandenhoeck & Ruprecht 2017).

[7] After taking power in a bloodless coup in 1908, the Young Turks issued two foreign loans. The first, to provide the Turkish Treasury with funds to repay provisory advances, was mainly guaranteed from customs and indirect revenues to be paid to the *Banque Impériale Ottomane* (which had headed a consortium that issued the short-term loans in 1908), as well as from tithes collected by the *Administration de la Dette Publique Ottomane*. Renegotiation of its Russian debt in 1909 produced a conversion loan, guaranteed by revenues from tithes, which would be collected by the Finance Ministry itself. In 1911, a new loan by a French syndicate was to be guaranteed by customs and certain tithes, again collected and transferred to the *Banque Impériale Ottomane* by the Finance Ministry and not the *Administration de la Dette*, bur after French public opinion got enraged about the sale of German cruisers to Turkey, France's Finance Ministry made approval conditional on placing the debt service under foreign control. The

legal powers to interfere with state finances in order to guarantee the repayment of loans that had been extended by foreign investors or banks.

This chapter asks whether foreign creditors wished to deal differently with bankrupt states after the First World War than had been customary in the past. Because creditors could gain administrative control over pledged assets and monopolies, overseas lending in the nineteenth century was often intertwined with colonialist strategies and imperial spheres of interest. After the Second World War, sovereigns borrowed predominantly from commercial banks, but today, emergency and reconstruction loans in bankrupt or war-torn countries are the business of multilaterals such as the IMF or the World Bank. The practices of these multilateral institutions aspire to be more respectful of national sovereignty than nineteenth century creditors, and indeed they provide not only long-term loans far below market-level rates, but also prohibit the mortgaging of state assets as security. However, conditionality, the (foreign) control over when, how, and under what conditions the lent funds can be spent by the borrowing government, remains a powerful instrument in the hands of these international creditor institutions. Did the League of Nations, guardian of the sovereign rights of nation states, continue or break with such practices when it coordinated the first international loan to Austria? To what extent were some of the more progressive practices of current multilateral lenders present already in 1922?

The Austrian loan was marketed to private investors, enjoyed foreign state guarantees, was secured by Austrian state revenues and incurred foreign control over the usage of borrowed funds. The IMF, World Bank, and other multilaterals are since prohibited from demanding securities, and foreign state guarantees have been applied to only a dozen sovereign loans throughout history. And multilaterals today lend their own funds, but they still set the conditions for their release and oversee the agreed upon application of their loans. This constraint on fiscal sovereignty, creditor control of when and how bankrupt countries can spend emergency loans, therefore continues until this very day. In the nineteenth century, creditor representatives interfered rather freely and directly with the financial administration of some borrowing states. After the Second World War, the IMF's Structural Adjustment Programs (SAP) made the provision of funds conditional on balancing national accounts, but ultimately left the choice of methods to the borrowing government. Increasingly, multilateral lenders, aware of the need to protect the weakest and politically least influential strata of the population, seek to ensure that funds are used productively and the costs of austerity not get distributed too unevenly.

Turks rejected and subsequent negotiations to co-nominate two French functionaries to oversee the conduct of the Court of Audits and Finance Ministry failed. Eventually an Austro-German consortium of 32 banks made the loan, guaranteed by customs that were transferred directly to the *Deutsche Bank*, which was in charge of the loan service. G. Pougly, *Les Emprunts de l'Etat Ottoman* (Paris 1916).

In Austria, the League's interference differed both from pre-war and present-day practices in important ways: First and foremost, it was organized by the League of Nations and not, as in the past, by creditor representatives, because international cooperation and control promised to forestall any of the self-interested machinations associated with nineteenth-century lenders. To make control more effective and less prone to discord, it was further placed in the hands of a single, neutral General Commissioner and not, as had been standard practice, given to a multinational commission. But unlike today's multilaterals, which are able to raise and lend their own money, the League of Nations still had to convince private investors to part with their savings and so would invariably favour creditors' interests regardless of the legitimacy of debtors' concerns. Upholding and practising the necessary principle of conditionality, the League's intervention in Austria gave foreign control a new, multilateral form. Its inventive solution aimed to benefit everyone by curtailing the harmful and self-interested abuse of particularistic creditors in favour of international cooperation based on bargaining, negotiation, and compromise.

I. Foreign Control Comes to Austria

In 1920, Sir William Goode, British member of the Reparations Commission's Austrian Sub-Committee in Vienna, was among the first to air the idea of foreign financial control in Austria, proposing a large foreign loan, guaranteed by the Entente Powers and coupled with some form of control over Austria's public finances.[8] Putting Goode's rescue plan before the Allied Supreme (War) Council in January 1921, French Foreign Minister Aristide Briand proposed a loan of $40 million through foreign banks, coupled with control by the Reparations Commission.[9] Britain considered the Reparations Commission too political and preferred the private control of bankers or business representatives instead, perhaps working through the League of Nations. The Council thereupon agreed that a commission of financial advisers should implement control and oversee the issue of Austrian currency, but the plan was stillborn when bankers required foreign states' guarantees, which neither Britain nor France were willing to give.[10] When the Council

[8] 'Memorandum from the British Representative regarding financial measures urgently necessary.' 15 September 1920. Enclosed with The National Archive [hereafter NA], T 160 / 57 / 2073 / 1.

[9] NA, T 160 / 57 / 2073 / 1: *Note of a conversation between the Chancellor of the Exchequer, Sir Hugh Levick and Sir William Goode*, 24 November 1920 and *Cabinet Decision*, 17 December 1920; NA, T 160 / 57 / 2073 / 2: Telegram from Hardinge to King and Cabinet, 25 January 1921 and *Draft: British Secretary's notes of an Allied conference held in the Salle* [sic] *de l'Horloge, Quai d'Orsay, Paris, on Tuesday, January 25th, 1921 at 11 a.m.*; League of Nations Archive [hereafter LONA], S 143 'Credits Internationaux / International Credits in Austria (File II)': *Procès-Verbal de la Séance du 25 Janvier 1921*.

[10] NA, T 160 / 57 / 2073 / 2 'Austrian Reconstruction': *Report of the committee on Austria. —Secret*, 29 January 1921 and *Second Cabinet Decision*, 30 December 1920 as well as *Memo* by Waterlow, 1 March 1921; Archiv der Republik [herafter AdR], 1 Ges. London Polit. Berichte 1920–1923 / 9 / P: Letter from Franckenstein to Foreign Ministry, 8 February 1921.

thereupon reconvened in March, Britain's Chancellor of the Exchequer, Austen Chamberlain, set on referring the problem to the League of Nations, told the Austrian representative that no money would materialize without some control of Austrian finances, proposing that at first the League's Financial Committee assess the value of Austrian assets and relate its findings to potential banks.[11] The Austrians agreed to both, but expressed their preference for some future form of Allied control as opposed to one by private bankers.[12] The Austrian envoy thereafter visited the Foreign Office where he formally announced that once enough money was obtained to put Austria on its feet, his government would gladly accept foreign control of lent funds, but not in return for mere advances, and only under condition that chairmanship of the control commission did not go to Italy.[13]

The League of Nations, however, would set its own conditions before getting involved in sovereign borrowing. As one of its officials wrote, 'Austria ... is a rare opportunity for the League to do something positive, but we must act with considerable caution.'[14] To avoid a scheme that placed too great a responsibility on the League, the international organization would only endeavour 'to coordinate, bring people together and exhibit methods'. But although Britain's delegate to the Economic Committee suggested a loan coupled to a committee of financial advisers, appointed by Austria and not the League, the final proposal suggested that a control commission appointed by the League of Nations' Financial Committee supervise Austrian finances.[15] When the head of the League's Financial Secretariat Arthur Salter together with members of the Financial Committee visited Vienna in April 1921, the Austrian Finance Ministry's Herman Schwarzwald confirmed that in his view Austria's best remedy was foreign control, which would free its politicians from the onus of having to increase taxation themselves.[16] The Austrian

[11] NA, T 160 / 57 / 2073 / 3 'Austrian Reconstruction': *British Secretary's Draft Notes of a meeting on financial experts, Conference held in the board room, Treasury, on Saturday, 12th March, 1921 at 3.0. p.m.* and *British Secretary's Notes of an Allied Conference held in St. James' Palace, S.W., on Saturday, 12th March, 1921 at 12–45 p.m* as well as *British Secretary's Verbatim Notes of a meeting of financial experts, held in the board room, Treasury, on Thursday, 17th. March, 1921 at 11.15 a.m.*; AdR, 01/9, Ges. London / Telegramme 1920–1923 / Karton 18 / 'Hinaus 1921': Telegram from Franckenstein, 12 March 1921; AdR 67 / 41662/21: *Bericht des Bundesministers für Finanzen über die Londoner Reise.*

[12] AdR, 01/9, Ges. London, Telegramme 1920–1923, Karton 18 'Hinaus 1921': Telegram from Grimm to Vienna, 15 March 1921.

[13] NA, FO 371 / 7338 / C 9643: Lampson, *Statement handed to the Austrian Delegation by the Chancellor of the Exchequer at the Financial Experts' Meeting on Thursday, March 17, 1921, at 11 A.M.*

[14] LONA, S 143 / Credits Internationaux / International Credits in Austria (File II): *The League and Austria*, 7 February 1921.

[15] LONA, S 143, Credits Internationaux / International Credits in Austria (File II): Memo from Loveday to Nixon, 26 March 1921; LONA, A.34 (SdN 1298 A1–A35, October 1920–March 1921): Avenol, *International Credits in Austria—Note*, 16 April 1921; LONA, A.36 (SdN 1299 A36–A56, April–May 1921): *Memorandum on the Finances of Austria—Facts and Comments*, 1 April 1921. The League's economist Alexander Loveday argued that Austria would have to 'accept the position of a company in liquidation' and a controlling organ 'similar to the position of Lord Cromer in the early days of his administration in Egypt'.

[16] LONA, S 106 Sir Arthur Salter's Private Papers, Austria No. 3: Letter from Avenol to Blackett, 2 May 1921 and documents filed under 'Reports of Meetings and Evidence given to Commission in Vienna

Government itself was ready to accept foreign control in principle so that the Financial Committee, reconvening in London at the end of May 1921, proposed appointing a commission consisting of four foreigners and three Austrians, working through an agent residing in Vienna, who would control lent funds and the revenues from pledged securities.[17]

Finding a form and composition of foreign control that pleased all involved parties was one of the main obstacles to a foreign loan for Austria (among other hurdles not discussed here were the liens placed on Austrian assets by the treaty of Saint-Germain-en-Laye, the composition of foreign state guarantees and the Austrian programme of reforms).[18] 'Control by a private group of capitalists' had been rejected by Austria, the League would only participate in a scheme in which foreign governments were involved, but Britain was weary of foreign control becoming an instrument of French or Italian policy.[19] The British further favoured a neutral administrator appointed by a committee of control made up of a majority of neutrals, while the Italians and French preferred charging a committee made up of a Danish, British, French, Italian, and perhaps a US member.[20] As Bank of England Governor Montagu Norman put it, he favoured 'Austria for the Austrians' over 'Austria for the Entente', and naturally the League itself also opposed assistance to Austria becoming an instrument of foreign politics.[21] But the League's General Secretary still found that France was right to prefer a committee to a single controller, because the

[Avril 1921]'; AdR, 67 / 41662/21 *Memorandum abgegeben den 28. April 1921 an den österreichischen Bundesfinanzminister durch die Delegierten der Finanzkommission des Völkerbundes.*

[17] As the British envoy summed up a conversation with Austria's Chancellor: 'But the opinion prevailing amongst those whose judgment carries most weight is that no Government will be strong enough to effect much except under outside pressure. One and all are waiting for some kind of financial control as a corollary of the help from the League of Nations.' NA, T 160 / 58 / 2073 / 6 'Austrian Reconstruction': Letter from Lindley to Curzon, 1 July 1921; AdR, 67 41663/21: *An die Herren Delegierten des Finanzkomitees des Völkerbundes M.J. Avenol, Sir Drummond-Fraser und Staatsrat E. Glückstadt derzeit in Wien.* 9 May 1921; AdR, 67 / 65478/21: Riis Hansen, Memo, 26 July 1921; LONA, S 106 Sir Arthur Salter's Private Papers, Austria No.3 / 'Reports of Meetings and Evidence given to Commission in Vienna' [Avril 1921]: *Entrevue au Ministère des Affaires Etrangères 23. Avril 1921*; LONA, A. 34: *First Memorandum of the Delegates, April 23rd, 1921*, pp. 72–4; LONA, 1148 Autriche II Mai 1921: *Commission Provisoire économique et financière. Séction financière. 4ème Session. Londres. 3ème Réunion, 25 Mai 1921. à 10 heures 30, et 15 heures*, 535–545.

[18] LONA, S 108 Sir Arthur Salter's Private Papers / Austria No. 5: Letter from Nixon to Loveday, 12 July 1921. For a more comprehensive account see Nathan Marcus, *Austrian Reconstruction and the Collapse of Global Finance, 1921–1931* (Cambridge University Press 2018).

[19] LONA, S 108 Sir Arthur Salter's Private Papers, Austria No. 5. 'AUSTRIA—League of Nations' scheme for the financial Reconstruction of Austria': Letter from Nixon to Blackett, 11 July 1921.

[20] Bank of England Archive [hereafter BoE], OV / 28/52 'Austrian Rehabilitation': *Austria*, 6 July 1921.

[21] Initially, Norman had not insisted on a single controller and had agreed to a commission consisting of a representative of each France, Britain, Italy, and a neutral state. The League's Frank Nixon thought the best compromise was a commission of five, including also the United States or another neutral, to ensure the legitimate political claims of France and Italy, though leaving them in a minority. NA, T 160 / 58 / 2073 / 6 'Austrian Reconstruction': Letter from Norman to Balfour, 15 July 1921; BoE, OV / 28/52 'Austrian Rehabilitation': Nixon to Drummond, *Austrian Reconstruction. Note on Commission of Control*, 7 July 1921.

latter might personally hasten calls for unification with Germany, either willingly or simply by failing in his job.[22] Thus by the summer of 1921, the League informed the Austrian government that control would go to a committee, which the Austrian government insisted be not permitted to tamper with the administration of the state's pledged revenues, as such interference was inacceptable and unnecessary in a 'Kulturland' like Austria, and akin to 'financial dictatorship', which as it alleged, stood counter to the intentions of the League.[23]

Anticipating foreign assistance, Austria's currency had appreciated during the second quarter of 1921, but a strike by state workers in July compelled the government to raise their wages. Expected expenditures and deficits increased and a considerable depreciation of the crown spurred hyperinflation.[24] On 1 June 1921, one US dollar still cost 590 crowns, but just one month later it was priced at 750 crowns, and on 1 August, at 955 crowns. Austria's new Chancellor, Johann Schober, thought it indispensable that advances come forward to prevent a general strike and his government's collapse, and when his Finance Minister resigned in September, the US dollar already cost 2,518 Austrian crowns.[25] In October an Austrian railway strike stopped all train traffic with Hungary, at the Vienna Stock Exchange riots ensued, and Schober informed London that if advances were not officially pledged, his government would resign.[26] After restless workers terrorized the streets of Vienna's first district in December, looting shops and vandalizing hotels and cafés, the Austrian currency dropped to a record low of almost 10,000 crowns per US dollar. In January 1922, after food subsidies were cut, Chancellor Schober desperately appealed to Prime Minister Lloyd George for an advance of £3 million, while Austrian President Michael Hainisch addressed a personal entreaty to King George V himself.[27]

On 17 October 1921, the British envoy had already confidentially informed Chancellor Schober that a small British advance of £250,000 was being arranged.[28]

[22] BoE, OV / 28/52 'Austrian Rehabilitation': Letter from Drummond to Balfour, 10 July 1921; LONA, S 108 Sir Arthur Salter's Private Papers / Austria No. 5: Letter from Nixon to Avenol, 11 July 1921.

[23] Direct intervention, the Austrian government insisted, could only be granted after the body in charge of control discussed its agent's complaints with the Austrian government. AdR, 67 / 65478/ 21 'Ministerratsprotokoll Nr. 106': *Notiz für Herrn Riis-Hansen betr. die vorläufige Kontrolle in Oesterreich*, 26 July 1921; LONA, A.83 (SdN 1301 A81–A128, July–December 1921): *Note for Mr. Riis-Hansen regarding the provisional control in Austria*, 26 July 1921.

[24] NA, T 160 / 58 / 2073 / 6, 'Austrian Reconstruction': Letter from Lindley to Curzon, 28 July 1921, and letter from Schober to Lindley, 29 July 1921.

[25] NA, T 160 / 58 / 2073 / 6, 'Austrian Reconstruction': Telegram from Lindley to Foreign Office, 8 August 1921; AdR, 01 / 9, Ges. London, Telegramme 1920–1923, Karton 18, 'Hinaus 1921': Telegram from Franckenstein, 4 August 1921.

[26] NA, T 160 / 58 / 2073 / 6, 'Austrian Reconstruction': Letters from Waterlow to Curzon, 21 and 23 October 1921.

[27] NA, T 160 / 58 / 2073 / 7, 'Austrian Reconstruction,' Telegram from Keeling to Foreign Office, 2 December 1921; AdR, 01 / 9, Ges. London, Telegramme 1920–1923, Karton 18, 'III Herein 1922': Telegrams from Schober to Franckenstein, 24 January 1922; AdR, 1 Ges. London Polit. Berichte 1920–1923: Letter from Franckenstein to Lloyd George, 25 January 1922.

[28] AdR, 67 / 90001 / 21, 'Kreditvorschüsse': Note by Lindley for Schober, 17 October 1921, and letter from Schober to Lindley, 18 October 1921.

The Treasury considered advancing a further £2.5 million from funds that did not require parliamentary approval and in January 1922 notified Austria's envoy to London that such a step would necessarily incur British control of the money.[29] The Austrians accepted and within a fortnight Prime Minister Lloyd George announced that Britain would provide £2 million, with G. M. Young, a former British diplomat working at the Anglo-Austrian bank in Vienna, appointed the Treasury's representative in control of release of these funds.[30] The League of Nations, which was to assist in issuing a larger loan to repay advances, wanted to appoint its own agent in Vienna to initiate a system of cooperation with the Austrian government and jumpstart reforms.[31] Young, apprehensive about seeming a second 'Gessler', suggested that the League nominate him as its controller also, while stressing the importance of forcing the Austrian government to pursue austerity.[32] However, the Austrian government refused and would only welcome a League observer—and not a controller—so as to keep Geneva updated and advise the Austrian government on putting the British advances to good use, with no authority over the revenues earmarked as pledged securities for a future, larger loan.[33]

Rejecting a League controller in early 1922 put the scheme for a League-sponsored international loan to a rest. Above all, however, the League's plan had failed because the Reparations Commission could not agree to lift its liens, a precondition for any large loan that was to be secured by Austrian assets.[34] Although

[29] AdR, 1 Ges. London Polit. Berichte 1920–1923, 39 / P: Letter from Franckenstein to Foreign Ministry, 25 January 1922; NA, FO 371 / 7335 / C 1282: Letter from Franckenstein to Curzon, 25 January 1922.

[30] NA, FO 371 / 7335 / C 1962: Telegram from Foreign Office to Akers-Douglas, 9 February 1922, and / C 1975: Letters from Treasury to Foreign Office, 9 February 1922 and from Waterlow to Franckenstein 10 February 1922; AdR, 01 / 9, Ges. London, Polit. Berichte 1920–1923: Letter from Franckenstein to Foreign Ministry, 8 February 1922.

[31] LONA, 1151 Autriche II Février 1922, 71–75: *Extrait des procès-verbaux de la 6ème session du comité financier, 2ème séance, tenue à Londres, le 24 février à 10 et 16 h.*; LONA, Documents du Comité Financier, vol. V., A.146 (SdN 1302 A129–A169, January–May 1922): Letter from Ador to Franckenstein, 23 February 1922; AdR, 01 / 9, Ges. London, Karton 101, Finanzsachen 1920–1923, 'Rekonstruktion 1922': Telegram from Franckenstein to Chancellery, 24 February 1922; AdR, 01 / 9, Ges. London, Telegramme 1920–1923, Karton 18, 'III Hinaus 1922': Telegram from Franckenstein to Foreign Ministry, 25 February 1922.

[32] AdR, 1 Ges. London Polit. Berichte 1920–1923, 60/P: Letter from Franckenstein to Foreign Ministry, 13 February 1922; NA, FO 371 / 7336 / C 2835: Telegram from Young to Blackett, 26 February 1922.

[33] LONA, 1151 Autriche II Février 1922, 71–75: *Extrait des Procès-verbaux de la 6ème session du comité financier, 2ème séance, tenue à Londres, le 24 febrier* [sic] *à 10 et 16 h* and 95–102: P.V. 6 (Procès-verbaux de la 6ième session du CF): *Comité financier 6ème session, Londres, février–mars 1922. 6ème séance, 1. mars 1922 à 11 h. et 3 h.30*; LONA, Documents du Comité Financier, vol. V., A.151 (SdN 1302 A129–A169, January–May 1922): Letter from Ador to Grimm, 28 February 1922; AdR, 01/9, Ges. London, Telegramme 1920–1923, Karton 18, 'III Herein 1922': Telegram from Foreign Ministry to Franckenstein, 27 February 1922; AdR, 01/9, Ges. London, Telegramme 1920–1923, Karton 18, 'III Hinaus 1922': Telegram from Franckenstein to Aussenamt, 1 March 1922; AdR, Finanzen, Dpt. 17/ Frieden, Karton 84 'Englisch-amerik. Kreditverhandlungen in London': Communication from Goode to Schober, 1 March 1922.

[34] Italy promoted its own plan during the summer of 1922, consisting of a private loan, coupled with an Allied control commission chaired by Italy, but considered 'useless and disadvantageous' by the British Treasury. Arthur Balfour managed to convince Carlo Schanzer to drop the proposal and fall

France viewed the League scheme as a guarantee against Austrian unification with Germany, its overall focus had been on strengthening Czechoslovakia, while Britain had worked to oppose French and Italian attempts at politicizing foreign financial control in Austria.[35] For the League, meanwhile, any direct control of Austrian finances, as it had existed in Turkey, Egypt, or China, was quite impossible, too: 'Austria is not a nigger country so that neither Austria nor her neighbours will allow Austria to be humiliated by being handed over, as they would say, to the mercy of western capitalism.'[36] After Austria had failed to raise funds directly from a consortium of London banks during the first half of 1922, the League was called upon once more, and this time put its credo into action, thereby developing and providing a pioneering solution to Austria's financial predicaments.

II. The Birth of Multilateral Control

The diminished Austrian crown had weakened since April 1922 and over the summer the Austrian currency once again started losing value more rapidly. One US dollar cost 7,600 Austrian crowns in early April, and 8,200 in early May, but 21,000 in mid-June, and 42,000 at the end of July. After the Reparations Commission finally recommended the liberation of Austrian assets on 8 August 1922, Austria was placed back on the Supreme Council's agenda.[37] The Austrian government was again threatening to resign if no help was forthcoming, prophesizing that no other government could be constituted and the responsibility for Austria's destiny would be left that of the Allies alone.[38] Unperturbed by such a warning, French Prime Minister Raymond Poincaré proposed on the last evening of the conference to get rid of Austria by asking the League to reconsider the problem at its upcoming fall

in line with France and Britain. NA, FO 371 / 7338 / C 9866: Communication from Blackett to Foreign Office, 11 July 1922 and / C 8832: Letter from Lampson to Grigg, 21 June and from the Italian ambassador to Foreign Office, 19 June 1922; NA, T 160 / 58 / 2073 / 8 'Austrian Reconstruction': Letter from Blackett to Undersecretary of State, 10 July 1922; AdR, 01/9, Ges. London, Telegramme 1920–1923, Karton 18 'III Herein 1922': Telegram from Grünberger to Franckenstein, 25 June 1922; AdR, NPA, 286 Liasse Oesterreich 1921–1922 8/IV, 'Liasse Oesterreich 1921–1922': Telegram from Kwiatowski to Foreign Ministry, 19 June 1922, from Eichhoff to Foreign Ministry, 27 June 1922 and from Franckenstein to Foreign Ministry, 1 July 1922.

[35] LONA, S 108, Sir Arthur Salter's Private Papers, Austria No. 5: Letter from Nixon to Blackett, 11 July 1921; NA, T 160 / 58 / 2073 / 6, 'Austrian Reconstruction': Letter from Norman to Balfour, 15 July 1921.

[36] LONA, S 116 Sir Arthur Salter's Private Papers, No. 10 Correspondence Letter-book 1923–30. 'Correspondence 1922': Draft letter from Monnet to Dwight Murrow, 16 March 1922.

[37] AdR, 01/1, NPA 287 / 632 'Liasse Oesterreich 8/IV Sek Schmid Fol. 523–733': Letter from Schüller to Vienna, 4 August 1922; NA, FO 371 / 7338 / C 10080: Memo from Vansittart for Crowe, 12 July 1922 and / 7339 / C 11706: Extract of I.C.P. 253, *British Secretary's Notes of an Allied Conference held at 10 Downing Street, S.W., on Monday, 14th August, 1922, at 5 p.m.*

[38] AdR, NPA 287 'Liasse Oesterreich 8/IV Sek Schmid Fol. 523–733': Letter from Franckenstein to Lloyd George, 13 August 1922, also in NA, FO 371 / 7339 / C 11517.

session. Neither the Italians nor the British had any better ideas to offer and so the Austrians were informed that their plight would be dealt with in Geneva next month. Spurred into renewed action, the League of Nations Council instructed the Financial Committee to draft a report on how to solve Austria's financial crisis and placed the question of Austria on its General Assembly's upcoming agenda.[39]

An Austrian delegation travelled to the League in Geneva, headed by Chancellor Ignaz Seipel, who seemed 'very pleased that the Austrian question loomed so large in the proceeding.'[40] Invited to address the League Council on the afternoon of Wednesday, 6 September 1922, Seipel warned that Austrians faced cold and hunger and that without funds to arrest depreciation and buy time for reforms, his country would inevitably collapse. As long as Austrian sovereignty was respected, Seipel admitted, it was both natural and unavoidable that a large loan would incur foreign control. Hoping to help, the Council appointed an Austrian Sub-Committee, headed by Britain's Council member Arthur Balfour, which referred financial and economic questions to the Financial and Economic committees respectively, and asked the League's lawyers for a study on the question of foreign control.[41] The legal analysis they supplied pointed out that all precedents of financial control were to safeguard existing creditors' interests, whereas in Austria it was future lenders seeking protection.[42] Still, though control was necessary to insure the safety of lenders, it could also help the Austrian government implement unpopular reforms by conditioning the provision of funds on their realization.[43] The Austrian Chancellor seemed to agree. When he appeared before the Sub-Committee two weeks later, Chancellor Seipel explained that even though he preferred a single controller to a control commission, he wished that a League delegation start work in Vienna at once, whether as a commission of control, in the form of a small committee or personified in a single controller.[44]

[39] LONA, S 106 Sir Arthur Salter's Private Papers, Austria No.3 'Austria - Memoranda etc.': Letter from Avenol to Salter, 18 August 1922; LONA, Documents du Comité Financier, vol. VI., A.191, (SdN 1303 A170–A215, June–December 1922): Speech by the President of the Council, 31 August 1922; AdR, NPA, 286 Liasse Oesterreich 1921–1922 8/IV / 309 'Liasse Oesterreich 1921–1922': Letter from Eichhoff to Foreign Ministry, 5 September 1922; NA, FO 371 / 7340 / C 12402: Telegram from Balfour to Secretariat of Cabinet, 31 August 1922.

[40] NA, FO 371 / 7340 / C 12982: Letter from Phillpotts to Akers Douglas, 7 September 1922.

[41] Seconded to Geneva, the British Trade Attaché wrote back to Vienna that 'control, if it comes to pass, will be of a very rigorous character, and that Austria will be expected to effect economies of the most far-reaching nature. This, in my opinion, is all to the good. It is control that is wanted most in Austria, but I cannot see how it can be effective without a grant of loans of some kind which would form the sanction of it.' NA, FO 371 / 7340 / C 13332: Letter from Phillpotts to Akers-Douglas, 10 September 1922. LONA, C 36, Reconstruction financière de l'Autriche 1922–1925 'Mins: Aust. Comm. of Council (Sept) '22': *Procès-verbal provisoire de la première séance du Sous-Comité du Conseil tenue le Vendredi 8 septembre 1922, à 17 h.30.*; LONA, C./S.C.A./P.V.1: *Provisional Minutes of the First Meeting of the Sub-Committee of the Council held at 5.30 p.m. on Friday September 8th, 1922.*

[42] LONA, 1154 Autriche Septembre 1922: *Procès-verbal de la 2ème Séance du Sous-comité du Conseil tenue le lundi 11 septembre 1922 à 17 h. 30.*

[43] LONA, S106 Sir Arthur Salter's Private Papers, 'Austria No.3': Quesnay, *Position du Problème Autrichien*, 13 September 1922.

[44] LONA, 1154 Autriche Septembre 1922: *Procès-verbal provisoire de la 7e Séance du Sous-Comité du Conseil, chargé d'examiner la question de la reconstruction financière de l'Autriche, (Mercredi 27*

The Financial Committee's own investigations had determined that Austria could balance its budget within two years if given a loan, though the latter required foreign state guarantees and foreign control. It differentiated between two forms of control: one of the tobacco and customs revenues pledged to service the loan, and one of the loan money to be gradually transferred to the government. If the Austrians refused to implement agreed upon reforms, the controller would withhold the transfer of funds, thus indirectly vetoing administrative decisions by holding the 'keys of the cash-box'.[45] Charged thereupon by the Sub-Committee to prepare a more detailed proposal, the Financial Committee concluded that control would be in the League's own name via a single controller appointed by the League Council and not in the name of the guarantor states, whose interests would be looked after by a separate body.[46] It was at that point that Italy's representative obstructed the proceedings, declaring that his government wished a commission of guarantor state representatives in place of a single controller.[47] His British colleague countered that a single controller was a superior choice because control was to be restricted to the loan funds and pledged revenues, leaving the Austrian government in full charge of implementing its reforms. Other members pointed out that the cost of a permanent commission would be considerable, and that there could not be two separate bodies, both the League and the guarantor states, giving instructions. Finding themselves outnumbered, the Italians deceptively agreed to a compromise that foresaw a committee of guarantor states, which would receive the controller's personal reports, but have no right to give him direct instructions.[48]

The Italians, losing their battle on the Financial Committee, took the fight to the Council's Sub-Committee. On Friday 29 September 1922, its Italian member transmitted a communication from Rome that his government (embattled by Mussolini's fascists) would only guarantee its part of the loan if a committee of guarantor states exercised control.[49] Balfour, who had to report to the Council

Septembre 1922, à 16 heures); NA, FO 371 / 7341 / C 13845: Letter from Phillpots to Akers Douglas, 29 September 1922.

[45] Asked by the Italian member what the powers of Lord Cromer in Egypt had been, his British colleague answered that the former controller's powers had been purely advisory, but had been supported by a strong gendarmerie. LONA, 1154 Autriche Septembre 1922: *Eleventh Meeting held Monday, September 18th, 1922 at 10.30 a.m.* E.F.S./Finance/9th Session/P.V.11.

[46] LONA, 1154 Autriche Septembre 1922: *Procès-verbal de la 5ème Séance du Sous-Comité du Conseil chargé d'examiner la question de la reconstruction financière de l'Autriche, tenue le mardi, 19 septembre 1922, à 10.h.30.* and *Treizième séance tenue le mardi 19 septembre 1922, à 17 h.30.*; NA, FO 371 / 7341 / C 13399: Letter from Phillpotts to Akers Douglas, 20 September 1922.

[47] LONA, 1154 Autriche Septembre 1922: *15ème Séance tenue le lundi 25 septembre 1922, à 13h.30.* and *Sixteenth Meeting, Held, Tuesday, September 26th, 1922, at 3.30p.m.*

[48] LONA, 1154 Autriche Septembre 1922: *Sixteenth Meeting, Held, Tuesday, September 26th, 1922, at 3.30p.m.* and *Provisional Minutes of 21st Meeting, Held Tuesday, October 3rd at 11.30 a.m.*

[49] LONA, 1154 Autriche Septembre 1922: *Procès-verbal Provisoire de la 9ème séance du Sous-Comité du Conseil chargé d'examiner la question de la reconstitution financière de l'Autriche (Vendredi 29 septembre 1922 à 15 H.30).*

and General Assembly before the closing session the next day, retorted that all had agreed that control would be in the name of the League—whether as a commission or a single individual—and that Italy's brinkmanship not merely concerned the form of control, but was aimed at changing its very foundation. The Austrian people, Balfour explained, would certainly resent control exercised by foreign powers and too easily ascribe any harsh measures being implemented to the avarice of foreign capitalists. In the words of Czechoslovakia's Prime Minister Edvard Beneš, it was in fact the League itself that made control impartial and acceptable to Austria, 'Etat souverain', so that he would not approve of control led by national interests. After all, Austrian Chancellor Seipel himself had accepted control by the League of Nations precisely because it was the most effective, and a single controller because it was the least expensive.[50]

The following day on Saturday morning, a few hours before Balfour was to address the League of Nations Council, Italy's representative informed the Sub-Committee that his country's delegate to the Assembly was leaving for Rome to convince his government to agree to any Austrian plan they might finally adopt. Suspecting further prevarications, Balfour recalled that Italy had helped refer Austria to the League and warned that if it insisted now on taking control from the League, he would not hesitate to ask the British government to exclude Rome and take over its guarantees together with Prague and Paris.[51] Behind closed doors at noon, Balfour told the Council that due to the delay caused by the Italians he could only give a bare outline of the work of his Sub-Committee. Yet, so far, they had secured foreign state guarantees and decided that the League Council would appoint a single controller to assist the Austrian government in drafting and executing a programme of reforms and to oversee the use of loan funds and pledged revenues.[52]

Addressing the General Assembly that mid-afternoon, Balfour similarly regretted not being able to report on a 'completed transaction'.[53] In his words, it was, however, clear that Austria needed foreign assistance, and that since it was bankrupt there could be no loans without reforms and proof that Austria adopted 'sound financial principles'. The loan would be guaranteed by foreign states, and the inevitable 'external influence acting in co-operation with the Austrian Government' would be accompanied by a declaration from the guarantors that they had no selfish motives. In his view, interference with Austrian sovereignty, or its economic and financial independence, was not possible 'under the new system'. The recent

[50] NA, FO 371 / 7341 / C 13845: Letter from Phillpots to Akers Douglas, 30 September 1922. LONA, 1154 Autriche Septembre 1922 (n 49).

[51] NA, FO 371 / 7342 / C 14058: Letter from Phillpotts to Akers Douglas, 30 September 1922; LONA, C./S.C.A./P.V.10.

[52] LONA, C./S.C.A./P.V.16.

[53] 'Twenty-Fifth Plenary Meeting, Saturday, September 30th, 1922, at 3 p.m.' in League of Nations, *Financial Restoration of Austria* (Geneva 1922), 25–30.

Italian manoeuvring had shown how enticing foreign control still was to countries willing to use it for their own political goals. The League of Nations had to ensure now that international interests would prevail over those of particular lenders or guarantors.

As Balfour finalized his statement before the General Assembly, the Financial Committee was holding a meeting in search of a last-minute compromise with Italy.[54] Gabriel Hanotaux, the French Council member, had earlier proposed that to please Rome, the Committee of Guarantor States could be made to meet more frequently or by request of any of its members. His Italian colleague, Guglielmo Imperiali, accepted the sop, under the condition that the committee be renamed Committee of Control, while the controller himself be given the new title General Commissioner instead.[55] This change in nomenclature was pure cosmetics, however, since the League Council would still appoint the General Commissioner, and he alone would be in charge of implementing control.[56] And despite the new terminology, the Control Committee of Guarantor States was given no direct authority over the General Commissioner. Its members, however, received the right to veto any new foreign borrowing, which eventually did allow Italy to pressure Austria financially in order to get its way in South Tyrol later in the decade.[57] But control itself was to go to a neutral, appointed by and reporting to the League of Nations Council, with no other body or state being authorized to give him instructions.

Even at the time, the League of Nations was accused of acting as a defender of imperialism, helping to uphold colonialist practice. National minority groups in Europe soon deplored how their rights were trampled with League acquiescence, as did administered peoples living in mandate territories. In Austria, where the League went on to oversee economic reconstruction from 1922 to 1926, socialists vocally accused the League of prioritizing foreign interests over the actual needs of the Austrian economy. Rather than assess the truth of these accusations or the outcome of Austrian reconstruction, this chapter studied whether those involved in drafting the specifics of the League's economic intervention were sensitive to such allegations and acted upon them. The minutes of the League's Financial

[54] LONA, 1154 Autriche Septembre 1922: *Twentieth Meeting Held on Saturday, September 30th, at 11.45 a.m.*

[55] LONA, S 59, M. DE BORDES Files, Box 6, Austria 1922–1926 'Various Papers September 1922 & 1921': *Note on a Conversation between various Members of the Financial Committee* by de Bordes, 30 September 1922.

[56] At a subsequent, private meeting it was agreed that the chairmanship of that renamed Control Commission would go to Italy. NA, FO 371 / 7341 / C 13987: Letter from Phillpots to Akers Douglas, 4 October 1922. LONA, 1154 Autriche Septembre 1922: *Procès-verbal provisoire de la douzième séance du Sous-Comité du Conseil chargé d'examiner la question de la reconstruction financière de l'Autriche (Mercredi, 4 octobre 1922, à 10 h. 30).*

[57] Nathan Marcus, 'Austria's Minority in South Tyrol and the Foreign Loan of 1930' in Christoph Kreutzmüller and others (eds), *National Economies: Volks-Wirtschaft, Racism and Economy in Europe between the Wars (1918–1939/45)* (Cambridge Scholars Publishing 2015).

Committee, staffed with experts and charged with planning the mechanisms governing international economic oversight, reveal that most envisioned a reformed system of controlled lending that would at least appear to be sensitive to Austrian sovereignty. The outcome was a system of limited control, one that did not push the narrow interests of creditors and guarantors, but the wider interests of the international community.

The new system differed mainly in that the rules and conditions were now set by the League of Nations and were no longer prone to easy and opportunistic abuse by individualistic states. Before the First World War, creditors had taken all sorts of measures to secure repayment of their loans, some of which interfered considerably with domestic policy and arguably served the selfish goals of foreign creditors, be they bankers or governments. Since the money came from private investors, the Austrian loan also required pledged assets, foreign state guarantees, and a competitive interest rate. But from now on emergency lending to sovereign states would be directed by a set of rules that had been established and could only be changed through international negotiation, agreement, and cooperation. Ideologically, the League officials certainly ascribed to a very specific economic world view, and saw no alternatives to balanced budgets and lean administrations. But the implementation of such steps was left to the borrowing government and not to foreign representatives, and the General Commissioner was not going to be responsible to creditors or guarantor states, but to the League of Nations Council alone.

III. The Reisseck-Kreuzeck Loan Agreement of 1954

By providing multilaterals such as the IMF and World Bank with their own capital, post-Second World War planners allowed these lending institutions to do away with pledged state assets to secure sovereign loans. Since money no longer needed to be raised from private investors, these multilaterals could provide loans to bankrupt states at much cheaper rates and without excessively onerous conditions. But conditionality and control naturally remained. In 1954, the Republic of Austria guaranteed a loan equivalent of $12 million (in Swiss Francs and Italian Lire) from the Bank for Reconstruction and Development (as the World Bank was initially called) to the Draukraftwerke (Drau River Power Company) and the Austrian Electric Power Corporation in order to pay for construction of the Reisseck-Kreuzeck hydroelectric project in southern Austria.[58] The agreement between the Bank and the Austrian government, dated 19 July 1954, consisted of merely five

[58] International Bank for Reconstruction and Development, *Ninth Annual Report 1953–1954* (Washington 1954). The project had been started in 1947. The remaining work, to be completed by 1958, included quadrupling the generating capacity, dams, pumping stations and other civil works. About one-third of the power produced would be exported to Italy under a long-term contract.

articles spread over seven pages. The Austrian government guaranteed repayment as well as free access for Bank representatives to any area within its territory related to the project. The loan itself had no lien on any state assets, but since it was not a pure sovereign loan (Austria was only guarantor), the two companies mortgaged some of their properties as well as future revenues from selling electricity to Italy.[59] Moreover, the borrowers had to commit to spend the loan exclusively on a pre-agreed list of machines and other goods needed to carry out the large project.[60]

Austria's post-Second World War loan thus continued the practice of creditor control over the release and usage of borrowed funds. Since the Bank could finance the loan, which in any case was much smaller, with its own capital and did not have to market bonds to private investors, control was more limited and less visible than in the case of the League's post-First World War loan. Certainly the Reisseck-Kreuzeck project raised less vocal criticism and accusations of financial dictatorship than the League's intervention had thirty years earlier. If in Geneva the League still had to battle an individualistic Italy, vying to secure its national interests to the detriment of others, the benefits of international cooperation governing sovereign lending were by now more credible and accepted. Trying to keep foreign lending by impoverished states free from competitive politics, the League had aimed to create a system of control that satisfied the legitimate demands of private investors to secure repayment of their lent funds, without placing the sovereign debtor at the mercy of creditor states' particularistic interests. Sure, similar aims had already governed comparable efforts by the United States and Great-Britain when negotiation international loans to China in 1918.[61] But it was the League that institutionalized these ideals in the early 1920s and made them palatable to sovereign debtors, changing the rules of external borrowing by sovereign states and, following the Second World War, leaving it to the multilaterals to put them into continued and continuously developing practice.

Thus, when following Austria-Hungary's defeat in the First World War foreign financial control reached the ruined state of Austria, its practices differed materially from those that had governed sovereign borrowing before the Great War. Vienna's perceived position as the frontier of western culture and civilization made it worth saving, but the same logic also demanded a new form of foreign control. But it was not just the expectable outrage from Austrians at being 'colonized' that favoured

[59] *Guarantee Agreement (Reisseck-Kreuzeck Project) between Republic of Austria and International Bank for Reconstruction and Development, dated July 19, 1954*:<http://documents.banquemondiale.org/curated/fr/603751468209672038/pdf/Loan-0102-Austria-Reisseck-Kreuzeck-Project-Guarantee-Agreement.pdf> accessed 24 March 2019.

[60] *Loan Agreement (Reisseck-Kreuzeck Project) between International Bank for Reconstruction and Development and Österreichische Elektrizitätswirtschafts-Aktiengesellschaft (Verbundgesellschaft) and Österreichische Draukraftwerke Aktiengesellschaft, dated July 19, 1954*: <http://documents.banquemondiale.org/curated/fr/715631468008422470/pdf/Loan-0102-Austria-Reisseck-Kreuzeck-Project-Loan-Agreement.pdf> accessed 24 March 2019.

[61] *The Consortium. The Official Text of the Four-Power Agreement for a Loan to China and Relevant Documents* (Carnegie Endowment for International Peace 1921).

handing control to the League of Nations, but more importantly perhaps, it was the fear of single countries, such as Italy, abusing their creditor position to extend their sphere of influence into Austria and thereby awakening the ire of Austrians or its neighbours. To prevent destabilizing intrusions from lenders, the control over borrowed funds and pledged revenues was not, as in earlier cases, put into the hands of a commission, but given to a single person. Unlike in the past, neither creditor states, banks, nor bondholder representatives were in charge of setting the rules of control and implementing them, but rather the League of Nations Council in cooperation with the Austrian government. This was an important break with the imperialist colonial practices that had governed sovereign lending in the pre-war world, when lending banks or states' possessed the power of control and often dangerously abused it to serve their foreign policy interests. Control was now placed in the hands of technocrats who ostensibly represented the League of Nations and not their home countries, while conflicts among the guaranteeing creditor states or bondholder representatives were to be resolved through peaceful negotiation at conferences that would be hosted outside of Austria and far away from Vienna.

6

Hungary and the League of Nations

A Forced Marriage

Zoltán Peterecz

I. The Aftermath of the First World War

One of the major results of the Paris Peace Treaties was the birth of the League of Nations, a new endeavour for an international organization to maintain peace and collective security through negotiation and public opinion. Although the organization lacked important major powers among its ranks and, therefore, came up short as a true international body, it was still a big leap forward in contrast to earlier times. While traditional powers—Great Britain and France in particular—enjoyed a larger influence within the League, many older and brand new smaller states looked with hope to the organization, putting their faith in the League's uncharted power to provide various forms of protection. There were states, however, that only reluctantly conformed to the new international realities. One such country was Hungary, whose love-and-hate affair with the League of Nations stood out in Central Europe. Yet for geopolitical, economic, and financial reasons, Hungary found a *modus vivendi* with the League of Nations in the interwar years.

After the First World War, Hungary found itself at the crossroads of internationalism. As successor to an empire, with a thousand-year-long history of a more or less intact Hungarian kingdom, Hungarians felt vindicated that they should at last enjoy total independence again. On the other hand, of course, thanks to the peace treaties, Hungary found itself severely punished, and a large number of ethnic Hungarians were detached from the state, together with formerly Hungarian territories. As a result, on the international stage, a traditionally highly nationalistic Hungarian desire had to accept and also use the internationalist idea, if for no other reason than for the vast number of Hungarians living now as minorities in neighbouring unfriendly states. Thence Hungary's paradoxical situation concerning the hub of the new Europe: it wanted to be both within and without the League of Nations. It wished to be a member state as this provided a possible route out of its dismal financial situation while ostensibly offering protection to Hungarian minorities beyond the new Hungarian borders. At the same time, however, Hungary was inclined to lead its own nationalistic, conservative, and often racist politics within its boundaries according to its own agenda. The two aims were time and

Zoltán Peterecz, *Hungary and the League of Nations* In: *Remaking Central Europe*. Edited by: Peter Becker and Natasha Wheatley, Oxford University Press (2020). © the many contributors. DOI: 10.1093/oso/9780198854685.003.0007

again inherently in conflict with each other. It is no wonder that the case of Hungary caused many a headache to the League of Nations. Hungary proved to be a really 'reluctant internationalist' actor in the post- First World War Europe.[1] It is also worth emphasizing that Hungary had been part of a long-standing empire. True, it always held the junior position and, for a long time, outright subjugation was its role. But especially within the Austro-Hungarian Empire after 1867, it practised a high-handed and imperial attitude towards its many minorities. Slovaks, Romanians, and Serbs were resentful of the Hungarian oppressive minority policy, and many of them saw independence as the only solution to cast off the Hungarian yoke. After the First World War, Hungary found itself surrounded with countries that formerly had made up many of its oppressed minorities. Furthermore, now the Little Entente, with French backing, could freely express and practise anti-Hungarian propaganda and agenda. Therefore, Hungary needed to adjust psychologically to a new situation where from a leading position it found itself in an inferior place and somewhat at the mercy of the successor states. So, questions of nationality collided with that of trans-nationality and inter-nationality here. To make things worse, the country experienced revolutions in quick succession after the Armistice in the fall of 1918 and during the Bolshevik coup in 1919, the latter led by Béla Kun establishing communist rule in Hungary. From a political point of view, this was a disaster for the country: it became an international pariah. After the defeat of the Bolshevist regime in the summer of 1919 and the subsequent Romanian occupation of half of the country including Budapest, Hungary faced newer humiliation and setback in the form of the peace treaty. The Treaty of Trianon, signed on 4 June 1920, was a grave blow to Hungary and sealed its fate for a long time to come.[2] To the shock of the whole nation, the treaty detached huge Hungarian ethnic blocs, which was due to nothing else but serving the wishes of the neighbouring Slavic countries and Romania as well as a broader geopolitical imperative to contain political hotspots. Both the territory and population of Hungary was reduced to one-third of its pre-war size, and an estimated 3,000,000 ethnic Hungarians remained in the successor states. These states—Czechoslovakia, Romania, and the Kingdom of Serbs, Croats, and Slovenes (officially Yugoslavia from 1929)—were obviously antagonistic to Hungary, and their main aim was 'a common policy against

[1] The term comes from the workgroup led by Jessica Reinisch, whose work can be followed at <http://www.bbk.ac.uk/reluctantinternationalists/>.

[2] About the Treaty of Trianon, see, for example, H. W. V. Temperley (ed), *A History of the Peace Conference of Paris* (vol. 5, Henry Frowde and Hodder & Stoughton 1921); Sándor Taraszovics, 'American Peace Preparations during World War I and the Shaping of the New Hungary' in Ignác Romsics (ed), *20th Century Hungary and the Great Powers* (Social Science Monographs, Atlantic Research and Publications Inc. 1994); Francis Deák, *Hungary at the Paris Peace Conference: The Diplomatic History of the Treaty of Trianon* (Columbia University Press 1942). The literature of the Peace Treaties is abundant and seemingly never-ending. The two latest works of value are Margaret MacMillan, *Peacemakers: The Paris Peace Conference of 1919 and Its Attempt to End War* (Random House 2002) and, from Hungarian perspectives, Bryan Cartledge, *Mihály Károlyi & István Bethlen: Hungary* (Haus Publishing Ltd 2009).

Hungary', which 'must be merely part of a broader political conception'.[3] The war, communist rule, losses due to the Romanian occupation, and the Peace Treaty had further consequences. Hungary was much weakened from an economic point of view due to the devastation it had been subjected to, and the fact that it lost most of its raw material and industry.[4] The devastated circumstances were exacerbated by the flood of Hungarian refugees from the territory of old Hungary. Moreover, the text of the peace treaty declared that Hungary would have to pay reparations for a period of thirty years starting from 1 May 1921, although the sum of it was not specified.[5] Article 180 declared that 'the first charge upon all the assets and revenues of Hungary shall be the cost of reparation'.[6] This, in practice, rendered any chance of borrowing money from abroad impossible, and was a major source of runaway inflation in the coming years. The Hungarian Assembly reluctantly ratified the Treaty on 13 November 1920, but the wording expressed the whole nation's sentiment: '[I]t considers the peace document as being based on false data, unjust and contrary to the interests of humanity [...] the National Assembly assents to its ratification solely because of [...] irresistible pressure.'[7] It is little surprise that the American minister described the Hungarian foreign policy outlook as 'anxious expectancy' and 'watchful waiting'.[8] In fact, the next two decades of Hungarian foreign policy was riveted around the question of revision of the Trianon Treaty, and this mood defined Hungarian foreign policy to a very large extent. Thus, Hungary's international isolation, the draconian peace treaty forced on the country, and also the dethronement act coming from international pressure in the wake of Charles's two failed coup attempts in 1921, proved all too clearly to Hungarian leaders the necessity of belonging to the League of Nations, which on paper promised some kind of protection against (from a Hungarian perspective) punitive acts of this sort.[9] In tension with these aspirations, Hungary's new and conservative governments did not cherish the idea of international pressure brought against them, particularly when their legislative acts questioned norms accepted elsewhere,

[3] Eduard Beneš, 'The Little Entente' (September 1922) 1/1 Foreign Affairs 69. Beneš called the first of these treaties 'a "*defensive convention*" against the Hungarian menace.' Ibid, 68. Emphasis in the original text. See also: Thomas Garrigue Masaryk, *The Making of a State: Memories and Observations, 1914–1918* (Frederick A. Stokes Co 1927).

[4] See, for example, Joseph Rothschild, *East Central Europe between the Two World Wars* (University of Washington Press 1974) 156, 167; C. A. McCartney, *Hungary and Her Successors: The Treaty of Trianon and Its Consequences, 1919–1937* (Oxford University Press 1937) 463; Derek H. Aldcroft, *From Versailles to Wall Street, 1919–1929* (Allen Lane, Penguin Books Ltd 1977) 28; M. C. Kaser and E. A. Radice (eds), *The Economic History of Eastern Europe, 1919–1975* (vol. 1, Clarendon Press 1985).

[5] Temperley, *Peace Conference* (n 2) 219.

[6] Ibid, 235.

[7] Deák, *Hungary at the Paris Peace Conference* (n 2) 337. The Treaty came into force on 26 July 1921.

[8] Theodore Brentano to Charles Evans Hughes, 20 September, and 1 October 1922, 864.00/511 and 864.00/517, Microcopy No. 708, Roll 6, Affairs of Austria-Hungary and Hungary, 1912–1929, National Archives and Records Administration (NARA). Washington, D.C., USA.

[9] In more detail about the events and diplomacy of the Karlist coup attempts, in Magda Ádám, *A Kisantant és Európa, 1920–1929* [*The Little Entente and Europe 1920–1929*] (Akadémiai Kiadó 1989) 39–112, and Admiral Nicholas Horthy, *Memoirs* (Hutchinson 1957) 139–152.

especially anti-Jewish legislation and restricted franchise. Hungary had to manoeuvre carefully between its long-term foreign policy aims and the requirements of the domestic political landscape, so often in conflict with one another. With this background, it is understandable why the financial reconstruction of Hungary via the good offices of the League of Nations came into being, and why it was a momentous event in the life of the country in the interwar years. This chapter will put into focus the debate surrounding the launch of the reconstruction effort in Hungary, its international implications, the relationship between Hungary and the League of Nations in the 1920s, and will give some comparison between the Austrian and the Hungarian financial reconstructions.

II. The Financial Reconstruction of Hungary

The new post-war Hungarian era was started under the leadership of Admiral Miklós Horthy, whom the National Assembly overwhelmingly elected to be Regent on 1 March 1920, a position in which he remained until 1944. Notwithstanding a new and conservative leadership, the above mentioned grave problems remained, and under such circumstances Hungary had to rely on outside charity to a large degree. Similarly to Austria and other Central and Eastern European countries, Hungary was provided with relief.[10] In all likelihood due to the Bolshevik takeover, however, the country received only a fraction of what other recipient countries were given. While the whole region received relief to the extent of almost $500 million, the sum given to Hungary was a meagre $9.3 million.[11] It was clear that Hungary needed political consolidation without which the country would stand no chance of rehabilitation of any kind. The real change took place when István Bethlen became Hungary's new Prime Minister on 14 April 1921:[12] his political approach was very practical and realistic. As he put it, 'What I say and what I do depend on the requirements of foreign and domestic policy. My policies are shaped by the circumstances.'[13] Bethlen already after the war tried to establish good relations with Great Britain, because he saw in that country the possibility of securing a counterweight against the successor countries and the French

[10] In more detail about the ARA's work in Hungary, see Tibor Glant, 'Herbert Hoover and Hungary, 1918–1923' (2002) 8/2 Hungarian Journal of English and American Studies 95. On the general Central and Eastern European relief work, which in the greatest part was provided by American sources, see Herbert Hoover, *The Memoirs of Herbert Hoover, Volume 1: Years of Adventure 1874–1920* (The Macmillan Company 1951) 282–430.

[11] Kaser and Radice, *The Economic History of Eastern Europe* (n 4) 387. Glant gives the worth of supplies as $220 million and Hungary's share as 1.3%. He adds that this small amount was still seventy times as much as what Hungary was given in the armistice period. Glant, 'Herbert Hoover and Hungary' (n 10) 99.

[12] The latest and best biography on Bethlen is Ignác Romsics, *István Bethlen: A Great Conservative Statesman of Hungary, 1874–1946* (Social Science Monographs 1995).

[13] Romsics, *István Bethlen* (n 12) 156.

hegemonic aims in the Danubian basin. Although right after the war British diplomacy did not support him, after his becoming the prime minister of Hungary, the British minister in Budapest sent a report in which he praised Bethlen's programme speech for its liberal and realist character and wrote that 'every effort should be made to help in the consolidation of the country'.[14] This kind of attitude was what Hungary counted on. If Great Britain once decided that Hungary should be helped, it practically meant that help was within reach. Therefore, it was no coincidence that Hungary was trying to put emphasis on the Anglo-Saxon orientation, but in order to enjoy British backing, Hungary first needed to become a member of the League of Nations, and this was the pivotal foreign policy question of the first years of the 1920s. When the League of Nations was born in 1919, quite logically it centred around the victorious nations and their allies, together with some neutral countries—the enemy states were not invited to the organization. Shortly after the peace treaties were concluded, however, the door of the League slowly opened to the defeated countries as well. Austria and Bulgaria were admitted to the League in December 1920, and it seemed only a matter of time before both Hungary and Germany could also qualify for membership. Still, there were no guarantees. In fact, Hungary had tried twice to be accepted to the new supranational organization, without success. In May 1921, Hungary had asked admittance only to ask for postponement on account of Charles's return and the havoc it created.[15] When the question of Hungary's possible admittance was on the agenda again in the fall session of 1922, the situation was favourable. Out of the three members of the Little Entente, it was Yugoslavia that was the most opposed to the Hungarian membership. But the unofficial leader of the alliance, Eduard Beneš, the Czechoslovakian foreign minister and an influential diplomat in western countries, was against such an idea, because he knew that supposedly Hungary's place was already assured.[16] Beneš must have been informed from British sources that Great Britain wanted to see Hungary in the family of the League of Nations and would have taken issue if, due to petty fussing, Hungary had remained outside. So, on 18 September 1922, the Assembly voted unanimously to admit Hungary to the League.[17] This was an important step from the point of view of Hungary's political status. Upon becoming

[14] Quoted in Romsics, *István Bethlen* (n 12) 153.

[15] Nicolas Bánffy to Eric Drummond, 23 May 1921, File 13039, Report of the Sixth Committee to the Assembly, 26 September 1921, and Resolution adopted by the Assembly, 30 September 1921, File 16180, Section 28, Admissions to the League, Box 1453, League of Nations Archives, 1919–1927, Geneva, Switzerland.

[16] Árpád Hornyák, *Magyar-jugoszláv diplomáciai kapcsolatok, 1918–1927* [Hungarian- Yugoslav Diplomatic Relations, 1918–1927] (Forum Könyvkiadó 2004) 115–116.

[17] Report of the First Sub-Committee (of the Sixth Committee of the Third Assembly of the League of Nations), 14 September 1922, File 23483, League of Nations Archives. In more detail about Hungary's entry into the League of Nations, see, Mária Ormos, 'Magyarország belépése a Nemzetek Szövetségébe' ['Hungary's Entry to the League of Nations'] (1957) 91/1 Századok 235. Ádám, *A kisantant és Európa 1920–1929* (n 9) 215–216; Juhász Gyula, *Magyarország külpolitikája 1919–1945* [Hungary's Foreign Policy 1919–1945] (3rd edition, Akadémiai Kiadó 1988) 89–94.

a member of the most important international political body of the day, Hungary stepped out of the political isolation it had been subjected to since the end of the war. This change was the key to significant possibilities: it meant an automatic protection against the Little Entente and Hungary could keep the minority question on the agenda.[18] Naturally, belonging to the League also meant seemingly giving up some room for manoeuvre in the international political arena, but realistically speaking this last point was moot at the time, and the benefits were much larger to Hungary within than without the League. Also, in belonging to the League, the door opened for Hungary to have the chance to find support for its plans and causes. First of all, the Hungarian government sought British political backing on the continent. It was well known that within the League of Nations Great Britain and France vied for leadership, and although Hungary needed to be on good terms with France as well, Hungary gravitated to the seemingly larger influence of the British. In addition, Britain was of the opinion that it could not allow Hungary to 'go under financially'.[19] One might say that internationalism for Hungary during this period meant selective inter-nationalism, meaning that the main bridge to the League of Nations and through it the European arena was Great Britain. Relations with Britain and success via British help proved to be the Hungarian internationalist outlook. Hungary could also count on British backing in the quest to re-establish financial normality. Hungary's economic and financial situation was very weak, and climbing out of this hole was the country's top priority. The production of almost all of the industries had sharply fallen since pre-war years. In the 1922/23 financial year, for example, the production of sugar was 30 per cent, of beer it was 15 per cent, of alcohol it was 40 per cent, and of coal it was 45 per cent compared to ten years earlier.[20] Agricultural production gave the backbone to Hungary's exports, but since its output was meagre, the volume in foreign trade was negative as well, between 200 and 300 million gold crowns ($40–60 million).[21] The financial leverage of the state was diminishing year by year, and the budget deficit was substantial.[22] Under such circumstances it was inevitable that Hungary needed to do something significant, and to many it was clear that the remedy should take the

[18] Hungary brought up already the question of the Hungarian minorities in the successor states during the Genoa Conference. Bethlen sent an urgent plea to the Conference to pass the Hungarian problem onto the League, which, thanks to the opposition of France and the Little Entente, led to no result. Meeting of the First Session of the First (Political) Commission held on 11 April 1922, at 10.30 a.m., DBFP, First Series, 19: 360–361; Meeting of the Inviting Powers to the Genoa Conference held on 10 May 1922, at 11 a.m., at the Palazzo Reale, Annex N, ibid, 836–837.

[19] Lampson's note on 22 February 1923, C3081/942/21, 8861, FO371, TNA.

[20] 9/VIII/2/Appendix 12, Various Data on the Output of Hungary's Industries, 56, K 275, The Semi-official Papers of Finance Minister Kállay Tibor (hereafter cited as Kállay Papers), 1901–1941, HNA.

[21] 6/V/7, The Volume of Foreign Trade, and the Industrial and Agricultural Output of Hungary, 1920–1923/1, ibid.

[22] 'Annual Report on Hungary' in Balfour to MacDonald, 23 May 1924, C8423/8423/21, 9914, FO371, TNA.

form of a foreign loan.[23] As Bethlen put it in a speech in Hungary, 'Our financial situation is serious. From our revenues we cannot cover our expenditures. It will be a long time before we achieve this goal with hard work. In this work without foreign help we cannot reach the goal.'[24]

The Hungarian government first thought they would try to raise a loan outside the League of Nations through private channels. The Hungarians had tried to secure a British or American loan on various occasions, but the question of reparations and the diminished economic and financial capacity of the country made it impossible to deal with the issue in detail.[25] Thomas Hohler, the British minister in Budapest, warned the Foreign Office of a possible crisis on account of the tragic economic situation and thought that a loan would be 'the only remedy' because 'it is certain that prevention is better than cure'.[26] If Great Britain thought that Hungary should be helped, they also believed that such aid ought to come through the League of Nations.[27] This was the only forum through which the reparation question could be solved and that was the precondition of a possible loan from either British or American financial circles. For some time, given the unenthusiastic Hungarian mentality concerning the internationalist agenda, the idea of turning to the League was unappealing to the Hungarian government. Hungary did not want to submit its finances to any kind of supervision. After the Treaty of Trianon, the ruling mood of the country was that of revision and not of further weakening of Hungarian sovereignty. With shorn territory and decreased population, Hungary clung onto every possible aspect of independence. Because a League loan would have meant strict outside control, which the Hungarians correctly saw as a factor in diminishing state sovereignty, Hungary sought a different solution. Since it seemed that only Great

[23] The first comprehensive work of the surrounding of the loan, albeit with a political angle and chiefly relying on the sources available in Hungary at the time, was György Magos, *Az amerikai imperialisták szerepe a Horthy fasizmus stabilizásában, 1924–1929.* [*The Role of the American Imperialists in the Stabilization of the Horthy Fascism, 1924–1929*] (Akadémiai Kaidó 1952). A decade later a somewhat more balanced work came out, Mária Ormos, *Az 1924. évi magyar államkölcsön megszerzése* [Raising the Hungarian State Loan of 1924] (Akadémiai Kiadó 1964). The latest study on the League loan to Hungary with an emphasis on the British role is Miklós Lojkó, *Meddling in Middle Europe* (Central European University Press 2006) 81–126. The most comprehensive studies from the technical point of view are those of György Péteri, *Revolutionary Twenties and Global Monetary Regime* (University of Trondheim 1995) and György Péteri, *Global Monetary Regime and National Central Banking. The Case of Hungary, 1921–1929* (Social Science Monographs 2002). The freshest monograph that puts Jeremiah Smith, Jr. and the whole reconstruction in the focus is Zoltán Peterecz, *Jeremiah Smith, Jr. and Hungary, 1924–1926: the United States, the League of Nations, and the Financial Reconstruction of Hungary* (Versita 2013).

[24] *Magyar Hírlap*, 28 March 1922.

[25] Lojkó, *Meddling in Middle Europe* (n 23) 73–74, 77–78; Péter Sipos, 'Teleki Pál párizsi és londoni útja 1921-ben és a magyar külpolitikai orientáció [Pál Teleki's Journey to Paris and London]' in Gergely Jenő (ed), *A hosszú tizenkilencedik és a rövid huszadik század* [*The Long Nineteenth and the Short Twentieth Centuries*] (ELTE BTK 2000). Max Warburg to Schossberger, 23 November 1922, 9/X./232, K 275, Kállay Papers, HNA. Also quoted in Péteri, *Global Monetary Regime* (n 23) 17; Joy to Schossberger, 1 December 1922, ibid, X./233.; Széchenyi to Daruváry, 4 February 1923, 9/VIII/5 Plan for a foreign (Swiss, British, American, and French) loan, 3–4, ibid; Steiger to Kállay, 15 January 1923, ibid/5.

[26] Hohler to Curzon, 2 March 1923, DBFP, First Series, 24:531–32.

[27] Szapáry to Daruváry, 28 March 1923, 9/VIII/5/11, K 275, Kállay Papers, HNA.

Britain took up the Hungarian problem, and British dominance was tangible in both the Financial Committee of the League and in the whole organization, it was therefore crucial for Hungary to have British backing. It would be misleading to believe, however, that the British were zealously working for the Hungarian cause, but their overall policy required a stabilized Central Europe of which Hungary was a key country. Otto Niemeyer, Controller of Finance at the British Treasury and member of the Financial Committee of the League of Nations, produced a subsequently oft-quoted line in connection with this policy that illuminates the British thinking very well: 'If we could tie up another loose end in this way [League loan to Hungary along the lines of the Austrian scheme] we should I believe, extend and increase our consolidation in South East Europe. I hope the Foreign Office approve these notions and if so that you will do anything you can to push them.'[28] In the light of such thinking, it is not surprising that they were 'prepared to support the scheme' and 'genuinely anxious to set [Hungary] upon the right rails'.[29] The British recommended that Hungary turn to the League for advice, to be ready to accept a scenario similar to the Austrian case, and to go to the Reparations Commission first, since it was the key to freeing the liens for a possible loan.[30] Hungary had little room for manoeuvring and by mid-April the Bethlen government was ready to accept League control if none of the Little Entente countries performed such a role; they also made it clear that they would not take any steps contrary to Britain's wishes.[31] With this new attitude taken, the possibility of a loan was a realistic expectation, but first the Reparations Commission had to be convinced that Hungary should not pay reparation for the period of a loan. According to this new course, Hungary appeared before the Reparations Commission of the League of Nations on 5 May 1923. Bethlen asked the Commission to suspend the treaty charges and help Hungary financially by virtue of a loan in which case Hungary would be happy to follow the advice of the Financial Committee.[32] With this step, Hungary handed over the decision to the League of Nations. Since in the Reparations Commission France and the Little Entente were in majority, it was little wonder that they did not assent to the Hungarian plea. The following resolution was born: 'Not to oppose, in principle, the request of the Hungarian Government that the charge be temporarily raised for certain revenues of Hungary, which may be needed as security for

[28] Niemeyer to Lampson, 16 March 1923, OV33/70, BoE. Also quoted in Péteri, *Global Monetary Regime* (n 23) 51; Péteri, *Revolutionary Twenties* (n 23) 168; Lojkó, *Meddling in Middle Europe* (n 23) 83.

[29] Butler's minute, 21 March 1923, C4996/942/21, ibid; Curzon to Hohler, 13 April, 1923, DBFP, First Series, 24:583.

[30] Summary of conversation between Lampson and Ruttkay, 6 April 1923, C6281/942/21, 8861, FO371, TNA; Curzon to Hohler, 13 April, 1923, DBFP, First Series, 24:583.

[31] Hohler to Curzon, 17 April 1923, DBFP, First Series, 24:591–93.

[32] Speech of Count Bethlen before the Reparation Commission, 5 May 1293, Communiqués from Kallay and Bethlen. Doc. No. 28903, Registry Files, R. 296, LNA.

authorised loans, but [. . .] a fixed part of which would be assigned to reparation.'[33] The Commission's condition that part of the loan should go to reparations would have rendered the whole plan undoable, which was obviously what the successor countries wanted to achieve. Bethlen and the government found themselves in a difficult situation. Montagu Norman, Governor of the Bank of England, however, stood behind the Hungarian case and the British started to use their financial clout too in order to achieve the desired outcome. All the successor countries needed financial help and this could be only provided by Great Britain, which was no stranger to using hardball tactics with them. Notwithstanding the very diplomatic terms the British used, the Czechs, the Romanians, and the Yugoslavs were blackmailed by the British to support the Hungarian scheme.[34] Norman made clear what these states had in store: 'There is no money for the Czechs (or Roumanians) till Hungary has release from reparation—which was prevented last month by Little Entente. Benes is free to come to London, but the City takes no part in his domestic politics and is not ready to talk future loans.'[35] In fact, the British foreign policy establishment sent an ill-disguised message to the countries concerned when Lord Curzon said in the House of Lords on 25 July 1923:

> We are giving our full support to the appeal of Hungary. [. . .] We desire to prevent the financial collapse of Hungary, with its incalculable consequences. We desire to see in force a complete scheme of reconstruction. [. . .] We earnestly hope, therefore, that the Reparations Commission will reconsider their decision of May last and will refer the question without delay to the League of Nations.[36]

The pressure on the Little Entente worked. After some wrangling, Beneš agreed to meet Bethlen in early September in Geneva, and at the headquarters of the League of Nations an agreement was reached. The most important element was that Bethlen accepted the idea of a reduced time and money for reconstruction together with a controller of the League, while the Little Entente became more cooperative

[33] Reparation Commission Minutes, 23 May 1923, ibid. The text of the resolution of the Reparation Commission of 23 May 1923, can also be found in 122/ 6/706–707, K 69, Economic Policy Department, HNA.

[34] Foreign Office Memorandum on Hungary, 24 August 1923, C14677/942/21, 8865, FO371, TNA; Dering to Curzon, 18 October 1923, and Treasury to Foreign Office, 13 November 1923, DBFP, First Series, 24:884; Memo of conversation between M. Milojevics, Yugoslav minister at Budapest and Sir William Goode at the S. H. S. Legation, Budapest, 30 June 1923, 9/VIII/5/95, K 275, Kállay Papers, HNA.

[35] Norman's Diary Entries, 5 July 1923, ADM34/12, BoE. See also Norman to Gaspard Farrer, 25 May 1923, OV33/70, BoE; Norman to Niemeyer, 7 June 1923, Norman to Eyre Crowe, 27 June 1923, and Norman to Niemeyer, 5 July 1923, G3/179, BoE.

[36] *British Parliament Diaries, 32nd Parliament, 2nd Session, vol. 54, House of Lords* (London: His Majesty's Stationery Office 1922) 1364–1365. Curzon also warned Hungary to follow a more conciliatory policy towards its neighbours. Ibid, 1365–1366. About the British backing of the Hungarian reconstruction, see Gábor Bátonyi, *Britain and Central Europe, 1918–1933* (Clarendon Press 1999) 128–148.

in the questions of reparations.[37] In the next few months agreements were hammered out between the various parties, and the Financial Committee submitted its report to the League Council in which they suggested the following: inflation must be stopped, a point of which was achievable with the setting up an independent Bank of Issue; balance of the budget must be reached by 30 June 1926; and all this by the help of a reconstruction loan of 250 million gold crowns ($50 million), the control of which would be practised through a Commissioner-General as in the case of Austria.[38] Five meetings in December produced the two Protocols to be signed later. Instead of reparations, the Protocols spoke of 'treaty charges', which was not to exceed 10 million gold crowns ($2 million) on an annual average during the amortization of the loan, and in the first five years after 1926 was to be substantially less.[39]

The British feared what the failure of securing a foreign loan would mean to Hungarian domestic policies. In their view, Bethlen's fall would mean the rise of 'the most undesirable extremists [. . .] If this forecast should be true it would portend a period of inexpert adventure and experiment, which would be full of danger to the peace of Europe'.[40] Thus, for the British the battle was one regarding the future of the whole continent. Without the Hungarian piece, the Austrian scheme was almost useless. They used all of their influence to win this fight, and after varying hardball tactics and friendly discourse, the British were finally triumphant. The decision on 21 February 1924 was a victory of diplomatic skill and perseverance. The compromise reached declared that certain specified assets for the Hungarian loan were released, and the reparation question was also agreed. According to the decision by the Reparations Commission, Hungary was to pay a sum of annually 10 million gold crowns in a twenty-year period starting after the reconstruction period. For the time being, this prospect was acceptable for the Bethlen government as well, which hoped that eventually they would be able to avoid paying reparations altogether. The now-finalized Protocols also said that financial control would be re-established if Hungary did not pay according to the scheme. This formula seemed at last to satisfy all the parties and it was only a matter of time before all the signatures were given.[41] The two Protocols provided for every possible aspect of the loan. Protocol No. I. was a political one in which the parties undertook to 'respect the political independence, the territorial integrity and the sovereignty of Hungary', while Hungary undertook 'strictly and loyally to fulfil the obligations

[37] Goode to Niemeyer, 26 September 1923, 8/VII. The Material of the Negotiations of the League Loan. VII/3/20, K 275, Kállay Papers, HNA; Ormos, *Az 1924. évi magyar államkölcsön megszerzése* (n 23) 71–81.

[38] Report of the Financial Committee to the Council, 30 November 1923, Report to the Council on the 12th Session of the Financial Committee. Doc. No. 32475, Registry Files, R. 297, LNA.

[39] 1st Session of the Committee of the Council, Paris. December 1923. Doc. No. 32636, Registry Files, R. 297, LNA.

[40] Hohler to Curzon, 3 January 1924, ibid, 10.

[41] Minutes of the meeting on 14 March 1924. Doc. No. 34921, Registry Files, R. 299, LNA.

contained in the said Treaty, and in particular the military clauses, as also the other international agreements'.[42] Protocol No. II. contained the technical details.[43]

All that remained now was the necessary legal act of the National Assembly passing the reconstruction bill. On 27 March, Bethlen submitted the package to the National Assembly, where debate, sometimes fierce in tone, lasted three weeks often in sixteen-hour sessions before it was passed on 18 April.[44] The political opposition criticized the whole scheme, mainly for subjecting the country's sovereignty to outside rule. This was a clearly visible symptom of how the political discourse expressed the deeply seated nationalist concern: while they wished to be helped financially, since it was obvious that from its own efforts Hungary could not solve the critical situation, many in Hungary wished to achieve this without weakening Hungarian sovereignty to the slightest degree. Despite the criticism of the political opposition, however, the passing was never in danger due to the majority of Bethlen's Unified Party. One of the key elements of sovereignty and control was the future League controller. The Austrian case had already shown that the person in charge played a key role in the financial reconstruction effort, both technically and politically. In light of this, the search for a suitable Commissioner-General had already begun in the last weeks of 1923. Hungary wanted to avoid giving the financial supervisor an Austria-like level control, which they judged far too strict and broad. During a dinner in September 1923 hosted by Joseph Avenol, Deputy Secretary General of the League, where the topic of discussion was the Hungarian case, Bethlen raised the question of the future Commissioner and said his powers should be more limited than Arthur Zimmerman's in Austria, which, in his view, amounted to those of a foreign dictator.[45] Being politically shrewd, the Bethlen government had already started to make steps towards securing a prominent American for the role. It seemed to them that if an American were named Commissioner, the doors of the private American banks would open and the United States would play a large role in securing the needed loan, while a larger American presence would possibly dilute some of the League control as well. For political reasons, the League was also inclined to have an American to fulfil the post in Hungary. After several possible candidates, the League officially invited Jeremiah Smith, Jr. to become Commissioner-General for Hungary until June 1926.[46] True to its nature, the Hungarian government first antagonized Smith's candidacy. In addition to concerns about Smith's standing, his name created some confusion in Hungary, leading to further problems. Not well versed in New England local culture, the Hungarian leaders suspected that Smith might be a Jew,

[42] League of Nations, *The Financial Reconstruction of Hungary*, 80–81 (n 23).
[43] Ibid, 81–92.
[44] *National Assembly Diary, 1922–27* (vol. 22, Athenaeum Nyomda, 1924) 60–68, 237, 268–289, 299–315, 317–341, 343–397, 399–452; 23:1–153, 163–241, 243–333, 335–426, 437–510.
[45] Lojkó, *Meddling in Middle Europe* (n 23) 94.
[46] Salter to Smith, 5 April 1924, Doc. No. 33315, Registry Files, R. 298, LNA.

and accepting him as a League Commissioner would have been a political impossibility for Bethlen. Only after being convinced that Smith was not of Jewish descent did the Hungarian government finally approve of his nomination, a fact that the British Consul General happily conveyed to London.[47]

The subscription began in London by Baring Brothers & Co., Rothschild and Son, and J. Henry Schroder & Co. on 2 July 1924, and the very next day in New York by the consortium led by Speyer & Co. After so much worry, the news was more than welcome that in the two most important places the loan was a huge success.[48] Until mid-August, subscription had taken place in the other countries as well. If not without obstacles, the League of Nations achieved what it had set out to do. This satisfaction was reflected in Henry Strakosch's message of the Financial Committee of the League of Nations when the London issue had started: 'The League has done its duty, and now it rests with the Hungarians to make a real success of the plan of Reconstruction.'[49] What Hungary really expected from the League endeavour with an American as Commissioner-General was twofold: political protection against especially the Little Entente, and a flood of American capital. It saw the future secured in these two elements, at least in the short run. Naturally, reparations were still to be paid later on, but if the country regained its financial and economic stability, its financial and later economic health, then a realistic revision of the Trianon Treaty might be on the agenda. Consequently, Hungarian internationalism on the surface was working towards the long-term aim of undermining the new European order of which the League of Nations was the hub and pivot.

III. Consequences and Comparisons

The reconstruction period overall was a successful one and represented the high point in the relationship between Hungary and the League of Nations. Smith's monthly reports could almost only speak of improving financial circumstances, which was good news for everyone concerned. The most serious issue came towards the end of the rehabilitation period, in early 1926, in the form of the franc forgery scandal. On 14 December 1925, a Hungarian officer was arrested in the Netherlands when trying to pay with a forged 1,000 French franc note. From the end of January, Bethlen was also compromised, but Horthy, Albert Apponyi, Great Britain, and Italy were all backing him. First, some officials in the French foreign

[47] Hohler to MacDonald, 5 April 1924, C5704/37/21, 9907, FO371, TNA. In more detail about anti-Semitism in Hungary in the interwar period, see Nathaniel Katzburg, *Hungary and the Jews. Policy and Legislation 1920–1943* (Bar-Ilan University 1981).

[48] Strakosch to Smith, 2 July 1924, C.III (4) Correspondence—Sir Henry Strakosch, C. 111, Financial Reconstruction of Hungary, LNA. Felkin to Salter, 4 July 1924, Dossier concerning the American tranche. Doc. No. 37289, Registry Files, R. 413, LNA.

[49] Strakosch to Smith, 2 July 1924, C.III (4) Correspondence—Sir Henry Strakosch, C. 111, Financial Reconstruction of Hungary, LNA.

political establishment wanted to make use of the scandal and cause a government crisis or change in Hungary, but nothing came of it and during the League session in March, the franc forgery was not dealt with officially.[50] But the Little Entente and France wished to use the problem of the franc forgery as a possible card against Hungary, so the issue came up again in the League headquarters. So, it can be stated that Hungary's neighbours were just as much against the League agenda in Central Europe by trying to stem the successful conclusion of the financial reconstruction effort in Hungary. In early June during the summer Assembly of the League of Nations, the focus of deliberations was the termination of the control of finances both in Austria and Hungary. In fact, it was no secret that the French were planning to ask for postponement of the termination of control precisely because of the forgery scandal.[51] The British, however, were determined not to let the French have their way and put off the decision about lifting the control in Hungary till September.[52] Finally, in its report to the Council, the Committee stated that in its examination of the financial position of Hungary it 'considered the financial and economic data furnished to it [and] it does not consider that such circumstances as the franc forgeries (entirely deplorable as they were) have affected the financial position of the country'.[53] It is important to note that the termination of the post of the Commissioner-General did not mean the end of supervision of Hungarian finances. Control over the revenues from the assets assigned for the service of the loan and over the balance of the loan remained in place after 30 June 1926. The key person to act as the bridge between the League of Nations, the Trustees, and the Hungarian government would be the American Royall Tyler, who had been acting as Smith's deputy for more than two years. After the successful termination of the programme, Hungary enjoyed its highest point since the war. Although League control remained in place, it was more nominal and informational than during the Smith era. Tyler was to stay for another three years. As an official League representative, his opinion well captures the positive atmosphere in Hungary at the end of the summer of 1926. As Tyler put it, capital investments 'have not ceased to soar. Besides, the crops are good this year, as good as last or better; the Hungarian beat the Swedish champion swimmer in the 100 yards after the Swede had swum every other possible distance, the Hungarians beat the others at water polo, there are lots of foreigners here admiring Bpest and the prowess of the Hungarian swimmers,

[50] More about the scandal in detail, see Ignác Romsics, 'Franciaország, Bethlen és a frankhamisítás [France, Bethlen, and the Franc Forgery]' (1983) 26 Történelmi Szemle 67. Finally, the alleged perpetrators got their not-too-heavy sentences in the summer.

[51] Ross to Niemeyer, 3 June 1926, C6375/443/21, 11369, FO371, TNA.

[52] Crewe to Chamberlain, 2 June 1926, C6443/433/21 and Niemeyer to Lampson, June 4 1926, C6392/443/21, 11370, FO371, TNA.

[53] Report of the Financial Committee to the Council, 6 June 1926, Financial Reconstruction of Hungary, Deliberations at the 40th Session of the Council, June 1926. Doc. No. 52083, Registry Files, R. 302, LNA.

and everything looks rosy in the extreme'.[54] Also, the steady reduction of the number of the state employees continued, although this policy was a mixed bag. Usually, people were laid off in the lower echelons, which did not affect the budget appreciably, but on paper the Hungarian government had done and even more than what it was supposed to do. As Tyler also noted, the whole structure was outdated and inadequate for Hungary's present needs, and the demands for higher salaries by the state employees placed an almost crushing burden on the yearly budget of the country.[55] More than half of Hungary's budget went for salaries and pensions of these employees. But the upward curve lasted only for another two and a half years, and from then on it was never as good as before, and Hungary was able to stem the financial storm only until 1931. It is worth taking a closer look at the similarities and differences between the Austrian and Hungarian financial reconstructions, which served the same aim: to integrate the defeated Central European countries into the post-war European order, thereby improving their financial situation so that these two countries could become politically stable international players.

Because of Austria's especially dire circumstances, its geographical proximity to Western Europe, and because politically it was both 'safer' and more important than Hungary, the League of Nations picked Austria as the showcase and prototype of financial reconstruction under League aegis. Only after the Austrian programme was successfully launched, did the League start dealing with Hungary in earnest. Many things were very similar in both undertakings: the whole reconstruction programme was under the guidance of the League of Nations—the international organization drew up the plan, put in place League supervision in the form of a commissioner-general, and tried to make sure that the international money market could raise the amount needed for the said programmes; the reconstruction programmes were financial in technical terms, but were in reality just as much politically motivated—it was a major aim to pacify the Central European area, and if east from Germany was working and stable states were found, it was hoped to achieve a smoother integration of Germany back into the European order. Additionally, these states had to serve as part of a buffer zone in case of a Bolshevik onslaught from the east, and the recent history of both countries gave reason to be concerned; in both cases Great Britain was the unquestionable leader—the financial reconstruction of Austria and Hungary served larger British aims in the region from political and commercial perspectives alike; and, most importantly perhaps, at the end of the day both programmes produced the desired results—a balanced budget, a new and independent central bank, a stable currency, a string of modest financial reforms, a burst in bilateral commercial agreements, a modest rise in the standard of living, political stability, and the flow of investment capital, mainly

[54] Tyler to A. H. Siepmann, 26 August 1926, Correspondence with A. H. Siepmann, 1926–1929, Thompson Todd Collection, Australia.

[55] Tyler to Siepmann, 23 March 1927, ibid.

from overseas. It is also important to mention that the Austrian and Hungarian reconstructions were actually forerunners of the German rehabilitation programme, which became known as the Dawes Plan, and took place outside the framework of the League of Nations. In the pan-European picture, Germany was the most important element both in a political and economic sense. Thus the German financial rehabilitation commenced almost immediately after the first two successful rehabilitation programmes—though mainly under American tutelage. It is not without interest that the tools and techniques that were pioneered in the Central European financial reconstructions, subsequently became forms of western hegemony in the developing world.[56]

There were, however, significant differences as well: Austria received an international loan of 650 million Crowns ($125 million), more than twice the amount that Hungary received, although 20 per cent of it had to be repaid immediately because of the British, French, and Czech debts (the League judged Austria in a more dire situation from the financial point of view, while the question of the *Anschluss* made the propping up of the Austrian state all the more imperative); while Hungary had to meet certain reparation obligations during the twenty-year amortization period, Austria was exempted from these for twenty years; Austria had to lay off 100,000 people, while Hungary only had to dismiss 15,000; the time of the reconstruction lasted four years in the case of Austria compared to the basically two years in Hungary (Hungary's programme was launched on smoother rails partly thanks to the Austrian experience and financially the challenge was also smaller); the personality of the commissioners-general was also an important difference (while Alfred Zimmerman proved to be autocratic, inflexible, and often antagonistic to Austrian perspectives, Smith created trust and, aside from minor incidents, his tenure in Budapest was picture-perfect, especially considering how much Hungarians were against outside control). While the Austrian currency became dollar-based, the Hungarian crown was adjusted to the British pound—an outright desire of Montagu Norman. Moreover, the Austrians initially attempted to deceive the League of Nations and defrauded quite a large amount, which led to some serious tension, while the Hungarian government, albeit not gladly, collaborated loyally in all respects.[57] In Austria the League of Nations even approved the raising of expenditure, while no such measures were necessary in Hungary. Although the formal control did not cease in either of the countries upon the departure of the high commissioners, the position of consultant in the Austrian National Bank was extended by three years, as opposed to the Hungarian situation where Harry Siepmann of the Bank of England gladly left along with Smith at the end of the financial reconstruction.

[56] On the last point a project is being carried out by a group headed by James Mark of Exeter, UK.
[57] Leithers to Niemeyer, 7 February 1925, BoE, OV9/437.

Perhaps the saddest similarity between the Austrian and Hungarian reconstructions was the lack of a well-conceived follow-up financial policy after the initial success, and by the early 1930s both countries ran into huge debt. One of the reasons was the amount of debt on the excessive loans, while another was the global economic crisis. From this point on there was no way out, regardless of the resolution of the Lausanne Conference in 1932 which suspended reparation payments that later were even terminated. Although in the mid-1930s there was some consolidation in banking, both countries were quickly drawn into the German orbit and the Second World War, which definitively put an end to the opportunity of financial recovery. Austria and the Austrian National Bank lost its independence through the annexation by Nazi Germany, while in Hungary the independence of the National Bank of Hungary was also subjected to revisionist endeavours, and was lost even before the war broke out.

IV. Thorny Issues between the League and Hungary

It is also useful to point out that when it came to the political relations with the League after the reconstruction period, Hungary's case proved thorny on more than one occasion. In the summer of 1928, for instance, both the so-called Optants and the Szentgotthárd (St. Gotthard) questions were on the Council's agenda. Both problems are good illustrations of the fact that despite the financial aid that Hungary had received from the League of Nations, Hungary still felt disappointed in the League. At the same time, the cases also show how careful the international organization wished to be in troublesome cases.

The Optants question was a long-lasting and thorny issue for the League. The Romanian government promulgated a law in 1921, in which they basically confiscated Hungarians' lands there. Hungary claimed that this Romanian law was violating certain aspects of the Treaty of Trianon, whereas the Romanians argued that their state's sovereignty came first before the protection of another treaty. In 1923 Hungary turned to the League for help in establishing which party was right. That is how a long and arduous but fruitless legal process began that refused to go away for seven years. The League tried to mediate but it was futile, and the Romanian government disputed the jurisdiction of the Rumanian-Hungarian Mixed Arbitral Tribunal in the question. Romania wanted to connect the Optants question with that of reparations. The issue was problematic from a domestic point of view in both countries, and the League wished not to intervene on either party's behalf. A diplomat well summarized the significance of the issue. Although he thought it was not 'a transcendentally important question "per se", but it is indisputable that it is a salient factor in the scrutiny and appraisal of the League by the smaller nations'.[58] In the end, a solution was achieved but it was a mixed success. In April 1930 the two governments at last agreed that Hungarian claimants were to receive 240 million gold crowns ($50 million), while Hungary agreed to pay an annual 13.5 million gold crowns from 1943 until 1966. This sum is often seen as a final act of reparations, but technically it was to liquidate other claims such as costs of the occupying forces, costs of bringing home Hungarian Prisoners of War (POWs) and internees, Yugoslavia's claim for unshipped coal, compensation for Czechoslovakia for Hungarian Soviet troops' movements on its territory, etc. Soon, however, the incoming depression made the long process practically unimportant, since Hungary ceased to pay its international debts from 1931, while the Lausanne Treaty of 1932 suspended all payments of reparations.[59]

As for the Szentgotthárd affair, in January 1928, at the border town of Szentgotthárd, the Austrian customs officers stopped a train going from Italy allegedly to Poland. In five of the wagons weapons were found which were listed in the official customs documents as machine components. Soon it was clear that the shipment was for Hungary, a clear violation of the Treaty of Trianon, which forbade any arming the Hungarian army. The shipment actually was a manifestation of the much improved and friendly relations between Italy and Hungary to the detriment and at the expense of Yugoslavia. Somewhat thanks to French backing, the Little Entente countries began a mainly propaganda outcry against Hungary.[60] Amid such calls, the League initiated an investigation and discussed the affair in the March Assembly.[61] The Hungarian government had auctioned the now disabled weapons in February, hoping to defuse the scandal. The League set up a Committee of Three, which suggested a strictly technical investigation in Hungary. Based upon the report of a seven-member League delegation that carried out the investigation in April in Hungary, the League Assembly in June deemed the affair closed without finding Hungary at fault.[62]

[58] J. Butler Wright to Frank B. Kellogg, 10 November 1927, 864.00/709, Austria-Hungary and Hungary, 1912–1929, Microcopy No. 708, Roll 8, NARA.

[59] On the Optants question, see Francis Deák, *The Hungarian–Rumanian Land Dispute* (Columbia University Press 1928); Ferenc Matheovics, *A magyar–román birtokper* [The Hungarian-Romanian Optants Case] (Grill Károly 1929); Elek Nagy, *Magyarország és a Népszövetség* [Hungary and the League of Nations] (Franklin Társulat 1930) 57–82; Gábor Aradi, 'A San Remo-i tárgyalások magyarországi előkészülete [The Hungarian Preparations for the San Remo Talks]' (2002) 52/3 Levéltári Szemle 24; Holly Case, *Between States: The Transylvanian Question and the European Idea during the Second World War* (Stanford University Press 2009) 27–30.

[60] The British Minister opined to his American colleague that the French 'rarely fail to improve an opportunity to counsel the members of the Little Entente to magnify small incidents'. J. Butler Wright to Frank B. Kellogg, 9 March 1928, 864.00 PR/4, Affairs of Austria-Hungary and Hungary, 1912–1929. Microcopy No. 708, Roll 10, NARA.

[61] League of Nations, *Official Journal*, 9th Year, No. 4 (April 1928) Forty-ninth Session of the Council 387–397.

[62] League of Nations, *Official Journal*, 9th Year, No. 7 (July 1928) Fiftieth Session of the Council 905–918 and 1009–1021. On the Szentgotthárd incident, also see Zsiga Tibor, *A szentgotthárdi fegyverbotrány*, [The Szentgotthárd Arms Scandal] (Pannon Műhely Kft. 1990); Zsiga Tibor, 'A szentgotthárdi fegyverbotrány [The Szentgotthárd Arms Scandal]' Vol. 35, No. 1, 2008, 14–23; Ildikó Császár, 'A

In light of such affairs it is no wonder that Hungary did not find in the League of Nations what it had been looking for, while often it seemed that Geneva was a good platform to attack Hungary. A good example how the official Hungarian political establishment looked at the League of Nations can be found in various government publications. One such example is the *Külügyi Szemle* (*Foreign Review*), the semi-official foreign policy views of the Hungarian government. It was not surprising to read of a 'stern, inflexible and one-sided League of Nations', which 'in its composition and work as of today is the insurance company of the winners and their preys, which institution keeps at bay every rightful complaint, every reform attempt, and every attempt to change the peace decrees in a more just and reasonable way'.[63] Although this opinion may be too harsh and one-sided, another Hungarian example from the same year seems more genuine, especially in light of the Optants question: The League of Nations' 'proceedings are hesitating, it dares accept resolutions only rarely, it favours political aspects to legal ones, which leads to a situation that the trust on part of the small states has been shaken [. . .] the issues that it deals with are stalled and, therefore, final act on them are belated. The large part of those feuds that are dealt with happens only in name but not in deed'.[64] These charges of belatedness and ineffectiveness document the Hungarian, and possibly other small countries', perception that the League's bureaucratic multilateralism was maladapted to the most pressing political challenges of the new order in Central Europe. The fragile small states that populated this region were the most sensitive to this problem, therefore, it is understandable that to some of them internationalism was part of the problem, and not the solution. Obviously the Hungarian political leadership and the public at large, as the above-mentioned opinions attest, were dissatisfied with what the League might offer to Hungary.

For all this disappointment and discontent, Hungary again identified the League as the last resort for financial help when the economic outlook grew desperate in the wake of the 1929 recession. Bethlen's ten-year reign came to an end in the wake of the crisis. In early September 1931, the Hungarian government formerly requested help from the League. The following month the Financial Committee met in Budapest to study the situation on the ground and realized that it was grave indeed. Tyler, who had already stated earlier that only the League could avert financial catastrophe in Hungary, was appointed one more time to remain in Hungary as Representative of the Finance Committee of the League, and he stayed another six

szentgotthárdi fegyverszállítási botrány sajtóvisszhangja [The Press Echo of the Szentgotthárd Arms Scandal]' (2013) 68/6 Vasi Szemle 579.

[63] Paikert Alajos, 'A Népszövetségi Ligák jelentősége [The Significance of the League of Nations]' (Magyar Külügyi Társaság 1929) VI/1 Külügyi Szemle 67.

[64] László Vince Weninger, 'Népszövetség [League of Nations]' (Magyar Külügyi Társasá 1929) VI/1 Külügyi Szemle 104.

years in Hungary.[65] The Hungarian Government declared transfer moratorium in the end of December 1931, and refused to pay its debts on all loans except for the 1924 League Loan, but the next spring transfer was discontinued on this obligation as well. American minsters accredited to Budapest spoke of 'the desperate nature of the present plight of Hungary', and of 'no justification for optimism at this time with regard to the economic outlook'.[66] However, despite help from the League through the newly established Bank for International Settlements, Hungary could not manage to climb back to a more normal financial status until the end of 1935, and in 1938 the League decided to cease its financial control over Hungary.

During these years the League of Nations provided the setting for another political showdown between Hungary and its opponents, this time mainly Yugoslavia. This latest issue, or scandal, was the assassination of King Alexander of Yugoslavia in Marseille, in October 1934, in which Louis Barthou, the French foreign minister, was also killed. Foreign policy considerations played a large role why Hungary was implicated in the aftermath of the murder, although not very seriously. The Hungarian government secretly helped Croatian separatists (they were the Ustasha, a revolutionary organization fighting for separation from the freshly christened Yugoslavia), especially with a small camp close to the Hungarian-Yugoslav border from where these elements could strike at the central government of Yugoslavia in the early years of the 1930s. Under almost continuous pressure from Belgrade concerning the Ustasha enclave in Hungary, Budapest chose diplomatic attack to muddy the waters, and complained at the League of Nations about Yugoslavia and its treatment of ethnic Hungarians in the border region. This manoeuvre was a short-lived success, because the accused in the assassination all could be connected to Hungary in some form. Due to the power constellation in Europe at the time (endeavours to try to reach agreements about armament with Germany, the peaceful conduction of the Saar referendum, and the French-Italian rapprochement to balance the resurging Nazi Germany), Hungary was a comfortable scapegoat for many. On 22 November, Yugoslavia complained in Geneva about Hungary's involvement in the assassination. As usual, a compromise was hammered out mainly due to British and French persuasion, not to mention Italy that might have been really behind the assassination, and all parties accepted the Hungarian memorandum concerning the question.[67] In the second part of the

[65] Tyler's opinion in Enclosure to Nicholas Roosevelt to Henry L. Stimson, No. 408, 6 February 1933, Box 59: Dispatches from Hungary 1930–1933, Nicholas Roosevelt Papers, Syracuse, New York, USA.

[66] Nicholas Roosevelt to Henry L. Stimson, No. 233, 30 January 1932, Box 59: Dispatches from Hungary 1930–1933, Nicholas Roosevelt Papers; John F. Montgomery to Cordell Hull, 5 August 1933, 864.00P.R./68, Affairs of Hungary, 1930–1944. Microcopy No. 1206, Roll 3, NARA.

[67] The most thorough book concerning the Marseilles assassination and its aftermath both in Hungary and Europe, is still Mária Ormos, *Merénylet Marseille-ben* [Assassination in Marseilles] (2nd edition, Kossuth Könyvkiadó 1984). Another academic writing, relying mainly on sources other than those of Ormos, reaches the same conclusion. See Bennett Kovrig, 'Mediation by Obfuscation: The Resolution of the Marseille Crisis, October 1934 to May 1935' (March 1976) 19/1 The Historical Journal 191.

1930s, there were fewer and fewer reasons why Hungary wanted to remain within the ranks of the League of Nations. Its finances were more or less in order, but the crippling effects of the Great Depression were palpable all over Europe, and no substantial change could be hoped for. More importantly, Hungary's main aim in the interwar years was territorial revision and protection of Hungarian minority in the successor countries. It had become clear by the early 1930s that the League was not a partner in either of these endeavours, so the Hungarian leadership began to seek closer ties with Italy and Germany, those two countries that promised support for such Hungarian aims. Since Germany left the League of Nations in 1933, the orientation of Hungary increasingly abandoned any tethering to the League. Moreover, in Hungarian eyes, the League of Nations did not help to solve or even alleviate the burning minority question. The Hungarian governments' grievances led to no positive outcome concerning the millions of ethnic Hungarians in the Little Entente countries, therefore this offered another reason to leave the organization and try and pursue a freer foreign policy. As Hungary's long-time prime minister, István Bethlen, complained in 1925, the minority treaties had 'practically no value at all' given that 'the League of Nations had yet to pour life and meaning into them'.[68] Or, as he put it in a propaganda presentation in London in 1933:

> We have, made the most painful experience in the direction that the protection of the minorities has not the slightest sanction, since the guarantee of the League of Nations is worth even less than any written sanction. The League of Nations, in order to safeguard its prestige, had much better declare openly that in its present composition and structure it is not in a position to fulfil its duty in this direction; and it would be much better if that important international body would assume no responsibility for what is going on in the domain of minority protection in the world, instead of playing Pilate washing its hands and keeping in suspense these minorities who—while being continually put off—are being crucified in their very ancestral home.[69]

In addition, the League proved time and again impotent to restrain aggressor countries, which gave further impetus to Hungary to rely on Italian and German support in hope of regaining some of its lost territories. The end result was not surprising: on 11 April 1939 Hungary left the League of Nations, a step that was rather symbolic, because one can argue that Hungary had always been a half-hearted advocate and member despite the fact that it naturally paid lip service to the goals of the organization.[70]

[68] Quoted in Case, *Between States* (n 59) 29.

[69] István Bethlen, 'The Problem of Transylvania, London, 27 November 1933' in István Bethlen, *Treaty of Trianon and European Peace: Four Lectures Delivered in London in November, 1933, by Count Stephen Bethlen* (Longmans, Green and Co. 1934) 133.

[70] Csáky to the Secretary-General, April 11 1939, League of Nations, *Official Journal*, 20th Year, nos. 3–4 (March–April 1939) 205.

V. Conclusion

In conclusion, it must be stated that Hungary did not want to become a member of the League of Nations because it shared the underlying assumptions of the international organization. It did not necessarily believe in the brotherhood of countries, the just reasoning of an international organization, or the power of world opinion. The only reason why Hungary was forced onto this path was the sheer power of its interests. Hungarian political leaders realized that outside the League they had a next-to-no chance of achieving any of their hoped-for treaty revisions. While being a member of the organization did not guarantee any such possibility either, it at least gave a forum where Hungary could keep the minority question on the agenda and could enjoy a relative equality with its neighbours. Also, financial considerations played a large role, and since private channels did not offer the assistance Hungary imagined, there was no other option but to turn to the League for a loan. The League of Nations played an important role in the interwar history of Hungary. By providing certain safeguards for short-term growth, promising relative equality in the new European order, welcoming Hungary in the financial and economic system, and thereby hoping to neutralize Hungarian irredentist desires, on the surface the League managed to integrate Hungary into the new international system. Hungary has almost everything to gain from collaboration with Geneva and the neighbouring countries. Since it behaved for years in a way the League expected, the work apparently provided a more stable Central Europe after the collapse of the Habsburg Empire. Hungary's case is intriguing from this aspect. It had long fought for its independence and its centuries-long constitutional rights. Within the Austro-Hungarian Empire this was to a large degree achieved, but still short of the ultimate goal. It is an irony that becoming independent in the wake of the First World War, Hungary so quickly became embroiled in an alternate set of sovereignty-limiting schemes and mechanisms: now it was not the shared sovereignty of the emperor–king, but the supervised sovereignty of transnational financial governance. Hungary chose what its political leadership saw as its escape route: the country was willing to accept a state of weakened sovereignty in the short term in order to gain a stronger one it in the long term. A paradox was thus created: short-term internationalism pursuant to long-term anti-internationalism. The Hungarian case necessarily raises the question: can internationalized governance paradoxically be used to strengthen sovereign independence, or is such a project always already illusory? It can be safely concluded, however, that Hungary was working both for and against the League of Nations at the same time. The hard fact is that interests define what countries do, and the Hungarian attitude in the interwar years was a perfect example. Once in the League of Nations, Hungary tried to use all the leverage of such a position, with varying success. As with all the issues raised in this chapter, the conclusion must be that the forced marriage of the League and Hungary ended with a predictable divorce.

7

On the Fraught Internationalism of Intellectuals

Alfons Dopsch, Austria, and the League's Intellectual Cooperation Programme

Johannes Feichtinger[*]

In 1922, the Assembly of the League of Nations approved the Council's 1921 proposal to establish an advisory committee both to 'promote practical intellectual co-operation' and to improve the technical tools of work at the international level.[1] The International Committee on Intellectual Cooperation (ICIC) was not included in the League of Nations Covenant, but was instead established at the instigation of the 1920 Nobel Peace Prize laureate Léon Bourgeois. It was expected to continue the policy of 'practical internationalism'[2] advanced by private and unofficial international associations in the nineteenth century. Before the First World War, the intellectual internationalization movement limited itself to science and scholarship and only rarely relied on government support. Postwar democratization, the increase in international organization and the rapid development of institutionalized research helped proponents of cooperation to realize that intellectual work required both a broader scope of action and governmental support. In this respect, the interwar intellectual cooperation movement followed a different path than the nineteenth-century international associations[3]—it proved to be a new mode of extended international governance that transgressed the narrow academic field and included action in the sphere of the arts, libraries, archives, museums, and film.[4] The foundation for this new mode of international intellectual governance was laid by the Geneva-based ICIC after the First World War. The ICIC paved the

* I would like to thank Natasha Wheatley and Peter Becker for their valuable suggestions for revising this chapter.

1 Alfred Zimmern, 'The League and International Intellectual Co-operation' in H. Milford (ed), *The Problems of Peace: Lectures delivered at the Geneva Institute of International Relations at the Palais des Nations, August 1926* (Oxford University Press 1927) 144, 145.

2 Jan Kolasa, *International Intellectual Cooperation: The League Experience and the Beginnings of UNESCO* (Zakład Narodowy im. Ossolińskich 1962) 15.

3 See Daniel Gorman, *International Cooperation in the Early Twentieth Century* (New Approaches to International History, Bloomsbury Academic 2019) 39–65.

4 See Daniel Laqua, 'Transnational intellectual cooperation, the League of Nations, and the problem of order' (2011) 6 Journal of Global History 223, 237.

Johannes Feichtinger, *On the Fraught Internationalism of Intellectuals* In: *Remaking Central Europe*.
Edited by: Peter Becker and Natasha Wheatley, Oxford University Press (2020). © the many contributors.
DOI: 10.1093/oso/9780198854685.003.0008

way for the activities that would be continued by the United Nations Educational, Scientific and Cultural Organization (UNESCO) on an expanded basis after 1945. From the beginning, the ICIC consisted of twelve full members—eminent scholars including Collège de France philosopher Henri Bergson, Oxford classicist Gilbert Murray, Sorbonne professor of physics Marie Curie, and Albert Einstein—and one corresponding member, the renowned Viennese historian Alfons Dopsch.

This chapter investigates both Dopsch's expectations and the frustrations he would experience in his collaboration with the ICIC, as well as the lasting effects he was able to achieve through the reform of this League Committee—a reform he himself instituted and that resulted in the inclusion of non-academic agendas in the ICIC's activities.

Although characterized as a non-governmental agency,[5] the ICIC supported the League of Nations in establishing a peaceful postwar order. In particular, it was tasked with satisfying the needs of individual governments, state-based institutional agents, and the novel intergovernmental intellectual regime. To each of these, internationalization offered new assets: the exchange of people, books, and ideas on an institutional basis; the opportunity to advance international conventions through government agreements; and the establishment of international intellectual institutions. The ICIC thus established itself as a broker between the League, individual states, and their leading intellectual actors, who were encouraged to form nation-based sub-organizations. From 1922 onwards, the first national committees were set up in the dozen newly founded states in Central Europe in which intellectual life was most at peril in the wake of the First World War. The successor states of the former Habsburg lands and beyond proved to be an appropriate arena for the ICIC's initial operation as a newly established body, and the serious crisis of Austrian intellectual life in particular helped to build up its capacity and tools for operation.

This chapter will show how the Austrian case decisively shaped the future character of the League's intellectual cooperation programme. The Geneva initiative raised great expectations in Austria, since the newly established republic was facing a serious situation. Politically isolated and economically ruined, it was threatened with total collapse of its intellectual life. The League initiative allowed Austrian intellectual and cultural actors to develop new visions of a rebirth of the cultural life that had flourished until the First World War. They believed that securing international funding was key to this rebirth. It was the ICIC that commissioned Alfons Dopsch (1868–1953), a historian at the University of Vienna, to serve as intermediary between the League and the Austrian intellectual world. As a distinguished member of both the University of Vienna and the Austrian Academy of Sciences, he had a well-developed local network of agents in the academic world

[5] Kolasa, *International Intellectual Cooperation* (n 2) 3, 164.

at his disposal, and this network grew even further after he received international recognition for his ground-breaking, optimistic book *The Economic and Social Foundations of European Civilization*, published in two volumes between 1918 and 1920.[6] Dopsch was considered the best choice for both Austria and the League—and once appointed as corresponding member of the ICIC, he began his work immediately.

This chapter provides a relational history of the development of international intellectual cooperation between Austria and the League. Although this was originally not envisaged, the composition of the ICIC demonstrated that international collaboration was increasingly transgressing the narrow field of science and scholarship. The following paragraphs will show how Alfons Dopsch's initiatives inspired the new scheme of action drafted by the ICIC from late 1923 onwards and framed the future strategic focus of intellectual cooperation in the new European intellectual order—including the new area of cultural heritage and its institutions such as libraries, archives, and museums, which had a rich imperial tradition in Vienna. We will also see how interwar intellectual cooperation subsequently informed the work of the ICIC's successor organization, UNESCO. However, the Austrian case also demonstrates that the international organization of intellectual collaboration brought forth disappointment, since the hopes of international financial support remained unfulfilled. This chapter explores the changing fortunes of international intellectual cooperation from a regional point of view, aiming to illuminate the finer nuances of both the opportunities and the realities related to the newly internationalized organization of intellectual experts. It also highlights the irreconcilable discrepancy between the national and international as well as the different scopes of action at work in the latter: while Dopsch received only guarded support from the Austrian government, his work was made even more difficult by the various often contradictory objectives of the League of Nations. The League's harsh economic recovery programme for Austria paid no regard to the ICIC's objective of restoring cultural life. All this placed Dopsch in a double bind that ultimately left him in a difficult predicament. A research approach oriented around regions, actors, and institutions can help us to reconstruct the 'international' of intellectual cooperation in the making.

6 Alfons Dopsch, *Wirtschaftliche und soziale Grundlagen der europäischen Kulturentwicklung aus der Zeit von Caesar bis auf Karl den Großen*. 2 vols. (2nd edn, L.W. Seidel & Sohn 1923–24). The book was also published in English, Italian, and Russian.

I. Austria's Efforts in International Academic Cooperation Before and After the First World War

The state system of higher learning in late Habsburg Austria was characterized by its diverse structure[7]: in addition to the University of Vienna, the Austrian part of the Habsburg Monarchy operated twenty universities and state colleges for technology, economy, veterinary medicine, arts, and music, as well as a great number of influential learned societies, libraries, and museums, and the Imperial Academy of Sciences in Vienna. Its internationally oriented members crossed territorial, scientific, and institutional boundaries in the pursuit of their research. Inspired by a cooperation agreement between the Austrian and German Academies of Sciences, steps were taken to establish the first International Association of Academies (IAA), which was eventually founded in 1899. The IAA brought together academic institutions from Europe, Asia, and the USA to solve urgent scientific problems of international import through cooperative research. The prewar Habsburg intellectual landscape can be characterized as a dynamic and rapidly developing hotbed of liberal cutting-edge research; this state of affairs would come to a sudden end in 1914 with the outbreak of the First World War, however.[8]

The International Association of Academies was not formally dissolved after the war, but instead replaced by two new organizations: the International Research Council (IRC, for the natural sciences) and the International Union of Academies (UIA, for the humanities and social sciences), which were founded in 1919 at a congress in Brussels. Since the IAA was not re-established, the Cartel of German Academies and Learned Societies (including the Academy of Sciences in Vienna) established in 1893 came to play a key role in cross-national academic cooperation in Central Europe following the First World War. However, this cross-national cooperation was now confined to Austria and Germany. Both states joined the Brussels-based UIA with considerable delay in 1935, but refused to join the IRC (later renamed the International Council of Scientific Unions) due to the exclusion clause adopted by the London Conference of Inter-Allied Scientific Academies in the fall of 1918, which barred Germany and Austria from international scientific organizations. The Academy of Sciences in Vienna never reassumed the role it had played on the eve of the First World War as one of the world's leading international

[7] See Johannes Feichtinger, 'Die verletzte Autonomie. Wissenschaft und ihre Struktur in Wien 1848 bis 1938' in Katharina Kniefacz, Elisabeth Nemeth, Herbert Posch, and Friedrich Stadler (eds), *Universität—Forschung—Lehre. Themen und Perspektiven im langen 20. Jahrhundert* (650 Jahre Universität Wien—Aufbruch ins neue Jahrhundert 1, Vandenhoeck und Ruprecht 2015).

[8] See Johannes Feichtinger, 'Der „edle geistige Militarismus'. Die Kaiserliche Akademie der Wissenschaften in Wien im Ersten Weltkrieg' in Claude Debru (ed), *Akademien im Kriege. Académies en Guerre. Academies in War* (Acta Historica Leopoldina 75, Wissenschaftliche Verlagsgesellschaft 2019); Johannes Feichtinger, 'Österreichische Akademie der Wissenschaften' in Matthias Berg and Jens Thiel (eds), *Europäische Wissenschaftsakademien im 'Krieg der Geister'. Reden und Dokumente 1914 bis 1920* (Acta Historica Leopoldina 72, Wissenschaftliche Verlagsgesellschaft 2018).

academic brokers. In the interwar period, international relations between learned societies continued to be disrupted by prejudice, mistrust, and violations (such as exclusions of members in enemy states) resulting from the recent conflict. As a result, the liberal Austrian agents of learning felt an indissoluble affinity for a reunited Austro-Germany, and they showed open solidarity with their academic fellows in the German Reich. Both communities suffered from the international academic isolation that forced the Austrian academic community to become even closer to the German Reich, which funded Austria's interwar research system to a large extent.[9] However, the Austrian academic elite also recognized that the international League initiative for intellectual cooperation offered a unique opportunity to overcome this isolation without offending their key German alliance partner.

II. The League's International Cooperation Agency in the Making

The International Committee on Intellectual Cooperation—incidentally the last body ever established by the League of Nations—met for the first time in August 1922. Its twelve members were selected with due care from different countries on grounds of their scientific and scholarly distinction. They were neither representatives of the countries they came from nor delegates of their governments. Rather, they were independent but eminent academics whose work was approved by the Council and the Assembly of the League. It has been shown that the committee members were trusted to contain Communist influence on national and international affairs, suppressing 'any truly revolutionary thought' by cultivating a form of intellectual international of illustrious minds.[10]

The Committee met twice a year in Geneva, and it had staff working under League Under Secretary General Inazō Nitobe (1862–1933) at its disposal at the Secretariat. The formulation of its task was vague and mainly addressed the international issue of academic cooperation, which in fact initially remained restricted to Europe. At its first session, the members of the ICIC (except for Einstein, who was otherwise engaged) decided to recommend two activities to the League Council: studying the conditions of intellectual life in the various countries, and subsequently providing assistance to the nation-states in which intellectual life was endangered. Following this initial recommendation, the ICIC's secretary Oskar Halecki (1891–1973), a polyglot Polish historian with a focus on Central Europe, independently conducted surveys on intellectual life in twelve Central European

[9] See Silke Fengler and Günther Luxbacher, 'Aufrechterhaltung der gemeinsamen Kultur'. Die Deutsche Forschungsgemeinschaft und die Österreichisch-Deutsche Wissenschaftshilfe in der Zwischenkriegszeit' (2011) 4 Berichte zur Wissenschaftsgeschichte 303.

[10] Kolasa, *International Intellectual Cooperation* (n 2) 163–166.

member states of the League[11] before national committees were established in the most distressed areas of the region. These were created either by universities (in Bulgaria, Estonia, Greece, Latvia, and Lithuania), under the auspices of Academies of Sciences (in Czechoslovakia, Hungary, Romania, and Yugoslavia), by foundations for the promotion of scientific work (in Poland), or by individuals of high academic standing (in Austria). The Austrian Committee was one of the first to be founded, namely on 28 April 1923 at the initiative of Alfons Dopsch. It was believed that the Austrian state was at risk of a complete collapse of intellectual life, and Dopsch had been commissioned by the ICIC in October 1922 to carry out a survey of intellectual life in Austria, which he completed within a year. At around the same time, precisely on 4 November 1922, the League Council itself launched an international appeal for immediate help on Austria's behalf. This appeal evinced sympathy in several countries—Great Britain, India, Japan, and the USA—and resulted in material support. No substantial assistance was provided by the ICIC itself, however; at least not immediately, and not in the financial form the intellectual world in Austria so eagerly hoped for. Rather, it would take over a year for the League of Nations to draw up a new scheme for action. This scheme included a decisive shift in the ICIC's policy: starting in the mid-1920s, the scope of the ICIC's primary activity—cross-border cooperation—was expanded from the field of academia, its common focus since the nineteenth century, to that of culture and cultural heritage issues, which were thus accorded an international infrastructure for the first time.

In view of Austria's tradition of liberal scholarship and culture, Dopsch's Vienna-based ICIC subcommittee immediately assumed responsibility for both higher education and the broader world of arts and letters, libraries, archives, and museums. It included luminaries from the academic, cultural, and cultural heritage worlds. In the Habsburg-ruled domains, scholarly, cultural, and museum activities had traditionally been interrelated: in 1849, for example, the Imperial Royal Mining Museum became Vienna's Imperial Royal Geological Institute, and the Natural History Museum in Vienna established several divisions to initiate and perform research in cooperation with the Imperial Royal Geological Institute and the Imperial Academy of Sciences. The imperial collections of natural and artistic artefacts, manuscripts, and books were traditionally the primary sites of research,

[11] See Andrzej M. Brzeziński, 'Oskar Halecki—the advocate of Central and Eastern European countries in the International Committee on Intellectual Cooperation of the League of Nations (1922–1925)' (2013) 48 Studies into the History of Russia and Central-Eastern Europe [Studia z Dziejów Rosji i Europy Środkowo-Wschodniej] 5, 12; Andrzej M. Brzeziński, 'Sprawy polskie w działalności Oskara Haleckiego—sekretarza Komisji Międzynarodowej Współpracy Intelektualnej Ligi Narodów (1922–1924) [Polish Issues in the Activity of Oskar Halecki as a Secretary of the International Committee on Intellectual Cooperation of the League of Nations]' in Małgorzata Dąbrowska (ed), *Oskar Halecki i jego wizja Europy* [Oscar Halecki and His Vision of Europe] (Instytut Pamięci Narodowej 2012); Małgorzata Morawiec, 'Oskar Halecki' in Heinz Duchhardt, Małgorzata Morawiec, Wolfgang Schmale, and Winfried Schulze (eds), *Europa-Historiker. Ein biographisches Handbuch*, Vol. 1 (Vandenhoeck & Ruprecht 2006).

and public education was an integral part of the activities of the learned societies and the University of Vienna from the mid-nineteenth century onwards. Austria's most famous archivist, the poet laureate Franz Grillparzer (1791–1872), was appointed as full member of the Academy of Sciences in 1847.

One basic assumption discussed in this chapter is the postulation that the ICIC's shift to a broader scope of activity resulted from the creative adoption of intellectual practices and understandings from the Habsburg lands—that is, that Austria had a formative influence on the ICIC's level of activity, its agenda, and the new structure of international cooperation it would subsequently develop. The new agenda included non-academic areas such as museums, and the new structure involved the establishment of national committees, for which Dopsch's Vienna branch served as a role model. Originally not envisaged by the international representatives in Geneva, the 1923 reform brought about the abovementioned new scheme of action which included, among other changes, novel forms and techniques of cross-national exchange and a more inclusive strategy with greater mass appeal. These allowed the League's intellectual cooperation programme to be revived in the new guise of UNESCO following the Second World War. The idea of today's UNESCO National Commissions, a network of 199 national cooperating bodies, arose from the need to base the ICIC's post-1918 initiative on nation-based committees intended 'to build peace through international cooperation in Education, the Sciences and Culture'.[12] In this way, Dopsch's appointment was formative for the future activities of the ICIC. How and why he came into this privileged position without ever being appointed as a full member of the ICIC will become clear over the course of the following pages.

III. Dopsch's Invitation

On 26 October 1922, a letter was sent to Vienna-based historian Alfons Dopsch that would have a huge impact on his professional life. In this letter, the Secretary-General of the League of Nations, Eric Drummond (1876–1951), invited Dopsch to accept the position of corresponding member of the newly established International Committee on Intellectual Cooperation at the League of Nations in Geneva.[13] The offer was based on a resolution adopted by the League Council on 4 October 1922 to invite the ICIC to 'choose an Austrian correspondent to keep

[12] See UNESCO in brief https://en.unesco.org/about-us/introducing-unesco, and https://en.unesco.org/countries/national-commissions. Accessed 15 February 2020. Jean-Jacques Renoliet, *L'UNESCO oubliée: La Société des Nations et la coopération intellectuelle (1919–1946)* (Paris: Publications de la Sorbonne 1999); Jo-Anne Pemberton, 'The changing shape of intellectual cooperation: From the League of Nations to UNESCO' [2012] Australian Journal of Politics and History.

[13] The ICIC was established in 1921 based on a resolution passed by the League Assembly on 18 December 1920.

the Committee informed of the needs of intellectual life in his country'[14] and conduct a more detailed survey there. The League Council considered Austria in particular to be a country whose previously fully developed intellectual life had been completely shattered by the war. The internal communication of the League Secretariat shows that the decision to appoint Alfons Dopsch as correspondent was made for several reasons. When the League Council discussed the composition of its advisory committee, Dopsch's candidature as a regular member of the ICIC was strongly supported by Léon Bourgeois, the first elected president of the League Council. Because the number of regular committee members had been strictly limited to twelve, however, Dopsch—'un savant très distingué' who had been shortlisted for regular membership—was recommended as a corresponding member. He was still actively involved in international intellectual cooperation, an issue on which he liaised with the League Secretariat as rector of the University of Vienna. The Japanese Under-Secretary-General of the League of Nations, Inazō Nitobe, pointed to Dopsch's two-volume work on *The Economic and Social Foundations of European Civilization*, which had gone out of print immediately after publication, as evidence of his scientific excellence.[15]

Before Dopsch was officially invited as corresponding member, the ICIC's secretary Oskar Halecki visited Vienna to submit the offer of the position to him. The post comprised the tasks of organizing the enquiry into the situation of intellectual work in Austria, which would be published as a pamphlet under the auspices of the League of Nations, and informing the ICIC about the urgent needs of scholars and scientific institutions in Austria.[16] The meeting with Halecki, which Dopsch arranged at his Seminar for Economic and Cultural History at the University of Vienna, was also attended by the most eminent representatives of the Austrian academic world: Oswald Redlich, president of the Academy of Sciences; Emil Reisch, dean of the philosophical faculty of the University of Vienna, who was present on behalf of the rector; Emil Artmann, rector of the Vienna College of Technology (today TU Wien—Vienna University of Technology); Hans Sperl, president of the Austrian Federation of Intellectual Workers; and Gustav Walker, who represented the Austrian League of Nations Society. Halecki reported that the participants 'expressed their deepest thanks for the sympathy which the Committee had shown to Austria'. Moreover, the meeting apparently left the impression of a 'general agreement that the choice of Mr. Dopsch as Austrian correspondent was the best possible'.[17] Having been offered 10,000 Swiss francs for his services, expenses and the

[14] League of Nations. Intellectual Co-operation. Resolutions proposed by M. Hanotaux and adopted by the Council on 4 October 1922, 5 October 1922. League of Nations Archive Geneva (LNA) 24013.

[15] See correspondence between Inazō Nitobe and Henri Bergson, 5 and 11 October 1922. LNA 24013.

[16] Oskar Halecki. Report as of October 1922. LNA 24013.

[17] Ibid.

publication of a pamphlet on the situation of intellectual life in Austria,[18] Dopsch accepted the invitation Drummond had issued on behalf of Henri Bergson (1859–1941), the president of the League Committee, in a letter dated 31 October 1922. He stated:

> I shall be honored to assume the outlined functions since I sincerely hope to be able to improve the deplorable situation of all those who are involved in intellectual work in Austria. I am prepared to pursue the work required by the Committee. [. . .] I will keep the Committee informed of the needs of intellectual life in Austria, but also provide information and reports in regard to any requests which may be addressed to the League Committee by Austrian institutions and individuals, and further to organize the enquiry on the situation of intellectual workers in Austria, which—according to the friendly message of Prof. Halecki—will be instituted by the Committee. The results will be compiled in a pamphlet.[19]

IV. Who was Alfons Dopsch?

Fritz Fellner considered Alfons Dopsch 'the most eminent Austrian historian',[20] renowned for his 'spirited revision of Western European medieval history'.[21] Joseph A. Schumpeter once called Dopsch 'one of the greatest economic historians of that period [. . .] who contributed to our knowledge of the economic and social institutions and processes of the Middle Ages more than economists ever did'.[22] Dopsch received numerous international academic awards and elected memberships in learned societies, mainly for two reasons: his internationalizing attitude, and the publication of a two-volume book in 1918 and 1920 entitled *The Economic and Social Foundations of European Civilization*.[23] He was appointed as full professor at the University of Vienna in 1900. After serving as rector of the University of Vienna in 1920–21, he declined two offers of chairs at the Universities of Berlin and Munich in favour of a post at the head of an institute, the Seminar for Economic and

[18] Ibid. Dopsch himself received a remuneration of 3,000 francs for the period from 1 November 1922 to 31 August 1923. Oskar Halecki to Sir Herbert Ames, Financial Director of the League of Nations, 10 November 1922. LNA 24013.

[19] Eric Drummond to Alfons Dopsch, 26 October 1922, and Alfons Dopsch to Eric Drummond, 31 October 1922. LNA 24013.

[20] Fritz Fellner, 'Alfons Dopsch' in Lucian Boia et al. (eds), *Great Historians of the Modern Age: An International Dictionary* (Greenwood Press 1991) 49, 49.

[21] Robert F. Forrest, 'Dopsch, Alfons' in *Encyclopedia of Historians and Historical Writing. Vol. 1* (Dearborn 1999) 319.

[22] Joseph A. Schumpeter, *History of Economic Analysis* (Routledge 2006) 750, 776. Peter Schöttler reminds us that Dopsch 'was the only Austrian and one of the few German-speaking historians who were in touch with the [school of] Annales'. Peter Schöttler, 'Lucie Varga—eine österreichische Historikerin im Umkreis der „Annales' (1904–1941)' in Peter Schöttler (ed), Lucie Varga, *Zeitenwende. Mentalitätshistorische Studien 1936–1939* (Suhrkamp 1991) 20.

[23] The book was also published in English, Italian, and Russian.

Cultural History at the University of Vienna, with a dedicated academic assistant at his disposal.[24] Without doubt, Dopsch was a key figure in the late Habsburg and Austrian academic landscape.

Despite his internationalizing attitude, however, he never denied his affiliation with the liberal Greater-German and Catholic-conservative academic milieus, in both of which he was well-connected. 'Born on German-Bohemian soil' in Lobsitz an der Elbe on 14 June 1868, he defined himself as an Austrian of German descent. In his 1925 autobiography, he stated: 'At that time, my political convictions were already avowedly Greater German. We were fascinated by Germany's greatness, and enthused by the idea of unifying all Germans in a common state. I got to know Dresden and Berlin before Prague and Vienna.'[25] Dopsch's strong commitment to a greater German state was also accompanied by anti-Semitic and anti-Slavic attitudes,[26] which he did not conceal. In his autobiography, he traced his critical attitude to source interpretation from his upbringing close to the German-Slavic linguistic border, where he had grown accustomed to responding to 'Slavonic mendacity and duplicity with suspicion, to always keep my eyes open and to accept the affirmations and promises of the enemy (*gegnerische Versicherungen*) only with caution and scepticism.'[27]

In 1889, Dopsch was among the founding members of the Akademischer Verein deutscher Historiker in Wien.[28] While Austria 'struggled for its existence', he participated in the intellectual war effort by lecturing at the Reichsdeutsche Waffenbrüderliche Vereinigung (Imperial German Association of Brothers in Arms) in Berlin in 1917 as well as in Brussels at the invitation of the German Army Administration in 1918. After the collapse of the Empire, he directed a large share of his academic work towards defending the rights of the German-speaking population of Bohemia and Moravia, usually referred to as 'Sudeten Germans'.[29] His nationalist, anti-Slavic attitude is manifest in some of the works he published while participating in the re-internationalization of intellectual life. In 1919, Dopsch put out a booklet, a book chapter and a pamphlet on the Germans in Bohemia,

[24] See Thomas Buchner, 'Alfons Dopsch (1868–1953). Die „Mannigfaltigkeit der Verhältnisse" in Karel Hruza (ed), *Österreichische Historiker 1900–1945* (Böhlau 2008) 155, 162; Thomas Winkelbauer, *Das Fach Geschichte an der Universität Wien* (V&R unipress 2018) 210–218; Anna Vollrath, 'Alfons Dopsch' in Hans-Ulrich Wehler (ed), *Deutsche Historiker Vol. 7* (Vandenhoeck und Ruprecht 1980) 39, 39.

[25] Alfons Dopsch, 'Selbstdarstellung' in Sigrid H. Steinberg (ed), *Die Geschichtswissenschaft der Gegenwart in Selbstdarstellungen Vol. 1* (Meiner 1925) 51, 52.

[26] See Reto Heinzel, *Theodor Mayer. Ein Mittelalterhistoriker im Banne des „Volkstums" 1920–1960* (Schöningh 2016) 30; see also in particular Winkelbauer, *Das Fach Geschichte an der Universität Wien* (n 24) 126.

[27] Dopsch, 'Selbstdarstellung' (n 25) 55.

[28] See Dopsch, 'Selbstdarstellung' (n 25) 58. Dopsch calls it 'Verein deutscher Historiker an der Wiener Universität'. See Winkelbauer, *Das Fach Geschichte an der Universität Wien* (n 24) 150–167, Buchner, 'Dopsch' (n 24) 160; Heinzel, *Theodor Mayer* (n 26) 29.

[29] See Dopsch, 'Selbstdarstellung' (n 25) 84.

whose existence he traced back to the medieval period[30] using historical arguments to defend their 'roots' in his home region.[31] He never joined the National Socialist Party, however, and in 1945 even suggested that 'Party members should automatically be deprived of the honourable position of being a member of the Academy [of Sciences]'.[32] Dopsch himself had been appointed to the Academy in Vienna as corresponding member in 1903 and as ordinary member in 1909 at the recommendation of leading historians and scholars of the time, which made him its longest-serving member in 1945.[33] When his proposal for automatic exclusion of Nazi Party members was threatened with rejection, he withdrew the motion,[34] which had provided him with a unique opportunity to settle an old score: Dopsch's rivals at the Historical Seminar, who were the driving force behind his premature retirement in 1936 and the hostile takeover of his Seminar for Economic and Cultural History, were apparently profiteers of the Nazi regime—not least at the Academy of Sciences, of which they were elected members. One may assume that this was Dopsch's primary motivation for attempting to deprive them of this supreme academic honour.

Dopsch's main achievements for the Academy included the collection and editing of the Carolingian diplomas as part of the *Monumenta Germaniae Historica* as well as the publication of the *Österreichische Urbaria* and the *Österreichische Weisthümer*. He was a member of the Vereinigte Weistümer und Urbaria-Commission for half a century and elected as its chairman in 1922. On his eightieth birthday in 1948, Dopsch was lauded by the Presiding Committee of the Academy for having been 'the first to apply strict historical-philological and palaeographical-diplomatic methods to the analysis of this group of sources, thereby making

[30] Alfons Dopsch, *Die historische Stellung der Deutschen in Böhmen* (Deutsch-Österreichische Staatsdruckerei 1919), published in English as *The Historical Position of the Germans in Bohemia* (Deutsch-Österreichische Staatsdruckerei 1919); Alfons Dopsch, 'Die historische Stellung der Deutschen in Böhmen' in Rudolph Lodgman, Landeshauptmann für Deutschböhmen (ed), *Deutschböhmen* (Ullstein & Co 1919); Alfons Dopsch, *Die historische Stellung der Deutschen in Böhmen* (Flugblätter für Deutschösterreichs Recht 6, Hölder 1919); Heinzel, *Theodor Mayer* (n 26) 29.

[31] Alfons Dopsch, 'Die historische Stellung der Deutschen in Böhmen und Mähren' in Wilhelm Volz (ed), *Der ostdeutsche Volksboden. Aufsätze zu den Fragen des Ostens* (Hirt 1926); Alfons Dopsch, 'Germanische Altsiedlungen in Böhmen' in Heinrich Swoboda (ed), *Epitymbion. Konvolut von verschiedenen historischen Beiträgen, Heinrich Svoboda dargebracht* (Stiepel 1927).

[32] Archive of the Austrian Academy of Sciences (AAAS), Minutes of the General Assembly of 22 June 1945 (A 995). Annex: Dopsch to Späth on 16 June 1945.

[33] Dopsch's promoters included Gustav Winter, director of the k.u.k. Haus-, Hof- und Staatsarchiv; Engelbert Mühlbacher, director of the Institute for Austrian Historical Research; Oswald Redlich, full professor of history and historical auxiliary sciences; Konstantin Jireček, professor of Slavic philology and archaeology; Otto Zallinger, full professor of German law and Austrian history of law; Emil von Ottenthal, full professor of history and historical auxiliary sciences; Joseph Seemüller, professor of German language and literature at the University of Vienna; and Anton Schönbach, professor of German language and literature at the University of Graz. See AAAS, personal file Alfons Dopsch, Congratulatory letter.

[34] See Johannes Feichtinger, Herbert Matis, Stefan Sienell, and Heidemarie Uhl (eds), *The Academy of Sciences in Vienna 1938 to 1945* (Austrian Academy of Sciences Press 2014) 121; 163–166.

scientific analysis of the rent rolls possible for the first time'.[35] It was his scientific approach to these 'antiquities' that led not only to the renewal of the discipline of early medieval economic history but also to his authoritative work *The Economic and Social Foundations of European Civilization*.[36] Although Dopsch's interdisciplinary approach was fairly unusual among German-speaking historians,[37] the international significance of his *Foundations* was recognized from the outset, since its author resolved the ongoing argument in contemporary medieval studies about whether the transition from antiquity to the Middle Ages took place in continuity or in a series of disruptions.[38]

Dopsch was the first historian to reject the theory of a sharp break in European civilization and promote the idea of a continuing process of evolution from Caesar to Charlemagne. Relying on detailed research comprising archaeological, linguistic, and legal source material, he concluded that the 'Germans did not behave as enemies of culture, destroying and abolishing Roman civilization; on the contrary they preserved and developed it. [...] The Roman world was won by the Germans from within, by a peaceful penetration which went on for centuries, during which they absorbed its culture, and even, to a considerable extent, took over its administration'.[39] This implied that there was not a 'fall' of Rome; nor was there a so-called Carolingian renaissance whose foundations had not already been thoroughly laid during the Merovingian period—a period previous historians had largely neglected.

Using a plethora of sources, Dopsch set down the cornerstones for the view of the foundation of European civilization as a continuous process of adoption and 'reciprocal exchange' of artefacts as well as legal and administrative knowledge and practices between the Roman and Germanic cultures. This transition process was characterized not by destruction but by transmission, mixing, and blending, and Dopsch understood it as the result of acquisitions from the East, the West, the South, and the North.[40] The available sources provided evidence for this notion of continuity. From Dopsch's point of view, which was so richly informed by and thoroughly grounded in the sources, the historical process was neither interrupted by individual events nor could it be divided into clearly distinct, self-contained epochs and spaces. Associated as he was with other open-minded Viennese fin-de-siècle

[35] AAAS, Personal file 'Alfons Dopsch. Congratulatory letter, 3' also printed in ÖAW: *Almanach für das Jahr 1949* (Holzhausens Nachfolger 1950) 322–325.

[36] See Winkelbauer, *Das Fach Geschichte an der Universität Wien* (n 24) 122–125.

[37] See August Loehr, 'Die Pflege der wirtschaftsgeschichtlichen und technischen Denkmale in Österreich' (1948) 2 Österreichische Zeitschrift für Denkmalpflege (Prof. Dr. A. Dopsch zum 80. Geburtstag) 1, 1.

[38] For further details see Buchner, 'Dopsch' (n 24) 168–178.

[39] Alfons Dopsch, *The Economic and Social Foundations of European Civilization* (Harcourt, Brace and Co. 1937) 386.

[40] See Alfons Dopsch, 'Vorwort' in Alfons Dopsch, *Wirtschaftliche und soziale Grundlagen der Europäischen Kulturentwicklung. Aus der Zeit von Caesar bis auf Karl den Großen. Vol. 1* (L.W. Seidel & Sohn 1918) VIII. This preface is not included in the English version.

historians of culture (such as Franz Wickhoff and Alois Riegl), Dopsch may in retrospect be considered one of the first scholars to anticipate recent innovative historical approaches such as shared, interconnected, and relational histories, which are widely employed today.[41]

Dopsch's influential work set the stage for that of two other Catholic historians, both of whom argued from a nationalist, anti-Communist viewpoint: the Mussolini-admiring Swiss literature professor Gonzague de Reynold (1880–1970) with his eight-volume work *La Formation de l'Europe*, published between 1944 and 1957, and the Catholic and conservative Polish history professor Oskar Halecki, author of *The Limits and Divisions of European History* (1950). Both de Reynold and Halecki referred to Dopsch, and we may assume that each of them advocated for Dopsch's personal involvement in the ICIC as a result of their reverence for and trust in him: Gonzague de Reynold as one of the twelve members of the ICIC advisory committee, and Oskar Halecki as the secretary of the ICIC. With the support of Marie Curie, de Reynold proposed Dopsch as corresponding member of the ICIC and as its Austrian rapporteur[42] during the very first ICIC session, and as mentioned above, it was Halecki who would eventually informally extend the invitation to Dopsch.

It is notable that, during the final months of the First World War and in its aftermath, Dopsch appealed for the 'inner consistency and international structure'[43] of cultural evolution in Vienna, where he was confronted with the ongoing nationalization process. In his inaugural speech as rector, entitled *The Reconstruction of Europe after the Fall of the Ancient World* and delivered on 26 October 1920 at the University of Vienna, he referred once again to his central argument that the referenced transition process was characterized by continuity and not by a sharp cultural break as the humanists had argued. In his speech, Dopsch emphasized certain similarities between the past and the dreadful conditions prevailing in contemporary Austria. He concluded:

> Nevertheless, I do not want to speak pessimistically today of a decline of civilisation. Precisely this historical approach instead enables us, so I believe, to proclaim good tidings [*frohe Botschaft*], and especially to be a guiding star for the future for

[41] On the Habsburg Central European epistemological approach in scholarship and science, see Johannes Feichtinger, *Wissenschaft als reflexives Projekt. Von Bolzano über Freud zu Kelsen: Österreichische Wissenschaftsgeschichte 1848–1918* (Transcript 2010); Johannes Feichtinger, 'Kakanian Mélange, Habsburg Central Europe and the Shift from the Study of Identity to the Study of Similarity' in Anil Bhatti and Dorothee Kimmich (eds), *Similarity: A Paradigm for Culture Theory* (Tulika Books and Columbia University Press 2018); Johannes Feichtinger, 'Intellectual Affinities: Ernst Mach, Sigmund Freud, Hans Kelsen and the Austrian Anti-Essentialist Approach to Science and Scholarship' in Ian Bryan, Peter Langford, and John McGarry (eds), *The Foundation of the Juridico-Political: Concept Formation in Hans Kelsen and Max Weber* (Routledge 2016).

[42] Marie Curie initially proposed Stefan Meyer, the director of the Institute of Radium Research (Academy of Sciences), whom she had known well for years, for the position of Austrian correspondent.

[43] Dopsch, Vorwort (n 40) IX.

> you, my dear young colleagues. You are the new generation who will have to carry out the upcoming reconstruction effort or, at the least, to play a decisive role in it. Show yourselves worthy of your ancient German ancestors.[44]

Dopsch's optimistic idea that this decline could also provide an opportunity for a fresh start would prove to be a crucial argument—and one that would open many new doors for him, not least in the context of intellectual internationalism.

V. Dopsch's Move

Using the budget provided by the League, Dopsch hired Dr Herbert Patzelt, the brother of his student and close collaborator Erna Patzelt, as his assistant and set up a new office equipped with its own telephone line. As we know from Dopsch's bi-monthly reports to the League Committee, he was fully occupied with promoting Austrian intellectual work and workers [*Geistesarbeiter*] in Geneva during the following year. As a first measure, he established a book and periodicals exchange programme between the Austrian National Library and international institutions (such as the Department of Scientific and Industrial Exchange in London, the Chemical Society of London, and the University of Calcutta) that were willing to send their publications for scientific use in Austria. He also handled financial gifts from the Kyushu Imperial University of Japan to the University of Vienna. Next he conducted an in-depth questionnaire-based survey on intellectual life in Austria as part of the general enquiry organized by the Geneva Committee. The survey included more than 450 persons and institutions in Vienna and the provinces—among them academic and scientific societies, universities, libraries, archives, museums, and prominent individual artists and writers. The number of questionnaires sent out to recipients across Austria is surprising when compared to other countries: only twelve questionnaires were sent out in Bulgaria, 30 in Yugoslavia, 50 in Romania, 52 in Greece, 140 in Hungary and 200 in Czechoslovakia. By processing such a high number of questionnaires, Dopsch clearly intended to signify the existence of an outstandingly developed intellectual landscape in Austria—even though it was deemed to be in great distress. Based on this source material, he produced a detailed study of intellectual life in the new Austrian Republic. The pamphlet was a mere fifty pages long, and was published in French and English in 1924 under the title *Conditions of Intellectual Work and Workers [in Austria]*.[45] Both the study and its impressive source material are practically unknown in Austria today.

[44] Alfons Dopsch, 'Der Wiederaufbau Europas nach dem Untergange der Alten Welt. Inaugurationsrede' in *Die feierliche Inauguration des Rektors der Wiener Universität für das Studienjahr 1920/21, am 26. Oktober 1920* (University in-house-publisher 1920) 61, 65; 80.

[45] Alfons Dopsch, *League of Nations. Committee on Intellectual Co-operation. Enquiry into the Conditions of Intellectual Work. Intellectual Life in the Various Countries. Austria. Conditions of Intellectual Work and Workers* (League of Nations 1924).

Last but not least, Dopsch formed the Austrian national committee of the ICIC, which he dubbed the Österreichische Landeskommission für geistige Zusammenarbeit, Wien—Zentrale Völkerbund Genf, under his chairmanship. It was composed of eminent intellectuals representing its leading institutions.[46]

The inaugural meeting was held on 28 April 1923 at Dopsch's Seminar at the University of Vienna. At the very beginning, its members adopted a joint statement asserting that they considered themselves representatives of (Greater) Germany, performing intellectual work in cooperation with their colleagues in the 'Reich'. Three resolutions were adopted and communicated to the ICIC at Geneva: the first referred to the dismissal of academic officials from public collections, museums, and libraries as a result of the reform programme directed in Austria under the auspices of the League of Nations. The second pertained to the protection of cultural property and the rejection of 'unjustified demands' of the successor states asking for objects from Austrian archives, museums, and collections, and the third was related to international exchange programmes for academic personnel, the nomination of experts to international sub-committees and other League organizations, and the recommendation of delegates to congresses and meetings under the auspices of the League. It is not clear to what extent the Austrian National Committee actually contributed to implementing these measures, however. What is certain is that public collections, museums, and libraries remained in operation and that the international exchange of personnel and publications was extended to institutions outside of academia. The eminent Austrian historian Alphons Lhotsky later praised Dopsch for his informational work thanks to which 'the European public soon began to recognise the serious consequences of significant damage to the Austrian cultural monument holdings'.[47]

As Dopsch soon discovered, however, his initiatives would receive only minimal support from the Austrian government—and none from the Vienna-based League Commissioner-General of Austrian Finances, Alfred Rudolf Zimmermann. Within the ICIC, it was tacitly understood that 'any vexed questions'—for instance,

[46] The founding members of the Vienna committee included Josef Bick (director general of the Austrian National Library), Arnold Durig (professor of physiology, University of Vienna), August Loehr (Federal Monuments Office), Joseph Marx (president of the Music Academy, Vienna), Hans Sperl (professor of law and governmental sciences), Gustav Walker (professor of civil law), Ferdinand Schmutzer (rector of the Academy of Fine Arts, Vienna), Emil Artmann (rector of the Vienna College of Technology), and Richard Wettstein (professor of botany and vice-president of the Academy of Sciences). At the committee's second meeting, Anton Wildgans, poet and former director of the Vienna Burgtheater, and Alfred Roller, co-founder of the Viennese Secession and later its president, were co-opted. The composition of the committee chaired by Alfons Dopsch reads like a who-is-who of the mostly Catholic, conservative and German-oriented intellectual elite of interwar Austria. For the minutes of its meetings (1923–1938), see the Dopsch Papers at the Archive of the University of Vienna (AUV) and the papers of August Loehr at the AAAS.

[47] Alphons Lhotsky, 'Die Verteidigung der Wiener Sammlungen kultur- und naturhistorischer Denkmäler durch die Erste Republik' (1955) 63 Mitteilungen des Instituts für Österreichische Geschichtsforschung 614, 626.

the issue of providing financial assistance—'should be avoided'.[48] As a result, Oscar Halecki was forced to tell the eminent representatives of Austrian intellectual life convened for the meeting at the University of Vienna in October 1922 that 'unfortunately the Committee has no money to spend for directly assisting intellectual workers in any country'.[49]

VI. The ICIC Breaks New Ground

In the first year of its existence, the ICIC operated in declaratory mode without taking any visible initiatives. It limited its activities to surveying the needs of intellectual life in the newly established Central European states, and especially in Austria. As it was not included in the League of Nations Covenant, its authority was based solely on resolutions adopted by the Assembly in 1921, measures laid down by the Council in 1922, and the authority of its individual members. The ICIC's scope was restricted by the hierarchical structure of the League organization, a lack of League funding, and the logic of the postwar order, which was shaped by the League's ambivalent stance towards the successor states of the former enemy powers. Patricia Clavin speaks of an 'elite victors' club',[50] while Daniel Laqua formulates the 'key problem' the ICIC had to deal with as follows: while the Committee was a 'vessel for efforts to create [a new international] order [. . .], intellectual cooperation relied on the very structures that it sought to transform'.[51] The ICIC thus shirked the most sensitive issue at hand, namely the providing of financial assistance to states whose intellectual life suffered from a catastrophic lack of funding, but which were regarded as successors of the former enemies. Against this background, the Norwegian ICIC member Kristine Bonnevie (1872–1948), who is renowned to this day as Norway's first female professor and the first female member of the Norwegian Academy of Science and Letters, raised an awkward question at the ICIC's second session on 27 July 1923. She enquired whether the Committee on Intellectual Cooperation had ever made 'any appeals [. . .] with the view to raising funds'.[52] Another Committee member, Goldsworthy Lowes Dickinson (1862–1932), a Fellow of King's College in Cambridge and peace activist, supported Bonnevie's question and put forth resolutions with the following contents: firstly, what was most urgently needed was the provision of material assistance to the universities in the war-torn countries of Europe; secondly, the

48 Committee on Intellectual Co-operation (ICIC). Minutes of the Second Session, July 26th to August 2nd, 1923, Geneva, 1 September 1923. LNA.

49 Oskar Halecki. Report as of October 1922. LNA 24013.

50 Patricia Clavin, 'The Austrian Hunger Crisis and the Genesis of International Organization after the First World War' (2014) 90/2 International Affairs 265, 277.

51 Laqua, Transnational Intellectual Cooperation (n 4) 226.

52 ICIC. Minutes of the Second Session, 19.

Committee should seek to raise money for distribution by appealing to universities, institutions, and societies in the USA and the less distressed countries of Europe; and thirdly, it should consider asking the League of Nations Council to intercede with state governments.[53]

The chairman, Henri Bergson, felt it necessary to tell Lowes Dickinson that neither asking for nor distributing money had been the Committee's responsibility up to that point, and added that such an appeal might give rise to criticism. Lowes Dickinson was adamant, however, presenting his proposal as 'a very happy innovation'.[54] Despite attempts from some members to stifle it with the argument 'that the Committee had considered intellectual rather than pecuniary assistance as its chief programme',[55] the Committee finally decided upon 'immediate action', that is 'to issue an appeal for funds'.[56] Rather than stopping at merely showing 'international solidarity',[57] the League Committee drew up 'a systematic scheme of action'[58] that heralded a new era in international intellectual cooperation.

The foundation of the scheme was twofold: forming national committees in those countries that had suffered as a result of the war as well as those whose intellectual life had been less severely affected by the crisis, and raising and distributing funds for pecuniary assistance.[59] This new scheme was ultimately approved by the League Council in December 1923. In 1924, League secretary-general Eric Drummond asked the governments of the member states 'to be good enough to consider the possibility of forming a national committee' and 'to lend their moral and financial support to these national committees'.[60] New national committees were subsequently set up in the 'more favoured' countries in Europe and around the world; for example in Australia, Belgium, Brazil, Cuba, Finland, France, Japan, Norway, Sweden, Switzerland, and the USA. Finally, an appeal was issued on behalf of the national committees on intellectual cooperation, which were intended to distribute the allocated funds.[61]

It has hitherto not been fully recognized that Dopsch's move outlined above contributed significantly to the reform of international intellectual cooperation practices and their future strategic focus. In March 1923, Oskar Halecki praised Dopsch in the Krakow-based journal *Contemporary Review* for submitting

[53] Ibid, 19.
[54] Ibid, 19.
[55] Ibid, 19.
[56] Ibid, 21.
[57] Ibid, 19.
[58] League of Nations. Secretary-General. Draft letter to the Governments, 2 January 1924. LNA 31902.
[59] See ICIC. Minutes of the Second Session, 21.
[60] League of Nations. Secretary-General. Draft letter to the Governments, 2 January 1924. LNA 31902.
[61] See League of Nations, *League of Nations. Intellectual Co-operation Organization. National Committees on Intellectual Co-operation* (League of Nations 1937). The German committee was established in 1928, and by 1938, there were more than fifty national committees.

'noteworthy applications' to the ICIC.[62] In the run-up to the Committee's second session in the summer of that year, Dopsch (as corresponding member) demanded that the ICIC replace the policy of proclamation with a scheme of action. The full members Bonnevie and Lowes Dickinson took up this initiative, with the result that the new policy was ultimately adopted. ICIC secretary Halecki, on the other hand, agreed with those members who attempted to stifle the proposal with the argument that 'the Committee had considered intellectual rather than pecuniary assistance as its chief programme'.[63] Although well acquainted with the needs of the individual Central European states, Halecki reaffirmed the ICIC's initial policy of enquiry and promotion of intellectual exchange rather than financial assistance as the appropriate tool for the Central European countries. Since the 'majority […] owed their independence to the late war', Halecki pointed out in his (somewhat biased) report that the Central European states had undergone an 'extraordinary development (creation of new universities, learned societies, research institutions, libraries, etc.)'.[64] He promoted the idea of intellectual rather than pecuniary assistance, which would 'allow these countries to come out of their isolation by means of exchanges of professors and students, above all, of books and periodicals'.[65] In their specific approaches concerning suitable means of assistance, Dopsch and Halecki thus replicated the divergent postwar experiences within the region as a whole. The Austrian Republic inherited the fully developed intellectual life of the Habsburg Empire; its intellectual elites were faced with the trauma of a dissolved Empire and a threat to intellectual institutions and actors that needed to be rescued via external funding. The Republic of Poland had newly emerged as an independent state; its intellectual elite revelled in the triumph of national rebirth. For one-and-a-half centuries, Poland's intellectual community in particular had been partitioned between Russia, Prussia, and Austria. Positioned as it was at the *Borderlands of Western Civilization*,[66] Halecki noted 'a spontaneous desire for relief and for collaboration with the great Western countries' to prevent 'acute disappointment'. Thus to him 'the question was not so much one of financial support as of intellectual assistance'.[67]

In the first year of its existence, the Geneva Committee primarily carried out research on science- and scholarship-related issues. The ICIC was composed of representatives of the academic world, and its work was done within three subcommittees for bibliography, inter-university relations, and intellectual property.

[62] Oskar Halecki, 'Komisja Współpracy Umysłowej [Commission for Intellectual Cooperation] II' (1923) 12 *Przegląd Współczesny* [Contemporary Review] 28, 35, see also Brzeziński, 'Oskar Halecki' (n 11) 10–11.

[63] ICIC. Minutes of the Second Session, 11.

[64] Ibid, 11.

[65] Ibid, 12.

[66] See Oskar Halecki, *Borderlands of Western Civilization: A History of East Central Europe* (Ronald Press 1952).

[67] ICIC. Minutes of the Second Session, 12.

Dopsch was involved in establishing the ICIC in his capacity as rector of the University of Vienna, and he proposed a broad agenda of international cultural cooperation to be pursued by the new League body from the very beginning. On 23 June 1921, the Austrian chancellor Josef Schober submitted a scheme of future work drafted by Franz Matsch, son of the famous Viennese art nouveau painter of the same name, and approved by Alfons Dopsch and Oswald Redlich, the president of the Academy of Sciences in Vienna. Matsch, who was attached to the League of Nations office at the Austrian Ministry of Foreign Affairs,[68] and the two other men argued for the establishment of an independent body whose 'business would be to encourage and to organize discussion and cooperation between the leading men in the spheres of art, literature, music, trade, industry, science education etc.' The underlying idea of this comprehensive approach was that 'international peace' and a 'sincere understanding among the nations' could only be achieved if the body to be formed were able to inspire 'the great masses' with the 'League spirit'.[69] Ultimately, the approach proposed by Matsch, Dopsch, and Redlich was not reflected in the initial composition of the ICIC. Its twelve full members included only eminent academics but no representatives of cultural life. In the course of his work at the ICIC, Dopsch nevertheless worked relentlessly to promote his proposed approach—and as mentioned above, the Austrian National Committee included representatives from both the academic and cultural heritage spheres from the outset. In retrospect, we can now see that the Austrian committee played a significant part in the ICIC's focal shift from international academic cooperation to the internationalization of cultural affairs.[70] The innovative idea of applying the principle of cross-border cooperation to the cultural heritage sphere became reality when the French government offered funds to establish a new International Institute of Intellectual Cooperation (IIIC) operating at the disposal of the Geneva Committee and as its executive instrument. The Paris-based Institute opened in 1926 and worked on a wide range of academic and non-academic subjects including international issues relating to music, literature, and the arts, as well as international relations between museums. In the same year, the IIIC established an International Museums Office (Office international des musées). Furthermore, in 1928, the International Educational Cinematographic Institute (IECI)—also part of the League—was founded in Rome.[71] The Paris Institute was one outcome of the new scheme of action drawn up by the ICIC in 1923.

[68] See Franz von Matsch, *Die Tätigkeit und Organisation des Völkerbundes* (In-house-publisher 1921).

[69] Johann Schober to James Eric Drummond, 29 July 1921 (including an 'Explanatory Statement' on 'International Intellectual Cooperation'). Dossiers. LNA 1-7, 1922.

[70] See August Loehr, 'Bericht über die Österreichische Landeskommission für geistige Zusammenarbeit' [1937]. AAAS, 'August Loehr Papers' (n 46); August Loehr, 'Internationale Zusammenarbeit auf dem Gebiete der Numismatik' (1936) 29 *Numismatische Zeitschrift* 3, 4–5.

[71] See Zimmern, 'The League and International Intellectual Co-operation' (n 1) 147; *The International Institute of Intellectual Co-operation* (IIIC 1930) 10.

Finally, Dopsch also helped to pave the way for German cooperation, in particular through the International Committee of Historical Sciences (ICHS) established in Geneva in 1926. After the First World War, Germany was excluded from many international (scientific) endeavours. Since Austria had joined the League and its bodies in 1920, Dopsch was ideally suited for the key role of intermediator and arbiter. In 1923, Austrian historians were invited to the international historical congress at Brussels but refused to attend out of solidarity with their German colleagues, who were not invited. With the endorsement of Halecki and the ICIC, Dopsch enabled the Association of German Historians to participate in the upcoming international congress in Oslo in 1928—a first since 1913. Dopsch had received assurance from the ICHS that German would be recognized as an official conference language. Germany also joined the International Committee of Historical Sciences,[72] with Dopsch elected vice-president (alongside president Henri Pirenne),[73] a position he held until 1933.

VII. Epilogue: Dopsch's Anger with the ICIC

In 1923, Alfons Dopsch was invited to attend the ICIC's second session in Geneva, scheduled for the end of July. This session would be the ground-breaking meeting in which the Committee adopted its new mode of action (see above). On his way to Geneva, Dopsch spent his summer holidays in Vill, on the outskirts of Innsbruck. But while he was there, his amicable understanding with the ICIC came to a sudden end. Rather than continuing on to Geneva, Dopsch returned to Vienna and threatened to resign as Austrian correspondent if the Geneva Committee failed to provide generous support for the intellectual workers of Austria.[74]

In June 1923, three copies of his lengthy study on intellectual life in Austria in German, English, and French reached the Secretariat of the League in Geneva. The trigger for this dispatch was a letter Dopsch received from Inazō Nitobe, Under-Secretary-General of the League, in which he was asked to write a short, 5,500-word resumé of his study for presentation at the session of the ICIC. Dopsch misunderstood Nitobe's request, assuming that the abstract was to replace the printed pamphlet, which he had originally been told could run to eighty pages.[75] In

72 See Karl Dietrich Erdmann, *Toward a Global Community of Historians: The International Historical Congresses and the International Committee of Historical Sciences, 1898–2000* (Berghahn Books 2005) 80, 102–103, 105, 109.

73 Dopsch agreed with Henri Pirenne in denying the break between Roman and early medieval civilization. However, he disagreed with Pirenne's belief that there was a break at the time of the Arab invasion. The 'Pirenne thesis' was elaborated by the Belgian historian in an address given at the international congress of historians in Oslo in 1928. See Rudolf Neck, 'Alfons Dopsch und seine Schule' in Wolf Frühauf (ed), *Wissenschaft und Weltbild. Festschrift für Hertha Firnberg* (Europaverlag 1975) 369, 374–375; and Buchner, 'Dopsch' (n 24) 163.

74 Alfons Dopsch to Inazō Nitobe, 15 August 1923. LNA 24013.

75 See Inazō Nitobe to Alfons Dopsch, 28 June 1923, and Dopsch's reply on 3 July 1923. LNA 24013.

addition, immediately before he left for Geneva, Dopsch was told that negotiations in preparation of the second session of the ICIC had already begun on 23 July 1923, whereas he had been invited to attend from 26 July. The late invitation made him suspicious that he was being treated like a second-rate member of the committee. In a letter to Nitobe on 25 July, Dopsch expressed his anger about the situation:

> When I was elected a member of the Commission internationale de coopération intellectuelle in the autumn of 1922, this happened without any application on my part. [...] Although I dedicated myself with zeal to the good cause, unfortunately, I had to experience one disappointment after another. I was only elected a 'corresponding member' at the time, this exceptional position over against the other members being motivated by the fact that a numerus clausus had to be respected. As soon as a post became free, I was supposed to move into it. However, when Einstein left his position, not I, but a Dutchman was elected full member. I personally overlooked this affront in the interest of serving the good cause for its own sake. [...] When I had finished my report, I found out to my great surprise that Dr Martin had been commissioned in Geneva to write a special report on the situation of the musicians in Austria. But I was officially informed that only a short extract of my report was to be printed, [... although] 80 quarto pages were promised. Furthermore, I found out at the last minute that proceedings of the special commission would begin on 23 July, whereas I was invited from the 26th onwards. [...] Finally, my situation in Vienna and with regard to my Austrian colleagues also became increasingly unpleasant, since to this day nothing has happened in response to the various requests and petitions made in the course of the year.[76]

In a letter dated 23 August 1923, Dopsch renewed and aggravated his accusations: he justified his threat of resignation with the deep disappointment felt by the very same Austrian institutions that had expected immediate financial support from the Committee after filling in the questionnaires Dopsch had sent them. Although the sources do not document this directly, it is clear that he had come under pressure from the Austrian institutions, which were disappointed by the fact that he had been unable to benefit them in his capacity as mediator, albeit by no fault of his own. He therefore blamed the Geneva Committee for lacking a systematic scheme of action, pointing out that a policy of resolutions could be no substitute for practical action to achieve results. It was during the very ICIC session Dopsch's anger caused him to miss, however, that Kristin Bonnevie put his dilemma into words with the following statement: 'It should not be forgotten that many universities were working with a reduced staff and would not willingly reply

[76] Alfons Dopsch to Inazō Nitobe, 25 July 1923. LNA 24013.

to questionnaires addressed to them for the purpose of carrying out an enquiry, which did not immediately show promise of some practical result.'[77]

Bonnevie was referring to the rigorous stabilization policy the League had imposed on Austria with the 'Geneva Protocol': for the granting of loans to Austria, the government had agreed to hand over state finance to an intergovernmental body, which appointed Alfred Rudolf Zimmermann, the anti-communist former mayor of Rotterdam, as Commissioner-General of Austrian Finances. Zimmermann's reduction of state expenditure had a direct impact on Austrian universities, museums, public collections, libraries, and archives, which saw massive reductions in staff and material equipment. Some 50,000 civil servants were dismissed in total.[78] When Dopsch had approached the Commissioner-General, the latter had 'systematically denied support even for the most urgent necessities' in the field of intellectual work.[79]

Drummond's abovementioned appeal to the League's member states had at least some effect: although there was immediate no offer of substantial financial assistance for the Austrian intellectual workers, Dopsch was at least able to garner 10 to 20 million crowns from the Austrian government for the running of the Austrian national committee. The appeal also produced unexpected drawbacks that the members of the Vienna Committee complained of time and again, however. Newspapers reported on considerable private aid for Austrian universities, giving rise to the mistaken belief both at home and abroad that Austria's universities had been saved. At the same time, the League widely disseminated the view that Austria had entered a recovery phase, and proclaimed its effort to restore balance to the national budget a success. It is not surprising that the Austrian National Committee strongly protested this policy of spreading misinformation about Austria's economic recovery. A memorandum entitled *On the Situation of the Scientific Institutions and Enterprises in Austria in the Year 1925* was written to clarify the origins of the false assumption that the Austrian university system had made a decisive recovery from its precarious situation.[80] The memorandum argued that cultural life had in no way benefited from the stabilization policy implemented by the League. Rather, it showed that the annual higher education budget allocated by the League amounted to only 36 per cent of the prewar budget, and that this reduction placed the Austrian university system in a permanent state of emergency.

Dopsch was in a tricky situation. He had promoted an international initiative that had promised to aid his country's intellectual culture but effectively ended up harming it. He ultimately decided not to resign his post as mediator, although he

77 ICIC. Minutes of the Second Session, 17.

78 See Clavin, 'The Austrian Hunger Crisis' (n 50) 276–277.

79 Alfons Dopsch to Inazō Nitobe, 15 August 1923. LNA 24013.

80 AUV, Dopsch Papers. Protocol. Ninth meeting of the Landeskommission für geistige Zusammenarbeit, Vienna, 4 December 1925, and Denkschrift ueber die Lage der wissenschaftlichen Institute und Unternehmungen in Oesterreich im Jahre 1925.

openly expressed his outrage at the actions of the ICIC to the head of the legal section of the Austrian Federation of the League of Nations:

> As chairman of the Austrian national committee, which is a branch of the League's Commission Internationale de Coopération Intellectuelle, I have had to undergo the very worst [*allerübelsten*] experiences. Even the very best recommendations are not taken into consideration […]. The Geneva Commission and its executive Institute founded and funded in Paris by the French government are overwhelmingly serving the political goals of France and its vassal states, especially the Little Entente. The so-called representatives of German science, Einstein and Schulze-Gaevernitz, were elected without the knowledge of the German scientific community and do not have its support, but rather are entirely isolated. […] What must be considered a disadvantage, however, to intellectual work in Austria is the misleading representation of the state of Austrian intellectual work that the Geneva Commission has publicly disseminated in its writings. This state has not at all improved. […] The misrepresentation of the Geneva Commission has caused us to lose almost all the financial support from outside Austria that once kept our head above water. These and other similar facts have not only caused great resentment within the Austrian national committee, but also strengthened our conviction that this kind of intellectual cooperation is completely worthless for us.[81]

VIII. Conclusion

Looking back on the work of the International Committee on Intellectual Cooperation, one may arrive at rather an ambivalent assessment of its effect. On the one hand, it paved the way for Austria's early reintegration into the system of intellectual cooperation after the First World War. On the other, the cooperation scheme did not make a decisive improvement to the deplorable situation of Austria's intellectual workers. Dopsch was an attractive recruitment for the ICIC, since he had published a well-received two-volume book on the foundations of European civilization in 1918 and 1920 in which he stressed the optimistic idea of historical continuity through peaceful interaction and reciprocal exchange.

Dopsch worked hard to obtain his secure position at the heart of Austrian academia. His trailblazing research on hitherto untapped medieval source material and his nationalist political convictions, which gave him access to the tightly knit pan-German network of Austrian professional academics, both contributed significantly to his soaring academic career in Vienna and facilitated his future

[81] Alfons Dopsch to Josef Kunz, 24 November 1925. AUV, Dopsch Papers (n 80).

involvement in international intellectual cooperation. It was Dopsch's firm position as a nationalist scholar that paved the way for his integration into the new, international network of academics that was being established after the war. This network included members who today are increasingly viewed as internationalists-cum-nationalists of conservative and Catholic conviction. It was Oskar Halecki and Gonzague de Reynold who were decisive in advocating Dopsch's membership in the ICIC, and he made good use of his status. His activities in Vienna helped to prepare the return of German scholars onto the international stage and shaped the future actions and strategic focus of international cooperation on a grand scale. Yet Dopsch never concealed his frustration about how the League's programme unfolded, and his complaints brought about a shift in the ICIC's policy from mere resolutions and recommendations to concrete action. For the first time, the ICIC extended its main scope of activity—international cooperation—from academia into the cultural heritage sphere. In view of the rich imperial tradition of promoting cultural life, Dopsch's Vienna branch of the ICIC felt responsible for the fields of both academia and culture—and their institutions such as universities, libraries, archives, and museums—from its inception. This shift in international intellectual cooperation, which took place in the mid-1920s, paved the way for the strategy UNESCO would adopt after 1945. After the Second World War, Dopsch lived to see UNESCO remake the international order afresh, including the reestablishment of his masterpiece as the Austrian UNESCO Commission for International Intellectual Cooperation.

PART II
REMAKING TERRITORIES AND BORDERS

8

Remaking Mobility

International Conferences and the Emergence of the Modern Passport System

*Peter Becker**

I. Introduction

In 1927, Sigismund Gargas, a migration expert of Polish descent, mused about the emergence of the postwar passport system. Born in 1876, he had experienced the almost unrestricted mobility for people of at least modest means within Western and Central Europe before the First World War—an experience closely connected to the 'general ascendance of political and economic liberalism' in the last decades of the nineteenth century. Seen from the vantage point of the 1920s, these open borders represented conditions akin to a 'fairy tale'—except for those individuals who had been mistreated as prospective emigrants by imperial authorities before the war and who likely framed their experience more as a nightmare than a fable.[1]

Gargas traced the origins of the modern passport system to the autocratic regime of Russian Tsarism and to wartime practices of closed borders and the systematic control of individual mobility.[2] The interruption of the flow of people and goods was one of the many challenges for postwar states, and there is a widely shared consensus that the modern passport system, which endured until the implementation of the Schengen Agreement, was born out of the political, social, and economic catastrophe brought about by the Great War.[3] It is true that the Conference on Passports, Customs Formalities and Through Tickets convened by the League of Nations in Paris in October 1920 defined an international standard for travel

* I would like to thank Patricia Clavin, David Petruccelli, Martin Schaffner, Glenda Sluga, and Natasha Wheatley for their invaluable comments.

[1] Sigismund Gargas, *Das internationale Passproblem* (Haag 1927) 18; cf. Tara Zahra, 'Travel agents on trial: Policing mobility in East Central Europe, 1889–1989' (2004) 223 Past and Present 161, 163 and 168–173, where she presents the administrative hurdles placed in the way of peasants heading towards the US as emigrants.

[2] Gargas, *Passproblem* (n 1) 17.

[3] Cf. Craig Robertson, *The Passport in America: The History of a Document* (Oxford University Press 2015) 219; Mark B. Salter, *Rights of Passage. The Passport in International Relations* (Boulder 2003) 78; George F. Kohn, 'The organization and the work of the League of Nations' (1924) 114/1 The Annals of the American Academy of Political and Social Science 5, 49.

Peter Becker, *Remaking Mobility* In: *Remaking Central Europe*. Edited by: Peter Becker and Natasha Wheatley, Oxford University Press (2020). © the many contributors. DOI: 10.1093/oso/9780198854685.003.0009

documents and worked hard to win over postwar states to implement it. If we look more closely at state measures and policies related to the developments in passport practices, however, it is much less plausible to claim the birth of a 'globally standardized passport system'[4] in 1920 and attribute this achievement to the League.

In his historical account of the passport in America, Craig Robertson argues that the League conferences 'ended up cementing the wartime system', and although this may be taking the argument too far, there is nevertheless a grain of truth in his statement. The new passport regime resembled the wartime conditions for individual mobility far more closely than the prewar ones. Still, the modalities for individual mobility during the interwar years differed from the travel restrictions put in place during the war. Compared to the modern, standardized passport system that emerged during the 1920s, travel restrictions during the Great War were a monstrous travesty, with exit visas for citizens and foreigners, passports issued for single journeys, and a costly and cumbersome process of applying for travel documents.[5]

The League as an institutional pillar of a new international order was also not particularly eager to create a modern regime of restrictions to individual mobility. Instead, it was an outspoken supporter of a return to the prewar conditions of open borders. The League organized two major international conferences on the topic, one in 1920 and one in 1926, and supported the Austrian government in convening the regional conference in Graz in 1922. Its bodies urged states to abolish the passport system as soon as possible, and they were encouraged in this endeavour by influential institutions like the International Chamber of Commerce (ICC)[6] as well as by public opinion.

In his book, Gargas identified the successor states of the Habsburg monarchy as part of the vanguard in the struggle against travel restrictions:

> The first active reaction began, characteristically, in an area that had formed a coherent whole before the war, particularly in terms of economic and customs policy including passport law, where the trips that became more of an inter-state journey after the war had the character of domestic travel: in the lands of the former Austro-Hungarian Empire.[7]

The breakup of the Dual Monarchy into individual nation states left these new states with 'phantom borders' that limited their integration efforts through the divisive effects of different social, legal, and political practices.[8] The defunct monarchy

[4] Cf. Sina Arnold, Sebastian Bischoff, and Jana König, 'Postnationale Potenziale: Praktiken jenseits der Nation' (2018) 68/48 APuZ 27, 30.

[5] Cf. Robertson, *Passport* (n 3) 219.

[6] On the position of the ICC, cf. Gargas, *Passproblem* (n 1) 21.

[7] Gargas, *Passproblem* (n 1) 18.

[8] Cf. Hannes Grandits, Beatrice von Hirschhausen, Claudia Kraft, Dietmar Müller, and Thomas Serrier, ‚Phantomgrenzen im östlichen Europa: Eine wissenschaftliche Positionierung', in Hannes

did indeed have a remarkable afterlife in 'concrete aspects of society and political culture', as Claire Morelon observes.[9] This posed an equally difficult challenge for the new states as the sudden establishment of borders, which cut through and broke up close-knit networks of social, family, and economic ties within relatively highly developed regions. The conference in Graz brought together the successor states of Austria-Hungary in a first attempt to facilitate the movement of people across the new state borders. While it was unable to fulfil its ambitious goals of abolishing passport and visa formalities, it nevertheless made a significant contribution to the emergence of the modern, standardized passport regime.

The mentioned conferences were occasions for the member states and experts of the League as well as representatives of business interests to debate a consensual strategy for facilitating individual mobility as part of an attempt to revive communication and transit after the war. Compared to the dramatic changes in international relations, the breakup of empires, ideological challenges from the left and right, and endemic economic problems at the national and international level, however, the passport question was a rather secondary issue. For several years, it was unclear how the governance of individual mobility would be reorganized. Immediately after the war, the French government even 'refrained from a particular and costly change to the national passport [...] "as there is reason to believe that the passport will presently be abolished"'.[10]

Looking at the results of the international congresses organized under the auspices of the League of Nations, the mission to abolish passports was obviously not accomplished, and the modern, standardized passport system ultimately emerged instead of the intended return to open borders. This system was based on the authority of states to control the movement of their own populations as well as that of foreigners who wished to enter them. The key position of states within this new governance of mobility placed stateless persons in a hopeless situation: lacking the protection and support of a government vis-à-vis other states, they were trapped. In concrete terms, they could not apply for travel documents and were thus unable to venture into countries with better opportunities for themselves and their families. To help Russian and Armenian refugees out of this impasse, Fridtjof Nansen, the high commissioner of the League's refugee organization, proposed a 'certificate delivered by national authorities on the recommendation of the High Commissioner [...] which was accepted as the equivalent of a passport by more

Grandits, Beatrice von Hirschhausen, Claudia Kraft, Dietmar Müller, and Thomas Serrier (eds), *Phantomgrenzen: Räume und Akteure in der Zeit neu denken* (Wallstein 2015) 13.

[9] Claire Morelon, 'Introduction' in Paul Miller and Claire Morelon (eds), *Embers of Empire: Continuity and Rupture in the Habsburg Successor States after 1918* (Berghahn 2018) 1, 6.

[10] Sara Kalm, 'Standardizing Movements: The International Passport Conferences of the 1920s' [2017/8] STANCE Working Papers Series 24.

than fifty countries'. This so-called Nansen passport was formally adopted at a conference in Geneva in July 1922.[11]

We should not be too quick to frame the contest between open borders and the standardized passport regime in terms of the opposition between liberal internationalism and 'Old-Worldism', however.[12] The Old World could not serve this purpose, since it actually stood for open borders. The representatives of the states rejecting the abolition of passports were not attempting to turn back time, nor were they simply short-sighted nationalists. They were responding to the complex reality of the early postwar years.

The Kingdom of Serbs, Croats, and Slovenes (or Kingdom of SHS for short), as well as Romania, to provide two examples from the Habsburg successor states, were driven by concerns about political stability under the daunting conditions of demobilization, political turmoil in the region, and severe economic problems.[13] The challenge of integrating legally, politically, and to some extent, ethnically diverse territories, was aggravated by fear of the national and political 'other', which war propaganda and the experience of wartime oppression against the Slavic population in the Habsburg Monarchy had imprinted strongly in the minds of the people. This almost paranoid attitude was not restricted to the successor states of Austria-Hungary, however, as the representative of Latvia—a state with an imperial past that had been a battleground for Polish and Soviet troops—made very clear during the 1926 conference: he strictly refused a change to the process of issuing of transit visas, arguing that 'any alteration of its [Latvia's] present method might lead to the introduction within its borders of a second Trojan horse.'[14]

Even great powers with strong liberal records were hesitant to return to the prewar system. Charles R. Pusta from Estonia, the president of the passport conference convened in Geneva in May 1926, proved this in his concluding remarks by referring to the position of a 'very great power, which had always been famed for its liberal institutions and its great respect for the rights of all mankind'. The representative of Great Britain, the power Pusta was alluding to, 'had told the Conference with laudable frankness that it was impossible to revert to prewar conditions'.[15]

[11] Frank Paul Walters, *A History of the League of Nations* (Oxford University Press 1952) 188; cf. also James C. Hathaway, 'The evolution of refugee status in international law, 1920–1950' (1984) 33 The International and Comparative Law Quarterly 348, 351–357; on the treatment of Armenian refugees, cf. Keith David Watenpaugh, *Bread From Stones: The Middle East and the Making of Modern Humanitarianism* (University of California Press 2015) 167–175.

[12] On the derailment of liberalism as a key question of interwar historiography, cf. Adam Tooze, *The Deluge: The Great War and the Remaking of Global Order, 1916–1931* (Penguin 2015) Introduction–II.

[13] Cf. Morelon, 'Introduction' (n 9) 5; on the broader picture, cf. Ronald Findlay and Kevin H. O'Rourke, *Power and Plenty: Trade, War, and the World Economy in the Second Millennium Princeton* (University Press, 2009) Ch. 8.

[14] League of Nations, *Organisation for Communications and Transit, Passport Conference, held at Geneva from May 12th to 18th, 1926* (Publications of the League of Nations 1926) 35.

[15] Ibid, 70.

The stakes in regard to the reduction of control over individual mobility were obviously high. Looking at the agreements achieved at the conferences convened by the League, we are confronted with a modern passport scheme whose appeal lay mainly in its standardization across the globe. Indeed, bringing passport regulations—especially the practices of issuance and control—into line internationally was the primary, though perhaps not the desired result. Why did the majority of delegates ultimately resist the call of the League, the preferences of influential business bodies, and the desire of the general public to abandon the war-inspired passport system? To understand the preference for standardizing the existing practices, we must also investigate the economic, technological, and political circumstances that passports were embedded in.

II. The League of Nations and the New Passport Regime

The birth of the modern passport regime is rarely framed as the outcome of a heroic struggle against the dark forces of segregation and deglobalization. Rather, it is portrayed as the unhappy outcome of an even more unfortunate war that led governments to depart from the widely practised freedom of movement of people, goods, and capital.[16] The war ended this freedom and made foreigners 'more and more intelligible by the documents they carried', as John Torpey observes.[17] During the war, the belligerent states began to use the various instruments for controlling and managing mobility that were later inherited by postwar governments and employed for the more or less 'remote control' of individual mobility.[18]

When the First World War and the 'shallow, fragile peace that was the interwar period'[19] gave birth to a new passport regime, the League of Nations seemed to have acted as its midwife. The League felt competent in this matter because Article 23 of its Covenant defined the 'freedom of communications and of transit' as one of its policy objectives.[20] This article authorized the League to take action for the purpose of 'coping with the vastly increased complexity of international relations in the normal spheres of peaceful life. Problems of finance and trade, of transport by land, sea, and air, of the prevention of disease and the promotion of health, of social evils such as prostitution or the drug traffic—these and others were breaking across the limits of national frontiers'.[21]

[16] Already the Balkan War of 1912 anticipated some of the restrictions about to come during the Great War. See Ivan Kosnica, 'Citizenship in Croatia-Slavonia during the First World War' (2017) 8 Journal on European History of Law 62.

[17] John Torpey, 'The Great War and the Birth of the Modern Passport Systems' in Jane Caplan and John Torpey (eds), *Documenting Individual Identity. The Development of State Practices in the Modern World* (Princeton University Press 2001) 256, 258.

[18] Ibid, 260.

[19] Ibid, 263.

[20] Cf. Salter, *Passport* (n 3) 79.

[21] Walters, *History* (n 11) 42f.

A number of auxiliary agencies were established to face these challenges, among them the Communications and Transit Organization run by Robert Haas as the director of the League Secretariat. Frank Paul Walters, the League's former deputy secretary general, described the extraordinary position of this organization within the League: membership was open to states that were not League members, and the Committee for Communications and Transit, which was charged with organizing conferences and following up on their recommendations, was appointed in part by the League's Council and in part by the general assembly of the League's Communications and Transit Organization.[22]

Formally established by a resolution of the League Assembly on 9 December 1920, the Committee provided the institutional basis for pursuing the rebuilding of transport and communication systems.[23] According to Walters, passport and visa questions were among the 'matters of secondary importance' for which the committee produced 'useful results'.[24] They nevertheless had a high priority for the League in terms of the facilitation of worldwide trade.[25] Sara Kalm underscores this point with reference to the timing of the first conference on passports, which was convened even before the first Assembly of the League.[26]

The strong commitment to restoring freedom of mobility positioned the League at odds with the existing passport regime, however. The resolutions and comments in preparation of the conferences in 1920 and 1926 show that the League was keener on abolishing travel restrictions than on successfully establishing a standardized system of mobility control. Delivery of this system was only a weak compromise dictated by dire circumstances, and especially by the security concerns of a great number of states. These concerns were omnipresent but generally considered rather transient, as we can see from the statement by the Italian delegate in 1926: 'Until Italy was convinced beyond all doubt that every reason for the compulsory use of passports had disappeared, it could not vote in favour of their abolition.'[27]

When the first passport conference in 1920 failed to deliver the envisioned return to prewar conditions, there still remained some hope that the new passport regime would not survive its infancy. This at least seems to be indicated by the resolution adopted in Paris:

[22] Cf. League of Nations, Advisory and Technical Committee for Communication and Transit. Procès-Verbal of the First Session, 25.–28.7.1921, C. 358.M.254.1921, VIII, 2; League of Nations, *The Committees of the League of Nations. Classified List and Essential facts* (Publications of the League of Nations 1945) 33.

[23] Cf. Arthur Sweetser, 'The first year and a half of the League of Nations' [1921] Annals of the American Academy of Political and Social Science 21, 23.

[24] Walters, *History* (n 11) 180.

[25] Kalm, 'Standardizing Movements' (n 10) 26 (quote) and 29.

[26] Ibid, 23.

[27] League of Nations, *Passport Conference* (n 14) 16.

> Being of the opinion, further, that the legitimate concern of every Government for the safeguarding of its security and rights prohibits, for the time being, the total abolition of restrictions and that complete return to pre-war conditions which the Conference hopes, nevertheless, to see gradually re-established in the near future.[28]

The League did not intend to leave this desired gradual shift back towards open borders to the free will of governments, however, and the Committee for Communications and Transit took its task to 'ascertain progress made with the ratification of Conventions' seriously. It immediately began to contact governments in order to collect information on the implementation of the recommendations made by the passport conference in Paris.[29] As director of the Communications and Transit Organization's secretariat, Robert Haas used this intelligence to put moral pressure on the member states during later meetings in the hope that confronting them with the statements about steps allegedly taken would persuade them to further decrease travel restrictions.[30]

The efforts of the Committee for Communications and Transit must be viewed within the wider context of initiatives to rekindle regional economies, for which the League operated in close communication and even cooperation with other actors. The Portorose Conference is a good case in point:[31] representatives of the successor states of the Dual Monarchy met between late October and late November 1921[32] to engage in multilateral negotiations on their infrastructural heritage from the monarchy and on 'the technical issues associated with the economic dismemberment of Austria-Hungary and the region's potential economic re-unification'.[33] They were strongly encouraged by the allied powers, who attended as observers and feared the political and economic costs of destabilization in the region.[34] The League was present insofar as the successor states were continuing at a regional level the negotiations initiated during a conference convened in Barcelona by the Committee for Communications and Transit in March and April 1921.

[28] League of Nations, *Conference on Passports, Customs Formalities, and Through Tickets* (League of Nations 1920) 1; cf. also Salter, *Passport* (n 3) 78f.

[29] Committee for Communication and Transit, Procès-Verbal of the First Session, Annex 3: Memorandum on the Work of the Provisional Committee for Communications and Transit, 22.

[30] Cf. letter from Robert Haas to the president of the International Conference on Passports in Graz, 16 January 1922, AdR Wien, AAng, BKA-AA VR (Völkerrecht, Abt. 15), Karton 195, 4002–4c, 1922.

[31] For a profound discussion of the conference and its results, cf. Jürgen Nautz, *Die österreichische Handelspolitik der Nachkriegszeit 1918 bis 1923: Die Handelsvertragsbeziehungen zu den Nachfolgestaaten* (Böhlau 1994) 306–327.

[32] On the structure and organization of the conference, including some remarks on protocol questions, cf. Mildred Moulton, *A Structural View of the Conference as an Organ of International Government* (DPhil thesis, New York University 1929) 66–69.

[33] Donald A. Hempson III, 'New to the game: Czechs, economic unions, and the diplomacy of contested zones' (2013) 35 The International History Review 256, 267.

[34] Cf. Nautz, *Handelspolitik* (n 31) 306.

The focus of the Portorose Conference was primarily on traffic barriers to transportation and communication networks, especially those pertaining to the rolling stock of the former Habsburg railway.[35] The conference was hampered by the fact that 'none of the delegates was empowered to commit his government', however, as participant observer William Goode mused.[36] Its results were ambivalent, and it did not succeed in removing trade barriers and replacing them with treaties based on the principle of nondiscrimination.[37] Austria, Hungary, and Italy failed to win support for their bid for a free-trade zone,[38] with the Little Entente following the foreign policy line of Beneš obstructing those plans. Instead, they secured an agreement concerning a new tariff system for the region based on bilateral treaties.[39]

The conference nevertheless managed to establish standards for postal services and telecommunication. It also settled open questions regarding the management of the railway systems the successor states had inherited from the Dual Monarchy.[40] In the policy field of infrastructure, the conference fully lived up to the expectations.[41] The close connection between tariffs, import and export restrictions, trains, and passports was clearly visible in its programme, with a discussion scheduled on the facilitation of the transport of goods and people across the newly created borders. There was ultimately not enough time in Portorose for this agenda item, however, and the discussion was postponed to a later meeting. The regional conference in Graz, convened by the Austrian government in close collaboration with the League in January 1922, served this purpose.

[35] Hempson, 'New to the game' (n 33) 259.

[36] William Goode, 'Austria' (1922) 1 Journal of the Birth Institute of International Affairs 325, 37.

[37] On the broader political and economic context of this failure, cf. Findley and O'Rourke, *Power and Plenty* (n 13) 443f.

[38] On the call for a full customs union in Central Europe after the crisis of the 1930s, cf. Vladimir Goněc, '"New Central Europe" in Co-operating and United Europe: Czechoslovak Ideas in the 1920s and 1930s and Attempts at Co-ordination with Austrian and Hungarian Ideas' in Wilfried Loth and Nicolae Paun (eds), *Disintegration and Integration in East-Central Europe: 1919—post-1989* (Nomos 2014) 78, 82.

[39] Cf. Hempson, 'New to the game' (n 33) 268f; Anne Orde, 'Baring brothers, the Bank of England, the British Government and the Czechoslovak State Loan of 1922' (1991) 106/418 The English Historical Review 27, 36.

[40] On the institutional precursors like the Comité de circulation du material roulants dans l'Europe Centrale, cf. Paul Mechtler, 'Internationale Verflechtung der österreichischen Eisenbahnen am Anfang der Ersten Republik: Die Trennung des altösterreichischen Eisenbahnwesens nach dem Zusammenbruch der Donaumonarchie' (1964/65) 17/18 Mitteilungen des Österreichischen Staatsarchivs 399, 410–412. Mechtler also underlines the long time it took to complete the distribution of rolling stock, which was only completed in 1933 (419).

[41] From the nucleus of regional cooperation, the International Union of Railways (UIC) finally emerged at the conferences of Genua and Paris in 1922: cf. Paul Véron, 'Railway Integration in Europe: UIC—A Key Player in East-West Railway Integration' in Ralf Roth and Henry Jacolin (eds), *Eastern European Railways in Transition: Nineteenth to Twenty-First Centuries* (Routledge 2016) 243, 246–248.

III. Passports in the Lands of the Former Habsburg Monarchy

The 1920 passport conference in Paris had invited 'adjacent states' to 'enter into mutual agreements with a view to exempting from passport formalities all classes of people holding papers which in practice can be taken as a guarantee of their identity'. This primarily meant railway officers and other functionaries on cross-border duty. In addition, governments agreed to notify the League of Nations of any changes regarding passport and customs formalities at border stations and on international railway systems.[42] Following up on these recommendations and the suggestion of the Portorose Conference, the representatives of the successor states met in Graz for the second of seven conferences on this policy issue to be convened under the auspices of the League of Nations.[43]

The successor states had many good reasons to drastically reduce travel restrictions, and the conference in Graz thus began with great ambitions—but it would ultimately generate only very meagre results. The reason for this failure can be explained with another observation by Gargas, who stated that wartime rule was the 'expression of general and mutual mistrust, the mistrust of the states among themselves, the mistrust of the state towards foreign nationals, and indeed of the state towards its own nationals'.[44] While this certainly applied to all belligerent states, it was particularly true for the Dual Monarchy, where the military 'created a system of distrust that permeated society and government', as John Deak and Jonathan Gumz argue.[45] The military had prominently targeted the Slavic population and their political leaders, resulting in ruptures that endured into the postwar period and represented one of the main stumbling blocks preventing the return to the prewar system of free individual mobility within the realm of the former Habsburg Monarchy.

The lands of the former Habsburg State suffered strongly from the new travel regime. They had gone from an integrated region with free movement of people, goods, and capital to a region with tightly controlled borders and highly restricted communication, transit, and travel. A return to open borders and closer regional collaboration was prevented by the strong preferences for bilateral treaties.[46]

[42] Advisory and Technical Committee for Communication and Transit, Passport Conference. Preparatory Documents: Resolution adopted by the Conference on Passports, Customs Formalities and Through Tickets in Paris on 21 October 1920, C.641.M.230.1925.VIII, 3.

[43] Cf. 'Passport' in Edmund Jan Ozmańczyk and Anthony Mango (eds), Encyclopedia of the United Nations and International Agreements (Vol. 3, 3rd edn, Routledge 2003) 1770.

[44] Gargas, *Passproblem* (n 1) 14f.

[45] John Deak and Jonathan E. Gumz, 'How to break a state: The Habsburg monarchy's internal war, 1914–1918' (2017) 122 AHR 1105, 1122 (quote) and 1133.

[46] Cf. Michael G. Spencer and Peter M. Garber, 'The Dissolution of the Austro-Hungarian Empire: Lessons for Currency Reform' (1992) 92/66 IMF Working Papers chap. II; cf. also Kalman de Buday, 'Foreign loans in Central Europe' (1934) 174 The Annals of the American Academy of Political and Social Science 22, 23. This was an affront to liberal multilateralism, cf. Raw Abdelal, *National Purpose in the World Economy: Post-Soviet States in Comparative Perspective* (Cornell University Press 2001) 158.

The Austrian government, being rather a lame duck during the negotiations because of its severe financial crisis, nevertheless attempted to keep the multilateral option open.

The successor states of Austria-Hungary were caught in the inherent contradiction between economic rationality and political hostility. A telling event was the resignation of Johann Schober as chancellor of the Austrian Republic on 26 January 1922 as a result of the Treaty of Lana (16 December 1921) between Czechoslovakia and Austria. In this agreement, the Austrian government guaranteed the borders between the two states and received a rather favourable trade agreement in turn. This was sufficient for the Greater German People's Party to entertain far-reaching suspicions of Austria shifting towards the Little Entente and thus becoming alienated from his former German ally. It left the government as a consequence, and the subsequent political crisis overshadowed the passport conference in Graz.

Passport controls and visa requirements among the successor states must be seen in the context of this ideologically and politically highly charged situation. In Austria, there was nevertheless a clear intent to reduce obstacles for travel within the region, and a joint memorandum sent to the League of Nations by the Austrian Chambers of Commerce as early as 1920 was one of the first initiatives in this context. The document complained about travel restrictions and customs formalities that were being handled in the most hostile and bureaucratic manner: 'Travelling from Vienna to Prague today is fraught with more difficulties than leaving the continent entirely'.[47] Similar experiences were reported by Hungarian travellers wishing to travel to neighbouring states whose newly defined borders remained contested by the Budapest government.[48] The prospects for travel in the future were bleak, as the principle of retorsion to restrictions put in place by other states had the potential to generate vicious circles from which only multilateral agreements could provide an escape.[49]

The report by the Austrian parliament's Budget Committee on Foreign Policy took up the issue of travel restrictions in 1921. It was clearly in line with business and tourism interests as well as with the visions of the League when it bemoaned that prewar conditions concerning the mobility of people and goods had not yet been reestablished. Although the Austrian government was aiming to liberate trade and personal mobility from the restrictions of the passport regime, as the report argued, freedom of movement was being hampered by other governments unwilling to give up the control potential of the new system. The report foresaw

[47] *Appell der wirtschaftlichen Korporationen Österreichs an den Völkerbund* (Verlag der Niederösterreichischen Handels- und Gewerbekammer 1920) 18: 'Eine Reise von Wien nach Prag ist heute mit größeren Schwierigkeiten verbunden, wie ein Verlassen des Kontinents.'

[48] Cf. 'Report of the Hungarian delegation' in Paßvisaabkommen, Protokolle der Konferenzsitzungen, AdR, BKA AA Zl. 16448–4b/1922, 13.

[49] The representatives of the Czechoslovakian and the Hungarian government threatened more than once to introduce retaliatory measures if, for example, the fees for controlling passports or the collection of information on applicants for entrance visas were continued: Paßvisaabkommen (n 48) 35.

significant changes in the near future with the implementation of the resolutions of the 1920 League conference.[50] To increase pressure in this direction, the Social Democrat representative to the committee, Deutsch, introduced a motion to the plenary session requesting the government to immediately enter into negotiations with neighbouring states in order to 'abolish the harassing passport controls at border crossings'. The motion was accepted.[51]

This domestic political initiative coincided with the Foreign Office's efforts to convene a conference on 16–27 January 1922 in Graz under the auspices of the Committee for Communications and Transit. The strong interest of the League in this regional conference is evidenced by a note sent to the Austrian Foreign Service by Robert Haas, which included an attachment with information about the implementation of the recommendations of the 1920 conference by individual states. This material was eventually used by the Austrian consul general Robert Lukes in his role as president of the Graz conference to exert rhetorical pressure on Romania and the Kingdom of SHS. In exchange, the Austrian government communicated the protocols of the conference to the League and had the resulting treaty registered in Geneva.[52]

Several governments approached the meeting in Graz in a more low-key manner than the Portorose Conference, as is apparent from the lineup of participants. Austria and Hungary were present with three, Czechoslovakia with four, and Italy with five representatives. Poland, on the other hand, sent only two and the Kingdom of SHS only one delegate. The single Romanian representative arrived more than a week after the talks had started.

Austria took the initiative and proposed a general abolition of obligatory passport and visa requirements for travel within and between the successor states, with the exception of immigration from 'certain eastern states, from where a numerous but unwanted immigration has been observed'.[53] This would have essentially recreated the free travel zone of the Dual Monarchy with certain restrictions pertaining to Jewish migrants from former Galicia, and would have represented a similar push for further integration as the one occurring in the Benelux countries with the inclusion of France.

Conference president Lukes pursued a double strategy: he introduced the abolition of passport and visa requirements as the preferred choice of his government while using the enforcement of the recommendations of the Paris conference as a fallback position. This approach was quite successful, and the creation of a free travel zone was met with general acclaim—though only for a time in the as yet

[50] Cf. Budget Report for the 3rd Session of Parliament, meeting on December 12, 1921, ch. 8 (Interior and Education), Beilage 628, 13.

[51] Budget Report, 6; 74. Session of the Parliament on Dec. 12, 1921, 2556.

[52] Cf. letter from Robert Haas to the president of the International Conference on Passports in Graz, January 16, 1922, AdR Wien, AAng, BKA-AA VR (Völkerrecht, Abt. 15), Karton 195, 4002–4c, 1922.

[53] Cf. Mechtler, 'Internationale Verflechtung' (n 40) 425.

unspecified future. The final agreement of the conference came nowhere near the ambitious goals of the Austrian government, however: at the end, the participating countries merely agreed to implement the resolutions of the 1920 conference in slightly modified form—few minor changes were requested for the form of the standardized passport and the validity of passports.

In addition, the resolution adopted by the Graz conference stipulated a simplification of formalities at border crossings as well as free visas for participants in international sports competitions and scientific and art congresses. It was also agreed to abolish all charges for the inspection of passports at the border, even though the Austrian and Hungarian representatives lobbied fervently to maintain them for the control of passports in moving trains.[54] Access to visas was also simplified, with preliminary enquiries being abandoned and the costs for visas waived for applicants whose income could only just maintain their families. Personal appearance before the visa authorities could likewise be dispensed with, and applicants were no longer required to prove the necessity of their intended journey.[55]

These results were not easily achieved, however, with Lukes having to overcome several major challenges. One was the absence of the Romanian delegate, who arrived very late and only after multiple telegraphic requests to the Romanian government. After finally turning up, he had no authorization to commit his government. The same was true for the representative of the Kingdom of SHS, who could not even produce a written accreditation from Belgrade. For this reason, they both remained silent and passive during the discussions, and signed the treaty only 'ad referendum'.

The conference tackled all the issues in the resolution adopted by the Paris conference in 1920, with the representatives in Graz going over the suggested measures point by point and discussing their applicability. There was one additional concern addressed with determination by the Austrian and Hungarian delegates: the practice of the Kingdom of SHS of having its consular agencies inquire back home concerning individual applicants for entrance visas. Italian consulates likewise checked back with Rome before issuing visas for certain applicants, explaining this measure with a fear of immigration of workers that would present a challenge to an already heavily strained labour market. The final agreement limited preliminary inquiries on individuals by consular agencies to threats to national security, public health, and the labour market. This clause, as well as the other additional clauses compared to the Paris resolution, was also adopted by the League conference in 1926.

From this perspective, the conference in Graz can be considered a success. Its agreement provided a strong impact for the future standardization process even

[54] 'Proces-Verbal de la sixieme seance pleniere' in Paßvisaabkommen (n 48) 34.

[55] Cf. BGBl 194/1922; League of Nations, *Passport Conference* (n 15) Annex 1: Agreement concluded between Austria, Czechoslovakia, Hungary, Italy, Poland, Romania, and the Kingdom of Serbs, Croats, and Slovenes regarding Passports and Visas, 72–74.

though it was not binding for the Kingdom of SHS and Romania. One year after the conference, Foreign Minister Grünberger still complained about the handling of visa requests from Austrian citizens by Yugoslavian authorities. They were still asking for information even from local administrations in some cases. According to Grünberger, this process could take weeks, sometimes even months, and in many cases ended in refusal.[56] Grünberger's complaint hints at the political problems that may have prevented Belgrade from considering a liberalization of cross-border travel.

The main victims of the rigid passport regime were former 'German' inhabitants of the region now belonging to the Kingdom of SHS. These Austrian citizens obviously posed a serious threat—if not to the government in Belgrade, then at least to Slovenian regional political elites. The nationalist struggle under the monarchy and the brutal harassment of the Slovenian population during the war still loomed ominously over the German nationalists.[57] Federal Chancellor Johann Schober made this point in parliament on 10 December 1921. He considered the harassment of Austrian citizens by the border police of the Kingdom of Serbs, Croats and Slovenes to be the result of Belgrade's failure to implement its policy against the will of local elites, whose mentality was based on the nationality struggles of the late Dual Monarchy.[58]

This reading is corroborated by the Hungarian government's reply to the questionnaire sent out by the preparatory committee for the League conference in 1926. Hungary criticized 'the practice of submitting to a preliminary enquiry the requests for visas of whole categories of Hungarian nationals […] This practice greatly hinders the passage of persons between Hungary and the neighbouring States and also produces unfortunate incidents'.[59] The tense situation between Hungary and his neighbours was not least due to the openly revisionist policy of the Budapest government, which labelled certain Hungarian citizens—mainly the optants and Croatian extremists—as security risks for which a rigid passport regime seemed to provide a solution.

The successor states would have been ideal candidates for stronger regional cooperation within and outside the framework of the League of Nations; they would have needed only to return to prewar practices. This was precisely the reason why

[56] Cf. 'Rede Außenminister Grünberg vor dem Ausschuss für Äußeres, Wien 1.3.1923' in *Außenpolitische Dokumente der Republik Österreich, Bd. 5: Unter der Finanzkontrolle des Völkerbundes, 7. November 1922 bis 15. Juni 1926*, 113, 119. Since the Kingdom of SHS was not willing to implement the resolutions of the Graz conference, the Austrian government strove to facilitate travel in the border region through bilateral negotiations: Rede Außenminister Grünberg (n 56) 120.

[57] Cf. Deak and Gumz, 'How to Break a State' (n 45) 1118–1121.

[58] Plenary Session of the Parliament, 12 December 1921, 2480. The regional political elite in Styria and Carinthia did not exhibit a different approach either. On their rather obstructionist take, cf. Mechtler, 'Internationale Verflechtung' (n 40) 423.

[59] League of Nations, Advisory and Technical Committee for Communication and Transit. Replies of the Governments to the Questionnaire regarding Passport Regulations, 10.7.1925, C. 405.M.143.1925. VIII, 35.

a far-reaching rapprochement was impossible, however—for the prewar practices had been fraught with questions of political dominance and national preference from which many of the successor states wished to free themselves. Collaboration was thus still possible but limited to bilateral negotiations—a strategy strongly preferred by the Czechoslovakian government. Austria pushed for a multilateral approach with regard to the passport regime, but it was a lame duck in international and national politics by the time of the Graz conference. With a financial disaster looming in the not too distant future and German nationalist ideology limiting its international policy options, the Austrian government was not a strong player by that time. Neither was Hungary.

What does the Graz conference tell us about the obstacles on the way towards a liberal passport regime? For one thing, the desire for freedom of movement was more than counterbalanced by the need for control. This remained a dominant theme at the conference in 1926 as well, where control of the labour market, the entrance of political subversives, and the destinations of the respective state's own inhabitants were considered indispensable requirements for most governments.

IV. The Conference of 1926: Standardization Accomplished?

A second major conference on the topic of passports was convened in Geneva on 12–18 May 1926. Its president, Charles R. Pusta from Estonia, summarized the results optimistically. At the beginning of his concluding remarks, he referred to the expectations of the League's Assembly and Council, which had called for the conference to abolish passports and return to prewar conditions. The agreements reached during nine meetings full of constructive but nevertheless heated debates were far from this objective, however, as Pusta had to concede. Representatives of powers 'proud of their liberal traditions and respect for individual rights' found it 'impossible to revert to prewar conditions'. The conference had nevertheless been no failure, for most of the participating states had proven ready and willing 'to try to regulate existing conditions'.[60] The result was an important step towards the standardized, modern passport system.

Pusta did not simply gloss over the disappointing results of the conference, however. His assessment was based on the acknowledgment that the League was not in a position to force states onto a specific course. It was the same consideration that had already limited the recommendations of the Committee for Communications and Transit for the conference to those with at least a chance of being accepted, as M. de Aguero y Bethancourt, the Cuban representative to the Committee and

60 League of Nations, *Passport Conference* (n 14) 70.

later vice-president of the 1926 conference had emphasized during a preparatory meeting in 1925.[61]

To fully appreciate the results of the conference, we therefore need to take into consideration the decision-making process, which was as complex as the governance structure of the League itself. The League's Assembly claimed a role in proceedings, as did the Council and the Committee for Communications and Transit. In fact, the Council played the decisive role since it convened the conference—though only after the Committee had laid the foundations for it.[62] The League's Assembly and Council were made up of delegates of the same states that also dispatched representatives to the Geneva conference. This did not mean that they would pursue the same strategies, however: to provide only one example, the British government's delegate to Geneva opposed the recommendations of the Council and Assembly, which had previously been supported by British delegates.[63]

The representative of the International Chamber of Commerce referred to this decision-making process while engaging with the position of the British delegate. In its own proposal, which called for the abolition of compulsory passports in the near future, the ICC considered itself to be 'in conformity with the resolution adopted by the Assembly of the League of Nations, and had moreover met with the approval of the British representative'.[64] The president of the conference also used his position to bring the institutional memory to bear on the more recalcitrant discussants. When the British, Turkish, Romanian, and Swiss delegates declared that their governments would not be able to accept the clause concerning the gradual abolition of the passport system, Pusta 'drew the attention of the Conference to the resolution adopted by the Sixth Assembly of the League of Nations [. . .]. The draft recommendation submitted to the Conference only differed from the resolution [. . .] as it indicated the means of achieving the total abolition of the passport system'.[65]

These attempts to reveal the inconsistency between the positions of governments at different steps of the decision-making process remained futile in that they were unable to sway the opposition towards a return to prewar conditions. They did, however, shed additional light on the internationalist character of the passport

[61] Minutes of the Third Session of the Sub-Committee on the Passport regime, Paris, 2–5 October 1925, League of Nations, Advisory and Technical Committee for Communication and Transit, C.699.M.252.1925.VIII, 4.

[62] Cf. Note by the Secretary General: Convening of a Passport Conference, 17 November 1925, C.707.1925.VIII.

[63] The negotiations on the abolishment of trade barriers followed the same principle of public support and practical-political resistance: cf. Findlay and O'Rourke, *Power and Plenty* (n 13) 444.

[64] League of Nations, *Passport Conference* (n 14) 19.

[65] League of Nations, *Passport Conference* (n 14) 44. On the role of institutional memory in the preparatory discussions of the Committee for Communications and Transit, cf. Minutes of the Third Session (n 61) 5, where the French delegate warded off the proposal of the Italian delegate to discontinue the use of French as the second language in passports with reference to the resolutions of the 1920 conference.

conference of 1926. It was during this event that governments negotiated the future of the passport system in concrete and not merely abstract terms. The discrepancy between political statements in the League Assembly and positions held at the conference can be explained by this logic: the British government could easily identify with the concept of open borders in relatively general terms, but it was unwilling to give up its concrete possibilities for control.

At the conference, the British delegate staunchly defended the right of governments to perform border controls, stating that they facilitated the work of immigration officers and helped the authorities to control the travels of British subjects.[66] When the draft resolution included the clause 'that the general control of travellers at the frontier should be gradually discontinued', he asked that his government's reservation 'be printed as a footnote to the resolutions of the Conference and not merely recorded in the Minutes, which had not such a wide circulation'.[67] To avoid this extraordinary measure, Pusta suggested a vote by roll call on the clause. This sequence provides us with a snapshot view of the attitudes of individual states towards a more liberal border regime.

The states supporting a gradual discontinuation of border controls were Austria, Czechoslovakia, Estonia, France, the Free City of Danzig, Germany, Switzerland, Uruguay, Brazil, and China. Their representatives displayed a rather liberal approach to passport control during the entire conference. Austria and Czechoslovakia lobbied for a more user-friendly passport regime to support their tourism and export-oriented industry. Until the conference, both states had failed to achieve significant steps in this direction, however. France and Estonia were part of two different free travel zones, and Switzerland maintained its prewar internationalist orientation[68] as one of the champions of bilateral agreements to reduce restrictions for the crossing of its borders. Together with the French and Estonian participants, the German delegate was part of the sub-committee that drafted the resolution. In addition, the German state strongly supported the introduction of identity cards as a less costly document to be used for crossing state borders—a system already in use in China.

The second group, that is, the states opting against a gradual abolition of border controls, were less coherent in terms of their positions. Belgium and the Netherlands were part of the free travel zone of the Benelux countries. Poland had introduced the proposal to abolish passports as a general rule at the beginning of the conference[69] but voted against the gradual discontinuation of border controls. Great Britain was heralded as the great defender of liberal political values, yet was unable to support a gradual liberalization of border controls. It was seconded by

66 Cf. Salter, *Passport* (n 3) 79f.

67 League of Nations, *Passport Conference* (n 14) 55.

68 Cf. Madeleine Herren, *Hintertüren zur Macht. Internationalismus und modernisierungsorientierte Außenpolitik in Belgien, der Schweiz und den USA 1865–1914* (Oldenbourg 2000) 215–370.

69 League of Nations, *Passport Conference* (n 14) 13.

the members of the Commonwealth. Italy defended passports and border controls as the pinnacle of the sovereign state while radically decreasing travel requirements for wealthy tourists from France and Switzerland.[70]

What can we learn from the debates and voting strategies at the conference? It is obvious that even governments with a strong interest in reduced state control over individual travel were unable to envision a radical change in the near future. The optimistic outlook of an imminent return to prewar conditions, which had still been present in the resolution of the 1920 conference, was abandoned for good in 1926. This was certainly not the result expected by the League of Nations as host of the conference.

How, then, should we assess the results achieved in Geneva? Did the conference simply 'cement the wartime system', as Robertson argues?[71] From my point of view, the results need to be viewed in more differentiated terms. The wartime system was quite different from the mobility regime after 1926 in its more restrictive and much less standardized form. And while the expectations for a return to the prewar system as supported by business interests, media, and declamatory expressions of state governments were not irrational, they were nevertheless out of touch with practical state interests. The results of the conference must be weighed against this complicated political situation—and from this perspective, the conference was certainly not the 'failure of its doctrine of liberal internationalism in the postwar era of economic nationalism'.[72]

V. Conclusion

The end of the Great War was the beginning of a struggle for a new political, economic, and cultural order and the corresponding reconfiguration of international relations. The League of Nations played an important but not decisive role in this endeavour by providing a platform for technical coordination and political negotiation. The rebuilding of infrastructure and communications was one of the crucial tasks after the war, and the League acted as a facilitator in this regard. Part of this mission was the normalization of travel regimes, for the war had brought the policy of open borders to an abrupt end and vested states with wide-ranging powers to control the movements of people. Peace allowed for the resurfacing of visions of free and unimpeded travel across Europe—especially for people with at least modest means.

The League of Nations and the newly created Committee on Communications and Transit took on the challenge of orchestrating the desired shift back to the

[70] League of Nations, *Passport Conference* (n 14) 56.
[71] Robertson, *Passport* (n 3) 219.
[72] Robertson, *Passport* (n 3) 220.

open borders of the prewar years. Three conferences later in 1926, however, it had become obvious that the League would not be able to muster the support of a sufficiently large number of states to accomplish this goal. Even self-styled liberal governments like the British clung to the possibilities of controlling mobility that the war had afforded them. Looking at the successor states of the Habsburg monarchy, their resistance to returning to the prewar mobility regime was not simply an irrational pursuit of politically unstable governments. They, too, had to respond to the challenging realities of the postwar years, and under the new conditions, multilateral agreements were an option only in strictly limited technical questions such as the management of rolling stock for the railways inherited from the monarchy. The notion of unrestricted mobility of individuals, on the other hand, bore too heavy a political burden for agreements of this kind to be concluded.

What role could the League play, then? It could provide an institutional platform for a new international regime[73] in which the collection of evidence, the structuring of discussions and problem-solving within its decision-making bodies, and the inclusion of non-state actors were decisive elements. The passport conference of 1926 clearly shows that the League's room for manoeuvre was limited, but also that certain achievements were possible within these limits. The president of the conference and the secretary of the Committee for Communications and Transit were able to steer the debates towards resolutions that most of the states would be able to accept. They generated sufficient pressure to sway recalcitrant governments in the direction of an increasingly standardized passport system—and while this did not radically change the restrictive mobility system, it nevertheless created opportunities for states to later revise their passport systems.

I would therefore argue that the League provided institutional spaces for the collection of information, for collective decision making, and for an institutional memory of past resolutions. The Geneva Passport Conference of 1926 was prepared in precisely this manner: it was preceded by two other conferences and the work of a preparatory committee. The result of these preparations were resolutions adopted by the League Council and Assembly. In parallel to this political work, the League initiated a fact-finding mission on passport regulations by sending out a questionnaire to its member states. The debates during the conference and their results clearly show the League's limitations as well as opportunities for pursuing a liberal mobility regime within an institutional setting in which where internationalist, trans-nationalist, and multi-nationalist features coexisted.[74]

This outcome prefigured mobility practices up until the Schengen agreement, and millions of people on the move for purposes of work, adventure, or intellectual

[73] On the international regime, cf. Shah M. Tarzi, 'Neorealism, Neoliberalism, and the International System' (2004) 41 International Studies 115.

[74] Patricia Clavin, 'Defining Transnationalism' (2005) 14/4 Contemporary European History 421, 425f.

pursuits became accustomed to it. The open border situation of the prewar period vanished into oblivion despite the League of Nations' struggle to commit states to return to it. This would not necessarily have meant turning the clock backwards, however: it would have been a further step towards open borders and open markets. In pursuing this goal, the League lived up to its mission to further collaboration and communication on a global scale. When it eventually became clear that the original plan could not be implemented, the League had to content itself with the role of midwife for a modern, standardized passport system—which was not the realist alternative to liberal internationalism but an important achievement in its own right, as Swedish political scientist Sara Kalm argues.[75] However, it redefined the role of the League from that of an active promoter of further global integration to that of an agent of deglobalization.

[75] Kalm, 'Standardizing Movements' (n 10) 1, 29.

9

International Commerce in the Wake of Empire

Central European Economic Integration between National and Imperial Sovereignty

Madeleine Dungy

In the final years of the Austro-Hungarian Empire, Richard Riedl, an influential Austrian bureaucrat, developed sweeping plans for a Central European economic union managed by a German commercial elite. This vision fit into a world of empires in which specific nationalities were singled out as agents of progress within large power blocs. The First World War shook but did not shatter this outlook. It precipitated the collapse of the Austro-Hungarian Empire along with a string of other continental empires across Eurasia. The Habsburg lands were divided among a collection of new sovereign nation-states, each anxious to affirm its independence and to sever economic and cultural ties to Vienna. Riedl sought to counter this fragmentation by translating his ambitions for a unified *Mitteleuropa* from an imperial framework to the League of Nations. He used the League's multilateral toolkit to devise an innovative regime of trans-border commercial rights that anticipated many of the features and tensions in our current system of global capitalism. His story reveals how regional concerns about the commercial disintegration of the Habsburg Empire were encoded in the sprawling Economic and Financial Organization that assumed an increasingly prominent position in the general operations of the League of Nations.[1] Riedl's case also highlights how the 'problem of Germany' complicated the insertion of the Habsburg successor states into the League's multilateral framework.[2] After 1918, Riedl openly advocated union with Germany, *Anschluss*, and this commitment was both a source of leverage and a handicap in Vienna and Geneva.

[1] Patricia Clavin, *Securing the World Economy: The Reinvention of the League of Nations, 1920–1946* (Oxford University Press 2013) (hereafter Clavin, *Securing the World Economy*).

[2] Peter Stirk shows that Germany was a fundamental sticking point in interwar plans for regional unity in Central and Eastern Europe; it was too powerful to be included and too powerful to be left out. See Peter MR Stirk, 'Ideas of Economic Integration in Interwar Mitteleuropa' in Peter MR Stirk (ed), *Mitteleuropa: history and prospects* (Edinburgh University Press 1994) 89–90 (hereafter Stirk, 'Economic Integration in Interwar Mitteleuropa').

Madeleine Dungy, *International Commerce in the Wake of Empire* In: *Remaking Central Europe*. Edited by: Peter Becker and Natasha Wheatley, Oxford University Press (2020). © the many contributors.
DOI: 10.1093/oso/9780198854685.003.0010

Riedl used the Vienna Chamber of Commerce and the International Chamber of Commerce to participate in League trade policy from outside Austrian ministerial structures. Using these back channels, he wrote an ambitious League treaty protecting the legal rights of foreign commercial agents, the Draft Convention on the Treatment of Foreigners. In continuity with Riedl's pre-war efforts to cultivate an Austrian commercial elite, this treaty proposed to unfetter trade networks from employment regulations that impeded their mobility. Riedl devised this formula specifically to support Viennese trading houses, but the Austrian government ultimately rejected it. Austrian immigration officials opposed Riedl's treaty as an unwelcome infringement on their authority to protect the large number of unemployed professionals in the national labour market. In sum, Riedl used the League to pursue an imperial vision that aimed to extend the influence of the Vienna-based commercial elite across Central and Eastern Europe. The Austrian Republic refused to support this vision and instead adopted a national perspective focused on enforcing economic solidarity within its narrow territorial borders. The conflict between Riedl and his government demonstrates how the League's Economic and Financial Organization shaped the transition from empires to nation-states in Central and Eastern Europe by intervening in the regulatory relationship between business networks and governments. The League of Nations was a support structure both for state sovereignty and for transnational market forces, creating a fundamental tension in technical initiatives that addressed both of these goals.[3]

I. Building an Austrian Commercial Elite Before the First World War

Prior to the war, Richard Riedl was one of Austria's most influential commercial bureaucrats. From 1890 to 1910 he worked for the Vienna Chamber of Commerce, where he was promoted to its highest-ranking administrative position, First Secretary.[4] In 1910, he was appointed to be the Director of the Commercial Policy Department in the Austrian Ministry of Commerce. One of Riedl's main responsibilities in both the Vienna Chamber of Commerce and the Ministry of Commerce was to promote exports by cultivating a mobile and cohesive Austrian commercial elite. A central institutional base for this effort was the Vienna Trade Museum.[5]

[3] Susan Pedersen, 'Back to the League of Nations' (2007) 112 The American Historical Review 1091; Glenda Sluga, *Internationalism in the Age of Nationalism* (University of Pennsylvania Press 2013) 49–61 (hereafter Sluga, *Internationalism*).

[4] Before the war, the full name of the Vienna Chamber of Commerce was the *Niederösterreichischer Handels- und Gewerbe Kammer*. In 1920 its name was changed to the *Wiener Kammer für Handel, Gewerbe, und Industrie*.

[5] 'Maßnahmen auf dem Gebiet der Exporförderung' *Die Industrie* (Vienna, 8 January 1910) 4–5; *Das Handelsmuseum in Wien. Darstellung Seiner Gründung Und Entwicklung, 1874–1919* (Handelsmuseum in Wien 1920) 25 (hereafter *Das Handelsmuseum in Wien*); Gerald Horst Brettner-Messler, 'Richard

The Trade Museum was a product of nineteenth-century aspirations for European commercial and cultural expansion. It was the first of a series of trade museums created from the 1870s to the 1890s on the basis of commercial samples gathered at World's Fairs, including the Brussels Commercial Museum, the London Imperial Institute, and the Philadelphia Commercial Museum. The Vienna Trade Museum was originally established to house the collections of the Oriental Section of the 1873 Vienna World's Fair. It was then transformed into a general Trade Museum in 1886 for the purpose of exhibiting products made by foreign producers that were selling well on international markets so that local firms could replicate them.[6]

While trade museums of the 1880s and 1890s focused on goods, the next generation of trade-promoting institutions established around 1900 focused on people and information. The French National Office of Foreign Trade and the Commercial Intelligence Branch of the British Board of Trade, founded in 1898 and 1899 respectively, were the models for this new type of information office. Both institutions were supported by large networks of dedicated correspondents. They marked a shift from things to people that reflected a reconceptualization of international markets as abstract spaces for competition among rival 'organizations' rather than concrete collections of wares on offer.[7] The Vienna Trade Museum was transformed into an information office in line with these trends. In 1898 it established an Export Academy to train young businessmen and began to sell its collection of commercial samples and applied arts to make space for teaching activities.[8] Today the Export Academy has become the prestigious Vienna University of Economics and Business (*Wirtschaftsuniversität Wien*).

Beginning around 1900, the Austrian Ministry of Commerce also began to support trade networks directly. It established foreign 'branch offices' for the Trade Museum by designating representatives of large Viennese trading houses to serve as official correspondents. The Ministry also disbursed stipends to enable Austrian firms to establish new subsidiaries abroad. Stipend recipients had to submit regular

Riedl—ein liberaler Imperialist: Biographische Studie zu Handelspolitik und "Mitteleuropa"-Gedanken in Monarchie und Erster Republik' (PhD, University of Vienna 1998) 21–70 (hereafter Brettner-Messler, 'Richard Riedl—ein liberaler Imperialist').

[6] *Das Handelsmuseum in Wien* (n 5) 9–13; Christian Meyer, *Exportförderungspolitik in Österreich: von der Privilegienwirtschaft zum objektiven Förderungssystem* (Böhlau 1991) 65–74 (hereafter Meyer, *Exportförderungspolitik*); Séverine Antigone Marin, 'Introducing Small Firms to International Markets: The Debates over the Commercial Museums in France and Germany 1880–1910' in Hartmut Berghoff, Philip Scranton, and Uwe Spiekermann (eds), *The Rise of Marketing and Market Research* (Palgrave Macmillan 2012) 127–152; Dave Muddiman, 'A Brain Centre of Empire: Commercial and Industrial Intelligence at the Imperial Institute, 1886–1903' in Toni Weller (ed), *Information History in the Modern World: Histories of the Information Age* (Palgrave Macmillan 2011) 108–129.

[7] Dave Muddiman, 'From Display to Data: The Commercial Museum and the Beginnings of Business Information, 1870–1914' in W Boyd Rayward (ed), *Information Beyond Borders: International, Cultural and Intellectual Exchange in the Belle Époque* (Ashgate Publishing Company 2014) 263–282.

[8] *Das Handelsmuseum in Wien* (n 5) 17, 22–23; Meyer, *Exportförderungspolitik* (n 6) 115–119.

reports accounting for the citizenship of their employees as well as the origins of the goods they sold.[9] These measures to ensure that Austrian trade networks were *really* Austrian were more invasive than export-promoting policies in other European states and reflected a perception that Austria had fallen behind its competitors. Richard Riedl was centrally involved in constructing the elaborate mechanisms to enforce patriotic solidarity in the Austrian commercial community, and this experience confronted him with frequent reminders of Austria's weakness on foreign markets.[10] Lacking alternative candidates, the Ministry was often forced to appoint correspondents who were junior partners in German or British collaborative ventures and who could not be relied upon to promote Austrian goods preferentially.[11] Efforts to develop Austria's Adriatic port of Trieste also produced only modest results.[12] Thus in the run-up to the First World War, Riedl faced mounting evidence that Austria was struggling to establish a global commercial infrastructure that could compete with expanding European maritime empires. His preoccupation with consolidating Austrian influence in Central and Eastern Europe in partnership with Germany can be interpreted, in part, as a response to this failure to break into overseas markets.

II. Patriotism and Commercial Expansion in a Multinational Empire

Internal conflicts over trade policy within the Dual Monarchy also persuaded Riedl that more forceful leadership from Vienna-based Germans was needed. The Austrian Ministry of Commerce had to contend with competing commercial centres in the Austrian half of the Empire, notably Trieste and Prague. Nationalist leaders in these cities developed their own trade institutions that often diverged from policy defined in Vienna.[13] The most fundamental conflict was, however, with Budapest. According to the terms of the 1865 agreement that established the Dual Monarchy, Austria and Hungary each had separate Ministries of Commerce but shared a diplomatic service. Thus, although Austria and Hungary often competed

[9] Entwurf eines Uebereinkommens betr. Expositurn des k.k. österr. Handelsmuseums in Rio de Janeiro, Buenos-Aires, Montreal, Calcutta (10 November 1908) ÖStA, AVA, k.k. Handelsministerium/Allgemeine Registratur/1218; Wiedererrichtung der ho. Expositur in Bombay und Erneuerung des bestehenden Expositurabkommens mit der Firma A. Janowitzer, Wien (29 September 1911) ÖStA, AVA, k.k. Handelsministerium/Allgemeine Registratur/1185.

[10] 'Maßnahmen auf dem Gebiet der Exportfürderung' *Die Industrie* (Vienna, 8 January 1910) 2; Meyer, *Exportförderungspolitik* (n 6) 76.

[11] Abschrift eines Berichtes des k.u.k. Generalkonsulates in Shanghai (5 April 1911); k. und k. oesterr. —ungar. Consulat to Handelsministerium (10 February, 1908) ÖStA, AVA, Handelsministerium/Allgemeine Registratur/1218.

[12] Richard Riedl, *Die Industrie Österreichs während des Krieges* (Carnegie Endownment for International Peace 1932) 25 (hereafter Riedl, *Die Industrie Österreichs*).

[13] Meyer, *Exportförderungspolitik* (n 6) 76–78.

for the same export markets, especially in the Balkans, they had to rely on shared consuls and embassies. Moreover, the two halves of the Monarchy had very different priorities, as Austria had sizeable manufacturing and service sectors, while Hungary was more focused on agriculture and food processing.[14]

As a German nationalist, Riedl was an outlier in the Austrian Ministry of Commerce. Ministerial officials pledged loyalty to the Emperor, and most were careful to avoid explicitly associating Austrian patriotism with a particular ethnolinguistic profile.[15] In contrast, Riedl unambiguously promoted a vision of Austrian commercial expansion driven by ethnic Germans. He occupied a prominent position in bourgeois nationalist circles. As a student, he had been a leading member of the university fraternity movement. In 1908 he cooperated with other fraternity alumni to establish the German Club in Vienna as a non-party social venue for German nationalists, serving as the organization's first chairman.[16]

While most forms of nationalism fit uneasily in most areas of Habsburg bureaucracy, there was a particularly sharp tension between Riedl's German nationalism and his efforts to develop Austrian trade institutions. During this period, German nationalism in Austria was closely associated with anti-Semitism. At the same time, Jews played a very prominent role in the country's foreign trade and finance and identified strongly with German culture, particularly in Vienna.[17] Riedl responded by adopting different attitudes towards Jews in different settings. He actively supported the exclusion of Jews from fraternity-based nationalist networks.[18] In the Vienna Chamber of Commerce and the Ministry of Commerce, he conformed to the more pragmatic anti-Semitism that prevailed there. Jews who had valuable expertise or personal connections could gain limited access to these institutions.[19] Riedl collaborated with many colleagues and even many German nationalists who had a Jewish background. He notably had ties to the historian Heinrich Friedjung, who came from a Jewish family in Moravia. Like Riedl, Friedjung advocated a pan-German continental bloc as a counterweight to European maritime empires.[20] In fact, Riedl's appointment in the Ministry of Commerce can be attributed to his

[14] 'Industrieller Klub. 28. Monatsversammlung. Handelskammersekretär Richard Riedl' *Die Industrie* (Vienna, 15 February 1908) 4.

[15] Arnold Suppan, '"Germans" in the Habsburg Empire: Language, Imperial Ideology, National Identity, and Assimilation' in Charles W Ingrao and Franz AJ Szabo (eds), *The Germans and the East* (Purdue University Press 2008) 162–163 (hereafter Suppan, '"Germans" in the Habsburg Empire').

[16] Brettner-Messler, 'Richard Riedl—ein liberaler Imperialist' (n 5) 12–20, 41–45.

[17] Steven Beller, 'Germans and Jews as Central European and "Mitteleuropäisch" Elites' in Peter MR Stirk (ed), *Mitteleuropa: History and Prospects* (Edinburgh University Press 1994) 75–76, 78; Monika Richarz, 'Berufliche und soziale Struktur' in Steven M Lowenstein and others (eds), *Deutsch-jüdische Geschichte in der Neuzeit: Umstrittene Integration 1871 - 1918* (CH Beck 1997) 55.

[18] Karl Beck, *Wiener akaemische Burschenschaft Albia, 1870–1930* (Wiener akadem. Burschenschaft "Albia" 1930) 63–75.

[19] Peter Pulzer, 'Rechtliche Gleichstellung und öffentliches Leben' in Steven M Lowenstein and others (eds), *Deutsch-jüdische Geschichte in der Neuzeit: Umstrittene Integration 1871–1918* (CH Beck 1997) 186.

[20] Heinrich Friedjung, *Das Zeitalter des Imperialismus, 1884–1914* (Neufeld und Henius 1919).

membership alongside the Ministry's director in Friedjung's Oriental Committee, which promoted Austro-German control of the Balkans.[21]

Riedl was also fixated on the Balkans and argued that Austria should seek to establish itself there as an 'intermediary between kindred Germany and the Orient'. He emphasized that Germany's efforts to develop its influence in the Middle East (for example through the Berlin-Bagdad Railway) left Austria 'only a short time' to act.[22] As these quotes indicate, Riedl remained committed to the preservation of the Habsburg Empire as an independent regional actor and did not seek formal union with Germany before 1918. This vision of Central Europe conformed to the preferences of German leaders from Bismarck to Bülow.[23]

As the Ottoman Empire was driven from Europe during the Balkan Wars, Riedl proposed to establish a vast economic and political bloc dominated by Germany and Austria-Hungary to take its place. His most ambitious attempt to realize this goal was a customs union between Romania and Austria-Hungary. He hoped this would lead to the formation of a larger union that would also include Germany. Advocates of an assertive Balkan policy, including Franz Ferdinand and the military chief of staff, Franz Conrad von Hötzendorf, favoured Riedl's plan and authorized him to travel to Romania to explore its implementation following the First Balkan War.[24]

Riedl supported the formation of a German-dominated *Mitteleuropa* in order to counter-balance large European colonial empires. He emphasized, however, that his regional vision would be implemented through treaties among sovereign states rather than formal colonial subordination, anticipating his later efforts to encode regional hierarchy in international trade law. He presented his planned customs union with Romania as:

> [A] decisive step towards the goals of uniting central European states in a great whole dominating access to the East, of establishing a solid foundation for the peace of the continent, and of countering the expansionary policies of colonial states the with the power of a Central European organization reposing on free treaty commitments among nations.[25]

It should be noted that while many other Austrian leaders also tried to present abstention from formal colonial rule as a virtuous choice for a more chaste 'free-trade

[21] Brettner-Messler, 'Richard Riedl—ein liberaler Imperialist' (n 5) 59–60.

[22] 'Industrieller Klub. 28. Monatsversammlung. Handelskammersekretär Richard Riedl' *Die Industrie* (Vienna, 15 February 1908) 4.

[23] Suppan, '"Germans" in the Habsburg Empire' (n 15) 172–173; Brettner-Messler, 'Richard Riedl—ein liberaler Imperialist' (n 5) 41.

[24] Brettner-Messler, 'Richard Riedl—ein liberaler Imperialist' (n 5) 148–153; Dörte Löding, 'Deutschlands und Österreich-Ungarns Balkanpolitik von 1912–1914 unter Besonderer Berücksichtigung ihrer Wirtschaftsinteressen' (PhD, University of Hamburg 1969) 93–95.

[25] Quoted in Brettner-Messler, 'Richard Riedl—ein liberaler Imperialist' (n 5) 148.

imperialism', Austrian companies and institutions did not avoid involvement in the violent and oppressive aspects of maritime empire during this period. A growing body of scholarship has revealed the myriad ways in which Austria participated in European imperial expansion in the late-nineteenth century, although the country did not have formal overseas colonies.[26]

III. The First World War and the Politics of Imperial Power Blocs

In 1914, the formation of an expansive system of Allied economic warfare encompassing the British and French empires spurred Riedl to try to transform the wartime alliance between Germany and Austria-Hungary into a permanent economic bond. Through his work for the Ministry of Commerce during the early months of the war, Riedl saw first-hand the tightening of the Allies' commercial vise around Central and Eastern Europe. Although the blockade was primarily directed against Germany, it also had a profound impact on the Austrian economy, which relied heavily on trade through German ports. In fall 1914, Riedl coordinated the trans-shipment of key commodities through Germany and also helped establish centralized distribution structures (*Zentralen*) that mirrored those in Germany to allocate this material. Thus, in the first months of the war, Riedl took stock of Austria-Hungary's critical dependence on the German trade system for strategic supplies and sought to institutionally enforce solidarity between the two states.[27]

In the early years of the war, Riedl emerged as one of the leading advocates for a customs union between Germany and Austria-Hungary. He circulated a Customs Union Treaty that proposed to unite Austria-Hungary and Germany behind a common external tariff and to integrate their commercial laws and administration.[28] This arrangement would be open to other states from the Baltic to the Balkans, forming a vast continental bloc with Germany and Austria-Hungary at its

[26] Walter Sauer (ed), *K.u.k. kolonial - Habsburgermonarchie und europäische Herrschaft in Afrika* (Böhlau 2002); Florian Krobb (ed), 'Colonial Austria: Austria and the Overseas' special issue of *Austrian Studies* (2012) 20. On the dark underbelly of Austrian 'free-trade imperialism' during the *Belle Époque*, see Alison Frank, 'The Children of the Desert and the Laws of the Sea: Austria, Great Britain, the Ottoman Empire, and the Mediterranean Slave Trade in the Nineteenth Century' (2012) 117 The American Historical Review 410.

[27] Riedl, *Die Industrie Österreichs* (n 12) 24–26; Brettner-Messler, 'Richard Riedl—ein liberaler Imperialist' (n 5) 261–265; Alexander Watson, *Ring of Steel: Germany and Austria-Hungary at War, 1914–1918* (Allen Lane 2014) 208 (hereafter Watson, *Ring of Steel*).

[28] Richard Riedl, Entwurf eines Zollvereinsvertrages (March 1915) ÖStA, Haus-, Hof-, und Staatsarchiv (hereafter HHStA), Nachlass Baerenreither (hereafter NL Baerenreither)/30; Richard Kapp, 'The Failure of the Diplomatic Negotiations between Germany and Austria-Hungary for a Customs Union, 1915–1916' (PhD, University of Toronto 1977) 132–143 (hereafter Kapp, 'Customs Union'); Jan Vermeiren, *The First World War and German National Identity: The Dual Alliance at War* (Cambridge University Press 2016) 173–174 (hereafter Vermeiren, *German National Identity*).

core. It would also be connected to the wider world through trade treaties, negotiated collectively.[29] Riedl remained committed this vision of regional integration as a bridge to the world economy through the end of the 1920s, but he transferred it from an imperial to an international framework.

In 1915, Riedl incorporated his plan for a customs union into an influential proposal for political and economic cooperation in Central Europe the *Denkschrift aus Deutsch-Österreich* (Memorandum from German-Austria). The *Denkshrift* was written by a group of officials and intellectuals who gathered around Heinrich Friedjung. They were also in contact with Friedrich Naumann whose more broadly popular *Mitteleuropa* was published in Germany around the same, but the two texts had very different emphases and audiences.[30] Naumann disdained technical detail, arguing that it was a waste of time to 'tinker too much with tariff laws' because 'first we must ensure that we have the great masses behind us'.[31] In contrast, the *Denkschrift* offered precise administrative and legal prescriptions and was only published for private circulation. It justified Central European union on the basis of the wartime transformation of international law:

> The security and the expansion of internationality (*Internationalität*) was the prerequisite for the independence of a large number of states, which, if dependent solely on their own resources, could not have developed. The war brought an end to this system of medium or small economic bodies that want to be called independent and yet are not self-reliant. We have witnessed – a mockery of the most widely recognized international law – the trampling of the principles of the protection of private property, of trade and transit and of neutrality. In such a manner, the life-giving internationality was taken from small governmental and economic bodies. Even after the conclusion of peace, a reversal is highly unlikely ... power as such will play an even greater role in relations among countries than before. Therein lies an undeniable incentive for the two empires of the centre of Europe to establish and develop their military and economic union.[32]

Riedl carried a distrust of 'internationality' through the 1920s. Although he supported the League of Nations as a framework for multilateral economic cooperation, he continued to insist that a small country like the Austrian Republic must be absorbed into an intervening European unit. He never believed that universal international institutions offered a substitute for regional ones, and he supported

[29] Besprechung bei Kaz. Dr. Marchet (4 May 1915); Sitzung bei Exz. Marchet (5 May 1915) ÖStA, HHStA, NL Baerenreither/30.

[30] Kapp, 'Customs Union' (n 28) 149–155; Brettner-Messler, 'Richard Riedl—ein liberaler Imperialist' (n 5) 222–228; Watson, *Ring of Steel* (n 27) 263.

[31] II. Sitzung (26 March 1915) ÖStA, HHStA, NL Baerenreither/30.

[32] *Denkschrift Aus Deutsch-Österreich* (Hirzel 1915) 71. Glenda Sluga shows that before 1914 'internationality' was understood as an infrastructural, legal, and cultural framework for nation-states. See Sluga, *Internationalism* (n 3) 12–17.

the League only insofar as he believed that it would be possible to create European and Austro-German substructures within it.

In 1915–1916, the *Denkschrift aus Deutsch-Österreich* circulated widely in Austrian and German official circles and notably made a strong impression on Hötzendorf and the German Chancellor Theobald von Bethmann-Hollweg. Along with many other top officials in Germany and Austria-Hungary, they had begun to consider the formation of a permanent Central European customs union as a wartime measure, in order to defuse tensions concerning the fate of foreign territory occupied by the Central Powers, in particular Russian Poland.[33] Yet, although many officials in Austria-Hungary may have been willing to accept an economic union with Germany in response to these geopolitical exigencies, they were unwilling to support it as a ploy to reinforce the cultural and political influence of Austrian Germans within the Dual Monarchy. This was the position taken by Karl von Stürgkh, the Austrian Minister President, and István Tisza, the Hungarian Prime Minister. In contrast, Bethmann-Hollweg responded positively to German nationalist propaganda from Vienna, especially the *Denkschrift aus Deutsch-Österreich*, and explicitly linked partnership with Austria-Hungary to ideals of pan-German cultural solidarity. This raised Tisza's hackles and doomed the project. Alexander Spitzmüller, the Austrian Minister of Commerce at the time, complained:

> There were certain undercurrents in the top levels of the Austrian bureaucracy that combined the economic reorganization of Central Europe with national-imperialist plans and thereby compromised this program, which otherwise was fully justified in economic and geopolitical terms.[34]

After the botched negotiations for a customs union in 1915–1916, Spitzmüller and other Austrian leaders excluded Riedl from high-level diplomatic negotiations with the German Reich through the end of the war in order to limit the influence of German nationalism.[35]

[33] Georges-Henri Soutou, *L' or et le sang: les buts de guerre économiques de la Première Guerre mondiale* (Fayard 1989) 39–43, 82–85.

[34] Quoted in Kapp, 'Customs Union' (n 28) 282. Jan Vermeiren explains that most Germans who favoured the formation of an economic *Mitteleuropa* during the First World War were motivated by general geopolitical calculations rather than a sense of cultural or political solidarity with German-speakers outside the German Reich. See Vermeiren, *German National Identity* (n 28) 120–145.

[35] Kapp, 'Customs Union' (n 28) 195–283; Heinrich Wildner, *1915/1916. Das etwas andere Lesebuch zum 1. Weltkrieg. Heinrich Wildner: Tagebuch* (Rudolf Agstner ed, Lit Verlag 2014) 196 (hereafter Wildner, *Tagebuch*).

IV. The End of Empire

Ironically, it was the collapse of the Austro-Hungarian Empire, which turned Riedl's vision of a united *Mitteluropa* on its head, that brought Riedl back into the inner-corridors of power in Vienna. In the fall of 1918, the Austro-Hungarian Empire splintered into eight new or reconfigured nation-states. These successor states largely resumed pre-war patterns of exchange immediately after the war, but a combination of structural weakness and restrictive policy began to significantly dampen regional trade by the middle of the decade.[36] Riedl regarded the economic disintegration of the Habsburg Empire as a catastrophic aberration that would have to be reversed, and he focused his professional energies on this goal for the duration of the 1920s. He wrote:

> the countries in the Eastern part of Central Europe belonged before the War, wholly or in part, to the large economic units of the Austro-Hungarian Monarchy and the Russian Empire and were only torn out of this connection by the Peace treaties. In the place of an economic unit a system of mutual seclusion through prohibitions and customs duties came abruptly into force. Seven thousand kilometers of new customs frontiers were created and eight new economic territories, some extremely small, came into being. In an age of large scale production the maintenance of these conditions is tantamount to the prohibition of resort to modern methods of production.[37]

At the close of the war, Riedl took for granted that rump Austria, initially called German Austria, would simply join rump Germany. The leaders of the new Austrian government shared this aspiration and included Riedl in their efforts to prepare an Austro-German political union, *Anschluss*, immediately after the war. In early 1919 Riedl travelled with a state delegation to Berlin to negotiate the economic sections of a secret Berlin Protocol for union between the new Austrian and German republics. He proposed a full customs union between Austria and Germany but also insisted on Austria's right to conclude separate treaties with the other Habsburg successor states. This would enable Austria to preserve an independent sphere of influence and continue to function as gateway between east and west, even after uniting with Germany.[38]

[36] Jürgen P Nautz, *Die österreichische Handelspolitik der Nachkriegszeit 1918 bis 1923: Die Handelsvertragsbeziehungen zu den Nachfolgestaaten* (Böhlau 1994) (hereafter Nautz, *Die österreichische Handelspolitik der Nachkriegszeit*); Drahomír Jančík and Herbert Matis, "Eine neue Wirtschaftsordnung für Mitteleuropa ... ' Mitteleuropäische Wirtschaftskonzeptionen in der Zwischenkriegszeit' in Alice Teichova and Herbert Matis (eds), *Österreich und die Tschechoslowakei 1919–1938: die wirtschaftliche Neuordnung in Zentraleuropa in der Zwischenkriegszeit* (Böhlau 1996) 330.

[37] Richard Riedl, *Exceptions to the Most-Favoured Nation Treatment* (PS King 1931) 17–18 (hereafter Riedl, *Most-Favoured Nation*).

[38] Brettner-Messler, 'Richard Riedl—ein liberaler Imperialist' (n 5) 198.

Austro-German union was desirable partly because it would allow for a geographic division of labour in which Austrian commercial institutions could focus on coordinating trade with the other imperial successor states, relying on Germany for access to global markets. Under Riedl's leadership, the Vienna Trade Museum sought to negotiate an arrangement along these lines with an analogous German institution.[39] After 1918, the Trade Museum retained only forty-six of its 500 pre-war correspondents.[40] Thus, the reduced Austrian Republic was more dependent on foreign trade than Austria-Hungary had been but had a more limited institutional base to support that trade. Riedl looked to Germany to bridge this organizational gap.

Riedl initially regarded the League as a roadblock to his regional plans because the Paris Peace Treaties explicitly proscribed *Anschluss*. He argued this prohibition both violated Wilson's principle of national self-determination and undercut the ethnic hierarchies that bound Central Europe together. He concluded that self-determination was a ploy to fragment the region and subordinate it to foreign economic control:

> [W]ith this idealistic phrase, he [Wilson] hides the eminently materialistic aspiration to place more than a third of the inhabited world in a condition of permanent economic atomization, perhaps in a progressive fragmentation, confusion, and conflict, so that it will be possible for the more organized political and economic bodies of the world to dominate here without using the force of arms.[41]

Riedl insisted that the Habsburg successor states would only be able to compete commercially with the United States and with European colonial empires if they reunited. He believed that this reintegration could only happen under Austro-German leadership and so did not see the League as a viable framework for it until Germany joined as a member in 1926.

V. Richard Riedl in Berlin

Riedl was appointed to serve as the Austrian Minister to Berlin from 1921 to 1925.[42] During this time, he developed a close relationship with German internationalist

[39] Information für den Herrn Staatsekretär für Handel und Gewerbe, Industrie und Bauten, betreffend die finanzielle Lage des Handelsmuseums (4 August 1920) ÖStA, AVA, Nachlass Richard Riedl (hereafter NL Riedl)/74.

[40] Meyer, *Exportförderungspolitik* (n 6) 132.

[41] Richard Riedl, 'Die Wirtschaftspolitik der Entente und Wilsons vor dem Frieden' (1920) 45 Deutsche Review 97, 117.

[42] As Minister to Berlin (*Gesandter in Berlin*), Riedl was the most senior Austrian diplomat in Germany. Starting in 1918, Austria sent only a Minister and not an Ambassador as the head of its diplomatic mission to Germany to signal that the separation between the two states was temporary. See Rudolf Agstner, *130 Jahre Osterreichische Botschaft Berlin* (Philo 2003) 55–59.

circles, business leaders, and foreign policy officials. Under their influence, he subsumed his vision of Austro-German unity within a broader programme of multilateral economic cooperation based on engagement with the League of Nations.

Riedl shifted from a Central European to a pan-European orientation in response to the Franco-Belgian occupation of German Ruhr industrial region in in 1923. For Riedl, this episode demonstrated the critical importance of Franco-German reconciliation. During the occupation, he wrote a draft treaty for a United States of Europe, which he sent to German leaders including Gustav Stresemann, who was soon to become Foreign Minister.[43] Stresemann later wrote, 'the idea of the united states of Europe was first presented to me by the local Minister from Austria, Mr. Dr. [sic] Riedl'. Stresemann affirmed that, 'I would not commit myself politically to this idea as far as Riedl does'. However, he agreed that Germany should work to minimize the impact of 'borders, passports, and tariffs' in Europe because these measures would consolidate the post-war territorial status-quo and impede Stresemann's long-term goal of establishing a 'nationally unified' Germany including Austria and the Danzig corridor.[44] When he began his six-year tenure as Germany's Foreign Minister during the Ruhr crisis, Stresemann initiated a new policy of reparations fulfilment and cooperation with France, Britain, and the United States. This led to the 1924 Dawes reparations settlement and the 1925 Locarno Treaties, which guaranteed the Franco-German border. Riedl supported Stresemann's more conciliatory foreign policy, and the two developed a very friendly relationship. During his time in Berlin, Riedl also established ties the German League of Nations Association, which collaborated closely with the German Foreign Office. Riedl wrote his plan for a 'United States of Europe' with a jurist from this association.[45] Riedl's tenure as the Austrian Minister to Berlin coincided with the campaign for German accession to the League.[46] After this goal was attained in 1926, Riedl accepted the principle that Austro-German union should be pursued through the League of Nations, rather than in opposition to it.

After he retired as Austrian Minister to Berlin in 1925, Riedl returned to the Vienna Chamber of Commerce, where he had begun his career. In the 1920s, the leaders of the Vienna Chamber shared Riedl's twin commitments to free trade and Austro-German rapprochement. In spring 1926, Riedl assumed leadership for the Chamber's policy in both areas. He became the General Secretary of the Austrian National Committee of the International Chamber of Commerce (ICC),

[43] Richard Riedl, *Die Vereinigten Staaten von Europa als konstruktives Problem* (Dt Schutzbund Verl 1926) (hereafter Riedl, *Die Vereinigten Staaten von Europa*); Brettner-Messler, 'Richard Riedl—ein liberaler Imperialist' (n 5) 321–322.

[44] Quoted in Walter Lipgens, 'Europäische Einigungsidee 1923–1930 und Briands Europaplan im Urteil der Deutschen Akten' (1966) 203 Historische Zeitschrift 64.

[45] Riedl, *Die Vereinigten Staaten von Europa* (n 43) 4.

[46] On the internationalist networks that developed in the early 1920s in connection with the German campaign to join the League, see Joachim Wintzer, *Deutschland und der Völkerbund, 1918–1926* (Schöningh 2006).

an umbrella business organization that worked closely with the League. He was also appointed Delegate to the Austrian Chambers of Commerce for the Extension of the Economic Area, a position dedicated to promoting Austro-German collaboration. In this role, Riedl coordinated efforts by different private associations to promote rapprochement with Germany and also prepared semi-annual joint meetings of the Austrian and German chambers of commerce.[47] The overarching goal of this work was to bring about de facto *Anschluss* by gradually aligning Austrian and German economic legislation. The Austrian chambers of commerce had been pursuing this strategy since the early 1920s.[48] Riedl's engagement with the League of Nations and the ICC was, in part, an attempt to anchor bilateral Austro-German legal integration in a broader, multilateral framework.

Riedl's vision of European solidarity retained remnants of imperial hierarchy—he proposed that Austria and Germany band together with industrialized West European states in order to open up markets to the East. Riedl condemned 'the endeavours of the new States in Eastern and South Eastern Europe to develop as extensively as possible their home production and to become self-supporting through shutting out foreign competition'.[49] In order to buffer his plans from the other successor states' anticipated objections, Riedl proposed to exclude most of them from the initial rule-making process. He argued that multilateral negotiations should be limited, in the first instance, to 'states which in a certain sense form a geographical unit and which in regard to their cultural and economic development stand closer to one another'.[50] In Riedl's plan, these states would first establish common norms amongst themselves and would then extend those norms eastward.

Riedl persuaded the leaders of the Vienna Chamber of Commerce to subsume their ambitions for Austro-German unity within this broader hierarchical vision of trade liberalization. His first act upon returning to the Chamber was to draft a fifty-page 'Action Plan' outlining an elaborate scheme to promote bilateral Austro-German integration within a multilateral framework.[51] Riedl remained committed to *Anschluss* as a long-term objective but urged caution. In the 1920s a wide segment of the Austrian public supported *Anschluss*.[52] At the same time, many

[47] Peter Fischer, 'Die österreichischen Handelskammern und der Anschluß an Deutschland. Zur Strategie der "Politik der kleinen Mittel" 1925 bis 1934', in *Das Juliabkommen von 1936; Vorgeschichte, Hintergründe und Folgen* (R. Oldenbourg Verlag 1977), 299–314; Brettner-Messler, 'Richard Riedl—ein liberaler Imperialist' (n 5) 350.

[48] Jürgen Nautz, 'Tarifvertragsrecht Und "Anschluss." Das Projekt Einer Gemeinsamen Tarifrechtsreform in Deutschland Und Österreich 1919–1931' (1991) 31 Archiv für Sozialgeschichte 123.

[49] *Collective Treaties Facilitating International Commerce in Europe. Report of the Austrian National Committee to the Committee on Trade Barriers* (Vernay 1926) 3.

[50] Richard Riedl, *A Collective Treaty Relating to a Common Upper Limit of Customs Charges and to Reciprocal Most-favoured Nation Treatment* (Vernay 1927) 8.

[51] Richard Riedl, Denkschrift über die Möglichkeiten einer Erweiterung des Österreichischen Wirtschaftsgebietes (April 1926) ÖStA, AVA, NL Riedl/80.

[52] Julie Thorpe, 'Pan-Germanism after Empire: Austrian "Germandom" at Home and Abroad' in Günter Bischof, Fritz Plasser, and Peter Berger (eds), *From Empire to Republic: Post-World War I Austria* (UNO Press; Innsbruck University Press 2010) 257–262; Erin R Hochman, *Imagining a Greater Germany: Republican Nationalism and the Idea of Anschluss* (Cornell University Press 2016) 38–41.

business leaders, including many in the Vienna Chamber of Commerce, feared competition from German firms and preferred to join a 'Danubian' grouping with the other successor states.[53] In the 1920s, the leading official advocate for a Danubian union was the Czechoslovak Foreign Minister, Edvard Beneš. He explicitly repudiated post-imperial regional hierarchies, calling for a free association of equals.[54] In contrast, Riedl hoped to use German backing in order to claim a dominant position in the former Habsburg lands, while ensuring that Austria retained an independent regional role as an intermediary between Germany and the East. To balance these goals, he argued that Austrian leaders should prioritize general pan-European cooperation without foreclosing a future union with Germany:

> Our approach must not appear to be a threat to European interests but rather must serve to advance them. It should not be limited to reciprocal relations between Austria and Germany, but rather must organically incorporate efforts in favor of an economic rapprochement of European countries with the goal of establishing a preferably <u>large economic area in Europe.</u> This is by no means camouflage, but rather an earnest attempt to end the present state of economic fragmentation and incoherence, in which the whole of Europe, but perhaps Austria worst of all, suffers. [original emphasis][55]

Riedl noted that the Paris Peace Treaties allowed for *Anschluss* with the consent of the League Council and suggested that Austria and Germany might be able to secure that consent by demonstrating a sustained commitment to wider multilateral cooperation.[56]

Even stalwart opponents of *Anschluss* in internationalist circles were willing to work with Riedl because he accepted the strictures of international institutions. French diplomatic reports indicate that Riedl was seen as a useful partner precisely because he was a credible German nationalist and therefore could mobilize Austrian business leaders who supported *Anschluss* around a relatively moderate course that passed through League channels.[57] He assured a French member of the ICC that 'while among his followers there might be known partisans of Anschluss, they will not use underhand methods [*moyens détournés*] to achieve their goal'.[58]

[53] Herbert Matis, 'Wirtschaftliche Mitteleuropa-Konzeptionen in der Zwischenkriegszeit. Der Plan einer "Donauföderation"' in Richard Georg Plaschka and others (eds), *Mitteleuropa-Konzeptionen in der ersten Hälfte des 20. Jahrhunderts* (Verl der Österr Akad der Wiss 1994) 249–251.

[54] Arnold Suppan, 'Mitteleuropa Konzeptionen zwischen Restauration und Anschluss' in Richard Georg Plaschka and others (eds), *Mitteleuropa-Konzeptionen in der ersten Hälfte des 20. Jahrhunderts* (Verl der Österr Akad der Wiss 1994) 185.

[55] Richard Riedl, Denkschrift über die Möglichkeiten einer Erweiterung des Österreichischen Wirtschaftsgebietes (April 1926) ÖStA, AVA, NL Riedl/80.

[56] Richard Riedl, Einführungsmemorandum für die Arbeiten des (22er) Zollunions-Ausschusses der 'Deutsch-Oesterreichischen Arbietsgemeinschaft' (undated) ÖStA, AVA, NL Riedl/86.

[57] Lucien Coquet to Monsieur de Clauzel (17 November 1930) Archives diplomatiques du Ministère des Affaires Étrangères, La Corneuve (hereafter AMAE), Rélations commerciales/Information/47.

[58] Maurice Beaumarchais to Aristide Briand (8 July 1926) AMAE, Société des Nations/1197.

German leaders also valued Riedl because of his dual commitment to pan-German solidarity and international law.

In the 1920s, most German leaders, including Stresemann, considered rapprochement with Austria to be a low priority. They focused on developing markets in Western Europe and overseas and on restoring Germany's status as a fully sovereign great power.[59] Yet although German leaders were not eager to pursue *Anschluss*, they also did not want to see Austria join a regional grouping with the other successor states that would block German access to the Eastern Mediterranean.[60] Riedl could be relied upon to do his very best to thwart such 'Danubian' schemes without making too much noise about *Anschluss*. Indeed, he had to resign from his post as the Austrian Minister to Berlin in 1925 because he worked to undermine a Danubian plan favoured by the Austrian Minister of Foreign Affairs (this episode also helped confirm his reputation as an unreliable maverick in Vienna's ministerial circles).[61] Although Riedl resolutely opposed regional solutions that precluded *Anschluss*, he was willing to couch his aspirations for Austro-German unity the neutral language of multilateral cooperation. The leader of the German chambers of commerce, Eduard Hamm, warmly praised Riedl's vision because it had 'the tremendous advantage of not being a specifically Austro-German scheme, but rather a general European plan.'[62] In the late 1920s, Riedl continued to work with Hamm as well as the leaders of the main German industrial association, the *Reichsverband der Deutschen Industrie*. Stresemann reported that he also had 'repeated discussions about economic policy', with Riedl, who he considered to play 'a leading role in Austrian economic life.'[63] Riedl was a valuable asset for German leaders because his position in the Vienna Chamber of Commerce gave him a power base outside the ministerial apparatus from which he could work against government policies inimical to German interests.

In particular, Riedl offered a counterweight to Richard Schüller, the top trade official in the Austrian government. Schüller's regional trade strategy primarily focused on cooperation with Italy rather than with Germany.[64] Riedl categorically rejected Schüller's Austro-Italian projects because he had long viewed Italian

[59] Matthias Schulz, *Deutschland, der Völkerbund und die Frage der europäischen Wirtschaftsordnung, 1925–1933* (Krämer 1997) 71–76; Susan Pedersen, *The Guardians: The League of Nations and the Crisis of Empire* (Oxford University Press 2015) 195–237.

[60] Anne Orde, 'The Origins of the German-Austrian Customs Union Affair of 1931' (1980) 13 Central European History 34, 37.

[61] Telegram, Stresemann to Vienna (24 January 1925), Politisches Archiv des Auswärtigen Amts, Berlin (hereafter PA AA), Politische Abteilung II/R 73239; Brettner-Messler, 'Richard Riedl—ein liberaler Imperialist' (n 5) 348.

[62] Protokoll über die Sitzung in Salzburg am 18. Mai 1926 über Fragen europäischer Handelspolitik (18 May 1926) ÖstA, AVA/NL Riedl/80.

[63] Aus der Niederschrift über die politischen Aussprachen in Wien am 14. November 1927 (14 November 1927) PA AA, Politische Abteilung II/R 30357.

[64] Jürgen Nautz, 'Historisches Einführung' in Richard Schüller, *Unterhändler des Vertrauens: aus den nachgelassenen Schriften von Sektionschef Dr. Richard Schüller* (Jürgen Nautz ed, R. Oldenbourg Verlag 1990).

expansionary ambitions in the Adriatic as one of the greatest threats to Austrian regional influence.[65] Riedl and Schüller also had a longstanding professional rivalry. In 1909, Riedl had been appointed to serve as a department head in the Austrian Ministry of Commerce over Schüller. At the time, Schüller had been the most technically competent candidate for the position within the ministerial hierarchy, but was not promoted partly due to his Jewish background.[66] The tables turned during the war, when Riedl was marginalized because of his ties to divisive German nationalists, while Schüller rose to prominence.[67] In the interwar period, Schüller became the Austria's top trade negotiator.[68] In 1926, he was appointed to represent Austria in the League Economic Committee, although according reports in Berlin, Riedl sought this appointment himself and would have been preferred over Schüller by German leaders.[69]

Despite the fact that he did not have a seat on the Economic Committee, Riedl's position in the Vienna Chamber of Commerce helped him establish close ties to the League. In the 1920s, the Vienna Chamber became a central hub for managing Austria's shifting role in regional trade networks and was consulted by League officials as authoritative source of information.[70] In 1923, as a measure of fiscal economy, the Ministry of Commerce transferred the key export-promoting organs of the Trade Museum to the Vienna Chamber's Foreign Trade Service.[71] The Chamber also became a prominent centre for economic theory due to the activities of its Secretary, Ludwig von Mises. Mises used the Chamber's headquarters to hold a prestigious seminar and run an Institute for Business-Cycle Research, together with Friedrich Hayek. This intellectual activity helped enhance the reputation of the Vienna Chamber in League circles.[72] In 1925, Pietro Stoppani, the

[65] Brettner-Messler, 'Richard Riedl—ein liberaler Imperialist' (n 5) 53–54, 220. Richard Riedl, Denkschrift über die Möglichkeiten einer Erweiterung des Österreichischen Wirtschaftsgebietes (April 1926) ÖStA, AVA, NL Riedl/80.

[66] Brettner-Messler, 'Richard Riedl—ein liberaler Imperialist' (n 5) 59–60.

[67] Wildner, *Tagebuch* (n 35) 167, 196.

[68] On Schüller's career as Austria's trade negotiator, see Richard Schüller, *Unterhändler des Vertrauens: aus den nachgelassenen Schriften von Sektionschef Dr. Richard Schüller* (Jürgen Nautz ed, R. Oldenbourg Verlag 1990).

[69] Hemmen to Trendelenburg (5 December 1926) Deutsches Bundesarchiv, Lichterfelde/R 3101/1951.

[70] Untitled report on a meeting of British, French, Italian and US commercial attachés with the president of the Vienna Chamber of Commerce (21 December 1922) Archives of the League of Nations, Geneva (hereafter LON), C 40, 7/3 and report from the Vienna Chamber of Commerce, Crise économique et finances publiques (23 August 1924) LON, C 41, 7/14; Meyer, *Exportförderungspolitik* (n 6) 141–142.

[71] Uebersicht über die Institutionen in Oesterreich zur Pflege der Aussenhandelsförderung (February 1929) ÖStA, Archiv der Republik (hereafter AdR), Handel und Verkehr/Allgemeine Reihe/3309; Regina Leuchtenmüller, 'Die Wirtschaftskammer Österreich. Ihre besondere Entstehung unter besonderer Rücksichtnahme der Außenhandelsstellen' (PhD, Johannes Kepler University 1995) 50; Franz Geißler, *Österreichs Handelskammer-Organisation in der Zwischenkriegszeit. Ein Idee auf dem Prüfstand* (Österreichischer Wirtschaftsverlag 1977) 10–13, 49–52.

[72] Alexander Hörtlehner, 'Ludwig von Mises und die Österreichische Handelskammerorganisation' (1981) 28 Wirtschaftspolitische Blätter 140–146; Quinn Slobodian, *Globalists: The End of Empire and the Birth of Neoliberalism* (Harvard University Press 2018) 48–49, 66 (hereafter Slobodian, *Globalists*).

main Secretariat official responsible for trade policy, praised the Vienna Chamber as an 'institution remarkable for its organization and its seriousness'.[73] Stoppani became Riedl's primary contact in the Secretariat and a key supporter of his multilateral projects. Stoppani and other Secretariat officials gave Riedl a warm welcome in part because they considered trade liberalization in Central Europe to be an essential complement to the League's currency-stabilization loans to Austria and Hungary in 1922 and 1924.[74]

Riedl's efforts to cultivate ties to the ICC and the League of Nations in the second half of the 1920s can be understood as an attempt to compensate for his alienation in official policy-making structures in Vienna. Yet because he was operating as an independent agent, Riedl ended up devising a policy formula that his own government ultimately rejected. The porous structure of the League's Economic and Financial Organization enabled outside experts like Riedl to bypass national ministerial hierarchies. This dynamic muddied the policy-making process even in established states like France and Britain. It may have had a stronger impact in Austria where there was a large surplus of former imperial bureaucrats such as Riedl mixing with a large volume of international officials.[75]

VI. Riedl's 'Safeguards for International Trade'

Riedl's engagement in the ICC and the League in the late-1920s focused on easing regulatory restrictions on foreign commercial agents. This was the first step in the 'Action Plan' for Austro-German rapprochement that Riedl wrote after he returned to Vienna in 1926. He decided to start with this issue partly because it was a high priority for the Vienna Chamber of Commerce and partly because it was already a core agenda item in the League and the ICC. Riedl predicted that it would be easy to rally political support in Vienna and Geneva for multilateral norms protecting trade networks, but underestimated how difficult it would be to disentangle the complex linkages between trade and migration.

The League's trade body, the Economic Committee, had been debating international standards governing the legal rights of foreign commercial agents since

[73] Pietro Stoppani, Notes pour Sir Arthur Salter (19 March 1925) AMAE, Papiers d'Agent Joseph Avenol/19, 92. Stoppani's personnel file reveals his central role in League trade policy (LON, S 888/3392). On his wider biography, see Elisabetta Tollardo, *Fascist Italy and the League of Nations, 1922–1935* (Palgrave Macmillan 2016) 220–222.

[74] Walter Layton and Charles Rist, The Economic Situation of Austria, Report Presented to the Council of the League of Nations, League of Nations Doc. C.440(1).M162(1).1925.11 (1925), 31; Clavin, *Securing the World Economy* (n 1) 27–31, 39; Nathan Marcus, *Austrian Reconstruction and the Collapse of Global Finance, 1921–1931* (Harvard University Press 2018) 193–195, 226–227, 236–237.

[75] Patricia Clavin and Jens Wilhelm Wessels, 'Transnationalism and the League of Nations: Understanding the Work of Its Economic and Financial Organisation' (2005) 14 Contemporary European History 465.

the early 1920s.[76] In 1923 and 1925, it issued non-binding recommendations concerning the rights of foreign nationals and firms in fiscal matters, property transactions, judicial protection, and access to professions.[77] These recommendations carefully avoided immigration policy, covering only individuals and firms who had already been admitted to a foreign country and authorized to exercise an economic activity. Thus, the League did not address the many restrictions that governments imposed during the admission process. Representatives from Czechoslovakia, France, the United Kingdom, and the British Dominions had argued that any attempt to address the sensitive 'question of admission' would mire the League's fledgling Economic Committee in toxic controversy.[78] In 1926, Riedl proposed to substitute the Economic Committee's non-binding recommendations on the 'treatment of foreigners' with a multilateral treaty imposing uniform international standards, but he decided to abide by the previous decision to exclude the 'question of admission'.[79]

The occasion for Riedl's normative push was the World Economic Conference, a large gathering of experts hosted by the League in 1927. Officials in the Secretariat used this event to consolidate ties to organizational partners, including the ICC.[80] Riedl took advantage of the new structures of cooperation linking the ICC to the League in the run-up to the 1927 conference to gain a foothold in Geneva. He was able to use these channels to write a Draft Convention on the Treatment of Foreigners that responded to the specific geopolitical and technical priorities of the Vienna Chamber of Commerce. His case highlights the affinities between Austrian imperialism and multilateral efforts to support international commerce in the 1920s.[81]

[76] Jasper Kauth shows that states' efforts to protect their nationals' legal rights abroad primarily focused on supporting trade networks both before and after the First World War. This explains why 'the treatment of foreigners' was dealt with as an economic issue and not a political issue in the League. See Jasper Theodor Kauth, 'Fremdenrecht und Völkerbund: Das Scheitern der International Conference on the Treatment of Foreigners 1929' (2018) 56 Archiv des Völkerrechts 205–212, 217–220 (hereafter Kauth, 'Fremdenrecht und Völkerbund').

[77] Traitement des ressortissants étrangers et des entreprises étrangères, rapport du Comité Économique (15 May 1923) PA AA, Rechtsabteilung/R 54262; Rapport du Comité Économique au Conseil (10 June 1925) PA AA, Rechtsabteilung/R 54262.

[78] Sub-Committee on the Equitable Treatment of Commerce. Second Session. Fourth Meeting (5 September 1922); Sub-Committee on the Equitable Treatment of Commerce. Second Session. Seventh Meeting (8 September 1922) LON, R/307, 10/23134/6105.

[79] Untitled, undated (notes on the ICC Sub-Committee on the Treatment of Foreigners beginning 'In Anbetracht der besonderen Schwierigkeiten') ÖStA, AVA, NL Riedl/132.

[80] George Ridgeway, *Merchants of Peace: Twenty Years of Business Diplomacy through the International Chamber of Commerce, 1919–1938* (Columbia University Press 1938) 227–231 (hereafter Ridgeway, *Merchants of Peace*); Michele d'Alessandro, 'Global Economic Governance and the Private Sector: The League of Nations' Experiment in the 1920s' in Christof Dejung and Niels P Petersson (eds), *The Foundations of Worldwide Economic Integration: Power, Institutions, and Global Markets, 1850–1930* (Cambridge University Press 2013); Slobodian, *Globalists* (n 65) 37–41.

[81] In *Globalists* (n 65), Quinn Slobodian also presents Austrian post-imperial politics as a key factor in multilateral trade liberalization during this period and specifically emphasizes the role of Riedl. He does not, however, assess how Riedl's deep commitment to pan-German nationalism structured his international engagement. The Vienna Chamber of Commerce, which is at the heart of Slobodian's

At the World Economic Conference, Riedl called for a fundamental shift from bilateral to multilateral trade policy. In June 1926, Riedl presented a lengthy memorandum to the ICC outlining a series of multi-party trade agreements that would gradually replace existing bilateral treaties. It was a condensed version of his 1926 'Action Plan', stripped of overt references to *Anschluss*.[82] Riedl's ideas fell on fertile soil, as leaders in both the ICC and the League were keenly interested in multilateral treaties in the years surrounding the World Economic Conference.[83]

Riedl's ICC memorandum on multilateralism circulated widely and made a strong impression on Pietro Stoppani, who was responsible for coordinating the World Economic Conference. Stoppani requested that ICC leaders give Riedl's recommendations particular consideration, writing that among the various documents they collected in preparation for the conference, 'the one that contains very definite seeds for future development is the Austrian report'.[84] The ICC appointed Riedl to serve as the chair of a Sub-Committee on the Treatment of Foreigners and on Legal and Social Discriminations.[85] In this role, he produced a pair of draft conventions, which the ICC submitted to the 1927 conference. Riedl's first treaty covered passport and visa procedures as well as the right of establishment, and the second treaty addressed foreign nationals' legal rights.[86] At the conference, an ICC representative helped secure a formal resolution endorsing Riedl's proposal for a multilateral treaty. The conference cut out Riedl's recommendations concerning passports and visas, however, because these issues were already covered by an ongoing standardization effort led by the League Transit Organization.[87]

Immediately following the World Economic Conference, the ICC appointed Riedl and the Economic Committee appointed Daniel Serruys, its French member,

story, was a central hub for the bourgeois *Anschluss* movement in interwar Austria. Riedl's plans for Central European multilateral cooperation were not simply a microcosm for a wider global order. There was a fundamental tension between the logic of regional blocs and universal markets, as evidenced in Riedl's interventions in League debates about the most-favoured nation principle. See Riedl, *Most-Favoured Nation* (n 37).

82 Much of the text of the German version of Riedl's ICC memorandum was lifted verbatim from his spring 1926 'Action Plan' for *Anschluss*. Compare Denkschrift über die Möglichkeiten einer Erweiterung des Österreichischen Wirtschaftsgebietes (April 1926) ÖStA, AVA, NL Riedl/80 and Richard Riedl, Kollektivverträge zur Erleichterung des internationalen Handels in Europa (Vernay 1926).

83 The Economic Committee tried to negotiate many multilateral treaties in the late 1920s but achieved only modest results. Constrained by the League's commitment to a universal application of the most-favoured-nation principle, the Economic Committee faced the difficult task of devising uniform multilateral rules for the whole world. See Clavin, *Securing the World Economy* (n 1) 44–45.

84 Pietro Stoppani to Édouard Dolléans (1 July 1926) LON, R 529, 10C/51057/46431.

85 Ridgeway, *Merchants of Peace* (n 80) 227–229; Chambre de Commerce Internationale, Commission des Entraves au Commerce, Première Session de la Comission Générale (23–24 February 1927) ÖStA, AVA, NL Riedl/134.

86 'Treatment of Foreigners and Legal and Social Discriminations,' in *International Chamber of Commerce Report of the Trade Barriers Committee presented of the Preparatory Committee of the Economic Conference of the League of Nations* (Herbert Clarke 1926), 14–15.

87 Actes de la Conférence Économique Internationale tenue à Genève du 4 au 23 Mai 1927, Vol. 1, League of Nations Doc. C.356.M.129.1927.II (1927), 35–36.

to write a new Draft Convention on the Treatment of Foreigners (hereafter, Draft Convention).[88] Pietro Stoppani coordinated the drafting process and made Riedl the primary author. Stoppani dispatched a League lawyer to Vienna to write the initial text with Riedl, which they then finalized with Serruys in Geneva.[89]

The resulting Draft Convention proposed to eliminate a wide range of legal obstacles and tax penalties that placed foreign nationals at a disadvantage in the negotiation and execution of contracts, the use of transport infrastructure, the creation of subsidiaries, the selection of personnel, and the acquisition and management of property.[90] It was also a bid to transform the League of Nations into the guarantor of an international regulatory order that covered all these areas of policy and therefore reached deep into national legislation.

The Draft Convention included series of blanket protections, 'safeguards for international trade', which aimed to attenuate the impact of immigration controls on foreign commerce without directly addressing the thorny 'question of admission'.[91] The 'safeguards' affirmed that foreign commercial agents covered by the treaty had a right to buy, sell, and deliver goods regardless of their immigration and residency status.[92] In sum, rather than making it easier for commercial agents to live and work in foreign countries, Riedl proposed to expand the range of activities that they could perform as non-resident foreigners.

The 'safeguards for international trade' were tailored to the particular demands of the Vienna Chamber of Commerce. The Vienna Chamber represented many trading houses as well as many specialty, high-value-added industries that depended on mobile commercial intermediaries for export sales. In the 1920s, the fragmentation of the Habsburg Empire made Vienna into a central regional nexus for transit trade, but Austrian exporters still had trouble accessing neighbouring markets.[93] Vienna trading houses complained that after the war, new licensing and registration requirements had been used to exclude them from wide spheres of commercial activity in the former Austro-Hungarian Empire. For example, in Poland, Czechoslovakia, and Hungary, foreign traders were required to obtain licences in order to place or accept orders and in order to access many forms of physical commercial infrastructure such as ports, exhibition spaces, and warehouses. Foreigners were often only eligible to for these licences if they first established

[88] For more detail on the role of Serruys, see Madeleine Dungy 'Writing Multilateral Trade Rules in the League of Nations' (forthcoming) Contemporary European History.

[89] Pietro Stoppani to Richard Riedl (20 October 1927) LON, R 405, 10/60780/29200; Charles Smets to Richard Riedl (1 December 1927) ÖStA, AVA, NL Riedl/115.

[90] Draft Convention on the Treatment of Foreigners, League of Nations Doc. C.174.M53.1928.II (1928) (hereafter Draft Convention).

[91] Although the Draft Convention did not address admission (the heart of migration policy), Jasper Kauth shows that it nevertheless stirred passions related to the heated population politics in Central and Eastern Europe concerning refugees and minorities. See Kauth, 'Fremdenrecht und Völkerbund' (n 76) 202, 216–217.

[92] Articles 1–5, Draft Convention (n 90).

[93] Nautz, *Die österreichische Handelspolitik der Nachkriegszeit* (n 36) 87–88.

residency and registered with the local chamber of commerce. This meant that that Viennese firms frequently had to operate through local partners in order to conduct routine transactions.[94] The 'safeguards for international trade' were designed to bypass these restrictions.[95]

New licensing requirements for foreign commercial agents were part of the national segmentation of the Central European economy after the collapse Austro-Hungarian Empire. In the early 1920s, restrictions on multinational trade networks went hand-in-hand with broader programmes of nationalization and 'nostrification', which aimed to place local industrial and financial organizations in the hands of loyal citizens.[96] Licensing and registration requirements can also be understood as a symmetrical response to the pre-war efforts by Riedl and other Austrian officials to establish a patriotic commercial elite to support a concerted programme of political and economic expansion. The Draft Convention would break this symmetry. The 'safeguards for international trade' required that Austrian commercial agents be treated as neutral 'foreigners' protected by an international legal structure rather than citizens of a particular country, supported by a national trade-promoting apparatus. This formula made national borders rather one-sided: they became barriers to be breached from without but not ramparts to be defended from within. Unsurprisingly, the Draft Convention elicited strong protest from the other successor states, especially Poland and Czechoslovakia. At an early stage, the association of Czechoslovak chambers of commerce told the ICC:

> With regard to the treatment of foreign nationals, the implementation of the whole liberal system must be done in such a way that free trade and free development proceed hand in hand with the freedom and security of states. The previous development and the particular relations of individual states must also be considered.[97]

[94] Die Zentrale zur Frage der Behandlungen der fremder Angehöriger (March 1926), PA AA, Sonderreferat Wirtschaft/R 118543; 'Gegen die Besteuerung der österreichischen Geschäftsreisenden in Polen' *Der Reisende Kaufmann* (Vienna, 1 May 1928) 3; 'Die ungarischen handelskammern gegen die österreichischen Reisenden' *Der Reisende Kaufmann* (Vienna, 1 August 1928); Sub-Committee on the Equitable Treatment of Commerce. Second Session. Sixth Meeting (6 September 1922) LON, R 307, 10/23134/6105.

[95] Although League debates focused on trade restrictions as the main impediment to Austrian exports, structural factors also played an important role. Many Austrian manufacturers simply were not competitive outside the protected Habsburg market, and their former customers had lower purchasing power in the 1920s due to declining agricultural prices. See Stirk, 'Economic Integration in Interwar Mitteleuropa' (n 2) 94; Jens-Wilhelm Wessels, *Economic Policy and Microeconomic Performance in Inter-War Europe: The Case of Austria, 1918–1928* (Franz Steiner Verlag 2007) 143–155.

[96] On 'nostrification' in the successor states, see Alice Teichova, *An Economic Background to Munich: International Business and Czechoslovakia 1918–1938* (Cambridge University Press 1974) 97–98, 119–121, 339–340.

[97] Die Zentrale zur Frage der Behandlungen der fremder Angehöriger (March 1926), PA AA, Sonderreferat Wirtschaft/R 118543.

This argument—that trade networks in Central Europe simply could not be regulated through abstract international norms that disregarded the specific historical relations between individual successor states—was a fundamental repudiation of the League's move to multilateralism in the 1920s.[98]

VII. Foreign Trade and Labour Mobility in Austria

The Austrian government also turned against the Draft Convention, although it was written to serve the particular needs of Austrian exporters. Opposition to the project came chiefly from Austrian immigration officials. They were concerned that provisions facilitating the employment of commercial elites would have a disproportionate impact in Austria, which had a top-heavy labour market with a large number of skilled professionals.

When the Draft Convention was submitted to a general diplomatic conference for a final review in 1929, the Austrian delegation led by Schüller helped eviscerate it. Along with the majority of the other forty-nine delegations assembled, the Austrians arrived at the conference with a long list of amendments that would bring the Draft Convention in line with existing national legislation.[99] Over three weeks of negotiations, the conference considered roughly four hundred amendments and produced a series of elaborate compromises.[100] Belgian and Dutch delegations then abruptly shut down negotiations by announcing that they would not sign a convention that incorporated the proposed amendments. The president of the conference, the Belgian jurist Albert Devèze, complained that the conference had attempted to accommodate too many country-specific reservations resulting in 'restrictive texts which would be appropriate to the worst possible situation which could be contemplated'.[101]

Devèze recommended that the majority decisions taken at the conference be discarded and that the original draft text written by Riedl and Serruys be adopted with minimal modifications. A second conference could then meet to consider whether individual countries might be granted special, temporary exemptions from specific articles. These exemptions would be phased out over time under League

[98] Comité Économique. Observations sur le projet de convention concernant le traitement des étrangers. Observations communiquées par M. Dolezal (2 April 1928), LON, R 2776, 10D/295/338; Observations du Comité National Polonais sur le projet de convention relative au traitement des étrangers (13 June 1929) PA AA, Rechtsabteilung/R 54265; Société des Nations, Comité Économique, 27ème session. Procès-verbal de la première séance (15 January 1929) ÖStA, AdR, Auswärtige Angelegenheiten/Handelspolitik/1166.

[99] Untitled and undated report (begins 'Artikel. 1, Absatz. 1'), ÖStA, AdR, Auswärtige Angelegenheiten/Handelspolitik/1163.

[100] Georg Martius, Schlußbericht über den Verlauf der ersten Tagung der Konferenz über die Behandlung der Ausländer (6 December 1929) PA AA, Referat Völkerbund/R 96707.

[101] Proceedings of the International Conference on the Treatment of Foreigners, League of Nations Doc. C.97.M.23.1930.II (1930), 67 (hereafter Proceedings).

supervision. Daniel Serruys and the Belgian, Dutch, and German delegations supported Devèze's proposal as a path to 'liberal progress' led by Western Europe.[102] Riedl also took this view. He had long favoured a two-speed rule-making process in the League.[103] Through the Draft Convention the capital-exporting, trade-dependent states of Western Europe converged with Riedl's pan-German imperialism to support a more sharply hierarchical regime of international economic regulation. Austria, however, opted out.

The majority of the national delegations assembled, including the Austrians, rejected Devèze's hierarchical solution in favour of a consensus-based procedure recommended by the Italians. The Italian delegation suggested that the League ask governments to prepare an exhaustive list of objections to the Draft Convention, which would then be circulated in preparation for a second conference. This would bury the project in amendments and counter-amendments indefinitely, but most of the conference participants preferred a more inclusive if slower League negotiating process.[104]

Although the conference officially endorsed the Italian procedure, Devèze used his discretion as the conference president to pursue the two-stage negotiating process that he preferred. In 1930–1931, he met in Geneva with representatives from six other West European states four times to negotiate a new treaty text, to be presented to the wider League membership as a fait accompli. This procedure contravened the majority decisions taken at the 1929 conference. Nevertheless, the League Secretariat provided administrative support, marking an evolution away from principles of unanimity towards a multi-speed governing process that continued in the 1930s.[105] The Austrian government refused to participate in Devèze's new round of smaller treaty negotiations. Riedl privately expressed his support for the new negotiations, affirming that he 'had always pleaded for the conclusion of a "restrained union"' that would include only 'the most advanced states'. He had little power to influence Austrian ministerial decisions, however.[106]

Opposition to further Austrian participation in the project came from the Migration Office (*Wanderungsamt*). This institution was initially conceived to regulate migrants' departure but shifted its focus to movement into Austria over the course of the 1920s. Interwar Austria faced a peculiar problem of high unemployment and high immigration. Migration patterns established in Austria-Hungary

[102] Proceedings (n 100) 67–69, 84–85.

[103] Riedl explicitly outlined this strategy in his 1926 'Action Plan' for the Vienna Chamber of Commerce (ÖStA/AVA/Nl Riedl/80). He presented it in the more neutral language of multilateral co-operation in Richard Riedl, *Rapport sur le Projet d'une Convention Internationale relative au Traitement des Étrangers* (Paris: International Chamber of Commerce 1929), 17.

[104] Proceedings (n 100), 67–91.

[105] The meeting minutes and working papers related to Devèze's second round of negotiations in 1930–1931 can be found in PA AA, Rechtsabteilung, boxes R 54269–54279 and LON box R 2885, dossier 10D/23109.

[106] Richard Riedl to Charles Smets (30 October 1930) LON, R 2885, 10D/23109/23109.

continued to bring foreign workers from the successor states into the Austrian Republic in the 1920s despite widespread joblessness. In response, the Austrian parliament passed a law in 1925 requiring employers to obtain licences for foreign workers in many categories.[107] Crucially, these licensing requirements were internal laws and were not part of Austria's external admission regime. Initial admission to Austria automatically conferred a right to engage in economic activity, but access to employment was restricted afterwards through local licences. In contrast, most of the other successor states imposed restrictions on employment during the admission process. The Migration Office expressed concern that Riedl's treaty would require Austria to loosen its internal labour-market controls, while many other signatory states would be free to preserve or even strengthen restrictions applied during the admission process, as this phase of the migration trajectory was excluded from the treaty. In its commentary on the Draft Convention submitted to League Secretariat, the Austrian government declared that this problem made it impossible for Austria to participate in the project unless it contained a uniform definition of 'admission'.[108]

This report also insisted that the employment provisions in the Draft Convention would have a disproportionate impact on the Austrian labour market. The convention's chapter on the 'Exercise of Trade, Industry and Occupation' guaranteed foreign nationals' equal access to professions requiring a certification and it also stipulated that foreign nationals and firms that operated abroad must be allowed to select employees 'for the management of their establishments and for the transaction of their business' without regard to nationality.[109] Riedl and Serruys wrote this chapter in consultation with the International Labour Organization (ILO). They agreed to assign the ILO authority for the general question of labour mobility. This meant that the Economic Committee's work on the treatment of foreign nationals would cover only salaried 'employees', but not wage-earning 'workers'.[110] The Austrian government's report on the Draft Convention argued that this distinction was less relevant in Austria than elsewhere:

> Austria is afflicted with appalling unemployment; like other countries it has thus been obliged to take measures to protect the national labour force against excessive foreign competition; given that the unemployed are not only found

[107] Peter Becker, 'Governance of Migration in the Habsburg Monarchy and the Republic of Austria' in Peri E. Arnold (ed), *National Approaches to the Administration of International Migration* (IOS Press 2010) 48 (hereafter Becker, 'Governance of Migration').

[108] Observations du Gouvernement fédéral autrichien concernant la documentation relative aux travaux de la Conférence Internationale sur le Traitement des Étrangers (28 May 1930) PA AA, R 54270.

[109] *International Conference on the Treatment of Foreigners, Preparatory Documents*, C.36.M.21.1929. II (1929), 4–5.

[110] Montel to Meyer (3 December 1929) ÖStA, AdR/Handel und Verkehr/1163.

> in the labour force, properly speaking, but also in all categories of salaried employees, the protection of the national labour market must also extend to these categories.[111]

Thus, the Austrian government wanted to preserve domestic protections for the same category of people—highly qualified commercial professionals—that Riedl was trying to protect abroad. Riedl remained committed to an imperial perspective and sought to project Austrian economic influence in Central and Eastern Europe, while the Austrian Republic asserted its sovereign prerogative to promote economic cohesion within its territory.

It was ironic that the Migration Office was the main source of opposition to Riedl's Draft Convention because Riedl had himself helped create this institution. In 1911, Riedl presided over a commission on migration that proposed to create a central information office to monitor emigrants leaving Austria.[112] This legislation was interrupted by the war, but after 1918 Riedl helped to establish the planned Migration Office in the Trade Museum of the Ministry of Commerce. It was moved to the Office of the Federal Chancellor around the same time as the Trade Museum's export-promoting organs were transferred from the Ministry of Commerce to the Vienna Chamber of Commerce.[113] Thus, the Draft Convention brought two pieces of the Austrian *Belle Époque* commercial bureaucracy that Riedl had helped build into conflict. In the Austria Republic, promoting exports and regulating migration had become conflicting policy priorities.

The divergent attitudes of the Vienna Chamber of Commerce and the Migration Office towards commercial agents' mobility partly reflects the links that these institutions developed to different international organizations during the course of the 1920s. While the Chamber established ties to the ICC and the League Economic Committee, which advocated free trade, the Migration Office interfaced with the ILO, which approached migration as a factor in employment policy.[114] The League Economic Committee supported Riedl's imperial vision that aimed to facilitate the activities of mobile Austrian commercial elites in the successor states, while the ILO helped enforce a national perspective focused on regulating domestic labour

[111] Observations du Gouvernement fédéral autrichien concernant la documentation relative aux travaux de la Conférence Internationale sur le Traitement des Étrangers (28 May 1930) PA AA, Rechtsabteilung/R 54270.

[112] The 1911 commission on migration focused on regulating the activities of shipping companies and emigration agents. Riedl was involved due to his responsibility for shipping policy. See Tara Zahra, *The Great Departure: Mass Migration from Eastern Europe and the Making of the Free World* (WW Norton & Company 2016) 23–64; Becker, 'Governance of Migration' (n 107) 46–47; Brettner-Messler, 'Richard Riedl—ein liberaler Imperialist' (n 5) 170; Richard Riedl, *Die Organisation der Auswanderung in Österreich. Bericht über die vorläufigen Ergebnisse der im k.k. Handelsministerium durchgeführeten Untersuchung* (k.k Hof- und Staatsdruckerei 1913).

[113] Becker 'Governance of Migration' (n 107) 47.

[114] Ibid; Heinrich Montel to Albert Thomas (16 November 1925) Archive of the International Labour Office, Geneva, E 2/1/5 A-C, R 232629.

markets. This demonstrates how the different branches of the League 'multiverse' could foster conflicting policy approaches at the national and regional level.[115]

VIII. Conclusion

The Draft Convention on the Treatment of Foreigners was not implemented as a multilateral treaty, but portions of it were transferred to bilateral agreements including the employment provisions that caused controversy in Austria.[116] The Draft Convention can thus be understood as part of a broader evolution towards a more indirect rule-making procedure in the League. Over the course of the 1930s, League economic norms were increasingly implemented through bilateral rather than multilateral treaties. For example, a set of model agreements on double taxation served as the basis for roughly one hundred bilateral treaties in the 1930s, establishing the foundation of modern international tax law.[117] By adopting a more flexible approach to regulation, the League was able define more ambitious multilateral standards aligned with the current practice of the most commercially developed states and allow governments to implement those norms gradually at their own pace. Writing in 1938, Alexander Loveday, one of the League's top economic officials, reflected:

> We are in fact gradually moving from a system of general conventions to the system of applying to each problem the procedure which seems most likely to result in business being done – in business being done, not universally [. . .] but between those States where there is a desire to do business.[118]

In the second half of the twentieth century this mode of hierarchical but indirect norm-setting played a central role in international economic governance. The League's Draft Convention on the Treatment of Foreigners was an early phase in the long twentieth-century movement to use international rules to protect border-spanning business networks. This movement stretches forward to the Organisation for Economic Co-operation and Development's (OECD's) Fair and Equitable Treatment Standard and the World Trade Organization's (WTO's)

115 On the League of Nations as a 'multiverse,' see Clavin, *Securing the World Economy* (n 1) 11–46.

116 Convention d'établissement et de travail entre la Belgique et les Pays-Bas (signed 20 February 1933) 3824 LNTS art 1–10; Luxembourg et Pays-Bas, Convention d'établissement et de travail entre le Grand-Duché de Luxembourg et le Royaume des Pays Bas (signed 1 April 1933) 4130 LNTS art 1–10; Commercial Policy in the Interwar Period: International Proposals and National Policies, League of Nations Doc. II. Economic and Financial 1942.II.A.6 (1942), 27; Mona Pinchis, 'The Ancestry of "Equitable Treatment" in Trade' [2014] The Journal of World Investment & Trade 13, 29 n 93.

117 Alexander Loveday, 'The Economic and Financial Activities of the League' (1938) 17 International Affairs 788, 790 (hereafter Loveday, 'Economic and Financial Activities'); Sunita Jogarajan, *Double Taxation and the League of Nations* (Cambridge University Press 2018).

118 Loveday, 'Economic and Financial Activities' (n 117) 789.

General Agreement on Trade in Services. Like the Draft Convention, both sets of norms were first defined multilaterally and then shifted to a more flexible bilateral basis.[119]

The Draft Convention highlights the significance of trade relations among the Habsburg successor states in the League chapter of the history of international commercial regulation. This treaty can be traced back to Richard Riedl's commitment to build a Central European bloc bound together by a mobile German commercial elite. This commitment predated the First World War and survived the collapse of the Austro-Hungarian Empire in 1918. In the 1920s, Riedl refashioned his regional vision using the new League idiom of international law, multilateral treaties, and neutral foreigners. He received considerable support for his repackaged imperialism in the ICC and the League, even as he became increasingly estranged from the Austrian government. Austrian immigration officials ultimately rejected Riedl's treaty and embraced a national outlook emphasizing economic solidarity within the borders of the republic. Imperial legacies developed their own momentum in the League of Nations, propelling an ambitious regime of transborder commercial rights that left behind the heart of the empire.

119 Sandra Lavenex and Flavia Jurje, 'The Migration-Trade Nexus: Migration Provisions in Trade Agreements' in Leila Simona Talani and Simon McMahon (eds), *Handbook of the International Political Economy of Migration* (Edward Elgar 2015) 267–274; Theodore Kill, 'Don't Cross the Streams: Past and Present Overstatement of Customary International Law in Connection with Conventional Fair and Equitable Treatment Obligations' (2008) 106 Michigan Law Review 853, 874–879.

10

Fighting the Scourge of International Crime

The Internationalization of Policing and Criminal Law in Interwar Europe

David Petruccelli

The interwar period occupies a strange place in the history of internationalism, the belief that international cooperation can peacefully resolve shared problems. For the first time, the idea gained a permanent institutional expression in the League of Nations, which transformed Geneva into a meeting ground where politicians, diplomats, and representatives of various international organizations dealt with problems previously confined to the sovereign sphere of states. At the same time, the prewar trend towards globalization that had nourished internationalist thought unravelled between the wars. The successive shocks of the First World War and the Great Depression effectively severed the lines of trade, movement, and communication that had characterized earlier decades and promoted a nationalist turn across Europe and much of the globe.[1] The interwar period, then, witnessed both the flourishing of international institutions and unprecedented constraints on the flow of people, goods, and capital.

The tension between internationalist ideals and a nationalist zeitgeist helps explain the derision heaped upon the League in its own time and in the decades since. Already during its lifetime, the League's liberal internationalism faced trenchant criticism from both right and left. What linked such critics as Carl Schmitt and E.H. Carr was the conviction that the League's liberal internationalist ideology was anachronistic, which, by obscuring the underlying political logic of international relations, threatened to create more conflict and bloodshed.[2] It is only in the past decade or so that historians have begun to challenge the dominant view of the League as naïve and utopian. Scholars have recently moved beyond the questions of war and peace to examine the way that the League provided novel forms of

[1] Harold James, *The End of Globalization: Lessons from the Great Depression* (Harvard University Press 2001); Robert Bryce, *The Great Interwar Crisis and the Collapse of Globalization* (Palgrave Macmillan 2009). On the specific restrictions on the movement of people brought by the war, see John Torpey, *The Invention of the Passport: Surveillance, Citizenship and the State* (Cambridge University Press 2000) 111–143.

[2] E.H. Carr, *The Twenty Years' Crisis: An Introduction to the Study of International Relations* (Palgrave Macmillan 2001); Carl Schmitt, *The Concept of the Political* (George Schwab tr., University of Chicago Press 1995) 56–57.

David Petruccelli, *Fighting the Scourge of International Crime* In: *Remaking Central Europe*. Edited by: Peter Becker and Natasha Wheatley, Oxford University Press (2020). © the many contributors.
DOI: 10.1093/oso/9780198854685.003.0011

international governance in a range of fields. Its brand of liberal internationalism, inherited from its American, British, and to a lesser extent French founders, was not divorced from but often served as a tool for exercising political power.[3]

One of the most trenchant lines of critique of the League's interwar internationalism has focused on the extent to which it both emerged out of and supported the European imperial project. This builds on recent scholarship that has revealed the extent to which nineteenth-century liberal ideas of trade and civilizational progress provided ideological justification for colonial expansion at the height of European imperialism.[4] A field long taken to be emblematic of liberal internationalism, international law, had developed not only out of an effort to develop norms and rules for interactions between sovereign western states but also to justify the subjugation of peoples around the globe in the name of civilization. Despite the anticolonial appeal of Woodrow Wilson's promise of national self-determination, the League Covenant also sprang from the pen of noted imperialists like the South African Jan Smuts. In a range of fields, but most notably in its mandates system that was set up to provide international governance for the non-European territories of the Ottoman and German empires, the League perpetuated the underlying logic and practices of European imperialism from the prewar era.[5] What makes this critique so powerful is its uncovering of the hypocrisy at the heart of the League; its liberal internationalist rhetoric provided justification for distinctly illiberal practices.

This chapter will suggest a different perspective on the work of the League of Nations. It starts not with the liberal intellectual and political traditions that characterized its founding, but by looking at thinkers at first at the periphery of League circles who gradually pushed a new problem towards the centre of its activities. These thinkers were police officials and experts in penal law from Central and Eastern Europe, and the problem was international crime. Though several issues that we would now think of as international crimes fell within the League's remit, notably the traffic in women and the drug trade, these issues were at first principally treated as social problems in line with prewar liberal internationalist activists.

[3] For a still-relevant overview of the recent literature on the League, see Susan Pedersen, 'Back to the League of Nations' (Oct. 2007) 122/4 American Historical Review 1091. On the connections between liberal internationalism and political power, see Glenda Sluga, *Internationalism in the Age of Nationalism* (University of Pennsylvania Press 2013); Mark Mazower, *Governing the World: The History of an Idea, 1815 to the Present* (Penguin Books 2012).

[4] Jennifer Pitts, *A Turn to Empire: The Rise of Imperial Liberalism in Britain and France* (Princeton University Press 2005); Uday Singh Mehta, *Liberalism and Empire: A Study in Nineteenth-Century British Liberal Thought* (University of Chicago Press 1999).

[5] Susan Pedersen, *The Guardians: The League of Nations and the Crisis of Empire* (Oxford University Press 2015); Antony Anghie, *Imperialism, Sovereignty and the Making of International Law* (Cambridge University Press 2007); Mark Mazower, *No Enchanted Palace: The End of Empire and the Ideological Origins of the United Nations* (Princeton University Press 2009) especially 28–103. For a more positive account of the League's liberal imperial internationalism, see Daniel Gorman, *The Emergence of International Society in the 1920s* (Cambridge University Press 2012).

The administration in Geneva resisted efforts to extend its mandate to include crime more broadly and to think of these problems principally as crimes. It was only in the 1930s that the issue of international crime occupied an increasingly prominent role in League activities, largely through the activism of two groups that had engaged in a protracted effort to push Geneva to take on the problem of international crime.[6] Examining the origins of these groups and their success in the 1930s suggests a more complex conception of interwar internationalism, one that moves beyond the customary emphasis on the tensions between imperialism and liberalism at the heart of League activities.

The law enforcement officials of the International Criminal Police Commission and jurists of the movement to unify penal law internationally developed international schemes in response to the bitter realities of political and social collapse in Central and Eastern Europe during and after the First World War. It was not an imperial but a post-imperial internationalism, which sought to grapple with the challenges facing a region of new states emerging from the collapse of the Russian, German, Austro-Hungarian, and Ottoman empires. It was an internationalism of necessity, for many of the thinkers despaired of the continued political existence of their respective states. And it would come to be an illiberal internationalism, one that sought variously to roll back, circumvent, and supersede key elements of the liberalism that had pervaded legal thought and policing in the nineteenth century and that served as a founding ideal for the League of Nations. In the 1930s, as the League's liberal internationalist agenda faltered, their ideas gained traction in Geneva.

The founders of the International Criminal Police Commission (ICPC), established in Vienna in 1923 and today known as Interpol, claimed that their organization was the realization of long-held aspirations of European police. This was, on one level, true. The ICPC's cherished programme for the centralization and specialization of national police offices freed from political and administrative restrictions on direct communication between each other and with an international office established in Vienna drew on ideas in circulation in police circles for decades. It tapped into particularly extensive prewar discussions among Central European police officials about the need for reforms in response to the 'international criminal' who took advantage of railroads, telegraphs, and other modern technologies while police were hamstrung by tightly drawn borders to their jurisdictions.[7]

A landmark moment in prewar efforts to internationalize policing had come at the 1905 meeting of the International Penal Union *(International Kriminalistische Vereinigung)*, an organization bringing together jurists and police officials from

[6] For a broad overview of the League's work on international crime, see Paul Knepper, *International Crime in the 20th Century: The League of Nations Era, 1919–1939* (Palgrave Macmillan 2011).

[7] Jens Jäger, *Verfolgung durch Verwaltung: Internationales Verbrechen und internationale Polizeikooperation, 1880–1933* (UVK Verlagsgesellschaft mbH 2006); Mathieu Deflem, *Policing World Society: Historical Foundations of International Police Cooperation* (Oxford University Press 2002).

across Europe to discuss reforms to penal law and policing. At this meeting, two German offices called for the centralization of national policing, direct international communication between police forces outside of diplomatic channels, and streamlined extradition procedures.[8] For German and Austrian officials, the internationalization of policing through this kind of informal administrative exchange capitalized on their preeminence in the maintenance of criminal catalogues recognized by foreign observers in the years before the First World War.[9] It also provided a solution to the decentralization of policing that vexed officers in German and the Habsburg Monarchy, who looked enviously to their counterparts in France. Internationalization of policing provided justification for centralization of state police apparatuses, though protracted efforts in Germany and the Habsburg Monarchy failed to produce national police forces.[10]

Yet the ICPC had not been founded before the war, at a time seemingly more propitious to international cooperation between police forces. The commission's existence, and many aspects of its agenda, reflected the specific context of its birth, a city (Vienna) and region (Eastern and Central Europe) wracked by war, revolution, and imperial collapse.[11] Social dislocation, political unrest, refugees streaming westwards from the collapsed Russian empire, and the collapse of governmental authority led to fears of revolution and cross-border crime in the years after the First World War. Counterfeiters, speculators, and bands of thieves and robbers proliferated amidst the chaos of postwar Central and Eastern Europe, unimpeded by the shifting and porous new national boundaries that crisscrossed the region. Reflecting on the new face of crime in the years after 1918, one police official noted that, 'All of Europe, or at least Central Europe, is in a sense internationalized'.[12] Even as cross-border crime seemed to be uniquely threatening, the

[8] Heinrich Lindenau, 'Das internationale Verbrechertum und seine Bekämpfung' (1906) 30 Mitteilungen der Internationalen Kriminalistischen Vereinigung 192; G.A. Hopff, 'Das internationale Verbrechertum und seine Bekämpfung' ibid, 206, 240–246.

[9] Raymond D. Fosdick, *European Police Systems* (Century 1915) 317.

[10] For examples of efforts to create a national German police force, see Curt Weiss, 'Ein Musterhaftes Zentral-Polizeiblatt' (1911) 41 Archiv für Kriminal-Anthropologie und Kriminalistik 110; Paul Richard Koettig, 'Zur Reform unserer Kriminalpolizei. Reichs- und Landeskriminalpolizei. Ein allgemeiner Deutscher Polizeikongress' (1910) 40 Archiv für Kriminal-Anthropologie und Kriminalistik 177; Robert Heindl, 'Reichskriminalpolizei' (1910) 40 Archiv für Kriminal-Anthropologie und Kriminalistik 368. On centralization of Austrian police, Anton Walitschek, 'Die Entwicklung der Polizei-Organization und des Polizeirechtes in Österreich von 1850–1930' in Hermann Oberhummer (ed), *Die Wiener Polizei: Neue Beiträge zur Geschichte des Sicherheitswesens in Den Ländern der Ehemaligen österreichisch-unagarischen Monarchie* (Gerlach & Wiedling 1938) 2, 296–298.

[11] For accounts of the postwar chaos emphasizing the violence, see Robet Gerwarth, *The Vanquished: Why the First World War Failed to End* (Farrar, Straus, and Giroux 2016); Robert Gerwarth and John Horne (eds), *War in Peace: Paramilitary Violence in Europe after the Great War* (Oxford University Press 2012); Peter Gatrell, 'War after the War: Conflicts, 1919–23' in John Horne (ed), *A Companion to World War I* (Wiley-Blackwell 2010); Christoph Mick, 'Vielerlei Kriege: Osteuropa, 1918–1921' in Dietrich Beyrau, Michael Hochgeschwender and Dieter Langewiesche (eds), *Formen des Krieges. Von der Antike bis zur Gegenwart* (Ferdinand Schöningh 2007); Alexander V. Prusin, *The Lands Between: Conflict in the East European Borderlands, 1870–1992* (Oxford University Press 2010) 72–97.

[12] Internationale Kriminalpolizeiliche Kommission, *Der Internationale Polizeikongreß in Wien*, 16.

police were remarkably ill equipped to deal with it, as the war and revolutions had disrupted old lines of communication and lasting political antagonisms hindered cooperation.

In these conditions, the president of the Vienna police, Johannes Schober sought to build ties with counterparts in neighbouring states. Schober used the prestige he gained from keeping order during the tumultuous postwar years as a springboard for a political career that led him twice to the chancellorship of Austria (1921–1922 and 1929–30), in addition to stints as vice chancellor and foreign minister.[13] Schober's Austria faced an existential crisis. One of seven interwar states made wholly or partly of territories from the collapsed Habsburg Monarchy, many of its citizens doubted that it was capable of independent existence. The notion that the unloved republic was *lebensunfähig*, or unfit to live, took root among much of its population.[14] In a 1922 article addressed to foreign audiences, Schober laid out this line of reasoning when he argued, 'The peace treaty of St. Germain has bestowed independence on this new Austria, and at the same time shut her off hermetically from the territories which had supported her with the necessities of life. At the same time it forbade the union with Germany […] and so robbed her of the fundamental conditions to guarantee an independent existence'.[15] Schober was both a monarchist who mourned the passing of the Habsburg Empire and a pan-Germanist favouring a closer union with Austria's northern neighbour. He was also a pragmatist, however, who recognized the need to accept the new European territorial order. He viewed his chief political task as promoting closer integration of Austria with its neighbours. In his first term as chancellor, he reached territorial and trade agreements with Hungary and Czechoslovakia, and in his second chancellorship worked with his counterpart in Berlin to develop an ill-fated plan for an Austro-German Customs Union.[16]

Internationalization of policing represented another route towards regional integration. In 1923, Schober held an international police congress in Vienna to discuss the problem of cross-border crime in the region. As he later recalled, he had hoped initially 'to interest the successor states and the other neighbors of Austria in the congress' in order to improve regional police cooperation.[17] In the event, the congress exceeded his modest aims. It was, in the words of one participant, 'a

[13] Rainer Hubert, *Schober, 'Arbeitermörder' und 'Hort der Republik': Biographie eines Gestrigen* (Böhlau 1990) 42–61; Hsia-Huey Liang, *The Rise of the Modern Police and the European State System* (Cambridge University Press 1992) 220–221.

[14] Bruce F. Pauley, 'The Social and Economic Background of Austria's *Lebensunfähigkeit*' in Anson Rabinbach (ed), *The Austrian Socialist Experiment: Social Democracy and Austromarxism, 1918–1934* (Westview Press 1985).

[15] Hans Schober, 'The Austrian Problem' (November 1922) 84/11 Advocate of Peace through Justice 374, 376.

[16] Hubert, *Schober* (n 13) 108–126; Anne Orde, 'The Origins of the German-Austrian Customs Union Affair of 1931' (March 1980) 13/1 Central European History 34.

[17] Johannes Schober, 'Ein Epilog zum Internationalen Polizeikongress in Wien' (1923) 1 PA Wien, Interpol.

truly international congress', with delegates from such far-flung countries as Egypt, the United States, and Japan, though the densest concentration were from Central Europe.[18] Despite its broad attendance, the ICPC, founded at the conference, was at first a largely a regional organization. Police officials from Austria, Germany, and the successor states of the Habsburg Empire numerically dominated the commission throughout the interwar period, most dramatically in its early years. Of the forty-six members of the ICPC in 1927, nine were from Germany, five from Austria, and a further eleven from the Habsburg successor states Czechoslovakia, Romania, and Yugoslavia, as well as the Free City of Danzig (an autonomous city-state separated from Germany at the end of the First World War).[19] By 1934, the ICPC had fifty-eight members, of whom twelve were from Germany, five from Austria, and fourteen from the successor states and Danzig.[20]

Viewed narrowly, the ICPC was an association of police officials who gathered periodically to discuss techniques and pendant cases. But its founders also hoped to promote a concrete agenda encouraging informal administrative exchange between police officials that circumvented political and legal channels while maintain a scrupulous respect for national sovereignty, reflecting the realities of a region riven by mutual antagonisms. In order to establish an institutional presence, Schober turned to his subordinate, the Vienna police official Bruno Schultz, who oversaw the construction of a series of catalogues on known international offenders in an International Bureau attached to the Vienna police. Though it welcomed files from around the world, the catalogues of the International Bureau similarly reflected the commission's immediate geographic context. Criminals from the region and specific offences preoccupying Central European police officials seem to have been overrepresented in the files.[21]

Despite the ICPC's roots in Central European concerns and goals, its founders harboured broader aspirations to organize international policing across Europe, and even globally. They sought to bring Western European and non-European police forces into active engagement with the commission, obtain official recognition by member government for its work, and have a seat at discussions at the League

[18] Friedrich Johannes Palitzsch, *Die Bekämpfung des Internationalen Verbrechertums* (Meissner 1926) 49. Of the 142 participants, the largest contingent came from Austria (71 delegates). The next largest delegations came from the successor states Czechoslovakia (16), Yugoslavia (9), and Hungary (5), followed by neighbouring Germany (4), Italy (4), and the Netherlands (3). Denmark, Egypt, France, Latvia, Romania, Sweden, and Switzerland each sent 2 delegates, while the United States, Fiume, Greece, Japan, Poland, and Turkey were each represented by one delegate. See Internationale kriminalpolizeiliche Kommission, *Der Internationale Polizeikongreß in Wien (3. bis 7. September 1923): Stenographisches Protokoll der Verhandlungen* (Selbstverlag der 'Öffentlichen Sicherheit' Polizei-Rundschau 1923) 3–4.

[19] Internationale kriminalpolizeiliche Kommission, *Die Internationale Zusammenarbeit auf kriminalpolizeilichem Gebiete*, 1st edn, 11–12.

[20] Internationale kriminalpolizeiliche Kommission, *Die Internationale Zusammenarbeit auf kriminalpolizeilichem Gebiete* (2nd edn, 1934) 24–26.

[21] Jäger, *Verfolgung durch Verwaltung* (n 7) 353.

of Nations over issues related to criminal policy.[22] By the late 1920s, however, the commission remained principally regional in its focus and activities.

There was a second agenda on international crime also coalescing outside of the League of Nations in the 1920s, promoted not by police officials but by jurists from Central and Eastern Europe. Like the ICPC's vision of police cooperation, the movement to unify criminal law internationally built on prewar ideas. International law had emerged in the last third of the nineteenth century as an academic discipline aligned with the era's liberal spirit. Its proponents viewed law as the embodiment of progress in international relations, using it both to organize interstate relations between so-called 'civilized' states and to justify colonial subjugation of 'uncivilized' states.[23] International criminal law, by contrast, had developed out of a specific critique of liberal legal theory. The International Penal Union founded in 1888 by the German Franz von Liszt, the Dutch Gerardus Antonius van Hamel, and the Belgian Adolphe Prins, was one of the most important organizations in Europe pushing for the infusion of modern sociological theory into the development of penal law and for the synchronization of legal norms around common ideas about crime and punishment. Chief among these ideas was the argument that criminal law should be reoriented from a focus on the individual culpability of offenders and on the protection of individuals' rights, core liberal principles, to an emphasis on the interests of society.[24] Along with a number of Italian jurists who formed what came to be known as the 'Italian school', the International Penal Union was a site of important legal thinking that contributed to a broad wave of penal reform in the late nineteenth and early twentieth centuries.

The war fractured the International Penal Union. While the German, Dutch, and Swiss national groups carried on their activities, its French members declared the organization defunct. In 1922, they invited 'loyally pacific countries', specifically excluding opponents during the war, to participate in a new organization

[22] Schober already announced the founding of the ICPC's central collection on counterfeiting to the League in 1924. See Bruno Schultz, 'Bericht des Referenten des Verwaltungsausschusses, Report from 1st ICPC Meeting, Vienna 1924 (1924) 6 PA Wien, Interpol; Oskar Dressler, 'Geschäftsbericht des Sekretariates der Internationalen kriminalpolizeilichen Kommission in Wien, 13 May 1924' (1924) PA Wien, Interpol. For a broader discussion of efforts to gain League acceptance, see Internationale kriminalpolizeiliche Kommission, *Die Internationale Zusammenarbeit auf kriminalpolizeilichem Gebiete* (1934) 112.

[23] Martti Koskiennemi, *The Gentle Civilizer of Nations: The Rise and Fall of International Law 1870–1960* (Cambridge University Press 2001) 66–177.

[24] On the International Penal Union, see Elisabeth Bellmann, *Die Internationale Kriminalistische Vereinigung (1889–1933)* (Lang 1994); Sylvia Kesper-Biermann, 'Wissenschaftlicher Ideenaustausch und „kriminalpolitische Propaganda": Die Internationale Kriminalistische Vereinigung (1889–1937) und der Strafvollzug' in Désiree Schauz and Sabine Freitag (eds), *Verbrecher im Visier der Experten: Kriminalpolitik zwischen Wissenschaft und Praxis im 19. und frühen 20. Jahrhundert* (Franz Steiner Verlag 2007). On both, see Mark Lewis, *The Birth of the New Justice: The Internationalization of Crime and Punishment, 1919–1950* (Oxford University Press 2014) 31–33; David von Mayenburg, 'Mitteleuropäische Strafrechtsvereinheitlichung—Internationale Zusammenarbeit versus Großraumkonzeption (1914–1933)' in Vanessa Duss et al. (ed), *Rechtstransfer in der Geschichte, Legal Transfer in History* (Martin Meidenbauer 2006).

called the International Association of Penal Law (*Association internationale de Droit Pénal,* or AIDP), which held its first meeting in Brussels in 1926.[25] Jurists in this organization developed new ideas about international penal law in response to the challenges of the war and the need to build a stable postwar order.

The Romanian jurist Vespasien V. Pella emerged as a leading voice within the AIDP. Like many jurists of his day, Pella was disappointed by the Paris peace settlement. His country had been one of the chief victors of the war and postwar turmoil, seizing a large swathe of territory from Hungary. For Pella, as for many jurists in the AIDP, the postwar settlement failed to provide satisfactory guarantees to the new and expanded states of Eastern Europe. He had shared the hopes of many jurists, inspired by Wilsonian calls for a new international order founded on principles of justice rather than power, that the peace settlement would put into place a robust body of international criminal law backed by the threat of force. British and American officials had established the League of Nations to operate through the force of public opinion rather than law, and they showed little interest in giving it enforcement mechanisms. Pella worked with other members of the AIDP to develop plans for an international criminal court to prosecute crimes of war and aggression, not only to punish the First World War's perpetrators but also to provide a legal defence for the new status quo. Such ideas failed to take hold. By mid-decade, Pella had turned an increasing share of his attention to the gradual unification of penal law internationally.[26]

Like the ICPC, the movement to unify penal law reconfigured prewar ideas in response to the challenges facing post-imperial Central and Eastern Europe. The new and expanded states of the region grappled with the legal chaos that had resulted from the integration into new or expanded states of territories with diverse and often incompatible legal codes. Many of these states sought to codify new penal codes in order to tackle this problem and to symbolically reaffirm the unity of their territories.[27] In 1927, at Pella's initiative, jurists mostly from Eastern and Central Europe gathered in Warsaw to develop common norms to write into their penal codes. This was the first of seven international congresses for the unification of penal law held before the Second World War. Though these conferences would come to include members from across and outside Europe, the movement's most

[25] Aufzeichnung, Barch R 901/27042, 2–3; Bellmann, *Die Internationale Kriminalistische* (n 24) 143–145.

[26] Lewis, *The Birth of the New Justice* (n 24) 78–117; Daniel Marc Segesser, *Recht statt Rache oder Rache durch Recht?. Die Ahndung von Kriegsverbrechen in der internationalen fachwissenschaftlichen Debatte 1872–1945* (Ferdinand Schöningh Verlag 2010) 241–261.

[27] Vespasien V. Pella, *La coopération des États dans la lutte contre le faux monnayage: Rapport et projet de convention présentés à la Sociètè des nations* (Pedone 1928) 21; Pierre Tzocoff, *Les Conférences Internationales d'Unification du Droit Pénal* (Impr. G. Thomas 1936) 12–13; Lewis, *The Birth of the New Justice* (n 24) 193–194.

influential members remained jurists from Poland, Romania, and Yugoslavia, as well as France and Belgium.[28]

For Pella and his peers, the international unification of penal law represented not an abandonment of their goals of building a body of criminal law overseen by an international court, but rather a means of preparing the ground for this through the gradual extension of common legal norms.[29] As Pella explained at the 1927 meeting, the ground for international criminal law must be 'first prepared by the extension to a more and more expansive group of states of common fundamental principles' of criminal law.[30] If the geographic expansion from a core of Eastern and Central European states represented one route towards a unified set of legal norms, Pella and his peers also sought to develop common legal norms from the top down aimed at a small but growing set of offences recognized as inherently 'international'. At the unification conference in Warsaw in 1927, the participants made a list of offences fit for broad international action, which included counterfeiting, slavery, the traffic in women, the drug trade, the distribution of pornographic images, and several other offences.[31] Many of these issues already fell within the remit of the League.

What Pella and his peers offered was a new conceptualization of these problems as international offences best tackled through unified criminal law. In a 1927 speech to the Assembly of the League of Nations as a representative of Romania, Pella underscored the need for concerted action against pressing international offences, arguing 'if we remember that ordinary criminality [. . .] closely follows the changes and the constantly growing internationalisation of contemporary social life—while becoming international itself too—we at once see the absolute necessity of seeking other methods of protecting society against international criminals'.[32] In 1928, Pella founded the International Bureau for the Unification of Penal Law, in which he served as secretary general. This bureau advocated for the unification movement at the League of Nations, particularly with reference to these international offences, but it had little success in its first years of operation.[33]

[28] Emil Rappaport, *Le problème de l'unification internationele du droit penal* (Revue Pénitentiaire de Pologne 1929) 4–5; Emil Stanisław Rappaport, *V Konferencja międzynarodowa unifikacji prawa karnego a jej poprzedniczki (garść wspomnień, wrażen i myśli 1927–1933)* (Drukarni Polskiej Ludomira Mazurkiewicza 1934) 8.

[29] Tzocoff, *Les Conférences* (n 27) 31–32.

[30] Rappaport, *Le problème de l'unification* (n 28); Emil Rappaport, Vespasien V. Pella, and Michel Potulicki (eds), *Actes de la 1 Conférence Internationale d'Unification du Droit Pénal* (Recueil Sirey 1929) 54.

[31] Ibid, 131–133.

[32] 'Records of the Eighth Ordinary Session of the Assembly, Plenary Meetings, Text of the Debates' (1927) 54 *League of Nations Official Journal, Special Supplement* 208.

[33] German representative at the League of Nations to Martius, Auswärtiges Amt, Berlin, 23 October 1929, 3, Barch R 901/78019; Rappaport, *Le problème*, 3–5; Buero, 'Congrés International de Droit Pénal', 21 October 1929, League of Nations Archives, Geneva, Switzerland R 3292 13117/510.

As they set about building the ICPC and unification movement, Johannes Schober, Vespasien V. Pella, and their associates drew on prewar ideas, but this should not obscure the radical break brought by the war and the collapse of empire in Central and Eastern Europe. Efforts to internationalize policing and the integration of sociological perspectives into penal law had deep roots. Yet the form and aims of these interwar programmes reflected the political and social upheaval that had followed imperial collapse and gained urgency in connection with broader geostrategic concepts for a Central and Eastern Europe emerging from the rubble of Europe's collapsed land empires. Johannes Schober had accepted the postwar status quo tentatively, but he continued to doubt the long-term viability of the state. The ICPC's informal system of police cooperation outside of legal or diplomatic frameworks addressed pressing concerns about cross-border crime after the war, stabilizing the precarious position of the Austrian Republic. But it also left the door open for future territorial revisions. For members of the unification movement, by contrast, the internationalization of penal law aimed at securing the postwar order. If schemes for codification around common legal norms answered the pressing need to impose unified systems onto the fractured post-imperial legal landscape, the longer term goal remained a body of international criminal law capable of averting future aggression. For the Eastern and Central European jurists and their French and Belgian allies, the forces of revisionism not only in Germany but also in Hungary and Austria, represented a threat that only a robust system of international penal law could deter.

The ICPC and unification movement both represented post-imperial internationalist projects, looking to the international sphere for novel ways to manage a new European order after the collapse of the Russia, Ottoman, Habsburg, and German empires, but the fundamental disagreement over the territorial status quo prevented cooperation between them for most of the 1920s. Nor did either group have much success influencing policymaking in Geneva, despite efforts to make common cause around issues of international concern. Bureaucrats in Geneva showed little interest in the problem of international crime despite repeated entreaties from both groups. And their brand of post-imperial internationalism was a poor fit for the imperial internationalist visions of the League's founders, represented not only in their approach to overseas territories but also their paternalistic attitude towards the new states of Central and Eastern Europe. This was initially viewed more as a region where new geopolitical visions could be imposed and experiments in international administration carried out than as a source of new international projects in its own right.[34]

[34] An important example of this Great Power paternalism was the minority rights system imposed on the states on Eastern and Central Europe at the Paris Peace Conference. See especially Carole Fink, *Defending the Rights of Others: The Great Powers, the Jews, and International Minority Protection, 1878–1938* (Cambridge University Press 2004); Mark Mazower, 'Minorities and the League of Nations in Interwar Europe' (1997) 126 Daedalus 47–61.

It was a major counterfeiting case and the subsequent drafting of an international convention concluded in 1929 that inspired cooperation between the ICPC and unification movement and opened the door for both to pursue their programmes through the League of Nations. The case involved a group of Hungarian nationalists who had counterfeited large quantities of French banknotes in a bid to weaken France's currency and to damage the credibility of its treaty system in Eastern Europe, where it had aligned itself with the status quo powers Romania, Czechoslovakia, and Yugoslavia against the powers of revision. The plot was laughable in execution. A clerk in a currency exchange bureau in The Hague had recognized as false the first forged note that a co-conspirator sought to put into circulation. Quick action by the Dutch and French police had traced the plan back to the chief plotters in Hungary, but investigations by French and Hungarian authorities soon faltered in the face of stonewalling by the authorities. With strong suspicions that top government officials in Hungary and rightwing circles in Austria and Germany had been involved in the plan, Paris at first sought to use its high-profile investigations of the case to promote democratic change within Hungary and to discredit revisionism in the region. When this failed, the French government proposed that the League of Nations oversee the drafting of an international convention on counterfeiting.[35]

The Hungarian banknote affair underscored the grave threat that criminal enterprises originating in Central and Eastern Europe could represent for international efforts to bring stability to the continent. The 1920s were years of rampant inflation in Europe, which sapped the authority of many governments, including the one in Paris. Widespread counterfeiting, especially in Central and Eastern Europe, undermined the credibility of already unstable currencies and raised the spectre of broader political crisis. The forgery of money had been at the centre of the agenda of the ICPC since its early meetings. Catalogues on counterfeiting currencies and counterfeiters had formed the nucleus of the International Bureau that Bruno Schultz developed in Vienna.[36] Pella had also recognized the threat that counterfeiting could represent to efforts at European stabilization, having warned about it in 1921 and 1925.[37] In the face of a criminal plot hatched in Central Europe that seemed to threaten the broader political and economic stabilization of Europe, the claims that international crime demanded international action gained credibility.

35 David Petruccelli, 'Banknotes from the Underground: Counterfeiting and the International Order in Interwar Europe' (2015) 51/3 Journal of Contemporary History 507.

36 R. Heindl, 'Der Internationale Polizeikongreß in Wien' (1924) 76 Archiv für Kriminologie 23–6, 29–30. Internationale kriminalpolizeiliche Kommission, *Der Internationale Polizeikongreß in Wien* (1926) 87–93; Bruno Schultz, 'Die Organisation des Internationalen Bureaus' 3, Barch R 3001/6334, document 87.

37 C.G. Disesco, 'Un nouveau crime international commis pour la premieère fois en Hongrie et prevu d'une manière imaginative depuis environ cinq anneés' (14 February 1926) 7 Dreptul; Legislatiune—Doctrina—Jurisprudenta—Economia Politica 53, in League of Nations Archives, Geneva, Switzerland, R 451 10/52185/52010; Vespasien V. Pella, *La criminalité collective des états et la droit pénal de l'avenir* (Imprimerie de l'État 1925) 257–258.

The counterfeiting plot also brought these projects into alignment with France's broader geopolitical agenda. Many in Paris had been disappointed by the insistence of British and American diplomats that the League worked through public opinion and deliberation between governments rather than legal mandates backed by the threat of force.[38] The call for a counterfeiting convention tied into earlier proposals for a legalistic League of Nations.

The drafting of the counterfeiting convention opened the door for Schober and Pella to influence policymaking in Geneva. The League secretariat invited both men to take part in the deliberations, and they remained involved from its inception in 1927 until its signing two years later.[39] The convention brought the police and jurists together in a common effort to combat international crime. It prompted Pella to reorganize the International Bureau for the Unification of Penal Law in 1932, not as a small set of jurists but as a pressure group representing several other international organizations, including the ICPC, that would influence the League's work against a range of international crimes.[40] Finally, the convention provided a template for subsequent conventions that would reconceptualize problems already within the remit of the League as international crimes, most prominently the drug traffic and traffic in women and children.

The League had continued long traditions of transnational engagement against the traffic in women and the drug trade. 'White slavery', as sex trafficking was commonly known before the war, had first come to public attention through the activism of the so-called 'abolitionists', who rejected the state regulation of prostitution then common in most of the world as indicative of society's sexual exploitation of women more broadly. Lurid accounts of white slavery sparked a public panic across the globe. By the early twentieth century, multiple overlapping groups of transnational activists pushed governments to stop the white slave trade, leading to two international treaties in 1904 and 1912.[41] Drug controls also had their root

[38] Zara Steiner, *The Lights that Failed: European International History, 1919–1933* (Oxford University Press 2005) 32–34, 40–46.

[39] The full minutes of the 1929 conference, along with supporting documents and final convention, is in League of Nations, 'Proceedings of the International Conference for the Adoption of a Convention for the Suppression of Counterfeiting Currency, Geneva, April 9th to 20th, 1929' 1 March 1930 [LND C.328.M.114.1929.II].

[40] Vespasien V. Pella, 'Unification du Droit Penal et Cooperation des etats dans la lutte contre la criminalite. Réunion des Représentants des Organisations internationales consultées par la Société des Nations' (8 May 1932) Bundesarchiv Berlin, R 901/27039, 167–180; League of Nations, 'Gradual Unification of Criminal Law and Co-Operation of States in the Prevention and Suppression of Crime' (30 May 1933) League of Nations Document A.7.1933.V., 8–9.

[41] On the origins of abolitionism in Britain, see especially Judith R. Walkowitz, *Prostitution and Victorian Society: Women, Class, and the State* (Cambridge University Press 1980). On the internationalization of anti-trafficking efforts, see 17/2 Women's History Review, special issue: Gender, Religion and Politics; Josephine Butler's Campaigns in International Perspective (2008); Anne Summers, 'Which Women? What Europe? Josephine Butler and the International Abolitionist Federation' (2006) 1/62 History Workshop Journal 214; Jens Jäger, 'International Police Co-operation and the Associations for the Fight against White Slavery' (2002) 38/2–3 Paedegogica Historica 565; Stephanie Limoncelli, *The Politics of Trafficking: The First International Movement to Combat the Sexual Exploitation of Women* (Stanford University Press 2010) especially 42–70.

in global advocacy groups protesting the trade in opium to East Asia, particularly China. This activism paid dividends by the early twentieth century, leading Britain, a chief exporter of opium to China, to commit itself to reducing the trade, and the United States to call international conferences on the issue, leading to the Hague Opium Convention of 1912 that laid the legal foundations of modern drug controls. At the suggestion of Britain, which hoped to counter the growing clout of German pharmaceutical firms, the convention committed adherents not only to control the trade of opium for smoking but also pharmaceutical narcotics such as cocaine, morphine, and heroin, which until then were easily accessible medical goods in much of the world.[42] In 1919, as the peacemakers gathered in Paris to work out an agreement to end the First World War, so too did representatives of these transnational advocacy networks, who managed to have both issues written into the Covenant of the League of Nations.

The League of Nations became the centre of global activism against both the traffic in women and children and the drug trade between the wars. In the case of the traffic in women, the League oversaw the drafting of a new convention in 1921, which consolidated prewar treaties, officially replaced the term 'white slavery' with 'traffic in women and children', invited countries to submit annual reports on the trade, and urged the League to set up an advisory committee on the problem, which held its first meeting the following year. This committee, which brought together state representatives and representatives of voluntary organizations, became an important centre in the interwar women's movement. At the committee's proposal, the League tasked a group of social scientists with carrying out a massive study into the extent and nature of the traffic. The experts' report, published in 1927, was based on flawed analysis of incomplete data, but the study was widely hailed as proving the existence of a large-scale traffic in women. It framed the trade as an international crime, driven by vast networks of pimps, procurers, and traffickers, but emphasized the need to fight the roots causes, including poverty, lack of education and opportunities for young women, and especially the state toleration of brothels in some countries, which met their demand for prostitutes by looking abroad. The experts proposed a raft of solutions to address these problems, such as improving the plight of poor women, tighter migration restrictions, and improved policing and welfare, but its principal conclusion was that the state toleration of brothels in some countries created the global demand for prostitutes. The study seemed to prove the abolitionist premise, and its proposal structured the League's engagement in the issue until the early 1930s.[43]

[42] On the anti-opium movement, see Peter D. Lowes, *The Genesis of International Narcotics Control* (Libraire Droz 1966) 58–78; Arnold H. Taylor, *American Diplomacy and the Narcotics Traffic, 1900–1939* (Duke University Press 1969) 20–46; Kathleen L. Lodwick, *Crusaders against Opium: Protestant Missionaries in China, 1874–1917* (University Press of Kentucky 1996).

[43] League of Nations, 'Report of the Special Body of Experts on Traffic in Women and Children, Part One' 17 February 1927, League of Nations Document C.52.M.52.1927.IV. (C.T.F.E./Experts/55). There is a large and expanding literature on the League's anti-trafficking activities. For critical views

The League of Nations played a critical role in the birth of the global drug control regime which transformed goods that had been lightly regulated before the war into strictly controlled narcotics. As with the traffic in women and children, the League of Nations established an advisory committee that met at least once a year to analyse the nature of the trade in drugs and to recommend policies to bring it under control. The representative of Britain, the Home Office bureaucrat Malcolm Delevingne, took the lead in shaping the emerging drug control regime. Because Britain's imperial holdings in East Asia continued to derive significant revenues from the trade in opium throughout the 1920s, Delevingne pursued a policy in Geneva aiming at imposing international controls on pharmaceutical narcotics mostly produced on continental Europe, effectively continuing his country's prewar agenda. The key to Delevingne's drug diplomacy was his effective use of the levers of publicity that the League of Nations offered him. He publicized a series of criminal cases where European pharmaceutical narcotics were intercepted being smuggled to East Asia and the Americas and used the international outrage to convince a broad group of states to draft and ratify two conventions, signed in 1925 and 1931, which effectively limited global pharmaceutical output of the narcotics morphine, heroin, and cocaine.[44]

The League's campaigns against the traffic in women and the drug trade had much in common. Both built on prewar efforts and were pushed into the League Covenant by global civil society groups with roots in the nineteenth century. In both cases, British officials and voluntary associations played a leading role, reflecting a British conception of the League as a body that would effect global reform through open deliberations and public opinion. One reason for the predominance of London was the capable leadership of the British Rachel Crowdy,

of the League's efforts, see Jean-Michel Chaumont, *Le mythe de la traite des Blanches: enquête sur la fabrication d'un fléau* (la Découverte 2009); Magaly Rodríguez García, 'The League of Nations and the Moral Recruitment of Women' (2012) 57 International Review of Social History, Special Issue 97; Paul Knepper, *International Crime in the 20th Century: The League of Nations Era, 1919–1939* (Palgrave Macmillan 2011) 86–113; Paul Knepper, 'The 'White Slave Trade' and the Music Hall Affair in 1930s Malta' (2009) 44 Journal of Contemporary History 205; Stephen Legg, '"The Life of Individuals as well as of Nations": International Law and the League of Nations' Anti-Trafficking Governmentalities' (Sept. 2012) 25/3 Leiden Journal of International Law 647. For more positive assessments of the League's goals, see Daniel Gorman, 'Empire, Internationalism, and the Campaign against the Traffic in Women and Children in the 1920s' (2008) 19/2 Twentieth Century British History 186; Katarina Leppänen, 'Movement of Women: Trafficking in the Intewar Era' (2007) 30/6 Women's Studies International Forum 523; Barbara Metzger, 'Towards an International Human Rights Regime during the Interwar Years: The League of Nations´ Combat of the Traffic in Women and Children' in Kevin Grant, Philippa Levine, and Frank Trentmann (eds), *Beyond Sovereignty: Britain, Empire and Transnationalism, c. 1880–1950* (Palgrave Macmillan 2007); Jessica R. Pliley, 'Claims to Protection: The Rise and Fall of Feminist Abolitionism in the League of Nations' Committee on the Traffic in Women and Children, 1919–1936' (2010) 22/4 Journal of Women's History 90.

[44] On the League's activities on drug control, see especially William B. McAllister, *Drug Diplomacy in the Twentieth Century: An International History* (Routledge 2000) especially 41–155; Kathryn Meyer and Terry Parssinen, *Webs of Smoke: Smugglers, Warlords, Spies, and the History of the International Drug Trade* (Rowman & Littlefield 1998) especially 15–35.

head until 1931 of the section of the League administration that tackled both the traffic in women and the drug trade.[45] And in both cases, the League committees sought to draw world attention to an international crime in order to generate momentum for ambitious reforms aimed at resolving deep-seated social problems. The traffic in women became a vehicle for abolitionists to argue for doing away with regulated prostitution globally, while the illicit drug trade was used to push through ambitious regulations on pharmaceutical output. Despite the effective use of public opinion to see through reform, however, there was little evidence that the underlying problems had disappeared, and in the case of illicit drugs seemed only to have grown more intractable as traffickers cut off from pharmaceutical supplies turned to producing their own drugs.

In the 1930s, emboldened by their success in drafting the counterfeiting convention, the jurists of Pella's movement and the police officials in the ICPC offered an alternative agenda, proposing legal and administrative frameworks for waging a sustained campaign against these problems reconceptualized principally as international crimes rather than ill-defined social problems. In 1930, in response to a request from the ICPC pointing to its work on the counterfeiting convention, the League's advisory committee on the traffic in women and children invited a representative from the commission to begin drafting an international convention targeting *souteneurs*, or pimps. The convention wound its way through multiple drafting committees over the following decade, with active participation after 1933 of Vespasien Pella and his unification movement. The proposed convention met resistance from abolitionists, who viewed it as a sideshow to the debate over regulated brothels, but the ICPC and unification movement propelled it forward, folding increasingly ambitious measures aimed at a range of third parties organizing prostitution into an instrument modelled on the 1929 counterfeiting convention's measures against crime. The conference planned for 1940 was called off due to the war, but the convention was picked up by the United Nations and signed with modest changes in 1949 as the United Nations Convention for the Suppression of the Traffic in Persons and the Exploitation of the Prostitution of Others.[46]

The international treatment of narcotics also became increasingly a matter of criminal policy in the 1930s, as officials in Geneva recognized that controls on pharmaceutical output had not stamped out the illicit trade but had simply driven production underground. The chief architect of the commission's International

[45] Gorman, *The Emergence of International Society in the 1920s* (n 5) 60–69. See also Rachel Crowdy, 'The Humanitarian Activities of the League of Nations' (May 1927) 6/3 Journal of the Royal Institute of International Affairs 153.

[46] For the history of this document, see Report of the Secretary-General, 'Draft Convention of 1937 for Suppressing the Exploitation of the Prostitution of Others' 10 February 1948 [UN Document E/CN.5/41]. The text of the final convention is available at United Nations, Convention for the Suppression of the Traffic in Persons and of the Exploitation of the Prostitution of Others, accessed 10 April 2014: <http://www.ohchr.org/Documents/ProfessionalInterest/trafficpersons.pdf>.

Bureau, Bruno Schultz, secured a seat on the League's Advisory Committee on Opium and Other Dangerous Drugs as a representative of Austria in 1931. He immediately pressed for a new convention targeting traffickers in drugs modelled explicitly on the 1929 counterfeiting convention, presenting a letter he had solicited from Pella endorsing the project.[47] Schultz and other members of the ICPC assisted in revising the draft convention, which was finalized and signed at an international conference in 1936. The resulting international convention, which remains in force, never counted as many adherents as the League's previous two treaties to control drugs, but it marked an important shift in the global treatment of narcotics from an emphasis on the licit manufacture to controlling the illicit trade through policing and criminalization. This would underpin the United Nations' approach to drug control that would be enshrined in the landmark 1961 Single Convention on Narcotic Drugs.[48]

The international conventions on *souteneurs* and the illicit drug trade revealed the growing influence of ideas about international criminals that had been promoted by the ICPC and the unification movement since the 1920s. The agenda on international crime inverted the League's work in the 1920s. The international criminal, embodied by the pimp and drug trafficker, was no longer justification for broader social reform efforts but the principal target of international action. These efforts capitalized on the success of voluntary organizations, government bureaucrats, and League officials in pushing these issues onto the global agenda and on the failures of these groups to fulfil their promised solutions to the problem of sex trafficking and illicit drug use. The abolition of state-regulated prostitution in an expanding circle of states did not bring an end to migratory prostitution, just as the control of pharmaceutical drug production did little to hamper the global flows of narcotics. The replacement of vague social reform movements with concrete measures to fight international crime also found traction in the 1930s due to a broader ideological shift, as economic crisis and mounting nationalism eroded the liberal impulses of the internationalism of the 1920s. In the 1930s, both the jurists of the unification movement and the police of the ICPC were increasingly conceiving of their agendas on international crime as alternatives to the liberal order of the previous decades.

The jurists of the unification movement formulated a sophisticated legal critique of the liberal legal order to push for a reorientation of international law. They drew on prewar ideas of 'social defence' that sought to overturn the traditional liberal emphasis legal equality and individual rights by prioritizing the interests of society over those of the individual in the formulation of penal law.[49] Pella transposed this

[47] Pella to Schultz, 22 April 1932, BKA-I / SR 4739 zl. 178.746/1932.

[48] David Bewley-Taylor and Martin Jelsma, 'Regime Change: Re-visiting the 1961 Single Convention on Narcotic Drugs' (2012) 23 International Journal of Drug Policy 72, 74.

[49] Lewis, *The Birth of the New Justice* (n 24) 22–23, 113–115. On the measures of security (*mesures de sûreté*), see especially Tzocoff, *Les Conférences* (n 27) 55–72. For a discussion of ideas of social defence

concept onto the international sphere. Criminals for him were 'beings inadaptable to the general and permanent conditions of social life' and therefore demanded a concerted international effort through the unification of legal principles. He resisted constitutional protections offered by many states to ordinary criminals by arguing that 'it is not the citizen, but the person with asocial tendencies' that criminal sanctions aim to punish.[50] This idea guided Pella's work drafting the convention on counterfeiting and *souteneurs*.

In the 1930s, jurists affiliated with the unification movement were increasingly explicit that their vision of international criminal law was meant to replace older liberal traditions. In 1931, the young Polish Jewish jurist affiliated with the unification movement, Raphael Lemkin, wrote in a report prepared for an international conference for the unification of penal law that international law traditionally followed liberal precepts, but 'such liberalism must vanish when the good that is sacrificed is important to all. Such is the situation when the acts of the offender create a common danger'.[51] Four years later, Lemkin's mentor, the Polish vice president of Pella's International Bureau for the Unification of Penal Law, Emil Stanisław Rappaport, called for a new theory of law that would form a basis for a new social form that would represent a 'middle ground' between 'individualistic liberal democracies' and 'new authoritarianism' represented by Nazi Germany and Soviet Russia.[52] They were seeking an illiberal internationalism founded on a different kind of law, then, but one that eschewed the radicalism of fascism and communism.

For the police officials of the ICPC, internationalization offered a means of circumventing the rule of law at home that they viewed as protecting criminals. Their model of policing was based on the informal administrative exchange about suspected offenders outside of official diplomatic or legal channels. They justified this move away from political oversight with appeals to the urgency and delicacy of international exchange. They used a combination international surveillance, harassment, and expulsion to target individuals identified as international criminals, overwhelmingly displaced Eastern Europeans, Jews, and Roma who did not fit easily into the new world of nation-states and therefore lacked the protections that states afforded their citizens. The police official Bruno Schultz captured this spirit in a 1931 address to the League of Nations, arguing 'this is a question of cosmopolitan criminals, who know neither nationality nor morality, spread unfortunately to the entire civilized world, a scourge of all humanity'.[53] This approach was compatible with that of the

in Fascist Italy, see Tiago Pires Marques, *Crime and the Fascist State, 1850–1940* (Pickering & Chato 2013) especially 69–108.

[50] Pella, 'Unification du Droit Penal' (n 40) 12, 13.

[51] Raphaël Lemkin, *Terrorism: Rapport* (Libraire du Recueil Sirey 1931) 10.

[52] Emil Stanisław Rappaport, *Media via Kodeksu Karnego Polskiego* (Skład Główny w Księgarni F. Hoesicka 1935) 5.

[53] Schultz's statement is in ÖStA AdR BKA-I / SR 4439, zl. 143.961/1931-20/g.

unification movement, looking to internationalization to circumvent traditional liberal protections constraining police power while also placing faith in, and working to codify, a new body of law. By the late 1930s, important voices within the ICPC, including many of its Austrian officials, had come out for a more radical position, aligning themselves with the efforts of police in Nazi Germany who sought expansive powers of preventive detention in order to build a new kind of state that was no longer characterized by the rule of law.[54] By this point, the League was politically in disarray, though it continued to carry out its technical functions, including the fight against the traffic in women and children and the drug trade.

Considering the evolution of the League's efforts to fight the traffic in women and the illicit drug trade opens new perspectives on the work of this organization. This entails a broadening of our traditional geographic horizons to bring Eastern and Central Europeans into a story of interwar international society traditionally dominated by Western European and American thinkers and politicians. The League's engagement against these activities initially followed the liberal prewar agenda of voluntary associations centred in Western Europe, to be sure, but by the 1930s, its programme increasingly reflected a very different internationalist vision emanating from Central and Eastern Europe. The police officials of the ICPC and the jurists of the movement to unify penal law internationally reconfigured prewar ideas for the urgent task of building a more stable postwar East Central Europe. The convulsive transformation of the region from a world of empires to one of nation-states demanded new forms of international cooperation. They sought to grant far-reaching powers to the international community to coercively solve shared problems and to override domestic liberal traditions. If this was a distinctively post-imperial version of internationalism, then, it was also an illiberal internationalism in practice as well as theory. The League of Nations is most often remembered today as embodying the folly of a utopian brand of liberal internationalism, but two of its most remarkable and enduring achievements—the construction of the global drug prohibition regime and the institutionalization of legal and administrative norms for dealing with human trafficking—were as much products of illiberal impulses as liberal ones.

[54] For discussions of 'preventive policing' that would empower law enforcement to detain and intern individuals without due process, see Bruno Schultz, 'Mesures répressives et préventives à l'égard d'actes préparatoires à des crimes et délits graves et à l'égard de toute autre conduite dangereuse qui laisse apparaître une intention criminelle' (1937) Report from 13th ICPC Meeting, London, Schweizerisches Bundesarchiv, Berne E 4326 A 1991/157, Bd. 1; Bruno Schultz, 'Die Bekämpfung von Vorbereitungshandlungen schweren Verbrechen und von sonstigem gefährlichen Verhalten, das verbrecherischen Willen erkennen läßt. Abschließender Bericht' (1939) Report Prepared for 15th Planned ICPC Meeting, Berlin, ibid, Bd. 2. On the National Socialist theories of policing, see especially Ulrich Herbert, *Best: Biographische Studien über Radikalismus, Weltanschauung und Vernunft, 1903–1989* (Verlag J.H.W. Dietz Nachfolger 1996) 133–203; Michael Wildt, *Generation des Unbedingten: Des Führungskorps des Reichssicherheitshauptamtes* (Hamburger Edition 2002) especially 209–282. For an insightful early analysis of the uneasy coexistence in Nazi Germany of a lawless police state ('Prerogative State') and a state of law ('Normative State') in Nazi Germany, see Ernst Fraenkel, *The Dual State: A Contribution to the Theory of Dictatorship* (E.A. Shils tr., Octagon Books 1969).

11

Nation, Internationalism, and the Policies against Trafficking in Girls and Women after the Fall of the Habsburg Empire

Martina Steer

'Austria-Hungary not only has the liveliest export trade, but also does brisk domestic trade in human merchandise. Since it serves as a link between Orient and Occident, it is of great importance as a transfer country.'[1] The author of these words, Martha (later Karl) Baer, a German-Jewish social worker and Zionist, described the Habsburg Monarchy in its entirety as the central hub of human trafficking. Common opinion at the time considered only Galicia, the Polish part of the empire, along with Bukovina and the frontier area of Romania to be the European hotspots of sex trade, however—and certainly not Styria or Tyrol in the West.[2] This was primarily due to the eastern region's large impoverished Jewish population. Similar allegations were raised against other parts of the formerly Polish territory, such as Warsaw and the *Kresy*, the eastern borderlands annexed by Russia, in which Jews lived in economic misery as well. While Jews were accused of buying and selling Christian girls, their detractors deliberately distorted the facts by neglecting to mention that the majority of prostitutes were in fact Jewish girls and women. Edward Bristow rightly hinted that these allegations represented a sexualized version of the ritual murder charge.[3]

But it was not only anti-Semites who imputed a disproportionate share in international human trafficking to Polish Jewry. Jewish activists in Western Europe likewise exaggerated the role of Polish Jews as procurers and pimps, although they did stress that it was primarily Jewish women who were forced to work as prostitutes and thus represented the victims of these activities.[4] Jewish welfare and feminist organizations such as the *B'nai B'rith* lodge of Hamburg, or the German *Jüdischer Frauenbund*, the Jewish Women's League, or the French-Austrian *Baronin Clara*

[1] Martha Baer, *Der Internationale Mädchenhandel* (Hermann Seemann Nachf. 1908).
[2] Keely Stauter-Halsted, *The Devil's Chain: Prostitution and Social Control in Partitioned Poland* (Cornell University Press 2015) 117–136.
[3] Edward Bristow, *Prostitution and Prejudice: The Jewish Fight against White Slavery, 1870–1939* (Schocken 1983) 75–80.
[4] Ibid.

Martina Steer, *Nation, Internationalism, and the Policies against Trafficking in Girls and Women after the Fall of the Habsburg Empire* In: *Remaking Central Europe.* Edited by: Peter Becker and Natasha Wheatley, Oxford University Press (2020). © the many contributors. DOI: 10.1093/oso/9780198854685.003.0012

von Hirsch-Kaiser-Jubiläums-Stiftung zur Unterstützung von Knaben und Mädchen in Österreich, concentrated their activities on Galicia. They sent delegates—social and feminist activists such as Baer—to the eastern borderlands of the empire to report on the situation, and they also engaged in practical work: to save Jewish girls and young women from prostitution and inhibit human trafficking, they established networks of schools and other educational institutions and campaigned against a misogynistic Jewish marriage law.

Baer's statement on the Habsburg Monarchy's role in human trafficking is indicative of the considerable international attention that the sexual abuse and exploitation of girls and women had attracted since the end of the nineteenth century. Numerous reports and pieces of information on the euphemistically termed 'white slavery' or human trafficking in Europe, South America, and the Middle East fuelled public hysteria regarding the danger faced by innocent young women, the spread of venereal diseases, and the degeneration of the body politic in general in nearly all European countries. This societal fear gave rise to the anti-trafficking movement.[5]

Some researchers have rightly argued that the preoccupation with prostitution and human trafficking subsided in most European countries after the war. The social and cultural uprooting of soldiers and persons on the home front alike, along with the massive population movements during and after the war, had suspended mechanisms of social monitoring and contributed to shifts in moral standards and long-term sexual behaviour trends.[6] Especially in the eastern war zones, the sexual needs of men in the armed forces fostered prostitution, which occurred clandestinely as well as under regulation by the military leadership.[7]

Despite a changing attitude towards prostitution, one of the successor states of Austria-Hungary, the Republic of Poland, continued to struggle with its image as the European hotspot of human trafficking during the interwar years. Prostitution and human trafficking were still generally perceived as activities monopolized by Polish Jews. While this perception tarnished the new republic's reputation as a civilized society, it also concurred with the Polish narrative of national victimhood. At the same time, the newly established League of Nations placed prostitution—and especially human trafficking—among the key issues on its social agenda. It is therefore no surprise that a League of Nations report published in 1927 shows that international institutions continued to view Poland as the European centre of human trafficking.[8]

[5] For an account of the first anti-trafficking movement, see Stephanie A. Limoncelli, *The Politics of Trafficking: The First International Movement to Combat the Sexual Exploitation of Women* (Stanford University Press 2010).

[6] Cf. Dagmar Herzog, *Sexuality in Europe: A Twentieth-Century History* (Cambridge University Press 2011) 47.

[7] Sven Rößler, *Reglementierung der Sexualität? Frontbordelle und "wilde" Prostitution im Ersten Weltkrieg* (Grin 2009).

[8] H. Wilson Harris, *Human Merchandise: A Study of the International Traffic in Women* (Ernest Benn 1928) 129.

Consequently, the topic of prostitution and human trafficking in Poland constitutes a worthwhile path for exploring the interaction between the recently acquired national sovereignty of a post-Habsburg state and the new world order after the First World War—the 'new internationalism' with the League of Nations as its pivotal force. Investigating Poland's various governmental and non-governmental activities against prostitution and human trafficking during the interwar years, along with its stance on the League of Nations' recommendations on the issue, sheds light on how a nation state came to terms with a problem inherited from its predecessors, as well as how it dealt with commitments resulting from its newly acquired position as a sovereign actor in the realm of interwar international politics.

The selected topic is of particular interest for several reasons. Firstly, due to its tripartite division between Russia, Germany, and Austria, Poland had been an arena for international interests and activities concerning the sex trade long before the war and the 'new internationalism' that would follow it. Secondly, the issue continued to be crucial during the struggle of Polish political agents for national integrity. Thirdly, although the preoccupation with prostitution and human trafficking in Poland outlived the empires, the national and international, governmental, and non-governmental agents and responsibilities changed. Examining the developments relating to prostitution and human trafficking in Poland can thus help us to understand not only how the social and political legacy of the empires shaped the interdependency between national politics and international governance (and vice versa), but also how the civil society of a new nation state dealt with an 'old' problem.

This chapter shows how, on the one hand, reestablished Poland came into the focus of the League of Nations and its anti-trafficking efforts and agencies. Though reluctant to implement the provisions of international treaties, such as the minority rights stipulated by the Little Treaty of Versailles, the Polish government did transact certain recommendations by the League of Nations' agencies concerning human trafficking. On the other hand, the prewar international endeavours to save girls and women from prostitution, which had focused primarily on Galicia, came to an end with the national sovereignty of Poland. Foreign organizations ceased their relief efforts and withdrew from the country for various reasons, and domestic governmental and non-governmental institutions making use of the opportunities provided by a democratic state took their place.

I. Anti-trafficking Activism in Tripartite Poland

Before exploring the various policies and strategies for combating prostitution and human trafficking in Poland, the following section will delineate the situation in Central Europe at the dawn of the twentieth century. At the time, the ubiquitous disconcertment over prostitution and human trafficking and their effects on society led to the establishment of various international and national movements with differing views on women and political goals.[9] The largest of these organizations were the London-based International Abolitionist Federation and the International Association for the Suppression of the White Slave Traffic. According to Limoncelli, the members of the Federation tended towards a feminist stance and championed women's rights within the framework of an international humanitarian network. The Association, on the other hand, belonged to the moral reform camp. It consisted of dedicated women who did not subscribe to feminist views as well as men who were concerned with the issue in a professional function, such as doctors, lawyers, etc.[10] National organizations such as the German *Jüdischer Frauenbund* and its charismatic leader Bertha Pappenheim fought at a smaller scale, but were no less active.[11] After persistent campaigning along with numerous conferences and meetings, the International Agreement for the Suppression of the White Slave Traffic was signed by thirteen states in 1904.[12] It was the first multilateral agreement to address the issue of prostitution and human trafficking.[13]

Split up between Prussia, the Russian Empire, and the Habsburg Empire in the late eighteenth century, Poland did not exist as a state at the time. Nevertheless, the dangers of prostitution and human trafficking played a prominent role in the debate about the composition of a Polish national community. By the end of the nineteenth century, nationalists had increasingly begun defining the nation in terms of Catholicism and middle-class morality. This excluded Jews and women whose lifestyles did not conform to those standards; they were accused of spreading venereal diseases and thereby destroying the Polish body politic. The impacts of prostitution and human trafficking thus became a central topic in the demarcation of the tripartite nation.[14] Especially after the Lwów trial in 1892, during which twenty-seven Jewish traffickers were convicted for procuring girls and women, the narrative of the Polish nation as a victim of Jewish criminal activities facilitated by imperialist conditions became preeminent.[15] The crusade against human trafficking became part of the struggle for political independence and against the alleged influence of foreign powers.

The policies and activities aimed at controlling the sex trade in prewar Poland varied among the occupying powers. The Austro-Hungarian government signed

[9] Cf. e.g. Julia Ann Laite, 'The Association for Moral and Social Hygiene: Abolitionism and Prostitution Law in Britain (1915–1959)' (2008) 17/2 Women's History Review 207.

[10] Limoncelli, *The Politics* (n 5) 44–45.

[11] Marion Kaplan, *The Jewish Feminist Movement in Germany: The Campaigns of the Jüdischer Frauenbund, 1904–1938* (Greenwood Press 1979).

[12] The initial signatory states were Belgium, Denmark, the German Empire, France, Great Britain, Italy, the Netherlands, Norway, Portugal, Russia, Sweden, Spain, and Switzerland. Austria-Hungary signed in 1905.

[13] Österreichisches Reichsgesetzblatt (1905) 695.

[14] Stauter-Halsted, *The Devil's Chain* (n 2) 169–196.

[15] Keely Stauter-Halsted, '"A Generation of Monsters": Jews, Prostitution, and Racial Purity in the 1892 L'viv White Slavery Trial' (2006) 38 Austrian History Yearbook 25.

the Agreement for the Suppression of the White Slave Traffic in 1905 and established the *Zentralstelle zur Überwachung des Mädchenhandels* (Central Office for the Monitoring of Traffic in Girls) in the same year. The Agreement committed its signatory states to surveilling and controlling the mobility and migration of lower-class girls and young women. In keeping with its overall paternalistic character, it authorized the police to monitor locations of 'suspicious' female mobility like railway stations and ports. Job agencies came under scrutiny as well. In 1910, Austria-Hungary also signed the International Convention for the Suppression of the White Slave Traffic, which sought to establish trafficking itself as an international crime.

With the support of the central government, activists such as police physician and anti-Semite Josef Schrank established the *Österreichische Liga zur Bekämpfung des Mädchenhandels* (Austrian League for Combating Traffic in Girls) in Vienna in 1902.[16] Writer and teacher Celestina Truxa served as its general secretary from 1904, and Viennese banker Nathaniel Meyer Freiherr von Rothschild was its most generous donor.[17] Non-Jews and Jews worked side-by-side. Implementing the regulations of the Agreement of 1904, they primarily attempted to control the mobility of lower-class females by distributing pamphlets warning of the dangers faced by travelling women, patrolling train stations, and circulating information about missing women in Austria-Hungary and Russia.[18]

Besides these efforts, Austrian governmental and non-governmental agents were not overly active in combating the sex trade in Galicia or elsewhere in the empire. In fact, the government did next to nothing to eradicate poverty, illiteracy, and religious fundamentalism as the structural causes of prostitution und human trafficking. In 1903, Jewish and non-Jewish activists including members of the local Jewish community, several delegates from the German *Hilfsverein der Deutschen Juden* (Relief Society of German Jews), rabbis from Germany, Galicia, Romania, and Vienna, Jewish deputies from Galicia and Silesia, the chairman of the local Catholic League against Human Trafficking, and Pappenheim met in Lwów. The speakers emphasized the severity of the problem and suggested preventive measures like improving Jewish primary education and establishing a Jewish employment agency.[19] A local chapter of the Austrian League was founded, but whether any measures were actually implemented is unknown.[20]

Interestingly, Austrian Jewish (women's) organizations began to show interest in the Eastern European Jews and their problems only when thousands of refugees

16 Daniel M. Vyleta, *Crime, Jews and News: Vienna 1895–1914* (Berghahn 2007) 58–61.

17 *Bericht der Österreichischen Liga zur Bekämpfung des Mädchenhandels über das Vereinsjahr 1908 und Generalversammlungs-Protokoll vom 18. Mai 1909* (Bondi 1909) 40. The history of the League has yet to be written.

18 Stauter-Halsted, *The Devil's Chain* (n 2) 208–209.

19 *Czernowitzer Tagblatt* 1/192 (18 September 1903) 3.

20 Stauter-Halsted, *The Devil's Chain* (n 2) 208.

from Galicia and Bukovina started to arrive in Vienna during the war. Viennese Jewish women organized aid and welfare institutions such as soup kitchens, a nursery, and a vocational school for female refugees in order to protect them from 'undesired idleness'.[21] But unlike their German-Jewish counterparts, they never campaigned against the sex trade nor travelled to the East themselves to assess the situation there—neither within Austria-Hungary nor from postwar Austria.

The lion's share of preventive work to improve the miserable situation of Galician Jews and put an end to prostitution and human trafficking came from abroad. Since the second half of the nineteenth century, the Austrian part of tripartite Poland was one of the foremost targets of international Jewish philanthropic organizations. Major institutions such as the *Alliance Israélite Universelle*, the *Baron Hirsch-Stiftung zur Beförderung des Volksschulunterrichtes im Königreiche Galizien und Lodomerien mit dem Grossherzogthume Krakau und im Herzogthume Bukowina* (Baron Hirsch Foundation for the Promotion of Elementary School Teaching in the Kingdom of Galicia and Lodomeria with the Grand Duchy of Kraków and in the Duchy of Bukovina), or the Jewish Colonization Association pursued different strategies to improve the dire living conditions of Eastern European Jewry, though all of them promoted education.[22] They filled a void resulting from the negligence of the Austrian educational department, which undertook practically no efforts for the education of Jews in Galicia. Western Jewish organizations established schools of various levels and types, from kindergartens to high schools and vocational schools, as well as financing and organizing preparatory training for emigration.[23] Besides the fact that these organizations catered first and foremost to boys and young men, however (as Pappenheim correctly pointed out), traditional Jewish groups like the Hassidim feared what they called 'polonization', that is, the assimilation of their children.[24] Reflecting the gender norms of the Western European middle class, whose men were supposed to be the sole breadwinners while women stayed at home, the practicability of the philanthropic efforts focusing on males was limited for traditional Jewish communities, where women often earned the family's living and men devoted themselves to the study of religious texts.

As a consequence, Pappenheim and other female Jewish activists and aid organizations from Germany and France, like Karl/Martha Baer and the *Baronin Clara von Hirsch-Kaiser-Jubiläums-Stiftung zur Unterstützung von Knaben und Mädchen*

[21] Clara Fischer, 'An die jüdischen Mädchen und Frauen' (1915) 32/46 Dr. Bloch's oesterreichische Wochenschrift. Centralorgan für die gesammten Interessen des Judenthums 855.

[22] André Kaspi, *Histoire de l'Alliance israélite universelle—De 1860 à nos jours* (Armand Colin 2010); Theodore Norman, *An Outstretched Arm: A History of the Jewish Colonization Association* (Routledge 1985).

[23] Kazimierz Rędziński, *Fundacyjne szkolnictwo żydowskie w Galicji w latach 1881–1918* (Wyższa Szkoła Pedagogiczna 1999).

[24] Bertha Pappenheim and Sara Rabinowitsch, *Zur Lage der jüdischen Bevölkerung in Galizien. Reiseeindrücke und Vorschläge zur Besserung der Verhältnisse* (Neuer Frankfurter Verlag 1904) 14; *Bericht des Curatoriums der Baron Hirsch-Stiftung* (1902) 8.

in Österreich (Baroness Clara von Hirsch Imperial Jubilee Foundation for the Support of Boys and Girls in Austria), targeted girls and young women with their activities.

Baroness Clara von Hirsch, a Belgian philanthropist and widow of Maurice von Hirsch, had established her eponymous foundation in 1899 in honour of the fiftieth year of Emperor Franz Joseph's regency.[25] Endowed with 1,500,000 florins, the baroness' trust operated under the wing of her late husband's *Baron-Hirsch-Stiftung*, focusing exclusively on the education of girls despite its name. Starting with the most basic aid, it provided free clothing and lunches for children and established vocational schools for Jewish girls in numerous towns in Galicia, including Tarnów, Kolomea, Bohorodchany, and Buchachz. By 1904, the foundation was operating forty-nine educational institutions with 7,859 students.[26] In keeping with the contemporary bourgeois perception of useful skills for female members of the lower class, the Hirsch schools trained girls and women as domestics. It should therefore come as no surprise that Pappenheim praised the educational network as 'oases in the desert'.[27]

Another important endeavour was launched by the Hamburg *B'nai B'rith* lodge in cooperation with its local lodge in Lwów. Between 1904 and 1906, the aforementioned Martha Baer informed women about the danger of human trafficking and established several institutions to support Jewish women, including a nursery, a self-help association for female workers, an employment agency for domestics, and an information service for female migrants.[28] Having escaped the sheer poverty and close-knit networks of traditional community life in the shtetls, many women were overwhelmed by the anonymity and harshness of life in the city. Without education or at least vocational training, they could easily be lured into prostitution by procurers and pimps.

That these foreign activists by no means abandoned western social and gender norms of the middle class is evidenced by a dispute between Pappenheim and the most prominent female Jewish activist in Galicia, the Zionist Róża Melcerowa. Pappenheim was touring Galicia in 1903 on behalf of the international *Jüdisches Zweigkomitee zur Bekämpfung des Mädchenhandels* (Jewish Committee for the Suppression of White Slavery) and the *Frankfurter Israelitischer Hilfsverein* (Frankfurt Israelite Relief Organization) with the aim of collecting first-hand information on prostitution and human trafficking in the region and developing best practices to improve the situation. She met Melcerowa, one of the most prominent Zionists and Jewish feminists in the Habsburg Monarchy, in Tarnopol.

[25] Baron Hirsch-Stiftung, *Stiftbrief und Regulativ der Baronin Clara von Hirsch-Kaiser-Jubiläums-Stiftung* (M. Waizner & Sohn 1899) 5–8.

[26] *Zeitschrift für Demographie und Statistik der Juden* 3, 4 (April 1907) 64.

[27] Pappenheim and Rabinowitsch, *Zur Lage* (n 24) 11.

[28] Louis Maretzki, *Geschichte des Ordens Bne Briss in Deutschland, 1882–1907* (M. Cohn 1907) 222–223.

A charismatic and sought-after speaker, Melcerowa had founded several Zionist women's organizations such as the *Koło Kobiet Żydowskich we Lwówie* (Jewish Women's Circle in Lwów) and was striving to centralize female Zionist activities in Galicia and Bukovina. She had also been one of the few female delegates to the first Zionist World Congress in Basel in 1897 and had begun participating in the debate on the high rate of Eastern European Jewish women among prostitutes in Europe and beyond in its early stages.

Despite being an anti-Zionist herself, Pappenheim was pragmatic. She co-operated with Zionists and Zionist organizations on numerous occasions and did not categorically rule out Zionism as an option for Eastern European Jewry. After being confronted with Galician Jews, however, she criticized the Zionists for lacking a sense of reality. In the best tradition of a German Jew, she quite arrogantly described her Galician brothers and sisters in faith as dirty, lazy, and uneducated—in short, as uncivilized and thus unable to establish a state.[29] Dismissing the idea of creating a Jewish state in Palestine with these human resources as an unrealistic goal, she suggested proceeding step by step: first, the people were to be educated and trained professionally and morally so as to become proper *halutzim* (settlers). Only then could Jews become a 'nation among nations', Pappenheim claimed.[30]

Unsurprisingly, Melcerowa did not take well to Pappenheim's recommendations and in turn criticized what she considered a display of snotty behaviour by her guest from Germany. The Viennese Zionist paper *Die Welt* printed Melcerowa's harsh account of the visit, in which she mocked Pappenheim's attitude as far too lady-like and vilified her and her companion Sarah Rabinowitsch as mouthpieces of 'the rich Frankfurt Jews, the high and mighty Western patrons of the wretched Eastern Jews'.[31] She accused Pappenheim of lacking knowledge of the circumstances in Galicia and rejected her recommendations concerning preparatory work for emigration as completely useless for the specific case of Galician Jewry: 'Away from here! A different place to live and work—a home of our own—this is our only possibility of salvation.'[32] Although she fully agreed with Pappenheim in regard to the lack of work ethic and sufficient hygienic standards of lower-class Jewish girls, she considered a more severe form of 'training', promising a strict re-education programme for selected girls in Zionist households.[33] Melcerowa thus constructed an antagonism between the 'Eastern' approach of Zionism and the 'Western' approach of local social improvements. From her perspective, social reform represented a colonialistic and paternalistic affront to the character of Galician Jewry and was not an option.

[29] Cf. e.g. Pappenheim and Rabinowitsch, *Zur Lage* (n 24) 43–44.
[30] Bertha Pappenheim, 'Ein Besuch aus Frankfurt: Erwiderung' (3 July 1903) 7/27 Die Welt 15.
[31] Rosa Pomeranz, 'Ein Besuch aus Frankfurt a.M.' (19 June 1903) 7/25 Die Welt 4.
[32] Ibid, 5.
[33] Rosa Pomeranz, 'Jüdische Dienstboten' (21 September 1900) 4/38 Die Welt 3.

How much impact these prewar Western European activities in Galicia actually had remains debatable. They were met with considerable obstacles erected by an indifferent central government, persistent traditional Jewish lifestyles, and local activists who felt marginalized by the insensitive demeanour of Western Jews. But regardless of how suitable, appreciative of the local circumstances, or successful these non-governmental endeavours were, they could ultimately be no more than a drop in the ocean in light of the appalling situation of Galician Jewry struggling with the ambivalent effects of modernization, industrialization, and urbanization.

Still, it would be wrong to neglect the international outreach of these anti-trafficking organizations and disregard them as 'domestic pressure groups' whose 'interests and influence were targeted at a change at home', as some researchers have described them.[34] The German Jewish Women's League, the Hamburg *B'nai B'rith* lodge, and Clara von Hirsch's Franco-Austrian foundation became active in Habsburg Galicia precisely *because* they were aware of the transnational character of the political, social, and economic problems of Eastern European Jewry. Being part of the European middle class, they felt their morals and virtues endangered by the large and allegedly uncontrollable number of migrating poor and ill-educated girls and women during the period of industrialization and urbanization. Moreover, as Western European Jews, they suffered from the connection between Eastern European Jews and prostitution and human trafficking purported by anti-Semites all over the world.[35] But there was also a significant humanitarian aspect to their engagement, and feminist principles along with a sense of transnational 'solidarity with all Jews' motivated their efforts as well.[36]

Although Russia had signed the International Agreement for the Suppression of the White Slave Traffic immediately in 1904, Western philanthropy and relief work to save 'fallen' girls and young women encountered even less favourable conditions in the Russian part of Poland than in Galicia. A repressive Russian administration, the language barrier, and likely cultural animosities may have prevented philanthropists from abroad from becoming active on behalf of endangered Jewish women in Russia.

There were, however, several domestic initiatives supporting Jewish and non-Jewish women in need in the Russian part of Poland. Physician Jozef Zawadzki founded the *Chrešcijanskie Towarzystwo Ochrony Kobiet*, the Christian Society for the Protection of Women, in Warsaw in 1900. It was followed two years later by a Jewish counterpart, the *Żydowskie Towarzystwo Ochrony Kobiet* (Jewish Society for

[34] Cf. e.g. Daniel Gorman, 'Empire, Internationalism, and the Campaign against the Traffic in Women and Children in the 1920s' (2008) 19/2 20 Century British History 186, 187–188.

[35] Bertha Pappenheim, *Sisyphus-Arbeit. Reisebriefe aus den Jahren 1911 und 1912* (Linder Verlag 1924) 53.

[36] Martina Steer, 'Nation, Religion, Gender: The Triple Challenge of Middle-Class German-Jewish Women in World War I' (2015) 48/2 Central European History 176, 181.

the Protection of Women).[37] The more radical *Polskie Towarzystwo Abolicjonistow* (Polish Society of Abolitionists) was established in 1904.[38] These organizations campaigned against prostitution and human trafficking, and their members tried to approach women at train stations and other spots of alleged suspicious migration, albeit without much success.[39] Challenging the imperial Russian authorities by opposing state-regulated prostitution, they were unable to operate in public and had to be cautious.[40]

Practical relief work in the Russian and Prussian parts of Poland—for example, in Warsaw, Lublin, Poznań, or Silesia—was primarily provided by the church-based model of the local Magdalene asylums. Founded by women from the Polish gentry, the *Zaklad Opieki Najświętszej Maryi Panny* (Reformatory of the Holy Virgin Mary), commonly known as the *Magdalenki*, offered shelter to young working-class women who were in danger of going astray or already working as prostitutes.[41] According to the *Magdalenki* philosophy, such women had to be profoundly re-educated and their putative idleness replaced with a lifestyle conforming to middle-class virtues: disciplined, diligent, neat, and deeply religious. This could only be achieved by means of a strict regimen, and the rehabilitation programme thus included a busy daily schedule filled with manual labour. The asylums often operated laundries in addition to the mandatory religious education and prayers. After years of hard training, clients were supposed to leave the institutions morally purified and with the skills required for work as housemaids, laundresses, or seamstresses. Only few young women were willing to adapt to such a strict and arduous environment, however, and the *Magdalenki*'s impact—like that of other church-run facilities—would thus remain limited.

II. Nationalization of the Sex Trade in Postwar Poland

After the First World War and the subsequent collapse of the Habsburg Monarchy, Austria had to give up large parts of its territory. Although the successor state, the Republic of Austria, bemoaned this loss of dominion in general, it was not entirely unhappy to cede the empire's most backward region Galicia and its poor Jewish population. The resurrected Republic of Poland, on the other hand, regained much of its historical territory with the redrawing of borders and its reunification into a sovereign state, but as a consequence it also inherited the region's specific problems

[37] Stanisław Posner, *Nad Otchłanią: (w sprawie handlu żywym towarem)* (Księgarnia Naukowa 1903) 4–7.
[38] Stauter-Halsted, *The Devil's Chain* (n 2) 207.
[39] Elżbieta Mazur, *Dobroczynność w Warszawie XIX wieku* (Instytutu Archeologii i Etnologii PAN 1999) 77.
[40] Cf. e.g. Bristow, *Prostitution* (n 3) 69; 257–264.
[41] Stauter-Halsted, *The Devil's Chain* (n 2) 199–202.

related to the sex trade and 'white slavery', which were ubiquitous in Galicia, Warsaw, and the *Kresy*.

Before the First World War, the bulk of prostitution and human trafficking in Eastern Europe that involved Jews as prostitutes and procurers had fallen within the political purview of two large empires, Russia and Austria-Hungary. After the war, it became concentrated within the independent state of Poland, now home to the world's largest Jewish population. Having previously been an alleged 'Polish' problem, it had thereby turned into a real political concern for Poland as a state. Human trafficking would remain on the political agenda in the new country after the war, not least due to a general sense of political and social crisis.

The newly established republic struggled to overcome the deep-seated enmity between the formerly occupied territories and meld into a single political entity in keeping with the model of a modern European nation state. The obstacles were massive, however. Having been among the prime battlegrounds of the war, vast areas of the country were desolate, and it could barely feed its already poverty-stricken, primarily rural population. The economy lay in shambles and inflation ran high. Moreover, Poland was engaged in neighbourhood wars with Germany, Ukraine, and the Soviet Union until 1921. Politically, the new state lacked stability as well: governments often lasted no more than a few months and thus could not operate effectively. The economically and politically precarious situation led to a tremendous sense of insecurity—not least in moral terms—among the Polish population.[42] The fight against prostitution and human trafficking was therefore also intended to help heal the obvious wounds of Polish morality and strengthen the humiliated Polish national pride.

National fears against the background of alarming nationwide developments during the interwar years forced Polish officials to take action in a way that differed significantly from prewar times.[43] As a result of the disastrous economic situation, more and more non-Jewish women had begun working as prostitutes. It was readily apparent that these women were no longer primarily poor Jews baited with false promises of marriage or employment in South America but in fact members of various social classes and religions who consciously sought to alleviate their material hardship by working in the domestic sex business. Prostitution and human trafficking could thus no longer be shrugged off as 'Jewish' issues—they had to be viewed and tackled as national problems affecting wider strata of the population.

Other issues were the ongoing mass emigration of Poles of all confessions to the industrial centres of Western Europe and the United States since the late nineteenth century as well as the high death toll of the recent wars. Both developments fuelled public fears of demographic decline and depopulation, which in turn prompted

[42] Eva Plach, *The Clash of Moral Nations: Cultural Politics in Piłsudski's Poland, 1926–1935* (Ohio University Press 2006).

[43] Stauter-Halsted, *The Devil's Chain* (n 2) 313.

debates on eugenics.[44] One element of this discussion of eugenic ideas were concerns regarding the societal and monetary costs of venereal diseases. Local authorities and hospitals were responsible for the treatment of infected persons, and they were struggling to cope with the increasing burden.

In summary, prostitution, eugenics, venereal diseases, and human trafficking began to pervade Polish society more and more after the war. Like citizens of other successor states of the Habsburg Empire, Polish women and men were highly mobile and relatively active in the international sex trade. Realistically, the resulting problems could no longer be attributed solely to the activities of allegedly hostile foreign forces such as the Jews. The awareness among the population increased that all Poles, be they Jewish or non-Jewish, were involved and affected. Moreover, after the resurrection of Poland, the responsibility for the fight against prostitution and human trafficking and their negative effects could no longer be delegated to the authorities of the occupying powers of Russia, Germany, and the Habsburg Monarchy. Poland itself had to take action against an issue that was considered a major threat to the Polish body politic.

III. The 'New Internationalism' and Polish Politics

The concentration or 'nationalization' of a phenomenon in an emergent nation state seems logical after the collapse of a multinational empire such as Austria-Hungary and its subsequent partition into several independent nation states. The central government had been obliged to balance the interests of the empire as a whole with the particular interests of its provinces, and it had exhibited varying degrees of motivation and ability to tackle the specific problems of the provinces—often much to the discontent of the respective subjects. After the war, the new sovereign nation states were able to work on solving problems exclusively at the national level and in the best interest of their own populations.

Yet simultaneously the so-called 'new internationalism' took shape, with new international institutions and non-governmental organizations such as the League of Nations entering the stage of global politics.[45] The emergence of international non-governmental organizations (NGOs) obviously predated the First World War: organizations such as the Red Cross, the League of Peace and Freedom, or the International Association for the Suppression of the White Slave Traffic, had been founded during the late nineteenth century.[46] They were primarily European organizations, and governments usually staffed their national branches. The national

[44] Marius Turda, *The History of East-Central European Eugenics, 1900–1945: Sources and Commentaries* (Bloomsbury 2015) 73–126.
[45] Gorman, 'Empire' (n 34) 189.
[46] Akira Iriye, *Global Community: The Role of International Organizations in the Making of the Contemporary World* (California University Press 2002) 11–16.

sentiments and specific interests of these national branches therefore often determined the politics of the new international institutions in a complex interaction of national interests and international cooperation. While acting on an international stage, they were frequently responding to what they perceived as domestic problems. By contrast, the international organizations established during the interwar years—with the League of Nations representing the central and most powerful among them—were conceived as autonomous structures intended to act independently of national interests. Considered non-governmental, they aimed to keep national egoisms in check, to improve and govern the interaction between states, and to influence domestic politics—or more precisely, to exert pressure on individual countries. Conflicts between emergent nation states unwilling to relinquish any of their newly attained sovereignty and these new supranational structures and agents were inevitable, and Poland's reluctance to implement even the most basic minority rights for Jews as codified in the Little Treaty of Versailles of 1919 is a paradigmatic and well-researched example in this regard.[47]

Despite the 'nationalization' of the issue of the sex trade in Poland, prostitution and especially human trafficking remained an international problem. Consequently, the sex trade would become one of the major areas besides minority rights and other humanitarian concerns in which the 'new internationalism' was embodied. Article 23 of the 1919 Covenant of the League of Nations entrusted the supranational organization with supervising 'the execution of agreements with regard to the traffic in women and children',[48] and the League's Social Section soon began to collect data on anti-trafficking measures around the world.[49] In 1921, the League organized the Conference on the Traffic in Women and Children in Geneva, with Poland as one of thirty-four states sending delegates. The conference drafted the International Convention for the Suppression of the Traffic in Women and Children,[50] which urged its signatory states to raise the age of consent from twenty to twenty-one, outlaw the procurement of women, foster multilateral exchange of information on trafficking, issue regulations regarding the protection of young and female migrants, and enable the extradition of traffickers even 'in cases where there are no extradition Conventions in force' between the respective states.[51] Furthermore, it obligated every covenant state to submit an annual report on preventive measures taken.

The focus on 'traffic in women' referred to the limitation of the League's jurisdiction to the international arena, for it could only target the international mobility

[47] Cf. e.g. Carole Fink, *Defending the Rights of Others: The Great Powers, the Jews and International Minority Protection, 1878–1938* (Cambridge University Press 2004) 237–266.

[48] <https://history.state.gov/historicaldocuments/frus1919Parisv13/ch10subch1>.

[49] Gorman, 'Empire' (n 34) 72.

[50] <https://treaties.un.org/Pages/ViewDetails.aspx?src=TREATY&mtdsg_no=VII-3&chapter=7&lang=en>.

[51] International convention for the Suppression of the Traffic in Women and Children, 31 March 1922, 3–4, League of Nations, A.125 (2) 1921.IV.

of women. Lower-class women travelling alone were considered either victims to be protected or suspects to be persecuted. The League's member states were unable to agree on measures against prostitution, however. Due to intensive lobbying by regulationist states including Poland, the convention drafted in 1921 ignored prostitution and focused on transnational human trafficking as the prime target of international measures.

One year later, in 1922, the Advisory Committee on the Traffic in Women and Protection of Children, which consisted of nine delegates and representatives of five international social relief associations, was established and began to meet on a regular basis to discuss the reports from participating states.[52] Poland, one of the nine member states of the committee, appointed lawyer and publicist Stanisław Posner as its delegate.[53] The five non-governmental organizations represented were the International Bureau for the Suppression of the Traffic in Women and Children, the International Women's Organization, the International Catholic Association for the Protection of Girls, the Jewish Association for the Protection of Girls and Women, and the Protestant *Union internationale des Amies de la jeune fille*. Their inclusion is an indication of the increasing recognition of non-governmental organizations as relevant agents in the international realm.

Poland ratified the Convention of 1921 in 1924.[54] In accordance with its stipulations and despite the central role sex morals played in nationalist debates, the Polish government did not outlaw prostitution outright—however, it did away with the regulationist policies that had characterized the stance of the Russian and Habsburg Empires on the issue.[55] The country tried to follow an alternative path to dry out human trafficking and control venereal diseases. Even before signing the Convention, the government established the *Polski Komitet do Walki z Handlem Kobietami i Dziećmi* (Polish National Committee for the Suppression of the Traffic in Women and Children), and in 1922 the minister of health prohibited all sex establishments. During the following years, the authorities closed down brothel after brothel.[56]

A year later, the government launched a system of so-called 'neo-regulation' in which the medical sector bore responsibility for the oversight of prostitution.[57] Regulation and medical supervision of prostitutes were transferred from the police

[52] Daniel Gorman, *The Emergence of International Society in the 1920s* (Cambridge University Press 2012) 72.

[53] The other countries were Denmark, France, Great Britain, Italy, Japan, Romania, Spain, and Uruguay.

[54] <https://treaties.un.org/Pages/ViewDetails.aspx?src=TREATY&mtdsg_no=VII-3&chapter=7&lang=en>.

[55] As argued by Nancy Wingfield, *The World of Prostitution in Late Imperial Austria* (Oxford University Press 2017) 249.

[56] David Petrucelli, 'Pimps, Prostitutes and Policewomen: The Polish Women Police and the International Campaign against the Traffic in Women and Children between the World Wars' (2015) 24/3 Contemporary European History 333, 343.

[57] Stauter-Halsted, *The Devil's Chain* (n 2) 329.

authorities to the Ministry of Public Health, which also took over the vice squad. Local hospitals and their respective departments were now responsible for the registration of prostitutes. They tested for venereal diseases, withdrawing prostitutes from circulation in case of infection and ensuring they were appropriately treated. While this shift in responsibility did not amount to a legalization of prostitution, it nevertheless mitigated its criminal aspects.[58]

Although the League's Advisory Committee favoured an abolitionist strategy and sought to eradicate prostitution and its negative societal circumstances, its scope extended beyond the sex trade.[59] It concerned itself on a broader scale with women in precarious circumstances and attempted to improve the situation of female prisoners, female foreign workers, and migrating women in general. Part of this more general approach was the idea of employing women as police officers. As early as March 1923, at its second meeting, the committee suggested appointing women to the police force.[60] Despite intensive research and lobbying for policewomen, this notion of women working side by side and on equal footing with men in law enforcement was met with scepticism in the League's General Assembly. Conservative states such as Great Britain pointed out the importance of the alleged motherly nature of policewomen as a preventive measure against prostitution.[61] The General Assembly eventually passed a resolution recommending the employment of policewomen later in 1923, and the recently established Polish National Committee followed suit, attempting to convince the Polish authorities of the importance of female police officers in the fight against prostitution and human trafficking.[62] The lobbying was successful, and by 1925 the first twenty-four policewomen had begun patrolling the streets in Warsaw and Łódź.[63]

The task of these female officers was to ferret out clandestine brothels and unregistered sex workers, turn in procurers and traffickers, and ensure the registration and examination of prostitutes. Unlike their Western equivalents, who were relics of prewar times when women were referred to as 'women police assistants' but were in fact social workers as opposed to members of the regular police force, the Polish policewomen stood in the martial tradition of female fighters during the years of the national struggle for political sovereignty and territorial integrity.[64] Nevertheless, the launching of the female police force was based on the notion of 'spiritual motherhood' common in conservative feminist movements all

[58] Marzena Lipska-Toumi, *Prawo polskie wobec zjawiska prostytucji w latach 1918–1939* (KUL 2014) 227.

[59] Jessica R. Pliley, 'Claims to Protection: The Rise and Fall of Feminist Abolitionism in the League of Nations' Committee on the Traffic in Women and Children, 1919–1936' (Winter 2010) 22/4 Journal of Women's History 90, 93.

[60] League of Nations Document C.T.F.E. 509, 1–2.

[61] Petrucelli, 'Pimps' (n 56) 338.

[62] Polski Komitet Walki z Handlem Kobietami i Dzie´cmi (20 Nov. 1924) 236 AAN MOS 1–5.

[63] Petrucelli, 'Pimps' (n 56) 340.

[64] Kerry Segrave, *Policewomen: A History* (McFarland Publishing 1995) 116.

across Europe.[65] According to this ideology, every woman—mother or not—had motherly emotions and was consequently qualified to work in social professions. As mother figures, female police officers were thought to 'exercise a very great preventive influence' and could thus contribute to the national good.[66] Consequently, their assignment in the fight against prostitution and human trafficking resembled an important participation in the national endeavour for 'the moral rebirth of society'.[67]

The policewomen were also assigned to enforcing the increasingly restrictive Polish emigration policy. Driven by the fear of population decline, the government introduced regulations limiting the emigration of women to regions notorious for their role in the international sex trade, such as South America, during the 1920s.[68] The authorities were urged to issue only limited numbers of passports, especially to Jewish women, and railway stations and ports were patrolled.[69] This repressive monitoring and restriction of female migration was disguised as an anti-trafficking measure and alleged safeguarding of unprotected women, but its main purpose was to curtail emigration.[70] In this sense, it worsened the already desperate situation of poor, illiterate women from the countryside, small towns, and shtetls. Police and other authorities did not differentiate between labour migration and sex trafficking, thereby depriving those women of opportunities to legally seek employment abroad. This often left prostitution as the only possibility to make a living, and Jewish women in particular were driven into the networks of procurers and traffickers. The Polish migration policy's focus on women thus exacerbated the very problem it purported to be eliminating.

Poland's refusal to implement minority rights stipulated in the Little Treaty of Versailles likewise worsened the economic situation and was instrumental in promoting prostitution and human trafficking, as pointed out by journalist and minority rights activist Lucien Wolf.[71] Samuel Cohen, secretary of the London-based Jewish Association for the Protection of Girls, Women and Children, came to a similar conclusion. In 1926, he reported to the League of Nations that the denial of minority rights was forcing Jewish women in Poland (and Romania) into

[65] Still seminal on this topic for Germany and beyond is Ann Taylor Allen, 'Spiritual Motherhood: German Feminists and the Kindergarten Movement, 1848–1911' (1982) 22/3 History of Education Quarterly 319.

[66] League of Nations, Official Journal. Special Supplement No. 13. Records of the Fourth Assembly, Plenary Meetings, Text of the Debates (Geneva 1923) 52.

[67] 'Komendantka Policji Kobiecej' (15 January 1928) 2/3 Kobieta Współczesna: Ilustrowany Tygodnik Społeczno-Literacki 17.

[68] On emigration panics in Central Europe, see Tara Zahra, 'Travel Agents on Trial: Policing Mobility in East Central Europe, 1889–1989' (2014) 223/1 Past and Present 161.

[69] Protokuł konferencji informancyjnej w sprawie handle kobietami i dzie´cmi w Argentynie (24 September 1930) 192 AAN MOS 85–86.

[70] Anna Kicinger, *Polityka Emigracyjna II Rzeczpospolitej CEFMR Working Paper 4* (2005) 7–8. <http://www.cefmr.pan.pl/docs/cefmr_wp_2005-04.pdf>.

[71] Bristow, *Prostitution* (n 3) 288.

prostitution.[72] Wolf and Cohen very insightfully analysed the causal connection between the Polish failure to comply with the Little Treaty of Versailles and the desperate economic situation of Polish Jewry. The Polish government, for example, did not contribute financially to the Jewish school system and pursued a policy of institutional discrimination: a numerus clausus and other anti-Jewish regulations barred Jewish students from entering universities, public hospitals did not employ Jewish physicians and nurses, and the army and civilian service were likewise effectively inaccessible for Jews.

The government's selective commitment to fulfilling international obligations caused a paradoxical development: on the one hand, the country was willing to implement international regulations regarding human trafficking, but on the other it refused to adhere to an international treaty on minority rights. The coincidence of these opposing stances directly disadvantaged the Jewish population—and Jewish women in particular.

IV. Jewish Measures against the Sex Trade in Interwar Poland

As in prewar years, Jews had to rely on self-help when it came to fighting prostitution and human trafficking within their community. But in contrast to the prewar foreign endeavours, anti-trafficking initiatives in Poland were now domestic. The Jewish relief organizations from the West that had been working in Poland before the First World War had withdrawn from Galicia and other Polish regions at the outbreak of the war and had not returned after the armistice.

This withdrawal of foreign organizations occurred for several reasons. With the dissolution of Austria-Hungary and the redrawing of borders, the Vienna-based Franco-Austrian foundation of Baroness Clara von Hirsch, which had run numerous schools and educational facilities for girls and women in Galicia, abruptly lost access to its area of operation and ceased to exist as a result. It is unclear from the available sources whether its schools were shut down or taken over by another institution.

German organizations such as the Jewish Women's League had more complex motivations for giving up their commitment in the East, one of their former core missions. During the war, they had focused their resources on the military effort so as not to give rise to any doubts concerning their loyalty to the German Empire. After the war, they encountered virulent anti-Semitism in Germany unlike anything they had experienced before or would ever have expected. As a consequence, they continued to attend international anti-trafficking conferences but simultaneously shifted their primary focus to other issues such as the fight against

[72] League of Nations, TC. Minutes of the Sixth Session 25–30 April 1927, 123.

anti-Semitism and efforts promoting female suffrage in Jewish communities in Germany, hoping to divert the attention of anti-Semites.[73] Furthermore, the overall attitude towards Eastern European Jews held by people in Western Europe had changed during the war. Formerly considered backward and uncivilized masses, young Jewish intellectuals had since discovered them as the supposedly 'authentic' Jews, and they began to serve as inspiration for a renaissance of Jewish culture in the West.[74] Prewar German-Jewish strategies for fighting prostitution and human trafficking by social reform were therefore now considered outdated models in the West.

Instead, several local Polish Jewish initiatives had begun to address the causes of prostitution and human trafficking in the country during the war. Interestingly, like their prewar foreign forerunners, they held abolitionist notions and pursued a social reforming agenda. Identifying the extreme poverty and lack of education of the rural Jewish population, the lack of job opportunities for women, the adherence to traditional Judaism, and the uprooting of thousands of Jewish refugees as the main causes of prostitution and human trafficking in Poland, they established schools and other educational facilities in order to educate girls and women and help them to obtain professional qualifications. Two Galician initiatives of the interwar years are particularly worthy of mention in this regard: the activities led by the aforementioned Róża Melcerowa, and the *Beis Yaakov* movement established by Sarah Schenirer.

When Poland became an independent, democratic state that granted Jews equal rights and introduced women's suffrage, Melcerowa was elected as a member of the *Sejm* for the *Histradut ha Tsyonit be Poloniah* or the *Organizacja Syjonistyczna w Polsce* (Zionist Organization in Poland); she would remain a delegate until 1927. Despite her political commitment to Zionism, we can clearly observe a shift in her activities already during the war. Confronted with the massive influx of Jewish refugees to Lwów and Vienna, she began to organize soup kitchens, day-care centres, and other welfare institutions for the uprooted Jewish population from the borderlands.[75] This transformation of Melcerowa's activities continued after the war, with the goal of creating a Jewish home in Palestine for the suffering masses of Eastern European Jews taking a back seat to the so-called *Gegenwartsarbeit*, that is, the representation of Jewish interests in the respective country of residence.

Melcerowa's work as a member of the *Sejm* focused primarily on social work in Poland. Besides her activities in the *Komisja Pracy I Opieki Społecznej* (Commission for Work and Social Welfare) and other national welfare organizations, she

[73] Steer, 'Nation' (n 36) 186–187.

[74] See e.g. Michael Brenner, *The Renaissance of Jewish Culture in Weimar Germany* (Yale University Press 1998) 129–212.

[75] T. Schorrowa, 'Plon znojnego życia' in Koło Kobiet Żydowskich we Lwowie (ed), *Pamięci Róży Melzerowej* (1936) 35.

intensified her commitment to Jewish social work.[76] She founded a Jewish foster home in Lwów and established several associations that operated elementary schools and offered vocational training. Underprivileged Jewish girls and boys in danger of becoming delinquents or prostitutes were trained in 'useful' jobs as printers, shoemakers, embroiderers, or domestic workers—a programme Pappenheim and others had suggested and implemented long before the war and that Melcerowa had strongly disapproved of at the time.[77] After the war, she no longer employed her reputation to promote the Zionist cause, instead informing audiences of her lecture tours in Western Europe and the USA about her projects aiming to prevent girls and women from being lured into the arms of procurers—and collecting donations for her various endeavours. Instead of preaching *aliyah*, that is, emigration to Palestine, as the only promising path to alleviating the economic and social misery of Eastern European Jewry, she now campaigned for the improvement of the local situation of Jews in Poland.

The shift in Melcerowa's commitment requires explanation, for she had originally refused social reform as an approach to helping Galician Jews before the First World War, as evidenced by the abovementioned conflict between her and Pappenheim.[78] Given this unequivocal rejection of social reform based on a general ideological conflict, mutual distrust between Eastern and Western European Jewry, and personal dislike, what was it that caused Melcerowa to change her mind during and after the First World War and become a committed activist for social reform in Poland? She never offered an explanation herself, but taking a closer look at the shifting political situation may help to understand her change of heart.

Firstly, as mentioned above, the Polish government actively impeded the emigration of young Jewish women by restricting the issuance of passports and controlling the movement of women. In addition, the British administration of Mandatory Palestine defined quotas for immigration. Emigration to *Eretz Yisrael* thus became difficult or nearly impossible for many people—in particular for lower-class women—and it was only logical that Melcerowa began developing an alternative strategy to save women from prostitution.

Secondly, although the living conditions of the impoverished Polish Jewry were worsening, the Polish government refused to implement the minority rights codified in the Little Treaty of Versailles. The constitution of March 1921 guaranteed Polish Jews equal rights, however. In the democratic Republic of Poland, Jews and women now had suffrage—and therefore a historically unique opportunity for political participation that had not existed under the rule of the German and Russian

[76] Dietlind Hüchtker, *Geschichte als Performance. Politische Bewegungen in Galizien um 1900* (Campus 2014) 136–138.

[77] Maks Schaff, 'Wspomnienia' in Koło Kobiet Żydowskich we Lwowie (ed), *Pamięci Róży Melzerowej* (1936) 55.

[78] Elizabeth Loentz, *Let Me Continue to Speak the Truth: Bertha Pappenheim as Author and Activist* (Hebrew Union College University Press 2007) 82.

Empires and Austria-Hungary. As a result, hopes ran high and Jews dreamt of a second *rzeczpospolita*, a multiethnic and multinational Polish republic. Melcerowa was one of the many Polish Jews who took advantage of the opportunities the newly established democratic state offered to Jews and women. Her political activities as delegate to the *Sejm* and her numerous domestic social projects for girls and young women in danger reflected her reorientation from a national Jewish solution in Palestine towards the more pragmatic goal of a better future for Jews in Poland.

The political transformation in Poland also spurred other domestic initiatives supporting imperiled Jewish girls and young women. Like Melcerowa, Sarah Schenirer—the founder of the Orthodox educational network *Bais Yaakov* (House of Jacob)—made use of the opportunity to become active during the period of upheaval at the end of the war.[79] Born into a Hasidic family in Kraków in 1883, Schenirer received only minimal education and worked as a seamstress. She fled to Vienna during the First World War and returned to Kraków shortly before it ended. In Vienna, she was confronted with the dramatic effects that modernization, secularization, and acculturation had on traditional Jewry. She witnessed the vulnerability of uprooted Orthodox girls and women from Galicia and how easily they fell prey to marriage swindlers and procurers in their precarious situation.[80]

For Schenirer, herself a deeply religious person, the Orthodox Jewish understanding of the role of women was beyond reproach; she adhered to traditional 'feminine' values such as modesty, faith, and motherhood. Nevertheless, she saw the need for formal school education for girls and women in a rapidly changing world and sought to combine secular and religious education. With the blessing of the Hasidic Belzer *rebbe*, she opened the first *Bais Yaakov* elementary school for twenty-five students in Kraków in 1917.

Schenirer also promoted her idea in other cities with considerable success. During the interwar years, approximately 200 schools with a total of 38,000 students were established throughout Poland.[81] The local initiative became a nationwide movement when *Agudas Jisroel*, the umbrella organization of Orthodox Jewry, decided to support the schools in 1923. Until then, the *Aguda* had not developed a feasible strategy for combating human trafficking and prostitution despite the fact that Orthodox girls and young women were the primary victims of the sex trade. On the contrary, contemporaries noted how Orthodox Jewish leaders turned a blind eye to the problem or were reluctant to talk openly about it for fear of playing into the hands of anti-Semites. In several of her travel reports, Pappenheim had complained about the ignorance of local Jewish authorities and how her ideas

[79] Caroline Scharfer, 'Sarah Schenirer: Founder of the Beit Ya'akov Movement. Her Vision and Her Legacy' (2010) 23 Polin 269.

[80] Tracey Hayes Norrell, *For the Honor of Our Fatherland: German Jews on the Eastern Front during the Great War* (Lexington Books 2017) 95.

[81] Alexander Zusya Friedman, 'Foreword' in Hilel Seidman (ed), *Dos yidishe religyeze shul-vesn in di romn fun der poylisher gesetzgebung* (Horev 1937) 8.

on education and vocational training as a strategy against human trafficking were met with suspicion and resistance.

The *Aguda*'s change of opinion was not motivated by a revision of its stance on traditional Jewish gender roles. The organization remained suspicious of institutionalized religious education for girls and women and maintained its general refusal of secular studies, but given Poland's new constitution it had no choice other than to adapt to the new situation. As a lobby group of traditional Jewry, it had a comprehensible interest in being involved in politics, especially when it came to minority rights. The introduction of female suffrage meant that Orthodox women came into the focus of attention as potential voters: the *Aguda* began to support the agenda of *Bais Yaakov* and took out ads in the movement's journal calling for women to vote for the *Aguda* in elections.[82] As a result of this strategy, it became one of the most powerful Jewish organizations, with representatives in the *Sejm* and other councils at the regional and local levels.[83]

Furthermore, a February 1919 decree made school education for children between the ages of seven and fourteen mandatory in Poland. As an organization representing a close-knit community, the *Aguda* understandably wanted a say in the design of this compulsory education. The community's social and religious cohesion relied on a considerable degree of social control, and the *Aguda* therefore had a strong interest in preventing its members from being led astray through inappropriate schooling.

Under the aegis of the *Aguda*, the *Bais Yaakov* movement even managed to become a success in other Central European countries with a significant Orthodox Jewish population that were infamous as platforms of human trafficking. For example, it operated eighteen schools with more than 1,500 students in Lithuania, a further eighteen schools with almost 1,300 students in Romania, and eleven schools with 950 students in Austria.[84]

It is unclear whether the measures and activities by governmental and nongovernmental agents in Poland prevented girls and women from becoming prostitutes, improved the lot of existing prostitutes, or effectively combated human trafficking. Many anti-trafficking activists apparently doubted the success of their work. Melcerowa, for example—who had accomplished a lot by common standards—reported at the Jewish International Conference on the Suppression of the Traffic in Girls and Women held in London in 1927 that prostitution had 'increased enormously in the last 10 years' due to the disastrous economic situation of

[82] Agnieszka Oleszak, 'The Beit Ya'akov School in Krakow as an Encounter between East and West' (2011) 23 Polin 277, 281.

[83] Gershon C. Bacon, *The Politics of Tradition: Agudat Yisrael in Poland, 1916–1939* (The Magnes Press 1996).

[84] Yosef Friedenson, 'Batey hasefer levanto beyt-Yaakov bepolin' in Tzvi Sharfstein (ed), *Hahinukh veharabut ha-ivrit be-eyropa beyn shtey milkhamot ha'olam* (Ogen 1957) 71.

Polish Jewry.[85] Nevertheless, reliable data and numbers on these matters are hard to come by since the annual reports by the League's Advisory Committee did not include confessional statistics. Only the report issued in 1928 stated that seventeen of forty-eight discovered procurers were Jewish.[86] Existing research suggests that domestic prostitution and human trafficking increased in Poland during the late 1920s and 1930s despite intense governmental and non-governmental preventive activity.[87] The worsening economic situation and the introduction of restrictive immigration quotas in other countries forced more and more women into the domestic sex business.

But the case of Poland also demonstrates that after the dissolution of Austria-Hungary, the interaction between the 'new international order', the establishment of a supranational institution like the League of Nations and the emergence of multilateral international treaties, and the newly gained national sovereignty of a successor state of the Habsburg Empire generated an ambivalent situation for the Jewish minority.

Almost from its very beginning, the League of Nations addressed the issue of prostitution and human trafficking by changing policies concerning these problems fundamentally. On the one hand, the simple fact that the key supranational institution was dealing with the matter raised awareness for the transnational humanitarian aspect of the sex trade and supported a shift from domestic to international reform endeavours. Human trafficking became a topic of negotiations between international institutions and states. On the other hand, the League's anti-trafficking policy signified an increasing focus on the criminal side of procurement and trafficking, whereas prostitution and the actual problems of women that made them susceptible to entering the sex trade were neglected.

Despite the internationalization of the issue of prostitution and human trafficking, it became a national concern for resurrected Poland. Formerly tripartite and under the strict rule of three empires, it was now a sovereign nation state and had to assume responsibility for a phenomenon that was concentrated within its territory. The country pursued a neo-regulationist strategy with regard to prostitution and ratified all relevant international conventions as a member of the League of Nations. The national consciousness perceived prostitution and human trafficking as a severe threat to the body politic, and the Polish government was therefore willing to implement any and all anti-trafficking measures recommended by the League and its agencies.

[85] Jewish Association for the Protection of Girls and Women, *Official Report of the Jewish International Conference on the Suppression of the Traffic in Girls and Women* (Central Bureau, Jewish Association for the Protection of Girls and Women 1927) 28–30.

[86] League of Nations, Traffic in Women and Children. Summary of Annual Reports for 1928 (Geneva 1930) 9.

[87] Cf. e.g. Bristow, *Prostitution* (n 3) 290–294.

For Polish Jewry, those measures were a mixed blessing. On the one hand, the focus on procurers (Jewish or not) meant persecution of the true criminals of the sex business, and every conviction helped to protect Jewish women. But on the other hand, the strict monitoring of suspicious migrating young females and the restriction of migration itself represented acts of discrimination—particularly of Jewish women, who were more mobile than their non-Jewish counterparts. The tight regulations prevented them from seeking legal occupation abroad. Poland's reluctance to implement the minority rights laid down in the Little Treaty of Versailles, along with the systematic discrimination of Jews in the educational system and the labour market, aggravated the problem. Without useful education and skills and with almost no opportunities to legally earn a living at home or abroad, Jewish girls and women became easy victims for procurers.

This is where Jewish institutions came in. Before the war, it had been primarily Jewish organizations from abroad that had been active in the East. Besides pity due to the miserable living conditions of their fellow Jews, their efforts had been driven by an awareness of the transnational context of the issue: not only did Eastern European Jewish prostitutes in Western European brothels spur anti-Semitic attacks in their respective home countries, the alleged moral shortcomings of Eastern European Jewry were projected onto them as well. Foreign organizations, mostly from Germany and France, had actively campaigned against prostitution and human trafficking in Galicia and attempted to improve the lives of poor Jewish girls and women by establishing schools and other educational facilities. Naturally, the idea of civilizing the Jewish masses according to Western European standards and values was not always met with sympathy by Polish Jewry, especially by Zionists and Orthodox Jews. They dismissed social reform based on Western concepts as presumptuous and unrealistic.

During the war, foreign Jewish anti-trafficking activists withdrew from Galicia. They were replaced by domestic Jewish initiatives that stepped in and continued their work. Encouraged by the opportunities offered by a democratic state, they established several educational networks aimed at providing girls and women with usable skills to take up a profession within the country. The restrictive Polish emigration policy also contributed to a more realistic stance regarding the future of lower-class girls and women, especially in Zionist circles. Jewish anti-trafficking endeavours in Poland thus preserved their character of social reform, but were undertaken by a different group of agents and became less international than they had been under Habsburg rule.

12

The League of Nations and the Optants' Dispute in the Hungarian Borderlands

Romania, Yugoslavia, and Czechoslovakia

Antal Berkes

I. Introduction

It is a well-known fact that the collapse of empires goes hand in hand with the redistribution of wealth and the creation of new economic elites.[1] What happened to private property at the end of the Austro-Hungarian empire largely reflected the global search for the creation of new political and economic elites in political transitions—despite and against the existing property structure. As Austria-Hungary dissolved and new borders carved up its former territory, many found themselves on the 'wrong' side of these new sovereign boundaries. With the territory of historic Hungary reduced by two-thirds, Hungarians in particular frequently found themselves residing in the new or enlarged states of Czechoslovakia, Romania, and Yugoslavia. The peace treaties provided them with the possibility to opt for Hungarian nationality instead of the nationality of these successor states and move across the border to live in Hungary. However, the systematic agrarian reforms and land redistributions in the successor states meant that the decision to do so often entailed the loss of property—especially in the case of the large estates of the major Hungarian nobility. In this way, questions of new borders, citizenship, private property, state-building, nation-building, and social reform became intertwined. And perhaps unsurprisingly, this compound problem known as the optants' dispute would eventually develop into a major international controversy. It not only derailed bilateral diplomacy and became entangled with reparations negotiations, it also travelled through the entire spectrum of new international fora including the Council and the Minorities Section of the League of Nations

[1] See e.g. Yegor Gaidar, *Collapse of an Empire: Lessons for Modern Russia* (Brookings Institution Press 2010) 17; Yuriy Kulchik, Andrey Fadin, and Victor Sergeev, *Central Asia After the Empire* (Pluto Press 1996) 24.

Antal Berkes, *The League of Nations and the Optants' Dispute in the Hungarian Borderlands* In: *Remaking Central Europe*. Edited by: Peter Becker and Natasha Wheatley, Oxford University Press (2020). © the many contributors.
DOI: 10.1093/oso/9780198854685.003.0013

as well as the Mixed Arbitral Tribunals established by the peace treaties. The issue thus straddled the borders of the successor states as well as the jurisdiction of various international institutions—and by tracking its course through the various branches of the international system, we can observe the conjoined evolution of new states and the emerging international institutions, each carving out their place on the world stage.

With the fall of the Dual Monarchy, a considerable part of the Hungarian nobility in the annexed territories opted for Hungarian nationality instead of the nationality of the respective state of the Little Entente: Romania; the Kingdom of Serbs, Croats, and Slovenes (Yugoslavia); and Czechoslovakia. Since these so-called optants were required to transfer their place of residence to Hungary within one year,[2] thereby they necessarily lost physical contact with their lands, which became subject to radical agrarian reforms enacted by the Little Entente governments. Most of these lands were expropriated without due compensation—even though the Treaty of Trianon expressly protected the optants' right to immovable property owned in the successor state they were forced to leave.[3] Invoking the pertinent treaty provisions, the Hungarian optants began to contest the land reforms, demanding restitution and later compensation for their lost property before a series of national and international fora. They argued that the peace treaty guaranteed their right to retain their immovable property within the successor state they had resided in before the option. The Little Entente states, on the other hand, argued that their land reform laws constituted egalitarian provisions without any discrimination regarding nationality. The regional dispute initiated against the Little Entente governments by the Hungarian optants and their government became part of a global controversy pitting the protection of private property (reflecting individual interests) against the sovereign states' agrarian policies (reflecting community interests). Some regarded the optants' demand for protection against land expropriation as an international guarantee of the peace treaties in exchange for radical border changes, while others saw it as preferential treatment controverting the principle of equality with co-nationals before the law.

The League of Nations provided a framework for debating this conflict at both the levels of international law and politics. While ultimately unable to settle the dispute, its various mechanisms offered a global scene for the passionate rhetoric of the conflicting parties and their international allies. This chapter argues that when faced with the delicate choice between socio-economic community interests and the property interests of individuals, all League procedures had to maintain a careful balance between the two.

[2] Treaty of Peace Between the Allied and Associated Powers and Hungary and Protocol and Declaration, Signed at Trianon, 4 June 1920 (Treaty of Trianon), Article 63(3).

[3] Ibid, Article 63(4).

The following pages will review the different procedural strategies of the optants as well as the Hungarian and the Little Entente governments, along with the broad spectrum of international law and political mechanisms the League of Nations could provide. The fact that the optants' dispute remained on the League's agenda exerted political pressure on the concerned governments to engage in bilateral negotiations. The claims could ultimately only be settled outside the League, however, in the framework of the Eastern reparations conference. While the role of the dispute settlement mechanisms of the League of Nations in settling the optants' claims was comparatively minor, they nevertheless worked as a channel for preparing a compromise.

This contribution is structured as follows: section II examines the common elements of the land reforms initiated by the three Little Entente states, especially the economic necessity presented as an 'ethno-politicized' community interest to enact agrarian reform laws and the enforcement regime against formerly dominant national groups—in particular the Hungarian landowners opting for Hungarian nationality after the collapse of the Dual Monarchy. Section III presents the optants' search for arbitration with the League of Nations respectively with the various international dispute settlement mechanisms that victims of land reforms and their governments had recourse to. The conclusions address the significance of the Hungarian optants' struggle in the League of Nations beyond the strict micro- and diplomatic history, especially as an eminent example of the history of transnational civil societies and internationally coordinated lobbying.

II. Land Reforms in the Little Entente States

This section examines the common elements of the land reforms in the three states of the Little Entente, especially their radical social and political agenda (II.A), their discriminatory land expropriation regime (II.B), their biased land redistribution (II.C), and finally their impact on the Hungarian optants (II.D). The agenda cited by the Little Entente states to justify their land reforms was the compelling community interest, which clashed with individual interests of the expropriated owners and was subject to various appeals to international fora, as section III will explain.

A. Radical Land Reforms: A Social and Political Agenda

In reaction to the pressing social needs of the majority populations in the newly established successor states, political parties leading the independence movements in Czechoslovakia, Romania, and Yugoslavia all declared their political promise to enact radical land reforms. In Czechoslovakia, the Social Democrats and the National Socialists along with other left-wing parties and trade unions demanded a radical agrarian reform and large-scale socialization of industry.[4] The first prime minister of the new Czechoslovakian state, Karel Kramář, declared in December 1918 that 'it is necessary to take measures concerning the selling of the large estates in Slovakia, that the people there may see that we have in this respect as much socialistic sense as the Hungarians who suddenly promise the Slovaks immediate division and distribution of the large estates'.[5] On 6 January 1919, the Yugoslavian regent Alexander proclaimed his intent to find a 'just' solution to the agrarian question.[6] Juraj Demetrović, a Croatian politician, Royal Commissioner for Croatia between 1921 and 1922, Yugoslavian Minister of Commerce & Industry in 1930–1932, and subsequently Minister of Agriculture and Agrarian Reform in 1932–1934, overtly claimed in 1920 that 'Serbia must repeat what it did in 1830 during the liberation from Turkish rule, when it distributed the lands taken from the Turkish aghas and beys among the Serbian peasants'.[7] The declaration on the unification of Transylvania with Romania, adopted by the National Assembly of Romanians of Transylvania and Hungary in Alba Iulia on 1 December 1918, likewise expressly stipulated a land reform. Among their political demands, the drafters called for a 'radical agrarian reform' in which 'all assets, above all the large ones, will be inscribed'.[8]

The ruling parties initiated such schemes in order to address the special contextual pressures faced by their societies: firstly, the high proportion of landless peasants in all three successor states; secondly, following the events of the Russian Revolution, the fear among the ruling classes of a similar 'bolshevization';[9] and thirdly and finally, by allocating land to peasants of the dominant national community, the successor states aimed to create a new, loyal middle class.

At the same time, beyond addressing social inequalities, the agrarian reforms of the Little Entente states had a nationalist agenda—namely to destroy the economic power of the formerly dominant national communities of the Hungarians

[4] Jan Kuklík, *Czech Law in Historical Contexts* (Charles University in Prague, Karolinum Press 2015) 91.

[5] Lucy Elizabeth Textor, *Land Reform in Czechoslovakia* (George Allen & Unwin Limited 1923) 25.

[6] Enikő A. Sajti, *Hungarians in the Voivodina, 1918–1947* (Social Science Monographs 2003) 165–166.

[7] Juraj Demetrović, *Agrarna Reforma i Demokratska Stranka: Sve Uredbe i Naredbe o Agrarnoj Reformi u Jugoslaviji* (Sekretarijat Demokrat Stranke 1920) 7–9, cited in Imre Prokopy, 'A Jugoszláv Agrárreform [The Yugoslavian Agrarian Reform]' [1933] Magyar Kisebbség 295.

[8] Resolution of the Great National Assembly in Alba Iulia, 1 December 1918, English translation at <http://www.cimec.ro/Istorie/Unire/rezo_eng.htm> accessed 15 February 2020.

[9] Christian Giordano, 'The Ethnicization of Agrarian Reforms: The Case of Interwar Yugoslavia' (2014) 19 Martor: revue d'anthropologie du Musée du Paysan Roumain 31, 35. See in this sense also the Romanian government, fearing a transborder threat from the Bolshevik presence in Budapest: Romanian Embassy in France, Aide-mémoire, 5 December 1918, Correspondance diplomatique, Europe 1918–1940, Roumanie, France, Archives Diplomatiques du Ministère des Affaires Étrangères (ADMAE), 110CPCOM/41 (Microfilm P/17428).

and Germans (Czechoslovakia, Romania). The debates about the respective laws and their legislative drafts expressly recognized this intention. In Czechoslovakia, the director of the State Land Office, Karel Viskovsky, pointed out in March 1921 that 'the land reform in the Czechoslovakian Republic has not only an economic and social, but also a political and national character. [. . .] thus from the political and national point of view, the agrarian reform pursues the aim of restricting foreign colonization in the Czechoslovakian Republic'.[10]

The rapporteur for the Transylvanian land reform law in Romania, Minister of Agriculture Constantin Garoflid, recognized that 'most of the land in the hands of Hungarian medium-sized landowners must be removed; it must be given to Romanian peasants, even those who have enough cultivated land'.[11] Similarly, a deputy to the Romanian lower parliamentary chamber asserted that 'once the law enters into force, our villages and hamlets located on plains or on hills, in valleys or on the heights of mountains will no longer have to suffer the oppression of non-Romanian counts and owners'.[12] In other words, besides addressing social inequalities, the land reforms of the Little Entente states were deemed to provide historic justice by 'ethnicizing' landed property, that is by 'apportioning it preferably to the sole members of the "entitled nation" '.[13]

B. Discriminatory Land Expropriations and the Hungarian Optants

This 'ethnicization' of agrarian reforms was a common element in the sense that all three Little Entente governments enacted or enforced land expropriations in a manner that discriminated against national minorities.

In Romania, a key characteristic of the land reform was the radical differentiation between the agrarian reform law applicable to 'old' Romania and that applicable to the territories annexed from Hungary (Transylvania, Banat, Maramures, Crisania). In other words, the former Romanian Kingdom, Bessarabia, and the annexed Hungarian territories had different land distribution regimes. A decree

[10] Cited in Joseph L. Kunz, 'Consultation de M. Kunz Concernant Les Affaires Agraires Des Ressortissants Hongrois Devant Le Tribunal Arbitral Mixte' in *La réforme agraire Roumaine en Transylvanie devant la Justice Internationale et le Conseil de la Société des Nations: Quelques opinions*, vol. 1 (Aux éditions internationales 1928) 190.

[11] Report by the Minister of Agriculture, Constantin Garoflid, on the land reform law in Transylvania (translated by the author), Mémoire de la Ligue pour la protection des minorités nationales au sujet de la réforme agraire, de Roumanie, Publication de la Ligue pour la protection des minorités nationales de la Roumanie, Budapest, 1921, League of Nations (LoN), C-65-M-1922-I, 20.

[12] Preface by Dr. Aurèle Dobresco, member of parliament and of the Special Agrarian Council of the Romanian lower chamber (Dobrescu, Aurel, *Legea agrară pentru Transilvania, Banat, Crişana şi Maramureş*, Sibiu, 1922), Hungarian National Archives [MNL], K 143 [Pénzügyminisztériumi Levéltár, A Vegyes Döntőbíróságok mellett Működő Kormánymegbízottak Hivatala], 201. cs.

[13] Giordano, 'Ethnicization of Agrarian Reforms' (n 9) 34.

issued on 20 September 1919 stated that land estates belonging to citizens of foreign states, or to persons who were aliens by origin or by marriage or had become aliens in any other way, were to be expropriated except in cases where these provisions conflicted with those of the Peace Treaty of Trianon.[14]

As Hungarian statistics from the period indicate, rural property in Transylvania amounted to 3,321,991 hectares, 70 per cent of which were in the possession of small landowners (629,100 persons in total, 413,012 of whom were of Romanian nationality) and 10.8 per cent in the possession of large landowners. The Hungarian government concluded that the situation of the 2,700,000 inhabitants of Transylvania in no way called for a more radical agrarian reform than the one introduced in Romania.[15] Its memorandum protesting the Transylvanian land reform included various examples to prove the discriminatory nature of the measures, with 91.7 per cent of the affected landowners being Hungarian. In particular, it listed Hungarian small landowners who were expropriated while the estates of large landowners of Romanian origin in the same towns were left untouched by the land reform.[16]

Following the decree of 20 September 1919, a new law on the agrarian reform in Transylvania, Banat, Crisana, and Maramures was enacted on 30 July 1921.[17] In Article 6(c), this law ordered the expropriation of the immovable property in question on grounds of the absence of the respective owners. The same provision defined an absentee as 'one who was absent from the country from 1 December 1918 until the submission of this law without having any official mission abroad. Rural properties up to 50 jugars [~29 ha; 1 jugar = 0.5754 ha] are exempt'. As Hungarian petitioners complained, this period corresponded to the Romanian invasion of Transylvania following the armistice of 3 November 1918, when masses of Hungarians fled the territory.[18] The expropriation of absent owners appeared to contradict the provisions of the Treaty of Trianon, however. Under Article 63 of the latter, persons who had exercised their right to opt for Hungarian nationality rather than that of the successor state 'must within the succeeding twelve months transfer their place of residence to the State for which they have opted'.[19] The same

[14] Memorandum by the Hungarian Government dated 31 December 1920 on the subject of agrarian reforms carried out in Transylvania by the Romanian Government, Société des Nations, Minorités d'origine hongroise, Lettre du Président de la Conférence des ambassadeurs, en date du 15 avril 1921, et autres documents sur le même sujet, LoN, C.50.M.24.1921.I, 20 May 1921.

[15] Memorandum by the Hungarian Government dated 31 December 1920, regarding the Romanian agrarian reform, LoN, Hungarian minorities, Letter from the President of the Conference of Ambassadors, 15 April 1921, and other documents on the same topic, 41/12285/12285, 20 May 1921.

[16] Ibid.

[17] Legea nr. 3610/1921 pentru Reforma agrară din Transilvania, Banat, Crişana şi Maramureş, *Monitorul Oficial al României*, În vigoare de la 30 iulie 1921.

[18] Romanian land reform laws before the Hungarian-Romanian Mixed Arbitral Tribunal. Some types of cases. Memorandum submitted by various parties regarding the incompetence raised by the Romanian State, 95 p., LoN, S.106.1927.VII, Geneva, 7 March 1927, Archives of the League of Nations (ALoN), Section 2, box no. R 613, folder no. 28470, document no. 57989, 6.

[19] Treaty of Trianon (n 2), Article 63(3).

article also stated that the optants 'will be entitled to retain their immovable property in the territory of the other State where they had their place of residence before exercising their right to opt'.[20] Further aggravating the dire situation of the Transylvanian optants, the Romanian legislation adopted a new constitution that stipulated a prohibition of real property by foreign citizens in its Article 18.[21]

The Czechoslovakian agrarian reform had a similarly discriminatory effect regarding national minorities. Law No. 215 of 16 April 1919 provided that all large land properties had to be expropriated in favour of the state. Under this law and a further one, Law No. 329 of 8 April 1920, all landed property exceeding 150 ha in size and all other agrarian property exceeding 250 ha was considered large agrarian property. If such property was owned by a citizen of a foreign state, it was expropriated without any compensation.[22] In the territories annexed from the Kingdom of Hungary by Czechoslovakia, all large land properties with few exceptions were owned by Hungarians. Czechoslovakian owners were not affected by the agrarian reform, since they owned lands smaller than 250 ha. Furthermore, proportionally more land was expropriated in the Hungarian-inhabited regions of Slovakia than in the country-wide average as well.[23] This policy caused various noble families of Hungarian origin to lose their entire socioeconomic basis and become landless in Czechoslovakia without any compensation.[24]

As regards the Yugoslavian land reform, the pertinent decree of 25 February 1919 intended to distribute small estates for lease by peasants and provided that all land exceeding the area of 521 jugars (300 ha) on any estate could be used by the state for this purpose.[25] The seized lands were to be parcelled out to Yugoslavian citizens working in agriculture who did not own sufficient land to make a living, for cultivation until the enactment of a proper land reform law.[26]

The Hungarian government complained that a second Yugoslavian decree issued on 21 July 1919 excluded Hungarian landowners from collecting revenues from their landed estates and that 'these revenues are remitted to the State Treasury at Belgrade by the sequestrators, who are almost always officers of the

[20] Ibid, Article 63(4).

[21] Romanian Constitution of 1923, Monitorul Oficial, March 1923, no. 282/29, Article 18, available at <http://www.cdep.ro/pls/legis/legis_pck.htp_act_text?idt=1517> accessed 14 February 2020.

[22] Memorandum by the Hungarian Government dated 25 February 1921 regarding the consequences to Hungarian landowners of the agrarian laws recently passed in Czechoslovakia, LoN, Hungarian minorities, Letter from the President of the Conference of Ambassadors, 15 April 1921, and other documents on the same topic, C.50.M.24.1921.I, 20 May 1921.

[23] Hantos László, 'A gazdasági kérdés [The Economic Question]' in Borsody István (ed), *Magyarok Csehszlovákiában 1918–1938 [Hungarians in Czechoslovakia 1918–1938]* (Méry Ratio 2002) 82.

[24] The Hungarian Government provided several examples of the seriousness of the expropriation measures in Czechoslovakia, see Memorandum by the Hungarian Government dated 25 February 1921.

[25] Mária V. Kápolnás, 'Iratok a Bukovinai Székelyek Letelepítéséről És a Jugoszláv Földreform Revíziójáról [Documents on the Settlement of the Székelys of Bucovina and on the Revision of the Yugoslavian Land Reform]' (1987) 29 Agrártörténeti szemle = Historia rerum rusticarum 463, 470–471.

[26] József Berkes, 'A Jugoszláv Agrárreform És a Magyar Kisebbség [The Yugoslavian Agrarian Reform and the Hungarian Minority]' [1928] Magyar Kisebbség 362, 364.

Serb-Croat-Slovene Army'.[27] The owners of estates larger than 521 jugars were also prohibited from divesting their property, and the seized lands exceeding the threshold were either administered by the Yugoslavian authorities or given to peasants for provisional lease. Finally, a third agrarian decree issued on 16 September 1920 provided for the expropriation of the entire landed estates of individuals who were not present in Yugoslavia or leased the entirety of their land—and thus likewise primarily affected Hungarian landowners.[28] In other words, optants who left the territory of Yugoslavia could lose their landholdings irrespective of their size. This decree was intended to be enforced in particular within the regions annexed from Hungary: in Baranya, Bácska, and Banat.[29] Out of a total of 923 large land estates, 395 with a combined area of 383,240 jugars (220,516 ha), were expropriated from absent owners under its provisions, the majority of them Hungarian optants.[30]

The optants and the Hungarian government alleged that the Little Entente governments took discriminatory measures against Hungarian optants with minimal or no compensation as a common element of these land reforms, thereby running afoul of Article 250 of the Treaty of Trianon, which prohibited the retention or liquidation of private property.[31] Even though the agrarian reform regulations used a neutral language on the surface, their effects were clearly discriminatory against Hungarians.[32]

C. Biased Redistribution of Expropriated Land

A further common feature of the land reforms in the Little Entente was the preferential allocation of the expropriated land to the dominant national community: ethnic Czech, Romanian, and Serb beneficiaries were granted the seized lands disproportionately often compared to their relative shares in the overall populations.

Following the model of the first land reform in the Old Kingdom, the regional land reforms in Romania (Bessarabia and the annexed former Hungarian territories) included provisions prioritizing the 'national' elements of Romania. Accordingly, the land expropriated from the acquired territories—most of it along the borders—had to be assigned preferentially to former combatants, invalidated officials, and the orphans and widows of fallen soldiers. The official statistics on

[27] LoN, Hungarian minorities, Letter from the President of the Conference of Ambassadors, 15 April 1921, and other documents on the same topic, C.50.M24.1921.I, 20 May 1921, 4.

[28] Berkes, 'A Jugoszláv Agrárreform' (n 26) 364–365.

[29] Kápolnás, 'Bukovinai Székelyek Letelepítéséről' (n 25) 471.

[30] Berkes, 'A Jugoszláv Agrárreform' (n 26) 366.

[31] Treaty of Trianon, (n 2) Article 250.

[32] See the plea by the Hungarian delegate at the League of Nations, Count Albert Apponyi, Communication du Gouvernement Tchécoslovaque, LoN, C.491.1927.VII, 8.

15 September 1924 reported the number of peasants benefiting from land distribution in Transylvania as 335,073; of these, 246,695 (73.6%) were of Romanian origin, while 88,378 (36.3%) belonged to national minorities.[33] Among the non-Romanian beneficiaries, 20,950 (6.2% of all beneficiaries) were Germans (Swabians) and 55,422 (16.54%) were Hungarians. However, the overall proportion of national minorities in Transylvania was much higher at 42.7 per cent, according to the Romanian statistics.[34]

In Czechoslovakia, the Land Allocation Law of 30 January 1920 gave priority to satisfying the needs of peasants.[35] Those parcels of expropriated land that were not used for public welfare purposes, had to be distributed preferentially by the Land Office to privileged beneficiaries, which included small peasant proprietors, cottagers, craftsmen, farm and forest employees and persons without land, legionaries and soldiers in the Czechoslovakian Army, the dependents of those who had fallen for their country in the war or died as a result of war service, and war invalids.[36] According to the statistics of the League Secretariat, Germans were almost entirely excluded from the beneficiaries of the land distribution administered centrally by the Czechoslovakian Land Office, and Hungarians were underrepresented.[37] The Land Office also applied different distribution methods according to the national character of the respective region: it favoured settlement policies in regions inhabited overwhelmingly by national minorities—especially in the near vicinity of the Hungarian frontier—with a view to settling groups of loyal subjects there.[38]

In Yugoslavia, a decree on the distribution of land issued on 1 July 1920 stated that individuals of Hungarian or German origin could not be registered in the list of applicants for land distribution since they were not considered confirmed nationals of Yugoslavia.[39] Their uncertain status was explained with their right to choose their nationality until the deadline (26 January 1922) defined by the Treaty of Trianon. Therefore, when the major land distributions took place between 1919 and 1922, all members of the Hungarian and German minorities were excluded from the benefits of the land reform.[40] After 1923, in the region of Voivodina (the northern part of the Kingdom in the Pannonian Plain, composed of Syrmia, Bácska, and the Banat regions), statistics reported 405,345 landless peasants who could not benefit from the land distributions; with regard to their national

[33] *La réforme agraire et la protection de minorités*, confidential memorandum prepared by Mr P. de Azcarate, 1927, received by the Registry on 28 March 1927, ALoN, Section 41, box no. R 1701, folder no. 58382 (ALoN, *La réforme agraire et la protection de minorités*), 104–105.

[34] Ibid, 105.

[35] Alice Teichova, *The Czechoslovak Economy 1918–1980* (Routledge 2013) 28.

[36] Textor, *Land Reform in Czechoslovakia* (n 5) 70.

[37] ALoN, *La réforme agraire et la protection de minorités* (n 33) 126.

[38] Textor, *Land Reform in Czechoslovakia* (n 5) 91.

[39] Decrees no. 1.091 of 29 January 1920 and no. 10.185 of 1 July 1920; Prokopy, 'A Jugoszláv Agrárreform' (n 7) 299; Berkes, 'A Jugoszláv Agrárreform' (n 26) 367.

[40] Berkes, 'A Jugoszláv Agrárreform' (n 26), 367.

origins, 106,337 were Serbs and Croats, 147,003 were Hungarians, 75,623 were Germans, and 76,382 were of other nationalities.[41] The beneficiaries of the land distributions were all of Slavic origin: 205,805 individuals received land with a total area of 531,252 jugars; among them were 185,344 local Serbians, 17,780 persons originating from South Serbia and Lika, and a further 2,571 settlers from South Serbia.[42]

It was thus a common element of the land reforms in the states of the Little Entente that they discriminated against Hungarian landowners in terms of the size of the land expropriated from them as compared to Slovakian, German, Romanian, Serbian, or Croatian landowners. Furthermore, the expropriated lands were not entirely assigned to the beneficiaries: whereas the agrarian reform laws stipulated the allocation of land to citizens considered loyal, such as veterans, widows of fallen soldiers, public servants, and the like, administrative dysfunctionalities blocked the distribution of land parcels in numerous cases, leaving the respective areas uncultivated for many years after their expropriation. Nevertheless, the land redistributions in Romania and Czechoslovakia undoubtedly contributed to a more balanced ownership structure, whereas in Yugoslavia, Serbian families were prioritized to the detriment of other ethnic communities such as Croats, Macedonians, and Kosovars. The economic success of the land reforms was also contested due to the new owners' frequent lack of technical background and failure to invest into improving their farms' productivity. During the optants' disputes before the League of Nations, such pragmatic arguments were produced to undermine the legitimacy of the reforms.

D. Hungarian Optants as Victims of Land Reforms

The drafters of the Treaty of Trianon intended to ensure continuity for individuals affected by the collapse of Austria-Hungary by stipulating a legal entitlement to opt for a nationality different from that of the state of residence. They recognized the so-called right to option, which had already been used in the Treaty of Frankfurt marking the end of the Franco-Prussian War on 10 May 1871 to offer French inhabitants of Alsace-Lorraine the right to choose French rather than German nationality.[43] Similarly to most peace treaties concluded in Paris in 1919,[44] the Treaty of Trianon based the right of option on the principle of automaticity: individuals

[41] Ibid, 368.

[42] Ibid.

[43] L. Arnould, *De l'option Des Alsaciens-Lorrains Pour La Nationalité Française* (Berger-Levrault et Cie, Librairies-Éditeurs 1879).

[44] E.g. Treaty of Versailles, 28 June 1919, Articles 85 (residents in any of the territories recognised as forming part of the Czecho-Slovak State), 91 (German nationals habitually resident in territories recognized as forming part of Poland), 106 (German nationals habitually resident in the Free City of Danzig); Treaty of Saint-Germain-en-Laye, 10 September 1919, Articles 78–80.

automatically acquired the citizenship of the successor state in which they resided, with the option of choosing the nationality of their kin state instead. Any individual opting for the nationality of his or her kin state had to transfer his or her residence to that state. As the treaty stated:

> Persons over 18 years of age losing their Hungarian nationality and obtaining ipso facto a new nationality under Article 61 shall be entitled within a period of one year from the coming into force of the present Treaty to opt for the nationality of the State in which they possessed rights of citizenship before acquiring such rights in the territory transferred.
>
> Option by a husband will cover his wife and option by parents will cover their children under 18 years of age.
>
> Persons who have exercised the above right to opt must within the succeeding twelve months transfer their place of residence to the State for which they have opted.
>
> They will be entitled to retain their immovable property in the territory of the other State where they had their place of residence before exercising their right to opt.[45]

Under these provisions, optants were to retain real estate owned in their former state of residence despite changing their nationality and moving to their kin state. Together with the abovementioned Article 250 of the Treaty of Trianon, these regulations were designed to protect the optants' continued enjoyment of private property.

The deadline for exercising the right to opt was 26 July 1922, one year after the treaty entered into force. Until that date, around 20,000 persons from the three Little Entente states opted for Hungarian nationality in Budapest.[46] Most of them were refugees, peasants, or former public servants who refused to serve the new authorities and take an oath of loyalty, while only a tiny minority were landowners: some 350 large landowners from Romania opted for Hungarian citizenship and moved to Hungary between 1918 and 1921, and approximately 200 large landowners from Czechoslovakia did the same.[47] From Yugoslavia, forty-four Hungarian optant landowners are known who were expropriated as a result of the Yugoslavian land reform and benefited from compensation in the 1930s.[48]

45 Treaty of Trianon (n 2) Article 63(1)–(4).

46 'Eddig több mint huszezer állampolgársági igénylés történt Budapesten [Until now more than twenty thousand requests of citizenship have been submitted in Budapest]' *Pesti Hírlap* (11 June 1922) 6.

47 (4 February 1930) 120 MTI Házi Tájékoztató [Hungarian News Agency Confidential Bulletin].

48 Total amount of payment concluded in February 1943, Settlement of Romanian and Yugoslavian agrarian procedures, 1941, Hungarian National Archives [MNL], K 143 [Pénzügyminisztériumi Levéltár, A Vegyes Döntőbíróságok mellett Működő Kormánymegbízottak Hivatala], 204. cs.

The land reforms deprived the optant landowners of most of their livelihood and their homelands. Some of them lost their entire landed property to the expropriations and were forced to pursue civilian professions in Hungary,[49] while others—primarily the wealthiest aristocrats—held sufficiently large estates in Hungary to maintain their lifestyle. But whether they had to change their lifestyle or not, all of the optants were eager to demand either the restitution of their land or compensation for their property loss. After their claims were rejected by the Romanian, Czechoslovakian, and Yugoslavian authorities, they focused their attention on international mechanisms established in the new era of internationalization within the larger framework of the League of Nations.

III. Involvement of the League of Nations

Various dispute settlement mechanisms of the interwar period examined, discussed, negotiated, and eventually settled, the optants' dispute. The League of Nations was the primary negotiating forum for the affected optants and involved governments to dispute their views, but it was by no means the only one. Chronologically, the first multilateral fora invoked in this context were the Conference of Ambassadors and the Inter-Allied Control Commission for Hungary (see section III.A). Starting in 1923, the League Secretariat and especially the Minorities Section (see III.B) of the League began to follow the issue closely. After the Hungarian government appealed to the League Council in March 1923 (see III.C), the Council appointed a mediator (see III.D) whose mission ended unsuccessfully in September of the same year. Beyond the League, the optants sought recourse with the so-called Mixed Arbitral Tribunals (see III.E), but after the Hungarian-Romanian Mixed Arbitral Tribunal rendered its first admissibility decision in January 1927, the Romanian government blocked further procedures and invoked the League Council once again. This led to the second phase of the Council's proceedings: the appointment of the Committee of Three (see III.F), whose mediation efforts lasted until 1928. Ultimately, the optants' cases were settled outside the League of Nations in the framework of the diplomatic settlement of the Eastern reparations in 1929–1930 (see III.G). As the following sections will show, the clash between the collective national interests of the concerned states and the optants' individual interests galvanized a wide range of institutions dealing with international politics and/or international law.

[49] The prime ministers Count Pál Teleki and Count István Bethlen, for example, had to live off their civilian salaries.

A. Appeal to Multilateral Fora outside the League

The Hungarian government acted on behalf of its citizens and was the first to bring the optants issue to the attention of multilateral fora such as the Diplomatic Representatives of the Principal Allied Powers in Budapest, the Conference of Ambassadors, or the Inter-Allied Control Commission for Hungary. On 19 February 1920, Count Albert Apponyi, head of the Hungarian delegation to the Paris Peace Conference, protested the provisions of the Romanian decree of 10 September 1919 allowing the expropriation of real estate owned by foreign citizens.[50] Budapest sent further memoranda to the President of the Conference of Ambassadors on 31 December 1920 concerning Romania, on 25 February 1921 concerning Czechoslovakia, and again pertaining to Romania on 28 April 1921 and 22 August 1922.[51]

The main function of the Inter-Allied Control Commission for Hungary seated in Budapest was the military supervision of Hungary, and it thus had limited power in civilian matters. Nevertheless, the diplomatic protests against the Romanian expropriation measures provoked a certain echo from the representatives of the four participating governments of the USA, the UK, France, and Italy. For example, a memorandum sent by Count Teleki, the Hungarian Minister of Foreign Affairs, convinced the French delegate General Fouchet to urge his government to intervene and put pressure on the Romanian government to comply with the peace treaty.[52] In February 1921, the Inter-Allied Control Commission adopted a resolution according to which 'the President of the Conference of Ambassadors will informally draw the attention of Prince Ghika to the complaints of the Hungarian government regarding the measures taken by Romania in Transylvania'.[53] Prince Vladimir Ghika, member of the princely Ghika family and a Romanian diplomat and charity founder, was studying in France at the time with a view to being ordained as a Catholic priest.

Although an informal gathering with no executive power whatsoever unlike the Inter-Allied Control Commission, the Diplomatic Representatives of the Principal

[50] Cited in Communication of the Czechoslovakian Government, League of Nations, 16 September 1927, LoN, C.491.1927.VII, 7.

[51] Memorandum by the Hungarian Government dated 25 February 1921 regarding the consequences to the Hungarian landowners of the agrarian laws recently passed in Czechoslovakia, LoN, Hungarian minorities, Letter from the President of the Conference of Ambassadors, 15 April 1921, and other documents on the same topic, C.50.M24.1921.I, 20 May 1921, 4; Letter from the Hungarian Government to the High Commissioner, Paris, 28 April 1921, Correspondance diplomatique, Europe 1918–1940, Roumanie, ADMAE, 110CPCOM/41 (Microfilm P/17428), 202–209.

[52] Letter from M. Fouchet, High Commissioner of France in Hungary, to Aristide Briand, President of the Conference of Ambassadors, Budapest, 25 January 1921, Correspondance diplomatique, Europe 1918–1940, Roumanie, ADMAE, 110CPCOM/41 (Microfilm P/17428), 163–165.

[53] Resolution 106 (XII) of the Conference of Diplomatic Representatives of the Principal Allied Powers in Budapest, 17 February 1921, Correspondance diplomatique, Europe 1918–1940, Roumanie, ADMAE, 110CPCOM/41 (Microfilm P/17428), 187.

Allied Powers in Budapest also viewed the Hungarian complaints favourably. In a letter addressed to the President of the Conference of Ambassadors in May 1921, they noted that the land reform in Transylvania created harsher conditions for expropriated owners than the corresponding laws concerning other parts of Romania.[54] They considered the Romanian law to be 'inspired by the aim of limiting and annulling the right to property of the ethnic minorities in Transylvania'.[55] As a recommendation, the Diplomatic Representatives proposed that the Conference of Ambassadors should ask for clarification from the Romanian government and send a fact-finding mission to Transylvania.[56] After the Minority Treaty concluded with Romania entered into force in July 1921,[57] the President of the Conference of Ambassadors, Jules Cambon, decided to transmit all complaints related to Romania to the League of Nations, which was charged with supervising the Minority Treaties.[58]

This decision disappointed the Hungarian government: after the Conference of Ambassadors had formally declared itself incompetent in the case of the Transylvanian optants, the Hungarian prime minister Bethlen—himself a Transylvanian optant—convoked the Italian, French, and British ambassadors in Budapest. He explained to them the difference between complaints lodged under the Minority Treaties and complaints by Hungarian subjects such as the optants, which asserted a breach of the peace treaty.[59] Bethlen later even urged the ambassadors in Budapest and the Conference of Ambassadors as a whole to revise their decision not to act on the matter and exert pressure on the Romanian government.[60] While France was not convinced, the British and Italian governments were amenable to such action through the Conference of Ambassadors.[61] Likewise, when

[54] Letter from the Conference of Diplomatic Representatives of the Principal Allied Powers in Budapest to Mr. Jules Cambon, President of the Conference of Ambassadors, Budapest, 20 May 1921, Correspondance diplomatique, Europe 1918–1940, Roumanie, ADMAE, 110CPCOM/41 (Microfilm P/17428), 210–212.

[55] Ibid.

[56] Ibid.

[57] United States of America—Treaty between the Principal Allied and Associated Powers and Roumania, signed at Paris, 9 December 1919 [1921] LNTSer 63; 5 LNTS 335, registered on 21 July 1921.

[58] Letter from the President of the Conference of Ambassadors, Jules Cambon, to the Secretary-General of the League of Nations, Eric Drummond, Paris, 24 June 1921, LoN, C.230.M.168.1921.I.

[59] Telegram from the French ambassador in Budapest to the French Ministry of Foreign Affairs, Budapest, 7 September 1922, Correspondance diplomatique, Europe 1918–1940, Roumanie, ADMAE, 110CPCOM/43 (Microfilm P/17429), 5.

[60] Letter from Mr. Doulcet, French ambassador in Budapest, to Mr. Raymond Poincaré, President of the Council, Minister of Foreign Affairs, Budapest, 7 September 1922, Correspondance diplomatique, Europe 1918–1940, Roumanie, ADMAE, 110CPCOM/43 (Microfilm P/17429), 6–9.

[61] Letter from Mr. Doulcet, French ambassador in Budapest, to Mr. Raymond Poincaré, President of the Council, Minister of Foreign Affairs, Budapest, 21 September 1922, Correspondance diplomatique, Europe 1918–1940, Roumanie, ADMAE, 110CPCOM/43 (Microfilm P/17429), 11; Note on the visit of the Hungarian ambassador to Mr. de Peretti, 23 December 1922, Annex, Letter from Mr. Doulcet, French ambassador in Budapest, to Mr. Raymond Poincaré, President of the Council, Minister of Foreign Affairs, Budapest, 27 September 1922, Correspondance diplomatique, Europe 1918–1940, Roumanie, ADMAE, 110CPCOM/43 (Microfilm P/17429), 27.

the Conference examined the Hungarian memorandum once more in September 1922, the division between the French, who viewed the Transylvanian land reform law neutrally and refused any intervention in the matter, and the British, who wished to bring the matter before the League of Nations, persisted.[62] The views of the respective diplomats also extended to other individuals in similar situations, such as the Hungarian optants affected by the Czechoslovakian land reform.[63]

The Conference of Ambassadors finally adopted a compromise resolution in January 1923: while it did not refer the case to the League of Nations itself, it stated that if it were to be brought before the League by the Hungarian government, the Conference would be available to mediate—and that it would 'intervene in a friendly manner with the Romanian Government so as to ask it to suspend provisionally the confiscation of the properties of Hungarian citizens in Transylvania'.[64] Accordingly, acting as President of the Conference, Raymond Poincaré amiably suggested to the Romanian government to defer at least temporarily its expropriation or confiscation procedures, which could be considered a violation of minority rights.[65]

Until April 1923, when the Hungarian government officially involved the Council of the League of Nations in the Transylvanian optants' case, multilateral fora like the Inter-Allied Control Commission or the Conference of Ambassadors were the only channels of communication on the matter.

B. Minorities Petitions

Citizens of the Little Entente states belonging to national or ethnic minorities, especially to the formerly dominant nations (Hungarians, Germans, Saxons) were as harshly affected by discriminatory expropriation measures as those who opted for Hungarian nationality. Unlike optants, however, these nationals enjoyed protection under the Minority Treaties signed by each of the Little Entente countries.

[62] Note for the President of the Council, Hungarian expropriation in Transylvania, Annex, Letter from Mr. Doulcet, French ambassador in Budapest, to Mr. Raymond Poincaré, President of the Council, Minister of Foreign Affairs, Budapest, 27 September 1922, Correspondance diplomatique, Europe 1918–1940, Roumanie, ADMAE, 110CPCOM/43 (Microfilm P/17429), 30.

[63] Letter from Mr. Doulcet, French ambassador in Budapest, to Mr. Raymond Poincaré, President of the Council, Minister of Foreign Affairs, Budapest, 15 September 1922, Correspondance diplomatique, ADMAE, Service Française de Societé des Nations (SFSdN), vol. 285, P14480 (La Hongrie et la Roumanie, 1922–1923), 38; Memorandum by the British Ambassador in Paris, Paris, 26 December 1922, Correspondance diplomatique, ADMAE, Service Française de Societé des Nations (SFSdN), vol. 285, P14480 (La Hongrie et la Roumanie, 1922–1923), 40–41.

[64] Resolution by the Conference of Ambassadors. Expropriation of Hungarian properties in Transylvania, 24 January 1923, Correspondance diplomatique, ADMAE, SFSdN, vol. 285, P14480 (La Hongrie et la Roumanie, 1922–1923), 42.

[65] Letter from the President of the Conference of Ambassadors, Poincaré, to the Romanian ambassador in Paris, Mr. Antonescu, Paris, 9 April 1923, ALoN, Section 41, box no. R 1685, folder no. 7326, document no. 28216.

While optants could not submit minorities petitions since the mechanism was only open to nationals of the concerned state, minority landowners who chose to stay in the successor states could file complaints regarding the execution of the land reforms with the League of Nations. The Secretariat of the League—and especially its Minorities Section—carefully registered and noted the similarities between the lodged complaints concerning agrarian reforms.

The states bound by the Minority Treaties were relatively cooperative with the supervisory bodies, the so-called Committees of Three, constituted for each petition. The effectiveness of the mechanism was owed to the publicity of the conclusions of these Committees of Three once one of their members decided to end the secrecy of the procedure and use their power to bring the matter before the Council or the Permanent Court of International Justice.[66]

Minority members from the three Little Entente states submitted a large number of petitions throughout the interwar period. As soon as Hungary joined the League of Nations, its permanent representative unofficially transmitted various petitions from private individuals to the Secretariat with the request not to reveal the intervention of his government in their submission.[67] Among the minority petitions were various complaints related to the agrarian reforms enacted by the Little Entente governments.[68] While the case of the Transylvanian optants was technically submitted not as a minority petition but as a political issue, the Minorities Section of the League of Nations followed the matter closely and was involved in the Secretariat's mediation efforts.[69] The Hungarian agent acting as counsel in the optants case, László Gajzágó, discussed the topic with one of the key members of the Minorities Section, Pablo de Azcárate,[70] who assisted the Brussels negotiations in April 1923. The Romanian delegate Titulescu likewise consulted

[66] Francis Paul Walters, *A History of the League of Nations* (Oxford University Press 1952) 403–404.

[67] Note by the Secretary-General, Geneva, 20 November 1922, ALoN, Section 41, box no. R 1661, folder no. 12273, document no. 24456.

[68] E.g. Memorandum regarding the violations of law committed by the Romanian rule in Transylvania against national, religious and racial minorities, by the Society for the Protection of Minorities in Transylvania, LoN, C.65.M.21.1922.I; Letter from 20 December 1922, with an attached Memorandum on the request of German large landowners in Czechoslovakia regarding the execution of the land reform in Czechoslovakia, LoN, C.3.M.1.1923, C.782.1922.I; Protection of Minorities in Czechoslovakia, agrarian reform, 3 March 1925, LoN, C.95.1925.I; Petition by farmers of Hungarian race in the Banat and Transylvania (Roumania), 2 March 1925, LoN, C.113.1925.I; Protection of Minorities in Yugoslavia, petition by Doc Jean Bisaku, Don Etienne Kurti, and Don Louis Gashi concerning the situation of the Albanian minority in the Kingdom of Yugoslavia, 16 February 1933, LoN, C.129.1933.I, 6–10 and 20–21.

[69] Pablo de Azcárate, *League of Nations and National Minorities: An Experiment* (Eileen E. Brooke tr, 1945) 65.

[70] E.g. Note by Mr. Pablo de Azcarate, Minorities Section, for Mr. Erik Andreas Colban, director of the Minorities Section, 16 April 1923, ALoN, Section 41, box no. R 1685, folder no. 7326, document 27326; Aide-mémoire of a discussion with Mr. Gajzágó, 28 April 1923, ALoN, Section 41, box no. R 1685, folder no. 7326, document 28065; Letter from Mr. P. de Azcarate to Mr. Colban, Geneva, 2 May1923, ALoN, Section 41, box no. R 1685, folder no. 7326, document 28066.

with the Minorities Section multiple times regarding the case of the Transylvanian optants.[71]

A delegation of the League Secretariat composed of Erik Colban, Director of the Minorities Section, his colleague Pablo de Azcárate, and Marcel Hoden from the Office of the Secretary-General, even visited Romania in late July/early August 1923. Colban visited Romania again in May 1924 (including Transylvania) and October 1926, and his successor Pablo de Azcárate undertook journeys to the country in October 1930 and September 1932.[72] While some governments including the British urged for the first visit with a view to preventing a fait accompli in the ongoing land distribution,[73] the members of the Minorities Section did not discuss the optants cases very actively, instead focusing their fact-finding journeys on other minority problems like education or political rights.[74]

The more petitions concerning the land reforms the Minorities Section received, the more it recognized the systematic nature of the reported discriminations. This realization led Pablo de Azcárate to prepare a confidential study on the minority problems created by the land reforms in Latvia, Lithuania, Poland, Romania, and Czechoslovakia. As he remarked in his introduction, there was tension between the social need for agrarian reforms and the fact that the most seriously affected landowners of the adopted measures were the formerly dominant national and ethnic minorities.[75] Azcárate noted that the League was faced with the dilemma of choosing between two extremely dangerous positions: supporting the minorities' demands for equal treatment and thereby interfering with the domestic affairs of the states on the one hand, and closing its eyes to the matter and thus tacitly acquiescing to the employment of oppressive measures against minorities on the other. Either choice would entail considerable social and economic costs: the governments of the successor states justified the land reforms with social necessity, and by challenging them, the League risked causing a reluctance to address historic privileges and social inequalities, with the ultimate threat of a peasant rebellion.[76] As Azcárate observed, the League was forced to adopt a careful position:

[71] Note by Mr. Erik Andreas Colban, concerning a conversation between the Romanian delegate Mr. Titulescu and Mr. Colban, 21 April 1923, ALoN, Section 41, box no. R 1685, folder no. 7326, document 27326.

[72] See their reports published in Gheorghe Iancu, *Problema Minorităților Etnice Din România În Documente Ale Societății Națiunilor (1923–1932) = Le Problème Des Minorités Ethniques de La Roumanie Dans Des Documents de La Société Des Nations (1923–1932)* (Argonaut 2002).

[73] Letter from Miles W. Lampson of the Foreign Office to the Secretary-General of the LoN, Eric Drummond, London, 23 February 1923, ALoN, Section F° 75, box no. S 351—No. 6, folder no. 16.

[74] Iancu, *Problema Minorităților* (n 72) 72 (both the Romanian foreign minister Duca and Colban agreed that the Secretariat had sufficient information regarding the optants question and it should therefore not be addressed during their meeting).

[75] ALoN, *La réforme agraire et la protection de minorités* (n 33) 3–4.

[76] Ibid.

> Therefore, regarding these difficulties, the League of Nations preferred, in principle, not to oppose the governments in the enforcement of the land reform, however radical it may be (~~as this is a purely internal question in which it cannot intervene~~) [deleted in the original—A.B.], but nonetheless submit to a detailed and meticulous examination all complaints and petitions that were presented by different minorities regarding this topic, [and] any measure taken against a minority which would not have necessarily resulted from the historic situation described above. Pursuant to this criterion, the different Minorities committees have not considered it possible, until now, to present before the Council the entire land reform of a given country but at several occasions have examined and in some cases drawn the Council's attention to certain specific points raised in the matter of non-enforcement (~~see the case of the Hungarian settlers in Transylvania, and the points related to the land reform in Lithuania~~) [deleted in the original—A.B.].
>
> In principle, it would be possible to affirm that a land reform would seem to be challengeable only if it were possible to demonstrate, either in the text of its constitutive laws, or in their application, a differential treatment of the interested persons (owners of beneficiaries) belonging to minorities, which would be harmful to them.[77]

The phrases deleted by Azcárate also underline the institutional dilemma: to what degree could the League intervene in the agrarian policies of its member states? International law was traditionally based on state sovereignty and the existence of a *domaine réservé*, that is, matters solely within the domestic jurisdiction of a state and not subject to international norms.[78] However, international law experts of the period—including the Permanent Court of International Justice (PCIJ)—were increasingly interpreting the latter notion narrowly, with a scope depending 'upon the development of international relations'[79] and excluding questions regulated by international law[80] such as the protection of the private property of members of minorities and foreigners.

Azcárate's study could not identify any common recommendation applying to all land reforms, and so the approach taken by the Committees of Three consisted of case-by-case analysis and the difficult search for compromise solutions. Whereas it was easy to discern discrimination when a legislative text made a clear-cut distinction between the majority and the minority, violations of the Minority Treaties were more difficult to determine when textually neutral regulations were enforced in a discriminatory fashion to the detriment of a minority.[81]

77 Ibid.

78 *Covenant of the League of Nations* Article 15(8).

79 *Nationality Decrees Issued in Tunis and Morocco on Nov. 8th, 1921*, Advisory Opinion, 1923, PCIJ, Series B, No. 4, 23–24.

80 *Nationality Decrees Issued in Tunis and Morocco* (n 79) 23–24.

81 ALoN, *La réforme agraire et la protection de minorités* (n 33) 4.

Despite the meticulous documentation and mediation efforts of the Minorities Section to settle agrarian petitions satisfactorily, its members held differing points of view regarding the well-founded nature of the minorities' petitions. Erik Colban, the Norwegian director of the Minorities Section, for example, openly told Titulescu that he saw a likely discrimination against Hungarians in the execution of the Romanian land reform and thus considered the Hungarian claims to have a strong moral foundation.[82] Azcárate, however, who succeeded Colban as head of the Minorities Section in 1932, was sceptical concerning the general allegations of minorities against agrarian reforms and more inclined to regard the socioeconomic context, namely the fact that former landowners almost exclusively belonged to minority populations of the new successor states while the overwhelming majority of peasants belonged to the majority population.[83] The fact that the Hungarian press considered Colban an anti-minority and Azcárate a pro-minority agent within the League[84] suggests that both men separated their personal opinion strictly from their professional mandate. Furthermore, both Secretary-General Eric Drummond and Colban confirmed—despite several informal Romanian requests to the contrary—that the Secretariat could not influence the proceedings of the Committees of Three, which enjoyed full autonomy in dealing with the minority petitions.[85]

While the Minorities Section did not influence the diplomatic negotiations nor the final outcome of the optants cases, it was successful in assisting the Committees of Three in the settling of individual minority petitions from expropriated landowners such as those of the settlers from the Banat and Transylvania[86] or the Székely border guards.[87] In these cases, 'informal and friendly negotiations between a Committee of Three and the Government', which the Minorities Section considered 'a much more effective method than public discussion by the Council', were held.[88] The pragmatism of the Minorities Section shows that in a fierce battle over the legality of land reforms, even a body entrusted with protecting individual rights under multinational treaties could not enforce compliance without political compromises between individual and community interests.

82 Note by Mr. Erik Andreas Colban (n 70).

83 Azcárate, *League of Nations and National Minorities* (n 69) 62–63; Minute sheet, Note by Mr. P. de Azcarate to Mr. Colban, 9 January 1925, ALoN, Section F° 75, box no. S 351–No. 2, folder no. 16.

84 *MTI Archívum* [Hungarian News Agency Archives] 'Lapszemle' (27 May 1930) 17–18.

85 Minute sheet, Confidential, prepared by Mr. Colban, Geneva, 2 November 1925, ALoN, Section F° 75, box no. S 351 - No. 4, folder no. 16.

86 After various rounds of mediation efforts by the Minorities Section and the Committee of Three, the Romanian government offered the distribution of 700,000 gold francs to the colonists of Hungarian nationality in the Banat and Transylvania. Letter from the Romanian Government to the Secretary-General of the League, Geneva, 11 April 1928, *League of Nations O.J.* 798 (June 1928), 798–799.

87 Hungarian Minorities in Romania: Petition of 15 August 1931 by descendants of Székely border guards, Examination of the petition during the 66th session of the Council, January 1932, ALoN, Section 4, box no. R 2160, folder no. 3442, document no. 33230.

88 Report by the Committee instituted by the Council resolution of March 7th, 1929, 73; *League of Nations O.J., Spec. Supp.* 42 (1929), 59.

C. Appeal to the League Council by the Hungarian Government

The League of Nations was established with the aim 'to promote international co-operation and to achieve international peace and security',[89] and it was vested with various powers to prevent political matters from disturbing the peace.[90] Under Article 11 of its Covenant, members of the League had the right 'to bring to the attention of the Assembly or of the Council any circumstance whatever affecting international relations which threatens to disturb international peace or the good understanding between nations upon which peace depends'.[91] Land reforms affecting the property rights of foreign nationals could typically lead to such inter-state disputes jeopardizing peace and the good relations between nations: recourse was taken to this article over land reform issues on no fewer than seven occasions during the first decade of the League.[92]

As the Conference of Ambassadors regularly forwarded the Hungarian memoranda to the League Secretariat, the latter was already aware of the complaints as early as April 1921. At the time, the Secretariat did not consider the League of Nations competent in the Transylvanian optants case, as Romania had not yet ratified its Minority Treaty.[93] It nevertheless decided to proceed as though Romania had ratified the treaty and thus circulated the Hungarian memoranda among the member states of the Council.[94] It did the same with the memorandum of 25 February 1921 concerning Czechoslovakia, and with the complaints pertaining to Yugoslavia as well.

When the Hungarian government filed its grievance regarding the case of the optants with the League Secretariat on 15 March 1923,[95] the Secretariat's Legal Section examined the matter and decided that it did not fall under the regime of the Minority Treaty.[96] Since both the Hungarian and the Romanian government invoked Article 11(2) of the Covenant, however, they were bringing to the attention of the Council a circumstance 'affecting international relations which threatens to

[89] *Covenant of the League of Nations*, Preamble.

[90] Ibid, Articles 11–17.

[91] Ibid, Article 11(2).

[92] Kenneth Deacon, *Land Tenure and Nationalism in Eastern Europe, 1919–1929: Diplomatic Aspects of Agrarian Reform* (New York University 1949) 74 mentions only six occasions while omitting the seventh, namely that of the Hungarian Government on 15 March 1923.

[93] Note by Helmer Rosting, public servant of the Minorities Section, to the Secretary-General, Geneva, 28 April 1921, ALoN, Section 41, box no. R 1661, folder no. 12273; Note by Erik Colban concerning the note by Helmer Rosting, Geneva, 5 May 1921, ALoN, Section 41, box no. R 1661, folder no. 12273.

[94] Ibid; Opinion of Daniele Varé, Political Section, Geneva, 7 May 1921, ALoN, Section 41, box no. R 1661, folder no. 12273.

[95] Request from the Royal Hungarian Government to the Council of the League of Nations in accordance with Article 11 of the Covenant of the League of Nations, concerning the expropriation of immovable property belonging to Hungarians who have exercised the right to opt by the Kingdom of Romania contrary to the provisions of the Treaties, LoN, C.244.M.128.1923.I.

[96] Legal note on the Hungarian-Romanian question, prepared by Mr. Van Hamel, Geneva, 25 April 1923, 6 p., ALoN, Section 41, box no. R 1685, folder no. 7326, document 28065.

disturb international peace or the good understanding between nations'. The case of the Transylvanian optants therefore continued not as a minorities petition but as a political matter before the Council, in a diplomatic settlement procedure.

During this lengthy mediation procedure comprising two phases, the Council initially appointed a rapporteur in 1923 (see III.D) and then a Committee of Three in 1927–28 (see III.F). Although both of these mediation attempts proved unsuccessful, the debates and successive reports galvanised the international community and gave the optants some hope for a diplomatic solution.

D. Mediation by a Rapporteur

The Council discussed the case of the Transylvanian optants as a political matter for the first time during its session on 20–23 April 1923. The rapporteur appointed for the case, Mr. Adatci, the Japanese ambassador to Belgium, proposed to the Council to refer matter to the Permanent Court of International Justice, or alternatively to ask the Permanent Court for an advisory opinion. The Romanian delegate, Nicolae Titulescu, firmly refused both proposals as unacceptable and a possible threat to the agrarian reform.[97] As the consent of the involved states was required to establish the Permanent Court's jurisdiction and unanimous decisions were the rule in the Council,[98] no resolution could be adopted. Instead of a judicial settlement, the Council thus decided to remit the question 'for further consideration at the next session of the Council', expressing the hope 'that M. Adatci will continue to act as Rapporteur, and in the meantime trust[ing] that the Governments of Hungary and Roumania will direct their best efforts towards the attainment of an agreed solution'.[99]

Adatci began his mediation efforts by convoking a meeting of the parties in Brussels on 27 May 1923, with Count Csáky and Mr. Gajzágó representing Hungary, and Mr. Titulescu representing Romania. While the participants failed to reach an agreement, Adatci and Titulescu insisted on the Hungarian delegates signing record of the minutes of the meeting on the morning of their planned departure. This meeting record included a draft resolution with a point according to which 'the Treaty [of Trianon] does not preclude the expropriation of the property of optants for reasons of public welfare, including the social requirements of agrarian reform'.[100] While Gajzágó refused to sign the minutes, Csáky agreed to append his initials to the portion of the text of the draft resolution that had been

[97] *League of Nations O.J., Spec. Supp.* 212 (1920–1946) 212–215.
[98] *Covenant of the League of Nations* Article 5(1).
[99] *League of Nations O.J., Spec. Supp.* 212 (1920–1946) 215.
[100] League of Nations, Expropriation by the Roumanian Government of the property of Hungarian optants, Report by M. Adatci, Geneva, 6 June 1923, C.386.1923.VII, 5.

discussed, although he was fully aware that he was exceeding his powers and his government might not approve.[101]

After Adatci included the signed minutes with the draft resolution in his report, the Hungarian government repudiated Csáky.[102] The Hungarian delegate to the League Council, Count Apponyi, accordingly refused Adatci's draft resolution, while Titulescu was ready to accept it as reflecting the 'Brussels agreement'.[103] The Council finally adopted Adatci's report, stating that it had taken note of 'the various declarations contained in the minutes attached to the report of the Japanese representative, and hopes that both Governments will do their utmost to prevent the question of Hungarian optants from becoming a disturbing influence in the relations between the neighbouring two countries'.[104] It declared its hope that both states would make their best efforts to eliminate the misunderstanding, and that 'the Roumanian Government will remain faithful to the Treaty, and to the principle of justice upon which it declares that its agrarian legislation is founded, by giving proof of its goodwill in regard to the interests of the Hungarian optants'.[105]

While the Council, Adatci,[106] and contemporary legal commentators[107] did not accept the Hungarian government's attempt to disavow its plenipotentiary, Csáky's signature under the minutes ultimately did not influence the mediation proceedings. At the same time, the Council's resolution left the dispute unsettled until it was called upon again in 1927.

E. Appeal to the Mixed Arbitral Tribunals by the Optants

Beyond involving the Hungarian government, the optants and their representatives also sought recourse themselves with all available national and international jurisdictions. They sent petitions to courts of the expropriating successor state, to the League of Nations, and even to the Permanent Court of International Justice,[108] which only had jurisdiction over disputes between states. As a major remedy instituted by the Treaty of Trianon, claims made by Hungarian nationals under Article

[101] Explanation by Gajzágó, Memorandum by the Hungarian Government, League of Nations Council, 25th session, seventh meeting (public) held at 10 a.m. on 5 July 1923, ALoN, Section 2, box no. R 613, folder no. 28470, document no. 29633, 53–54.

[102] *League of Nations O.J.* 886 (August 1923) 886–894.

[103] *League of Nations O.J.* 904 (August 1923) 908.

[104] *League of Nations O.J., Spec. Supp.* 287 (1920–1946) 291.

[105] Ibid.

[106] *League of Nations O.J.* 886 (August 1923) 902.

[107] E.g. Jean Appleton, 'Histoire d'un conflit' in Yves de La Brière and Henri Capitant (eds), *La réforme agraire en Roumanie et les optants hongrois de Transylvanie devant la Société des Nations: (suite)* (Imprimerie du Palais 1928) 54.

[108] Letter from Mr. Hammarskjold, registrar of the PCIJ, to Mr. Eric Drummond, Secretary-General of the LoN, The Hague, 2 June 1924, ALoN, Section 2, box no. R 613, folder no. 28470, document no. 33380x.

250 of the treaty on the prohibition of retention or liquidation of private property could be submitted to the so-called Mixed Arbitral Tribunals (MATs) jointly established by Hungary and the Allied and Associated Powers.[109] The Mixed Arbitral Tribunals were not part of the League of Nations system itself, but were stipulated as dispute settlement bodies by the peace treaties. In the event of failure of a state to appoint the president or the two arbitrators for its MAT, however, such appointment was to be made by the Council of the League.[110]

The majority of Hungarian optants, almost 400 (389) litigants, brought their cases before the Hungarian-Romanian MAT in Paris in December 1923. They were represented by the same three Budapest-based advocates who had previously been appointed by the Hungarian government and were thus already well-versed in the subject matter.[111] Some 111 optants took action against Czechoslovakia at the Hungarian-Czechoslovakian MAT, while approximately 100 other families settled directly with the Czechoslovakian Land Office.[112] From Yugoslavia, seventy-eight optants brought their claims before the Hungarian-Yugoslavian MAT.[113]

While hundreds of optants thus initiated proceedings with the MATs, many others were unable to do so. This was due to a combination of the considerable procedural fees for the MATs,[114] the failure of some litigants to meet the deadline for filing their petitions with the tribunals (31 December 1924 for the Hungarian-Romanian MAT, 28 February 1925 for the Hungarian-Czechoslovakian MAT, and 31 December 1925 for the Hungarian-Yugoslavian MAT),[115] the distance to the seats of the MATs (Hungarian-Romanian and Hungarian-Yugoslavian MAT: Paris; Hungarian-Czechoslovakian MAT: The Hague), their procedural language (French), and the large number of forms to be submitted. The Hungarian government tried to facilitate litigation before the MATs by establishing an Office of Governmental Agents at the Mixed Arbitral Tribunals[116] led by the tried legal counsel of the Ministry of Foreign Affairs, László Gajzágó. This office provided generous legal aid and assistance to both the litigants and the MATs in Paris,[117] and

[109] Treaty of Trianon (n 2), Articles 239, 250.

[110] Ibid, Article 239(a)(2).

[111] The law firm of Lakatos and Császár or that of Aurél Egry.

[112] In 1930, Benes spoke of 101 optants asserting claims against Czechoslovakia. Declaration by Eduard Benes, *MTI Házi Tájékoztató* [Hungarian News Agency Confidential Bulletin], 4 February 1930, N° 120 (translated by the author). This number rose to 111 by 1937 according to Numerical list of all agrarian cases, around 1937, Listes des affaires—états généraux, AN, AJ/22/34.

[113] Numerical list of all agrarian cases (note 119).

[114] For example, procedural fees at the Hungarian-Romanian MAT varied from 50 francs (petitions pertaining to claims of up to 5000 francs) to 300 francs (petitions pertaining to claims between 750,000 and 1,000,000 francs). See Note du TAM roumano-hongrois sur les frais procéduraux, no date, Fonctionnement interne du Tribunal, Renseignement-Instructions, Archives Nationales de France (AN), AJ/22/30.

[115] *Délmagyarország* (6 January 1925) 4.

[116] (*Vegyes Döntöbíróságok mellett müködö Kormánymegbízottak Hivatala*) *MTI Archívum* [Hungarian News Agency Archives], 23 February 1924.

[117] Hungarian governmental order 2930/1925 on the legal aid provided at Mixed Arbitral Tribunals, 16 May 1925, *Rendeletek tára*, 1925, 59–61.

Gajzágó simultaneously worked to exempt as many litigants as possible from the procedural fees and disbursements on account of their social status.[118]

The optants proceedings before the three MATs were highly politicized and observed closely by academic and press commentators, and the involved parties employed high-ranking international law experts to plead their respective cases: renowned law professors like Joseph Barthélemy, Charles Dupuis, and Gilbert Gidel from the University of Paris, as well as René Brunet from the University of Caen, all of whom were advocates at the Cour de Paris, represented the Hungarian optants.[119] In 1927, Albert de Lapradelle, professor and legal counsel (*jurisconsulte*) at the Quai d'Orsay, provided an expert opinion to the Hungarian government on the issue of the Transylvanian optants. After publishing his legal position in the daily journal *Le Temps*, Lapradelle had to choose between maintaining his position at the Quai d'Orsay and his freedom to compile expert opinions for foreign governments; he chose the latter.[120] The governments of the Little Entente likewise engaged high-ranking experts, such as the former French President of the Republic Alexandre Millerand in his profession as advocate or two professors from the University of Paris, Jules Basdevant and Nicolas Politis—the latter being the Greek ambassador in Paris and former Minister of Foreign Affairs of Greece.[121]

Of the three MATs, it was the Hungarian-Romanian tribunal that rendered a first precedent in the optant cases. Following the failed initial mediation attempt by the League Council, some 350 Transylvanian optants filed petitions with the Hungarian-Romanian MAT between December 1923 and 10 January 1927. Because the MAT was kept busy dealing with its own structure and the organization of its work during 1924 and 1925, and in part also due to the illness of its president Cederkrantz and the dilatory tactic of the Romanian agent,[122] the first oral pleas in the agrarian cases could only be heard in late 1926. This second phase of the Transylvanian optant cases concluded with a first decision issued on 10 January 1927 in which the Hungarian-Romanian Mixed Arbitral Tribunal established its competence regarding the challenged measures of expropriation taken against optants. Concerning the cases *Archiduc Frédéric de Habsbourg-Lorraine v Romania*, *Emeric Kulin v Romania* and twenty other similar cases, the tribunal held that the challenged expropriation measures constituted liquidation without compensation

[118] Verbatim records of the sessions from 23 to 28 January 1925, AN, AJ/22/28 (Procédures).

[119] Letter from Mr. L. Gajzágó, general agent of the Hungarian government before the Hungarian-Romanian Mixed Arbitral Tribunal, to the President of the Hungarian-Romanian Mixed Arbitral Tribunal, Budapest, 14 December 1926, Fonctionnement interne du Tribunal, Correspondance, AN, AJ/22/30.

[120] Letter from the French Minister of Foreign Affairs, Aristide Briand, to de La Pradelle, 18 October 1927, ADMAE, Personnel, 2e série, vol. 687.

[121] *MTI Archívum* [Hungarian News Agency Archives], 'Napi hírek' 14 March 1927.

[122] Letter from Mr. Szent-István y to Mr. Gajzágó, Paris, 4 October 1925, report 29/res., Fonctionnement interne du Tribunal, Correspondance, AN, AJ/22/30.

and were thus prohibited by the peace treaty.[123] The MAT also concluded that the peace treaties, the legal basis for its competence, imposed necessary limitations on the successor states with regard to private property.

The repercussions of this decision went beyond the Hungarian-Romanian MAT: it opened the door to admissibility for all analogous agrarian cases and qualified expropriation measures as 'liquidation without compensation' in breach of the Treaty of Trianon. The tribunal's decision was not signed by the Romanian arbitrator and was sharply rejected by the countries of the Little Entente. It also gave rise to a long vacuum in the judicial procedure: the Romanian government ceased its participation in the proceedings and withdrew its arbitrator. With this withdrawal, the Romanian government effectively boycotted the operation of the Hungarian-Romanian MAT in agrarian cases for many years until the diplomatic settlement in 1930 (see section III.G, below). At the same time, Romania appealed to the League Council on the basis of Article 11(2) of the Covenant.[124] This action once again initiated the mechanism of diplomatic settlement of the dispute under the aegis of the League of Nations.

Meanwhile, the admissibility decision by the Hungarian-Romanian MAT was examined closely by the parties to the agrarian cases brought before the two other tribunals, the Hungarian-Czechoslovakian MAT and the Hungarian-Yugoslavian MAT. The Czechoslovakian government attempted to employ the Romanian arguments by claiming that any land reform was subject to state sovereignty and unrestricted by international law. At the same time, however, it began trying to negotiate friendly settlements with individual optants. A group of Hungarian petitioners whose 684 jugars (393.64 ha) of land located near Turiszakállas (*Sokolce*) had been expropriated by the Czechoslovakian authorities received an offer in the spring of 1927 to cede 100 jugars (57.55 ha) in favour of Czech settlers and a further 100 jugars in favour of Hungarian landless peasants at 30 per cent of the market price in exchange for exemption of the remainder of their land from expropriation.[125] This deal surprised commentators, as it contradicted the Prague government's firm insistence on the immutability of the land reform.[126] As for the court proceedings, on 31 January 1929, two years after the Hungarian-Romanian MAT's admissibility decisions, the Hungarian-Czechoslovakian MAT followed its example and declared itself competent concerning agrarian cases submitted by optants.[127]

[123] E.g. *Emeric Kulin v Romania*, no. 139, Hungarian-Romanian MAT, 10 January 1927, 7 *Recueil des Decisions des Tribunaux Arbitraux Mixtes Institués par les Traités de Paix* 138 1928; Decision of the Hungarian-Romanian Mixed Arbitral Tribunal on its competence, Paris, 10 January 1927, *Olivér Almay c. Etat roumain*, affaire no. 316, AN, AJ/22/38.

[124] *League of Nations O.J., Spec. Supp.* 226 (1920–1946) 226–232.

[125] 'Csehszlovákia követi a román példát [Czechoslovakia follows the Romanian example]' *Prágai Magyar Hírlap* (5 May 1927) 4.

[126] Ibid.

[127] Hungarian-Czechoslovakian Mixed Arbitral Tribunal, *Alexandre Pallavicini c. s. c. État tchécoslovaque*, No. 3, 31 January 1929, 8 *Recueil des Decisions des Tribunaux Arbitraux Mixtes Institués par les Traités de Paix* 713 1929; *Stephan de Bacsak c. Etat tchécoslovaque*, No. 218, 5 February 1929, 8 *Recueil des Decisions des Tribunaux Arbitraux Mixtes Institués par les Traités de Paix* 410 1929.

The Hungarian-Yugoslavian MAT rendered the same decision of admissibility in May 1929.[128] The decisions of the two other tribunals shocked Romanian diplomacy, as it held that this case law 'ruins the basis of our thesis on the abuse of power committed by the Hungarian-Romanian mixed tribunal, which by its decision of 1927 established its competence'.[129]

F. Mediation by the Committee of Three

The discussions between the Romanian and Hungarian delegates under the aegis of the League Council attracted much international attention as well as triggering interventions by the other Little Entente states. These debates were not merely about the Transylvanian optants or the proceedings at the MATs but about the legitimacy of the land reforms enacted in the Little Entente countries in general.[130] It was a sign of the matter's international importance that Edvard Beneš intervened in favour of the Romanian position not to appoint a new arbitrator to the MAT.[131] As he stressed:

> The agrarian reforms were a vital necessity for the countries of Central Europe. They ensured the social order and peace for the countries and nations that would otherwise socially suffer the revolutionary crises of bolshevism and be plunged into political anarchy [...]. By avoiding this, these nations saved themselves from a disaster, and they enabled the consolidation of the countries situated in the Western part of Europe.[132]

Beneš reiterated the Romanian government's position that the agrarian laws were written in neutral language and applied to nationals and foreign citizens equally.[133] It was in fact the opposite approach, he claimed—that is, the exemption of Hungarian subjects from the provisions of the agrarian laws—that would create a privilege and violate the sovereignty of the affected states.[134]

[128] Hungarian-Yugoslav Mixed Arbitral Tribunal, *Elisabeth Schmidt c. Etat serbe-croate-slovène*, 14 May 1929, no. 226, 1929 *Recueil des Decisions des Tribunaux Arbitraux Mixtes Institués par les Traités de Paix* 169; see identical decisions in the *Bödy* (no. 244), *Benyovsky* (no. 342), and *Meszaros* (no. 605) cases.

[129] Letter from the Romanian ambassador in Budapest, Vasile Grigorcea, to the Romanian Minister of Foreign Affairs, Budapest, 17 May 1929, Archives of the Ministry of Foreign Affairs of Romania (AMFA Romania), Fond Problema 11—Proprietăți ale statului și particularilor în străinătate și ale străinilor în România, Vol. 48–1929 (ianuarie-iunie) [translated from Romanian by the author].

[130] See in this sense e.g. Gustav Stresemann speaking about 'national vital interests', Second Meeting (Public), Geneva, 17 September 1927, *League of Nations O.J.* 1390 (October 1927), 1398; Jean Appleton, 'Les lois agraires roumaines et le traité de Trianon' *Le Temps* (10 September 1927) 2.

[131] Communication du Gouvernement tchécoslovaque, League of Nations, 16 September 1927, LoN, C.491.1927.VII.

[132] Ibid, 2–3 [translated from French by the author].

[133] Ibid, 9.

[134] Ibid, 11.

Both the Romanian and the Czechoslovakian government protested the decision of admissibility by the Hungarian-Romanian MAT, which they considered an 'excess of power'. The Hungarian government, however, asked the League Council to appoint two substitute arbitrators so as to guarantee the continued operation of the Hungarian-Romanian MAT. The Council, which had been called upon by Romania on 24 February 1927 under Article 11(2) of the Covenant, decided during its session on 7 March 1927 to task Sir Austen Chamberlain, the British Minister of Foreign Affairs, with preparing a report on the question. Chamberlain was to be assisted by the League representatives of Chile and Japan. The Committee of Three thus formed met several times and attempted to mediate between the parties. During its conciliation efforts, it compiled a report based on three principles that, according to the Committee, bound both Romania and Hungary under their status as signatories of the Treaty of Trianon. The three principles were as follows:

1. The provisions of the peace settlement effected after the war of 1914-18 do not exclude the application to Hungarian nationals (including those who have opted for Hungarian nationality) of a general scheme of agrarian reform.
2. There must be no inequality between Roumanians and Hungarians, either in the terms of the agrarian law or in the way in which it is enforced.
3. The words 'retention and liquidation' mentioned in Article 250, which relates only to the territories ceded by Hungary, apply solely to the measures taken against the property of a Hungarian in the said territories and in so far as such owner is a Hungarian national.[135]

The Committee of Three recommended that the Council should a) urge the two parties to adhere to the elaborated principles, and b) request Romania to reinstate its arbitrator at the Mixed Arbitral Tribunal.[136]

Out of the three principles, Hungary strongly opposed the second, that is, the principle of non-discrimination, arguing that the Treaty of Trianon had set up a 'preferential system' in favour of nationals of the defeated states, in this case Hungarians, that was more stringent than that protecting expropriated Romanians. Such a preferential treatment was certainly common in various Eastern countries at the time, especially in Asia in favour of Western nationals.[137] In Western European states, however, where the legal tradition granted foreigners less protection than the nationals of a state—as well as in American states, where foreigners

[135] Request by the Hungarian Government for appointment by the Council, in virtue of Article 239 of the Treaty of Trianon, of two deputy arbitrators for the Hungarian-Romanian Mixed Arbitral Tribunal, Report by the Committee of the Council, LoN, C.489.1927.VII, 10–11.

[136] Ibid, 12.

[137] René Cassin, 'La réforme agraire en Roumanie et les optants hongrois de Transylvanie devant la Société des Nations' in Yves de La Brière and Henri Capitant (eds), *La réforme agraire en Roumanie et les optants hongrois de Transylvanie devant la Société des Nations: (suite)* (Imprimerie du Palais 1928) 121.

enjoyed equality of treatment with the nationals—accepting a greater protection for foreigners than for nationals seemed a step backwards.[138]

The Council unanimously adopted the Chamberlain report, whose legal effect was only recommendatory, and appealed to the two governments 'to conform to the principles indicated therein'.[139] The Romanian government accepted and welcomed the resolution, as did the Czechoslovakian foreign minister Edvard Beneš, who considered it a victory for both Romania and Czechoslovakia.[140] Quite unsurprisingly, both the Czechoslovakian and Yugoslavian government invoked the three principles of the Chamberlain report as a point of reference in subsequent debates about their land reforms.[141]

In contrast to Romania, Hungary did not accept the three principles. In turn, when the Council urged Romania in April 1928 to reinstate its arbitrator to the Hungarian-Romanian MAT, which had been expanded to include two neutral judges,[142] Romania refused that proposal.[143] The eventual failure of the conciliation mechanism under the auspices of the League of Nations was not necessarily a consequence of the weakness of the League, however: a different international dispute concerning land reforms, the case of the German settlers in Poland, ended with an agreement concluded in June 1924 as a consequence of mediation by a Committee of Three (delegates from Brazil, Great Britain, and Italy) that intervened in Paris from March to June 1924.[144] This goes to show that friendly settlement was possible if both parties to such a dispute were interested in a compromise at the moment of the League's intervention.

G. Diplomatic Settlement of the Eastern Reparations

As a result of Hungary's opposition to the Chamberlain report and the Romanian refusal to accept a judicial procedure, the Council could only postpone the question during its September 1927 session, leaving it to negotiations between the involved parties and asking Chamberlain to continue to serve as rapporteur.[145] At

[138] Alvarez Alejandro, 'La réforme agraire: le litige hungaro-roumain devant le Conseil de la Société des Nations' in Brière and Capitant, *Réforme agraire en Roumanie* (n 137) 41.

[139] *League of Nations O.J.* 1378 (October 1927) 1413–1414.

[140] Letter from the Romanian ambassador in Prague to the Romanian Minister of Foreign Affairs, Ion I.G. Duca, 21 September 1927, AMFA Romania, Fond Problema 11–Proprietăţi ale statului şi particularilor în străinătate şi ale străinilor în România, vol. 39–1923–1928.

[141] E.g. Hungarian-Czechoslovakian Mixed Arbitral Tribunal, *Alexandre Pallavicini c. s. c. État tchécoslovaque*, No. 3, 31 January 1929, 8 *Recueil des Decisions des Tribunaux Arbitraux Mixtes Institués par les Traités de Paix* 713 1929, 720; *Stephan de Bacsak c. Etat tchécoslovaque*, No. 218, 5 February 1929, 8 *Recueil des Decisions des Tribunaux Arbitraux Mixtes Institués par les Traités de Paix* 410 1929, 417–418.

[142] *League of Nations O.J.* 436 (April 1928) 446.

[143] *League of Nations O.J.* 933 (July 1928) 933.

[144] Marie-Renée Mouton, 'La Société des Nations et la protection des minorités: exemple de la Transylvanie, 1920–1928' (Thèse de 3e cycle, Université Panthéon-Sorbonne 1969) 349, note 1.

[145] *League of Nations O.J.* 1378 (October 1927) 1413–1414.

its meeting on 9 March 1928, the Council then unanimously recommended—subject to acceptance by the parties—to add two persons who were to be nationals of neutral states during the war to the Hungarian-Romanian MAT, which would continue to hear the agrarian cases in its restructured form with five members.[146] While Hungary fully endorsed this recommendation, the Romanian government refused it. Faced with this blockage, the Council urged the parties to settle the protracted dispute 'by reciprocal concessions'.[147] The two governments thereupon initiated bilateral negotiations by way of diplomatic notes in the summer of 1928[148] followed by several rounds of negotiations in Abbazia (*Opatija*), San Remo, and Vienna between late 1928 and summer 1929; the delegations were led by Baron József Szterényi, former Hungarian Minister of Commerce, and the Romanian diplomat Constantin Langa-Răşcanu. During these talks, the parties agreed to ask the League Council to postpone the case until its next session.[149] After the meetings had reached a deadlock in autumn 1929[150] and the Little Entente governments had managed to channel all optant claims into the multilateral negotiations on the Eastern reparations, Hungary and Romania abandoned their bilateral talks.

In 1929, simultaneously with the question of the German reparations and the Young Plan, multilateral negotiations about the so-called Eastern reparations, that is, the non-German reparation obligations of Austria, Hungary, and Bulgaria, as well as the claims and liabilities of the successor states of the former Habsburg Empire began in The Hague. At the end of the first reparations conference, a special committee was appointed to prepare the settlement of the non-German reparations. Presided over by the French diplomat Alexandre Aron, this committee focused mainly on the Hungarian reparations.

The more the issue of the optants came to form part of the broader question of the Eastern reparations,[151] the more the governments of the Little Entente were ready to coordinate their negotiation strategy in the matter. In 1928, Titulescu set out on a round of diplomatic visits with a view to persuading Western governments to side with Romania. In order to prevent any obligation to pay out the optants, the governments of the Little Entente insisted from the very beginning of the talks that they would only support the Young Plan—or any other arrangement with Austria and Hungary—if the agreement to be concluded with Hungary fully protected

146 *League of Nations O.J.* 407 (April 1928) 446.

147 *League of Nations O.J.* 933 (July 1928) 934.

148 *League of Nations O.J.* 1588 (October 1928) 1588–1595.

149 Letter from the head of the Hungarian delegation to Mr. Constantin Langa-Rascano, extraordinary envoy and plenipotentiary minister of the Romanian government, San Remo, 19 February 1929, 3 p., Hungarian National Archives, K63 [Ministry of Foreign Affairs, Department of Political Affairs], no. 36 cs./ 2929-27/a-181.

150 *League of Nations O.J.* 1673 (November 1929) 1674.

151 See in this context in October 1929: Diplomatic note by the Hungarian Minister of Foreign Affairs for his diplomats in London and Paris, Budapest, 16 October 1929, Hungarian National Archives, K58-1929-185, K 58 [Cabinet of the Minister], no. 42. cs./1929.

them in regard to the agrarian disputes.[152] The non-German reparations committee proposed that annuities to be paid by Hungary after 31 December 1943 (the end of its regular payments as provisionally scheduled in 1924) should be collected in an international fund created to satisfy the optants' claims. These monies would therefore be granted to the optants, mainly Hungarian aristocrats. The Hungarian delegate refused the proposal, stating that the payments his country would agree to make after 1943 would not suffice to satisfy the optants' claims. After more than two months of talks (September to December 1929), the committee eventually concluded at its second conference at The Hague that it was impossible to arrive at an agreement.[153]

In January 1930, when another round of negotiations on the Eastern reparations was convoked in The Hague, it was Hungarian Prime Minister István Bethlen who participated personally. The Hungarian position was that its reparation debt would be entirely discharged by the payment of the twenty annuities to end in 1943, while the creditor states insisted that Hungary would have to make payments after 1943 and continuing until 1966.[154] The main agreement on the Eastern reparations was concluded in The Hague on 20 January, with four supplementary agreements 'relating to the obligations resulting from the Treaty of Trianon'—including the optants question—signed in Paris on April 28.[155]

These settlements reflected a compromise solution: Hungary agreed to pay an annuity of slightly more than half a million pounds sterling from 1944 until 1966, and the three Little Entente countries in turn consented to the continuation of the Mixed Arbitral Tribunals, each expanded with two neutral members.[156] All the powers involved were to collaborate in constituting two funds that would disburse the recompense awarded to Hungarian optants by the MATs: fund 'A' for the agrarian disputes, meaning the optants' claims regarding land reforms, and Fund 'B' for all other matters. Fund 'A', the so-called Agrarian Fund, would be covered by the payments to be made by Hungary after 1943 together with certain payments by Romania, Czechoslovakia, and Yugoslavia, as well as the shares of Belgium, France, Great Britain, Italy, Japan, and Portugal in the Hungarian payments up to 1943;[157] further contributions in the form of annuities were to be made by France, Italy, and Great Britain until 1966.[158] This system of co-payment into the Agrarian Fund meant that it was essentially the Western powers who financed the satisfaction of

[152] Etienne Weill-Raynal, *Les Réparations allemandes et la France III. L'application du plan Dawes, Le plan Younget la liquidation des réparations. Avril 1924–1936* (Nouvelles éditions Latines 1947) 577.

[153] Ibid.

[154] Royall Tyler, 'The Eastern Reparations Settlement' (1930) 9 Foreign Affairs 106, 115–116.

[155] Agreements relating to the obligations resulting from the Treaty of Trianon, Paris, 28 April 1930, *Recueil des Decisions des Tribunaux Arbitraux Mixtes Institues par les Traites de Paix*, 176–192.

[156] Tyler, 'Eastern Reparations Settlement' (n 154) 116.

[157] Agreements relating to the obligations resulting from the Treaty of Trianon (n 2), Agreement III, Article II(1).

[158] Ibid., Article II(3)–(4).

the optants claims in order to benefit from the annuities to be paid to them by the Little Entente states in return.[159] As for Yugoslavia, where the agrarian reform was still ongoing at the time, the Paris Agreements provided that the country should 'promulgate the definitive law [of agrarian reform] before 20th July 1931'.[160] The responsibilities of the respondent state before the MATs were no longer incumbent on the three Little Entente states but instead on the Agrarian Fund, which had legal personality.[161]

As a consequence of the agreements reached in The Hague and Paris, the matter of the Transylvanian optants was settled and the Council decided to remove it from its agenda.[162] The optants themselves were awarded compensation in bonds corresponding fairly to their actual losses by the MATs, which mostly decided in their favour.[163]

IV. Conclusions

The importance of the Hungarian optants' struggle for compensation transcended the immediate microhistory and regional history and provides an eminent example of the history of transnational civil societies and internationally coordinated lobbying.

The effects of the optants' claims against the three Little Entente governments undoubtedly crossed the borders of the former Habsburg Empire: the ensuing disputes drew attention to the discriminatory nature of contemporary land reform laws enacted by Central European states. While these transnational effects still require further research, some examples can be cited. The Hungarian petitioners, their government, and the commissioned advocates cooperated and coordinated their activity before the Mixed Arbitral Tribunals. Furthermore, both the Hungarian government and the Little Entente governments resorted to international campaigns comprising diplomatic talks, shuttle diplomacy, public opinion campaigns, massive use of academics and their scholarly works, etc. The Congress of National Minorities, an annual assembly of representatives of various national

[159] This intention was primarily focused on Czechoslovakia, which had liberation debts towards France. Weill-Raynal, *Réparations allemandes* (n 152) 586.

[160] Agreements relating to the obligations resulting from the Treaty of Trianon (n 2), Agreement II, Article 2(3).

[161] Weill-Raynal, *Réparations allemandes* (n 152) 577.

[162] *League of Nations O.J.* 498 (June 1930) 498.

[163] E.g. Decision of the Hungarian-Romanian Mixed Arbitral Tribunal, Paris, 15 December 1932, *Comte Jules Andrássy c. Etat roumain*, no. 332 (25,718 jugars expropriated, compensation of 4,350,560 gold crowns with interest granted), AN, AJ/22/38; Hungarian-Romanian Mixed Arbitral Tribunal, Paris, 8 April 1933, *Comte Etienne Bethlen c. Etat roumain*, no. 338, AN, AJ/22/46 (11,051 jugars expropriated, compensation of 2,643,680 gold crowns with interest granted for moral damage and a further 2,385,280 for lost profit).

minorities at the League of Nations beginning in 1925,[164] stated the explicit demand that no agrarian reform should affect any minorities' close relationship to their land and lead to their economic weakening.[165]

The final settlement was largely promoted by the long mediation efforts and debates under the aegis of the League of Nations: since the League's mechanisms could not impose a binding decision protecting either the socio-economic community interests or the individual optants' property interests, it practiced a culture of mutual concessions. The eventual acceptance of the compensation regime by the Little Entente states equated to an admittance of their violations of the Treaty of Trianon, while Hungary made financial concessions to place the deal within its reparation debts.

164 Sabine Bamberger-Stemmann, *Der Europäische Nationalitätenkongress 1925 bis 1938: nationale Minderheiten zwischen Lobbyistentum und Grossmachtinteressen* (Herder-Institut 2000).

165 Congress of European Nationalities (ed), *Sitzungsbericht des Kongresses der Organisierten Nationalen Gruppen in den Staaten Europas. Genf, 25–27 August 1926* (Braumüller 1926) 159.

13

Non-Territorial National Autonomy in Interwar European Minority Protection and Its Habsburg Legacies

Börries Kuzmany[*]

What is the relationship between ethnic diversity and sovereign territoriality? Central Europe was a bustling laboratory for this question both before and after the dissolution of the Habsburg Empire. The notion of minority rights overseen by an international organization like the League of Nations was one of the most striking innovations of the interwar international order. From the perspective of Central European activists, scholars, and politicians, however, this system emerged as just one possible response to an older problem concerning the form of rights and jurisdiction best suited to a region in which different ethnicities, languages, and religions were densely intermingled. In fact, various thinkers had developed a number of bold proposals that sought to redefine the relationship between rights and territory by forming national jurisdictions and communities on a corporate—and thus non-territorial—basis. This chapter traces the emergence of 'non-territorial autonomy', as this idea is referred to by scholars today, in the multinational Habsburg state and its translation into the area of interwar minority protection.

At the very heart of this idea was the aim of disentangling the state from the nation, thereby making non-territorial autonomy the exact opposite of what was considered the state of the art in 1918. Yet the true winner of the First World War was the idea of the nation state, which was realized even in those parts of Europe that had previously been ruled by the multinational Habsburg, Ottoman, and Romanov empires. New borders were demarcated according to historical, economic, and ethno-linguistic considerations. But the region's dense ethnic diversity meant that these new borders effectively simply created a set of smaller multinational states. According to their own legal definition, they were all nation states, however—even

* I would like to thank Marina Germane, Emanuel Dalle Mulle, and Natasha Wheatley for their very helpful remarks and suggestions, and Timo Aava for his help with Estonian sources. The research for this contribution was supported by funding from the European Research Council (ERC) within the project 'Non-territorial Autonomy: History of a Travelling Idea', no. 758015.

Börries Kuzmany, *Non-Territorial National Autonomy in Interwar European Minority Protection and Its Habsburg Legacies*
In: *Remaking Central Europe*. Edited by: Peter Becker and Natasha Wheatley, Oxford University Press (2020). © the many contributors. DOI: 10.1093/oso/9780198854685.003.0014

if they housed a twin-headed state nation like the Czecho-Slovaks or were home to a trinity of nations like the Kingdom of Serbs, Croats, and Slovenes. Any citizens not belonging to the titular state nation had the status of minority—for better or worse. Whereas a national minority is basically a deviation from the ideal type of the nation state, multinational states formally do not perceive their multilingual populations as minorities but as nationalities constituent to the state itself.[1] In both cases, arrangements to deal with national diversity must be found—and it is possible for a nation state to treat its minorities more liberally than a multinational state treats its nationalities.

The Habsburg Monarchy in particular had struggled with this very issue since the revolution of 1848. As if in a political laboratory, political thinkers and policymakers discussed and negotiated different options to deal with the empire's linguistic diversity, its fuzzy national dividing lines, and various national movements. While the principal equality of all languages and nationalities was accepted in the wider framework of civil liberties, the question of how—or whether at all—to reorganize the empire on national grounds was fiercely discussed.[2] The Hungarian publicist and politician József Eötvös (1813–1871) elaborated on two options for national reorganization, but eventually dismissed both of them. The first one would have been to redraw the internal borders of the Habsburg Empire according to national criteria and thereby grant national self-rule to the provinces thus defined; this has been labelled the 'territorial principle'. Eötvös's second option was to transfer cultural self-rule to national collectives that would be constituted by all members of a given national group—which meant organizing political community according to individuals' national belonging and was therefore labelled the 'personal principle' of national autonomy.[3]

[1] Ignaz Seipel, *Die geistigen Grundlagen der Minderheitenfrage. Vortrag gehalten im Minderheiteninstitute der Wiener Universität am 14. Jänner 1925* (Franz Deuticke 1925) 3. On the intricacies of the emergence of the term 'national minority' itself, cf. Anna Adorjáni and László Bence Bari, 'National Minority: The Emergence of the Concept in the Habsburg and International Legal Thought' (2019) 16/1 Acta Universitatis Sapientiae, European and Regional Studies.

[2] The Kremsier/Kroměříž draft constitution negotiated during the summer of 1848 stipulated the equality of all Austrian nationalities, and Emperor Francis Joseph proclaimed the same in the address during his ascendency to the throne on 2 December 1848. On the importance and acceptance of the principle of equality of all Habsburg nationalities, cf. Stourzh's seminal monograph: Gerald Stourzh, *Die Gleichberechtigung der Nationalitäten in der Verfassung und Verwaltung Österreichs 1848–1918* (Verlag der Österreichischen Akademie der Wissenschaften 1985).

[3] Joseph von Eötvös, *Über die Gleichberechtigung der Nationalitäten in Österreich* (C.A. Hartleben's Verlag 1850) 83–85, 90–92. A huge number of other contemporaries wrote about the Habsburg Empire's nationalities problems and suggested solutions as well. Following is a very small selection: Franz Palacký, 'Über Zentralisation und nationale Gleichberechtigung in Österreich' (23 December 1849) Národní Noviny; Adolph Fischhof, *Oesterreich und die Bürgschaften seines Bestands* (Wallichauffer´sche Buchhandlung 1869); Ludwig Gumplowicz, *Das Recht der Nationalitäten und Sprachen in Österreich-Ungarn* (Wagner 1879); Karl Hugelmann, *Das Recht der Nationalitäten in Österreich und das Staatsgrundgesetz über die allgemeinen Rechte der Staatsbürger. Zwei Vorträge, gehalten in der juristischen Gesellschaft zu Wien am 25. November und 16. Dezember 1879* (Styria 1880); Aurel Popovici, *Die Vereinigten Staaten von Groß-Österreich. Politische Studien zur Lösung der nationalen Fragen und staatrechtlichen Krisen in Österreich-Ungarn* (B. Elischer Nachfolger 1906);

In this chapter, I will explore the Habsburg legacy of non-territorial autonomy based on the personal principle in four steps. To begin with, I will sketch the practical and theoretical approaches to the concept as they developed in Habsburg Austria during the last fifty years of its existence, that is, the implementations of non-territorial arrangements in several provinces that arose from pragmatic and administrative considerations as well as the theoretical notions elaborated mainly by Austro-Marxist thinkers. The second section of this chapter scrutinizes the first steps of non-territorial autonomy into the sphere of international minority protection. In the wider setting of the Paris Peace Conference, different protagonists promoted or rejected this form of collective rights. In the third section, I will investigate how intensively the non-territorial autonomy ideas that had developed in imperial Austria were received and adapted in Central and Eastern Europe before and after the Russian Revolutions of 1917. The next section contains an analysis of how transnational minority activists—who were well-acquainted with the idea's Austrian roots—approached non-territorial autonomy as a solution to Europe's minority issues, not least because they were unsatisfied with the minority protection system established by the League of Nations. The two final sections of this chapter highlight the role of the continent's eastern parts within the post-war international order, portraying them as actors and contributors to the field of national diversity management and not as mere objects of considerations. The aim is not to suggest that these Central and Eastern European approaches were better or worse, but simply to include them in the greater picture.

I. Two Approaches to Non-Territorial Autonomy in Habsburg Austria

There are several ways to begin this story, but I would like to start with Rudolf Laun (1882–1975), a Prague-born legal scholar of international and civil law who had closely followed the nationalities question in Habsburg Austria during the last two decades before the war. In mid-January 1918, he wired his rather critical remarks on President Wilson's Fourteen Points to The Hague, where the *Central Organization for a Durable Peace* had asked him to assess Wilson's declaration. With reference to the tenth point concerning the autonomous development of the peoples of Austria-Hungary, Laun stated:

Edmund Bernatzik, *Über nationale Matriken. Inaugurationsrede gehalten von Edmund Bernatzik* (Manz 1910); Rudolf von Herrnritt, 'Die Ausgestaltung des österreichischen Nationalitätenrechtes durch den Ausgleich in Mähren und der Bukowina' (1914) 5&6 Österreichische Zeitschrift für öffentliches Recht; 'Die Stellung der Kronländer im Gefüge der österreichischen Verfassung. Eine Rundfrage' (1916) Special issue Österreichische Zeitschrift für öffentliches Recht.

> If Wilson wishes to afford the peoples of Austria-Hungary the opportunity for autonomous development, he is misinformed. He does not know, for example, of the Moravian and the so-called Budweis [Budějovice] Compromise, free and autonomous agreements between the equal Czech and German nation.[4]

What was Laun referring to in his statement? The Moravian Compromise was the first (in 1905), and the compromise in the Bohemian city of Budějovice/Budweis the last (1914), in a series of new provincial or municipal constitutions that aimed to realize national autonomy based on non-territorial arrangements; the other such agreements were concluded for Bukovina (1910), Bosnia-Herzegovina (1910), and Galicia (1914). All five cases were driven by two conditions: the need for a fairer political representation of each nationality, and the wish for a certain degree of national self-rule. They were basically negotiated by the conflict parties in the provinces themselves, yet Vienna invariably served as an importunate mediator. The results of the individual negotiations varied markedly given the different national settings, power relations, and general developments over time. Laun may have chosen these examples not only out of local patriotism for his native Bohemian lands, but supposedly also because the Moravia and Budějovice cases demonstrated the development the basic idea had seen within a decade.[5]

In the 1900 census, more than 70 per cent of Moravia's population had declared Czech to be their language of daily use, whereas only 28 per cent stated German. Yet due to the province's class system of franchise, people identifying as Germans had dominated the provincial diet, the executive authority, and the administration since the return to constitutionalism in the 1860s. By the turn of the century, however, the Czech bourgeoisie had grown and would have eventually reversed power relations. Under these circumstances, a national compromise became possible, and the results of the negotiations stipulated national quotas in the provincial diet and administration via non-territorial arrangements.[6]

[4] Austrian State's Archives/Haus-, Hof- und Staatarchiv (furthermore ÖStA/HHStA), Min. d. A., 25/23, 'Rudolph Laun writing to the ministry of foreign affairs, 13 January 1918, draft of a reply telegram, Jong Beekdonk, Bern, Bernerhof. The letter was published as a facsimile in Egmont Zechlin, 'Die „Zentralorganisation für einen dauernden Frieden" und die Mittelmächte. Ein Beitrag zur politischen Tätigkeit Rudolf Launs im Ersten Weltkrieg' in Forschungsstelle für Völkerrecht und ausländisches öffentliches Recht der Universität Hamburg (ed), *Festschrift für Rudolf Laun zu seinem achtzigsten Geburtstag* (Vandenhoeck & Ruprecht 1962) 448, 514.

[5] For a synopsis of these compromises, cf. Börries Kuzmany, Habsburg Austria: Experiments in Non-territorial Autonomy (2016) 15/1 Ethnopolitics.

[6] The most comprehensive study of the Moravian Compromise is still Horst Glassl, *Der Mährische Ausgleich* (Veröffentlichung des Sudetendeutschen Archivs 1, Fides 1967). The University of Brno organized a bilingual conference on the occasion of the centenary of the Moravian Compromise, cf. Lukás Fasora, Jiří Hanuš, and Jiří Malíř (eds), *Moravské vyrovnání z roku 1905 / Der Mährische Ausgleich von 1905* (Matice moravská 2006). The best delineation of the compromise in English is the as yet unpublished article by Jeremy King, cf. Jeremy King, 'Which Equality? Separate but Equal in Imperial Austria' (2010) Article Draft. Another English overview was published by Mills T. Kelly, 'Last Best Chance or Last Gasp? The Compromise of 1905 and Czech Politics in Moravia' (2003) 34 Austrian History Yearbook.

In order to avoid nationalist agitation during the election campaign, Moravia's politicians decided to reorganize the electorate not only according to five social classes—that is, the curiae of the big landowners, members of the chambers of commerce, urban taxpayers, rural taxpayers, and the common voters—but also according to national affiliation. Three of the five social curiae were thus divided into a Czech and a German section each. This meant that, even if they lived next to each other in the same village, a Czech voter from, for example, the curia of rural taxpayers (fourth curia) would only be allowed to vote for a Czech candidate in the Czech constituency, whereas his German neighbour could only choose among German nominees in the German electoral district of the fourth curia. For this purpose, the local authorities had to register every eligible voter in either the Czech or the German national register of the corresponding social curia. Given the situation in early twentieth-century Moravia, where many people did not identify along national but rather along social or confessional lines, the decision who should be registered in which national cadastre was often not as clear-cut as nationalists tried to assert.[7]

Yet every Moravian citizen except those belonging to the first curia, that is, the large estate owners, had to be registered, and there was a fixed number of delegates to be elected to the provincial parliament by each nationality: seventy-three Czechs, forty Germans, and thirty-eight major landowners. Once elected, each national parliamentary group could designate their envoys to each of the parliamentary committees and the provincial government. During the normal legislative process, they sat together, deciding jointly on political matters and—most importantly—agreeing on a budget. Autonomous agency existed primarily in the area of education, where the local, district, and provincial schoolboards were each divided into two separate bodies and the monolingual high schools were to be controlled by the respective co-national deputies of the provincial government.[8]

As indicated above, the landowner curia was not split into a German and a Czech section. This not only corresponded to the self-identification of these mostly high aristocrats but was also a political means of counterbalancing the nationalist interests with power loyal to the empire: with thirty-eight seats in the provincial

[7] Over the last fifteen years, a very rich research literature showing the ambiguity and fluidity of national identifications in the Habsburg Empire has developed. In her influential article, Tara Zahra coined this phenomenon as 'national indifference', cf. Tara Zahra, 'Imagined Noncommunities: National Indifference as a Category of Analysis' (2010) 69/1 Slavic Review. Yet the doyen of Habsburg nationalities policies, Gerald Stourzh, has remarked that this terminology is blurred in itself and might not be suitable as an analytical category, cf. Gerald Stourzh, 'The Ethnicizing of Politics and "National Indifference" in Late Imperial Austria' in Gerald Stourzh (ed), *Der Umfang der österreichischen Geschichte. Ausgewählte Studien 1990–2010* (Studien zu Politik und Verwaltung 99, Böhlau 2011).

[8] Glassl, *Der Mährische Ausgleich* (n 6) 197–198, 212, 214–216. The referenced legal text is: *Landesgesetz- und Verordnungsblatt für die Markgrafschaft Mähren 1906. I. Stück. Nr. 1–4. Gesetze vom 27. November 1905*. The German version of the provincial law gazette is available at the ALEX online law collection of the Austrian National Library <http://alex.onb.ac.at/cgi-content/alex?apm=0&aid=lma&datum=1906>.

diet, the noble landlords could always tip the scales.[9] Hence while the Moravian Compromise was—symbolically speaking—a first step towards non-territorially organized national autonomy, it was more of a consociational system in its real-life implementation.

The other case referred to by Rudolf Laun in his evaluation of Wilson's declaration was the national compromise concluded in the Bohemian city of Budějovice in February 1914. Owing to the outbreak of the First World War, this compromise was never legally enacted, however. While the basic elements of the Moravian Compromise were to be found in the Budějovice case as well, the latter agreement went much further. In contrast to the year 1905, there were no longer any nationally unaligned curiae, and every voter was registered according to nationality. In addition, the compromise was the first to provide financial autonomy to the two national groups within the municipal government.[10]

The years 1913 and 1914 were actually a very busy period in terms of negotiations for national self-rule based on non-territorial arrangements. The very same question of financial autonomy as in Budějovice was also one of the topics during the renegotiations to further develop the Moravian Compromise taking place in Brno/Brünn in February 1914.[11] The Galician Compromise, which became law less than three weeks before the beginning of the First World War, also stipulated non-territorial elements for the provincial electoral system. There was almost no autonomous agency for the national curiae within the provincial diet, however—only a blocking minority for the smaller national group, the Ruthenians.[12]

In this respect, the Budějovice Compromise came closer to the theoretical considerations of the Austro-Marxist thinkers Etbin Kristan, Karl Renner, and Otto Bauer, who had developed a model of national autonomy that was person-based instead of territory-based—or to be more precise, they were a mixture of both approaches.[13] Arguing that confessional wars had ended in Europe only after state

[9] Robert Luft, 'Die Mittelpartei des Mährischen Großgrundbesitzes. Zur Problematik des Ausgleichs in Mähren und Böhmen' in Ferdinand Seibt (ed), *Die Chance der Verständigung. Absichten und Ansätze zu übernationaler Zusammenarbeit in den böhmischen Ländern 1848–1918* (Oldenbourg 1987) 187, 218–219.

[10] Emil Brix, Der Böhmische Ausgleich in Budweis (1982) 24/2 Österreichische Osthefte 225–248. Jeremy King, *Budweisers into Czechs and Germans. A Local History of Bohemian Politics. 1848–1948* (Princeton University Press 2002) 137–147.

[11] Jiří Malíř, "Druhé' moravské vyrovnání z roku 1914' in Fasora, Hanuš and Malíř, *Moravské vyrovnání* (n 6) 87–102.

[12] I prefer the ethnonym 'Ruthenian' over the later 'Ukrainian' because it was used until the early twentieth century both in Austrian official terminology and by the people themselves. On the Galician Compromise cf. Börries Kuzmany, 'Der Galizische Ausgleich als Beispiel moderner Nationalitätenpolitik?' in Elisabeth Haid, Stephanie Weismann, and Burkhard Wöller (eds) *Galizien. Peripherie der Moderne—Moderne der Peripherie?* (Tagungen zur Ostmitteleuropaforschung 31, Herder-Institut 2013).

[13] Only two of the relevant Austro-Marxist's texts were translated into English: Karl Renner, 'State and Nation' in Ephraim Nimni (ed), *National-Cultural Autonomy and its Contemporary Critics* (New York 2005 [1899]); and Otto Bauer and Ephraim Nimni, *The Question of Nationalities and Social Democracy* (University of Minnesota Press 2000 [1907]). Neither Kristan's Slovenian nor German text,

and religion became disassociated, they claimed that national conflicts would come to an end only once the state separated from the nation. Their suggestion was thus the exact opposite of the idea of the nation state, yet in accordance with the idea of national self-determination. Both Austrian social democrats proposed a double structure for the entire monarchy: the first pillar would be organized around a central parliament elected by all citizens of the empire and responsible for general state affairs like infrastructure, foreign relations, police, military etc., while the second pillar would be formed by several national councils (German, Czech, Polish, etc.) responsible mainly for matters of culture and education. Via these national councils and their executive organs, all national groups would constitute themselves as legal entities with autonomous rights and duties.

For the second, the national pillar of state organization, Karl Renner suggested a bottom-up approach with autonomous administrative districts at its heart. Returning to a decades old idea, Renner suggested to dissolve the historical provinces and to split up Imperial Austria into monolingual districts as much as possible and give full political autonomy to these districts. According to Renner around 90 per cent of the population would end up in such nationally homogeneous districts, where national and political self-rule would coincide. The nation would thus become part of the state administration and thereby more democratic and more powerful.

Only the remaining 10 per cent of the Austrian districts would be constituted as bi- or mulit-lingual. Here, all inhabitants of the district would have to enrol in national registers. For general political matters all district inhabitants would elect a joint district council. In addition to this political district council, each national group would elect its separate national district diets responsible for all cultural matters. These national district diets would later delegate representatives to the above-mentioned overarching national councils.[14]

While Renner and Bauer were never able to convince their own Austrian Social Democratic Workers' Party of their concept, many other political activists read their writings attentively. Most important were the reception and adaptations by Jewish socialists, who popularized the Austro-Marxist non-territorial autonomy model in the leftist political camp of Central and Eastern Europe before the First

in which he argued for a radical non-territorial autonomy approach, was translated into English: Etbin Kristan [Anonymus], 'Avtonomija', 1 January 1898, Delavec. Etbin Kristan, 'Nationalismus und Sozialismus in Oesterreich' (1898) 2/2 Akademie. Organ der socialistischen Jugend. Renner's most important book and its second and revised edition are also not available in English: Karl Renner [Pseud. Rudolf Springer], *Der Kampf der österreichischen Nationen um den Staat. Das nationale Problem als Verfassungs- und Verwaltungsfrage* (Deuticke 1902); Karl Renner, *Das Selbstbestimmungsrecht der Nationen. In besonderer Anwendung auf Oesterreich. Zugleich zweite, vollständig umgearbeitete Auflage von des Verfassers Buch 'Der Kampf der österreichischen Nation um den Staat'* (Deuticke 1918).

[14] This is the basic model as it was designed in Renner's 1902 book, cf. Renner [Springer], *Der Kampf der österreichischen Nationen um den Staat* (n 13).

World War.[15] At the end of the war, non-territorial autonomy was demanded, discussed and partly implemented in many of the newly created nation states. One crucial change had occurred with reference to the Austrian experiences; however, non-territorial autonomy was no longer intended to organize national diversity within a given state in its entirety but was now proposed as a tool for the protection of minorities. In this regard, returning to the activity of Rudolf Laun within the Central Organization for a Durable Peace seems sensible.

II. Non-Territorial Autonomy's First Steps in the Arena of International Minority Protection

The Central Organization for a Durable Peace, established in the Netherlands, was an initiative of intellectuals from neutral states who were attempting to design a just political order that would prevent future wars. In its 1915 minimum programme, the members agreed on nine points including the principle of non-annexation of territories against the will of the local population as well as the protection of national, religious, and linguistic minorities.[16] During the following year, important legal scholars from different parts of Europe discussed this programme in written statements.[17] Rudolf Laun actively participated in the Central Organization's written debates and meetings. Despite some serious criticism,[18] he considered the overall treatment of national groups in Austria to be far better than in any other state, and he encouraged Austria to openly present its nationalities legislation as a strength and not as a deficit in the international public arena. The German sociologist Franz Oppenheimer likewise painted a rather positive picture of the Habsburg Austrian experiences in his statement, referring in particular to the model of (non-territorial) national autonomy as conceived in the writings of Karl Renner and embodied in the Moravian and Bukovinian Compromises.[19] Digesting the various statements, Norwegian historian and later politician Halvda Koht, the leader of the Central Organization's internal expert commission, lauded the Habsburg Empire's achievements in the handling of national diversity and its early approaches to national autonomy.[20]

[15] Cf. e.g. Roni Gechtman, 'Conceptualizing National-Cultural Autonomy: From the Austro-Marxists to the Jewish Labor Bund' in Dan Diner (ed), *Simon Dubnow Jahrbuch, vol. 4* (Vandenhoeck & Ruprecht 2005) 17.

[16] Organisation pour une paix durable (ed), *Une paix durable. Commentaire officiel pour un programme minimum* (The Hague 1915) 7–8.

[17] They were published in four volumes: Organisation centrale pour un paix durable (ed), *Recueil des Rapports sur les différents points du Programme Minimum* (The Hague 1916–1918).

[18] Rudolf Laun, 'Das Nationalitätenrecht als internationales Problem' (1917) 4 & 5 Österreichische Zeitschrift für öffentliches Recht 397.

[19] Franz Oppenheimer, 'Nationale Autonomie' in Organisation centrale pour un paix durable (ed), *Recueil des Rapports sur les différents points du Programme Minimum, 4 vols.* (The Hague 1918) 74.

[20] Halvdan Koht (ed), *Avant-Projet d'un Traité général relatif aux Droits des Minorités nationales. Rapport présenté par H. Koht* (The Hague 1917).

After several meetings during the war, the Central Organization arranged the so-called Bern meeting of the 'League of Nations' in March 1919—an association not to be confused with the 'real' League of Nations that would come into being a year later. The participants in this summit unanimously agreed on a draft of an International Treaty on the Protection of National Minorities and forwarded it to the Paris Peace Conference. The author of this treaty was Rudolf Laun, and its text was based on his knowledge of the Habsburg experiences. Most notably, Laun suggested in Articles 16 and 17 that the collective of persons registered of their own accord in a single national cadastre should constitute a legal entity with autonomous agency in cultural affairs, including the right to levy taxes on its members:[21]

> § 16. If there exists in a municipality [...] a national minority that is manifestly recorded in a national cadastre, then all people registered in the national cadastre form a public corporate body.
>
> § 17. This corporate body is entitled [...] to regulate the following affairs by means of self-elected organs:
>
> 2. create schools and educational facilities in which instruction occurs in the language of the national minority;
>
> 3. form national confessional organisations [...];
>
> 6. collect national contributions in the sense of direct taxes for the abovementioned affairs from those persons who, according to the cadastre, belong to the national minority.

The Paris Peace Conference entirely ignored this proposal, and the eventually established League of Nations also rejected the idea of non-territorial autonomy since Europe's new political order was built around the nation state and strongly disapproved of any ethno-national group rights.[22] Even though individuals and organizations had the right to inform the League Council about violations of the rights stipulated in the minority treaties, members of the Council could only become active in cases where the national rights of individuals were at stake.[23]

[21] Rudolf Laun, *Entwurf eines internationalen Vertrages über den Schutz nationaler Minderheiten. Vorgelegt der Berner Völkerbundkonferenz, März 1919* (Haymann 1920).

[22] David James Smith and John Hiden, *Ethnic Diversity and the Nation State: National Cultural Autonomy Revisited* (Routledge 2012) 22.

[23] There is a plethora of secondary literature on the minority protection system of the League of Nations. One of the earliest concise descriptions is Julius Stone, *International Guarantees of Minority Rights: Procedure of the Council of the League of Nations in Theory and Practice* (Oxford University Press 1932). For other comprehensive descriptions, cf. Christoph Gütermann, *Das Minderheitenschutzverfahren des Völkerbundes* (Schriften zum Völkerrecht 63, Duncker & Humblot 1979); Martin Scheuermann, *Minderheitenschutz contra Konfliktverhütung? Die Minderheitenpolitik des Völkerbundes in den zwanziger Jahren* (Materialien und Studien zur Ostmitteleuropa-Forschung 6, Herder-Institut 2000) 26–29. For more specific information on strategies of minority groups petitioning with the League of Nations, cf. Stefan Dyroff, 'Der Platz der Völkerbundbeschwerde in den politischen Strategien nationaler Minderheiten. Positionen aus dem Kreis des 'Europäischen

This is not the full story, however. Forms of corporative rights were at least discussed in Paris when it came to Jewish issues. Even though Jews certainly did not sit at the table of the victorious powers, Jewish organizations were able to exercise a certain influence.[24] This was possible firstly because they were not among the vanquished, and secondly because US president Woodrow Wilson considered Jews to be the paradigmatic minority population whose rights the new international order would have to safeguard.[25] But there were two competing Jewish claims: the first formed around the French-dominated Alliance Israélite Universelle and the British Joint Foreign Committee, which actively lobbied for an international guarantee of Jewish civil and confessional rights. On the other side were the Zionists, who had gathered in Copenhagen in October 1918 to vote on a manifesto including three basic demands: a Jewish homeland in Palestine, national autonomy for Eastern European Jews, and a Jewish representation in a future League of Nations.[26]

Zionist groups from Eastern Europe gathered again in London in February 1919 to coordinate their demand for recognition as a national group with the right to national autonomy before the peace talks in Paris began. Their most important ally became the American Jewish Congress, which by the end of 1918 had found a compromise among its members to seek equality for Jews throughout the world in either an individual rights approach or a collective one; the corresponding declaration is often referred to as the Jewish Bill of Rights.[27] In mid-March 1919, the American Jewish Congress and Zionist activists established the Committee of Jewish Delegations,[28] which was represented at the peace conference by the Americans Julien W. Mack and Louis Marshall. Mack and Marshall actively lobbied with David Hunter Miller, an American diplomat and confidant on minority issues of Edward M. House, who in turn was one of Wilson's closest advisors.[29]

Central and Eastern Europeans, however, led the Committee's programmatic commission—first and foremost in the shape of its secretary general Leo Motzkin, a long-term Zionist activist and ardent promoter of the colonization of Palestine

Nationalitätenkongresses" in Mathias Beer and Stefan Dyroff (eds), *Politische Strategien nationaler Minderheiten in der Zwischenkriegszeit* (De Gruyter 2014) 27–56.

[24] This influence has been discussed (and exaggerated) very frequently. For an early and still valuable assessment, cf. Oscar I. Janowsky, *The Jews and Minority Rights* (Columbia University Press 1933).

[25] Erwin Viefhaus, *Die Minderheitenfrage und die Entstehung der Minderheitenschutzverträge auf der Pariser Friedenskonferenz 1919. Eine Studie zur Geschichte des Nationalitätenproblems im 19. und 20. Jahrhundert* (Marburger Ostforschungen 11, Holzner 1960) 112.

[26] Simon Rabinovitch, *Jewish Rights, National Rites: Nationalism and Autonomy in Late Imperial and Revolutionary Russia* (Stanford Studies in Jewish History and Culture, Stanford University Press 2014) 257–263.

[27] Julian W. Mack, 'Le congrès juif américain' in Comité des Délégations Juives auprès de la Conference de la Paix (ed), *Les droits nationaux des Juifs en Europe Orientale. Recueil d'etudes* (Beresniak & Fils 1919) 28–30.

[28] In 1936, the Committee became the World Jewish Congress.

[29] Viefhaus, *Minderheitenfrage* (n 25) 78–92. Carole Fink, *Defending the Rights of Others: The Great Powers, the Jews, and International Minority Protection, 1878–1939* (Cambridge University Press 2004) 126–205.

as well as the fostering of a Jewish national sentiment in Europe. Already a decade earlier, Motzkin had suggested some form of collective cultural autonomy for the Arab population in a future Jewish province under Ottoman and European protection, and he also seems to have been aware of the Austro-Marxist writings of the first decade of the twentieth century.[30] Although Zionists in Central and Eastern Europe were in strict opposition to the Yiddishist and atheist agenda of Jewish leftist parties, they agreed with them on the need for collective rights and national autonomy for Jews in the diaspora, at least after the 1906 conventions of Russian Zionist organizations—and they equally acknowledged borrowings from Renner and Bauer.[31] Socialist parties like the Jewish Labour Bund had previously already adopted programmes that represented adapted versions of the Austro-Marxist non-territorial autonomy.[32] What was more, the liberal Folkist Party of Jewish historian and thinker Simon Dubnov had customized the traditional Jewish community autonomy patterns to the needs of a modern Jewish nation. The model of Jewish autonomy existing in the early modern Polish-Lithuanian Commonwealth had been based on the Jewish community, the *kehillah*, along with a non-territorial assembly uniting representatives from all parts of the country, the *Vaad arba aratsot* or Council of Four Lands.[33]

Leo Motzkin's right hand and the actual editor of the Committee's guideline of arguments for the peace conference was Leon Reich, one of the five vice-presidents of the Committee and the man responsible for propagandizing its positions.[34] Reich was an early Zionist activist in Austrian Galicia, and the idea of corporative Jewish national self-rule must have come to him quite naturally. A mere five years earlier, Polish and Ukrainian politicians in Galicia had negotiated a national compromise that built on the experiences made with the Moravian Compromise.

[30] Frank Nesemann, 'Minderheitendiplomatie—Leo Motzkin zwischen Imperien und Nationen' in Dan Diner (ed), *Synchrone Welten: Zeitenräume jüdischer Geschichte* (Vandenhoek & Ruprecht 2005) 147, 154–157.

[31] Jolanta Żyndul, *Panstwo w Panstwie? Autonomia narodowo-kulturalna w Europie Srodkowo-wschodnej w XX wieku* (Wydawnictwo DiG 2000) 18–32.

[32] Cf. Gechtman 'Conceptualizing' (n 15); and Roni Gechtman, 'National-Cultural Autonomy and 'Neutralism': Vladimir Medem's Marxist Analysis of the National Question, 1903–1920' (2007) 3/1 Socialist Studies / Études socialistes 69.

[33] Recent studies have elaborated Simon Dubnov's ideas in general, cf. Rabinovitch, *Jewish Rights* (n 26); Anke Hilbrenner, *Diaspora-Nationalismus. Zur Geschichtskonstruktion Simon Dubnows* (Schriften des Simon-Dubnow-Institutes 7, Vandenhoeck & Ruprecht 2007); and Grit Jilek, *Nation ohne Territorium. Über die Organisierung der jüdischen Diaspora bei Simon Dubnow* (Schriftenreihe der Sektion Politische Theorien und Ideengeschichte in der Deutschen Vereinigung für Politische Wissenschaft 24, Nomos 2013).

[34] On Reich in general, cf. ÖBL, <http://www.biographien.ac.at/oebl/oebl_R/Reich_Leon_1879_1929.xml>>. The guideline was published in French: Comité des Délégations Juives auprès de la Conference de la Paix (ed), *Les droits nationaux des Juifs en Europe Orientale. Recueil d'etudes* (Beresniak & Fils 1919). Leon Reich, 'Das Komitee der jüdischen Delegationen in Paris' (1920/1921) 5/8–9 Der Jude. Eine Monatsschrift 439, 441.

Much to the discontent of Jewish nationalists, however, the Galician Compromise of 1914 had not recognized Jews as one of the registered nations.[35]

Leon Reich was given the opportunity to speak before the peace conference's influential Subcommittee for Polish Affairs as a representative of East Galician Jewry, and he elaborated on the importance of Jewish national autonomy for the region.[36] His contribution to the Committee of Jewish Delegations' argumentative guidelines is perhaps the most revealing example of how the Jewish delegation used former Austrian non-territorial autonomy approaches in Paris. Reich openly referred to Karl Renner, honouring his inventive propositions to remodel the Habsburg Empire into a federation of corporative nationalities and attempting to portray these ideas as the analogous predecessors of Wilson's principles:

> In the old Austrian Empire, Karl Renner preached in numerous academic books and newspaper articles the importance of transforming the unitary state with its central power into a federal state based on the autonomy of its diverse nations. And since the borders of each country in no way correspond to the territories inhabited by the members of each nation, who are distributed unevenly across all of the territories, it is impossible to conceive of national autonomy as territorial autonomy, only as national-personal [autonomy] by giving each inhabitant the possibility to declare to which nation he desires to belong and to opt equally for the dominance of his choice.
>
> This very precisely developed theory is in its consequences nothing else than Wilson's principle, which is accepted by all victorious and defeated powers and embodies the protection of ethnic minorities.[37]

In the same guideline document, Leo Motzkin formulated the demands of the Committee of Jewish Delegations, which were likewise focused on non-territorial autonomy. Among other measures, he called for the following in the second set of demands: II.a, the recognition of Jews as an ethnic community; II.c, proportional representation in all legal organs via national curiae; II.f, obligatory membership of all Jews in the Jewish community and the right of the latter to impose taxes on its members; and II.g, the establishment of a Jewish body exercising authority across the entire country.[38]

[35] Börries Kuzmany, 'The Rise and Limits of Participation: The Political Representation of Galicia's Urban Jewry from the Josephine Era to the 1914 Electoral Reform' (2015) 42/2–3 East Central Europe 216, 230–240.

[36] Reich, 'Komitee' (n 34) 445.

[37] Léon Reich, 'La situation des Juifs en Pologne et leurs revendications' in Comité des Délégations Juives auprès de la Conference de la Paix (ed), *Les droits nationaux des Juifs en Europe Orientale. Recueil d'etudes* (Beresniak & Fils 1919) 36, 38–39.

[38] Leo Motzkin, 'Les revendications nationales des Juifs' in Comité des Délégations Juives auprès de la Conference de la Paix (ed), *Les droits nationaux des Juifs en Europe Orientale. Recueil d'etudes* (Beresniak & Fils 1919) 7, 22–23.

By April 1919, it was clear that any plans to incorporate minority protection directly in the statutes of the League of Nations had failed—but also that the League would sign separate bilateral minority treaties with Poland and other newly established or enlarged states in Central and Eastern Europe. Based on Motzkin's demands and Reich's elaborations, Louis Marshall and Julien Mack sketched a minority treaty that they intensely discussed with David Miller, the aforementioned American diplomat. They eventually convinced him of their vision that Eastern European Jewry needed national group rights, and together they elaborated a draft treaty suggesting the recognition of minorities as 'distinct public corporations' with the right to tax members and proportional representation based on electoral colleges, as well as the right of each individual to withdraw from the minority.[39]

Shortly after receiving the draft, President Wilson read Miller's suggestion in the Council of Four meeting on 1 May 1919. Wilson and Lloyd George decidedly rejected any form of national autonomy. Miller therefore could not even proffer collective corporative rights within the peace conference's minority commission meetings a few days later, and separate electoral colleges were repudiated *expressis verbis*.[40] Attempting to convince the minority commission, the Committee of Jewish Delegations submitted—once more in vain—a final draft treaty and a memorandum on 10 May. Therein it underlined the need to urge Poland to recognize 'the several national minorities in its populations as constituting distinct, autonomous organizations, and as such having equally the right to establish, manage, and control their schools and their religious, educational, charitable, and social institutions.'[41]

Eventually, the Polish Minority Treaty—which later became the prototype for similar treaties concluded with other Central and East European countries—stipulated no corporative rights for minorities. And where it did guarantee some sort of collective rights, it employed rather awkward vocabulary to circumscribe the subjects it referred to, avoiding the term 'national' minorities in particular. Instead, it spoke of 'Polish nationals who belong to racial, religious or linguistic minorities' or, in an even more complicated phrasing, of 'Polish nationals of other than Polish speech.' On the one hand, this can be interpreted as a tacit concession to Poland's general discontent at being forced to sign a minority treaty at all.[42] But on the other hand, it also reflected the unwillingness to introduce into international law other subjects than states and their respective citizens. The treaties thus targeted national groups as subjects while simultaneously concealing them—an

[39] David H. Miller, *My Diary: At the Conference of Paris. With Documents* (vol. IX, New York 1924) 194, cited in Viefhaus, *Minderheitenfrage* (n 25) 151.
[40] Viefhaus, *Minderheitenfrage* (n 25) 151–165.
[41] This document is cited in full in the annex to Viefhaus, *Minderheitenfrage* (n 25) 228, 229.
[42] Fink, *Defending the Rights of Others* (n 29) 258–259.

approach heavily criticized by a legal scholar with acknowledged expertise in national group rights: Rudolf Laun.[43]

How come, then, that so many scholars and policy-makers claim to this day that the minority treaties were an example of collective rights that was replaced by a focus on individual human rights because the League of Nations' minority policy was ultimately a failure?[44] The reason may lie in the impreciseness of the term 'collective rights', which can be interpreted in a very broad and controversial sense,[45] and a purported dichotomy between individual and group rights.[46] Indeed, those who argue that the League of Nations had installed a collective rights system seem to interpret minority rights themselves as collective rights, since a national minority is constituted by definition by a group of people numerically inferior to the majority population. Yet it would be simplistic to term all rights designed for members of specific groups 'collective rights'. Rather, I suggest applying the differentiation developed by legal scholar Yvonne Donders to the minority treaties. Donders distinguishes between 1) community or group rights, where the holder of the rights is a collective entity as such; 2) communal rights, where the holder is an individual recognized as a member of a collective entity; and 3) individual rights with a collective dimension.[47]

Transferring these considerations to the minority treaties,[48] we might say that they were largely spelled out in the spirit of individual rights with a collective dimension, thus placing them in Donders' third category. Yet some provisions can be understood as falling into to the second category, that is, communal rights: among other civil liberties, Article 7 guaranteed the use of a person's mother tongue before the courts; Article 8 gave all members of a racial, religious, or linguistic minority

[43] Natasha Wheatley, 'Spectral Legal Personality in Interwar International Law: On New Ways of Not Being a State' (2017) 35/3 Law and History Review 753, 776–777. Wheatly also points to another contemporary scholar, Alfred Verdross, who lamented the absence of a legal definition of 'minority' as a collective bearer of rights, cf. Alfred Verdross, *Völkerrecht* (Springer 1937).

[44] This direct causation is not entirely obvious. Mark Mazower critically evaluates the moralistic overtone that accompanied the post-Second World War II human rights narrative, yet he also wrongly refers to the minority treaties as collective rights. Cf. Mark Mazower, 'The Strange Triumph of Human Rights' (2004) 47/2 The Historical Journal 379.

[45] Philip V. Ramaga, 'The Group Concept in Minority Protection' (1993) 15/3 Human Rights Quarterly 575, 582–584.

[46] Joseph Marko, *Autonomie und Integration. Rechtsinstitute des Nationalitätenrechts im funktionalen Vergleich* (Studien zu Politik und Verwaltung 51, Böhlau 1995) 199.

[47] Yvonne Donders, 'Foundations of Collective Cultural Rights in International Human Rights Law' in Andrzej Jakubowski (ed), *Cultural Rights as Collective Rights: An International Law Perspective* (Leiden 2016) 87, 89–90. I would like to thank Marina Germane for making me aware of this article and discussing its applicability to the minority treaties. Before Donders other scholars also pleaded for a more nuanced application of the term collective rights, e.g. Peter Jones, 'Human Rights, Group Rights, and Peoples' Rights' (1990) 21/1 Human Rights Quarterly 80. Marko, ibid, 195–427 distinguishes between cases where legal norms stipulate 1) minority peoples are legal personalities, 2) the protection of the very existence of groups, 3) the de facto existence of groups in order to ensure individual human rights.

[48] For the text of the Polish Minority Treaty, cf. Clive Perry (ed), *The Consolidated Treaty Series* (Vol. 225, Oceana Publications 1919) 412–424.

the right to manage and control private social and educational establishments; Article 9 recognized the rights of members of minorities to an equitable share of public funds for their educational, religious, or charitable institutions; Article 12 stipulated that the victorious powers were to guarantee these provisions for minority members. From my point of view, Article 11, which prohibits forcing Jews to violate their Sabbath rules, is somewhere between Donders' second and third category. The fact that the subject of the provision are Jews and thus members of a collective entity points to the second type. However, the phrasing of the article as well as the fact that the protection of the Sabbath was a long-standing determination to guarantee religious freedom, which is clearly an individual right with a collective dimension, rather supports a reading in the sense of Donders' third type of collective rights.

In no article, however, was the minority itself as a corporate group the holder of autonomous rights as suggested in Donders' first type of collective rights—the form of arrangement that would come closest to the idea of non-territorial autonomy. Only Article 10 regulating Jewish education could potentially also be interpreted on a corporate rights basis, as it mentioned 'educational committees' to be appointed by the 'Jewish communities of Poland'. Whether these communities were to be the traditional religious community bodies or some other national corporative bodies yet to be established was not specified.[49]

Non-territorial autonomy and Habsburg experiences also came to the fore in two other cases at the Paris Peace Conference. The first was the memorandum on the March 1919 mission of the American referee on Czechoslovakia, Archibald Coolidge, which included two contradictory reports: the paper drafted by Coolidge himself argued that Czechoslovakia's future borders should follow the national principle as closely as possible. At the same time, it criticized another report written by Robert Kerner that strongly supported the historical, economic, and military arguments of the Czechoslovak government but suggested a decentralized nation state 'giving full protection to German minorities on some such basis as the Moravian nation-Register system'.[50] This reference to the 1905 Moravian Compromise obviously represented Kerner's personal opinion, since the Czechoslovak delegation had never referred to earlier Austrian experiences. The latter was quite understandable, as Czechoslovakia was trying to position itself as the national and thus democratic counter-thesis to the Habsburg Empire. Yet in his influential 1918 book *The New Europe: The Slav Standpoint*, Tomáš G. Masaryk briefly referenced Renner's and Bauer's non-territorial autonomy model explicitly—only to largely dismiss it. He stated that every developed nation

[49] Reich, 'Komitee' (n 34) 443.

[50] 'Professor R. J. Kerner to Professor A. C. Coolidge' in United States Department of State (ed), *Papers Relating to Foreign Relations of the United States. The Paris Peace Conference, 1919* (US Government Printing Office 1947) 337, 340.

would sooner or later seek to found its own nation state and that even honestly implemented 'national autonomy'—applying the terminology used in the Habsburg Empire—would not be sufficient for this purpose; it could at most be applied to small and scattered minorities.[51]

Karl Renner was the leader of the Austrian delegation to the Paris Peace Conference, and Rudolf Laun was one of its counsellors. Yet their long-standing expertise and knowledge of Habsburg Austrian approaches to non-territorial autonomy seem not to have played any role in 1919, despite the fact that Renner had published a reworked version of his influential 1902 book outlining non-territorial autonomy as late as 1918. Only at one point in Austria's written reply to the treaty draft do we find a reference to it: the delegation suggested that, in the event that the German-speaking areas of Bohemia and Moravia should not become a part of Austria, Czechoslovakia should introduce a comprehensive territorial autonomy based on national cantons; only if such a cantonal system were likewise not applied should a 'national autonomy' be granted.[52]

The German government referred to cultural autonomy at least to some extent in its unavailing correspondence with the allied powers. The German international law specialist Theodor Niemeyer[53] had drafted a statute for a future League of Nations[54] in January 1919 that mentioned a national cadastre system for dispersed minority groups rather as an aside.[55] Yet the extensive but ultimately futile German response to the conditions of the allied powers in late May 1919 clearly demanded the protection of Germans outside Germany's future borders: 'It would be well if a still more completely cultural autonomy could be procured, on the basis of national land registers.'[56]

As it was, because the Paris Peace Conference considered the protection of Jews a matter that needed to be addressed, it conceded something akin to party status to Jewry—that is, Jewish delegates were at least heard. Indeed, representatives of the Committee of Jewish Delegations made serious efforts to table non-territorial autonomy with its corporate rights approach at the conference, in particular when it came to the drafting of the bilateral minority treaty prototype with Poland. They not only proved to be familiar with Habsburg experiences in their discussions with diplomats, but—as Jews were considered to have been 'on the good side of

[51] Tomáš G. Masaryk, *The New Europe: The Slav Standpoint* (Eyre & Spottiswoode 1918) 81–83.

[52] *Bericht über die Tätigkeit der deutschösterreichischen Friedensdelegation in St. Germain-en-Laye.* Vol 1 (Deutschösterreichische Staatsdruckerei 1919), Annex 47, Partie III, Section III, Annexe a, Régime cantonal dans l'État Tchéco-Slovaque, 338, 341.

[53] On Niemeyer, cf. Hans Wehberg, 'Theodor Niemeyer' (1939) 39/5–6 Die Friedens-Warte 238, 239.

[54] The American diplomat David H. Miller must have known about Niemeyer's draft; at least it can be found in his collection of documents. Cf. Miller, *My Diary* (n 39) Vol. IV, Doc. 248, Art. 33a, 294.

[55] 'Proposals of the German Government for the Establishment of a League of Nations' in United States Department of State (ed), *Papers Relating to Foreign Relations of the United States. The Paris Peace Conference, 1919* (Vol. VI, Washington 1946) 765, chapter VII, 772.

[56] 'Observations of the German Delegation on the Conditions of Peace' in United States Department of State, ibid, 800, 823.

the war'—the members of the Committee of Jewish Delegations did not have to fear that their outspoken and favourable references to Austro-Marxist conceptions would detract from their goals.

III. Developments in Interwar Nation States

Another careful reader of Rudolf Laun's draft treaty on national minorities was the Baltic German activist Werner Hasselblatt. In a much later Festschrift in Laun's honour, he admitted how influential Laun's writings had been for the drafting of Estonia's and Latvia's non-territorial minority protection regulations. Hasselblatt also mentioned Renner's general ideas but conceded that he had been only vaguely familiar with them in the early 1920s, whereas Laun's draft had been directly accessible to him.[57]

While this may be true for Hasselblatt individually, non-territorial autonomy was in fact one of the options for managing the multinational Russian Empire that had been discussed since the failed revolution of 1905. And although the discussion in Russia was also influenced by concrete Habsburg-Austrian developments in various provinces, it gave rather more regard to the theoretical elaborations of the Austro-Marxists. Considering how many socialists in the Russian Empire were able to read German—in some regions, they were apparently influenced as much by German as by Russian theoretical texts[58]—it is remarkable how quickly Austro-Marxist treatises were translated. As early as 1906, a Russian translation of the minutes of the 1899 Brünn/Brno convention of the Austrian Social Democrat Party was published in Kyiv. It was at this convention that Etbin Kristan had (unsuccessfully) proposed for the first time in the name of the South Slavic section of the party to include non-territorial autonomy in the official party programme. Three years later, in 1909, two key books—Renner's 1902 *The Struggles of the Austrian Nations over the State* and Bauer's 1907 *The Question of Nationalities and Social Democracy*—were published in Russian translations as well.[59]

The intense interest with which Austrian developments were received in Russia is also exemplified by two other publications. In 1910, A. I. Kastel'janskij edited a more than 800-page collection of articles entitled *Forms of the National Movement in Contemporary States*, which dedicated around 300 pages to the Habsburg

[57] Werner Hasselblatt, 'Kulturautonomie. Ein Erinnerungsblatt für Professor Rudolf Laun' in Gustaf C. Hernmarck (ed), *Festschrift zu Ehren von Rudolf Laun anläßlich der Vollendung seines 65. Lebensjahres am 1. Januar 1947* (J. P. Toth 1948) 32, 34–35.

[58] For the importance of German socialist thinking in Latvia, cf. Marina Germane, 'Pēteris Stučka and the National Question' (2013) 44/3 Journal of Baltic Studies 1, 4.

[59] The Russian titles of these three publications are: *Debaty po nacional'nomu voprosu na brjunnskom partejtage* (Serp 1906 [1899]); Karl Renner [Rudol'f Špringer], *Nacional'naja problema. Bor'ba nacional'nostej v Avstrii* (Krasand 1909 [2010]); and Otto Bauėr, *Nacional'nyj vopros i social-demokratija* (Serp 1909 [1907]).

Empire. He invited important Austrian protagonists to contribute to the volume, including Karl Renner himself, who wrote on the general evolution of the national question in Austria-Hungary. Among the ten chapters dedicated to the various nationalities of the empire, we find the abovementioned Etbin Kristan elaborating on the South Slavs; the Moravian lawyer Alfred Fischel writing thirty pages about the Germans in the Bohemian lands, including a three-page explanation of the central elements of the Moravian Compromise; and Nathan Birnbaum (under the pseudonym of Mathias Acher) reflecting on the Jews' ambiguous position in the nationalities struggles.[60]

Another contributor, Engelprecht Pernerstorfer, who had actually been one of delegates to dismiss non-territorial autonomy at the Brünn convention, wrote the following appreciatory acknowledgement in his concluding note to the editor: 'I would really not have thought that the reading public in Russia is acquainted to such an extent with the Austrian national relations, and especially because of this I felt obliged to describe the external twists in greatest detail.'[61]

The second and even more influential publication was Josef Stalin's *Marxism and the National Question*. At Lenin's request to critically study the Habsburg nationality policies, Stalin had spent two months in Vienna in early 1913. His lengthy article dedicated an entire chapter to national-cultural autonomy, in which he heavily criticized the Austro-Marxist model as reactionary and false.[62]

While Stalin ostensibly dressed down Renner and Bauer, the real addressee of his text was the Jewish Labour Bund in Lithuania, Poland, and Russia. The Bund was founded in October 1897 as a socialist party dedicated to the economic, political, and cultural interests of the Jewish proletariat. When the Russian Social Democratic Labour Party (RSDRP) was established in March 1898, the Bund initially joined it, but after the RSDRP attempted to eliminate the Bund's autonomous structures within the party in 1903, the Bundist delegates left the party only to eventually merge with it again in 1906. Bundist thinkers like Vladimir Kosovskij and Vladimir Medem had been among the first to adopt the Austro-Marxist ideas of non-territorial autonomy and adapt them to the circumstances in the Russian Empire.[63] They also attempted to get the RSDRP to formulate a national

[60] A. I. Kasteljanskij (ed), *Formy nacional'nogo dviženija v sovremmennych gosudarstvach. Avstro-Vengrija. Rossija. Germanija* (Obščestvennaja Pol'za 1910).

[61] Engelbert Pernerstorfer, 'Nacional'nyj vopros i socialdemokratija v Avstrii' in A. I. Kasteljanskij (ed), *Formy nacional'nogo dviženija v sovremmennych gosudarstvach. Avstro-Vengrija. Rossija. Germanija* (Obščestvennaja Pol'za 1910) 801, 817.

[62] Joseph V. Stalin, 'Marxism and the National Question' in Joseph Stalin (ed) *Works. Volume 2, 1907–1913* (Foreign Languages Publishing House 1953 [1913]) 300, 331–344.

[63] Their first contributions were in Yiddish and thus addressed the Jewish political arena. Vladimir Kosovski, *Tsu der frage vegn der natsyonal-kultureler oytonomye un iberboyung di ruslendishe sotsyal-demokratishe arbeter-partey ofy federative yesoydes* (New York 1901). Vladimir Medem, *Di natsyonale frage un di sotsyal-demokratie* (Di velt 1906). Both men, but especially Medem, also engaged in the Russian discussion. For the adoption and adaptations of Austro-Marxist ideas by the Bund, cf. Roni Gechtman, 'Conceptualizing National-Cultural Autonomy: From the Austro-Marxists to the Jewish Labor Bund', *Simon Dubnow Jahrbuch* (vol. 4, Leipzig 2005) 17–49.

programme based on the Bundist vision, which could be realized only after the final split between Bolsheviks and Mensheviks in 1912. Propelled by the Bund, the entire party spectrum of the democratic political left (e.g. Mensheviks, Social Revolutionaries, etc.) had eventually accepted non-territorial autonomy as a desirable solution to Russia's nationality problems by the time of outbreak of the revolution in 1917.[64]

Yet the year 1917 also offered many new options. Even though ethno-federalist ideas had been circulating in Russia after the 1905 revolution, they had hardly been considered realistically implementable in the near future.[65] After the March Revolution in 1917, many non-Russian political protagonists quickly began planning a reorganization of Russia based on national territorial units. In this regard, Ukrainian politicians were among the loudest voices, and they convened a Congress of Representatives of the Peoples and Regions of Russia in September 1917 in Kyiv.[66] Among the ninety-three delegates, the largest groups with nine to ten envoys each were Jews, Latvians, Tatars, Lithuanians, and Ukrainians. In its resolutions, the Congress not only demanded a federalized Russian Republic based on national territories but also called for non-territorial autonomy for national groups dispersed across Russia.[67]

The Bolshevik coup in November 1917 gave developments yet another spin, however. Finland, Latvia, Poland, Estonia, Lithuania, and Ukraine declared their independence over the course of 1918, with the latter three of these new nation states promising non-territorial autonomy provisions for the national minorities within their territories. The first state to make good on its promise was the Ukrainian People's Republic: mere hours before its declaration of independence, the Ukrainian assembly passed a law on national-personal autonomy for the Russian, Jewish, and Polish minorities.[68] After the unanimous adoption of the law,

[64] Irina V. Nam, 'Nacional'naja programma Bunda: korrektivy 1917 goda' (2003) 3/276 Vestnik Tomskogo gosudarstvennogo universiteta, Serija Istorija. Kraevedenie. Ėtnologija. Archeologija 83, 86–88.

[65] For the Ukrainian national movement, cf. the writings of Mychajlo Hruševs'kyj, e.g. Michail Gruševskij, *Nacional'nyj vopros i avtonomija* (Obščestvennaja Pol'za 1907 [1906]). For the national movements in the Baltics, cf. Kaarel Piirimäe, 'Federalism in the Baltic: Interpretations of Self-Determination and Sovereignty in Estonia in the First Half of the Twentieth Century' (2012) 39/2-3 East Central Europe 237–265.

[66] On this meeting in general, cf. H.D., Hulenovyč, 'Z"izd narodiv Rosiji u Kyjevi (veresen' 1917 r.)' (1994) 6 Ukrajins'kyj istoryčnyj žurnal 83–84. CDAVO, 1115-1-7, 1–6, Protokol. S"ezd predstavitelej Narodov i Oblastej, stremjaščichsja k federativnomu pereustrojstvu Rossijskoj Respubliki, Kyiv, 6–15 September 1917.

[67] The resolutions are published in: Vladyslav F. Verstjuk (ed), *Ukrajins'ka Central'na Rada. Dokumenty i materialy; u dvoch tomach* (vol. 1, Kiev 1997) doc. 127, 15 September 1917, Postanovy Z"jizdu Narodiv, 307–312.

[68] For the only article on the making of the law in English, cf. George Liber, 'Ukrainian Nationalism and the 1918 law on national personal autonomy' (1987) 15/1 Nationalities Papers: The Journal of Nationalism and Ethnicity 22–42. There is hardly any analytical research literature in Ukrainian either. The best legal description of the law itself and its creation is perhaps Natalja V. Čebotok, *Deržavna etnonacional'na polityka v Ukrajiny u 1917–1921 rr.* (unprinted PhilD thesis, University of Kyiv 2005) 64–84.

Moyshe Zilberfarb, who was the minister of Jewish affairs in the Ukrainian government and had actually drafted the bill, lauded it and mentioned that such a solution had first been approved at the Brünn party convention of the Austrian Social Democrats.[69]

Although Zilberfarb understandably referred to the imperial Austrian roots of the Ukrainian law, he disregarded the fact that the delegates at Brünn had only *discussed* non-territorial autonomy for the first time but had not actually accepted it as their official national programme. This misinterpretation can be found in other places as well, for example, in a series of articles on the idea of non-territorial autonomy published by the Estonian historian and socialist politician Hans Kruus during the summer of 1917. Kruus nevertheless demonstrated a thorough knowledge of the origins of the idea, as he not only referred to the Austro-Marxists and the Bund but also correctly pointed to the aforementioned national curiae in the abortive 1871 Bohemian Compromise, which he perceived to be the very first seeds of non-territorial national autonomy provisions.[70]

The interwar Baltic states are actually the most interesting cases in regard to non-territorial autonomy—or cultural autonomy, as it was usually termed in the interwar period. All three countries professed their intent to grant collective autonomy rights to their national minorities. The first to make such a statement on 24 February 1918 was Estonia in its independence manifesto *To the Peoples of Estonia*, whose second article promised cultural autonomy to the new country's minorities.[71] The same promise was included in the Estonian constitution drafted in 1920, but it would take five more years before a provisional law on cultural autonomy was passed and implemented by the Estonian parliament.[72]

The driving force behind the Estonian cultural autonomy law was the Baltic German minority, which consisted mostly of big landowners, urban white-collar workers and craftsmen. The German large estate owners had suffered most from the radical Estonian agrarian reform of 1919 and lost their dominant position within the region's political and economic life. Supporters and opponents of corporative minority legislation were to be found across the entire Estonian political spectrum. The leader of Estonia's Agrarian Party and later authoritarian head of

[69] Verstjuk: *Ukrajins'ka Central'na Rada*, vol. 2, doc. 46, 9 January 1918, Materialy zasidannja Maloji Rady, 98–99.

[70] Hans Kruus, '[Rahvusautonoomia] Rahwuskultuuriline autonoomia' (22.7.1917), 48 Töö Lipp: sotsialistlik ajaleht 2.

[71] The manifesto is printed in German in: Ago Pajur, 'Die Geburt des estnischen Unabhängigkeitsmanifests 1918' (2006) 1 Forschungen zur baltischen Geschichte 136, 160–162. An online English version can be found at: <https://www.president.ee/en/republic-of-estonia/declaration-of-independence/index.html>.

[72] Cornelius Hasselblatt, *Minderheitenpolitik in Estland. Rechtsentwicklung und Rechtswirklichkeit 1918–1995* (Baltos Lankos 1996) 31. Kaido Laurits, 'Die deutschbaltische Minderheit in der Republik Estland von 1918 bis 1940' (2010) 19 Nordost-Archiv. Zeitschrift für Regionalgeschichte 71, 72–74. Kari Alenius, 'Birth of Cultural Autonomy in Estonia: How, Why, and for Whom?' (2007) 38/4 Journal of Baltic Studies 445.

state Konstantin Päts strongly endorsed the idea, as did the social democrat Karl Ast, who justified his support in a parliamentary session in 1923 with reference to the Austro-Marxists and the fact that the existing European minority protection was hardly democratic:[73]

> The Social Democrats are pleased that this law has been put forward since it derives from the work of Springer and Bauer. We would be happy to see Estonia become a modern democracy, which in its approach to the national question applies a set of principles wholly different to those employed by the old democracies. We already know that the latter offer no cause for celebration as far as the development of the national question is concerned. Despite everything that was said before and during the Versailles treaty, European democracy has done nothing as far as peoples' rights to self-determination are concerned; rather, old methods still prevail to the same extent.[74]

Eventually, the Baltic German elite was still influential enough to have a cultural autonomy law for Estonia's Germans, Jews, Russians, and Swedes passed in 1925. The act was designed around the needs of the Germans, and the latter two groups never even implemented the stipulated autonomous institutions. While some researchers suggest that cultural autonomy for Estonia's tiny Jewish minority was an unintended by-product of the state's complex relationship with the Germans living in the country,[75] the Estonian Jews should not be disregarded as independent actors. They were well aware of the idea of non-territorial autonomy and convinced of its usefulness for their community. At a gathering of Jewish communal representatives in Tallinn in 1919, Hirsh (Grigorij) Aisenstadt, the later long-term head of the autonomous Jewish Cultural Council, communicated 'the ideas of Renner and Bauer, stressing as key principles the belonging of an autonomous minority to the state in which it resides and the "inviolable" unity of the citizen body.'[76] The minimum numerical threshold needed to apply the cultural law was originally set at 4,000 potential members. It was only during the concrete negotiations for the drafting of the bill in 1925 that this threshold was eventually lowered to 3,000 in order to make the law applicable to the Jewish minority as well.[77]

In contrast to Estonia, Latvia's declaration of independence issued on 18 November 1918 guaranteed cultural and national rights and a fair share in the government to ethnic minorities—although it did not explicitly mention any specific

[73] Smith and Hiden, *Ethnic Diversity* (n 23) 34–35.

[74] Karl Ast in: I Riigikogu: IX istungjärk: [11. jaan. - 9. märts 1923]: protokollid nr. 185–221: (Tallinn 1923), 2062, cited according to Smith and Hiden, ibid, 35.

[75] Cf. Anton Weiss-Wendt, *On the Margins: About the History of Jews in Estonia* (Central European University Press 2017) ch. 2, 69–93.

[76] Smith and Hiden, *Ethnic Diversity* (n 23) 33.

[77] Hasselblatt, *Minderheitenpolitik* (n 72) 51.

form of autonomy.[78] This does not imply, however, that non-territorial autonomy was unfamiliar to either the majority or the minority populations. Latvians actively participated in the abovementioned 1917 Kyiv meeting, and Latvian socialists had repeatedly referred to the Austro-Marxists already prior to the country's independence.[79] Indeed, during the first years of its independence the new state was very much inclined toward the idea of Latvia being not an ethnic but a civic nation. When the Latvian parliament passed a law on the educational system of minorities that provided them with a wide range of self-rule in December 1919, minority protagonists hoped that this would be but a first step.[80] Further measures were never taken, however, and neither of the bills proposed by advocates of non-territorial autonomy—one by Baltic German lawyer Paul Schieman and one by Jewish lawyer Max Laserson—were passed by the Latvian parliament.[81]

The situation was slightly different in Lithuania, since unlike Estonia and Latvia it was not clear whether a future Lithuanian state should be a multinational one with a large territory similar to the early modern Grand Duchy of Lithuania or a smaller ethnic Lithuanian state. Poland as well as Soviet Russia contested the proposed territory and borders when Lithuania declared independence on 18 February 1918. Ethnic Lithuanians were in search of allies to support their national and territorial claims, in particular those to the Vilnius/Wilno region occupied by Polish forces. Cooperation between Lithuanian national and Jewish national protagonists had already begun long before the First World War, and this fact led the Lithuanian parliamentary assembly to not only admit three Zionists to its provisional government in mid-December 1918 but also to accept their demand for non-territorial autonomy.[82]

78 'Politische Plattform des Volksrates Lettlands. Angenommen am 17. November 1918' in Herder-Institut (ed), *Dokumente und Materialien zur ostmitteleuropäischen Geschichte. Themenmodul 'Lettland in der Zwischenkriegszeit'* <https://www.herder-institut.de/resolve/qid/1343.html>, accessed 14 April 2020.

79 Marina Germane, 'Latvia as a Civic Nation: The Interwar Experiment' in David J. Smith and Matthew Kott (eds), *Latvia—A Work in Progress? One Hundred Years of State- and Nation-Building* (Ibidem 2017) 55, 57–58. Helene Dopkewitsch, *Die Entwicklung des lettländischen Staatsgedankens bis 1918* (H. R. Engelmann 1936) 17–20.

80 Marina Germane, *The History of the Idea of Latvians as a Civic Nation, 1850–1940* (unprinted DPhil thesis, University of Glasgow 2013) ch. V, 272–280.

81 Kaspar Näf, 'Die nationale Autonomie Karl Renners als Vorbild für die jüdische Kulturautonomie in Litauen und Lettland während der Zwischenkriegszeit' in Vanessa Duss (ed), *Rechtstransfer in der Geschichte / Legal Transfer in History* (Jahrbuch für junge Rechtsgeschichte, Peter Lang 2006) 64, 76–79. On the ambiguous relationship between Laserson and Schiemann on minority issues, cf. Marina Germane's forthcoming article Marina Germane, '"A Melancholy Enterprise?": Revisiting German and Jewish Minorities' Cooperation in Interwar Europe'.

82 Šarūnas Liekis, *A State within a State? Jewish Autonomy in Lithuania, 1918–1925* (Versus Aureus 2003) 42–79. The volume edited by Sirutavičius and Staliūnas points to many forms of interethnic co-operation in general, cf. Vladas Sirutavičius and Darius Staliūnas (eds), *A Pragmatic Alliance: Jewish-Lithuanian Political Cooperation at the Beginning of the 20th Century* (Central European University Press 2011). Besides the Jewish Ministry, there was also a Belarusian Secretariat within the Lithuanian government until 1924; cf. Tomasz Błaszczak, *Białorusini w Republice Litewskiej 1918–1940* (Białoruskie Towarzystwo Historyczne 2017) chapter 2.

To further strengthen this strategic alliance, the Lithuanian government sent a declaration to the abovementioned Committee of Jewish Delegations at the Paris Peace Conference in August 1919 wherein it promised to grant Lithuania's Jews non-territorial autonomy. Many of the eight points of this declaration of intent used a wording very similar to that of the Austro-Marxists, for example, those referring to the national curiae, the sphere of competence of the autonomous organs, or the autonomous organs' status as state organs. Indeed, one of the earliest analysts of Jewish autonomy in Lithuania, Leyb Garfunkel, underlined that its very idea derived from Karl Renner.[83] Despite these promising beginnings, however, Jewish autonomy in Lithuania was already being hampered in 1922, and by early 1926—that is, even before the authoritarian coup—the autonomous Jewish communities had been abolished.[84]

It would nevertheless be simplistic to reduce the cultural autonomy law for Jews in Lithuania to the influence of Austro-Marxist theories and Bundist intermediation. Equally important was Simon Dubnov's abovementioned concept of a modernization of Poland-Lithuania's Jewish self-rule. Jewish activists throughout Central and Eastern Europe—whether leftist or rightist, Zionist or Bundist, religious or atheist—were always aware of this early modern legacy. Non-territorial cultural autonomy for Jews conceived as a modern nation thus came to these protagonists quite naturally.[85]

In conclusion of this subchapter, I wish to stress the fact that minority activists in all countries generally observed the minority rights developments in other countries closely. Naturally, they were interested in all forms of legal arrangements including non-territorial autonomy provisions—as shown by the following example: three weeks after the Ukrainian Peoples' Republic had passed its law on national-personal autonomy in January 1918, the executive committee of the Austrian Zionists sent a letter congratulating and thanking the Ukrainian government for its far-sighted decision.[86] A Baltic German newspaper in Tallinn later also elaborated on the pioneering character of the Ukrainian law, and the abovementioned Lithuanian-Jewish advocate Leyb Garfunkel likewise dedicated several paragraphs to the developments in Ukraine.[87]

[83] Leyb Garfunkel, *Di idishe natsyonale avtonomye in Lite. Aroysgegebn durkh dem idishn natsyonalrat* (Bak un tankes 1920) 5. Garfunkel also prints the text of the declaration of the Lithuanian government, dated 5 August 1919, 31–33.

[84] Samuel Gringauz, 'The Jewish National Autonomy in Lithuania (1918–1925)' [1952] Jewish Social Studies 225–246. Smith and Hiden, *Ethnic Diversity* (n 23) 29–30. The most thorough study of Jewish non-territorial autonomy in Lithuania is Liekis, *State within a State?* (n 82).

[85] Rabinovitch has demonstrated the omnipresence of the idea of national autonomy in Jewish modern political thought, cf. Rabinovitch, *Jewish Rights, National Rites* (n 26). See also Żyndul, *Panstwo w Panstwie?* (n 31) 17–52.

[86] ÖStA/HHStA, Ministerium d. Äußeren, PL Akten, K. 193, Letter from the executive committee of the Austrian Zionists to the government of the Ukrainian Peoples' Republic, Vienna, 12 February 1918.

[87] Völkische Autonomie in der Ukraine, in: Revaler Bote, 18.02.1920, 1. Garfunkel, *Idishe natsyonale avotonomye* (n 83) 11–13.

IV. Developments in the Interwar International Arena of Minority Protection

This interest in minority rights developments in other countries, coupled with the increasing disappointment of many people with the minority rights regimes as implemented by their own home countries and supervised by the League of Nations, led to a surge in inter- and transnational minority protection activism during the 1920s. This activism was transnational not only in the sense of coordinated action by specific national groups across Europe, but also in the sense that it brought together stakeholders from different national minorities. An initial form of transnational organizations like the Committee of Jewish Delegations or the *Verband deutscher Volksgruppen* established in 1922 already existed or originated quite quickly. By the mid-1920s, however, the time was ripe for a second form of transnational minority activism. The Baltic German publicist and politician Ewald Ammende initiated a pan-European lobby group that was to speak on behalf of all of the continent's national minorities: the Congress of European Nationalities. During the thirteen years of its existence, it brought together more than 200 minority representatives from various European countries, with Germans, Jews, Catalans, Ukrainians, and Hungarians being the most numerous groups. Perhaps the most active members were the Baltic German and Zionist activists—the latter at least until the Congress began leaning more and more towards racist and Nazi ideology after 1933.[88]

While there was consensus that national minorities formed a collective and had to be protected against denationalization, the resolutions of the Congress' first meeting in Geneva in August 1925 stated that only the members of a given minority group should be allowed to decide whether they actually wished to establish national-cultural self-rule for themselves. The Congress insisted that membership in any minority register had to be a free choice for each individual concerned. A respective resolution stipulated that:

1. the constitution and implementation of national-cultural self-administration, respectively the emergence of corresponding associations, is subject to the approval of the minorities within whose volition the decision-making concerning this matter lies,

[88] Sabine Bamberger-Stemmann, *Der Europäische Nationalitätenkongreß 1925 bis 1938. Nationale Minderheiten zwischen Lobbyistentum und Großmachtinteressen* (Materialien und Studien zur Ostmitteleuropa-Forschung 7, Herder-Institut 2000) 60–78; 104–125. On Ammende's interesting biography, cf. Martyn Housden, *On Their Own Behalf: Ewald Ammende, Europe's National Minorities and the Campaign for Cultural Autonomy 1920–1936* (On the Boundary of Two Worlds, Rodopi 2014). For a study on the Congress in English, cf. Ulrike von Hirschhausen, 'From Minority Protection to Border Revisionism: The European Nationality Congress, 1925–38' in Martin Conway and Kiran Klaus Patel (eds), *Europeanization in the Twentieth Century* (Palgrave Macmillan 2010) 87.

2. the free affirmation of a nationality by the individual and, if a national register is created, the accedence to that register may be neither disputed nor verified, must be protected by law, and may not form grounds for any disadvantages in public life for the individual or the entirety of the national group,
3. the State and all compulsory corporate bodies that provide cultural functions using public funds are obligated to contribute financially to this self-administration in the same proportion as they contribute to the cultural life of the majority nation.[89]

The resolution was delivered by one of the Congress's most active protagonists—and a man we have encountered before: Leo Motzkin. Already as a leading member of the Committee of Jewish Delegations at the Paris Peace Conference, he had argued in favour of corporative non-territorial rights for Jews. He continued to strongly support the idea and was an attentive observer of developments in Europe; in 1926, for instance, he congratulated the Estonian Jews on implementing the country's law on cultural autonomy for their community.[90]

The Estonian example played an important role for the Congress of European Nationalities in general. This was in part because the Congress's initiator Ewald Ammende as well as the editor of its semi-official mouthpiece *Nation und Staat*, Werner Hasselblatt, were Estonian citizens, and in part because Estonia's cultural autonomy law was widely perceived as an achievement and frequently presented as a model. Numerous articles in minority journals and other publications across Europe testify to this fact.[91] Most prominent in this respect may be the survey initiated by Ammende in 1930/31, when he asked a wide range of Estonian protagonists—including left-wing and right-wing, majority and minority politicians—to share their opinions on the country's experiences with non-territorial autonomy. The predominantly positive evaluation was presented at the Congress' annual convention in Geneva in 1931.[92] Eventually, the Congress even

[89] *Sitzungsbericht des Kongresses der organisierten nationalen Gruppen in den Staaten Europas. Genf, 25.–27. August 1926* (Wilhelm Braumüller 1927) 69–70.

[90] The telegram was printed in the publication on the occasion of the tenth jubilee of the Jewish cultural autonomy, cf. *E. V. Juudi Vähemusrahvuse Kultuuromavalitsuse juubeli album* (Juudi Kultuurvalitsus 1936) 11.

[91] Estonia's non-territorial autonomy law was particularly well received by German and Jewish activists, cf. e.g. 'Die Kuturautonomiepläne der Juden und Russen in Estland' (1925) I Kulturwille. Zeitschrift für Minderheitenkultur und -politik; Friedrich von Poll, *Das Kulturautonomiegesetz der Republik Estland und seine Bedeutung für das europäische Minderheitenproblem* (unprinted DPhil thesis, Universität Würzburg 1926); Moritz Mintz, *Die nationale Autonomie im System des Minderheitenrechts unter besonderer Berücksichtigung der Rechtsentwicklung in den baltischen Randstaaten* (Walters und Rapa 1927); Fritz Cohn, *Nationale Minderheiten und kulturelle Autonomien: mit besonderer Berücksichtigung des Estnischen Kultur-Autonomiegesetzes vom 5. Februar 1925* (unprinted DPhil thesis, Universität Breslau 1929); Werner Hasselblatt, 'Hat sich die Kulturautonomie bewährt?' (1930) 4 Nation und Staat 441; Max Laserson, 'Das Minoritätenrecht der Baltischen Staaten' (1931) 2/1 Zeitschrift für ausländisches öffentliches Recht und Völkerrecht 401–429.

[92] *Sitzungsbericht des Kongresses der organisierten nationalen Gruppen in den Staaten Europas. Genf, 29.–31. August 1931* (Wilhelm Braumüller 1932).

called upon the League of Nations to recommend corporative minority systems to all European nation states.[93] As we will see in the next but one paragraph, the League's reaction to this proposal was bluntly dismissive.

Yet we should also not perceive the Congress of European Nationalities as a unitary block, for not all of its protagonists were such staunch supporters of non-territorial autonomy as the leading figures Ewald Ammende, Paul Schiemann, Leo Motzkin, and Max Laserson. On the one hand, representatives of small and economically weak minorities like the German Sorbs or the Austrian Slovenes feared that only few of their members would be willing to register in a national cadastre and that they would never be able to finance autonomous structures.[94] On the other hand, minority groups living in smaller and more compactly delimited areas, like the Sudeten Germans or the Hungarian-speaking Szeklers in Romania, preferred territorial autonomy. Ammende considered such wishes illusionary, as he was certain that the governments of unitary nation states would perceive territorial autonomy as a first step towards secession, in particular where territories adjacent to a minority's kinstate were concerned. This danger of any form of territorial autonomy being interpreted as a precursor to territorial revision was not mitigated by the fact that the Congress admitted any minority representatives only under the condition that they renounced any potential changes to borders.[95]

The internal disagreement was taken up by Ludvig Krabbe, deputy director of the League of Nations' minorities section, when he was officially commissioned to examine cultural autonomy on behalf of the League in 1931. He dismissed the idea as a general tool for minority protection and criticized the way in which the dominant protagonists of the Congress of European Nationalities was attempting to promote cultural autonomy as the ultimate and universal solution to all minority problems.[96] Yet the underlying reason for his critical remarks may have been the fact that the League of Nations and the Nationalities Congress had fundamentally opposing approaches to national diversity within states, as reflected in the very terminology of their names: the Congress had *nationalities* as its agents, whereas the League had a *minorities* section—and national minorities could exist only were a nation state existed. While the League of Nations thus insisted that there could be no further legal body between the individual and the state, the Congress wished to introduce the ethnic nation as an additional corporate legal entity with rights

[93] 'VII. Sitzungsbericht des Kongresses der organisierten nationalen Gruppen in den Staaten Europas', cited in Glasul Minorităţilor / La voix des minorités / Die Stimme der Minderheiten, Sept. 1931, no. 1, 297–298.

[94] Żyndul, *Panstwo w Panstwie?* (n 31) 203. On Sorbs in Germany, cf. in particular Bamberger-Stemmann, *Nationalitätenkongreß* (n 88) 176–177; on Slovenes in Austria, cf. Valentin Einspieler, *Verhandlungen über die der slowenischen Minderheit angebotene Kulturautonomie 1925–1930. Beitrag zur Geschichte der Slowenen in Kärnten* (Verlag des Geschichtsvereines für Kärnten 1980) 60–62.

[95] David J. Smith, Marina Germane, and Martyn Housden, '"Forgotten Europeans": Transnational Minority Activism in the Age of European Integration' (2018) 24/1 Nations and Nationalism 1, 7.

[96] Housden, *On Their Own Behalf* (n 88) 246–249.

and duties in specific, delineated matters like education and culture. Although originally conceived by Austro-Marxist theoreticians and liberal legal scholars in the Habsburg empire as well as by minority activists in the Baltic states as a tool to increase democratic participation, the idea of an ethnic nation possessing legal personhood with autonomous agency was one that far-right and Nazi ideologists could easily get behind.[97]

V. In Lieu of a Conclusion

Non-territorial autonomy was widely discussed in many different languages in interwar Europe, and the Habsburg origins of the concept were familiar to most of the protagonists in one way or another. Although three important countries—the Soviet Union, Great Britain, and France—were barely involved for different reasons, it was nevertheless a true trans-European discussion. The Soviet Union refuted non-territorial autonomy on ideological terms and therefore hardly became involved in the debate.[98] In France, however, we can find at least two scholars who were very well informed about the notion and origins of non-territorial autonomy. Not surprisingly, one of them was an Alsatian—Robert Redslob, a law professor at the University of Strasbourg and fierce critic of the concept.[99] The other was the French diplomat Jacques Fouques Duparc, who worked at the League of Nations between 1921 and 1924 and dedicated an entire chapter to Karl Renner in his book, which is maybe one of the best early histories of minority protection.[100]

Although German protagonists certainly dominated the interwar discourse on non-territorial autonomy, policy-makers and legal scholars from the north, south, east, and west of Europe conversed about how to deal with national diversity in journals like *Kulturwehr, Glasul Minorităților, Magyar Kisebbség* or, most importantly, *Nation und Staat*. These publications served as transnational platforms for

[97] Natasha Wheatley, 'Making Nations into Legal Persons between Imperial and International Law: Scenes from a Central European History of Group Rights' (2018) 28 Duke Journal of Comparative & International Law 481, see in particular the final section, 493–494. The ongoing ERC project 'Non-territorial Autonomy: History of a Travelling Idea' specifically investigates the claim that non-territorial corporate autonomy was translatable through the entire political spectrum from the far left to the far right.

[98] Besides some forms of de facto implementations of non-territorial autonomy arrangements, Matthias Battis shows that there was even a limited discussion on the topic during the 1920s in his forthcoming article, cf. Battis, *Matthias: On Common Ground—Soviet Nationalities Policy and the Austro-Marxist Premise.*

[99] Robert Redslob, 'Le principe des nationalités' [1931] Recueil des Cours de l'Académie de droit international (1931) 37/III, see in particular chapter IV, Les solutions possible, sub-chapter II.B, Autonomie des groups éthniques, 50–57.

[100] Jacques Fouques Duparc, *La protection des minorités de race, de langue et de religion* (Dalloz 1922), in particular chapter III, 'Les difficultés du problème (Les précédents autrichiens; la formule de M. Renner)' 43–53. Another scarcely received book is Dragoljub Krstić's doctoral thesis published in 1924, cf. Dragolioub Krstich, *Les minorités, l'état et la communauté internationale* (Libraire Arthur Rousseau 1924).

the discussion of national minority issues, where ideas could be exchanged, criticized, and adapted to local circumstances. In conclusion, I would like to reference a multi-part contribution published in *Nation und Staat* between 1935 and 1936 by Austrian legal scholar Karl Braunias: 'The Further Development of Old Austrian Nationalities Law After the War'.[101] Braunias observed continuities of the idea of non-territorial autonomy as developed in the Habsburg Empire in several cases. On the one hand, he pointed out the general influence that Austro-Marxist thinking had on Eastern European socialist movements, particularly in imperial Russia. On the other hand, he mentioned several cases in interwar Europe that directly or vaguely involved corporate rights for nationalities—most prominently Estonia's 1925 cultural autonomy law.[102]

With Braunias's article, my chapter comes full circle, for I initially argued that both kinds of Habsburg Austrian experiences with non-territorial autonomy influenced developments during the interwar period: the national compromises in the provinces of Moravia, Bukovina, Bosnia-Herzegovina, and Galicia as well as the Austro-Marxists' theoretical elaborations. This legacy crystallized for the first time in the context of the 1919 Paris Peace Conference, where Zionist activists lobbied for corporate rights for Jews based on non-territorial arrangements. In general, we can hardly overstate the importance of Jewish protagonists, Zionist and non-Zionist alike, for translating the idea of non-territorial autonomy to the needs of Eastern European minorities before and after the First World War.

Despite the fact that the Paris Peace Conference—and eventually the League of Nations as well—disregarded corporate minority rights, non-territorial autonomy was discussed or even (temporarily) implemented in several newly established nation states in Central and Eastern Europe during the interwar period. Debates about non-territorial autonomy did not occur in a void, and in one way or another, most discussants were familiar with the idea's origins as well as with developments in other European countries. Sometimes they were also active in the transnational arena of minority protection, for example by participating in the annual meetings of the Congress of European Nationalities. Many protagonists involved in the interwar discussion of non-territorial autonomy thus either knew each other in person or were at least familiar with each other's writings. Through this entangled intellectual space, the idea of non-territorial autonomy found its way from late imperial Austria into the post-Habsburg period—and although its voyage sometimes followed direct lines, it very often occurred via indirect and winding paths.

[101] Karl Braunias, 'Die Fortentwicklung des altösterreichischen Nationalitätenrechtes nach dem Kriege' (1935–36) 9 Nation und Staat 226–238, 288–301, 358–370, 578–589.

[102] Ibid, (1936) 9/6 364–367.

14
Beyond the League of Nations
Public Debates on International Relations in Czechoslovakia during the Interwar Period

Sarah Lemmen

I. Introduction

The date of the Czechoslovak Republic's declaration of independence, 28 October 1918, was mostly of symbolic significance. The size of the country's territory and its borders were still provisional and in flux, although the order of the day was to settle these matters quickly so as to present an orderly and stable entity to the international community that would eventually decide on the fate and shape of Central Europe.[1] It is symptomatic for the time—and a further indication of the improvised timing of the declaration of independence—that neither the president nor some of his most senior staff had yet returned to the newly declared republic from their wartime exile: the large procession in Prague welcoming president Tomáš G. Masaryk with military honours would eventually take place in December of the same year.

The absence of the most senior state representatives at such a crucial time also points to another aspect, namely that at its core, the founding of the Czechoslovak Republic in 1918 had been an international endeavour. The new state had already been lobbied for across Europe and the USA during the First World War by—among others—its future president, Tomáš G. Masaryk, and Edvard Beneš, who would shape Czechoslovak foreign affairs as foreign minister for more than fifteen years; it was based on the Pittsburgh Agreement between representatives of the Czech and Slovak exiles in the United States that demanded 'a Union of the Czechs and Slovaks in an independent state made up of the Bohemian lands and Slovakia',[2]

[1] Dagmar Perman, *The Shaping of the Czechoslovak State, Diplomatic History of the Boundaries of Czechoslovakia, 1914–1920* (Brill 1962) 67–70; Mary Heimann, *Czechoslovakia, The State That Failed* (Yale University Press 2009) 42.

[2] Martin Votruba, 'Pittsburgh Agreement' in *Slovak Studies Program*, University of Pittsburgh <http,//www.pitt.edu/~votruba/qsonhist/pittsburghagreement.html>, accessed 27 September 2020.

Sarah Lemmen, *Beyond the League of Nations* In: *Remaking Central Europe*. Edited by: Peter Becker and Natasha Wheatley, Oxford University Press (2020). © the many contributors. DOI: 10.1093/oso/9780198854685.003.0015

and the Czechoslovak declaration of independence was drafted in Washington, D.C. before sovereign statehood was eventually announced by the National Committee on 28 October 1918. The new country was finally approved by the victorious powers during the Paris Peace Conference in 1919. Both the existence and the shape of the Czechoslovak Republic were thus results of international efforts.[3]

This focus on international relations was dominant not just during the founding process of the republic but throughout the entire interwar period. The fate of the new republic was thought to depend on resilient diplomatic and economic networks as well as on international goodwill, and international relations were understood to be key to its security—and even existence—throughout the interwar period. This outlook was underlined most dramatically in the moment when the international safety net eventually failed with the signing of the Munich Agreement in 1938, which led to the disseverance of the Czechoslovak Republic and eventually to its occupation by the German Reich and dissolvement in 1939.

But this was a distant future in the days after the First World War. Early on, Czechoslovakia was invested in expanding its international network as an important safety measure for the stability of the postwar order, as demonstrated most prominently by its founding memberships in the League of Nations and the so-called Little Entente. This co-constitution of national and international orders was common practice among states in general. It was, however, of particular relevance to those countries founded in the post-imperial sphere of the interwar years. Born into a period with a strong focus on international law, order, and organization, the existence of these states was largely dependent on their international standing. In this context, the Czechoslovak Republic with its excellent conditions in terms of size, economic strength, political power, and international approval provides a notable example in regard to its international outreach, which was molded to some degree on imperial models and in other parts mirrored the country's self-image as a 'small nation'.

I argue that this narrative of international relations for the sake of national sovereignty and as measures of security and advancement for the new republic can be told from a broader perspective beyond the narrow understanding of the political workings of the Ministry of Foreign Affairs. The interwar period features various examples of political, economic, and cultural relations on a global scale that were considered vital and fundamental to the aspirations of the new state.

Based on this assumption, this chapter traces examples of worldwide outreach and public debates pertaining to the global standing of Czechoslovakia and its international links—economic, political, and cultural—during the interwar period. Politicians, journalists, economists, and other professionals described the

[3] The rushed 'Declaration of Independence' as well as the coup on 28 October that occurred without the consent or even knowledge of Tomáš G. Masaryk or Edvard Beneš is touched upon in Heimann, *Czechoslovakia* (n 1) 36–39.

standing of this new country in a globalizing world in speech and in writing and contemplated possible paths for further development.

By contrast, the academic focus on Czechoslovak international relations—both in a narrow and in a broader understanding—has hitherto generally been placed on (Central) European regional relations. In terms of international security, the alliance between Czechoslovakia, Romania, and Yugoslavia—known as the Little Entente—has likely been the object of more academic scrutiny than Czechoslovak membership in the League of Nations.[4] Concerning economic relations, research has concentrated mainly on the most important trade partners such as neighbouring Germany, the former Habsburg territories, and the Balkans,[5] and the most-studied political relations are likewise those with Czechoslovakia's immediate neighbours.[6]

This general regional focus on European or often only Central European relations certainly highlights the most influential aspects of Czechoslovak political, economic, and cultural ties. However, it also omits other facets that might provide a different understanding of Czechoslovakia's role and position in an international context. Shifting the academic gaze to Czechoslovak relations with Africa, Asia, or the Americas—or to a truly global context—brings into focus different aims and a different narrative of the Czechoslovak Republic during the interwar period. While this further-reaching narrative cannot and must not replace the regional narrative, it can certainly serve to complement it.

In the following, I will first outline some specifics of the founding of the Czechoslovak Republic and its attention to international affairs before discussing four instances of Czechoslovak global outreach beyond the European continent—in the realm of international politics and alliances, in both the diplomatic and

[4] The Little Entente is discussed e.g. in Andrzej Essen, 'Malá dohoda jako nástroj československé zahraniční politiky' in Jaroslav Valenta, Emil Voráček, and Josef Harna (eds), *Československo 1918–1938, Osudy demokracie ve střední Evropě. Sborník z mezinárodní vědecké konference, díl 2* (Institute of History of the Czech Academy of Sciences 1999) 562–565; Zdeněk Sládek, *Malá dohoda 1919–1938, její hospodářské, politické a vojenské komponenty* (Karolinum 2000). The Czechoslovak relations to the League of Nations are discussed from various perspectives in Eduard Kubů, 'Ziele und Handicaps der Politik von Edvard Beneš im Völkerbund' in Hans Lemberg, Michaela Marek, Zdeněk Beneš, and Dušan Kováč (eds), *Suche nach Sicherheit in stürmischer Zeit. Tschechen, Slowaken und Deutsche im System der internationalen Beziehungen der ersten Hälfte des 20. Jahrhunderts* (Klartext 2009) 45–80; Gyula Popély, 'Mezinárodní ochrana menšin, Československo a Společnost národů' (1991) 7/19 Střední Evropa. Revue pro středoevropskou kulturu a politiku 58–73; Zuzana Trávníčková, 'Edvard Beneš a Společnost národů' in Zdeněk Veselý et al. (eds), *Edvard Beneš. Československo. Evropa* (Professional Publishing 2005) 56–64.

[5] Cf. e.g. Eduard Kubů and Jaroslav Pátek (eds), *Mýtus a realita hospodářské vyspělosti Československa mezi světovými válkami* (Karolinum 2000); Vlastislav Lacina, *Zlatá léta Československého Hopodářství 1918–1929* (Historický Ústav AV ČR 2000); Alice Teichova, *Wirtschaftsgeschichte der Tschechoslowakei 1918–1980* (Böhlau 1988).

[6] Cf. e.g. Jindřich Dejmek, *Československo, jeho sousedé a velmoci ve XX. století (1918–1992)* (Centrum pro ekonomiku a politiku 2002); Antonín Klimek and Eduard Kubů, *Československá zahraniční politika 1918–1938. Kapitoly z dějin mezinárodních vztahů* (ISE—Institut pro středoevropskou kulturu a politiku 1995); Antonín Klimek, *Diplomatie am Scheideweg, Außenpolitik der Tschechoslowakei 1918–1938* (Orbis 1989).

economic spheres, in the area of colonial debates, and finally in regard to relations with the Orient as a specific case study—and elaborating on the relevance of these global relations for Czechoslovakia's understanding of its standing and changing position throughout the interwar period.

II. The New State and Its Global Outreach

The Paris Peace Conference was a resounding success for the Czechoslovak delegation led by Edvard Beneš. By the time the peace treaties were signed, the Czechoslovak Republic was not only an internationally recognized state, but Beneš and his delegation had received virtually everything they had asked for:[7] with the Bohemian crown lands, Slovakia, and Subcarpathian Ruthenia, Czechoslovakia inherited a fifth of the territory and a quarter of the population of the former Austro-Hungarian Empire, thereby becoming the latter's largest successor state by population and the second largest by area. The new country could also boast around 40 per cent of the national product and two- thirds of the industrial production of the former empire (including the so called 'armory of the monarchy').[8] This initial economic position placed Czechoslovakia among the fifteen strongest national economies globally. What was more, the Czechoslovak delegation was able to convince the world leaders in Paris of their 'Europeanness' and therefore of their rationality, their efficiency and—most importantly—their adherence to democracy.[9] In short, the Czechoslovak Republic was a symbol of triumph of the new international order. This reassuring position aroused hopes of becoming a significant economic and political power in Europe, taking over the leading role in the region of Central Europe from Vienna.[10]

With this overwhelming initial success, the Czechoslovak Republic was committed to international relations from the outset. Only strong international ties were thought to secure the postwar order in Central Europe—and thus the borders of Czechoslovakia—and a global outreach was considered necessary to ensure the state's economic thriving. The towering foreign minister Edvard Beneš was convinced that even 'our domestic affairs will be influenced more by foreign

[7] Andrea Orzoff, *Battle for the Castle, The Myth of Czechoslovakia in Europe, 1914–1948* (Oxford University Press 2009) 137; Ivan T. Berend, *Decades of Crisis, Central and Eastern Europe before World War II* (University of California Press 2001) 166.

[8] Jiří Kosta, 'Die tschechoslowakische Wirtschaft im ersten Jahrzehnt nach der Staatsgründung' in Hans Lemberg and Peter Heumos (eds), *Das Jahr 1919 in der Tschechoslowakei und in Ostmitteleuropa* (Oldenbourg 1993) 63–91, here 63; Vlastislav Lacina, *Formování československé ekonomiky 1918–1923* (Academia 1990) 170–171.

[9] Orzoff, *Battle for the Castle* (n 7) 9.

[10] Zdeněk Sládek, 'Edvard Beneš a malá dohoda' in Vladimîr Goněc (ed), *Edvard Beneš a středoevropská politika* (Masarykova univerzita v Brně 1998) 21–41, here 23.

affairs than elsewhere',[11] since he saw the security and prosperity of Czechoslovakia tightly linked to the security of Europe and beyond.[12]

This relevance of international relations was reflected in the size of the Ministry of Foreign Affairs, which—as historians Antonín Klimek and Eduard Kubů suggest—may appear excessive compared to the dimensions of the country itself.[13] The tasks of foreign policy, however, were understood in a very broad sense and comprised diplomatic, economic, and security issues as well as aspects of cultural propaganda.[14] As we will see, in the realm of classical foreign policy this included bilateral agreements with other European countries and membership in European and global alliances to protect the postwar order[15] as well as the creation and expansion of diplomatic relations on a global scale.[16] It also meant, as historian Andrea Orzoff notes, the creation of 'a global Czech [!] presence, whether personal or textual':[17] one of the missions of the third division of the ministry ('intelligence division') was 'to persuade the world—especially the West—of the moral and strategic necessity of Czechoslovakia's continued existence'.[18]

This outreach to 'the world' in diplomatic, economic, and cultural terms was not only a means of guaranteeing the existence and furthering the ambitions of the Czechoslovak Republic; 'the world' was also where answers to domestic problems were sought and found. Global outreach was part and parcel of Czechoslovak political, economic, and cultural thinking, and it was also a prerequisite for becoming the 'great power' Czechoslovakia aspired to be.

A. The Quest for Global Security: The League of Nations

The young Czechoslovak Republic was only too aware of its precarious geographic position as well as its disputed borders. The main task of the Czechoslovak foreign policy was therefore to integrate the republic as an independent entity into the international system to ensure the safety of the state—a key challenge for any small country with powerful neighbours.[19] Under the leadership of foreign minister

[11] As quoted in Klimek and Kubů, *Československá zahraniční politika* (n 6) 9.

[12] Sládek, 'Edvard Beneš a malá dohoda' (n 10) 34; Klimek and Kubů, *Československá zahraniční politika* (n 6) 9.

[13] The foreign ministry's size was criticized during the interwar period. Klimek and Kubů, *Československá zahraniční politika* (n 6) 9.

[14] Klimek and Kubů, *Československá zahraniční politika* (n 6) 13.

[15] Andrea Orzoff, 'Interwar Democracy and the League of Nations' in Nicholas Doumanis (ed), *The Oxford Handbook of European History, 1914–1945* (Oxford University Press 2016) 261–281, here 272.

[16] With the possible exception of the USA. Klimek and Kubů, *Československá zahraniční politika* (n 6) 10.

[17] Orzoff, *Battle for the Castle* (n 7) 151.

[18] Ibid, 4.

[19] Klimek and Kubů, *Československá zahraniční politika* (n 6) 7; Ivana Koutská (ed), *Českoslovenští diplomaté do roku 1945, studie a dokumenty* (Ústav pro soudobé dějiny AV ČR 2006) 100.

Edvard Beneš, the Czechoslovak Republic therefore began—in the assessment of Martin Zückert—'to punch well above its weight in international politics'.[20]

First and foremost, the foreign ministry sought to align Czechoslovakia with bilateral and regional agreements and contracts. The most important component of its international security system was arguably the Little Entente, an alliance between Czechoslovakia, Romania, and the Kingdom of Serbs, Croats, and Slovenes (later Yugoslavia) founded in 1920–21 as a shield against both the restoration of the Habsburg Empire and Hungarian revisionism.[21] At the European level, Czechoslovakia relied in particular on a binational defence alliance with France, which was to become the guarantor of the post-war order in Eastern and Central Europe.[22]

At the international and global levels, however, the country's hopes for maintaining peace and the post-war status quo were placed in the League of Nations, an organization whose foremost aim was 'to promote international coöperation and to safeguard international peace and security',[23] as Edvard Beneš summarized the introductory words of its Covenant. As a 'guardian of peace',[24] the League was mainly a support system for multinational diplomacy with primarily moral weight, and it always depended on the willingness of its member states—especially the most powerful ones.[25] Due to its structure and idealistic approach, the League was considered a 'great experiment'[26] even by its founders and supporters.

Internationally respected since the Paris peace talks, Edvard Beneš was intensively involved in establishing and leading the new organization; the various positions he held at the League gave him greater influence than the standing of the Czechoslovak Republic in international relations alone could account for.[27] His regular presence in Geneva—amounting to a total of more than two years spent in Switzerland—testifies not only to the importance he attributed to the League for the overall goal of securing Czechoslovakia's existence, but also to his influence

[20] Martin Zückert, 'National Concepts of Freedom and Government Pacification Policies, The Case of Czechoslovakia in the Transitional Period after 1918' (2008) 17/3 Contemporary European History 325–344, here 329–330.

[21] Essen, 'Malá dohoda jako nástroj' (n 4) 562.

[22] Petr Ort, 'Edvard Beneš a bezpečnost Evropy' in Veselý et al., *Edvard Beneš* (n 4) 65–69, here 66–67.

[23] Edvard Beneš, 'The League of Nations, Successes and Failures' (1932) 11/1 Foreign Affairs 66–80, here 66.

[24] Ibid, 75.

[25] Zara Steiner, *The Lights That Failed, European International History 1919–1933* (Oxford University Press 2005) 349.

[26] As phrased by Lord Robert Cecil, quoted in Steiner, ibid, 349.

[27] For example, his much-lauded leading role in crafting the 'Geneva Protocol' in 1925. Steiner, ibid, 380. On Czechoslovakia's considerable representation at the League of Nations, cf. also Jörg K. Hoensch, *Geschichte der Tschechoslowakei* (3rd edn, Kohlhammer 1992) 46. Similarly, Alexandr Ort, 'Koncepce československé zahraniční politiky' in Jaroslav Valenta, Emil Voráček and Josef Harna (eds), *Československo 1918–1938, Osudy demokracie ve střední Evropě. Sborník z mezinárodní vědecké konference, díl 2* (Historický ústav AV ČR 1999) 495–501, here 497.

exercised through this form of diplomacy:[28] owing to his dedication to the organization, he soon became known as 'the man of the League of Nations'.[29]

Beneš's commitment to the League remained high throughout the interwar period. Nevertheless, he always ascribed only moderate power and influence to it. During his period in office as foreign minister from 1918 until 1935, he wrote and spoke extensively about the international organization. In 1923, he acknowledged the limitations of the League of Nations while simultaneously emphasizing its moral authority and democratic ideals in a speech on the first five years of Czechoslovak foreign policy. He underscored that '[e]very democratic state must try to side with the League of Nations. The Czechoslovak Republic will therefore continue consistently and everywhere to carry out policies of peace and democracy in keeping with the intentions and ideas of the League of Nations'.[30]

During the 1920s, Czechoslovak relations with the League of Nations experienced some setbacks, such as the failed Geneva Protocol or the admission of Germany into the League at the expense of Czechoslovakia's (and Sweden's) positions in the League Council.[31] Nevertheless, Beneš still unambiguously called himself 'a friend and adherent of the League of Nations' in 1929 and recognized that in many instances, the 'peaceful settlement of international disputes is becoming the official method of political procedure'. He saw the League as an idealistic endeavour that would only be successful with essentially democratic members. However, he also cautioned against it becoming an institution representing only the political power players while ignoring the votes of smaller nations, and consequently against decisions affecting the interests of smaller nations being 'taken without hearing their opinion and without their consent'.[32] This was an acknowledgment of the realities of political powers even within an institution that adhered to democratic ideals, and it was a clear-sighted warning of what was to come in the 1930s.

In 1935, the year in which Edvard Beneš succeeded Tomáš G. Masaryk as president of the Czechoslovak Republic, he looked back once more at the aims and tasks of the League of Nations. Yet again he highlighted its importance for the Czechoslovak Republic, but by now it sounded more like a plea: 'A state like ours'—namely one that could not defend itself against potential political and military

[28] Kubů, 'Ziele und Handicaps' (n 4) 46. Cf. also Zuzana Trávníčková, 'Edvard Beneš a Společnost národů' in Veselý et al., *Edvard Beneš* (n 4) 56–64, here 57.

[29] Orzoff, 'Interwar Democracy' (n 15) 272.

[30] All translations from Czech to English by the author. Edvard Beneš, *Problémy nové Evropy a zahraniční politika československá. Projevy a úvahy z let 1919–1924* (Melantrich 1924) 273; here quoted from Trávníčková, 'Edvard Beneš a Společnost národů' (n 28) 57. In another speech three years later, Beneš highlighted the importance of the League of Nations especially for 'small states', since international organizations allowed a small state to gain 'a position from where it can defend itself against a large state'. This lecture by Beneš is quoted in Kubů, 'Ziele und Handicaps' (n 4) 74.

[31] Kubů, 'Ziele und Handicaps' (n 4) 54.

[32] Beneš, 'The League of Nations' (n 23) 74–76.

threats from neighbouring countries without foreign help—'must always and in everything have an institution of this kind at its side and must always use it for its interests and its politics'.[33] This was a call for an international policy of contracts and negotiations rather than of power play.

The League's mixed results in the resolution of conflicts and the hesitant engagement of its member states—which included the withdrawal of Germany, the unimpeded Italian aggression against Abyssinia, and finally Germany's unpunished occupation of the demilitarized zone of the Rhineland—eventually led Beneš to doubt the League's capacity to react appropriately to international crises.[34] The hopes of the early interwar period for a new global order based on agreements and mutual support rather than purely on power and aggression, with a mediating agency in times of conflict, remained a dream that would not materialize.

For Czechoslovakia, this realization would ultimately come in the shape of dramatic events. The Munich Agreement concluded between Germany, France, Great Britain, and Italy in September 1938 without so much as a consultation with Czechoslovak representatives permitted the German annexation of the Czechoslovak Sudetenland, which was not only home to more than 3.6 million inhabitants but was also of vital strategic and economic importance for Czechoslovakia. The League of Nations did not protest or interfere with this deal in any way.[35] Instead, it proposed 'the Czechoslovak people and Edvard Beneš' for the Nobel Peace Prize in 1938.[36] This was cold comfort in light of what was to come, for in March 1939, the German Reich invaded what was left of Czechoslovakia and installed a 'Protectorate Bohemia and Moravia' under German administration. The day after the invasion, Beneš wrote a note of protest to the League. It would be the last direct contact between the organization and the 'man of the League of Nations'.[37]

B. The Quest for Global Representation: Building a Diplomatic Network

The ardent Czechoslovak involvement with the League of Nations was clearly motivated by a sense that the organization offered protection for 'small states', as Beneš had emphasized in his speeches. Other contexts also indicate, however, that the concentration on international and global relations was seen as an attempt by the

[33] Trávníčková, 'Edvard Beneš a Společnost národů' (n 28) 63.

[34] Ibid. The general mood regarding the League of Nations was hardly more enthusiastic, with trust in the League having dwindled rapidly by the late 1930s. Steiner, *The Lights That Failed* (n 25) 371.

[35] Kubů, 'Ziele und Handicaps' (n 4) 46.

[36] Heimann, *Czechoslovakia* (n 1) 83.

[37] Kubů, 'Ziele und Handicaps' (n 4) 59.

thriving Czechoslovak Republic to position itself as a political or economic power in Central Europe and possibly succeed Vienna as the main player in the region.[38]

One of these attempts at internationalization was the creation of a global diplomatic network that was, as some historians have suggested, comparable in size to those of the great European powers.[39] It aimed not only at political representation with relevant political partners, but most importantly also at economic representation around the world.[40] This global diplomatic outreach occurred in several stages. During the first years of the republic's existence and in quick succession, official diplomatic relations were taken up in particular with close Western allies; embassies in France, Italy, and Great Britain opened as early as October 1918 and thus during the state-founding process, and relations with the USA—another important advocate of Czechoslovak independence—were officially established in 1919. Regional neighbours and strategic allies, including Yugoslavia and Romania as future fellow members of the Little Entente as well as neighbouring Poland, were contacted in 1919, while connections to the two important but considerably more challenging neighbours Germany and Austria were instituted in the first quarter of 1920. Another diplomatic entity deserves special mention in the context of this first phase of diplomatic outreach: as a founding member of the League of Nations, Czechoslovakia maintained a permanent diplomatic representation in Geneva from 1921.[41]

Following this initial consolidation of international diplomatic relations, other regions of the world were gradually incorporated into the Czechoslovak diplomatic network. During the first half of the 1920s, the Americas became a target of increased diplomatic attention with the establishment of an embassy in Brazil and consulates in Argentina and Canada in 1920, followed by Mexico in 1923 and Chile in 1925. Further Latin American countries were subsequently added to bring the total number of representations to seven by 1938.[42] To the east, Turkey was among the first countries to be diplomatically engaged (in 1919), while China, India, and Japan received Czechoslovak diplomatic representations in 1920. Lebanon and Palestine followed in 1926.[43] Diplomatic relations with the African

38 Sládek, 'Edvard Beneš a malá dohoda' (n 10) 23.

39 See the assessment by various historians including Jaroslav Olša jr., 'Českoslovenští diplomaté v černé Africe, 1918–1955. Počátky sítě československých zastupitelských úřadů na jih od Sahary' (2005) 2 Mezinárodní Vztahy 90–105. The size of the Czechoslovak diplomatic network—especially in Africa—exceeded that of other Eastern European countries, as stated in Petr Zídek, *Československo a francouzská Afrika 1948–1968* (Libri 2006) 17–19. The diplomatic network was already the subject of debate and criticism during the interwar period, as argued in Klimek and Kubů, *Československá zahraniční politika* (n 6) 13.

40 Zídek, ibid, 17–18.

41 Koutská, *Českoslovenští diplomaté do roku 1945* (n 19) 101.

42 Jindřich Dejmek, *Diplomacie Československa, díl 1, Nástin dějin ministerstva zahraničních věcí a diplomacie (1918–1992)* (Academia 2012) 44–49 and 61–63.

43 For general information on the expansion of the diplomatic network, cf. Dejmek, *Diplomacie Československa* (n 42) 36–52, including Table 1 showing existing diplomatic representations in the year 1922, 47–49, and Table 2 showing existing diplomatic representations in 1938, 61–63.

continent began with a consulate in Alexandria in 1920, which was followed by an embassy in Cairo in 1923. Further consulates were established in Algeria (1925), Tunisia (1925), South Africa (1926), and—comparatively late—in Morocco (1936).[44] While the initial map of official diplomatic representations did not include the majority of Africa, many regions were eventually covered by honorary consulates, which reached territories such as Mauretania, Niger, Senegal, and Togo in West Africa (in 1927), Southern and Northern Rhodesia as well as Swaziland in Southern Africa (in 1930), and finally Kenya, Tanzania, Uganda, and Zanzibar in East Africa (in 1937).[45]

This diplomatic outreach was aimed especially at representing Czechoslovak economic interests, and it covered considerably more ground than the networks of other Eastern European countries. In fact, the Czechoslovak Republic was the only country in the region to attempt to establish a global consular and diplomatic presence, which was generally the prerogative of world powers.[46] By 1938, Czechoslovakia had eighty-eight representations abroad, comprising thirty-five embassies and fifty-three consulates in forty-three countries—not including the honorary consulates.[47]

C. The Quest for a Global Economy

Czechoslovakia's diplomatic outreach not just to European or Western capitals but also—especially since the late 1920s—increasingly to regions in Africa, Asia, and Latin America was primarily motivated by economic considerations. The new state's growing interest in non-European markets was well-founded, though like the diplomatic or security issues discussed above, economic relations were mainly concentrated on (Central) Europe—especially during the first years of the interwar period. The pre-war relations, which had mostly been concentrated on markets inside the Habsburg monarchy and on neighbouring countries, were to be continued under the new Czechoslovak government as well, making the successor states of the monarchy as well as Germany the most important trading partners for the Czechoslovak Republic between the wars.[48] At the same time, however, the expansion of international trade was increasingly reaching overseas regions: above all, the

[44] Zídek, *Československo a francouzská Afrika* (n 39) 18.

[45] Olša, 'Českoslovenští diplomaté' (n 39) 102–104.

[46] As assessed in Olša, 'Českoslovenští diplomaté' (n 39) 90 and 99. This is also hinted at in Zídek, *Československo a francouzská Afrika* (n 39) 17.

[47] Koutská, *Českoslovenští diplomaté do roku 1945* (n 19) 101; Dejmek, *Diplomacie Československa* (n 42) 61–63.

[48] Cf. Table 14 in Alice Teichova, 'Die Tschechoslowakei 1918–1980' in Wolfram Fischer et al. (eds), *Handbuch der europäischen Wirtschafts- und Sozialgeschichte, Bd. 6, Europäische Wirtschafts- und Sozialgeschichte vom Ersten Weltkrieg bis zur Gegenwart* (Klett-Cotta 1987) 598–639, here 617.

USA became a key trading partner, with exports growing from 4.2 per cent in 1924 to 9.3 per cent in 1937.[49] Economic relations with Africa, Asia, and Latin America were strengthening as well: while Czechoslovak exports to markets in Africa, Asia, and the Americas (without the USA) made up 5.2 per cent of all exports in 1924, their percentage had already grown to 8.4 per cent in 1929.[50] The 1930s further increased the share of these non-European markets. On the one hand, this was because Czechoslovak enterprises were increasingly avoiding the strong German competition in the Balkans and searching for new opportunities overseas.[51] On the other hand, the collapse of the European markets during the Great Depression led to a growing relevance of non-European markets for Czechoslovak trade, with Argentina, Brazil, China, Egypt, Japan, and Turkey in particular coming into focus. In 1937, as much as 16 per cent of all Czechoslovak exports were being sent to these non-European regions,[52] lending them a relevant position in Czechoslovak economic considerations as markets that still had growth potential according to the experts of the time.

This trend of economic outreach to non-European markets was also taken up and discussed by the professional public. For instance, the Prague-based Oriental Institute organized a lecture series in the early 1930s to discuss potential markets in Asia. The lectures dealt with possible trade with China, Indonesia, or Malaysia, as well as with Czechoslovak products in the context of their global competition. Despite government efforts to establish a broad diplomatic network in non-European regions for economic support as described above, the undertone of these talks—irrespective of the country they focused on—was one of fundamental criticism of the lack of state structures aiding Czechoslovak firms abroad. In his lecture on the economic conditions on Java, for example, the engineer Rudolf Staněk criticized the constantly declining market share of Czechoslovakian products on the Indonesian island and argued that Czechoslovak exports to the region could be organized much more effectively.[53] Rudolf Cicvárek, who was considered an expert on economic conditions in Asia after having lived in East and Southeast Asia for almost two decades, complained about the slow establishment of Czechoslovak global trading networks after 1918, claiming that this lack of pace had cost Czechoslovak trade ten years in its attempts to establish itself on the global market.[54]

[49] At the same time, the percentage of Czechoslovak imports coming from the USA grew from 5.6% in 1924 to 8.7% in 1937. Ibid.

[50] This increase is even more impressive when focusing on imports from Africa, Asia, and the Americas (without the USA). The percentage of imports from these continents rose from 2.5% in 1924 to 8.4% in 1929. Teichova, 'Die Tschechoslowakei 1918–1980' (n 48) 616–617.

[51] Ibid.

[52] Lacina, *Zlatá léta československého hospodářství* (n 5) 70; Teichova, 'Die Tschechoslowakei 1918–1980' (n 48) 617.

[53] Rudolf Staněk, *Hospodářské poměry na Javě* (Orientální ústav 1933) 25.

[54] Rudolf Cicvárek, *Obchodní poměry ve východní Asii* (Orientální ústav 1931) 15.

Assertive engagement with non-European markets was viewed not only as a purely economic objective, however—it also offered a solution for urgent domestic problems such as the dramatic rise in unemployment during the 1930s. Rudolf Cicvárek, for example, saw the national promotion of foreign trade and the institutions conducting it as a necessity that 'was never as important as today, because without trading houses overseas it is impossible to increase industrial production and fight long-term unemployment. That is why I repeat: The increase of our industry and the increase of our prosperity is reliant solely on our powerful export firms.'[55]

These arguments were not specific to markets in the Orient as the abovementioned lecture series may suggest, however. In fact, virtually all world regions were considered important for economic trade—be they in Africa, Asia, or Latin America.[56] In 1928, Vladimír Kybal, an acknowledged specialist on Latin America and ambassador to Brazil from 1925 to 1927, argued for a consistent Czechoslovak economic policy regarding South America. The South American market, which according to Kybal offered 'endless marketing possibilities', was set to become an 'economic battlefield' between Europe and the USA. He continued in this martial rhetoric with a description of the 'battle' for this 'only truly free market of today'—a battle that would be fought with huge financial, technical, cultural, and colonial investments. Therefore,

> Czechoslovakia, a strongly export-oriented state, cannot idly stand by if it does not want its interests to be affected and its export opportunities threatened, because it is important *to gain, to keep, and to expand* our place under the South American sun with all our might and to thus secure our future in the global competition.[57]

In the same document, Kybal focused not only on the possibilities offered by South America but urged the public 'and mainly those concerned in industry, trade, labor force, and intellectuals' to liberate themselves from the idea of 'the self-sufficiency of a landlocked country' manifested in an exclusive focus on Berlin and Vienna—and possibly on Paris and London—and instead to 'maintain a truly global policy, which would include the entire world as an object of systematic and coordinated political, economic, and cultural action'. As was often the case with this type of advocacy of global outreach in economic, diplomatic, or cultural terms, his demand

[55] Cicvárek, ibid, 38. Similar arguments are made by Rudolf Kalina, *Hospodářské poměry v Mandžursku* (Orientální ústav 1931) 20.

[56] In addition to the mentioned treatises focusing on Asia or Latin America, the African continent as an economic opportunity was covered in František V. Foit, *Autem napříč Afrikou, deník jedinečné cesty z Prahy do Kapského města, díl 1* (V Praze 1932) XI–XVII, and Antonín Blahovský, *Hospodářské poměry v Jihoafrické Unii* (Česká společnost národohospodářská 1938).

[57] Italics in the original. Vlastimil Kybal, *Jižní Amerika a Československo, s přehledem obchodní, finanční a emigrační činnosti jiných národů* (Merkur 1928) 6.

was immediately followed by words of defence or explanation: such outreach to Latin America 'is not an overestimation of our powers, but rather indispensable for the confirmation of our independence'.[58] Kybal's statements once more showcase a subtle rift between the Czechoslovak Republic and the great European powers, which would never have been questioned for their involvement in global markets.

D. The Quest for Czechoslovak Colonies

A further attempt to find global solutions for domestic affairs was the advocacy of Czechoslovak colonies, primarily in African, Asian, and Latin American regions. In this debate, which came up repeatedly during the interwar period from the founding of the republic to its demise in 1938, the term 'colony' was used with various different meanings and graduations ranging from colonialism to mere settlements abroad, but its purpose was always to address issues such as high unemployment, overpopulation, or insufficient outlet markets.

The discussion on potential Czechoslovak colonies has so far garnered little academic interest—and indeed it was a small and somewhat marginal debate.[59] Nevertheless, it is encountered both in the public and in professional circles. Diplomats, journalists, and entrepreneurs contributed to it, and it was even discussed at the Paris Peace Conference.[60] More importantly, however, this focus on a project that was never realized offers insights into contemporary notions, wishes, priorities, and arguments, and enables an understanding of what was considered possible without any teleological hindsight. First and foremost, the debate shows clearly how experts and the public viewed the Czechoslovak Republic's position in a global context.

No matter what kinds of colonies were called for or where they were to be located—in Africa, Asia, or Latin America—they were generally envisioned to serve the same purposes: firstly, both in the sense of territorial acquisition and of settlements, colonies were thought to support domestic affairs by way of easing unemployment and other social problems through emigration while at the same time protecting emigrants from assimilating to other nations and therefore 'being

[58] Ibid, 11.

[59] Some historians have even described the calls for Czechoslovak colonies as 'absurd' or as marginal chauvinist demands by ultranationalists. Cf. Stefan Albrecht, 'Böhmen liegt am Meer. Bemühungen um den Aufbau einer eigenen tschechoslowakischen Hochseeschifffahrt in der Zwischenkriegszeit' (2004) 46/4 Österreichische Osthefte 515–534, here 516; Klimek and Kubů, *Československá zahraniční politika* (n 6) 24–25. For a more detailed analysis of the Czechoslovak calls for colonization, cf. Sarah Lemmen, *Tschechen auf Reisen. Repräsentationen der außereuropäischen Welt und nationale Identität in Ostmitteleuropa 1890–1938* (Böhlau 2018), especially 80–100.

[60] See the Memorandum o zájmu Československé republiky na mezinárodní úpravě otázky kolonií. Archiv Ministerstva zahraničních věcí, Pařížský archiv 1918–21, book 54, document 5210.

lost' to the Czechoslovak nation.[61] Secondly, these colonies were to become both secure outlets for Czechoslovak goods and preferential suppliers of raw materials, thus bolstering the national economy.[62] Thirdly, the debates about colonies broached the issue of Czechoslovakia's standing in Europe and in the world. In this context, colonies—understood as overseas territories under the political rule of Czechoslovakia—were depicted as a sign of a country's 'adulthood':[63] following the example of most Western European countries, colonies were to enhance the standing of the Czechoslovak Republic—albeit only in terms of prestige and not through exploitation.[64]

These key arguments in favour of Czechoslovak colonies appeared roughly in chronological order. The argument for a 'proper' colony under Czechoslovak rule as a form of prestige or as confirmation of the achievement of complete state sovereignty was primarily expressed during the founding period of the republic. As early as 1919, Jan Havlasa, journalist and later Czechoslovak ambassador to Brazil (1920–1924), wrote a manifest about 'Czech [!] colonies overseas'.[65] In his sixteen-page booklet, he referred to (uncited) newspaper articles discussing 'the possibility of transferring the African Togo to the Czechoslovak Republic', coming to the conclusion that this idea was 'not as absurd as it may look to many [readers]'.[66] A colony, he said, would not only strengthen Czechoslovak trade but could also absorb the majority of those who were poised to emigrate, and therefore keep them working '*for the ideological and economic improvement*' of the nation.[67] As potential areas for colonization, Havlasa proposed the former German colony of Togo or 'Czech West Africa' as a convenient supplier of cotton, as well as a 'Czech New Guinea' as a provider of cocoa and other raw materials and foods.[68] As a further option in the northern hemisphere, Havlasa suggested Russian Kamchatka—which from a strategic perspective was separated from Czechoslovakia 'only by a single, albeit enormous country'—as a source of metals and coal.[69]

In 1923, Vilém Němec, who had been living in North Africa for over twenty-five years, discussed the potential usefulness and prosperity of a Czechoslovak colony and proposed the lease of a region in Abyssinia comparable to the German

[61] This argument was used among others by Jan Havlasa, *České kolonie zámořské* (Naklad. spisů Jana Havlasy 1919) 13; Jan Kořínek, *Koloniální problémy zítřka* (Nákladem České společnosti národohospodářské 1939) 17; Vilém Němec, *Je-li nám třeba kolonisace?* (Ze zkušeností v Habeši) (Vilém Němec 1923) 5.

[62] Havlasa, ibid, 15; Němec, ibid, 5.

[63] Němec, ibid, 4.

[64] The difference between Czech colonization and that by Western European countries was discussed by Rudolf Cicvárek, *V čarovných tropech jest naše budoucnost* (Pražská akciová tiskárna 1929) 74; Alois Musil, 'Naše úkoly v orientalistice a v orientě' (1920) 27/3–4 Naše doba 9.

[65] Havlasa, *České kolonie zámořské* (n 61).

[66] Ibid, 12.

[67] Italics in the original. Havlasa, *České kolonie zámořské* (n 61) 13.

[68] Ibid, 15.

[69] Ibid, 14–15.

acquisition of territory from China in the nineteenth century. Like Havlasa, Němec stated economic (such as trade advantages and a constant supply of raw materials) and social aspects (such as a national destination for emigrants) as the main reasons for his advocacy of colonization. His ambitions were already somewhat more modest, however, with the territory he envisioned being comparable in size to 'our Těšín', a small town on the Polish-Czechoslovak border.[70]

In the late 1920s and early 1930s, talk of a political colony had become almost muted, but the economic and social advantages of an overseas settlement were still being considered. The focus was now less on prestige and more on practical solutions for urgent social issues at home. In 1929, the specialist on Asian affairs Rudolf Cicvárek joined the chorus of those calling for a Czechoslovak colony. His argument included the prevalent focus on economic advantages, but he spoke explicitly of a colony 'deserted of people' that would offer emigrants plenty of work opportunities. Cicvárek proceeded to distinguish his idea of Czechoslovak colonialism from that of Western European countries, as 'all European colonies are based on aggressiveness, imperialism and capitalism. Our colony should be the exact opposite.'[71]

Soon after the publication of Cicvárek's treatise, debates about emigration and overseas colonies virtually stopped with the onset of the economic crisis. Only in the late 1930s—and under very different circumstances—was the discourse on colonization rekindled to a degree. In 1939, the journalist and expert on Moroccan-Czechoslovak relations Jan Kořínek looked back somewhat wistfully upon the beginnings of the republic: 'We have longed for our own Czech colonies, where we could have settled and where we could have kept the surplus of our population for our nation. After the war this dream seemed to come true [...] but [eventually] no concrete action was taken.'[72] In keeping with the spirit of the time, instead of a colonial manifest, Kořínek published a 'Health Guide for Czechoslovak Tourists and Colonists in French North Africa', which prepared emigrants not for life in Czechoslovak colonies but nevertheless for colonial life overseas—and thus for an existence far away from the political turmoil in Central Europe.

E. 'As a Sovereign State, We Must Engage in International World Politics': The Founding of the Oriental Institute in Prague

As demonstrated above, public debate on national security, economy, and emigration in interwar Czechoslovakia went far beyond the purely regional context and pursued solutions in a global perspective. Similar debates accompanied the

70 Němec, *Je-li nám třeba kolonisace?* (n 61) 5.
71 Cicvárek, *V čarovných tropech jest naše budoucnost* (n 64), 74.
72 Kořínek, *Koloniální problémy zítřka* (n 61), 17.

establishment of the Oriental Institute (Orientální ústav) in Prague[73] during the early days of the republic. President Masaryk invited Orientalist Alois Musil to Prague to develop such an institution based on his experience with a similar institute founded in Vienna in 1916.[74] Musil presented his ideas on what an Oriental Institute in Prague should be in 1920 in an article entitled 'Our Tasks in Oriental Studies and in the Orient'.[75] In his endeavour for stronger Czechoslovak-Oriental relations, he appealed to researchers, merchants, manufacturers, state representatives, and individuals willing to emigrate. To Musil, it was essential for a sovereign state 'to engage in international world politics'.[76] Read inversely, this argument also confirms that the Czechoslovak Republic could be a truly sovereign state only if it engaged in world politics (rather than contenting itself with regional politics). In this context, the Orient—which was never defined geographically—held a special role:

> Our young state tries to prepare its relations with other countries, and therefore has to build the base for these relations at home. A central part of the regions important to us is the Orient, and [that means] both the Near East and the Far East. Especially the Near East is of great importance to us and always will be.[77]

This exceptional significance of the Orient for the Czechoslovak Republic manifested on three levels according to Musil. Firstly, he described the Orient as the perfect counterpart to Czechoslovakia in terms of economic needs, presenting it as indispensable for Czechoslovak exports and imports since it not only provided inexpensive raw materials but was also a viable market for Czechoslovak products—and thereby offering the same arguments that were used in the colonial debate.[78]

[73] For further information on the founding of the Oriental Institute and the debates accompanying it, cf. Sarah Lemmen, "Unsere Aufgaben in der Orientalistik und im Orient'—Die Gründung und die erste Dekade des Prager *Orientalischen Instituts* in der Zwischenkriegszeit' in Robert Born and Sarah Lemmen (eds), *Orientalismen in Ostmitteleuropa. Diskurse, Akteure und Disziplinen vom 19. Jahrhundert bis zum Zweiten Weltkrieg* (Postcolonial Studies 19, transcript 2014) 119–143.

[74] For information on the *k.k. österreichische Orient- und Überseegesellschaft*, cf. Karl Johannes Bauer, *Alois Musil. Theologe, Forscher, Gelehrter und Stammesscheich. Eine Darstellung seines Lebens im Dienste der österreichischen Forschung und der Verbindung der Monarchie mit dem türkischen und arabischen Orient* (DPhil thesis, University of Vienna 1984) 223–229. For more information on the illustrious Alois Musil—Arabist, theologian, professor of biblical studies and Arabic at the University of Vienna and later in Prague, discoverer of the desert castle of Qasr Amba, advisor to the imperial family, and Austrian adversary of the more famous British Thomas Edward 'Lawrence of Arabia' during the First World War, see as an introduction Karl Johannes Bauer, *Alois Musil, Wahrheitssucher in der Wüste* (Böhlau 1989). On Musil's time in Prague, see Pavel Žďarský, 'Alois Musil jako zakladatel československé orientalistiky, Z Vídně do Prahy' (2013) 68/1 Nový Orient 50–56.

[75] Alois Musil, 'Naše úkoly v orientalistice' (n 64) 2–20. Cf. also Jiří Bečka, 'Alois Musil, duchovní otec Orientálního ústavu' in Rudolf Veselý (ed), *Alois Musil—český vědec světového jména* (Rozpravy Orientalia 1, Globe 1995) 29–32, here 29.

[76] Musil, 'Naše úkoly v orientalistice' (n 64) 9.

[77] Ibid, 2.

[78] Ibid, 16.

Especially in economic terms, as Musil phrased it, only the Orient would be able to 'replace the colony we do not have, although we need one'.[79]

Secondly, Musil thought that Czechoslovakia could likewise play a unique role for the Orient. He declared that the republic, with its large numbers of unemployed workers and high demand for raw materials, would perfectly complement the Orient's lack of skilled workers and know-how as well as its surplus of commodities.[80] But even in economic terms, his train of thought went beyond this quasi-colonial perspective and effectively turned it into an anti-colonial argument: he claimed that at the time, that is, in 1920, the Czechoslovak Republic was the only perfect partner capable of tending to the needs of the Orient, especially in regard to skilled workers and expertise: while Great Britain, France, and Italy needed their populations for their own overseas territories and other countries were forced to employ foreigners themselves due to a lack of skilled workers, it was Czechoslovakia in particular which, with its 'surplus of people',[81] was ideally equipped to support the Orient. At the same time, Czechoslovakia's problems with unemployment and 'overpopulation' could be resolved through directed emigration. Similar to the arguments for a colony overseas, Musil stressed that emigrants would not assimilate in the Orient but rather maintain their Czech (or Slovak) identity.[82]

Other aspects would support Czechoslovak relations with the Orient even further: as a country without a fleet, and especially without a colonial history, Czechoslovakia would win the trust of the oriental countries easily: 'The Orient willingly accepts us, because it knows we have neither a political nor a religious hidden agenda.'[83] In this sense, Musil was sure, the Czechoslovak Republic would gain more favour in the Orient than any of the great European powers.

Musil also considered cultural and academic relations with the Orient essential besides economic ties, and he argued explicitly against 'constant' criticism that academic dealings with the Orient were 'exotic' and a luxury reserved only for 'rich Englishmen and Frenchmen'.[84] The Oriental Institute received support from a wide range of advocates and experts early on: President Masaryk not only instigated its foundation, but also contributed financial aid from his presidential funds.[85] Three ministries (Foreign Affairs, Education, and Trade) were involved in its planning and establishment, as were chambers of commerce, banks, and manufacturers as

79 Ibid, 16.
80 Ibid, 2.
81 Ibid.
82 Ibid.
83 Ibid, 3.
84 Ibid, 6.
85 Zdeněk Fafl and Vincenc Lesný (eds), *Věstník Orientálního ústavu v Praze za desítiletí 1928–1938, sv. 2* (Orientální ústav 1938) 34. Cf. also Jiří Bečka and Miloslav Krása, 'On the History of the Oriental Institute, 1922–1952' in Jiří Prosecký, Blahoslav Hruška, and Vladislav Dudák (eds), *The Oriental Institute Prague, Basic Information* (Czechoslovak Academy of Sciences 1991) 18–33, here 34.

well as leading Orientalists from Charles University in Prague. This spectrum of supporters and sponsors demonstrates the broad interest in a growing political, economic, and academic engagement with the Orient and—as can be assumed—beyond on a global scale.[86]

III. Conclusion: A Czechoslovak Outlook onto the World

In retrospect, the first Czechoslovak Republic has often been described as 'small' and occasionally as 'betrayed' or even 'failed'.[87] These assessments are usually based on the ultimate outcome of the interwar period, which would prove the country's internal politics as well as foreign affairs and international relations to be either insufficient or flawed. But close examination of the founding period as well as the state's course during the 1920s and 1930s suggests a different perspective on the international standing of the Czechoslovak Republic and the goals and hopes that were tied to it.

At the same time, by focusing not only on obvious relations to chiefly European countries but also on relations with African, Asian, or Latin American states, as well as by concentrating both on what was (active membership at the League of Nations; increase of trade with overseas markets) and on what could have been (expansion of a diplomatic network comparable in size to those of Western European powers; Czechoslovak settlements or actual colonies overseas), we achieve a better understanding of what the international standing of the Czechoslovak Republic was perceived to be or to become.

Early on, a clear focus was placed on international relations (political, economic, cultural) reaching far beyond the European continent. This included active membership in the League of Nations, a strong diplomatic representation in Africa, economic expansion to Latin America, and plans for the founding of settlements in Asia. The importance of this outreach for the republic was emphasized by an unusually large Ministry of Foreign Affairs. Taken individually, these efforts might be considered surprising or even 'absurd' and 'exotic'—a luxury only the great nations such as the British and the French could afford, as contemporaries and historians alike have opined.[88] Taken together and put into context, however, this striving for global outreach on various levels appears more coherent.

[86] Despite this profound support, however, and mainly due to conflicts among the various involved parties, the establishment of the institute was put on hold for several years. The efforts were intensified once more in 1927 before the inaugural meeting could finally be held in 1928. For a more detailed analysis on the founding period of the Oriental Institute in Prague, see Lemmen, 'Unsere Aufgaben in der Orientalistik und im Orient' (n 71).

[87] Elisabeth Bakke, *Doomed to Failure? The Czechoslovak Nation Project and the Slovak Autonomist Reaction 1919–1938* (series of dissertations submitted to the Department of Political Science, Faculty of Social Sciences, University of Oslo, No. 11/99, 1999); Heimann, *Czechoslovakia* (n 1).

[88] Albrecht, 'Böhmen liegt am Meer' (n 59) 516; Havlasa, *České kolonie zámořské* (n 61) 12; Klimek and Kubů, *Československá zahraniční politika* (n 6) 9; Musil, 'Naše úkoly v orientalistice' (n 64) 6.

The interwar years were a period of co-constitution not only of national and international orders, but also of national and imperial ones—and while the Czechoslovak Republic clearly represented one of these juxtapositions, it was reaching for the other.[89] Relatively small in size but strong in economic terms, Czechoslovakia exhibited characteristics of both a 'small country' and a regional power, and outreach at the supraregional or even global level in the realms of economy, diplomacy, and culture was pursued in both capacities. International relations were considered to be of utmost importance especially during the founding years of the republic. The large foreign ministry, the founding memberships in the League of Nations and the Little Entente, the plan for a diplomatic network larger than that of any other Eastern European country, and even the debates about the establishment of Czechoslovak colonies (although these were not endorsed by government officials) all underscore this argument. The Czechoslovak Republic's aspiration to succeed Austria as the regional political and economic power likewise emphasizes this assessment of the country's international standing.

By the early 1930s, some of these global ambitions had tempered noticeably. The call for colonies had been replaced by more humble stipulations of settlements abroad, and the global outreach now concentrated mainly on economic aspects, with respectable results in several overseas regions. By the end of the decade, the initial hopes and visions for Czechoslovakia's bright future had withered almost completely. The international outreach in the diplomatic, economic, and cultural spheres had not succeeded in securing the republic's prosperity or even its existence. Not even the League of Nations was able—or willing—to protect its former founding member. Relations to Africa, Asia, and the Americas changed dramatically as these regions lost their status as 'economic battlefield[s]'[90] for adventurous entrepreneurs and instead became safe havens for Czechoslovak refugees.[91]

By 1938, the highly promising Czechoslovak Republic of 1918, which had convinced the international community not only of its political and economic prospects but also of its democratic character and its inherent 'Europeanness', had been abandoned and reduced, in the words of British Prime Minister Neville Chamberlain, to 'a far away country [with] people of whom we know nothing'.[92]

[89] Cf. Susan Pedersen, *The Guardians, The League of Nations and the Crisis of Empire* (Oxford University Press 2015) for a convincing take on the interwar period as an imperial order.

[90] Kybal, *Jižní Amerika a Československo* (n 57), 6.

[91] Peter Heumos, *Die Emigration aus der Tschechoslowakei nach Westeuropa und dem Nahen Osten 1938–1945* (Oldenbourg 1989).

[92] As quoted in the article, 'Prime Minister on the Issues' *The Times* (28 September 1938) 10.

An Epilogue to the Making and Unmaking of Central Europe and Global Order

Patricia Clavin

In *Leviathan*, Thomas Hobbes gave us one of the earliest uses of the term 'epilogue' to denote the concluding part of a literary work.[1] This foundational text in the history of modern political thought on the 'reason of state' is an appropriate starting point here, because so many essays in the *Remaking of Central Europe* touch on Hobbesian themes of sovereignty, human agency, fear, and conflict. Moreover, the founding of the League of Nations, and its deep and varied impact on post-imperial Europe, facilitated the globalization of the nation state as the dominant mode of political organization, a trend too often taken as a given by political scientists.[2] As we see in the pages of this text, the pre-eminence of the nation state was not taken for granted in Central and Eastern Europe, in the way it has been subsequently in much international relations literature on the rise of global and regional institutions of global governance.[3]

The relationship between the League and Central Europe was foundational for the institution, the region, and the world. Much of the League of Nations' project of global ordering was directed at Central and Eastern Europe. The Paris Peace treaties that set the region's new territorial parameters were incorporated into the body of international law overseen by the League. The new states of Central and Eastern Europe were the League's squabbling foster children, and the organization's capacities, notably in the field of health, finance, and refugees grew directly out of the efforts to bring order to the region.[4] The League of Nations was first focused

[1] 'Epilogue, n.' *OED Online*, Oxford University Press, March 2020, <www.oed.com/view/Entry/63416>, accessed 25 May 2020.

[2] Thomas Hobbes, *Leviathan. Revised student edition* (Richard Tuck (ed), Cambridge University Press 1996) xiv.

[3] See e.g. Peter Evans, Dietrich Rueschemeyer, and Thelda Skocpol (eds), *Bringing the State Back In* (Cambridge University Press 1985) . Significantly, Skocpol identifies Polyani's *The Great Transformation* as a key reference in their project to theorize the locus of societal dynamics away from civil society to the state. See Theda Skocpol, 'Bringing the State Back In: Strategies of Analysis in Current Research' in Evans, Rueschemeyer, and Skocpol, ibid, 6.

[4] Patricia Clavin, *Securing the World Economy: The Reinvention of the League of Nations, 1920–1946* (Oxford University Press 2013) 12.

Patricia Clavin, *An Epilogue to the Making and Unmaking of Central Europe and Global Order* In: *Remaking Central Europe.* Edited by: Peter Becker and Natasha Wheatley, Oxford University Press (2020). © the many contributors.
DOI: 10.1093/oso/9780198854685.003.0016

on bringing order to European affairs. During the course of the twentieth century, this western regional system assumed global dominance. It was an era that ended early in the twenty-first century. By then the end of western dominance seemed irreversible. Relations between states were changing, with new powers emergent, notably 'Superpower China' and 'Rising India', with the structures of global capitalism in flux, and with new technologies—notably the internet—creating new, transnational forms of political mobilization.[5]

At the point at which the US-led world order appeared to be dissolving, Peter Becker and Natasha Wheatley draw out the four ways in which the *Remaking of Central Europe* shapes, and reflects, the building of the western international order in the era after 1918. Recognizing the order's liberal and illiberal characteristics, they deepen our understanding of a part of the world that lay at the centre of the League of Nations project. They identify the ghostly afterlives of the Habsburg imperial order in the League; and the (re)casting of the region, and its place in the trinity of nation, region, and the international that orders the globe.

The chapters develop emergent trends in the wider new literature on the League of Nations, and the other international organizations and transnational networks that worked with, or through, the League, addressing different elements of the League's agency, such as health, the policing of borders and people, and practices of financial oversight. Nationalization and internationalization move in lockstep, most overtly perhaps in the League's initiatives to stabilize and integrate national economies with the international one. In this volume, the programmatic features of Sluga's stress on the intellectual ties of national*ism* to international*ism*, by contrast, are rendered concrete.[6] The League and Central Europe were 'made' together. This shared history is a project of construction borne of policy, legal norms, scientific exchange, and bureaucratic performance. National borders and populations, central banks and public health schemes are just some of the examples of the national collectives fashioned by the laws and practices embodied in, and developed through, the League of Nations working as an international agent, and as a site of transnational exchange.

Here, epilogue will serve as prologue. I want to take the four central signposts of the roads travelled by this book to suggest some future directions for research that emerges from them, and that also inform my work. These are exploring international orders and global currents; recognizing the geography in geopolitics, a term usually taken to mean a crude form of power politics; and the return of global health as the primary concern of global governance.

[5] Andrew Hurrell, 'Power Transitions, Global Justice and the Virtues of Pluralism' (2013) 27/2 Ethics and International Affairs 189.

[6] Glenda Sluga, *Internationalism in the Age of Nationalism* (University of Pennsylvania Press 2013).

I. International Orders and Global Currents

The creation of the League of Nations changed the configuration of international order through its stress on open diplomacy, international law, institutionalized cooperation, and the multilateralism that came with it. Contemporaries regarded the permanent move to a 'world in conference' through institutionalized multilateralism as a radical step.[7] Historians have rather taken this move for granted since, yet it would be essential for the development of regional or post-imperial polities. The authors' use of the term 'international order' reflects the language of the period. The League existed in a time of inter-national relations. The hyphen in the concept is significant. International relations stood for the relations between states, and the emerging field of International Relations (IR) in the political sciences studied them in relation to understanding the origins and character of war and peace.

From studies of the West, we know that foundational chairs and taught courses in IR were strongly influenced by intellectual and practical developments at the League of Nations, with summer schools held at the new Graduate Institute in Geneva, and in other capitals and universities, notably Berlin, Cambridge, London, Paris, and New York.[8] The Nordic network, formulated as a 'peace tradition', was an analogous and equally important regional network.[9] As yet, the impact of other parts of the world, notably in Central and Eastern European universities and education, is much less clear. The volume offers suggestive evidence that figures such as Pirquet were influential League advocates and educationalists. My research into Anglo-Austrian exchanges, exploring the connections between the British nutritionist Harriet Chick and Pirquet, as well as the role of William Beveridge, Director of the London School of Economics (LSE) offer tantalizing insights into an under-appreciated network of exchange in political and social sciences.[10] Here is another afterlife of the Austro-Hungarian empire, reconnected, reinforced, and reshaped via the League, and associated Geneva-based institutions.

In December 1918, as part of his final duties for the Food Ministry, Beveridge agreed to serve as the British member of an Inter-Allied Mission of Relief of German Austria. Beveridge was one of the first international observers to witness the Austrian hunger crisis first hand. Like many progressive Liberals, he had been shaped by intellectual and political currents emanating from Central Europe before 1914. Now, the disastrous effects of the region's transition from imperial

[7] 'The World in Conference' (1920) 10/40 The Roundtable. The Commonwealth Journal of International Affairs 721.

[8] Jan Stöckmann, 'The formation of International Relations: ideas, practices and institutions, 1914–1940' (DPhil thesis, University of Oxford 2017).

[9] Helge Pharo, 'Norway's Peace Tradition Spanning 100 Years' (2005) 93/1 Scandinavian Review 15–23.

[10] For a preliminary taste, listen to 'Armistice 1918: Feeding the Peace', Broadcast on Radio 4, 11 November 2018 <https://www.bbc.co.uk/programmes/m00013tr>.

rule, and the encounters that followed left a further imprint. After meeting representatives of the new Austrian state on Christmas Eve, 1918, he recorded: 'I am ashamed before them as I used to be at going to interview beggars at the door at Toynbee [a reference to Toynbee Hall—East London settlement, where he had been warden]. For beggars they are—sans food, sans money, sans country, sans everything.'[11] Beveridge was one of the first outsiders to describe the crisis that captured the international imagination. Thereafter, he led annual summer study schools to Vienna and was a regular correspondent and supporter of many of Central Europe's leading Liberal intellectuals. These connections and his commitment led him to found and lead the Academic Assistance Council in 1933, which rescued imperiled academics from Central Europe. Today, renamed the Council for At-Risk Academics (CARA), this British organization continues to help scholars at risk around the world. Beveridge subsequently found employment at the LSE. He used his position as Director to help academics at risk from fascism sanctuary in the UK, exemplified by the famous case of Austrian economist Friederich Hayek. Beveridge employed him at the LSE. The work was a product of the continued reputation of Central European science and artistic life in the West. Pirquet was renowned in paediatrics, and had a lasting impact on the development of Anglo-American nutritional science as a result of the Austrian hunger crisis. His account complements the story of Alfons Dopsch and the League's Intellectual Cooperation Programme. In both cases, Pirquet and Dopsch's personal and professional circumstances were not necessarily enhanced by international engagement. At the same time, their histories indicate at least a partial international restoration of the esteemed reputation of Central European arts and letters, and scientific life that was so vibrant before July 1914. It suggests that fascism and the Second World War exacted more lasting damage on European scientific networks than the First World War, as key figures were pushed into exile in Britain and the United States, at the same time as US institutions, methods, and power was ascendant.[12] The effects on Britain were significant, with the Second World War breaking a century-long orientation of the physical and social scientific worlds away from Central Europe and towards the United States. The long-term implications of this disruption continued to be apparent in the twenty-first century.

[11] Private papers of William Beveridge, Archives of London School of Economics (hereafter LSE). LSE BEVERIDGE/10/2 'Diary of Visit to Vienna, Prag and Buda Pesth', December 1918–January 1919; W.H. Beveridge, 'Peace in Austria: A Study of Social and Industrial Conditions with a Programme for Reconstruction based on a Personal Visit to Austria', 7 February 1920.

[12] Johannes Feichtinger's essay suggests the International Commission on Intellectual Cooperation (ICIC) served as a node of reconnection for Austria in ways that revise the view the First World War permanently ruptured cooperation across the Allied and Central Power devised which is suggested by looking at the International Research Council and the International Union of Academies in their own right. Compare to Robert Fox, *Science without Frontiers: Cosmopolitanism and National Interests in the World of Learning, 1870–1940* (Corvallis 2016).

This new historical writing on the League has stressed that the organization's founding vision and impact was a world order organized around the primacy of the state, whether nation or empire. The co-existence of these two types of state models within the League, in particular, generated problems. It enabled powers who wanted to revise the Paris Peace Settlement, notably Germany and Italy, to demand the restoration of empire, at the same time as they challenged the quality of British and French imperial governance through the League. It was not just a consequence of the Permanent Mandates Commission that imperial rule was subject to intense public scrutiny.[13] The conflict inherent in this vision reverberated through all the sections and commissions. It resounded across all its fields of activities, in discussions over global trade regimes, debates in disarmament where military—especially naval—resources played a prominent role, and in League investigations into raw materials—in short, it affected the entire institutional body of the League of Nations.

The conflicting visions of sovereignty represented in the League reflected the character of global politics in the period. It is significant that while the 'have-not' wannabe imperial powers of Germany, Italy, and Japan both challenged and frustrated aspects of the League's work in the 1920s, but they articulated their frustrations in Geneva, and with reference to the legal treaties of the peace enshrined in the League. It was in the 1930s that these states moved aggressively against League-based norms thanks to the withdrawal of US capital after 1929, and devastating financial turbulence in 1931, in a process akin to developments worldwide after 2008. From 1929, nationalist leaders challenged the League across the range of its operations, from trade and health, through disarmament and the arbitration of international conflict.

At the same time, perspectives on the League from Central Europe showcased here complicates the binary picture of empire versus nation state, and general view of modern international relations that the latter is the natural heir to the former. As Lemmen shows, the new Czechoslovakian republic harboured imperial ambitions of its own. By contrast, the unwilling postcolonial states of Austria and Hungary did not hanker for the restitution of the Habsburg Empire in the ways that shaped German and Italian relations with the League; nor was the League able to contain all the effects that followed from Austro-Hungary's disintegration, even as the organization was shaped by its afterlives. The rapid and chaotic character of Austro-Hungary's dissolution shattered British commentators; an ominous portent for some of what the future might hold for empire as global recovery faltered after the First World War.[14]

13 Susan Pedersen, *The Guardians: The League of Nations and the Crisis of Empire* (Oxford University Press 2015) 1.

14 Record of General Correspondence of the Foreign Office, The National Archives, Kew London (Hereafter TNA FCO), TNA FCO 371/4647/C12705, Sir William Goode to the Chancellor of the Exchequer, 22 Nov. 1920; H.G. Wells, *Washington and the Riddle of the Peace* 4–5 (London 1922), 4–5.

Politics infused every facet of the League's work. Technical aspects of its work—in transportation, health, policing, finance, and trade—engaged with scientific and practical challenges of effecting cooperation. But the term 'technical' camouflaged political agendas contested within and beyond Geneva.[15] League internationalism, as the volume underlines, was universal in its claims, and particular in its outcomes. This was a striking feature of its work as the essays on its interventions in passports, trade law, and policing show. It was not confined to the League. It became a prominent characteristic of post-1945 international organizations too.

The chapters underscore how Central Europe and the League shaped one another. Throughout, the League's blend of liberal internationalism, was both confronted by, and in dialogue with, Communist and Fascist internationalist ambitions. We know this had local effects. In Geneva, Italian Fascists, for example, confronted liberal values in the Assembly Room of the Palais des Nations and in demonstrations on the streets; sometimes violently.[16] The chapters evoke other local to international interactions; the analysis could go further. For example, how far, and in what ways, do international ideas and practices play into local politics in the city or regional governments? How did the great cities of Vienna and Budapest respond to the League's loans and financial and oversight? And did international encounters inform urban and rural relations?

The Galician-born Max Beer was a prolific, yet often neglected, commentator of the relationship between local, national, and international Socialism and Liberalism. In 1921, he argued of Manchester and London, 'politically sovereign in the legislature, the workman is merely a hireling in the workshop; he can make and unmake Governments, but has no say whatever in the arrangement of his daily work'. Beer anticipated the poor's 'mentality' was now 'passing from politics to economics, and from economics to social ethics' on a local, national, and international level.[17] He was to be disappointed. By 1933, the League's move into economic and social questions frustrated and infuriated him because its 'narrow approach' left state power and capitalism intact.[18]

Contributors to *The Remaking of Central Europe* underline that contemporaries' understanding of international order were primarily state-centric. What is less clear is how the generation studied here understood and recognized the character, variation, and limits of states' power in the international realm. The problem preoccupied Raymond Aron, a French-Jewish political scientist, who taught at Cologne University in the early 1930s. His first book was preoccupied with the Nazis' rise to power. Thirty years later, by now a prominent journalist and public intellectual, his seminal 1962 text, *Peace and War: A Theory of International*

[15] Clavin, *Securing the World Economy* (n 4).
[16] Elisabetta Tollardo, *Fascist Italy and the League of Nations, 1922–1935* (Palgrave Macmillan 2016).
[17] Max Beer, *A History of British Socialism*, Vol.II (Harcourt, Brace and Howe 1921) 198–199.
[18] Max Beer, *The League on Trial: A Journey to Geneva* (Houghton Mifflin Company 1933) 166.

Relations, asked: '[U]nder what conditions would men [*sic*] divided in so many ways be able not merely to avoid destruction, but to live together relatively well on one planet?'[19] If Aron's question appeared Wilsonian, this stress on 'one planet' reflected the period's new sense of planetary vulnerability and inequality. Biologist Rachel Carson and British economist Barbara Ward, whose books were published in the same year as Aron's, captured these features of what would become calls for a new world order.[20] It marks the shift from notions of international to global order, and what in the twenty-first century we might more readily reference as the practices of global governance. The latter concept has been the focus of a great deal of work in IR over the past thirty years. It is understood to be a response to the challenge of generating collective action as a result of growing societal, ecological, and economic interdependence.[21] These processes of globalization led to an increasing need for coordination and cooperation.

Aron gave his readers a set of tools for thinking about international relations, delineating three core components that comprise the ability of one political unit to impose its will on another: territory, resources, and the collective capacity for action. His 'ideal type' was the United States, a vast country, bordered by oceans that protected it from invasion, and rich in natural resources. The USA's open economy, too, he argued, enabled it to assert its power globally in ways that no other state in the twentieth century was able to match. What was especially novel at the time was Aron's stress on the collective capacity for action of a state. He asked, how effectively could its people work together for a common cause or objective? The question invites us to explore the purpose of a country's international policy, and the goals underlying it, which, as we have seen in this volume, is not something that is separate from the domestic arena.

Aron stressed the primacy of politics in shaping the international order. Foreign policy was not some iron law of national interest that was immune to changes in government or ideology. His argument came back into vogue after 2003 as the early triumphalism of the post-Cold War years gave way to a new turbulence in international politics. But Aron's view of the world largely was one where states smash

[19] This was Stanley Hoffmann's reformulation of Aron's research question. Compare, Stanley Hoffmann, 'Conference Report on the Conditions of World Order' (1966), *Daedalus* 95:2, 456, with Raymond Aron, *Peace and War: A Theory of International Relations* (Doubleday & Co 1966), x.

[20] Rachel Carson, *Silent Spring* (Houghton Mifflin 1962); Barbara Ward, *The Rich Nations and the Poor Nations* (W. W. Norton & Company 1962).

[21] See Andrew Hurrell, *On Global Order: Power, Values, and the Constitution of International Society* (Oxford University Press 2007) 13–15, 95–120; James N. Rosenau and Ernst-Otto Czempiel (eds), *Governance without Government: Order and Change in World Politics* (Cambridge University Press 1992); Robert O. Keohane, *Power and Governance in a Partially Globalized World* (Routledge 2002). For the move from international cooperation to global governance in the practices of the League, see Patricia Clavin, 'The Ben Pimlott Memorial Lecture 2019. Britain and the Making of Global Order after 1919' (2020) hwaa007 Twentieth Century British History <https://doi.org/10.1093/tcbh/hwaa007>, accessed 27 May 2020. For a global ordering approaching to race after 1919, see, Musab Younis, 'The grand machinery of the world: race, global order and the black Atlantic' (DPhil thesis, University of Oxford 2017).

into one another like marbles in a net-bag. He had much less to say about how states related to—or were affected by—global currents embodied in financial markets or communicable disease; phenomena that disregarded or exploited borders. Unlike Carson and Ward, he did not have much to say about the limits of the planet itself either.

The period covered by *Remaking Central Europe*, like the world today, underscores that for all state leaders—whether they govern states that are powerful in the ways Aron described or not—the realm of their foreign relations is where they have the least control. Engagement with the international highlights the limits of their agency. Meanwhile, IR concepts have moved from international order to global order, defined by the relations between states, markets, and civil society; the language of war and peace recast as one of global challenges. Carson and Ward sketched out some of the global forces—transnational crosscurrents—that shifted the state-centric language of international order into debates about global challenges that shape our world today. These included climate change, nuclear proliferation, the spread of infectious diseases, and economic globalization.[22] This was global-order theorist Andrew Hurrell's list in 2007. It was remarkably prescient. After it, came the Credit Crunch in 2008, followed by nuclear crises in Asia and the Middle East, the Extinction Rebellion movement and the Covid-19 pandemic.

What is striking about these global challenges one hundred years on from the birth of the League is that then, as now, the most discernible voices seem to be those who challenge institutionalized cooperation. Their focus is not a particular treaty or policy recommendation. They reject international law, and the very notion of global governance. It is compelling, as Zoltán Peterecz has pointed out in the case of Hungary, to set out and compare the arguments of those for and against the League. History shows us the politics of global order are in reality rival attempts to find solutions to common dilemmas exemplified by the tension between promoting economic growth in the consumer economy versus the needs—and limits of the physical environment.

When it comes to imagining futures of global order out of the history of the world's first inter-governmental organization, we need to take seriously the League's recognition of common challenges in the midst of the crisis-filled 1930s. In short, 'of the need for a much larger degree of international collaboration than anything yet achieved'.[23] This approach was first and foremost found in the League's secretariat. These officials, many of whom spent most of their careers in the League's service, repeatedly sought to face different varieties of crises by effecting institutional reform, or by taking more radical steps. Ultimately, this included dissolving the League itself. These officials asked hard questions about the place and utility of

[22] Hurrell, ibid, 105.

[23] League of Nations Economic and Financial Committees, Report to the Council on the Word of the Joint Session (League of Nations August 1942) 22.

markets in global order; the character and composition of global health, whether in relation to disease control, clean water, or food supply; and the make-up and role played by the physical environment. These, and other questions, are central to the prospects of global order in the twenty-first century too.

Probing the 'Geo' in Geopolitics

New research has underlined how the League drew on nature in its aspirations to nurture global order. League planners and later, League architects hoped the clean air of the Alps would cleanse human bodies and pacify their spirits.[24] Some of the world's earliest environmental activist groups turned to Geneva, discussing and promoting laws for the natural world that became fundamental in the search for a sustainable planet.[25]

The natural environment is conspicuous in the fashioning Central European identity.[26] It has yet to surface prominently in its history in relation to the League. Physical geography in general, and topography in particular, loomed large in the peace-makers' approach to boundary-making in problematic relation to Wilson's conception of 'self-determination'.[27] A number of authors in this volume have drawn out the power and complexity of Central European identity politics. This was more than the assertion of national self-determination. Identity politics laid claim to a 'higher' set of values or priorities that empowered one particular community above the consideration of those beyond it. The new Republic of Austria, for one, had self-determination. Yet its identity politics wanted more. Geography—the physical features and asserted characteristics of the region—were part of these claims.[28] In the twenty-first century, these impulses are evident again in a series of nationalist moves against institutionalized co-operation, such as Brexit; in the criticisms levelled by US President Trump of the United Nations and the World Health Organization; and China's 'Belt and Road' initiative, which promotes co-operation but underscores a strong state as the guarantor of national security and an orderly world.[29] Together, these phenomena signal a return to geopolitics.

Since 1924, the term *geopolitics* itself has become shorthand for an approach to international relations that stresses the agency of the state in relation to geography,

[24] Ilaria Scaglia, *The Emotions of Internationalism: Feeling International Cooperation in the Alps in the Interwar Period* (Oxford University Press 2019).

[25] Omer Aloni, 'Back to the League of Nations—An Evaluation of the Environmental Regime, 1919–1939' (DPhil thesis, Tel-Aviv University 2018).

[26] David Blackbourn and James Retallack (eds), *Localism, Landscape and the Ambiguities of Place, German-Speaking Central Europe 1860–1930* (University of Toronto Press 2007).

[27] Volker Prott, *The Politics of Self-Determination* (Oxford University Press 2016).

[28] 'Geography', *Oxford English Dictionary* <https://www.oed.com/view/Entry/77757?redirectedFrom=geography#eid>, accessed 23 May 2020.

[29] Yongjin Zhang, 'Dynamism and Contention: understanding Chinese foreign policy under Xi Jinping' (July 2016) 92/4 International Affairs 769.

and the state's superiority as an organism, with powers independent of, and superior to, constituent groups or individuals. The term hangs like a poisonous cloud over Central Europe because of its associations with National Socialism. The genesis of geopolitics is identified with the retired general and honorary Professor in Munich, Karl Haushofer. Credited with coining the term *Lebensraum*, his influence on Hitler was at worst exaggerated, at best fictional. If the ideas of this 'pottering and slightly pathetic non-entity' are no longer central to the field of German geopolitical thought, the field's preoccupation with the relationship between geography, military defence, and economics resonated with the work of the League.[30] It begs questions of how far were these Central European schools of geopolitical inquiry in dialogue with the League, helping to shape the work of bodies such as the Economic Committee's Raw Materials Committee? What were the links between Central European geopolitical networks operating within the League networks, given that Carnegie Foundation helped fund bodies such as the Deutsche Hochschule für Politik, where geopolitics was a prominent field of enquiry?[31]

Geography did not determine the fate of nations the way proponents of *geopolitik* imagined. Börries Kuzmany's chapter (13) reminds us that claims for national autonomy need not be tied to territory. Yet many believed physical geography was important for a state's economic and strategic prospects, especially after the First World War. As Chapter 12 by Antal Berkes here underlines, this was particularly the case in the dramatic and complex physical and human geography of Central Europe. Here, I want to redirect our gaze on the materialist aspects of League's relations downwards, from its League's situation among Alpine summits that symbolized peace and health, towards the region's magisterial rivers and the challenges they posed for Central and Eastern European's relations with the League.

The 'freedom of the seas' was a core principle of Wilsonianism and the League's legal framework. The global order of 1919 marked a significant expansion of the juridical and geographic framework of international waters by including rivers. Central Europe was at the heart of the move. The transformation was set out by Georges Kaeckenbeeck, a Belgian member of the Legal Section of the League Secretariat. The global order was now distinguished between a national river lying wholly within the territory of one state and subject to its national jurisdiction, and an international river, defined as a body of water 'navigable from the sea that flowed through, or along, the territories of two or more states'.[32] This legal framework, incorporated into the League, drew extensively on the legal regime governing

[30] David Thomas Murphy, 'Hitler's Geostrategist? The Myth of Karl Haushofer and the "Institut für Geopolitik"' (2014) 76/1 the Historian 1–25; Nicola Bassoni, 'Karl Haushofer as a "Pioneer" of National Socialist Cultural Diplomacy in Fascist Italy' (2019) 52 Central European History 424–449.

[31] Detlev Lehnert, '"Politik als Wissenschaft": Beiträge zur Institutionalisierung einer Fachdisziplin in Forschung und Lehre der Deutschen Hochschule für Politik (1920–1933)' (1989) 30/3 Politische Vierteljahresschrift 443–465.

[32] Georges Kaeckenbeeck, *International Rivers: A Monograph Based on Diplomatic Documents* (Sweet & Maxwell 1918) 1.

European rivers—especially Central European ones—established in the nineteenth century. It generally followed precedents developed at the Congress of Vienna and subsequent Conferences in Berlin in 1878 and 1884–5, noting that these agreements also had implications for river governance in European colonies.[33]

Central and Eastern Europe comprised numerous riparian states, which is to say powers whose national boundaries bordered a major river. Kaeckenbeeck identified the core international challenges posed by rivers such as the Danube, the Elbe, and the Vistula in Central and Eastern Europe. New state boundaries marked the rivers into sections across several jurisdictions, at the same time as their 'organic unity' and 'physical entirety; needed to be preserved as it is most eminently and perfectly an economic instrument'.[34] International rivers were not just a problem for global governance. They represented, as well as created, the 'complexity of international relations' and global currents, and the intricate interdependence of the interests of all nations.[35]

Rivers in Europe were closed during and immediately after the First World War, while Kaeckenbeeck wrote his legal study as part of the historical information gathered by the British Foreign Office in preparation for peace-making. The challenge of reopening them were manifold given their militarization, the operations of the blockade and the multiplication of new states on the riverbanks. In the same way that the peace treaties and the practices of the League were unequal, so too were 'states occupying the banks of an international river are mostly not in a state of natural equality'. Crucially, the state at the mouth of the river held a 'master-position' that enabled it to control access to the sea, and the effects of this strategic advantage pushed the question of access and navigation on the river into international law.

Lawmakers were faced with two questions: who could navigate these rivers, and with what freedoms? By recognizing the rivers as international, states agreed to grant equal rights to all flags and to give international commissions the authority to uphold this principle and administer the rivers. Here I want to underscore that these globally derived legal norms—binding principles that governed relations among riparian states on the Mississippi, Saint Lawrence, the Amazon, and the River Plate were also influential—had discrete regional effects in ways we have yet to understand fully. Work on the League has shown how its institutions, norms, and practices were foundational for European institutions.[36] Here, I want

[33] The Congress of Vienna had not concerned itself explicitly with the Danube as Turkey was not deemed part of the European state system. Kaeckenbeeck, ibid, 30–40.

[34] Kaeckenbeeck, ibid, 2.

[35] Kaeckenbeeck, ibid, 2.

[36] Patricia Clavin, 'The League of Nations and Europe' in Robert Gerwarth (ed), *Twisted Paths: Europe, 1914–1945* (Oxford University Press 2007), 521–570; Robert Gerwarth (ed), *Twisted Paths: Europe, 1914*–1945 (Oxford University Press 2007); Patricia Clavin and Kiran Klaus Patel, 'The role of international organisations in europeanization: The case of the League of Nations and the European Economic Community' in Martin Conway and Kiran Klaus Patel (eds), *Europeanization in the Twentieth Century: Historical Approaches* (Palgrave Macmillan 2010); Kiran Klaus Patel and Wolfram Kaiser, 'Continuity and Change in European Cooperation during the Twentieth Century' (2018) 27/2 Contemporary European History 165–182.

to suggest that a forgotten history of the League's engagement with riparian governance holds the potential to add to our knowledge and understanding of how regions and global governance are fashioned in relation to the environment, and how nature has evolved in relation to human practices.[37] The approach demands a fusion of international and environmental history, and speaks also to local and global anxieties over water security in the twenty-first century.

II. The Return of the Plague Doctors

I am writing this epilogue in April 2020 at a new hinge-moment in history. It is too early to test the value of historian Peter Hennessy's prediction of a new historical marker BC and AC—Before and After Corona.[38] Nevertheless, the grave challenges the pandemic poses for global order presently prompts new questions of the formative years of global governance. Governments and the media are reaching for military analogies in the battle against the novel coronavirus. Many have reached for ready narratives of solidarity, resilience, and reconstruction cast during and after the Second World War. (The first peak of the pandemic coincided with the seventy-fifth anniversary of the Allied victory in Europe.) It is unhelpful to invoke military metaphors given the pandemic poses a shared global threat to humanity. Indeed, it harks back to the mid-century language of war and peace I explored earlier.

If we are to draw on military parallels, then it makes much more sense to compare 2020 to one hundred years ago as a way to understand the challenges of the present. The First World War and its chaotic aftermath, which was the seminal catastrophe of the twentieth century. As in 1914–1918, we conscripts in the fight against Covid-19 know little about the enemy, it is unclear how long we will need to 'fight', and we have no shared international war aims. Our commonality lies in 'fighting' an enemy we cannot see, and may not be able to defeat. We fight with old weapons, such as quarantine and plague-masks. Handwashing away germs currently is the most effective method of combat, invoking the discovery and practices of the nineteenth-century Austro-Hungarian physician scientist, Ignaz Semmelweis.[39] Semmelweiss is not just the father of hand hygiene. His intervention of the medical practice 'recognize–explain–act' is the base model of epidemiologically driven strategies to prevent infection. Much like the career of Pirquet, detailed in this

[37] New work on the transnational history of the Rhine is instructive here. See, for example, Vincent Langendijk, 'Europe's Rhine power: connections, borders and flows' (2016) 8/1 Water History 23–39.

[38] Peter Hennessy speaking on *Radio Four*, 'The World At One', reported by Jon Kelly, 'Coronavirus: The month everything changed', *BBC News Online*, 28 March 2020 <https://www.bbc.co.uk/news/stories-52066956>, accessed 26 July 2020).

[39] WHO Guidelines on Hand Hygiene in Health Care: First Global Patient Challenge Clear Care is Safer Care (WHO 2009) 49–51.

volume, the work of Semmelweiss drew medical practitioners and students from around the world to the heart of Europe, and informed and shaped scientific networks and international agency long after his lifetime.

We need to ask new questions of how the League wrestled with challenges that connected sovereignty to biopolitics and to markets. My research on Central and Eastern Europe and the League encouraged me to connect the challenge of hunger and financial crisis. The relationship between deprivation and some sort of monetary collapse is frequently characteristic of global famine crises but obscured to history because of disciplinary and methodological divides.[40] Research pulls in different directions with questions orientated around understanding the monetary and political causes of stabilizing financial instability, the history of scientific discovery and knowledge exchange, or recovering the social and cultural history of rural life.

Is it really the case, as Adam Tooze suggested, that Covid-19 has triggered the first economic crisis of the Anthropocene?[41] Even a cursory reading of the League's engagement with Central Europe in the aftermath of the First World War suggests it may not be. British and American financiers involved in trying to manage rapidly rising inflation and economic dislocation in Central and Eastern Europe were intently aware of the devastating impact of the 1918 influenza, typhus, and tuberculosis (TB) pandemics. Sara Silverstein underscores the importance of this history for the League and the region in this volume (Chapter 3). The spring of 2020 brought renewed interest and attention to the Spanish 'flu pandemic of 1918, yet over time the tuberculosis pandemic which ran alongside it was more enduring and deadly. It shares some characteristics with the Covid-19 pandemic that are worrying. I want to highlight two of them. The first is TB's devastating impact and persistence in the world's poorest communities. The second is that the fight against the disease required a global commitment to supporting local, community-based strategies, which included economic and financial support as well as better healthcare.[42]

The stress on local, national, and global interdependency that connected the fields of health, the economy, and their impact on gold order, was recognized by many figures associated with the League actors and Central and Eastern Europe. At the time, the impact of the TB pandemic there was well known. In October 1920, the International Union Against Tuberculosis and Lung Disease was founded,

[40] Patricia Clavin, 'The Austrian Hunger Crisis and the Genesis of International Organization after the First World War' (2014) 90/2 International Affairs 265–278.

[41] Adam Tooze, 'We are living through the first economic crisis of the Anthropocene', *The Guardian* (London, 7 May 2020).

[42] Salmaan Keshavjee, Aaron Shakow, and Tom Nicolson, 'The TB epidemic teaches us the battle against Covid-19 won't be won in hospitals alone', *The Guardian* (London, 30 April 2020). <https://www.theguardian.com/commentisfree/2020/apr/30/trust-tuberculosis-tackle-covid-19>, accessed 17 May 2020.

another product of the internationalist moment proclaimed by the League.[43] Its founding fathers, including Professor Léon Bernard, were instrumental in creating a League Epidemic Commission in 1920, and the League of Nations Health Organization the following year.[44]

Anecdotally, we know that many leaders and advisors pivotal in the forging of global order in the era of the two world wars, such Benjamin Strong, Governor of the Federal Reserve Bank of New York, and Secretary of State, Cordell Hull, secretly suffered from TB. But neither their personal contexts, nor the ways in which pandemic disease, and scientific practice cut across and shaped wider moves and structures in global governance has been connected by historians, or used to inform the present by IR.

One hundred years before Covid-19 in 2020, TB was an intractable and pervasive problem for which there was no vaccine, no diagnostic tools, and no cure. It was known to thrive in conditions of poverty, but no one was immune.[45] Is it really an accident that much of the language around the ailing global economy and increased prospects of international conflict in the era of the two world wars related to contagious disease?[46] Epidemic disease, then as now, triggered politically contested debates about the viability of long distance supply chains, and 'diseased' goods and people with profound implications for global order.

Historians may return to older preoccupations and subjects. Hobbes recognized the challenges posed by epidemic disease. We do not need to read as far as his epilogue to see it. The famous frontispiece by Thomas Bosse, with input from Hobbes, offered anamorphic representations of the text's core themes. The protective grand central figure of the Sovereign King whose body is literally and figuratively constituted by blurring together individual bodies of citizenry, also recognizes the threat posed by plague and pestilence.[47] Hobbes' sovereign body is represented to be

[43] Its origins lay also in the British Tuberculosis association whose publication *Tubercle* became an official journal with anonymous contributors working at the League of Red Cross Societies in Geneva. See, 'To Our Readers' (Oct.1920) II/1 Tubercle 14.

[44] The Epidemic Commission's genesis lay in the typhus epidemic in Central and Eastern Europe, notably in Poland and Russia. Georgia Dill, 'History of the health organization of the League of Nations' (DPhil thesis, Montana State University 1938) 13; Mara Aleksandra Balińska, 'Assistance and not mere relief: the Epidemic Commission of the League of Nations, 1920–1923' in Paul Weindling (ed), *International Health Organizations and Movements, 1918–1939* (Cambridge University Press 1995), 81–108. The International Union Against Tuberculosis and Lung Disease—now called The Union—and the WHO continue to work together on projects such as the Global Project on Surveillance for Anti-Tuberculosis Drug Resistance.

[45] Patricia Clavin, 'Men and Markets: Global Capital and the International Economy' in Glenda Sluga and Patricia Clavin (eds), *Internationalisms: A Twentieth-Century History* (Cambridge University Press 2017).

[46] For examples of the contagion literature, René Fry-McKibbin, Cody Yu-Ling Hsiao, and Chrismin Tang, 'Contagion and Global Financial Crisis: Lessons from Nine Crisis Episodes' (2013) 25/3 Open Economies Review 521570; Robert Peckham, 'Contagion: epidemiological models and financial crises' (2014) 36/1 Journal of Public Health 13–17.

[47] Francesca Falk, 'Hobbes' *Leviathan* und die aus dem Blick gefallenen Schnabelmasken' (2011) 39/247 Leviathan 247–266.

male. But women were prominent in the management and treatment of epidemics then as now. The wide-ranging social and political consequences of the war led to a flowering of progressive ideas for a new world order that recognized the rights of the vulnerable, and put social and economic security at their core. Through organizations such as the Women's League for Peace and Freedom, which, of course, had strong ties to Central Europe, women activists drew in other groups normally disadvantaged in the normal practice of international relations, for example student groups, such as the Student Christian Movement and the World Student Christian Federation. These associations embraced all the opportunities for campaigning and connections the new League of Nations appeared to afford.

The return of the 'plague doctors' to national and international prominence in the twenty-first century reminds us of the close connections between local and international activism, and the importance of private and public partnerships. The Austrian hunger crisis detailed here by Michael Burri (Chapter 2) inspired Eglantyne Jebb and her sister Dorothy Buxton to found the Save the Children Fund in April 1919. From there, the activities of this early non-governmental organization, reached out to the 'war stricken lands of Europe and Asia minor'.[48] It coordinated its operations with similar agencies across Europe and the British dominions, while at the same time, promoting the cause of child wellbeing and rights at the League of Nations.[49] These were founding moments in the modern history of humanitarianism. Its activists had a religious fervour, seeking to challenge states' visions and practices, and in demanding new knowledge and fresh perspectives that offered the opportunity to bind transnational civil society together in new ways.

In May 1922, an editorial of *The Record of the Save the Children Fund*, argued:

> It used to be said that the free press of England was the Fourth Estate of the Realm. There is need for a 'Fourth Estate' in the realm of international relations, an instrument which, without limitations of party or creed or nation, is free to reflect the human impulse of goodwill and to interpret it into action when the more formal organisations of Government are held back by considerations of tradition and policy and expediency.[50]

That perspective challenged a world order predicated solely on the principle of national sovereignty. The NGO's stress on the need for a 'fourth estate' to support global order also signaled an awareness of the complexity of the global and

[48] Records of the Save the Children Fund (hereafter SCF), Cadbury Research Archive, University of Birmingham. SCF, *The Record of the Save the Children Fund*, reel 1, vol. 1, October and December 1920. See also papers relating to Dorothy Buxton (hereafter SC/DB), SCR, DB/4/1-5, letters from E. Hobhouse (Vienna) to Buxton, 26 July 1920.

[49] SCF, 'The League of Nations and Child Distress: The Appointment of a High Commissioner Proposed', *The Record of the Save the Children Fund*, reel 1, vol.1 (January 1921) 51.

[50] SCF, 'Three Years', The Record of the Save the Children Fund, reel 1, vol. 2 (May 1922).

international system, and the interaction between its different domains: social, economic, and strategic. In 1945, the constitution of the United Nations Charter, notably Article 71 relating to the Economic and Social Council, stressed the new organization should make 'suitable arrangements for consultation with non-governmental organizations' and recognize NGOs in a way they had not been in 1919.[51] Their number and the range of NGO interests and activities proliferated. Arguably, their formal incorporation into the international system did not deliver all the benefits activists imagined it would had they been accorded the privilege of recognition in 1919. Moreover, questions over the role and character of the fourth estate in the global order became more pressing than ever in the digital age and the era of 'fake news'.[52]

It is hard to tell whether the global crosscurrents unleashed by—and embodied in—Covid-19 will provide a new moment of global re-ordering akin to 1919 and 1945, as some commentators predict. (The absence of 1989 in debates is significant: despite the end of the Cold War events, that year had only a limited impact on the institutions of the liberal order.) What is clear is that the history of world ordering in the era of the two world wars continues to play a pivotal role in how the powerful state actors of China and the USA think about the purpose of international organizations.[53] But the twenty-first century will not be determined solely by China any more than the twentieth was by the USA. The entangled history of the League in the making and unmaking of Central Europe reminds us of the capacity, and limits, of state agency. It also recovers the importance of forces that lie beyond the boundaries and control of the state. This history tells of the particular vulnerability of impoverished peoples to global challenges such as epidemic disease, hunger, disinformation, and transnational crime.

[51] Charter of the United Nations and Statue of the International Court of Justice (San Francisco, 1945), Article 71, 13 <https://treaties.un.org/doc/publication/ctc/uncharter.pdf>, accessed 25 May 2020.

[52] I am grateful to my colleagues Louise Fawcett, Andrew Hurrell, and Andrew Thompson for helpful conversations on the histories and futures of global order.

[53] Rosemary Foot, 'Remembering the past to secure the present: Versailles legacies in a resurgent China' (2019) 95/1 International Affairs 143; Edward Fishman, 'The World Order is Dead. Here's How to Build a New On for a Post-Coronavirus Era' *Politico* (3 May 2020) <https://www.politico.com/news/magazine/2020/05/03/the-post-coronavirus-world-order-230042>, accessed 25 May 2020.

Index

For the benefit of digital users, indexed terms that span two pages (e.g., 52–53) may, on occasion, appear on only one of those pages.